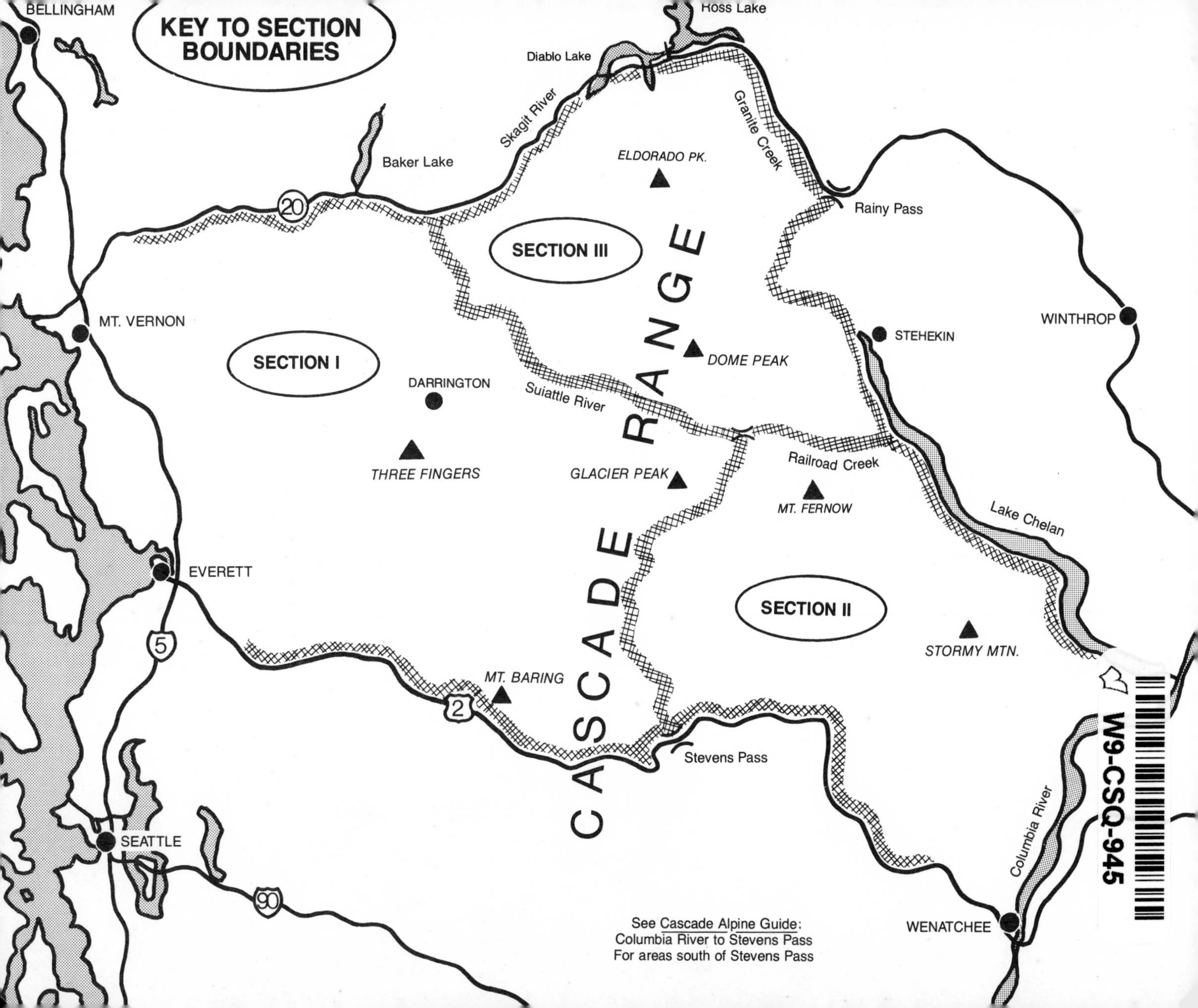
KEY TO SECTION BOUNDARIES
BELLINGHAM
Ross Lake
Diablo Lake
Skagit River
Baker Lake
20
Granite Creek
ELDORADO PK.
Rainy Pass
SECTION III
CASCADE RANGE
WINTHROP
MT. VERNON
STEHEKIN
SECTION I
DOME PEAK
DARRINGTON
Suiattle River
THREE FINGERS
GLACIER PEAK
Railroad Creek
MT. FERNOW
Lake Chelan
EVERETT
SECTION II
5
STORMY MTN.
MT. BARING
2
Stevens Pass
SEATTLE
90
Columbia River
WENATCHEE
See Cascade Alpine Guide:
Columbia River to Stevens Pass
For areas south of Stevens Pass

CASCADE ALPINE GUIDE

Property of

Bill Sipple

CASCADE ALPINE GUIDE

CLIMBING AND HIGH ROUTES

Stevens Pass to Rainy Pass

by ***FRED BECKEY***

THE MOUNTAINEERS *Seattle*

THE MOUNTAINEERS
ORGANIZED 1906

To explore and study the mountains, forests and watercourses of the Northwest;
To gather into permanent form the history and traditions of this region;
To preserve by the encouragement of protective legislation or otherwise the natural beauty of Northwest America;
To make explorations into these regions in fulfillment of the above purposes;
To encourage a spirit of good fellowship among all lovers of outdoor life.

First Edition 1977

The Mountaineers,
719 Pike Street, Seattle, Washington 98101

Manufactured in the United States of America

Library of Congress Catalog No. 77-82368
ISBN 0-916890-51-1

Published simultaneously in Canada by Mountain Craft, Box 5232, Vancouver, B.C. V6B 4B3

Photo overlays by John V.A.F. Neal

Maps and sketches by Gary Rands

TITLE PHOTO *MT. MAUDE, North Face*
JOHN V.A.F. NEAL

Contents

Acknowledgements

Prior to and during the preparation of this guidebook I incurred many literary and source obligations beyond those acknowledged here. A statement of appreciation to those who donated information and conducted earlier research is entirely inadequate, for this volume is patently enriched by many individual contributions. I trust some manner of vested interest in the final result will serve as an expression of my gratitude to persons not specifically named here.

Austin Post generously reviewed the material on glacial history and present glaciers in the North Cascades. Professor Joseph Vance patiently critiqued rough drafts concerning bedrock geology and made amendments from his wealth of knowledge of this region, and Rowland Tabor commented upon certain material related to geology and routes in his area of study. Parts of the manuscript related to glacial geology and geographic matters were reviewed at various stages of completion by William A. Long and Will F. Thompson. Philip Woodhouse was called upon several times to verify data and provide history of the Monte Cristo mines. Personnel from the Forest Service and National Park Service have been generous in reviewing mileages on approach routes and informing me of maintenance or other changes on roads and trails. Many dedicated climbers and hikers contributed to and criticized route information, and improved schematic topos. For this assistance I am particularly indebted to Roland Amundson, Bruce Bryant, Kenn Carpenter, Everett Darr, Les Davenport, Harold Deery, Nick Dodge, Joe Firey, Bill Fix, Brad Fowler, Bill Fryberger, Clark Gerhardt, Manuel Gonzalez, Robert Grant, Mike Heath, Anthony Hovey, Dallas Kloke, Ron Miller, Tom Miller, Dick McGowan, John V.A.F. Neal, Larry Penberthy, John Pollock, John Roper, Mickey Schurr, Rowland Tabor, Hermann Ulrichs, Joseph Vance, Dwight Watson, and Don Williamson.

Much of the historical research conducted for this volume is grounded in various libraries. The personnel of these institutions are to be thanked for much assistance in locating source material and providing reference suggestions. Among these were the staff of Government Documents and the Map Library, University of California at Los Angeles; National Archives, Washington; Bancroft Library of the University of California, Berkeley; Henry E. Huntington Library, San Marino; Special Collections Division and Regional Manuscripts Collection of the University of Washington; Western History Research Center of the University of Wyoming; Seattle Public Library; Oregon State Historical Society; Washington State Library, Olympia; Washoe County Library, Reno; and Vancouver, B.C. Public Library.

Considerable valuable material was obtained from the Minnesota Historical Society, St. Paul, including letters, records, and diaries related to railroad exploration. Lucile M. Kane, Curator of Manuscripts, patiently searched files and called my attention to the availability of documents which I did not know existed and which are still incompletely researched. Worthwhile research was done at Federal Records Center, Seattle, and at the library and photographic files of the U.S. Geological Survey, Tacoma. Valuable data from old maps was obtained from the U.S. Forest Service's cartographic files in Portland, and at the Washington-Northwest Room, Washington State Library, Olympia.

John V.A.F. Neal, artist and mountaineer, skillfully prepared the route markings on photographs, and Gary Rands, with patient devotion, has prepared exacting maps and schematic drawings.

The guidebook is not only a timely reference work but a fascinating collection of spectacular photography, and particular thanks for providing needed scenes is here given to Jeff Colehour, Ed Cooper, Harold Deery, Philip Leatherman, Tom Miller, John V.A.F. Neal, and Robert DeWitz of the U.S. Forest Service.

Special mention is due Austin Post for his high resolution aerial oblique photographs sponsored by the U.S. Geological Survey. In the field of international glaciology Post's name has become well known during the past 15 years in association with his magnificant photography of glaciers and their phenomena. The program of annual photo surveys of Western North American glaciers has fortunately included the Cascade Range, and some of his scenes as related to this study are shown. The pictures of Post are a tribute to the grandeur and complexity of a superb mountain wilderness. His camera has shown the beauty of sculptured cirques, ice-draped peaks, and ice-freed alp slopes, although photographs were specifically taken to record features of glaciation and changes in glacier activity.

The labors of the members of the Literary Fund Committee of The Mountaineers are much appreciated, and here special gratitude is due chairman John Pollock, for the many tasks of coordinating the publishing of this volume, Peggy Ferber for editorial assistance, and Duncan Kelso for coordinating photos and art.

FRED BECKEY

Preface

The mountains are here interpreted through word portrait, camera, artistry, and maps. This guidebook is in part an encyclopedia of natural features, but it can only give a brief image of a region or a peak, sometimes with emphasis applied to a feature of specific interest. An attempt to provide the same criterion of significance has been applied to climbs, yet some imbalance appears because of popularity or available knowledge. Some of the detailed information collected here has existed for some time, but has not been integrated into a single format to produce a digest of physical geographic features and human history on a regional scale.

The book also very briefly depicts the important known exploring and climbing history. To achieve the effect of personal experience, quotations are occasionally given from early narratives to lend a flavor of these times. Culture and technology has so separated us today from 100 years ago that it is hard to picture how vastly different the environment was then. While driving along the paved highway near Marblemount, it is difficult to imagine that within this time span a starving army expedition desperately hailed Indians across the Skagit River for a canoe.

While the author and publisher are both anxious to describe the most sensible, safest, and shortest routes to summits, this is not always possible because of lack of documentation or direct experience. Some of the research involved locating a wide variety of sources, and the consequent writing required the integration of a mass of detail, with some conflicting interpretation.

In the instances of some very recently or seldom-done routes, climbing would be better served if descriptions were checked before printing, but human limitations being what they are, it seems only practical in most doubtful cases to present the unverified route as accurately as available information permits, with the hope those repeating the way will send opinions and corrections to the publisher. It is freely admited that some seldom-done routes described here are as accurate as the memory and integrity of the report source. Where personal experience or a responsible report is lacking, the use of photgraphy has sometimes been adopted to suggest the probable best way; on some routes of limited use it simply is impossible to separate fact from interpretation every foot of the way. And finally, routes recorded after the publishing deadline will unfortunately be omitted until revision.

Various routes on a mountain are listed in clockwise direction following the most popular route as known. Directions such as "left" or "turn left" are used in the sense of direction of movement.

Each section of the volume lists the principal mountain trails and many connections which apply to alpine areas; some cross-country routes are shown, but many are left for the reader to discover. The road, trail, and cross-country information is signaled in the text by the symbol ♦ for referencing. Each section is prefaced by map references and ranger station locations.

A number of provisional names are used in the Cascades, and here acceptance has not always kept pace with exploration and subsequent chronicling. An effort has been made to choose and use the best adopted names in new situations, and to restore historic usage. For preliminary nomenclature, sometimes designating a feature by general location and without prejudice to a possibly unknown local name is preferable. Feature names can provide associations with history, and here American personal names are sometimes those of explorers. Streams, as in Alaska and British Columbia, are mostly derived from the Indian, but mountain names are predominantly descriptive or personal. Many Cascade feature names are derived from the Chinook jargon.

Some locations are defined only by elevation as shown on the most recent topographic map, pending a possible later naming. When a height is not shown as triangulated, it is given as the altitude of the highest contour of the most recent topographic map, with a plus. Some altitudes between contour lines are defined as estimated ("est.").

Abbreviations used are:

A.A.J.	*American Alpine Journal*
ATP	at time of publication
Hwy	highway
Crest Trail	Pacific National Scenic Crest Trail
F.S.	Forest Service station
R.S.	Ranger station
ft or ′	feet (altitude)
m	meters
mi.	mile or miles
hr, hrs	hour, hours
N, S, E, W, NW, etc.	compass points
km	kilometer (glacier length)
km^2	square kilometer (glacier area)
KB, LA	knife blade, lost arrow

The collection of pictures of the Cascades included herein amounts to 71 aerial oblique photographs and 61 of ground coverage. The visual content of the pictures goes beyond a mere collection of attractive scenic views. Each selection and sketch was chosen to pictorialize a specific vantage which would augment the text. The plan is to present a logical overview of the landscape portrayed in this volume. An impressive amount of information can be gained by interpreting the topography covered by the camera. Discrepancies in locations on maps and corresponding photographs are the result of distortion in the photographic image. Oblique photographs are not orthographically correct, whereas vertical photographs, ERTS images, and maps are nearly so.

While all of the significant peaks between the western foothills and Lake Chelan are covered from the air, not all of them are seen closely or from more than one direction. In some cases sketched scenes were designed to give a literal rendition not available in accessible photographs. While sketches are realistic, they are produced to emphasize chosen detail. Topos, which are schematic art diagrams, are used occasionally to clarify specific climbing problems.

Some areas or mountains are depicted cartographically in different attitudes. Important peaks are presented in detail for effective pinpointing of exact positions of features and routes when nomenclature needs amplification or additional detail is desirable. Two of the special maps are a unique combination of existing map sources, field reconnaissance, new nomenclature, research and climber contributions, and modern aerial photography. Some names and items not shown on government maps are presented on maps in this volume, based on the 1:24,000 and 1:62,500 scales of the topographic series of the U.S. Geological Survey. These maps summarize and correlate selected existing information possible within this framework. The appropriate topographic maps are important accessories to these maps, and should be taken on field trips.

Topographic maps can be ordered from:

Denver Distribution Section
U.S. Geological Survey
Federal Center, Bldg. 41
Denver, CO 80225

Maps regularly available in 15-minute quadrangles are also available as topographic prints at 1:24,000 scale in 7.5-minute units (one color with appropriate accuracy and contour interval).

Send requests to:

Western Mapping Center
U.S. Geological Survey
345 Middlefield Road
Menlo Park, CA 94025

A number of libraries have maps for reference use and most regional retail outdoor stores stock maps of the Cascade Range. It should be noted that some culture errors and discrepancies in feature names may exist on maps. Current planimetric maps are generally more reliable regarding trail and road locations, and are revised more frequently. Not all logging spurs and operational extensions are shown on even the most recent issues. The continual changes in roads and trails can only be shown on map revisions at interim periods. It should be noted that some of these changes will make established and recommended routes less advantageous.

National Forest Recreation Folder maps and Glacier Peak Wilderness maps can be obtained from forest headquarters in person or by mail, or from district ranger stations during business hours.

The Forest Service has special planimetric maps based on aerial photography, with contour lines superimposed, and up-to-date culture and drainage control noted. Maps are in 15-minute quadrangles, available through U.S. Forest Service, P.O. Box 3623, Portland, Oregon 97208.

Legend for photos

route
variation
hidden route
campsite ▲

Legend for sketches and maps

trail or route
route
major summit
minor summit
campsite ▲
campground
ridge
road
mine
structure ■

Introduction

GEOGRAPHIC ASPECTS

"Between Mount Baker and Mount Rainier a number of lesser peaks, presenting from the Strait of Fuca the form of a broken sierra, rise to the limits of perpetual snow. They have never been explored, but they appear, from some points of view, like skeletons of formerly more elevated volcanic mountains."

GEORGE GIBBS, 1873

source

Gibbs, George, "Physical Geography of the Northwestern Boundary of the United States." *Journal of American Geographical Society of New York,* Vol. 4 (1873), p. 358

The area encompassed by this volume is a transect from 47°44′ N latitude at Stevens Pass to 48°32′ at Rainy Pass, with the tangential additional terrain S to the Wenatchee River and N to 48°44′ at the S end of Ross Lake. Cross-range limits extend from the foothills E of Puget Sound to Lake Chelan.

The scenic diversity and majesty of the North Cascades is due to long-term geologic and climatic processes. The environment is a spectacular variety of terrain, climate, and vegetation within a great vertical relief pattern. Landforms identified include rugged serrate peaks, a major stratovolcano, subdued dome-shaped mountains, valley walls and mountain slopes trimmed by Neoglacial glacierization, complexes of talus and escarpments, stream terraces, areas of mass deposition, alluvial fans, and valley bottom alluvium.

The vast Plio-Pleistocene uparching of the Cascade Range, of a time not precisely known, probably occurred less than 6 million yrs ago, possibly much less. The present ruggedness of the range is due largely to ice modification of a highland already deeply dissected by rivers and streams. In Pleistocene time glaciers advanced and readvanced during each glacial age to deepen, widen, and straighten winding V-shaped river canyons and form hanging tributaries. Interlocking ridge spurs conforming to bedrock structures were generally removed in this process. Most of the tantalizing alpine scenery in the range today is the direct result of the last ice episode which ended an estimated 10,000 yrs ago. This glaciation magnified the alpine character of the range and resulted in steep-sided, U-shaped configurations. Ice streams moved down stream-erosional valleys, scouring bottoms, truncating flanks, and removing debris; as they retreated, they formed thick deposits of glacial drift. Valleys were left part-tilled with unassorted gravel, clay, and sand, overlain with stratified gravels into which streams re-excavated channels.

The mean altitude of peaks along the Cascade drainage divide ranges from about 5400 ft at latitude 47°50′ N to 6550 ft at latitude 48°00′ N. Both relief and mean altitude increase northward. Stevens Pass and Cady Pass are the lowest depressions on the divide. Local relief ranges from 650 ft in alluvial river bottoms near Darrington to over 10,500 ft at Glacier Peak. In many valleys relief changes of 6000 ft occur in a horizontal distance of 3 mi. Most ridges are separated by narrow, steep-walled valleys, whose floors are generally less than 3000 ft above sea level even near their headwaters.

Major W-draining valleys have been more deeply eroded than those E of the divide (except the Chelan Trough) and relief remains high to the range front. The floor of the North Fork of Skykomish River valley stands at an altitude of 1800 ft only 7 mi. from the drainage divide. By contrast, at comparative distances E of the divide valley floors generally lie at altitudes of more than 3000 ft. Only beyond the outer limits of glaciation, more than 30 mi. from the Cascade crest, does the floor of Wenatchee River valley fall below this altitude.

Bedrock structures, which have a northwesterly component, reflect the pronounced topographic grain.[1] Since topography in the Cascade Range is largely a function of bedrock structure and lithology, it plays a modifying role in cirque orientation. While cirques are distributed through a wide range of altitude, studies have shown a progressive eastward rise across the range in average floor altitude.[2] Mean altitude of ice-free cirques lies below the mean altitude of small glaciers, implying that cirque development occurred mainly when climate was more glacial than today, but less so than the closing phases of the last glaciation. The mean altitudes of glaciers tend to increase with continentality and a decrease in precipitation, and tend to increase with decreasing latitude. Likewise, the firn limits reflect the transmountain climatic regimes.

The Cascade Range shows the mark of severe alpine glaciation during the Pleistocene glacial ages. These began early in the Quaternary Period, over 600,000 yrs ago, and peaked several times when extensive summit icefields and systems of valley glaciers intermittently expanded and occupied most of the land surface in the North Cascades. During early Pleistocene time all principal valleys contained long glaciers.[3] Streams were superseded as valley-cutting agents, and these regions entered a new epoch in their history.

Two distinct episodes of late Pleistocene glaciation are recognized. First was the Cascade alpine glaciation (beginning of Fraser Glaciation), 17,000 to 21,000 yrs ago, which modified present river valleys.[4] Glacial lobes of the Cordilleran Ice Sheet advanced and retreated across the Puget Lowland, first crossing the border of Washington shortly after 20,000 yrs ago to reach a maximum stand about 15,000 yrs ago, then retreating by 10,000 yrs ago.[5] Rather curiously, in late Pleistocene time the mountain glaciers were relatively small though enormous ice sheets covered the lowland, and lobes of the Cordilleran ice in Canada extended southward E and W of the Cascade Range.[6]

In the second episode the last ice sheet pushed into all principal Cascade valleys to create morainal blockades which impounded long lakes. Then the ice sheet disappeared, largely by downwasting. The last Pleistocene glaciation was followed by warmer climate and an almost complete melting of North Cascade glaciers. The most significant climatic event after the last 15,000 yrs would have been that which started rapid demise of glaciers and marked changes from a glacial to an interglacial climatic regime.[7]

Late Neoglacial activity was characterized by at least two main intervals of glacier growth, the first culminating about 2800 to 2600 yrs ago.[8] A more recent period of advancing glaciers began approximately 600 yrs ago and peaked in the mid-19th century.[9] From the extent of barren zones, old maps, and fragmentary records it is clear that glacier retreat was rapid after about 1900. Recently deglaciated slabs and end moraines nearly devoid of vegetation indicate a rapid period of recession. From about 1910 to 1945 extensive retreat and stagnation of North Cascade glaciers appears to have been universal as elsewhere along the Pacific North. In the early 1950s a rejuvenation of glacier activity commenced, a remarkable change from catastrophic retreat due partly to cooler, wetter weather conditions. The strong glacier growth was of relatively short duration, and has been followed by a rough balance with years of growth and shrinkage generally cancelling each other for the majority of glaciers. A few glaciers responded to changed climate by advancing. The timing of readvance is partly a function of response rates of individual glaciers. Those advancing have common characteristics of location on steep slopes and relatively high mean altitude with respect to nearby steady-state glaciers. Retreating glaciers show characteristics of low gradient and relatively low mean altitude. Most Cascade glaciers are below the altitude zone of maximum snow accumulation and suffer accordingly in terms of nourishment. Still, the Cascades have a vast aggregate of ice, maintained by immense snowfall which provides an important water resource, since glaciers act as a solid state reservoir. While the contiguous United States has about 1100 glaciers covering 205 square mi., the North Cascades (N of Snoqualmie Pass) alone have 756 glaciers of a minimum 0.1 km² area. Some 267 km² of terrain currently is covered by ice.[10]

Streams which originate in the foothills usually have their greatest flow during the winter maximum rainfall and their lowest flows during summer, when the flow is largely maintained by ground seepage. Snow- and glacier-fed streams usually sustain the summer snow melt; the climax flow occurs in late spring and early summer.

Erroneous associations are often made between the Cascades and Alps of Europe. While the Alps have notable, impressive glaciers, they receive less snow, partly because of a more continental climate. The milder climate of the Cascades is distinctly more maritime; the Alps, which have more clear and cold weather than the Cascades, more closely resemble the Selkirks of Canada. In the Cascades the permafrost occurs about 2000 ft above timberline. Deep couloir dissection occurs, especially on the western side of the divide, because of the lack of protective permafrost. Cascade rock tends to be less cold than that of the Alps, so there is less of the dreaded verglas on climbs. In the American Rocky Mountains the permafrost line reaches to about timberline, usually near 10,000 ft. In both Canada and the Rockies of the United States couloir dissection apparently reaches only 20 to 30 ft, then tends to stop due to the permafrost. This has an important bearing on the common triangular shapes of mountains and their faces.

CLIMATE

The great forest
"its grandeur in an artistic sense is beyond description . . . Beneath the deep shade of the boughs, which, to one looking upward from beneath them, seem to mingle with the clouds—and during much of the prevailing misty weather this is literally true."

PROF. I.C. RUSSELL, 1898

source
Russell, I.C.
20th Annual Report, U.S. Geological Survey

The Pacific Northwest is covered by marine air in

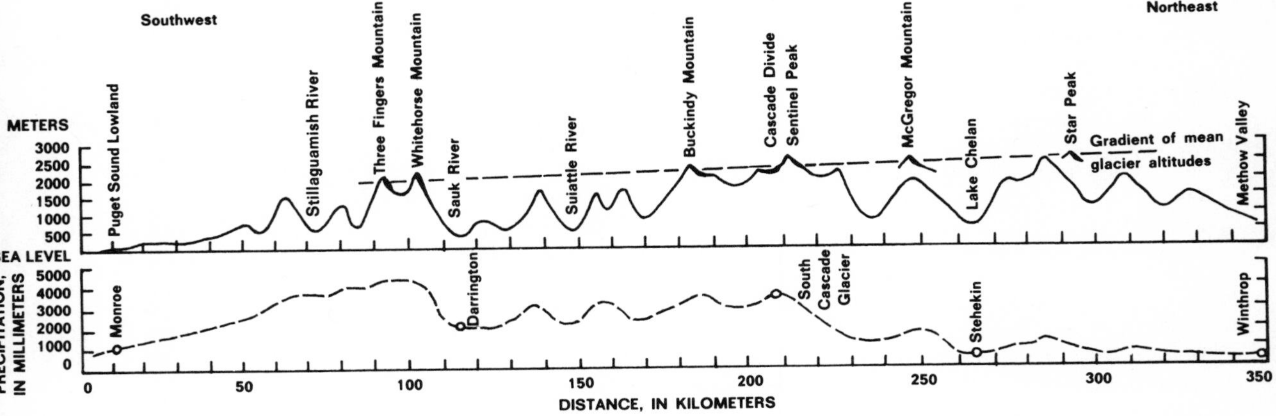

FIGURE 1.—SW-NE profile across the North Cascades showing topography, precipitation, and gradient of mean glacier altitudes. Short, heavier segments on topographic profile indicate glaciers. Precipitation is indicated by circles where measured and by dashed line where inferred from streamflow records. (Source: Inventory of Glaciers in the North Cascades, Washington; U.S. Geol. Survey Prof. Paper 705-A (1971), p. A5.)

which cyclonic storms are imbedded. Ocean storms are first intercepted by the Olympic Mountains and then the Cascade Range, which forms a major topographic barrier to the flow of air and divide the state into two contrasting climatic regions. Orographic lifting of moist marine air masses moving eastward produces generally increased precipitation with altitude; the forced lifting of this air by the range creates instability and cooling needed for condensation. Topographic shelter controls precipitation locally and mean minimum temperatures are reflected by these barriers. Variables in precipitation cannot always be related precisely to location.[11] The efficiency of topography varies in extracting moisture, but conditions on the W side of the range tend to prolonged cloudy periods, muted temperature extremes, and narrow diurnal fluctuations. Summer cloud cover averages 40 to 50 percent.

The climate in the North Cascades is typified by mild, equitable temperatures and moderate to heavy precipitation. The prevailing winds, ocean temperatures, and position and intensity of low and high pressure centers near the North Pacific work to prevent climatic extremes. Winters tend to be wet and cold, with cool and relatively dry summers. In late September and October the heavy autumn rains generally begin; by the last week of October it is not uncommon to find 18 in. of fresh snow on the higher passes; snow will usually remain until June.

Striking changes in climate take place along E-flowing drainages. Mean annual precipitation decreases rapidly with decreasing altitude and increasing distance from the range crest. Mean precipitation on the E side of the range is about one-half that of the W side.[12] Average annual precipitation ranges from more than 200 in. in some parts of the mountains near and W of the crest to less than 10 in. in the semiarid eastern margin.[13] Conditions do not favor thunderheads and resultant lightning on the windward slopes, but the E side is susceptible.

Generally July and August have less than 5 percent of the average total precipitation, which is heaviest during the winter months when it falls predominantly as snow. Such snowfall totals may accumulate heavily down to 2000 ft. A stormy winter can produce a total snowfall of 50 to 70 ft—with 20- to 30-ft snowpacks on the ground in the higher regions.[14] These depths, combined with precipitous gullies and cliffs, create extreme avalanche hazard in winter and spring.

The W side has moderate temperatures for its latitude.[15] Mountain temperatures seldom fall below 0°F. in winter or rise above 80°F. in summer, but the E side has greater extremes, both high and low. Both extremes occur with a high pressure system centered E or N and continental air mass spilling over the Cascades. Alternating semi-permanent high and low pressure cells over the North Pacific are strong climatic influences. The low pressure system reaches its maximum intensity in late fall and winter to produce a prevailing southwesterly flow of moist Pacific air resulting in a distinct rainy season. George Gibbs, in 1954, observed the proper season for an exploration of this district is at some time during the winter, when not much rain is expected. "The Indians recommend February."[16] By late spring the low pressure cell generally weakens, altering the pattern, and a high pressure system intensifies over much of the North Pacific, bringing a northwesterly flow of relative dry cool air.

HUMAN IMPACT

You are on your honor to treat the Cascades with respect.

Mountaineering has many facets, some of which will be overlooked by a reader of narrow interests. Guides are written not only for informative reasons, but for safety, historical, and traditional purposes. To protect the sport of climbing we must be aware of attitudes and values held by the climbing culture. It is hoped everyone will honor precedents that have been in focus. There are no referees.

Treat the forests and mountains as your own personal property—with a sense of ownership. We all have a share in these public lands. The perpetuation of the wilderness resource is largely dependent upon the sensitivity and behavior of the user.

Self-restraint and responsibility to the natural setting appear to depend in part on the awareness of the resource user of the consequences of his own actions. Most meadow regions are too fragile to withstand unlimited human usage; therefore we have a social as well as environmental crisis, one which must be solved if the Cascade Range is to remain the same for the next generation. Although in the richer soils of the urban and rural low-altitude parks and college campuses lawns appear to withstand the trampling of thousands, the fragile plants and grasses of the mountain meadow cannot survive such abuse.

A few reminders:

Use existing campsites.

Camp on the forest floor or on gravel bars; avoid meadow camping.

Camp away from any water; 200 ft is desirable in most

cases. Camping is now prohibited within 100 ft of designated lakes and up to ¼ mi. of some others. Look for specific restrictions on recreation folders and postings at ranger stations.

Do not construct tables, rock wall, etc. at campsites.

Do not build new firepits. Do not "ditch" tents.

Bury human wastes. Toilets should be made in soft soil a minimum of 300 ft away from camp and water. Dig a shallow hole and cover.

Do not cut boughs. Do not cut trees. Do not blaze trees or mark routes with ribbon-tape. Do not carve initials or use paint on any tree or rock.

Use liquid fuel or butane stoves for cooking to conserve limited wood supply, minimize fire hazard, and eliminate damage to the land surface.

Carry out all plastics, foil wrappers, cans, peels. Note: aluminum foil does not burn.

Keep soap, detergents, and pollutants out of lakes and streams. Do not wash dishes in lakes and streams.

Leave dogs at home. They disturb both others and wildlife.

Do not cut switchbacks on trails.

Do not smoke when hiking.

Give pack and saddle animals the right of way on trails; step downhill and stay still.

Do not collect plant or animal specimens without written authorization from land management agencies. No extraction of natural materials is allowed in national parks.

A Washington State fishing license is required for all persons over 16 yrs of age.

Motorized equipment of any sort is prohibited in wilderness areas as well as on many other trails.

Wilderness permits are required in the Glacier Peak Wilderness Area. These can be obtained in person at ranger stations, by mail, or by telephone arrangement. Otherwise campfire permits are not needed in national forests, but cars and packtrains are subject to special requirements if camping outside of a designated campground. During periods of extreme fire hazard, be prepared for special restrictions or forest closures.

Leave valuables at home. Empty cars are less attractive to theives. Unfortunately, prospecting by delinquents is a problem protective agencies have not been able to pace.

Report loss or injured persons to the nearest Forest Service station or to the County Sheriff.

Rock climbers should focus on the use of nondestructive protection to keep cliffs and mountain walls from suffering scarring. Priorities should begin with natural features, employing protection in the most natural and hammerless form feasible. Attempt to use slings over horns or natural chockstones, or tree runners (but examine brush for reliability), and chocks (nuts). To properly utilize natural protection carry many runners as links to the climbing rope.

Piton damage has reformed our philosophy of style. Yet conventional piton protection is sometimes within the realm of the best judgement, and continues to be useful on difficult aid, as fixed anchors, and in explorative climbing. The realities of the particular situation should be avaluated. The rope leader should maintain the integrity of an established route by refraining from using protection that is more damaging than originally used. The party should retreat if they find established protection and previous usages beyond their limit. Since bolts directly affect the entire climbing community, they should be used only if no alternatives exist, as a last resort that only the most experienced climbers should consider.

WILDERNESS TRAVEL

"The alder stems, about two inches thick, form a dense jungle, and as they grow parallel to the ground, owing to having been pressed down by snow when young, you must continually keep scrambling over a selection of them, and at the same time bend low enough to get under the next branch above: not being able to get your foot to the ground, you slip on the branches, and, do what you can, often tumble over in a helpless manner.

"Things are slightly better when your course is down a declevity parallel with the direction of the branches, for then you slide along gaily, checking your speed by hanging from the branches as they pass."

REV. W. SPOTSWOOD GREEN, 1889

source

Rev. W. Spotswood Green, "Explorations in the Glacier Regions of the Selkirk Range, British Columbia, in 1888." *Proceedings of the Royal Geographic Society*, March 1889. p. 165.

The Cascade Range can be savage in its elemental ruggedness. Though man has destroyed part of the integrity of this environment, the North Cascades are still an awesome experience, a complex of life and land developed over eons into a unique grandeur, which, despite all the maps, information, and photography in this guidebook, are bound to remain full of surprise. Pleasantry will prevail, but at their worst these mountains can be a brutal, treacherous paradise. No amount of words can substitute for good mountaineering judgement. It is always wise to study routes and one's progress in relation to weather and remaining daylight. Mental conditioning can help one adapt to the unknown. The varied character of climbing conditions in the Cascades tends to limit specialization, though skills are always valuable for technical situations. Physical condition is a vital factor in keeping a wide reserve of strength. A rapid weather change can turn a pleasant outing into a disaster.

Wear sturdy boots with lug soles and heavy duty wool socks. Take a wool hat and wool gloves. Do not hike in tennis shoes. Bright clothing is useful if one is lost. Keep a reserve of wool clothing and a rain parka in your rucksack.

On talus and moraine slopes watch for precarious boulders. Low and medium altitude rock frequently is covered with grass and moss, making climbing uniquely exasperating. When this cover is moist, simple technical problems can become very dangerous. Cascade rock tends to have much more lichen than ranges in continental climates.

When crossing snow gullies and snowfields, one danger is not always apparent: watch for thin surface snow that can readily break through, commonly at locations where running water beneath the snow has created a space for locally warmer air, and therefore invisible melting from beneath.

The diverse maintained trail system and other hiker paths follow heavily forested river valleys, cross mountain slopes, and traverse subalpine ridges and basins; many trails are not snow-free until July. While in early summer fallen trees, avalanche litter, and high water tend to make trail hiking more of a problem, in some years meadows may be deep in snow until August; upper valley routes may lead over the debris of massive avalanching. Although many foot bridges have been built for stream crossings, high water may wash out these and natural foot logs. The high water period occurs in May and June, but intense fall and winter rainstorms can create high runoff. When streams become murky torrents, and it is necessary to ford, bear in mind that where the river is swiftest and broadest it is also shallowest. It may be useful to recall a practice of the Chilkat Indians, as observed by Seton-Karr: in crossing they held onto a long pole in parties of five or six, the strongest man upstream to break the water's force. Indians seem to have preferred wading to fighting dense bush.

The North Cascades receive the full force of westerlies which are responsible for ice—and the impenetrable jungles of rain forest in such valleys as the Sultan, Sauk, Suiattle, and Cascade Rivers. Even in relatively clear forests prostrate tree trunks lie beneath living trees. Some persons obtain a sadistic joy in approaching the peaks without trail, but slide alder is difficult to traverse, for the weight and creep of snow mat the boughs downhill, and tracts of scrub Alaska cedar with drooping branches and second growth areas can be equally vexing. Rev. William Spotswood Green spoke of devil's club: ". . . whose thorns, if they penetrate the flesh, produce festering sores. . . . Picture yourself, then, with a 40-pound pack on your back, creeping along a slippery, fallen trunk, fending off the devil's club with an ice axe, wriggling under fallen trees, or eight feet from the ground on top of them, and you will have some idea of what travel in the Selkirks means."[17] Typical also of the North Cascades, such travel is bad enough in dry daytime conditions, but must worse when wet, and nearly impossible at night. If a valley route is brushy, consider using talus and alluvial fans on the flanks. Dense brush in creek bottoms often makes it advisable to gain altitude to ridges, then connect up high. Often on faint trails old blazes can be found: look for axe scars and for branch cuts between trees. (However do not blaze, tag, or flag cross-country routes; remove any such existing markers. Develop your own routefinding skills and do not spoil the unmarked wilderness.) Near timberline, old miner and sheepherder trails can often be located.

The larger animals are seldom a problem, but it is interesting that the Tlingit Indians say a bear runs down a mountain, never up, when it sees a man.

SELECTED REFERENCES

The following material gives helpful background for the region covered in this volume; other references of localized value will be noted in the copy.

Atkeson, Ray. *Northwest Heritage: The Cascade Range.* Portland, 1969.

Ayres, H.B. "The Washington Forest Reserve," *19th Annual Report U.S. Geological Survey, 1897-1898,* pt. 5, pp. 283-313.

Crowder, D.F. and Tabor, R.W. *Routes and Rocks: Hiker's Guide to the North Cascades from Glacier Peak to Lake Chelan.* Seattle, 1965.

Easterbrook, Don J. and Rahm, David A. *Landforms of Washington.* Bellingham, 1970.

English, Edith Hardin. "Plant Life of the Area Surrounding Glacier Peak," *Mountaineer*, 1958, pp. 28-39.

Hodges, L.K. *Mining in the Pacific Northwest.* Seattle, 1897.

Lyman, W.D. *The Columbia River.* Portland, 1963.

Manning, Harvey and Spring, Ira. *101 Hikes in the North Cascades.* Seattle.

Manning, Harvey H. *Wild Cascades: Forgotten Parkland.* San Francisco, 1965.

Marshall, Louise B. *High Trails, Guide to the Pacific Crest Trail in Washington.* Lynnwood, 1973.

McKee, Bates. *Cascadia: The Geologic Evolution of the Pacific Northwest.* New York, 1972.

Miller, Tom. *The North Cascades.* Seattle, 1964.

Patty, E.N. "The Metal Mines of Washington," *Washington Geologic Survey Bulletin 23*, (1921) pp. 279-289.

Post, Austin, et al. "Inventory of Glaciers in the North Cascades, Washington" *Geological Survey Professional Paper 705-A.* Washington, 1971.

Prater, Gene. *Snow Trails: Ski and Snowshoe Routes in the Cascades.* Seattle.

Sterling, E.M. *Trips and Trails, 1.* Seattle.

The American Alpine Journal. New York.

The Living Wilderness. Washington. Vol. 1, no. 1; vol. 16, no. 39; vol. 23, no. 26; vol. 24; vol. 39; vol. 70; vol. 74.

The Mazama. Portland.

The Mountaineer. Seattle.

National Geographic Magazine. Washington. March 1961.

National Parks Magazine. Washington. Vol. 30 (June 1956), pp. 125-170.

Off Belay. Renton.

Sierra Club Bulletin. San Francisco. Vol. 41, no. 12 (December 1956); vol. 42, no. 6 (June 1957).

Summit. Big Bear Lake. December 1962, pp. 8-11.

NOTES

[1]Stephen C. Porter, "Quaternary Glaciation in the Southern Part of the North Cascade Range," *Geol. Soc. America Bull.* (1975), p. 113 (preliminary paging). A study transect in the southern North Cascades shows a distinct northwesterly trending lineament of both valleys and ridges.

[2]*Ibid*, p. 114. Cirque floors near the western range front stand as low as 1000 m (3281′) whereas those at easterly limits of glaciation average at 1800 m (5900′). This corresponds to a similar range in mean altitudes for existing glaciers in the area studied, though the glaciers are about 500 m (1640′) higher. The study showed a concentration of NE distribution of cirques. Cirque orientation is affected by insolation factors, the effect of which is more pronounced with increasing altitude (p. 113).

[3]Porter, *op. cit.*, p. 42. The earliest references to Pleistocene glaciation in the North Cascades were published in the pioneer geologic studies by Russell (1898), Willis (1903), and Smith and Calkins (1906). Though they recognized evidence of glaciation, the extent of former valley glaciers was not accurately determined.

[4]Most detailed and some general characteristics of these glacial episodes remain unknown. Regional orographic snowlines during the maximum Late Pleistocene glaciation were probably at least 3000 feet lower than the present snowline. Cascade glacial advances were separated by intervening nonglacial periods. Geologic evidence of multiple glaciations in the higher portions of the range is varied and abundant. Glacial intervals are represented in the Cascades by Pleistocene drifts and Neoglacial drift. The older drifts represent major glaciations of the range prior to the Late Pleistocene. The drift deposit represents a depositional record associated with a succession of cirque and valley glaciers. Glaciated regions in the middle North Cascades have looped moraines on valley floors and a distinct upper limit of glacial drift on valley sides.

According to an estimate, alpine glaciers from the Cascades reached their maximum positions around 18,000 to 19,000 yrs ago, well before the culminating advance of the Puget Lobe in Western Washington (J.E. Armstrong, D.R. Crandell, D.J. Easterbrook, and J.B. Noble, "Late Pleistocene Stratigraphy and Chronology in Southwestern British Columbia and Northwestern Washington," *Geol. Soc. America Bull* 76 (1965): 321-330; see fig. 2).

[5]Don J. Easterbrook and Barbara Spross Hansen, "Stratigraphy and Palynology of Late Quaternary Sediments in Puget Lowland, Washington," *Geol. Soc. America Bull.* 85 (1974): 599.

[6]Porter, *op. cit.* Local alpine glaciers in the Coast Ranges and Interior Ranges and Rocky Mountains of British Columbia coalesced on high plateaus of the interior to form the central reservoir for the Cordilleran Ice Sheet.

Outlet glaciers discharged W along valleys transecting the Cascade Range and S along each side of the range, thereby invading the Puget and Okanogan lowlands (Dwight R. Crandell, "The Glacial History of Western Washington and Oregon," in Wright, H.E., Jr., and Frey, D.G., (eds.), *The Quaternary of the United States*, Princeton, N.J., 1965, pp. 341-353).

Many drift sheets record at least four advances of this ice sheet down the Puget lowlands. Striations show this ice sheet flowed generally S into the North Cascades (Richard B. Waitt, Jr., "Geomorphology and Glacial Geology of the Methow Drainage Basin, Eastern North Cascade Range, Washington," Ph.D. diss., Univ. of Washington, p. 5, citing R.W. Brock, 1902 and H.M.A. Rice, 1947). Although the greatest flux of Fraser (Late Wisconsin) cordilleran ice was in the lowlands, Cascade peaks were buried to an altitude of 8000 ft along the 49° parallel by the incursion of ice (Reginald A. Daly, "Geology of the North American Cordillera at the Forty-Ninth Parallel," *Canada Geol. Survey, Memoir 38,* pt. 2, Ottawa, 1912, p. 594). Alpine ice apparently then reached a maximum stand and began to retreat (Mackin, Crandell).

[7]Porter, *op. cit.*, p. 123. During this period floors of ice-free cirques in the southern North Cascades indicated nearly ice-free conditions by 6700 yrs ago. During this interval prior to Neoglacial ice advance there was a substantial rise in timberlines (implying milder climate); p. 121. Most of the Cascade crest was probably deglaciated and only a few small residual ice bodies persisted on the highest summits and the most sheltered cirques.

[8]Stephen C. Porter and George H. Denton, "Chronology of Neoglaciation in the North American Cordillera," *Amer. Jour. of Science* 265, no. 3 (1967): 202.

[9]Fresh rubbly sharp-crested moraines fronting existing glaciers extend beyond modern terminii. Such deposits also are found in cirques now devoid of glacier ice but lying at altitudes equal to or only slightly lower than nearby glaciers. This Neoglacial drift lacks extensive vegetation cover and shows its comparative recency.

[10]Austin Post, et al., "Inventory of Glaciers in the North Cascades, Washington," *U.S. Geol. Survey Prof. Paper 705-A* (Washington, 1971), p. A 1.

[11]The Olympic Mountains exert significant rain shadow effects. The wettest portion of the North Cascades are foothills and range front E of Everett (Lowell A. Rasmussen and Wendell V. Tangborn, "Hydrology of the North Cascades, Washington: Part I. Runoff, Precipitation, and Storage Characteristics," U.S. Geological Survey, Tacoma, 1975, p. 5 and fig. 3). The Sultan River drainage basin with a mean altitude of 890 m (2920′) has an average annual runoff of 3700 mm (averaged over the drainage basin)—the highest streamflow gaging (*ibid*). The most logical explanation is that this area catches the full sweep of the prevailing storm track in winter. However, neither precipitation nor runoff show a consistent relationship with altitude.

The Verlot area appears to be a location of unusual runoff in a region of comparably high runoff (p. 8). Verlot and Silverton record higher mean totals than other stations at comparable altitudes (more than valleys N and S such as the Snoqualmie, Skykomish, Sauk, Skagit, and Nooksack). Verlot shows a mean annual of 3420 mm (134.6″) and Silverton 3110 mm (122.4″), the highest of 37 stations (p. 23). That summer precipitation at the latitude of the Skykomish, Sultan, and South Fork Stillaguamish is higher than farther N is substantiated by another study (*Atlas, op. cit.*). Forest Service records compiled in the 1930s and 1940s showed 50 percent more precipitation in the South Fork than North Fork Stillaguamish valley (Darrington 80″, Verlot 120″).

[12]In summer the weaker storm systems do not penetrate the Cascade Range as deeply as in winter, so the seasonal distribution on the E side is even less (Rasmussen and Tangborn, *op. cit.*, p. 7, 19).

[13]Incomplete measurements give 170 in. annual precipitation for the Glacier Peak area; other studies show lower figures (Verlot, 1946, 144″; Monte Cristo, 7 yrs, 118″; Index, 12 yrs, 94″). An 1897 study by Martin Gorman may be relevant: an average snow depth of 60 in. at Stehekin increased to 96 in. at Bridge Creek (15 mi. nearer the divide); he estimated the area of Cascade Pass receives 150 in. mean annual precipitation. A recent study indicates the W slope of the North Cascades has 210 days of annual precipitation, but on the E slope there are less than 100 days (James F. Lahey, "Climates," in Richard M. Highsmith, Jr., ed., *Atlas of the Pacific Northwest*, Corvallis, 5th ed., 1973, p. 44). But more summer rainfall occurs in the North Cascades than in the southern portion because of different flow patterns of air. Spring windflow from the ocean is similar to that of winter, so the general pattern of spring precipitation is similar; but the mountains receive less total than in winter (50-70 percent) (*ibid*, p. 43).

[14]Autumn precipitation shows a marked increase over summer totals on windward slopes. Snowfall is frequently in excess of 300 in. annually and on certain occasions it exceeds 1000 in. annually (*ibid*).

[15]August is generally the warmest month in the mountains and January the coldest. Radiant solar input is greater on the E slope of the range, and here in the lee of the mountain pockets of nighttime radiational cooling tend to form. At the higher altitudes of the range there are fewer than 30 days of above-freezing daytime temperatures (*ibid*). Temperature means during a 1-yr recording at Monte Cristo showed a February average of 32°F. and an August average of 63°F. Winter cloudiness in the Cascades keeps average maximum temperatures uniform.

[16]Gibbs, *op. cit.*, p. 486; see Section I, footnote 46.

[17]Rev. W. Spotswood Green, "Explorations in the Glacier Regions of the Selkirk Range, British Columbia, in 1888," in *Proceedings of the Royal Geographic Society*, March 1889, p. 165.

SECTION I

West Side of Cascade Crest

STEVENS PASS AND SKYKOMISH RIVER TO SUIATTLE RIVER

"That the mountains of the Northwest will win world-wide renown for the beauty and interest of their glaciers, as well as for the magnificence of their scenery, is predicted by all who have scaled their dizzy heights."

PROF. I.C. RUSSELL, 1884

source

Russell, I.C., "Existing Glaciers of the United States" *5th Annual Report*, U.S. Geological Survey (1883-4), p. 341

This region of the Cascades, so dramatic from the Puget Sound Basin, is a complex intermingling of sharp-crested alpine peaks, ice-scoured cirques, glaciers both prominent and hidden, and the full complement of rich W-side forest and vegetation. Verdant meadow slopes, timberline conifers, rocky plunging glacial canyons, tarns, and frothy waterfalls add to the superlative natural setting. This is a landscape of natural contrasts, characterized everywhere by rugged alpine topography and deep drainage dissection which has evolved largely through the erosional activity of formerly extensive glaciers. Topography attributable to glacial erosion is characteristic of the entire transect W of the Cascade divide—a span of 30 to 40 mi. Within this region streams head in well-formed and snow-filled cirques that descend into deeper and wider trunk valleys having generally parabolic cross-profiles. Valley walls typically are smooth and abraded where ice-eroded, but higher nonglaciated crests often display rugged relief and evidence of frost shattering. The region truly sustains the great local relief and a quality of alpine landscape associated with the North Cascades. Relief remains high to the range front. Gently sloping glacial valleys have long tracts, deep into the range: the floor of the North Fork of the Sauk stands at an altitude of 2000 ft only 7½ mi. from the drainage divide; the North Fork Skykomish and the Suiattle exhibit similar statistics. Partly because of the vast forest mantle, the area's complex geology is hard to decipher. The principal lithologies include the granitic rocks of the Snoqualmie Batholith, quartzites, schists, slates, cherts, phyllite, gneiss and peridotite.

One of the great stratovolcanoes of the Cascades, ice-clad Glacier Peak, rises to its reigning height just W of the Cascade crest. Sloan Peak dominates the "Monte Cristo" subrange of extremely rugged peaks, as Whitehorse and Three Fingers stand supreme near Darrington, while along the Sauk River Pugh and White Chuck rise as lonely sentinels. In addition to these outstanding peaks there are dense concentrations of serrate crests and alpine peaks whose modest 5500 to 6500-ft altitudes belie their true porportions because of great local relief. The highly distinctive character of each peak, and their wholly different attitudes from each exposure are remarkable. These striking landforms are produced by the interaction of Pacific winds, ice, and geologic forces. The peaks of the seaward slope have been sculptured from highly metamorphosed sediments and are varied in rich tints. Free action of natural forces are reflected in warm tones of the landscape, with an almost dramatic contrast with the grey of the E-side slopes. The glare of the midday sun reduces the shadows and conceals the relief and grandeur of this rugged land; at the middle altitudes the harsh outlines are softened in contour and varied in color by the forests. But as I.C. Russell pointed out, "in the early morning light and at sunset the slanting light brings out mountain range after mountain range in bold relief."[1]

Moving inland to the Cascade mountain slope, the flat topography of the Puget Sound Basin changes to gradually rising, heavily wooded evergreen foothills which reach to timberline within as little as 17 mi. of tidewater. The flanking parade of gently outlined foothills assume a rugged character increasing on nearing the axis of the range. There are subordinate ranges—small orographic units—usually defined on the principle of continuity of crests. Nowhere in the Cascades are the waves of rugged and angular precipices that rise to narrow crests more apparent than on the seaward flank of this region. Even-crested ridges, so prevalent in the North Cascades (both above and below timberline) probably are caused by timberline inhibiting erosion of alpine crests sharply at certain levels. Accordant ridges (such as Lime Ridge, Meadow Mountain, and Cady Ridge) with only low summits and shallow cols are ridges truncated by headward expansion of alp slopes; the same accordance is present as a belt of alp slopes on faces of higher peaks in more rugged areas; here alp slopes are closely overshadowed by spectacularly youthful alpine crests. Such alp slopes were subject to strong undercutting by Pleistocene glaciers and have maintained themselves by constant surface renewal and headward migration at the expense of high ridges above.

One of the most distinctive features of the North Cascades is the widespread evidence of past and present glacier activity. Glaciation is an impressive process in the regional landscape evolution. Neighboring glaciated valleys generally are separated by serrate ridges. These associated landforms constitute evidence of a formerly extensive alpine style glaciation. The recent work of ice not only is apparent in sharp aretes and Matterhorn peak forms, but in moraines and outwash beds, and in the complicated derangement of drainage patterns.

Pleistocene glaciation seems to have been universal here, producing numerous small cirques with floors at alp slope levels and ice-gouged alpine lakes. In areas underlain by granitic and volcanic rocks, cirques commonly have distinct bedrock depressions that impound tarns. The entire region is noted for attractive alpine and subalpine lakes such as Goat, Blanca, Silver, Crater, Copper, Byrne, Twin, and the Lime-Rivord group, which fill cirques and troughs of vanished glaciers. The evidence points strongly to the conclusion that glaciation and mass-wasting have been primary processes in forming the moderated alp slopes. Post-glacial modification is topographically expressed by gullying, mass-wasting, and stream erosion. Wild rivers and streams are everywhere ceaselessly attacking this primitive region. Many cirque basins that formerly contained small residual valley and cirque glaciers are now devoid of ice and show no indication of having regenerated glaciers after post-glacial interlude.

Today's largest glaciers mantle Glacier Peak and the highland S. Other peaks hosting significant ice are Sloan, Columbia, Kyes, Cadet, Three Fingers, and Whitehorse.[2]

The natural boundaries of this section are relatively obvious: the valley of the W-flowing lower Skagit River separates it from the Skagit Ranges on the N, and the Skykomish River, in a smaller but equally well defined trench, provides demarcation on the S; the Sauk-Suiattle system to Suiattle Pass is herein an arbitrary division for convenience.

The boundary of the North Cascades can be defined largely on a geologic basis, for their rocks are primarly crystalline-intrusive granites and a large spectrum of metamorphic types. S of Snoqualmie Pass are younger sedimentary and volcanic rocks, giving support for the consensus view that here is where the North Cascades begin. But the boundary between the two geologic provinces can as logically be said to lie near the latitude of Stevens Pass. N of the Skykomish River, Stevens Pass, and Wenatchee River is a distinct geologic province—the boundary being a rough diagonal from latitude 48° N on the W side of 47°20′ on the E side of the range.

For example, when entering the trench of the Skykomish River from the W, one immediately notices the landscape to the N is generally more striking and rugged. The most prominent feature is the high mountain mass between the N and S forks, culminating in Gunn Peak and Mt. Baring. E and N of Gunn lies a steep bold series of ridges; the higher peaks are Merchant and Spire. Near the sources of both Skykomish forks are glacial cirques, often containing small rock-rimmed lakes surrounded by talus slopes.

Farther N, bordering the Stillaguamish and Sauk Rivers, the mountain architecture becomes even more climactic. The Monte Cristo-Big Four area encompasses wide glaciated basins near the center of a cluster of high peaks a few miles W of the Cascade divide. Confluent valley troughs tend to isolate subranges and massifs. Smaller troughs typically "hang" several hundred to over 2000 ft above the floor of the larger troughs. In this important subrange summit altitudes approach 6000 ft near Silverton and in a W-E progression rise to nearly 7800 ft at Sloan Peak. Dramatic local relief, from 4000 to 5500 ft, is the rule. Josiah E. Spurr, pioneer geologist, commented, "The valleys are narrow and deep, the slopes of the mountains so steep as often to appear inaccessible, and the higher mountains contain fields of perpetual snow and small glaciers."[3]

Most of the W side up to 5000 ft is heavily forested. Exceptions include natural snow or ice accumulation areas, recurring avalanche swaths, recently glaciated areas, steep low cirque walls and their associated talus, and low altitude rock exposures. Near creek bottoms an evergreen forest cover and ground moisture support a luxuriant growth of underbrush; a dense tangle of red alder, dwarf willow, vine maple, crab apple, black cottonwood, ferns, and devil's club with its broad, tropical-appearing leaves opposes travel. Thick evergreen avalanche scrub is common in disturbed locations; open slopes below about 3500 ft feature vine maple, a large flexible shrub, and spindly relative of the bigleaf maple. Heavy protective vegetal cover tends to restrict erosion and enhance development of powerful soil horizons. Mosses and ferns act as a forest carpet (studies have shown that the zone of maximum organic surface accumulation occurs between 4000 and 4500 ft in the western Cascades). Burned or logged areas support thick underbrush of salmonberry, blackberry, and huckleberry.

The size and diversity of the evergreen forests compare with that of the Coast Mountains of southern British Columbia. In virgin stands, great first tower in closed ranks, mingled with thick stands of giant, massive western red cedars often 25 to 30 ft in circumference near the ground, tapering rapidly from deeply fluted buttressed bases to spire-like points. Below about 3500 ft Douglas fir, western hemlock, noble fir, and western red cedar become the principal tree species. Mountain vegetation zones have long been described as related to latitude, and in the Cascades the Canadian zone is generally considered to range from 3000 to 5000 ft.[4] Here the subalpine fir is well represented, but Englemann spruce does not follow into the maritime climate; other dominants are mountain hemlock, Pacific silver fir, and Alaska cedar.

The alpine zone (Hudsonian), which includes those areas lying above timberline, in this sector of the range extends to about 6000 ft. The stunted species (usually alpine fir, mountain hemlock, and whitebark pine) predominate in very sparse cover characterized by discontinuous patches of trees. Here ground flora decreases in density with heather prevailing between alpine groves. At higher altitudes the trunks become more defective and twisted, the growth shorter and more branched. Near the limits of existence, isolated miniatures are found rooting among rocks, resisting the burden of snow and frequent storms. Shrubs and heather may form extensive mats among a variety of herbaceous plants.

In this zone are the lightly plant-covered expanses of alpine parks, with their dazzling floral displays. Some entire ridges, such as Meadow Mountain and Meander Meadow, are bedecked with dwarf lupine, phlox, anemone, fleabane, valerian, paintbrush, penstemon, and gold lily masses, and in summer attract intense bee and hummingbird activity.

The region still abounds with wildlife, despite all the human activity, and the mountain goat finds a habitat among high crags. Fortunately for its preservation poor access in the back country did not encourage recreational use of most of this section. In the 1930s the Glacier Peak Wilderness was outlined to include approximately 600,000 acres, but reduced a decade later. Although its 458,505-acre area is now more secure through legislation, truly unique areas still cry for inclusion. The wilderness was not set aside to preserve a single feature, but to insure the grandeur of forest and meadows contrasting with snow and ice of Glacier Peak.

In the Cascade Range climatic and topographic contrasts are reflected as extremes in natural hydrologic conditions. Much of the medium and high altitude precipitation falls as snow, and this has a significant bearing on the spring runoff pattern and on the drainage from perennial snow and glacier ice. Most mountain rivers discharge peak loads in late May and in June, and during the wet season in foothills, some rivers also record a November-December maximum. George Gibbs, one of the earliest explorers to study the natural features in the range, wrote in 1854 that rivers entering Puget Sound "swell greatly during heavy rains, or the melting of snow in the Cascades."[5] Meltwater from the snowpack and glaciers helps maintain a continual summer streamflow from the alpine regions and provides a reliable water supply for man's use.

The larger rivers in this section rise in the axial highlands or high western subranges of the Cascades to flow westward, issuing into Puget Sound. The NW trend of some rivers is due to established courses during Oligocene time which were controlled by a series of NW-trending ridges. As the Cascades were uplifted, rivers kept to pre-established courses and only the pattern of smaller tributaries is the result of more recent mountain building effort.

Characteristic of a well integrated drainage system in this region, the Skykomish River and its tributaries have deeply dissected an area, leaving an axial valley with steep slopes. At the confluence of the N and S forks, it is apparent that the N is equally the main river, but the other usually has been so considered and called the Skykomish without qualification, perhaps only because it was the more settled and traveled. The tributary Rapid River is really the main course of the S fork, but the name has not been attached to the whole stream. The Rapid takes the name Beckler and then joins the Tye to become the S fork. W of Index, glacial material, deposited in the mouth of the valley by the Puget Lobe, assumes considerable thickness and through this the river has re-excavated its channel to the present level. Along the lower river slopes evidence of Pleistocene glacial drift is seen up to 1000 ft above the valley bottom. Terrace remnants form a prominent bench above the river. Farther W the valley broadens into alluvial plains near Puget Sound.

The Suiattle and Sauk Rivers, joining to flow into the Skagit, are the major drainage courses in this section. The peculiarities of these axial valleys is that, instead of being at right angles to the main watershed, they form a confluence at an acute angle. Curiously the Sauk is now separated from the North Fork of the Stillaguamish at Darrington by only a 2-mi. flat, where once it had channelled its course. The Sauk once flowed W to Puget Sound, but abandoned its course because deeper channels were carved to the north by a Pleistocene glacier.[6] The northerly course of the Sauk is anomalous since it passes through a narrower valley. Ice from the N and W also reached into Squire Creek to produce spectacular scouring.

Glaciation formed other interesting drainage changes. Evidence supports the post-glacial drainage reversal of the Suiattle River system to the Skagit from a presumably earlier western course. The divide between the Skagit and present Suiattle was lowered by glaciers moving S and by continued stream erosion.

It is remarkable that the headwaters of both forks of the Stillaguamish are blocked off by low divides from the course of the Sauk. A peculiar and anomalous condition of the South Fork Stillaguamish valley exists in relation to the present position of Barlow Pass. The wider Stillaguamish trench continues E, across the low pass, occupied here by the NW-flowing South Fork of the Sauk. The orographic features of the upper Sauk are of importance, for the widest valley here is the Stillaguamish. This argues for original western outflow through Barlow Pass, from a large valley glacier during the Pleistocene.[7]

The Sauk has a remarkable course. Its N fork sources on the Cascade crest, but that tributary known as Cadet Creek could equally be considered the head. In its course it collects tributaries from both sides, the principal one being the S fork. The merged river trends NW for a distance, and in this portion of its course is joined by the White Chuck River from the E, and then continuing past Darrington comes so close to the head of the North Fork of the Stillaguamish that a portage was formerly made here. The Sauk then is joined by the Suiattle on its course to the Skagit River. The Sauk is a clear green river; the Suiattle and White Chuck are muddy colored from glacial silt and mud from deposits on Glacier Peak. A large local radial drainage pattern has developed around Glacier Peak. The Suiattle begins by running E of N, separated by Glacier Peak from the White Chuck, which has its headwaters on the volcano's W flanks. The Suiattle then curves W, with little trend N, and is joined by many tributaries from both sides before its flow meets the Sauk.

The principal valleys are an erosional feature of the Cascade Range that came into present form and evolved by successive stages in consequence of certain epochal events in orogenic history and in the glaciation of the range. The form of the major depressions was produced by earlier alpine glaciation, as indicated by the deep trough valleys. Immense alpine glaciers once carved their pathways W into the lowlands, invading river valleys and eroding over spurs and curves; the viscous ice tended to truncate features and leave steep triangular cliffs, the final result being valley straightening. Hanging side valleys are characteristic accessory features of deeply glaciated main streams. W-side valleys tend to be deeper than those on the E side, except Lake Chelan, and streams generally more turbid with glacial silt. Valley tracts extend far into the range.

During Pleistocene glacial succession the Puget Lobe advanced into the Puget Lowland at least four times. Alpine trunk glaciers expanded and united at lower extremities to assist in the formation of a large piedmont glacier which occupied Puget Sound.[8] Probably whenever full glacial conditions in British Columbia led to the development and advance of a major ice lobe in Western Washington concomitant glaciers existed in the adjacent North Cascades. By the time the Puget Lobe had reached its maximum extent W of the Cascades between 15,000 and 13,500 yrs ago, alpine glaciers had receded from lower valleys or had disappeared.[9] Sublobes of the ice sheet pushed into the lower ends of W-draining Cascade valleys, blocking drainage and depositing thick accumulations of drift.[10] The lateral continuity of morainal embankment deposits which block the lower ends of the principal valleys indicates that long lakes were ponded by the Puget Lobe in Cascade valleys which had been occupied before by alpine glaciers.[11] Morainal blockades occurred in each valley between the Nisqually and South Fork Stillaguamish valleys. Extensive lakebeds occupy the major valleys at lower elevations. When the Puget Lobe reached a maximum about 14,000 yrs ago the lake in the Skykomish valley was at 1800 ft altitude; prominent benches formed by lake fill remnants are visible.

Ice played an important part in developing the present topographic features of the smaller but equally well defined trench of the Sultan River. The U-shaped valley of the upper S fork is carved in quartz diorite. Four tributary streams—the N and S forks, Elk Creek and Williamson Creek—converge to form the main trunk in lower Sultan Basin. Here the valley floor is relatively broad in contrast to the narrow tributaries. At the lower end of the valley the river leaves the basin and plunges abruptly into a constricted canyon toward a confluence with the Skykomish River.

Evidence indicates that prior to invasion of the Puget Sound ice sheet glaciers moved down the forks of the Sultan, coalesced in the lower basin, and pushed westward through the present valley of the Pilchuck.[12] A deposit of glacial debris forms the low gravel ridge separating the Sultan and Pilchuck watersheds, a terminal moraine remnant of the ice front which thrust up the Pilchuck River valley and impounded the waters of the Sultan as a lake.[13] This glacial lake drained westward when the ice lobe forced a new channel flow. Erosive action by meltwater which flowed along the ice-marginal course eventually drained the lake and the postglacial Sultan River breached the delta moraine to establish this as the permanent outlet of Sultan Basin.[14]

Puget Sound ice also moved up other valleys; ice pushed inland as much as 7 mi. above the mouth of White Chuck River.[15]

Various modern glaciers exist W of the Cascade divide, the largest concentration W of Glacier Peak centering near Monte Cristo. Within the drainage basins of Glacier Creek, Cadet Creek, Elliott Creek, North Fork Sauk River and North Fork Skykomish River there are 27 glaciers covering some 5.7 km². A northwestern group of five small glaciers is concentrated between Whitehorse Mountain and Three Fingers along a N-S oriented subrange. The glaciers lie within an altitude range of 1370 m (4495′) to 2040 m (6693′) and have a mean altitude of about 1767 m (5798′).

The nebulous story of the North Cascades extends back more than 500 million yrs; the earlier chapters are still obscure. During the Late Paleozoic and much of the Mesozoic ancient marine sediments and volcanic rocks accumulated on the sea floor. During Cretaceous time there were vast changes, with uplift, faulting, and severe folding, so that these rocks were strongly deformed. W of the Straight Creek Fault they were involved in major overthrusts—the Shuksan and Church Mountain thrusts.[16] E of the Straight Creek Fault they were metamorphosed to schist and gneiss and intruded by igneous rocks of quartz dioritic composition.

In early Cenozoic time, after a major episode of uplift forming a mountain range and its destruction by erosion, sandstone, shale, and conglomerates of the Swauk formation were deposited across these older rocks. These sediments were folded and intruded by Cenozoic granodiorites and are now preserved only in a narrow belt extending from south of Skykomish to W of Darrington (J.A. Vance, personal commun.). The pre-Tertiary sedimentary and metamorphic rocks of the North Cascades together with scattered occurrences of Tertiary sedimentary and volcanic rocks have been widely invaded by Tertiary plutons[17] ranging from about 50 to 15 million yrs in age and predominantly granodioritic in composition. Hot magma rising from depth intruded the existing rocks, then solidified as major plutons such as Chilliwack, Cloudy Pass, Index, and Snoqualmie batholiths and associated smaller intrusive bodies. Intense heating altered the pre-existing rocks adjacent to the plutons causing recrystallization and hardening. These contact metamorphic rocks are more resistant to erosion than the adjacent intrusive rocks and typically form a zone of high peaks surrounding the granitic plutons (Vance).

Prior to the uplift of the Cascades (probably within the last 6 million yrs) volcanic rocks, the surface equivalents of the intrusive batholithic rocks, were probably much more extensive in the North Cascades than they are now after erosion. In the late Pliocene or early Pleistocene there was a vast uparching of the range on a S-plunging N-S axis. Uplift and subsequent glaciation resulted in extensive erosion and produced the major drainage patterns seen today. Rock types in this section are diverse due to quite complex bedrock geology. Summits comprise many rock structures. Del

Campo, Gothic, Sheep Gap, and Sperry lie in a narrow belt of indurated, folded, and tilted plant-bearing early Tertiary sandstones and shales of the Paleocene Swauk formation which extends from Crested Buttes on the S through Helena and Devils Peak to Jumbo and Higgins on the N. The Swauk rocks occur as steep open folds, whose axes parallel the N-NW regional trends formed during moderately strong Eocene deformation.[18]

The oldest rocks in the Sultan Basin-Silver Creek area are several volcanic and sedimentary rock formations. These were then intruded by early Oligocene granodiorites of the Index batholith and related rocks. The area was extensively mineralized and has been heavily prospected. Mineralized deposits crop out in similar geologic environment of the Monte Cristo area.[19] The Big Four-area peaks are composed mainly of altered sedimentary rocks, while the N face of Vesper Peak is quartz diorite of the Copper Lake stock. Three Fingers consists of deformed slates and sandstones, while Whitehorse is slightly metamorphosed lava and slates (Vance, written commun., 1975). This subrange features a series of strongly folded andesitic volcanic and sedimentary rocks. The Gunn Peak series (W of the Straight Creek and Evergreen Faults) is an extensive thick group of low grade metamorphic rocks, largely sedimentary in origin. It resembles the old metamorphic series of Sultan Basin. These metamorphosed sedimentary rocks are overthrust by highly metamorphosed gneiss and amphibolite which form the ragged summit ridges of Gunn, Merchant, Baring, and Iron (Vance).[20]

Sloan and Bedal Peaks and the summit of Mt. Pugh lie E of the Straight Creek Fault and are of gneissose quartz diorite which has intruded schists and migmatites of the Skagit Suite. Foggy Peak, also of the Monte Cristo stock, is adjacent to the black phyllite of the Gemini Peaks. Cadet, Kyes, Monte Cristo, Columbia, and Wilmans Peaks consist of thick horizontal beds of volcanic breccia which separate the Monte Cristo and Grotto plutons. In the area of the North Fork of Sauk River schist and Skagit gneiss-type migmatites are interlayered. The pre-Tertiary central schist belt extends near the Cascade crest along Indian Pass, White Pass, and N; the rocks are predominantly garnet-graphite-mica schist. NW of Glacier Peak similar schists are found.

Barlow Pass volcanics (probably Eocene) are an exposed series of volcanic rocks (predominantly andesite), with sedimentary interbeds; they were folded in Oligocene time.[21] Examples are Sheep Mountain, Silver Tip, Twin, and Stillaquamish Peaks. These volcanic rocks are over a mile thick and unconformably overlie the Swauk formation, which itself rests unconformably on the older rocks.

N of the main mass of the Index batholith, the satellite Squire Creek stock invaded pre-Tertiary and Tertiary rocks.[22] Granite emplacement set the stage for later shearing and mineralization. Following emplacement of Index plutonic rocks (Early Oligocene), recurrent deformation produced a strong E-W joint pattern in the quartz diorite.[23]

Transverse structural belts, which appear to have controlled the sulfide distribution, cut the regional grain of the Cascade system. These belts (predominantly NE-trending) provide an environment for base metal deposition and pass through many Cascade mining districts (Grant, p. 39). The principal mining locations in the range have been made along the contacts of granitic intrusions in an E-W sheeting system (Grant). These belts are characterized by echelon shear and fracture systems transversely traceable across the range for distances up to 70 mi. (the Glacier Peak structural belt currently can be traced from Silver Creek into the Methow Valley).[24]

In the late Pleistocene, Glacier Peak developed, one of a number of solitary large andesite stratovolcanoes along the axis of the modern Cascades. Recent volcanics are limited to Glacier Peak and to prominent terraces of reworked volcanic ash in the Suiattle and White Chuck River valleys.

As much of the history relates and nomenclature signifies, the entire region is noted for its mineral wealth. It is not surprising that most of the trails were originated by miners, trails that sometimes defy belief. Many summits were named for mines or to honor miners and settlers (Del Campo, Pugh, Gunn); others were evolved for appearance (Three Fingers) and some for natural phenomena (Foggy). A few names are commemorative (Liberty, Columbia).

Prospecting began in the Skykomish River drainage. Elisha Hubbard cut a trail in 1882 from Index to Galena to begin the Silver Creek boom, which climaxed in 1890 at Galena and Mineral City. Prospectors traced the mineral belt across divides to the Sultan, Troublesome Creek, and the Sauk drainage. In summer 1889 adventurous prospectors explored access into the Sauk River drainage. Reports differ about the sighting of the "Monte Cristo" riches.[25] Soon a frenzy of miners came in by way of Poodle Dog Pass from the Skykomish (18 mi. from Index via the mining camps of Galena and Mineral City),[26] and via the "Wilmans

(Pioneer) Trail" from the Sauk. By fall 1891 this winding narrow wagon road was completed to Monte Cristo;[27] at Sauk City on the Skagit River provisions were transferred from stern-wheelers to wagons bound for Monte Cristo. Homesteads soon blossomed along the route, and such key trading posts as Orient, at the forks of the Sauk, arose; among settlers in the valley of the Sauk were criminals accused of land fraud and killings. Not until 1891 did the Monte Cristo miners learn they could enter the basin by the S fork of the Stillaguamish; a railroad engineer, J.Q. Barlow, on a reconnaissance W of the Sauk River noted a hillside spring flowing in the opposite direction, then traced its course.[28] Mining interests financed a wagon road from Hartford and also the narrow puncheon wagon road built between Barlow Pass and Goat Lake in spring 1896 by a force of 70 men; the latter went beyond the lakehead through the bottomland toward the Penn Mine camp.[29]

The history of Monte Cristo is full of interest to a generation which looks back on the days of mining excitement with a kind of wonder. Monte Cristo was the first live mining camp on the W slopes of the Cascades. By 1891 there were 13 mines and 40 claims; an 1893 map shows the district had 211 claims. The area had timber for building and ample water power for drilling. Eastern capital was necessary for an enterprise of magnitude. In 1891 John D. Rockefeller became interested in the area, and his syndicate through Colby and Hoyt took over the leading mines (including the Pride and Mystery), for which they paid the Wilmans brothers $470,000.[30] Mining engineers sent to examine the exploratory tunnels concluded tonnage would be many times railroad, mining, and smelter costs, and production promised to be one of the greatest lead-silver mines on the western hemisphere. Among schemes were plans for tunnels to Goat Lake and Sultan Basin, a railroad across to Silver Creek, and a wagon road to the Okanogan district.

In a short time $2.7 million in silver and gold was taken out. Most of the heavy galena ore was shipped from the Mystery, 89, and Pride of the Mountain mines, served by an elaborate 6600-ft cable-bucket aerial tramway over Mystery Ridge to the townsite. Some 230 tons of ore were carried daily from mine tunnels to the five-level concentrator at the townsite;[31] loaded buckets pulled the empties back uphill on an endless cable.[32] The system was quite simple, though physically staggering considering the times and the topography. Accidents occurred frequently, including falls into ore chutes, slips from cliffs, and mishaps from collapsing timbers, explosions, rifles, railroading, and avalanches.[33]

The townsite plat of Monte Cristo appeared in the form of a huge revolver (a shape symbolic of the times), pointing NW to the junction of Glacier and '76 Creeks. At the height of the boom in 1894 such establishments as the Blazing Stump, a combination saloon, gambling hall, and brothel likely had some magnetism for miners who hiked over Ida Pass from the Goat Lake area.[34] The town had a population of well over 1000, ruled by one M.T.J. Cummins, the "Count of Monte Cristo."[35] Pollution was perhaps the least of local concerns: a report in 1894 on the river concluded, "concentrator tailings have changed the dark green water to murky white."

The Monte Cristo mines employed men summer and winter; in August 1893 150 men were reported to be working. In 1895 the mines employed 125 men, with a monthly payroll of about $10,500;[36] in July 1896 employment rose to 200. An estimate was made that management spent $3.5 million, giving direct and indirect employment to 600 persons.

To transport ore a standard gauge railroad was built over the bull trail, 42 mi. from Hartford to Monte Cristo, at an estimated cost of $1.8 million, reaching the townsite by fall 1893.[37] Some of the heavy machinery for the mines and trams could not be brought in until railroad completion.[38] Eventually recurrent floods, which damaged the roadway and destroyed bridges, hindering shipping and affecting profits, plus heavy penalties at the smelter for metallic impurities, put an end to the boom, and in the early 1900s most of the miners followed the gold rush to Alaska.[39]

The largest "way town" along the railroad, Silverton, showed a typical life expectancy: in 1897 it had five saloons, six hotels, and a town band. When the railroad failed due to the autumn 1897 floods, the town quickly deteriorated.[40] There was a mini-boom in the Monte Cristo area in 1900, when the railroad was rebuilt and some gold but little silver mined. Despite vast repairs the trip generally took 12 to 14 hrs one way. The Everett & Monte Cristo Railroad was purchased by the Northern Pacific in 1902 and operated for 10 yrs; later the line became the Hartford Eastern. For some years a passenger service was run with gas cars. After 1933 the only access to Monte Cristo was by horseback or foot.[41]

There has been little mining activity since the gold rush ended in the early 1900s, and now a small resort stands on the patented mining land at Monte Cristo. A popular diversion for hikers is to visit some of the abandoned mines in Glacier Basin, on the Wilmans Spires, in '76 Gulch, and near Mineral City and Silverton. Galena, formerly the local base of mining supplies, is now deserted. In the less visited locations, one may still find many relics of an unrecorded history.

Interesting references to the area include L.K. Hodges, *Mining in the Pacific Northwest*, Seattle, 1897; Margaret D. Hargrove, "Monte Cristo Outing, 1918," *Mountaineer*, 1918, pp. 7-22 (also pp. 23-32); Rosemary Wilkie, *A Broad Ledge of Gold*, Seattle, 1958; Henry L. Gray, *The Gold of Monte Cristo*, Seattle, 1969; *The Coast*, June 1902; "An Account of Monte Cristo," *Off Belay*, August 1973, pp. 7-27; Josiah E. Spurr, "The Ore Deposits of Monte Cristo, Washington," *22nd Annual Report U.S. Geological Survey, 1900-1901*, pt. 2 (Washington, 1901) pp. 785-865; W.S. Thyng, "The Metalliferous Resources of Washington Except Iron," *Annual Report for 1901, Washington Geol. Survey*, pt. 2, pp. 63-82; *Mazama* 55, No. 3 (1973), pp. 63-65; John MacDonald Wilmans Papers, University of Washington Library; Monte Cristo Mining Co. Papers, University of Washington Library.

The Index district principally mined copper ore, with some silver. Most ledges are fissure veins cutting the fundamental granite.[42] The principal producing mines were the Ethel, Sunset, Wilbur Index, and Copper Bell.[43]

In the Sultan Basin prospecting began after 1874; small scale placer operators recovered some gold deposits from gravel along the lower Sultan River as early as 1869, and later rich placers were found in the basin. The first major discovery was in 1891, when the 45 vein was found, but development of the area was linked to growth of transportation facilities, which came slowly.[44] In 1896 the 45 Mine became the first producer in the basin. To maintain production the operators built a 20-mile puncheon-construction road to connect the mine with the railroad near Sultan. This road opened the basin to horse-drawn wagons; feeder roads and trails were built. A trail was built over Marble Pass to Silverton and in 1897 a two stage aerial tram was begun.[45]

Whitehorse Mountain became the center of prospecting activity near Darrington, with the Buckeye Basin having 20 claims located before 1900 (gold, copper, silver, lead); the Buckeye Ledge was named by pioneers for their home state, Ohio. Gold Mountain and the W side of Jumbo Mountain were the site of numerous claims.

Relatively little is known regarding Indian routes used in hunting and trading, but it is logical to assume there were primitive trails in the valleys of the Sauk, White Chuck, Suiattle, Stillaguamish, and Skykomish. An outline map drawn by George Gibbs (1860) shows an existing horse trail from the Skagit River to Lake Wenatchee, probably via the North Fork of Sauk River and Indian Pass.[46] The report from the Northern Pacific Railroad reconnaissance of 1867 indicated Indians traversing the Cascades "selected for their trails the ground least obstructed by timber without regard to its elevation, showing that the trails are unreliable as guides to the best Passes."[47] The Indians who assisted on the railroad survey in 1870 were familiar with the Sauk route (the party met Chief Sosomkin at the Skagit Indian camp to obtain men for canoeing). Indians tended to take their canoes upriver as far as feasible, then to connect with trails and horse travel from the east slope.

Gibbs mentioned a whole set of independent tribes along the Cascades who rarely descended, and were intermediate in habits between coast and mountain tribes; those near passes owned a few horses.[48] The Sauk tribe lived on both sides of the Sauk River and at Sauk Prairie, where they met to dig roots. They had large houses at Buck Creek and Tenas Creek; their land went to the head of the Suiattle River. A.J. Treadway in 1867 (Trails, *op. cit.*, footnote 46) noted that Whowetkan's Camp on the Sauk, 3 mi. above the confluence of the Suiattle, was the last permanent Indian camp.

All principal river names were derived from changing Indian dialects. The word Stillaguamish has settled in its present form after long fluctuation in many different shapes, from the early Stolokwhamish through Stilaguamish.[49] The Skykomish has taken various names for some or all of its course. The name is an approximation of an Indian tribal name Sky-whamish.[50] The Suiattle River was called the Suiatl (A.J. Treadway) (or Suiathl—Bruseth Papers, 1st ed., p. 16) and the Sultan River was derived from the name of a local Indian chief, Tseul-tud. Pilchuck is derived from Pill-Chuck (red water).[51] The name Sauk is derived from Saakw, as shown on the U.S. North West Boundary Survey manuscript map; it has also been called the Sah-kee-me-hu branch of Skagit River. Some usages show the Sauk's S fork as Sakumchu Creek. Early maps did much course interpolation: there is a unique curve in the "Saakw" off the Skagit in the General Sherman map.[52] Boulder River was called Kal-ub and White Chuck River, DeKabub, meaning swift, roily water and boulders. Silver Creek was Nasukakum. In Chinook jargon Sitkum means one-half (one branch of the creek sinks into pumice in the dry season).

Sorting out the enigmatic reports of the early exploration history of the region has not been concluded, but much material from the railroad and military explorations has come to light. George Gibbs, associated with both the boundary and military explorations, did not visit the "Monte Cristo" peaks, but he refers to them on the U.S. North West Boundary Survey map (1866), as seen from near Port Townsend ("Peaks observed").

Surveys for the Northern Pacific Railroad in the Washington Division were placed under General James Tilton in 1867 to obtain definite information regarding the number and elevation of practicable passes for a railway over the Cascade Range. Reports indicate there was much reliance on the 1866 map for the survey of the Skykomish Pass to the Wenatchee River. W.H. Carlton was sent by Tilton from Olympia to examine Cady's Pass on September 19, 1867. Carlton followed the Indian trail from Snohomish, then planned to run a line of levels over the pass. He took the trail up the North Fork of Skykomish River and set mileposts from Snohomish City to the summit and partially opened the trail that year, then descended to the SE.[53]

The map with the Johnson report showed Cady's Pass as one of three practical passes for a railroad.[54] Carlton returned to state it would not do without a tunnel, but about 1 mi. S a pass was found (perhaps Saddle Gap) over which the line could be carried by grade.[55]

The survey up the Sauk River, the first known exploration by white men, was conducted under Tilton by Assistant Engineer A.J. Treadway in October 1867, the object being to locate a "Skagit Pass." The party went about 22 mi. above the Suiattle junction with Indians and a canoe, but high water and rain forced a retreat.[56] Tilton summarized that N of Cady's Pass "is a Pass leading from the We-nach-ee to the Saak branch of the Skagit, and another from the Skagit to lake Chelan, both of which are supposed to be more elevated than Cady's."[57]

The Cascades in this region underwent their first extensive scientific investigations beginning in 1895. In that year the geologist Bailey Willis traversed the W slope of the range from Snoqualmie Pass to Monte Cristo, during which he studied rock formations, the orogeny, and theorized on summit uniformity. In the field season of 1898 I.C. Russell traversed mountains and glaciers north from Indian Pass on a geologic reconnaissance.[58] He was the first to define the extent of glacierization in the North Cascades: he commented that from the summit of Glacier Peak 100 or 150 glaciers were noted S of the Canadian border, "but of these only a few in the immediate vicinity of Glacier Peak have been traversed."[59]

Between 1895 and 1902 the U.S. Geological Survey undertook the monumental project of mapping the Cascades from Snoqualmie Pass to near Cascade Pass. In fall 1895 a survey unit made their first trip from Skykomish River to Monte Cristo, using mules.[60] The Skykomish quadrangle was surveyed by parties under G.E. Hyde in 1897 and 1902; the Sauk and Stillaguamish quadrangles were mapped between July and October 1897 and in 1898 by Louis C. Fletcher and Thomas G. Gerdine; the Glacier Peak quadrangle and Suiattle River area was surveyed under Gerdine between 1897 and 1899; Fletcher between 1897 and 1899 surveyed a wide area near Darrington; W.C. Guerin surveyed the Beckler River area in 1902. Altitudes were determined by vertical angulation and marked on bolts set into rock used as plane table stations.[61] Such locations included Monte Cristo, Orient, Barlow, Silverton, and Pugh's Ranch (pp. 369-375). In the field season of 1897 H.B. Ayres, while conducting a forest resource study, noted prospecting, mining, and settlers' cabins on the Sultan, Sauk, and Stillaguamish Rivers and Williamson Creek.[62] In the lower valleys he noted there were small clearings and houses of split cedar on lands taken as squatter's claims (there were 18 such claims on the North Fork Stillaguamish River). Ayres cites pack trails along the Sultan, North Fork Sauk, and North Fork Stillaguamish Rivers, and Williamson, Silver, Martin, and Perry Creeks.[63] The report mentions many slash fires and extensive burns caused by gold seekers and settlers along the Sauk and Stillaguamish valleys (pp. 306-308 and pl. 100). On early trails, bridges were a constant problem; the heavy flood of the Sauk River in November 1897—a flood greater than any known in the tradition of the Indians (pp. 309-310)—was devastating to the railroad and settlers. The Settler's Bridge across the Skykomish River 2 mi. W of Index was the only way to reach claims in 1908. Solid timber bridges built across the White Chuck and North Fork Sauk Rivers in 1912 were used by pack trains.[64]

The early government maps, such as the Forest Reserve map of 1898, showed a limited number of features: mountains depicted were Pilchuck, Columbia, Glacier Peak, White Chuck, and Index (Baring);

Suiattle Pass, Indian Pass, Cady Pass and Cascade Summit were shown. A confusing feature of the map is that the drainages of both the Suiattle and White Chuck Rivers are shown N of Glacier Peak. The General Land Office map of 1909 added the following summits: White Horse, Jumbo, Red, Black, Higgins, Pugh, Helena, Vesper, Sloan (but omitted Columbia); the first Forest Service map (1913) added Three Fingers.

The lure of the supposedly rich Similkameen mines in British Columbia was the impetus to locate a trail route across the Cascades which would avoid packing from the heads of navigation on the Columbia and Fraser Rivers. Through the initiative of Snohomish pioneer E.C. Ferguson, Capt. Edward T. Cady and a companion named Parsons were sent on a scouting trek up Skykomish valley in fall 1859. Heavy snows drove them back, but they discovered "Cady's Pass."[65] Construction funded by subscriptions in 1860 enabled Cady and Ferguson to cross the pass with pack animals in August, but the trail project was dropped when gold prospects proved disappointing.[66] A map (Public Surveys in Washington Territory, 1868) shows the trail from Skywhamish River over Cady's Pass to Lake Wenatchee. Road building schemes were promoted by county officials, who hoped a highway would be constructed by a route other than Stevens Pass; a proposed Cady Pass crossing was studied by C.N. Bush, with J.A. Juleen and engineer A.B. Cutter.[67]

By 1890 a horse trail was built over Stevens Pass, the route eventually chosen for the line of the Great Northern Railroad. By the spring of that year it had been virtually decided that the Wenatchee River be adopted as the route from the Columbia, but the final selection was to be dependent on the conclusions of the explorations of John F. Stevens in 1890 and 1891.[68] In the winter of 1892-1893 many men worked at Stevens Pass to complete the line, a task of great hardship. The main line was completed near Scenic (then Madison) on January 6, 1893. During the first 7 yrs the trains crossed the pass by a series of switchbacks on a 4 percent grade. The original line location crossed N into Martin Creek with a large horseshoe curve, then made a steep rise to Wellington (name changed to Tye after the 1910 disaster).[69] By 1897 tunnel work began, completed in 1900 as a 2⅔-mi. tunnel beneath Stevens Pass, with portals at 3200 and 3400 ft. A series of immense snow sheds were built between Scenic and Wellington because of heavy winter snow accumulation. Construction of the lower Cascade Tunnel began in 1926 and ended in January 1929, employing workers housed in large camps at Scenic, Berne, and Mill Creek; the 7.79-mi. tunnel was the longest in the Western Hemisphere.[70]

CAMPGROUNDS

There are numerous campgrounds on the forest roads in this section. For locations see Mt. Baker-Snoqualmie National Forest maps or National Forest Campground Directory, which also lists facilities and usage fees.

RANGER STATIONS

Skykomish: on U.S. Hwy. No. 2, 1.5 mi. E of Skykomish. Skykomish, WA 98288; (206) 677-2414

Verlot: on Mountain Loop Hwy. No. 322, 11.4 mi. E of Granite Falls. Granite Falls, WA 98252; (206) 691-7791

Darrington: at N end of town, on main roadway. Darrington, WA 98241; (206) 436-1155

Suiattle F.S.: Suiattle River road, 1 mi. E of Buck Creek; summer only.

Baker River R.S.: Concrete, WA 98237; (206) 853-2851

FOREST HEADQUARTERS

Mt. Baker-Snoqualmie National Forest
1601 Second Ave.
Seattle, WA 98101
(206) 442-5400

National Parks Service—Forest Service Information Center
Room 110, 915 Second Ave.
Seattle, WA 98174
(206) 442-0170 or 442-5542

Wilderness permits issued at Ranger stations and the Information Center.

MAPS

U.S. Geological Survey Topographic

The North Cascades (1972)	1:250,000
Concrete (1955)	1:250,000
Sultan (1923)	1:62,500
Glacier Peak (1950)	1:62,500
Index (1957)	1:62,500
Silverton (1957)	1:62,500
Oso (1956)	1:62,500
Baring (1965)	1:24,000
Blanca Lake (1965)	1:24,000
Skykomish (1965)	1:24,000

Scenic (1965)	1:24,000
Evergreen Mountain (1966)	1:24,000
Captain Point (1966)	1:24,000
Benchmark Mountain (1965)	1:24,000
Darrington (1966)	1:24,000
Fortson (1966)	1:24,000
White Chuck Mountain (1966)	1:24,000
Pugh Mountain (1966)	1:24,000
Bedal (1966)	1:24,000
Sloan Peak (1966)	1:24,000
Monte Cristo (1966)	1:24,000
Finney Peak (1966)	1:24,000

U.S. Forest Service

Mt. Baker—Snoqualmie National Forest recreation map (½ in. to 1-mi. scale).
Glacier Peak Wilderness map (topographic)

U.S. Forest Service Planimetric

Stillaguamish #43
Glacier Peak #41, 42, 56, 57
Silverton #55
Skykomish #68, 69
Index #70

MT. PILCHUCK 5324′/1623 m

The word Pilchuck is derived from the Indian name of the river, meaning "red water;" the mountain's slopes were frequented by local tribes in search of game and berries. Because Pilchuck is located farther W than any similar summit in this region, it can readily be sighted from the Puget Sound Basin, and conversely offers an excellent view westward and along the range flanks from Mt. Baker to Mt. Rainier. Rock is granitic, similar to the Index batholith. Its position seems to make the mountain prone to aircraft accidents (in April 1948 a training plane hit the upper S slope, there was a crash in January 1952, and another in September 1964 on the lower W slope.

The U.S. Geological Survey used the summit for a triangulation station in 1898. The original lookout cabin was built in 1919, at which time the peak was reduced some 12 ft in height by blasting; the cabin was replaced in 1942, and manned until 1956. Much of Pilchuck became a State park in 1951 (the S slope and summit are State-owned) and the N slope managed by the Forest Service, and in 1963 a chair lift was built from Cedar Flat to 4300 ft. Roads extend high on the S slope, where there is also a summit trail. Toll road promotions began as early as 1937 and in the late 1940s a strong campaign was conducted by the American Legion for a summit road and three-story vista house.[71]

ROUTE: The popular 2-mi. summit trail hike begins at the W end of the parking lot and bypasses the ski area (see Mt. Pilchuck State Park Road♦). Beyond Little Saddle (4600′+, on the summit ridge) a left fork allows a boulder-scramble along the W ridge to the summit. The main trail winds to the summit by crossing the S slope to SE of the top. Warning: the N summit rim is an extensive cliff; scrambling has its dangers (fatal fall, August 1925). When the entire route is snow-covered a direct route is inviting, but does have steep snow sections where fatal slips have occurred.

A new trail system of about 12 mi. will link the mountain with the scenic subalpine lakes to the E, and connect with Williamson Creek road extensions on Bald Mountain. Near the E summit ridge 1¼ mi. from Pilchuck's summit, terraces hold five tarns and numerous ponds (Twenty Lakes Basin—about 4300′) in a ½-mi. span; two rock knobs on the summit ridge stand just N of the basin, the "East Knob" (5120′+) and "Eagles Nest." This is a picturesque trek for hikers, with a route connecting to Pinnacle Lake, but heather and soils are fragile—visitors must be careful of their impact. References: *101 Hikes*; Harry W. Higman and Earl J. Larrison, *Pilchuck—The Life of a Mountain*, Seattle, 1949.

BALD MOUNTAIN 4851′/1479 m

Bald is a subalpine ridge between Sultan Basin and Boardman Creek of the South Fork of Stillaguamish River. An isolated exposure of solid quartz diorite stock occurs W of the highest summit of this long ridge; here there are towers (4480′+) up to 200 ft high with good cracks. Winter and spring is the suggested time for a visit.

Take Pilchuck River Road♦ about 12 mi. to branch SL-P582 which bears NW; follow it about 1 mi. to old timber (Section 20) near the head of Pilchuck River (crosses two streams, then a clearcut by Billie K Creek). It appears best to hike from timber near this creek, then ascend northerly. Keep left to a heavy wooded slope (left of talus) and up it to gentle upper slopes. Here the E tower is farthest right on the ridge.

ROUTES: *West Tower.* An interesting stemming crack with paint, "Man's Chimney."

East Tower. This is harder to climb; the summit is a large block. First ascent by Gordon, Paul, Terry, and Leo Trelford in May 1972 by Spiral Route.

Climb to the notch left of the tower and take the narrow N-side ledge to a vertical crack; use aid to a 5.7 open book, continue to a 6-ft roof, then right onto a small dirty ledge. Take a gully, then reach a large ledge with trees on the W side of tower. Traverse the S face on this ledge to a steep gully. Climb up to a small fir on a ledge, then up a short slab (5.6);

then scramble to a broken area on the ridge, and a 12-ft jam crack to the summit. Rappel bolt atop.

RED MOUNTAIN 5738′/1749 m

Lack of imagination and originality were factors in the application of this common name to this isolated and seldom climbed pointed rock peak between the upper Sultan River's N fork and Elk Creek. This little-known Red is everywhere rugged; any route will provide formidable brush and cliff. On the W Red has much local relief, with long gullies and brushy slopes beneath a craggy summit face. The S and E flanks present precipitous summit barriers, as well as long brushy approaches. There is a N summit (5204′) ¾ mi. from the true summit, a part of the 3-mi.-long massif. The summit and NW ridge consist of weakly metamorphosed sedimentary and volcanic rocks which are cut by a NW-trending dike-like body of serpentinite (Joseph Vance, personal commun.). On the E all these rocks are intruded by granodiorite of the Index batholith.

Much mineral exploration has been done on Red's flanks, and the Florence Rea Mine above road's end is currently being operated. An aerial cable and trails lead to mine workings about ⅓ mi. W of the road.[72] The first ascent was by Anthony Hovey and Klindt Vielbig on October 4, 1958. Reference: A.A.J., 1959, p. 301.

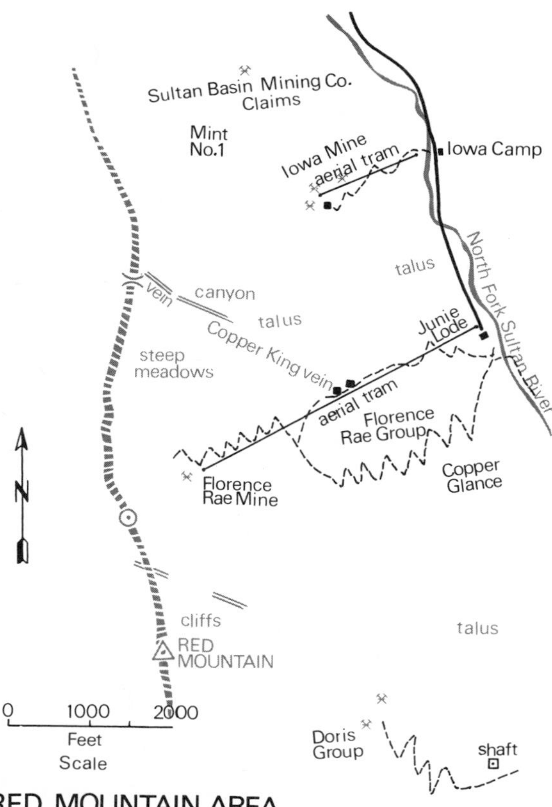

RED MOUNTAIN AREA
(from Carithers & Guard)

ROUTE: From the end of Sultan Basin Road♦ (2100′) find vague trail from mine shed, near lower watercourse slabs; it crosses a large fern-brush slope SE, then climbs near a creek to talus below upper eastern cliffs (if trail disappears, head for narrow timber band where tread should show). Climb gradually NW for ¾ mi. to a canyon (possible trail traces from adit at 4650 ft at head of talus going N ¼ mi. to a claim); ascend canyon edge to the lowest ridge saddle (est. 5000′). Cross to the W and contour steep open forest S below the crest to the first chute; here a delicate grass traverse to a tree, then vertical moss and roots. Continue contouring on easier terrain and then scree fields below the N peak crags to a wide scree chute where a cliff forces the route up to the prominent U-shaped notch at its head (on summit ridge). A short vertical cliff provides an initial difficulty, followed by two leads on very steep heather, then steep mixed rock-heather close to the N crest. Cross the S side of two gendarmes and scramble a few hundred ft to the summit. Grade II; class 4. Time: 5-7 hours. On descent: rappel the notch pitch.

MT. STICKNEY 5367′/1636 m

Stickney is a wooded frontal mountain located 3 mi. E of Wallace Lake (N of Wallace and Skykomish Rivers). It rises as a ridge with the summit at the eastern end, the first peak of prominence when driving up the Skykomish valley. Stickney was first named Prospect Mountain, but then dedicated to a prospector who spent years on nearby claims; it is said he went to Alaska in 1898 and was killed by wolves. The Sultan quadrangle of 1923 was the first to use the current name.

EAST RIDGE: Take Sultan Basin Road♦ and South Fork (Kromona Mine) branch to the crossing of the Middle Fork (just before the mill). An easy cross-country route can be taken to the N side of the mountain (1 mi. to E ridge saddle—est. 4400′). One beginning on the approach is to hike the short roadway, then continue S; to avoid brush use the rocky streambed if water level permits. The remainder is mostly heather slope beyond the forest zone. Time: 4 hours.

WEST RIDGE: This was once the popular route, but is now a poor choice because of road washouts, gates, and brush. From the Wallace River Road♦ at about 1500 ft hike on its continuation to 3800 ft on the mountain's W flank. A cross-country route leads past a small lake (est. 4200′), then along the main crest over several minor points to the summit.

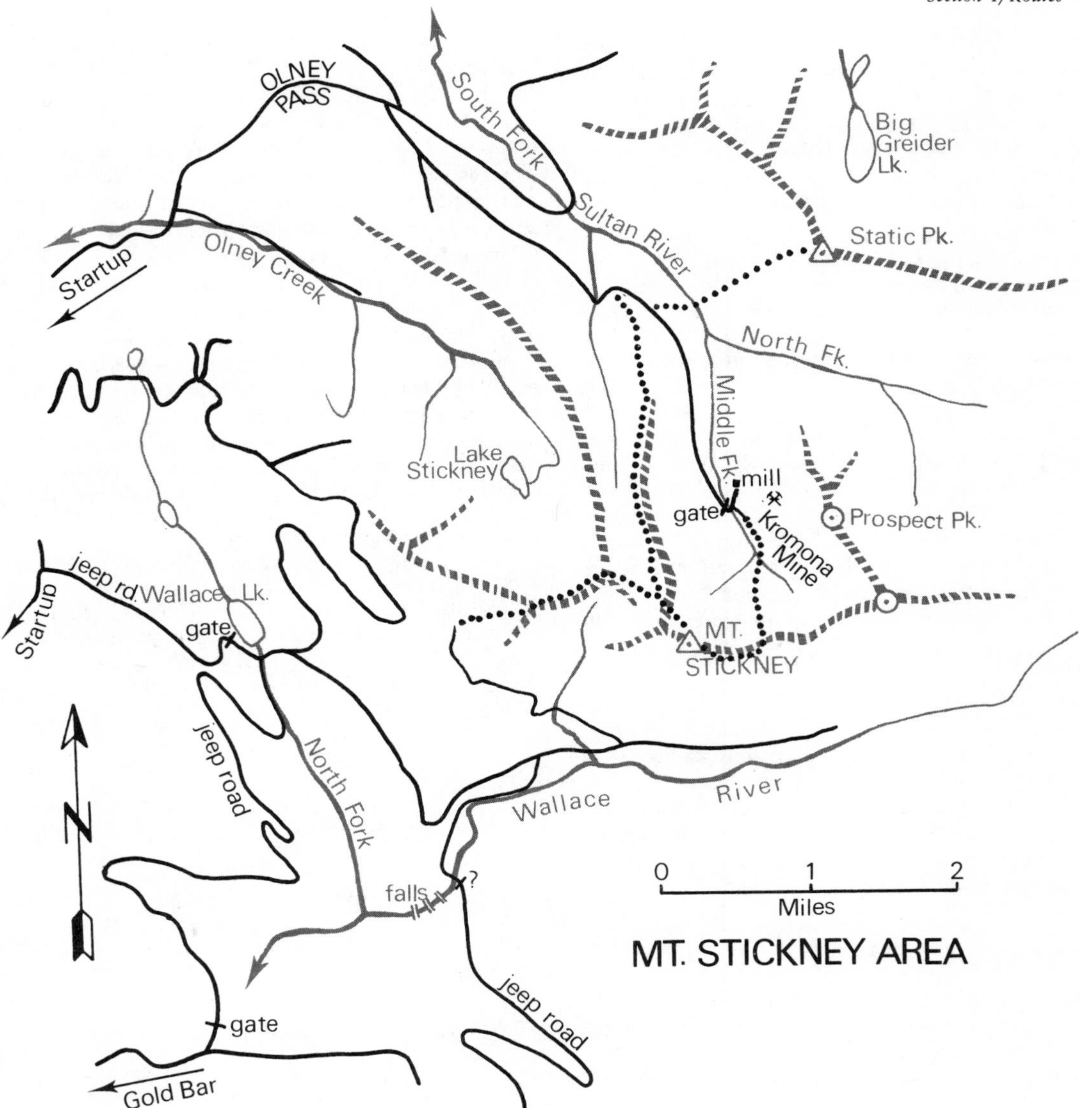

Before the last point keep N of the crest (possible snow), then ascend a little gully back to the crest for the final scramble. Time: 5-6 hours.

Logging road gates and bad road conditions have effectively closed off the formerly used route via Wallace Lake.

NORTH ROUTE: If the road is washed out at the South Fork crossing (see East Ridge) this is the suggested route. Follow the spur E of the South Fork to the mountain, then ascend the final NW side. An approach variation is to leave the road about 1¼ mi. farther, above the Middle Fork, and ascend W to the spur.

PROSPECT PEAK 4640′+/1414 m

This is a small but rocky peak of local interest 1½ mi. NE of Mt. Stickney. There appears to be a SW-facing wall of sound rock (quartz diorite) that may be of technical climbing interest. The route from Kromona Mine is speculative, but appears short and reasonable, with a short scramble above an alp slope. For driving directions toward the mine, see Sultan Basin Road♦.

STATIC PEAK 4905′/1495 m

This small pointed peak, not identified on maps, is located 3 mi. NNE of Mt. Stickney in Section 1; rock is quartz diorite. First ascent by Preston Bonney, Glen Watson, Monte Haun, Bob Hall, and Kenn Carpenter in May 1960. Reference: *A.A.J.*, 1961, pp. 367-368; *Mountaineer*, 1961, p. 103.

ROUTE: Drive the Kromona Mine branch of Sultan Basin Road♦ about 3 mi. (in Section 2) above where the S fork branches. To reach the river descend some 500 ft through timber just beyond the large clearcut, cross and then climb N (open timber) to the W shoulder. Here a 500-ft rocky ridge leads to the summit. Class 2-3. Time: 4 to 6 hours.

PEAK 5144 5144′/1568 m

Located about 3.3 mi. ENE of Mt. Stickney, this secondary summit lies between Salmon Creek and the South Fork of Sultan River. It has a small but obvious rock horn on the W end of a double-summit ridge. There is a gentle basin below the E ridge, which may be the best summit route. The upper portions of the Wallace River, Salmon Creek, or South Fork of the Sultan offer possible cross-country approaches.

PEAK 5335 5335′/1626 m

A small peak on the Elk Creek-South Fork Sultan River divide, 4½ mi. NE of Mt. Stickney, it is very rocky on the N with a spur extending N. Rock here and on nearby peaks is predominantly quartz diorite.

No known route. Possible approaches are from Elk Creek, Salmon Creek, the South Fork of the Sultan, or Boulder Lake; from Boulder Lake, an ascent then a slope traverse would lead to the N side.

MT. BARING 6125′/1867 m

Although Baring does not rise to unique height, sheer bulk and strategic position give it a dominating aspect from both distant and nearby vistas. Located NE of the town of Baring, the southern slopes are largely featureless forest and rock outcrops, with a long ridge jutting westward. The main summit is the N one; it is separated from the S summit (6010′) by a gap, and there is a lesser S peak at about 5800 ft.

The N face as seen in profile overhangs for about 2000 ft. No climbing route has yet been attempted, but where the face corners to the E above Barclay Lake, one of the most arduous climbing projects in the range took place. Baring offers excellent views of nearby peaks, but as a climb from the W or S it is largely a subalpine forest exercise. Spring is an advisable time if snow is firm, for then much brush is covered.

The peak was named "Index Mountain" in 1872 by Northern Pacific Railroad surveyors because of its outline from the W (this name appears on many old maps); in 1917 the new name Baring was proposed by The Mountaineers, who already had changed the nomenclature of West Index, across the Skykomish River, to Mt. Index. The first climb was made by John Charlton and Albert H. Sylvester on July 28, 1897 on a U.S. Geological Survey triangulation, via the S slope—a grueling climb with "great logs to climb over" (Albert H. Sylvester Papers, University of Washington Library, p. 8); the first winter ascent was made by Dan Davis on December 23, 1962.

NORTHWEST RIDGE: This has recently been accredited as the simplest route, and the one with least brush. Drive Barclay Creek Road♦ about ¼ mi. beyond Barclay Lake trailhead. A narrow gully comes downslope. Ascent SSW through the clearcut to the right of the gully, then timber and brush to the NW ridge (4000′). Turn left and take the wooded crest about ½ mi. (or its S side). Here (est. 4700′) cliffs block the way; drop to the right and contour ¼ mi. to bypass, then gain the ridge again. Then make a short drop to the small basin below the rocky chute leading to the V-gap between the two summits. Turn left and take the ridge NNE to the main summit; keep left of the final summit ridge. Class 2. Time: 4-5 hours.

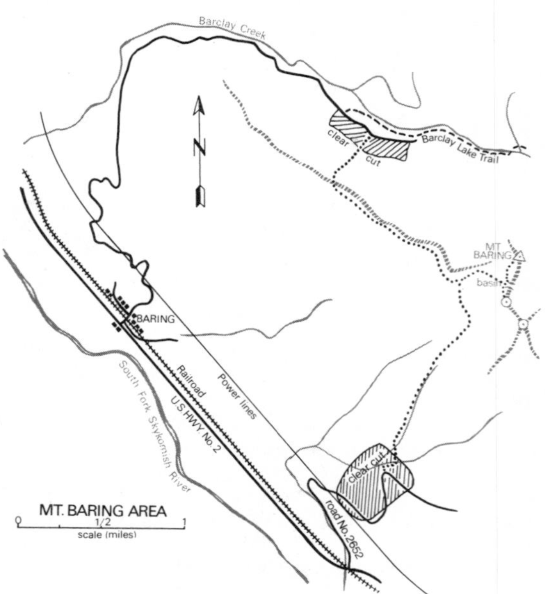

MT. BARING from west
JOHN V.A.F. NEAL

NORTH FACE—EAST CORNER: This face, directly above Barclay Lake and not visible from the highway, is in part a major buttress dividing the N and E faces. It was the object of considerable explorative climbing (seven attempts) in the 1950s before its conquest in 1960. The direct N face rises sheerly for nearly 3000 ft above Barclay Creek; "Dolomite Tower," a giant pillar, is merged against the face.

On Baring's NE the wall begins to steepen dramatically at 3400 ft (about 1000 ft above the lake), but offers some compromise because of its buttress form and three well defined ledges on upper levels. Farther E, the E face becomes a hostile-appearing basin followed by a smooth wall, less attractive as a route opportunity. A vexing problem of the route is the difficult, cliffy brush approach in the lower portion. Rock is massive, inconsistently fractured, and brittle.

The first 1000 ft of the route are largely brush and timber. The next 1300 ft involve two precipitous parallel brushy ribs separated by a large rock gully (often snow-filled) that eventually becomes a hideous chasm. The rock face above and N features four steps: 300, 400, 230, and 250 ft high, each separated by spacious ledges. The climb is certainly a great one, although it appears deflected, for one never climbs the upper wall direct.

In the summer of 1951 Pete Schoening and Richard Berge twice attempted the climb and reached just above the end of a 50-ft piton traverse ("Traverse of the Pioneers") on the third step. In 1952 Don (Claunch) Gordon, David Collins, and Paul Salness packed a heavy camp 1600 ft up, but only reached a limited distance higher. On July 19 the same year, Berge, Tom Miller, and Fred Beckey reached Dolomite Camp, and while descending in the dark at the edge of lower cliffs, Berge fell to his death. Schoening and Gordon reached the high point again in 1955, but progress was foiled by brittle rock and a scarcity of piton cracks. In 1957 Gordon and John Rupley halted at Dolomite Camp due to heat and lack of water, but in July 1959 Beckey, Gordon and Ed Cooper reached the high point and advanced 15-20 ft beyond, to place a needed bolt; time limits and heat forced a retreat. In June 1960 this team cut a "trail" through 2300 ft of bushy cliffs and with a few key fixed ropes left a week's food at Dolomite Camp. The final climb began on July 9; the next day Beckey in 4 hrs managed to place a poor bolt above the other, then had to return to work. Cooper and Gordon, with the aid of chromalloy blades not previously available, completed the ascent July 13.

Take Barclay Lake Trail♦ to the S end of the lake, then circle back about one-third its length. Ascend brush (keep right of low main canyon), then steep forest to the wide jungly rock wall. Make a right traverse across steep rocky forest to the gully between the parallel ribs. Climb brushy rock on left side of gully, eventually bearing left to the sharp ridge crest. Continue up rib to the level of a white blotch in the gully (Rockfall Point). Make a left traverse off the rib, into a bowl, then bear up and left to a bushy rock area on another rib. Ascend rib and a broad depression (below great upper chimneys).

Make a rightward rising traverse on bushy ledges to right rib and the first step's base; work around on cliffy brush to the N side (steepens here). The two-pitch step develops steeply; keep right of center for hardest portion (5.7); second

MT. BARING, North Face
ED COOPER

1 - Couloir Camp
2 - Rockfall Point
3 - Dolomite Camp
4 - Dolomite Tower
5 - Third Step

MT. BARING Upper Northeast Face from Dolomite Camp
ED COOPER

pitch located slightly right of first. On the second step, keep slightly left of center (some loose rock). Its first pitch ascends a nose crack to a bush about 20 ft left of a big white spot; second pitch bears left about 15 ft, then up, keeping slightly left of nose; higher rock eases and a few shrubs appear.

On the third step climb a short overhang (several aid pitons), then traverse left beneath an extensive roof to negotiate 40 ft (four aid pitons incl. a wide angle); continue bearing left for 10 ft past a narrow foot ledge (now about 60′ from belay), then up-right in a difficult vertical trough for 12 ft to blankness. Climb up and right a few slabby feet to 1-ft ledge at bolt (72′ to here). Use knife blades, small pitons (possibly stoppers) and several angles for about 40 ft or more (mostly aid); the last part is a vertical 10 ft angle crack that ends beneath a roof. From a poor blade pendulum 6 ft around the slight corner and climb obliquely left (a 15′ crux is a shallow groove—poor protection). Reach a good small ledge in recess for belay. A steep lead of mixed free and aid begins with 25 ft (possibly 40′), to bypass the corner of the nearest horizontal roof; continue up and left toward brush (final part is right-facing dihedral or on left edge). Walk 100 ft left on a ledge, then bear up and left about two easy pitches to avoid the caprock. Grade V; class 5.8 and A4 or A5 (four KB used). References: *A.A.J.*, 1952, p. 345; 1961, pp. 302-305 and pl. 63; *Mountaineer*, 1951, p. 40; 1961, pp. 25-27.

SOUTH SLOPE: Formerly the normal route, this direct approach has lost favor since construction of the Barclay Creek Road. Despite a moderate amount of brush and fallen timber the start from a logging road still makes this a sensible way to the summit. At 2.1 mi. SE of Baring, just beyond the railroad overpass, take road no. 2652 uphill to the second rightward hairpin (2 mi.). Hike a short dirt spur and the remainder of the large clearcut uphill and westward (est. 200 yds) across a stream gully. Continue bearing leftward in the open mature timber of continuous forest, climbing toward the upper portion of the prominent small stream gully which begins at timberline below the S peak. Unless the gully is filled with solid snow keep in timber to the end, then bear obliquely left on heather (grassy chute) and talus to work through a gap in rocks near the left end of the rock wall. Skirt cliffs to the ridge crest, then traverse the N side into the rocky basin and climb E to the V-gap (5520′+) for the final summit ascent. Time: 6 hours.

SOUTH PEAK

Make the ascent from the V-gap; class 3.

GUNN PEAK 6240′/1902 m

Named Gunn's Peak for pioneer miner Amos Gunn, this prominent landmark appears as a thumb from the Stevens Pass Hwy. Gunn is N of Barclay Creek, where differential erosion of an alpine crest has produced a jagged skyline culminating at Jumpoff Ridge on the NW. As a climb Gunn has attained reasonable popularity; spring or early summer is the best time. There are numerous old claims at various altitudes N of the peak (see Trout Creek Trail♦). The first ascent party of Dr. H.B. Hinman, Walter Eriksen, and Louis Lesh made the climb on their fifth attempt, on July 18, 1915, via Lewis Creek on the SW; rumor of a U.S.G.S. flagpole already placed proved unfounded.

ROUTE: From the Barclay Creek Road♦ at about 400 yds before the trailhead (2200′) cross the creek on a footlog to a bushy area. Climb NNE to the base of a large slide area with a creek which higher has a waterfall. Ascend timber on its W side via a meager trail to upper slopes where it works right across a dry stream (be sure to ascend left of waterfalls visible from road); here angle up to an obvious rock outcrop. Traverse right beneath it and continue climbing to dip on the ridge crest (5300′) via timber, a rocky rib, and a gully on left. Here the summit lies ½ mi. N.

Now traverse NW on N side of the ridge to the 5400-ft saddle just S of Gunn's summit and E of Gunn Lake. Climb a steep couloir near the right side of the rock face to the N. When it steepens, work up and right, then spiral counterclockwise E to N by use of a broad ledge. Class 3. Time: 6 hours.

Variation: A chimney above the couloir head offers a direct route; moderate class 5.

JUMPOFF RIDGE 6218′/1895 m

This high crest is really an extension of the Gunn massif, at 0.7 mi. NW, between Lewis and Bitter Creeks. The best approach is from the saddle S of Gunn's summit; then traverse W beneath the crest (no special difficulties).

MERCHANT PEAK 6113′/1863 m

Merchant is a bulky mountain 1.3 mi. SE of Gunn. Maps identify the summit at the E peak (5831′), but the true summit is ⅜ mi. NW; there is a less significant W peak (5730′) at 0.7 mi. NW of the summit. Merchant is an ideal late spring climb because of almost continual snow (most of the mountain can be glissaded), but even in late season there is only negligible brush. The peak is named for Andrew Merchant, who with Col. Benjamin Townsend made many claims in the upper W fork of Trout Creek. A small plane crash in 1965 gave the peak public notoriety.

SOUTH SIDE: A good route, but large groups invite trouble; rockfall is unavoidable in the upper portion of the gully.

Take Barclay Lake Trail♦ to stream bridge, crossing to the N side. Hike 100 yds upstream (the objective gully is not evident from the trail, but seen in about 50 yds through timber). Ascend large rockslide area to narrow (loose) slide gully. Continue about halfway up the mountainside (some rockfall unavoidable in upper part) where the chute bends left past a towering S cliff (waterfall enters from right). Take a sloping dirt ledge under the cliff (near waterfall) and follow it obliquely right (partly hidden). A small brush area leads to broad and moderate upper meadows (snowfields) which lead directly or just E of the summit. Time: 6 hours. Note: do not

MT. STICKNEY
GUNN PEAK
MT. PILCHUCK
Saddle to
Gunn Lake
Saddle to
Barclay Creek
Trout
Creek

take the gully between Gunn and Merchant. Reference: *Mountaineer*, 1958, pp. 104-105.

SOUTHEAST ROUTE: A long and tedious route beginning from a higher base. From Eagle Lake climb NW to the 4480-ft saddle between Merchant and Townsend. Contour W on the N slope rockslide ½ mi., past the E peak. There are several couloirs leading S toward the summit. Take the last one before reaching very steep rock on the contour. Ascend left to the ridge at 5600 ft. The final ascent westward is on the S side of the crest.

NORTH SIDE: An early season route. Take Trout Creek Trail♦ to the S fork junction (campsite; est. 2200′). Keep left of the creek, high in trees to minimize brush. From the tree fringe bear over stony area toward peak, then take a rocky creek bed. Reach center rocky area to right of second stream, then angle left up through bush to reach upper snowfield. A long finger bearing left leads to the eastern summit ridge. Time: 6 hours.

EAST PEAK: This summit is located ½ mi. W of Eagle Lake. Make the ascent directly from there via easy heather and rock. It is reported the climb is quite feasible from upper meadows of the normal main peak route.

MT. TOWNSEND 5936′/1809 m

Although lower than Gunn and Merchant, this summit is generally apparent because of fewer nearby peaks; named for Col. Benjamin T. Townsend, it is 1.8 mi. E of Merchant.

ROUTE: From Eagle Lake (see Barclay Lake Trail♦) ascend NE to the ridge at a 5360-ft saddle. Then hike ¾ mi. E along the gentle ridge (a bit of grass and scree). The route can be varied almost anywhere on the S slope, which is uniformly moderate. The summit is a rocky pile at the E end.

CONGLOMERATE POINT 5375′/1638 m

This minor summit rises closely S of Howard Lake, SE of North Fork of Skykomish River.

ROUTES: One could ascend the E side from Howard Lake, or ascend the long W slope from Trout Creek Trail♦.

IRON MOUNTAIN 5245′/1599 m

Iron is a minor peak between Trout and Howard Creeks, E of the North Fork Skykomish River.

ROUTE: An old mine road leads high on its W side. See Trout Creek Trail♦.

SPIRE PEAK 6213′/1894 m

The highest crest of Spire consists of three spires on a NW trend, on the Bear-Howard Creek divide. They rise in height from the SE, with the Northwest Spire highest. As viewed from the N this spire is twin-towered, the Central Spire quite slender, and the Southeast Spire bulky and craggy; there is generally a snowpatch beneath the spires. Several lesser crags stand on the ridge to the SE. A ridge point at ¾ mi. S is an extension of the crestline which maps identify as Spire Mountain. Reference: *Mountaineer*, 1934, p. 18.

The first ascent was made by Kenneth Chapman and Dwight W. Dean on May 22, 1934 (Northwest Spire).

ROUTE: The old Howard Creek mining trail leaves North Fork Skykomish River Road♦ at a small clearing 0.1 mi. W of the Howard Creek bridge (9½ mi.). Follow an abandoned logging grade to a subsidiary creek (Lost Creek), then cross it and continue about ¾ mi. to a cutover at Howard Creek. Find the abandoned trail in timber beyond and follow it, crossing to the E bank on a footbridge (good camp in first deep timber after cutover); trail ends in a clearing about 2¼ mi. from road. Continue to brush patches past timber, then follow main creekbed. Continue almost to valley head (est. 3200′, 4 hrs), then bear 90° toward saddle notch (4400′), Then head 60° up chute to ridge crest (est. 5600′) between Spire Peak and Spire Mountain. Drop 300 ft on E side, then traverse ½ mi. N, on the N side, to the small notch W of the Northwest Spire. The short climb uses the NW ridge. Class 3. Time: 8 hours.

Note: the original party climbed an open chimney on the N side, about 200 ft with a chockstone problem near its head, located close to the E end of the pinnacle (est. class 4).

Variation (West Flank): At about ½ mi. beyond trail's end note the first prominent gully which bears toward the apparent summit (right of a white gully and left of a tree-apex). Ascend it a series of lesser rockslide gullies, keeping left of a prominent pinnacle which comes into view about midway. An accident occurred in this area when a climbing student was hit by a boulder. Near the ridge crest a short rock pitch may be met, followed by heather and rock slope to the ridge notch W of the true summit. Drop across to the snowfield.

CENTRAL SPIRE est. 6200′/1890 m

The route uses a chimney on the NW side. First ascent by Karl Boyer, Lyman Boyer, and David Lind in 1938. A snow finger (possible snow block problems) lends to a chockstone on the W side of the summit. The route climbs the chockstone and then ascends loose, steep rock (unstable class 4); reported as two 75-ft leads.

SOUTHEAST SPIRE est. 6185′/1885 m

Reach by traversing beneath the other spires. Route is estimated class 3.

SPIRE MOUNTAIN 6065′/1847 m

From the S slope of the ridge crest between Spire Mountain and Peak, bear up easily to the broad summit.

EL CAPITAN 5327′/1624 m

One of the minor summits in the region, at the head of San Juan Creek nearly 3 mi. W of Beckler River. The W end of the formation is highest.

GUNN PEAK from Merchant Peak
JOHN V.A.F. NEAL

ADDISON RIDGE
FOGGY PK.
SLOAN PK.
SPIRE PK.
Central Spire
Southeast Spire
COLUMBIA PK.
MONTE CRISTO PK.
KYES PK.
SPIRE MTN.
North Fork Skykomish Valley
Howard Creek

ROUTE: No specific information is available ATP, but hard cross-country bushy travel should be anticipated to reach this summit. Logging roads from the NW offer the nearest approach (see Beckler River Road♦).

BEAR MOUNTAIN 5519′/1682 m

Bear is a rough rock peak of moderate height located about 1½ mi. W of Jack Pass and 1 mi. S of the North Fork Skykomish River. The upper W and E faces are quite sheer rock for the final 500 ft. The S summit is highest; there is a N summit (5480′) several hundred yds distant, and a still farther point at 5320 ft. Flanking rock appears quite massive and gray. First ascent by Kenn Carpenter and Herbert Denny on July 13, 1957.

ROUTE: Leave Beckler River Road♦ via spur road no. 2865 on the S side of the Skykomish River bridge; take it W to San Juan Creek (about 1 mi; park here). A track goes up and W; ascend forest along the creek to a point ENE of the summit. Here ascend a gully and steep timber toward the N peak; just beneath the final rock face angle left and up to the S peak (class 3). The short ridge spanning the peaks is sharp and broken, with an apparently difficult 40-ft step. It is best to climb the N peak on its SW side. Time: 8 hours.

NORTH PEAK

First ascent by Kenn Carpenter and Herbert Denny on September 8, 1956. North Ridge route: Linda Burns, Kenn Carpenter, Roger Gorham, and Tom Menzel on August 25, 1974. There are numerous rock bluffs in the timber; follow the ridge crest (good rock). There is one exposed narrow knife-edge sitting straddle of about 30 ft about 200 ft below the summit; class 3 and 4.

FLAPJACK POINT 5191′/1582 m

This summit is located 3 mi. W of Beckler River and NW of Eagle Rock.

ROUTE: Use Eagle Creek road no. 2632 and no. 2779 off Beckler River Road♦; after the road crosses Eagle Creek hike NE upslope (expect some bush). See also Eagle Rock.

EAGLE ROCK 5615′/1711 m

This summit is largely a timbered hill, but the E and S slopes are very rocky.

ROUTES: Begin on Eagle Creek road no. 2632, which leaves Beckler River Road♦ at about 1 mi. Road no. 2779 extends up the S slope of Eagle Creek and crosses to the N in Section 3 (5 mi.), then winds E to within a mi. of the summit. An alternative is to follow no. 2632 to the E of the summit; here a jeep trail reaches to about 3900 ft. Hike upslope, but keep to the N near the top to avoid the cliffy area.

BECKLER PEAK 5062′/1543 m

Both the moderate peak and the river take their name for E.H. Beckler, chief engineer of the Great Northern Railroad in 1892. The peak, the first summit E of Beckler River, is 2 mi. N of Tye River.

ROUTE: Use the approach for Mt. Fernow, but leave the road at about 6 mi. (2800′), then hike uphill. Expect some second growth. An alternative is to ascend the W ridge from the road's northern hairpin turn. Reference: *Trips and Trails 1.*

ALPINE BALDY 5200′+/1585 m

Located 2 mi. N of Tye River and SW of Mt. Fernow.

ROUTE: See approach for Mt. Fernow.

MT. FERNOW 6190′/1887 m

Fernow is of modest importance, but of local interest because of its solitary situation. Most of the peak is subalpine, but there are rock outcrops at the top. A series of lakes, the Mt. Fernow Potholes, lie about 1 mi. N.

SOUTHWEST ROUTE: This is a good spring or early summer trip. From 2 mi. E of Skykomish R.S. on U.S. Hwy. No. 2♦, take road no. 263 and E branch no. 2685 about 9 mi. (into Section 22 on S slope of Alpine Baldy). If the road is not passable to near this point, begin the ascent from the highway about 4½ mi. E of the ranger station. Ascend N over Alpine Baldy, then continue ENE on the ridge toward Fernow. The first major rock summit is not the true one and is best traversed right and across a shoulder. Then enter a wide gully, and ascend right to the summit. Time: 6 hours.

NORTHEAST ROUTE: Where Johnson Ridge Trail♦ turns NE to descend to Joan Lake, find an unmaintained trail descending S through meadows and bands of timber. The trail parallels the long S ridge of Scorpion for almost a mi., keeping about 100 ft below and a few hundred ft E of the heavy windfalls on the ridge crest. On the SE ridge of a 5183-ft high point, contour W to the ridge crest, following old blazes. Contour SE of the 5375-ft high point, W of the 5498-ft peak, then regain the ridgecrest to the saddle (5000′+) ⅓ mi. NE of Fernow. Continue on the N side of the crest across a small basin to a larger one at about 5600 ft. Ascend to about 5900 ft to a rock notch which leads to a ledge system across the E face. Cross the timbered SE ridge and contour to a gully which leads N then E to the summit. Class 3; time: 6 to 7 hours.

WINDY MOUNTAIN 5386′/1642 m

This moderate summit is located between Martin Creek and upper Tye River, N of Scenic.

ROUTE: Starting from the old highway, cross the railroad grade and find logging roads that go upslope N of Scenic. The travel is mostly burnt-over slope and bush. Ascents such as this are best in spring.

CAPTAIN POINT 5724′/1745 m

Located between Martin and Johnson Creeks, 5 mi.

SPIRE PEAK from southwest
JOHN V.A.F. NEAL

NW of Stevens Pass.

ROUTES: This summit can be approached via Martin Creek Road and the trail up Kelley Creek W of the summit. See Johnson Ridge Trail♦. From the SE ridge of the 5183-ft high point (see Mt. Fernow—Northeast Route), follow a ridge SSE 1 mi. to the summit, keeping just E of the crest to minimize brush.

SCORPION MOUNTAIN 5540′/1689 m

Another modest summit, S of Rapid River and 4½ mi. E of Beckler River.

ROUTE: The Johnson Ridge Trail♦ passes almost atop on the S slope.

EVERGREEN MOUNTAIN 5587′/1703 m

This small peak, N of Rapid River, is situated 2 mi. E of Beckler River.

ROUTE: To reach the 1½ mi. trail (4200′) to the summit lookout, use Evergreen Mountain Road, a fork of Beckler River Road♦, and follow forks to the SW end of the peak. Reference: *Trips and Trails 1.*

SILICA MOUNTAIN 5400′+/1646 m

This moderate summit is about 3 mi. E of Beckler River, N of Evergreen Creek.

ROUTE: Reach from Evergreen Mountain Road (see Beckler River Road♦); just walk up the stream about ½ mi. and bear NE upslope. Expect some bush.

FORTUNE MOUNTAIN 5903′/1799 m

A fine viewpoint to scan alpine topography to the N. Fortune is W of the Cascade crest about 2 mi. NW of Wenatchee Pass.

ROUTE: This summit is easily reached by a short hike from about 1 mi. SW of the junction of the Crest Trail♦ and Meadow Creek Trail♦. From near Fortune Ponds hike S upslope to the E summit ridge. The ascent could also be done from Meadow Creek Trail.

BENCHMARK MOUNTAIN 5816′/1773 m

Actually the highest part of West Cady Ridge, Benchmark is 1½ mi. SW of Cady Pass. The summit can be reached by trail. On August 11, 1887 Albert B. Rogers and his companion "Al" made the first ascent for the view (and saw Mt. Rainier); Albert B. Rogers Papers, University of Washington Library, p. 71.

ROUTE: See West Cady Ridge Trail♦. Benchmark can also be easily reached from the Crest Trail♦; see Trails, Section II.

SKYKOMISH PEAK 6368′/1941 m

A gentle summit on the Cascade crest 15 mi. NNW of Stevens Pass.

ROUTE: The summit is a short alpine stroll W from the Crest Trail♦ at about 2 mi. N of Cady Pass (at est. 5600′); see Trails, Section II.

MARBLE PEAK 5111′/1558 m

This minor peak 2 mi. S of Silverton has prominence because of the low level of the Stillaguamish valley; the N and E sides are steepest.

ROUTE: From Marble Pass♦ ascend W up steep timbered and rocky slopes, then easy rock. Time: 4 hours from either road.

WEST SIDE: Leave the Mountain Loop Hwy♦ about ⅓ mi. W of Silverton at a survey marker. Cross a log jam to an island; about 200 yds downstream leave the island and contour through brush parallel to the river until the creek draining Marble Gulch is crossed. Climb SE up a timbered ridge, keeping directly on the crest. Where it becomes rocky, contour right through open timber until the second large clearing is reached. Here the summit is an easy scramble east. Class 2. Time: 4 to 5 hours.

Note: this is a good winter or spring climb; avalanche exposure is minimal if gullies right of timbered ridge are avoided.

An alternate approach is longer: one could travel some 1½ mi. cross-country along the crest from Mallardy Ridge Trail No. 705.

HALL PEAK 5452′/1662 m

Hall is a secondary yet very rugged peak of asymmetric shape 2 mi. SE of Silverton. The precipitous N face is distinguished by a long slanting gully and rib that angle W to the upper N ridge. The peak is named for George Hall, the original 1891 settler of Silverton. In mining times the peak was estimated to be 8000 ft high—highest of the "group. known as the Big Four."[73] Old maps show Hall's N flank had numerous prospects; claims of the 45 Mine reached above 4500 ft on the S. It seems safe to assume prospectors were the first to reach the summit, but Art Winder claimed a solo first July 5, 1927.

WEST RIDGE: At Silverton (see Mountain Loop Hwy♦, 1521′) cross bridge and drive 0.2 mi. to spur end. Find Silver Gulch Trail on right and take to its end in 1½ mi. at minesites (est. 2400′). Ascend SE to the ridge on the W side of Hall (4600′) keeping well right of the NW face. There is a ridge of trees leading to a basin just beneath the first saddle W of the top (this saddle is E of minor humps toward Marble Pass). Then take the easy W ridge. Time: 6 hours.

Note: alternate approach is via Marble Pass.

SOUTHEAST RIDGE: From near the end of Williamson Creek Road♦ follow a timbered ridge to the W side of the Hall-Big Four saddle; follow the heathery SE ridge; no difficulties. Time: 6 hours.

Alternate Approach: See Big Four Mountain-Northwest

BIG FOUR MOUNTAIN from southwest
U.S. GEOLOGICAL SURVEY

GLACIER PK.
SLOAN PK.
CADET PK.
WIN PKS.
SHEEP MTN.
SPERRY PK.
South Peak
Barlow
Pass
BIG FOUR MTN.
S. E. Ridge
N.W. Ridge
S.W. Spur
VESPER
GLACIER
Copper
Lake

Ridge for route to the saddle; a shortcut can be taken climbing through bush above cliffs to gain a sloping snow finger and ledges that lead to the upper ridge.

SKUBI RIDGE: This is the N ridge, named for Steve Skubi, who died in an avalanche here in spring 1962. First ascent by Jim Carlson, Bob Marcy, George Mattson, and Kenn Carpenter on July 4, 1963. Reference: *A.A.J.*, 1964, pp. 173-174.

Reach the ridge from Silver Gulch (see West Ridge). The snow gully leads to the notch (4000′) on the N shoulder (S of hump 4271′); then climb rock into the high notch (est. 5200′); class 3 and 4 (the steep fatal avalanche gully is just below this notch). Climb 20 ft of class 5 (poor rock), then continue 300 ft (loose but easier).

BIG FOUR MOUNTAIN 6135′/1870 m

Big Four is the outstanding mountain flanking the South Fork Stillaguamish valley. It stands just 3 mi. SE of Silverton and features an immense N face that begins at the low altitude of 2000 ft and is often decorated with snowpatches and plumes of falling water. A small ice remnant ("Rucker's Glacier") remains at its foot—probably the lowest ice in the Cascades. The mountain is wedge-shaped, trending W to E, with five minor summit points on the backbone. There is a separated SE peak (5840′+) near the main summit mass, with a saddle at 5600 ft. As seen from Monte Cristo, this profile prompted the first name, the "Saddle Mountain" of the miners. Later the mountain acquired its name from the "4-shaped" decorative snowpatch high on the E face.

The mountain was a landmark to early prospectors, miners, and tourists who took the railroad into the area; from the former Big Four Inn many hiked to view the ice caves. Mining maps show claims high on the mountain, but the alpine nature of the mountain likely kept prospectors well beneath the summit. Rock is pre-Tertiary meta-sedimentary (sandstone and conglomerate).

The first ascent was made by Forest Farr and Art Winder on July 19, 1931 via the NW ridge (*Mountaineer Bull.* October 1931, p. 5); interestingly, a goat preceded them on most of the upper route. Winder and Norval Grigg had attempted an E side route from the Headlee Pass route on May 30, 1928, but were halted in a steep snow finger above a large snowfield and gully by rain, rockfall, and poor snow conditions. A report was made about a Swiss group climbing the frontal N or NW face in the late 1920s, but the completion of ascent is uncertain. The first winter climb of Big Four was made by Kenn Carpenter, Bob Marcy, and Ron Miller on February 10, 1963 via the SW buttress.

DRY CREEK ROUTE (East Face): This has become the most popular route because of directness; it is not certain which party first completed the route. In early summer beware of slide conditions in the upper gully and from adjacent snowpatches which may work loose from slabs. In the gully there is party-inflicted rockfall danger (wear hard hats); some snowpatches exist all summer in this area.

From the Mountain Loop Hwy♦ at 1.4 mi. E of Big Four campground (1718′) travel 200 yds directly to the river, then cross on a log jam. Hike upstream 150 yds, then inland 150 yds to detour a bog; then angle downstream to Dry Creek, which is taken to the lower cliff base. Bear right and ascend the far right side of the cliffs (much scrub cedar) about 700 ft to the talus cirque under the big rock headwall. Traverse left about 1500 ft (possible snowpatches) to the major right-slanting couloir that splits the E face of the mountain. Ascend the couloir's right side (possible schrund) to where the face broadens into a shallow rock basin (est. 5000′) just above the "4" snowpatch. Climb rock slope (watch rockfall) W near the right side of the face to the saddle in summit ridge. Then ascend reddish broken rock on the false summit; cross to the S side of the crest. Traverse easy minor points atop or on the N of the crest. Class 3. Time: 6-8 hours.

SOUTHWEST FACE: This is a long, broad and slabby face with a number of ribs and gullies above a flank of upper Williamson Creek drainage. A western depression, often snow-filled, is just S of the NW ridge; a deep narrow canyon cuts into the lower face, entering Copper Creek below the lake. The two main spurs on the face are (1) W spur to S of the western depression to reach the NW ridge beneath where the gradient levels to the summit points; (2) spur from exit of Copper Lake leading to the W summit points. Climbing history is uncertain. The winter climb used the SW spur to the summit ridge.

Several approach possibilities exist. From the Williamson Creek Road♦ walk to the far-right switchback (2500′), then head cross-country upstream rightward, but keep left of the W spur. Either climb directly up the spur or use the western depression farther upslope (some brush).

Or leave the path to Copper Lake (see Vesper Peak) at the pass above the lake exit—see (2) above. Climb directly E toward the mountain. Continue scrambling on steepening rock, circling above the spectacular red rock scar on N side of rib. A choice of gullies or face climbing provides routes (class 3 or 4) to the summit points joining the NW ridge. A direct finish looks more difficult.

NORTHWEST RIDGE: Recommended before mid-July; potentially dangerous in early season. From the Big Four Campground follow the old sidewalk SSW and continue on trail about ¼ mi. to the river (log bridge); follow trail and continuing dry creek beds ¾ mi. to the brushy cliff base beneath the Big Four-Hall saddle. Note: do not come too close to the Hall side; stay left of steepest lower cliffs and evergreen scrub.

Climb the lower cliff first slightly left, then right up dirt and brush slopes adjacent to a stream (some class 3) and then

BIG FOUR MOUNTAIN from northeast
ROLAND AMUNDSON

left toward a couloir; this ends in a steep obvious dirt-filled gully leading to the 4400-ft saddle. Now ascend the long NW ridge. At several hundred ft below the first summit avoid an exposed rock step by working around the S about 200 ft; drop to a little shelf, then ascend. Continue up easy heather and rock, then over or around the ridge humps to the more level but narrow sections that lead to the flat summit ridge. Class 3. Time: 8 hours.

Note: there is a rappel bolt in place on the lower cliff at a break just W of a waterfall.

Alternate Approach: Reach the saddle from the S. From Williamson Creek Road♦ (1800′) follow the old roadbed on foot to 2600 ft where it switchbacks left. Work up and right on a timbered ridge (NE) toward the saddle; expect brush.

NORTH FACE: The face of Big Four may have been climbed in the late 1920s by a Swiss party, but this is uncertain. An incomplete ascent was made in 1935 by Wolf Bauer and Jack Lowe, beginning on the rock headwall and climbing to within about 700 ft of the summit; a storm forced a descent by a traverse to the W. The first recorded ascent of this 4000-ft face was by Montgomery Johnson, Ken Prestrud, and Charles Welsh on August 16, 1942. Wesley Grande and Jack Kendrick climbed the face in August 1947, probably beginning closer to the highest part of the headwall. A winter climb via the gully E of the N rib was made January 4, 1974 by Rich Carlstad and Cal Folsom (*A.A.J.*, 1974, p. 142).

Approach the N face using the ice caves trail. The 1942

BIG FOUR MOUNTAIN, North Face
ROBERT J. De WITZ, U.S. FOREST SERVICE

ascent climbed the lower rock wall (E of the central headwall) to a shallow basin (class 4), where the climbing eases, then took the left (eastern) of the two N rock ribs. This rib is long, but generally easy (exposed class 3), and meets the ridge near the summit. Grade III. Time: 8-10 hours.

Variation: Take the western (more prominent) of the two N ribs; a class 4-5 section has been reported on this rib, which meets the ridge several hundred ft W of the summit.

Variation: Ascend the lower cliff below the basin on the far W, then traverse on a rising sloping shelf about ¼ mi. to the N rib. Partway up the rib a variation traverses left across the face to a left-bearing ramp. Ascend, then gradually climb up and rightward (rock or snow) to the summit.

Headwall Variation: 1947 route. This followed smooth water-worn granitic rock right of the waterfall four difficult pitches (two pitons used for safety); the climbing probably angled upward to the right, then led to the shallow basin and the eastern rock rib.

Headwall Variation: By Ben Guydelkon and Ron Miller July 17, 1973. This variation may be similar, the same, or a nearby line on the lower headwall as per the 1946 or 1947 ascent. This climb went to the highest point of the glacier remnant, where a 100-ft pedestal can be seen. Use laybacks, stemming and jams in the obvious and classic crack (5.7-5.8). From atop traverse 20 ft left and climb up to a belay. Traverse 30 ft right and up an open book; near its end climb right (5.8) to where the climbing eases (one lead of class 3 gains broad ledges). Climb a very strenuous brush cliff to the right of a secondary stream; an open basin is soon reached. Cross the stream and gain the rib to the left of the main N rib and follow to the top (class 3 and 4). Grade III. Class 5.8; all nuts.

NORTH FACE, TOWER ROUTE: This route lies E of the N headwall. First ascent by Ron Miller and Ben Guydelkon on July 25, 1971.

From the end of the ice caves trail traverse E to the NE side of the first tower (at a prominent gully). Scramble the gully (steep but well broken) to a broad ledge which bisects the tower. Follow the ledge about 100 ft past its crest (where original party roped). Begin in a chimney and work slightly right to the tower's W ridge (four leads). Some six more leads are required to reach the tower's summit. Rappel into the notch; descend E 200 ft to where the second tower may be gained at two obvious trees. About six leads will gain the summit of the second tower (good bivouac). The third tower is done directly on small face holds; beyond the tower a short overhanging knife-edge section (good protection) is climbed on the right side. Several more leads gain the end of the ridge of towers. Cross the snowfield to the rock band, staying well to the left of the large stream. Continue up the rock band for three leads, then cross stream at the rock bench. From here there are 14 leads on steep snow (unless dry) followed by a short walk to the summit. Grade IV. Class 5.6 or 5.7. References: *Mountaineer*, 1971, pp. 80-81; *A.A.J.*, 1972, p. 114.

SOUTH PEAK, SOUTHEAST RIDGE: Leave the Sunrise Mine Road♦ 0.1 mi. from its end, then descend logging slash and cross the several stream channels on logs. Climb W into the large cirque on the N of Sperry Peak; follow the narrowing couloir W, leaving it via a short, steep and slabby spur (class 4) to the S just below its upper end at est. 4000 ft. Climb WSW on gentle slopes to an obvious saddle and drop about 200 ft on the W side. Contour NW about ⅔ mi. beneath cliffs and slab, then ascend NE to the S ridge of a 5600-ft intermediate summit. Descend the N ridge to the S rib of the main summit (class 3 for 350′). Time: 7-8 hours. This route is really practical only in late spring when snow still fills the lower couloir but avalanche exposure has ended.

VESPER PEAK 6214′/1894 m

Vesper ranks with Big Four and Del Campo as one of the major frontal summits on the Sultan-South Fork Stillaguamish divide (2 mi. S of Big Four Mountain). The gentle S slopes can be distinctly seen from the highway hill S of Monroe; the SW slope features a large fault gully (S and SW slopes are meta-volcanics, with the contact near the top). From the E Vesper's quartz diorite presents a curious slab-like, pointed appearance; stock is a satellite of the Snoqualmie Batholith. The steep clean N face offers excellent technical routes. Currently the summit can be identified by a stop sign. Many parties use the connecting ridge to combine this ascent with that of Sperry.

Copper Lake nestles at the NW foot of Vesper. Most of the basin above the lake is filled with the narrow Vesper Glacier (1.3 km—5400′ to 3600′); to its SE is a smaller, parallel but broad ice remnant hanging on a sloping bench. In the area of the lake claims were

VESPER PEAK, North Face
MIKE HEATH

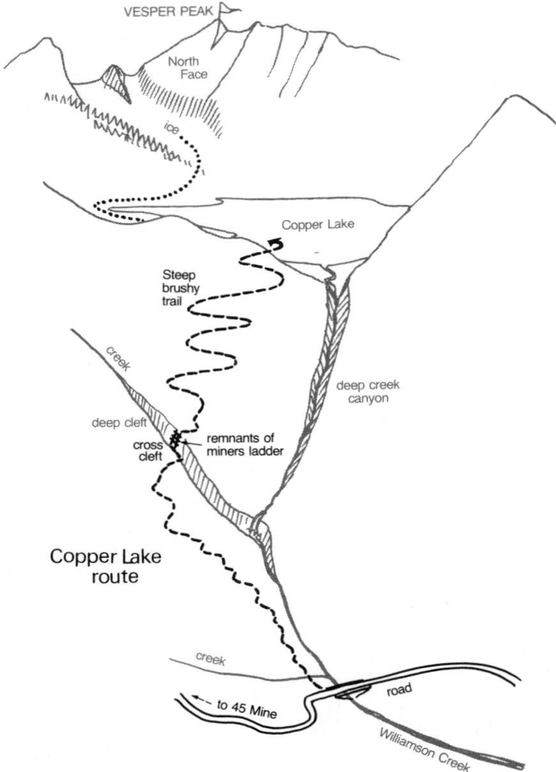

staked after the 45 Mine began its development in 1896. The "Garnet" prospect was staked at about 5500 ft ½ mi. W of the summit by miners from the early Sunrise Mine on Vesper Creek. Members of the 1918 Mountaineers outing climbed Vesper, but were likely preceded by prospectors and perhaps a geological survey party led by Thomas Gerdine. Reference: *Mountaineer*, 1918, p. 14.

Rough, brushy low peaks stand NW of Vesper: *Little Chief Peak* (est. 5280′/1609 m) is 1.6 mi. distant; an unnamed peak (est. 4800′) stands to the N of Little Chief on the W side of the lake.

EAST SLOPE: Use Vesper Creek Trail♦ to the small lake; a longer alternative is to use Sunrise Mine Trail♦ across Headlee Pass for a ¼-mi. traverse to the lake. Climb due W over heather and granite rockslides (snowpatches in early season) to the gradual slabs on Vesper's upper portion. Class 2. Time: 3 hours from the end of the mine road in Vesper Creek.

Northeast Approach: Skirt Copper Lake♦ on its N, then continue on open slopes to Vesper Glacier; ascend easily to the snow saddle (5440′+) NE of the summit. Turn S behind a knob to meet the E slope.

NORTH FACE

This moderately steep 800 to 900 ft face lacks regular-spaced jointing, and as a consequence is denied classic climbing lines. Yet the face has its appeal and affords solid, difficult rock climbing. There is a major ledge system at about two-thirds of the height from the glacier; steep but gullied rock beneath the ledge affords new opportunities. The upper face is a triangular-shaped slab that is divided by a dihedral: the eastern portion rises at an angle of about 60° while the western is of lower angle. Reach the face from the eastern snow notch via the East Slope approach or ascend the glacier (Northeast Approach).

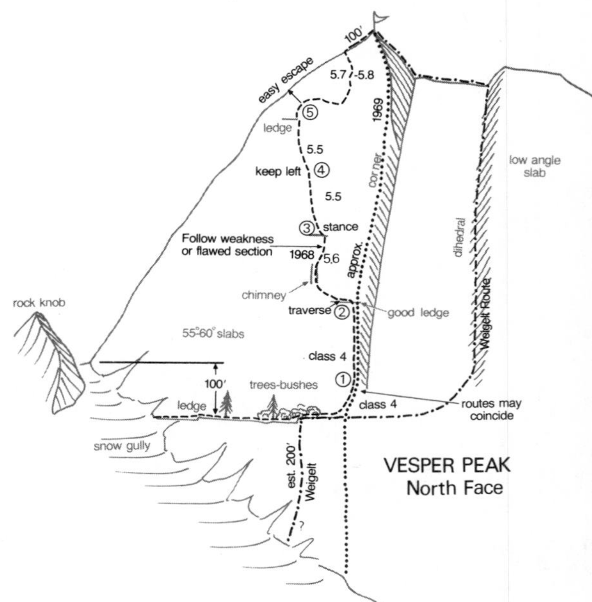

EAST SIDE: This route is near the center of the left-hand slab; first ascent by Bruce Garrett and Jim Langdon on July 21, 1968. The route enters from the eastern snow notch and traverses the big ledge to the 1969 route. After two class 4 leads ascend slabs leftward three pitches (class 5) through a definite flaw (the first of these pitches is a poorly protected traverse and small shallow chimney; last one follows a weakness—class 5.5). There is a possible leftward escape here. The final lead begins by a slight downward drop on a long rightward traverse; the lead was done 180 ft in tandem (hard, poor protection—bolts would be helpful). Grade II; class 5.7-5.8.

CENTRAL ROUTE: First ascent by B.J. Heath, Michael Heath, Tom Oas, and Bill Sumner on August 3, 1969. This route is completed on the western area of the left-hand upper slab.

Reach the glacier at the lowest point of the face. Climb

MONTE CRISTO to VESPER PEAK
PHILIP LEATHERMAN

GOTHIC PK.
Castle Rocks
MORNING STAR PK.
SPERRY PK.
LEWIS PK.
1972
1973
Weden Creek
South Fork Sauk River Valley
MONTE CRISTO

four leads (5.5 to 5.8). Scramble several hundred ft and belay one lead (5.6) to the scrub tree at the lower right-hand corner of the high-angle slab. Next climb a small overhang (5.4) and work up, right, along a heather ledge to its end. Climb up and right to edge of the slab on broken blocks (5.7). The next two leads are the crux: climb with poor protection to a bolt (est. 50 ft) and then up and right to a belay bolt (5.7). The next lead is about 70 ft with weak protection (5.8) and generally follows the W edge of the slab to the summit. Grade III; class 5.8. Piton or chock selection up to 1½″—including four KB. Time: 6 hours from glacier. References: *Mountaineer*, 1970, pp. 104-105; *A.A.J.*, 1970, p. 118.

WEIGELT ROUTE: First ascent by John Bonneville, Julie Brugger, Earl Hamilton, and Mark Weigelt in June 1970. From the snow notch descend 100 ft down glacier, round a buttress, then make a long traverse to an obvious dihedral system (crosses 1969 route). Ascend a broken gully to a ledge (a class 5 and a class 4 pitch). Third lead goes to a ledge by angling right. Begin fourth pitch with a mantle and up a gully (some loose rock) to a mossy ledge, then continue right across this exposed ledge. Sixth pitch climbs the dihedral and around corner to right (5.8 or 5.9 at several moves of face climbing at dihedral top); easy slabs farther right could be done. Then the summit scramble. Grade II; class 5.9. Time: 4 hours on rock. Selection: eight pitons up to 2″ and many chocks. Reference: *A.A.J.*, 1971, p. 342.

WEST SIDE: First ascent by Mac Harnois and Don Williamson on September 27, 1970. From the base of the face climb a steep defined buttress to the major ledge (three leads). Continue directly above for about six leads, mostly on clean 45° slab (well protected) to the ridge crest W of the summit; on the last two leads one is 50 ft W of the dihedral. A short scramble leads to the summit. Grade II; class 5.6. Time: 7 hours from Copper Lake. Reference: *A.A.J.*, 1971, pp. 342-343.

Note: the route's upper part can be met by traversing out the ledge.

SPERRY PEAK 6000′+/1829 m

Sperry is a rocky precipitous pyramid located on the same divide as Vesper, ¾ mi. E. The 5300-ft saddle on its W connects to a ridgepoint, from which the divide continues SW to Vesper.

Sperry is moderate only on its southern slopes. A NE ridge steeply divides adjoining faces; the E face is precipitous with deep gully systems; the WNW face is a pattern of vertical lines, a steep mixture of rock and scrub conifers. Rock is quartz diorite, generally sound.

The topographical map of 1905 showed a glacier 1 mi. in length and 1¼ mi. wide atop the slabs N of Sperry, but the ice area may have been overestimated; a vast denuded slab remains with only a vestige of this glacier. There is a small ice patch under the N face, between the N and NW ridges. A long vertically trending gully cuts down the N face to this ice. The peak is named for A.D. (Dick) Sperry, a Silverton prospector of the 1890s.

SOUTHWEST SLOPE: The S face has a rock band with a heather bench atop; above is the final rock pyramid. Take Vesper Creek Trail♦ to the small lake. Skirt it and climb easy rock to the W shoulder; then continue to the summit. Class 2. Time: 5 hours from road.

Note: one could traverse to Vesper Peak; follow the crest (lower portion is scrubby) to outflank the lower rock band.

WEST RIDGE: This route was first done July 4, 1927 by Norval Grigg and Art Winder on a traverse from Vesper Peak. It is possible to follow the ridge or make minor variances on the S; class 3.

NORTHWEST RIDGE: This narrow rock prow, ending on slabs, is a prominent feature on Sperry; it rises at the E edge of the glacier segment, and is bordered on its opposite side by the N face. First ascent by Anthony Hovey, Bob Mulfinger, and Charles Torko on July 15, 1965.

Approach as for Northeast Ridge route, but follow creek bed in center of basin; this leads directly to a gully that offers the best route to timberline and snow basin (denuded slab) to the W. Climb left onto the NW ridge and follow it to a point: here it joins the Southwest Slope route at about 200 ft below the summit. Class 3 and 4.

NORTHEAST RIDGE: This precipitous ridge corners the N and E faces; it levels near the summit, but remains very narrow. First ascent by Anthony Hovey and Don Keller in summer 1962.

From the end of Sunrise Mine Road♦ descend clearcut, then cross bottomland and brush to the forested branch valley emanating from the basin between Sperry and Big Four. Then climb brushy lower slopes of the N ridge to rock. Climb onto ridge on its E side (a harder variation begins from W). Ascend the ridge about 1000 ft (mostly class 3 and 4 with one short class 5 pitch at about two-thirds of the climb); here move around the right side to a very exposed and narrow ridge (difficult finger jam). Rock is generally sound. Grade II; class 4 and 5. Time: 8 hours from road.

EAST FACE—GULLY ROUTE: This face is characterized by slabby steep and brushy rock, deeply gully cut. The first ascent by Anthony Hovey and Gary Rose about July 1963 used a line that ends at a prominent notch on the NE ridge at about 300 ft below the summit.

Take Sunrise Mine Trail♦ to basin below Headlee Pass, then attack the E face directly via a prominent gully. At the beginning a snow moat may be hard to cross; the route used started on slabs, with fairly brushy class 3 and 4 (and steep heather, dirty rock). Bear up and right, then make a short rappel rightward into an open book (gully) just below where it ends. Slabs and a minor ridge system (?) trend N. The upper part of the climb is more exposed, but fractured and not too difficult; avoid more difficult rock directly beneath the summit and climb to NE ridge notch. Class 4. Time: 6-8 hours from road.

MORNING STAR and SPERRY PEAK from east
ROLAND AMUNDSON

VESPER PK.
MORNING STAR PK
SPERRY PK.
BIG FOUR MTN.
Northeast Ridge
Vega Tower
?
1963
1973
1972
East Side Route
Swauk Formation east-dipping bed

EAST FACE—NORTH RIB: This route takes the rib about 100 yds N of the Central Rib. The rib forms the left hand margin of the deep gully dividing the E face. The original climb was 13 leads and about 300 ft of class 3 in the middle portion. First ascent by Todd Bibler and Mark Thornton in October 1973.

Ascend from the boulders in the valley's upper basin to the apron several hundred ft above. After three leads of class 5 climbing off the apron, a long stretch of mixed brush and rock leads to a gendarme and ledge area (here the gully on right looks like a funnel). Now a rock fin (class 5) gradually sharpens to take the route to the broad part of the NE ridge just below the lower summit. Grade III. Time: 6 hours.

EAST FACE—CENTRAL RIB: The rib begins at the left end of the apron that spans the N half of the face. The route has about 20 pitches from the top of the apron to the upper NE ridge. First ascent by Mickey Schurr and Glen Cannon on July 2, 1972.

At entry to upper basin below Headlee Pass cross toward watercourse slabs; climb gully to their N, follow it through thicket, and ascend apron (class 3 ends). About 100 ft right of cliffs at upper left apron corner take chimney/gully up slabs. At first cul de sac work leftward out onto slabs, continuing up and left to second gully. Ease out of gully on right side of cul de sac over steep rock with short loose section near roof, continuing up to tree on right and back left to brush (tree density increases here). Fifth pitch climbs easily to tree atop right-slanting gully in evergreens. Go up and left through brush back to S edge of rib overlooking cliff. Angle through brush right to a broad dirt gully; ascend it to rock promonotory.

Descend along left side of promonotory to exposed gully; climb it to exposed notch above pinnacle terminating tree section, then up/right (clean face) to a belay at 60 ft. Tenth lead (5.7) goes up to right side of the offset, crosses left onto it and goes up a difficult crack capped by a problem bush. Next lead (5.8) passes lower overhang closely on its right up difficult slabs and groove, and finishes at recess below/left of large red overhang. Pitch 12: traverse moderate rock up leftward into scrub trees, then up left along rim at S rib edge. Go left around promonotory and ascend minor gully to its upper notch, then up enjoyable broken slabs. Pitch 16: ascend to top of crest (top of rib) and descend to notch adjacent to next pinnacle toward face, moving rightward and down onto bushy ramp perched above the N canyon. Follow ramp on rightward traverse of pinnacle to notch at base of steep upper face. Follow ramp continuation rightward and up with some difficult/strenuous bushwork. Turn upward and take moderate rock to gain NE ridge (possible snowcrest); follow to summit or traverse to W ridge. Grade III or IV. Class 5.8; recommend about 12 pitons (nothing over 1¼″) and a few small nuts. Time: 13 hours.

SOUTH RIDGE: This is quite feasible and interesting, but a seldom-used route. From Headlee Pass scramble to ridge base (or reach from just E of the lake). Follow generally easy rock, with one class 4 pitch just after a prominent notch about midpoint. Time: 2-3 hours from pass.

MORNING STAR PEAK 6020′/1835 m

This is a cliffy, thimble-shaped peak between Headlee Pass and Del Campo Peak 1¼ mi. SE of Sperry Peak. It was apparently named for the Morning Star group of claims on Silver Creek. As a climb and viewpoint it deserves more attention: there is no really easy way to the summit. First ascent by Sam Heller and a companion about 1940 (route unknown).

NORTH FACE: This is an interesting route, with the easiest trail approach, though not the simplest way to the summit. It is suggested that the route be studied on the approach; not recommended in adverse weather.

Take Sunrise Mine Trail♦ to the basin closely below Headlee Pass. then contour left around the head of the talus canyon on a large slanting rockslide about ¼ mi. to the NW of the summit. From here climb talus and broken rock in the basin, and gullies, to the crest of the NW ridge. Cross over and skirt N of summit cliffs to work around to the N or NE. Pleasant rock climbing leads to the top. Class 3 and 4. Time: 5 hours from road.

Variation: A slightly harder route starts from the base of the main summit cliff; climb the NW upper corner (class 4).

Variation: By Kenn Carpenter, Mark Haun, Monte Haun, and Dick Hill in July 1960. From Vesper Creek Trail♦ S of Headlee Pass reach the NW face via talus and a gully to the ridge connecting the pass. Skirt cliffs to the N ridge. Reference: *A.A.J.*, 1961, p. 367.

EAST SIDE: Leave Sunrise Mine Trail♦ at Manley's cabin. Keep on the N side of the stream about ½ mi. (old trail into the basin now vanished), then follow stream boulders for about ¾ mi. (easy). Ascend a boulderfield (snow in early season) rightward, keeping right of large slabs. Ascend rightward toward the summit formation, to meet the ridge about 400 ft below the summit at a saddle. Contour the basin on the SE side to reach the S ridge 200 ft under the summit for the final scramble. Class 3. Time: 4½ hours from road.

SOUTH ROUTE: First ascent by Anthony Hovey, Ed Parker, and Klindt Vielbig September 10, 1960. Leave Vesper Creek Trail♦ where it corners left. Travel in the opposite direction cross-country to the stream. Go down to the stream, then up watercourse, then along gully to a pool. Follow gentle snow slopes in the basin (pinnacles on left). Beyond the snow there is a short rock pitch, then continue to top of gully. Traverse to the N and then some scrambling leads to the summit. Class 3.

VEGA TOWER 5480′+/1670 m

This rock thumb is on the spur ¼ mi. N of Morning Star's summit. As seen from the W, Vega is the southern and higher of two rock eminences; both have steep walls with deep gullies on S flanks (there is also a 5440-ft tower N and a rock hump (5280′) with a steep E face). First ascent by Anthony Hovey, Klindt Vielbig, and Paul Williams on September 4, 1962.

Reach the tower by leaving the trail in the basin opposite Sperry; climb the obvious gully leading to the S notch below the final summit. A safety piton may be advisable at a gully chockstone. Scrambling on the NW side of the summit completes the climb (class 3). References: *Mountaineer*, 1962, p. 104; *A.A.J.*, 1962, p. 207.

LEWIS PEAK 5608′/1709 m

Lewis is a lower summit on a spur 1 mi. N of Del Campo. Its W slope features vast slabs; from the E it resembles a mound, but with cliffy, brushy terrain. The name comes from the Lewis brothers, early trappers and prospectors.

ROUTES: Begin as for Morning Star Peak—East Side, then continue to the lower W face. Traverse slabs via a gully to the N ridge, then follow 1000 ft to the summit.

A longer route is via the Del Campo-Lewis saddle: climb N ½ mi. along the crest; a short rappel is made at one place (see approach for Del Campo-North Spur).

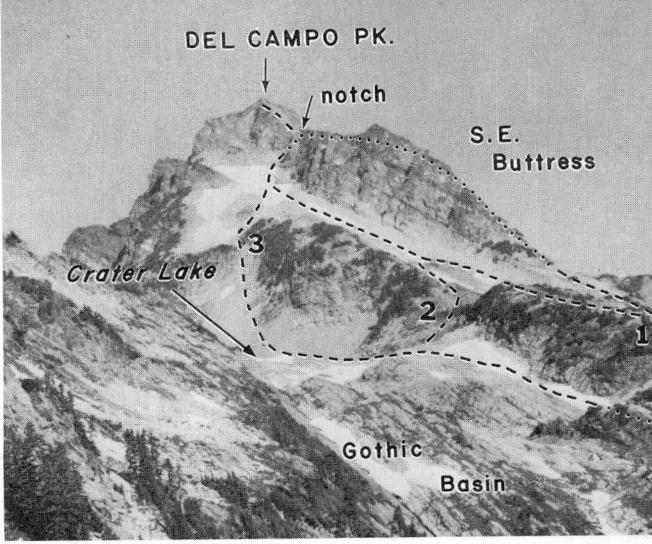

DEL CAMPO PEAK from Gothic Basin
JEFF COLEHOUR

DEL CAMPO PEAK 6610′/2015 m

This craggy and outstanding peak W of Monte Cristo is blessed with sound rock—very hard metamorphosed sandstone, shale, and conglomerate forming prominent E-dipping beds; one of these forms a picturesque ramp on the S face, often holding snow until late summer. These sedimentary beds were folded into a sharp V-shaped syncline between Del Campo and Lewis Peak and later were cooked by granodiorite of the Index batholith. The steepest flank of Del Campo is on the N, but the peak presents a rugged appearance from all vantages. The peak is located midway between the upper courses of the Sultan's N fork and Sauk's S fork. First called "Flag Peak," it was renamed for a mine on its slopes (the Del Campo group of three claims overlooking Crater Lake).[74]

The first ascent is uncertain, but documentation proves the summit was reached by J.A. Juleen, his wife, and two others in about 1912 on a photographic mission. Members of the large Mountaineer party August 6 and 7, 1918 reached the summit. Reference: *Mountaineer*, 1918, pp. 15-16.

SOUTH FACE: Follow the Weden Creek Trail♦ 3 mi. to Gothic Basin, just SE of 5200-ft Crater Lake. A path leads up to the lake, which lies in an alpine cirque; talus and snow lead to Foggy Pass, which separates Del Campo and Gothic Peaks. The summit of Del Campo lies ½ mi. to the NNW.

There are several ways to reach the rock of the upper S face: (1) the shortest is to leave the trail before the lake, where a creek and snow gully descend from the N (snow gully steepens as it trends WNW to S side of SE buttress); (2) start E of lake, then ascend a shoulder and rockslide to a small snowfield, keeping left of the steep SE buttress (promontory). Climb easy broken rock left of the gully which separates the main summit and promontory; (3) reach the snowfield by ascending talus from the lake, then go through a band of broken rock; (4) from Foggy Pass (5480′+) bear over to the upper S face, or make a climb on the SW corner.

On the upper S face climb mixed heather and rock to the summit. There are many variations, but a good route is to ascend to the high notch of the SE buttress; out of a gully here is a 30-ft step (class 4), then the summit is a scramble. Class 3 or 4. Time: 4 hours from road or 1 hour from lake.

SOUTHWEST ROUTE: A new route approximately on the SW buttress or W buttress was done on the fourth known ascent of the peak (June 10, 1933) by Don Blair, Willard Carr, Norval Grigg, and Art Winder, coming from Gothic Peak; the route was apparently class 4. An ascent on August 8, 1969 is recorded by Jon Bagg, George D. Brede, and D. Kruger via the W buttress, using one safety piton.

NORTHWEST FACE: Inconclusive reports make it uncertain if this route has been done as presented; hence the description should be taken as speculative. Take Sunrise Mine Trail♦ and continuation as for Morning Star Peak—East Side and continue to the upper basin of the S fork (mostly open talus). Reach the long narrow snowfield between the lower NW face and the Morning Star slabs, then ascend this snow basin to the crest extending from Morning Star. Continue several hundred ft until it is feasible to bear left through a break in the face to the lower part of the "G"-shaped ice patch. Climb to the left upper side about 200 ft from the summit where a natural exit left reaches rock; here the broken N spur continues to the summit (probably class 3 and 4). A steeper but possible finish may be from the top of the ice, then the headwall, working slightly left.

NORTH SPUR: First ascent by Jim Crooks, Bob Martin, and Dick Wille on June 25, 1940. The route taken may not follow the exact pattern of the description given, which is based on several reports and a study of photography. Use the route to upper basin as per Northwest Face. Ascend E ½ mi. to the saddle (est. 4800′) adjacent to Lewis Peak (or keep right of saddle in an open basin). On the sloping northern spur of Del Campo climb mixed slab, debris, and snow patches to where spur steepens; from here about 200 ft of rock to the summit. An alternative is to bear to the upper E face by bearing for the U-notch on the upper SE buttress; one could climb directly here or descend 50 ft and join the South Face route. Class 3 or 4, depending on completion taken. Time: 5 hours from road.

EAST FACE: Various ways to gain the upper face are described above. The face was attempted on September 25, 1935 by John Bissell and R.S. Eskenazi, who then completed the ascent by a detour. From the trail before reaching Gothic Basin hike up to the SE buttress at about 5600 ft. Ascend snow on the N of the buttress to moderately steep rock at about 400 ft beneath the summit. There are numerous class 3 and 4 opportunities on slabs, including taking the SE buttress. Broken rock just beneath the summit on the E face forms a slight central depression which in winter and spring is snow-filled.

GOTHIC PEAK 6213′/1894 m

Gothic is ½ mi. SW of Del Campo Peak and separated from it by Foggy Pass. The crestline to the SE connects to the Sheep Gap group of peaks. Two small satellite spires decorate the short crest immediately N of the summit. The 1918 *Mountaineer* (p. 16) perceptively describes this scene: "The mediaeval outline of Castle Rocks etched on the horizon."

Solid sandstone offers fine climbing pitches, especially on the E faces of the summits. One of the best examples of the conglomerate-argillite series occurs on the rugged W and S faces (Sultan River drainage) where about 2600 ft of the series is exposed above quartz diorite contact. This series is very resistant to weathering, so forms steep walls. The name honors William Gothic, an early prospector. The first ascent was made by Norval Grigg, Art Winder, Don Blair, and Willard Carr on June 10, 1934 (via W fork of Silver Creek). References: *Mountaineer*, 1934, p. 5; 1918, p. 16.

EAST SIDE: From Crater Lake (see Del Campo Peak) make a climbing traverse (snow or easy talus and rock) to beneath the E side of Castle Rocks. Continue beneath Gothic until SE of the summit. Then ascend the short SE ridge (class 2-3); harder pitches exist on the short E face. The spires of Castle Rock can be reached directly from the lake; a connection to the summits is facilitated by a band on the E; the final portions of the spires are easiest on the S. A popular program is to traverse Castle Rocks.

Alternate Approach: From Sultan Basin Road♦ at 26.3 mi. take a cat road E (opposite old buildings); becomes a miner's trail about 1 mi. long and ascends forest to the yellow talus gully on Gothic's S slope. Take the gully to ridge crest, then N to summit.

WEST FACE: The steep W face rounds into the even steeper S face. Deep chimney systems funnel into a stream that exits on the lower SW face into a brushy area. The climb is steep and rugged. First ascent by Anthony Hovey and Gary Rose on July 9, 1961.

From Sultan Basin Road♦ at 25.9 mi. (½ mi. before final bridge) start through brush to the creek bed ENE (dry in late season) which flows from the main gully to W of the summit; in early season the wet creek bed forces more travel through brush. When near the upper cliffy area beneath spires, work right on easy obvious slabs. Bear right over a shelf to a steepening rock gully, then climb rock and steep heather slopes, bearing rightward to the summit. Class 3 and 4. Time: 6 hours. References: *A.A.J.*, 1962, pp. 206-207; *Mountaineer*, 1962, p. 104.

Descent: A rib can be used parallel to Gothic Peak and about ½ mi. S.

SHEEP GAP MOUNTAIN 5819′/1774 m

The Sheep Gap group is a rugged massif of several striking rock peaks of the Swauk Formation between Weden Creek, the upper Sultan River, and Silver Creek's W fork. The bell-shaped highest peak is about ¼ mi. N of Sheep Gap and 1½ mi. SSE of Del Campo Peak; it features a high rounded spur on the SW, a pronounced couloir on the E, and a sheer western face. The entire S and E faces are especially steep; as a climb the mountain deserves more attention.

Sheep Gap's pointed N peak, ⅜ mi. distant, is climbed more often; a register intimating that this lower summit is "Sheep Gap" has been here, and published photographs have erroneously identified it as such. There is a sharp middle peaklet between the two highest peaks. The entire group was once labelled "Sheep Mountains" (goats mistaken for mountain sheep)[75] The first ascent (main peak) was made on July 9, 1933 by Don Blair, Willard Carr, Norval Grigg, and Art Winder, who reported "interesting rock." They approached from Mineral City; at the time there was a good mining trail along the N bank of Silver Creek's W fork. From an abandoned mine they contoured around the head of the basin and below the peak to the NW ridge, opposite the ridge with the hole.

Members of the original climbing party studied the peaks on their return from Gothic Peak. Because of imprecision of existing topographic maps they believed Sheep Gap was the peak at the ridge junction separat-

SULTAN-STILLAGUAMISH PEAKS from southeast
MARTIN JOHNSON

THREE FINGERS
WHITEHORSE MTN.
MT. BAKER
DEL CAMPO PK.
SPERRY PK.
GOTHIC PK.
LEWIS PK.
SHEEP GAP MTN.
North Pk.
Crater
Lake
am's Horn
trail
Weden Pass
Sheep
Gap

ing Gothic Basin, Silver Creek, and Sultan River drainages (now considered the N peak). After conferring with Forest Service personnel, they decided Sheep Gap was the quite striking peak seen from Mineral City, and easily identified by the large hole in the SE ridge (Art Winder, written commun., January 6, 1977).

MAIN PEAK

NORTH FACE—NORTH RIDGE: From Crater Lake (see Del Campo Peak) travel S on alpine terrain of upper Weden Creek (mostly meadows; about 5000′) and cross Weden Pass (est. 5100′; divide to West Fork Silver Creek), just NE of Sheep Gap's North Peak. Traverse around its E to the col (5240′) just N of the main peak. Then ascend steep heather and rock. The final portion was reported by the original party to be a fine rock ascent of a steep and narrow arete. Class 4. Time: est. 4 hours from lake. Note: descent feasible with rappels. The original approach route is no longer recommended because of underbrush; mining paths have vanished.

Alternate Approach: Drive Sultan Basin Road♦; park 0.4 mi. from its end, then hike 220 yds up logging left-fork to old trail. This follows left side of creek that leads into open basin NW of the mountain. At est. 4400 ft contour W below cliffs to gain ridge two saddles W of the middle peak. Follow the ridge toward the latter and contour up to the col N of the main peak (3½ hours).

SOUTH FACE: First ascent by Joan Firey, Joe Firey, Joe Hanson, and Anthony Hovey on October 4, 1959. Reach Sheep Gap (4600′+) from the W (Sultan Basin); the old mining trail to the Gap is largely vanished. Use the approach for South Crested Butte-North Ridge for about 1 mi.; ascend eastward (timber slopes) into a basin ending in slabs below the W face of the peak (keep right of wide avalanche swath). A rocky gully leads to Sheep Gap. Ascend NW on an oblique contour through trees, on slab and broken rock, working left around Ram's Horn into the steep slot leading behind it; the slot has short pitches of stemming and one small overhang (watch rockfall). Then bear left onto the main S face; climb a 40-ft chimney and on to where class 4 climbing begins. Climb a short pitch and on up to a notch leading to the final peak. Another pitch, a bit more scrambling, and the climb ends. Class 3 and 4. References: *Mountaineer*, 1960, p. 90; *A.A.J.*, 1960, p. 120.

Alternate Approach: It is possible to traverse under the E flank of the peak from the N approach (Weden Creek) and reach the S face.

NORTH PEAK 5683′/1732 m

ROUTE: The best route is the slabby NE ridge (a dipping conglomerate bed). A steep leaning tower can be avoided bypassing it on the W via a gully. Continue on the ridge. Class 2. Note: one could reach the N side via the saddle (5080′+) at ¼ mi. N of the peak via miner's trail from the Sultan (see Gothic Peak—West Face). Follow the creek to the valley head.

MIDDLE PEAK 5480′/1670 m

This small but sharp peak is simplest on the N.

RAM'S HORN 5400′+/1646 m

This is a subsidiary point located SSE of the main peak at about 200 yds from the S face. It has a flat top with some greenery; its S face rises sharply from Sheep Gap. References: *Mountaineer*, 1960, p. 90; *A.A.J.*, 1960, p. 120. The first ascent was made by two routes on October 18, 1959 by a group of five.

NORTHWEST ROUTE: By Cal Magnusson, William Stebbins, and Herb Swanson. From the junction of the main peak (NW side) a short scramble on slabby, mossy rock (class 3).

SOUTH RIDGE: By Anthony Hovey and Frank Tarver. The climb involves about 400 ft of class 4 and 5. From Sheep Gap scramble up dry watercourse to a notch overlooking the E face. Then class 3 leads up loose rock, then onto arete to the foot of a rock step. The next lead is steep; three pitons were used at about 50-ft level (belay). Then work down and across right to a small buttress (here one safety piton). Climb on good but loose holds; reach a tree and then a short slab. Then a series of easy shelves are done as the arete eases. A short wall leads to the top through a rock jungle.

CRESTED BUTTES

The Crested Buttes are an extremely rough and rocky ridge of sub-peaks, heavily forested on lower E and W slopes. They lie on a N-S axis, with a deep notch between the two peaks. The contact of the conglomerate-argillite series with intrusive quartz diorite is well exposed on these peaks. The more attractive summit is the pointed North Butte, located about ½ mi. S of Sheep Gap. This wedge-like peak has an impressive towerlike summit, protected by steep flanking chutes and cliffs; this is especially evident on the W, where there is a long rock wall. The eastern face is broad and steep; both N and S ridges are sharp crests.

The South Butte is about ½ mi. farther S, about ½ mi. N of 4600-ft Hard Pass. Its S ridge appears as the lowest profile; the upper W face is a rock wall above brush slopes. A gentler third peak (5241′) is S of Hard Pass, and still farther S is Mineral Butte; these two offer no climbing interest.

The peaks were named by the Lewis brothers, early trappers and prospectors. The Sultan Queen mine, later to become the Sultan King, was once an active operation on the W side of the Buttes. The claim group extends eastward from the head of the North Fork of the Sultan across the central saddle to the Silver Creek slope; the properties range in altitude from 3300 ft on each side of the divide to over 5000 ft on Crested Buttes, with a wide scattering of prospects. At one time a mining trail, well used by prospectors who staked claims in the pass area, led from Mineral City over Hard Pass to Elk Creek, and a trail to a mine in upper Elk Creek offered a route to Hard Pass from the W; these routes are essentially vanished. The peaks are relatively unknown to climbers and seldom visited.

NORTH CRESTED BUTTE 5318′/1621 m

The northern is the more rugged of the two buttes, which are both small but craggy peaks in a relatively inaccessible position. The first ascent was probably made by Anthony Hovey and Klindt Vielbig on October 25, 1958.

SOUTHEAST RIDGE: This ridge has less gradient than the N, but does steepen near the summit. Take route for South Crested Butte—South Ridge to the sharp pinnacle. Climb or rappel 60 ft into the basin and traverse ½ mi. N through scrub trees and occasional steep-sided streams to the long SE ridge. Follow a gully parallel and just S of the ridge until heather slopes and finally a sharp ridge is taken to the summit. About 1700 ft of scrambling (mostly class 2 and 3) and two class 4 moves. Time: 7 hours.

Note: the S ridge is blocked by a steep 100-ft step above the central saddle.

EAST FACE: Take route from Lake Gulch to the basin E of the South Butte. Contour upward and N along rockslides and some brush to round a rock shoulder on the North Butte (est. 3800′). N of the 40° slabs ascend a prominent gully (snow early season); the climb is fairly easy with one class 4 portion reported at exit to heather. Time: 7 hours.

NORTH RIDGE: First ascent route (on N-S traverse). Use the mine trail (see South Crested Butte—North Ridge) to reach the basin beneath the South Butte. Ascend NE and climb the steep right side of the chute to the notch between the two prominent pinnacles and the N ridge (3 hours on this section; slabs, brush dirt). The ridge features two steep steps with narrow crests; class 4 for about 600 ft (some steep heather and stunted trees). From the base of the summit tower .make a short class 3 scramble. Time: 5-7 hours. References: *Mountaineer*, 1959, p. 110; *A.A.J.*, 1959, p. 301.

SOUTH CRESTED BUTTE 5338′/1627 m

NORTH RIDGE: From the last bridge on Sultan Basin Road♦ (2095′) a trail begins as a cat-road parallel with the river's E bank. In about 1 mi., take the left trail fork (possibly brushy) up to the SE (central of three river forks to the no. 1 tunnel of the Sultan King property at 3800 ft—old trail distance was estimated at 3 mi. from road to claims) just W of the 4680 ft saddle between the two Buttes. Ascend talus and brush to the saddle, then brushy rock to the summit.

SOUTH RIDGE: Leave the road to Mineral City (see North Fork Skykomish River Road♦) at ¼ mi. N of Lake Gulch (about ¾ mi. S of Mineral City). Ascend the creek here ¼ mi., then a wooded slope and ridge to a sharp pinnacle at about 3800 ft in a basin below the peak. The climb is not difficult; take the E side and some low-angle rock on the S edge.

Alternate Approach: Leave the road at Lake Gulch (trail now vanished). Turn up steep wooded hillside N of creek (brush is light). Continue ascent until reaching a basin directly E of the South Butte. After leaving forest a short downscramble or rappel leads into the basin. Climb forest and bush to past Gulch Lakes (3638′) to the ridge S of the summit, close to Hard Pass.

MINERAL BUTTE 5255′/1602 m

This summit is 1 mi. SSW of Hard Pass, W of Silver Creek. The E slope is rough and steep; the S is the gentlest.

ROUTE: The best approach appears to be from Salmon Creek Road, a branch of North Fork Skykomish River Road♦. Expect some brush and second growth.

SCOTT PEAK 5288′/1612 m

Scott is smaller than Hubbart, but quite a rugged formation. The peak has a smooth sheet-red upper E face. The W and SW flanks are largely timbered except for the final crags. The name commemorates John Scott, who staked a claim near Galena in 1888 and within 3 yrs owned nine mines; one of his claims is the Great Scott, high on the peak. Galena was logically once called "Scott's Camp." The first winter ascent was apparently made by Albert Heath and Hermann F. Ulrichs in January or February 1935.

ROUTE: From about 0.7 mi. along the E side of Silver Creek Road (see Hubbart Peak) ascend the wooded SW ridge, which runs to 4400 ft, then flattens. Mixed timber and low-angle rock allows several completions; the most gradual are the NW and the S ridge.

HUBBART PEAK 5936′/1809 m

Hubbart is the high point of the rough divide between Silver and Troublesome Creeks, 2½ mi. N of the North Fork of Skykomish River. A second summit, at 5791 ft, is 2/5 mi. N of the summit, and Scott Peak ends the ridge's high crest at about 1 mi. S of the summit. Hubbart is quite steep and rocky on the E and SE, and largely wooded on the W. Rock is of granodiorite and Swauk sediments. At one time there were minesites in the area of all three upper branches of Troublesome Creek, and prospects on the W slope and close to the top of Hubbart.

The peak is of more interest in history than as a climb. Some sources say that from high on its northern slopes Joseph Pearsall saw the rich ore veins in the amphitheatre of the Sauk and immediately after this discovery made his much-quoted promise, "it is rich as

SILVER TIP PEAK, view north HERMANN F. ULRICHS COLLECTION, University of Washington Library

Monte Cristo." The peak with incorrect spelling is named for Elisha H. Hubbard, who in 1882 cut a trail from Index to Galena and located claims there. The peak soon became known as "Hubbart's Peak." The first winter ascent was made by Granville Jensen, Marion Marts, and Hermann F. Ulrichs on February 10, 1935 via the W slope.

ROUTES: Because of the dense natural brush of this area, and the abandonment of former mining trails, there is no simple approach to the summit. Of four possibilities, the first two seem best: (1) From the current end of the E side Silver Creek logging road (see North Fork Skykomish Road♦) work uphill and N to reach a spur between Quartz Creek and the next stream N; the spur leads moderately to the craggy summit area. If the road is extended this spur could be reached more directly; at present it may be equally well to bear toward the south summit ridge—see (2). Terrain is generally lightly wooded with occasional outcrops and the gradient is moderate. (2) From 200 ft W and below the top of Scott Peak descend about 100 ft N over a ridge. Traverse steep snow (or bare slopes) on the W, then diagonal toward the summit, generally keeping about 200 ft off the ridge. Appearances indicate it is soon best to stay near the ridge to avoid W-side slabs, except near the summit, where the W side seems most broken. (3) From the end of the logging spur switchbacks about 1 mi. E of Mineral City (4000′) ascend the ridge E to near timberline. Veer S into a small basin and follow a ramp S up onto the true summit ridge crest. Skirt under the top of the N peak (slabs) into a final basin NW of the summit; scrambling completes the climb. (4) An old mining path extended along the W bank of Troublesome Creek (road at 10½-mi. point); it is still possible to trace the path for about 2 mi. Here, shortly after reaching the third tributary, a trail led steeply to mines at the 3000-ft level. It might be possible to ascend to the final SW ridge of the summit (est. 5000′), then follow it. Immediately beneath the summit on the E is a steep, rocky, timbered area to avoid; approaches seem feasible via gullies on either flank.

SILVER TIP PEAK 6140′/1871 m

Popular "Silvertip" is about 1½ mi. SW of Monte Cristo, immediately W of Silver Lake. It has two E-running arms that flank the lake like a horseshoe. A lesser summit (5835′) points on a NW spur. Rock is andesite, lava, and tuff. The peak is dotted by numerous claims, and is named for the Silver Tip claim (the old and correct wording; *Mountaineer*, 1918, p. 21 and John MacDonald Wilmans Papers, University of Washington Library). Spurr's 1900 map shows National and Flag Peaks as lesser summits to the W.

Some sources state Pearsall and Peabody, with J.M. Wilmans, spotted the glistening ore veins on what is now the Wilmans Spires from Silver Tip's N ridge in

SILVER TIP PEAK and ADDISON RIDGE, view north

1889. Presumably this was on or near the fourth of July, since patriotic names as "76", "Liberty", and "Independence" were used in early claim naming. It is known a party from The Mountaineers climbed the peak in 1915. The first winter climb was by Hermann F. Ulrichs, Dan O'Brien, Albert Heath, and a companion on March 26, 1934.

ROUTE: See trail to Poodle Dog Pass♦. From the S side of Silver Lake (4260′) climb easy heather slopes to the southern arm, past the last trees, then hike W toward the lower S summit. Pass the E side below the ridge and traverse N to the saddle (5900′) at the base of the 100-ft summit crag. Begin on the S corner, toward a little step. Follow heathery rock working right to bypass a left-jutting horn, then back up and left on a slanting ramp; then a final steep 20-ft pitch—class 4. Time: 2 hours from the lake.

Note: make summit rappel from stumps.

Variation: Upper Northwest Ridge: Continue through the saddle and descend 100 ft. Traverse N about 600 ft on scree (or snow) on the W side of the summit crag to talus. Reach the 45°NW ridge, then ascend (class 3).

NORTHWEST RIDGE: First ascent by Ron Miller and Ben Guydelkon on August 22, 1970. Follow Weden Creek Road (a spur off Monte Cristo Road♦) past the mine to where it begins a descent; about 30 ft lower and left is a path which leads directly to the base of the NW ridge and a red tower (4920′). Begin here—the tower is the route's best rock. Use a bolt from its top for the rappel into the notch. The route is long and sometimes loose; some nuts and slings used. Grade II; class 5.5. Time: 11 hours. Reference: *A.A.J.*, 1971, p. 344.

NORTHEAST RIDGE: First ascent by Kenn Carpenter and Everett Mountaineer party of seven on October 16, 1960. From Silver Lake's N side traverse up to the NE ridge. Where it connects to the summit face climb directly up, but keep right along the crest of the N face. Class 3.

EAST FACE: First ascent by Dale Hardisty and Rich Carlstad on September 13, 1970. Bypass the lower cliffs above Silver Lake on the N ridge. Bear left and ascend the blank section of the summit block directly. The route was signed as "north face" in the register, and this may be more correct than "east face." Two solid leads; class 5.6. Time: 5 hours from road. Reference: *Mountaineer*, 1971, p. 80.

WILMANS PEAK GROUP

The steep, rocky crest trending SE between Glacier Basin and '76 Gulch on the divide from Monte Cristo to Columbia Peak has a long, continuing series of spires and peaks. Hodges elaborates on the frontal view: "Wilmans Peak is a bold, precipitous headland jutting out between Glacier and Seventy-Six gulches, which the ice has carved out to right and left of it."[76] The rock is layered volcanic breccia flows.

WEST WILMANS PEAK
East Wilmans Spire
West Spire
North Spire
N.W. Face
North Face

When the rich ore veins were spotted in 1889 they were first on "another mountain." This soon took the general name "Wilmans Peak," from the pioneer enterpreneurs the Wilmans brothers, and has often been misspelled "Wilmon" (maps still do so). It is time to restore the correct orthography.[77]

The crest groupings require separate nomenclature now for the purpose of identification; this was of course not necessary in mining times. The first group consists of three spectacular Wilmans Spires, often confused with the two Wilmans Peaks to the SE. The most striking is the thumb-shaped West Wilmans Peak (6840′+) ¼ mi. from East Wilmans Spire and ⅝ mi. from Columbia Peak. The slightly higher East Wilmans Peak (6880′+) is just less than ¼ mi. to the SE (toward Columbia), immediately NW of conspicuous Wilmans Gap (6480′+), where Wilmans and '76 Glaciers rise to 6400 ft on opposite flanks. This is the logical conclusion of the group; beyond the gap the crest spires are on the Columbia Peak ridge.

The two Wilmans Peaks are separated by a "V" notch (6480′) of perfectly triangular shape. The N face of the entire spire and peak group is quite precipitous and alpine, a steep rock facade above the level floor of Glacier Basin. Bedding planes are common; bedding of the breccias here is near horizontal.

The '76 Glacier, about ½ mi. in breadth, on the '76 Creek drainage, lies in the shallow basin between East Wilmans and Columbia Peaks. The Wilmans Glacier on the steeper Glacier Basin drainage clings to the N slope and extends to near Monte Cristo Pass; it is a slope (hanging) glacier which descends to 5550 ft; below the glacier is a narrow ice patch (base est. 4600′) in Glacier Basin, largely built from avalanched snow. One climbing reference, an article by Joseph Hazard in the *Mountaineer* of 1923, states "six of our men made a 'first ascent' of Wilman Peak." This ambiguous note leads to the speculation that the climb was of the West Peak, technically the simplest. But the implication exists that it was the climb of the North Spire, for another reference records its ascent by a party of six.

WILMANS SPIRES

The cluster of the three spiked Wilmans Spires form a remarkable scene on the divide leading SE of Monte Cristo. From here one sees the two summits of the western spire, which for the sake of simplicity are referred to as the "West" and "North" Spires. They are merely separate final summits of a single mass, divided from the slender East Spire by a quite narrow, deep gap (a pronounced joint-plane).[78] Rock is volcanic breccia: it is generally solid on W exposures, but steeper and eroded on respective E faces. When climbing either two or all of the spires on one tour, it is recommended that the East Spire be done last (use a rappel rather than an awkward climb out of the gap).

The N side of the spires falls steeply to Glacier Basin; immediately E of the East Spire the divide climbs abruptly toward West Wilmans Peak.

Many mining relics remain on the slopes of the Spires. Much of the technology of the Comet Mine, including the cable from the bunker to the "Count of Monte Cristo" is still there. Spire climbers would do well to pay homage to the efforts of the pioneer miners. Even a casual visit to the Comet Mine (5350′), will persuade one to believe all apocryphal stories.[79]

WILMANS PEAK and SPIRES from north
PHILIP LEATHERMAN

WEST WILMANS SPIRE 6233′ / 1900 m

This is the higher of the two western spires, virtually a unit with the North Spire; a small notch separates them. A short but sheer wall drops to the gap adjacent to the East Spire. The 1923 party which climbed the North Spire came within 50 ft. of the summit and felt that they could have continued but for rain. A story was circulated in early times that the Wilmans brothers offered $500 to anyone who could climb "either peak." The first ascent was made by William Herston and Keith Rankin in 1944.

ROUTE: After walking the roadway 0.6 mi., an extension of the Monte Cristo Road♦, cross the stream bridge and take "Glacier Street" to "Dumas Street." Turn left and hike toward Justice Mine, then bear right (ESE). Keep left of the big bushy cliff band and then find a break somewhere in the cliff.

A possible variation (not verified) is to traverse right beneath the first cliffs several hundred yds to the "Count" (est. 4800′); then a break turning 45° left appears feasible.

When the flatter part of the ridge is reached just NW of the spire, make a short traverse S on the W slope, then ascend the gully (class 2; may be snow-filled) to the small notch between the West and North Spires. At the notch climb a crack rightward on the corner to a good platform (90′, class 4). A hard move follows; keep right of corner via exposed face climbing (70′) to the summit. Class 5.2. Time: 5 hours.

Note: if descending to reach the East Spire: at about 200 ft below the small notch level, take the decided ledge circling the W face to its S edge just above SW cliffs (see Variation).

EAST FACE: First ascent by Patty Crooks, Wesley Grande, and Jim Wells on October 13, 1947. This steep new route was done during an episode when all three spires were done in a day, but which ended in tragedy when Wells was killed down-climbing after a rappel off the East Spire (*A.A.J.*, 1948, pp. 91-92). From the gap adjacent the East Spire climb the vertical wide chimney and following face to the small West-North Spire notch; two pitches, probably not too

well protected (class 4 and 5).

Variation: From the col (see East Spire), make a rising traverse 150 ft southward to a vertical rock band about 25 ft high (face climbing with some shrubbery handholds, hard class 4 or 5). This reaches a heathery ledge, which is used to circle to the W slope gully 100 ft below the notch. If using this variation as a descent to the col, traverse S on the first heather bench; a rappel is made at the vertical pitch.

NORTH WILMANS SPIRE est. 6075' / 1852 m

This is the shorter and easier of the two western spires. The first climbing party called it "West Peak," terming it strenuous, with "toe holds;" it was climbed in early September 1923 in 4 hours from the valley by Harold B. Sparks, Fairman B. Lee, Alex Fuchs, Bert Farqhuarson, Fred Huber, and Norman Huber. Reference: *Mountaineer Bull.*, November 1923.

ROUTE: From the high notch of the West Spire rock terraces lead to a final 30-ft pitch (class 3).

EAST WILMANS SPIRE 6120' / 1865 m

This spectacular erect spire rises 300 ft on the W and S, 200 ft on the E, and much farther on the N. The spire has become a fairly popular climb due to its appearance and reasonable access. First ascent by Fred Beckey and Herb Staley on August 19, 1945; first repeat was in 1948 by Art Holben and Mel Marcus. References: *Mountaineer*, 1946, pp. 45-46; *Mazama*, 32, No. 13 (1950), 33, 39; *A.A.J.*, 1946, p. 46, 1948, pp. 91-92.

Approaches: (1) Take the '76 Creek Trail♦ to Peabody Rock (est. ¾ mi.), then on to Lincoln Mine; go up a short hill to another level, and continue on trail to Peabody Mine. At about 1-mi. point (after leaving timber, near end of large rockslide) ascend obliquely right (open talus and slide alder) and climb a long dirt gully to just right of the "Count of Monte Cristo." Here, take a ramp angling right to the rocky spur of the Comet bunker. An obvious gully bears right to the 5960 ft gap just W of the Spire.

(2) An alternate route to the "Count" is to use a variation suggested for the West Spire.

(3) An alternate route above the "Count" works farther right to take the second gully toward the gap. Another variation is to traverse a total of about 700 yds E, then ascend a gully.

(4) From the floor of Glacier Basin♦ ascend a long rockslide, then a steep rocky right-slanting gully to the gap. This is the shortest approach to the gap, but most technical; often snow- or ice-filled (suggest crampons).

SOUTHWEST FACE: The S base is scrambled to the E notch. A section of the earlier rotten shelf is missing; ascend about 20 ft from the notch, then diagonal down to bypass the void. Traverse out on a sloping ledge obliquely to the far (W) corner. Then cross a short, steep slab rightward on the SW face and continue around the corner to a small, sloping platform on the face. A 1-in. jam crack near the right corner of a red wall is climbed until a ledge on the corner is reached (almost over notch). Then climb up and left on the SW corner, finally working back near the top (a final belay can be made at a broken area on the S face some 50 ft from the summit). The actual climb spans about 140 ft (one long lead from ledge; class 4 to 5.4). A selection of four pitons (horizontal variety), plus several chocks (to no. 8) is adequate. Time: 6 hours from road.

Variation: Lower Southwest Face: By Fred Beckey and Jack Schwabland on September 30, 1945. Begin at the western base of the S face, near the gap, and ascend directly to the summit over rather shattered rock. Keep left of the normal route for 1½ leads, then join; class 5.5.

Variation: Southwest Face: By David Collins, Don Gordon, and Paul Salness on September 16, 1951. Begin midway from the W gap to the start of the normal route. Difficult balance climbing reaches the broad ledge (est. 200′) or possibly the normal route at it highest point before the final short pitch; the upper half of the variation is hardest. Class 5. The first lead is poorly protected (no cracks).

Note: a climb done from the W base of the Spire on September 16, 1967 by Gary Glenn and Mike Heath probably is similar to the above variations, which are actually quite closely spaced (four pitons and three chocks used).

COUNT OF MONTE CRISTO est. 4800′/1463 m

This 85x30x20-ft monolith was noted by early miners by several names, including "Old Man of the Mountains." To reach see East Wilmans Spire approaches. First ascent by Eugene Dod, Earl Levin, and Bob Martin in June 1962.

ROUTE: Approach below and S of the inside notch, cross the notch and traverse behind to the overhanging W face. The route takes a crack near the NW corner (six aid pitons), then traverses up left across the N face (5.4); bolt atop for rappel.

EAST FACE ROUTE: By Mike Berman and Mark Weigelt, June 1966. Ascend a crack (easy class 5), then use two aid pitons; make a short tension left, then climb to the top.

WILMANS PEAKS

For topographic description, see Wilmans Peak Group. Approaches include: (1) from the gap at East Wilmans Spire; (2) from '76 Gulch via the major right-slanting gully under the Wilmans Peaks to the N edge of the '76 Glacier; (3) from Glacier Basin, up the Wilmans Glacier, through Wilmans Gap SE of the East Peak. Allow 6 hours for approach and ascent of either the West or East Peak. Combined climbs on the Wilmans Peaks and the ascent of Columbia Peak are occasionally done in a single day, since it is feasible to traverse either the '76 Glacier or talus beneath.

EAST WILMANS SPIRE
AL ERRINGTON

WEST WILMANS PEAK 6840′+ / 2085 m

This horn-summited rock peak is not the highest of the Wilmans Peaks, but from most positions appears to be the highest, and is the most prominent; in early nomenclature it was the summit referredto as Wilmans Peak. The first ascent may have been done by a Mountaineer party of six in 1923 (see *Mountaineer Bull.*, November 1923; *Mountaineer*, 1923, p. 61). Equally probable is that the first climb was done by Ben Spellar and Art Winder on either July 1 or 2, 1935 from a base camp at Mineral City.

MT. BAKER
MT. PUGH
SLOAN PK.
FOGGY PK.
North Pk.
Addison Ridge
CADET PK.
Ida Pass
Wilmans Spires
Wilmans Peaks
Comet Mine
MONTE CRISTO
gap
Broadway Ledge
Peabody Mine
SEVENTY SIX

WEST SHOULDER: Make a rockslide traverse from the shallow scree basin below and closely E of the East Wilmans Spire, going S until well past the upper notch. Then bear up slabby ramps to or near the shoulder high on the S side (it holds snow in early summer). Keep below the W ridge until about 100 ft from the summit; when the shoulder holds snow, take a snow finger or rock angling leftward to the skyline, then ascend directly. Class 2. Time: 6 hours from road.

Variation: Stay low on the traverse to keep beneath a horizontally curving wall; continue to just above a wall (last part of traverse is easy but exposed, through scrub conifers). When near the corner, climb directly up to the high S shoulder.

Variation: Broadway Ledge: First climbed by Nick Dodge, Jack Grauer, Dave Kuchler, Ted Lathrop, Jim Menzies, Lisle Walker, and Bob Wilson on July 4, 1965. The original party reached a high margin of the '76 Glacier from Columbia Peak (could also be reached from Wilmans Gap—see Sawhorse Tower), and crossed a hanging snowpatch (can be dangerous due to snow melt). Cross W onto the E end of the prominent narrow reddish ledge (bedding plane) which runs horizontally about 600 ft below the summit on the S face, and is nearly ¼ mi. in length. Do not ascend the first prominent gully, but traverse to the end, turn a corner, and locate the last chimney/gully at an apparent cul de sac. This chimney is rotten, with dirty chockstones; actually two sub-chimneys divided by a rib about 50 ft in height (climb either one). Above this junction follow easy heathered rock to the normal route and summit. Advise small party due to loose rock. Class 4. Reference: *Mazama*, vol. 47, no. 13 (1965), pp. 60-61.

NORTHWEST FACE: First ascent by Dan Davis and Dave Erickson in 1959. From Glacier Basin♦ ascend a large rockslide and climb into the slanting gully just beneath East Wilmans Spire. Part way climb out left, then up a long, broad, sloping ramp to a flat area under the summit, then directly up to the W edge of the final horn. Class 4.

NORTH FACE: First ascent by Dallas Kloke and Scott Masonholder on July 19, 1969. Begin at a rock finger projecting from the base of the face. About 250 ft up, work through a vertical brushy pitch and traverse right to easier rock. From a large ledge, make an ascending left traverse for 100 ft, then climb easy rock and heather to the base of a snowpatch. The key to the ascent is an 800-ft narrow rock gully which begins above the snow (solid; one or two pitons used). Above, climb on easy rock for about 500 ft to the base of the summit pyramid. From a ledge 120 ft below the top, climb the N side of the summit (well broken; 5.1). Grade II; class 5.6. Time: 6 hours from Glacier Basin. Reference: *A.A.J.*, 1971, p. 344.

SOUTHEAST FACE: A route to the summit was climbed by the 1935 party from near the notch adjacent to the East Peak or possibly beginning near the first portion of Broadway Ledge. The exact line of the route is not known, but the final pitch was via a shallow chimney; probably class 3 and 4. The 1935 party approached from Twin Lakes-'76 Creek divide and traversed below Columbia Peak. They climbed diagonally across the basin slope (partly snow and partly rock) to above the rock ribs which lead between the East and West Peaks. The descent was made directly down '76 Gulch.

EAST WILMANS PEAK 6880'+ / 2097 m

The highest point is at the NW end of the summit mass; two crags (6840'+) are closely SE. The best approach from the valley is via '76 Gulch—continue beyond gully of approach (1) to East Wilmans Spire—and ascend the gully and stream to the left edge of the '76 Glacier. It is also possible to come from Glacier Basin and the Wilmans Glacier through Wilmans Gap. It is practical to reach the peak from Poodle Dog Pass and the '76 Glacier (see Columbia Peak). Due to lack of records and confusion of summit nomenclature, climbing history is incomplete; however, on the 1970 climb no evidence of a previous visit was noted on the summit (it is possible this was the first climb).

LOWER NORTH FACE and NORTHWEST RIDGE: By Dallas Kloke on September 12, 1970. From Glacier Basin♦ climb talus, then make an ascending traverse on a snow ramp below the N face of the West Peak to the prominent gully that separates the two peaks. When a short distance up the gully (snow, early season) traverse left to easy rock and heather slopes, then continue to a second gully. Either climb it or the rib on the right to the notch (6480'+) between the peaks. Shortly above is a brief slab section (est. 75'—class 3), then scramble ridge crest to summit. Class 4. Time: 2 hours basin to summit.

Note: A non-documented approach to the notch seems very feasible from the lower NW end of '76 Glacier; scree (possible snowpatches) and a broad rock gully lead to the notch.

NORTH FACE: First ascent by Charles Raymond and Mickey Schurr in September 1971. Take the Lower North Face and Northwest Ridge route to the second gully. Then climb moderately steep mixed rock and heather on a tangent directly to the summit; if the climb is done in anything but dry conditions the exposure and vegetation would make the ascent considerably more difficult. Class 3 and 4.

INDEPENDENCE TOWER est. 6720'/2048 m

Independence Tower is one of the two smaller towers SE of Wilmans Gap, probably the first one; from the S side, it has a geometric blocky shape with a narrow base. First ascent by Dallas Kloke and Scott Masonholder on July 5, 1969.

Begin at the SE corner and use several pitons for aid. Traverse left for a few ft, then climb directly up steep and loose rock. Class 5.4 and A1. Reference: *A.A.J.*, 1971, p. 343.

Note: there may be an easier route via a short N rib.

MONTE CRISTO AREA from south
U.S. GEOLOGICAL SURVEY

COLUMBIA PEAK from northwest JEFF COLEHOUR

SAWHORSE TOWER est. 6960′/2121 m
This is the prominent rock point of the row of towers SE of Wilmans Gap and on the crest leading to Columbia Peak. First ascent by Dallas Kloke and Terry Stoupa on June 8, 1970.

From Glacier Basin♦ make an ascending traverse below the N face of East Wilmans Peak, then climb directly up the Wilmans Glacier to Wilmans Gap (6480′+); or approach the gap by obliquely ascending the glacier from Monte Cristo Pass, near its E margin (see Monte Cristo Peak—South Face). A short snow climb eastward leads to the base of the SW face of Sawhorse. There are four leads to the summit (class 4 and 5.1).

Note: the short SE corner (from a snow gully) appears possible. Reference: *A.A.J.*, 1971, p. 343.

COLUMBIA PEAK 7172′/2186 m

Columbia, one of the monarchs of the very compact "Monte Cristo" group of peaks, is located barely over 2 mi. from the old townsite. The peak's name—one of the first established and shown on area maps—was given by Monte Cristo railroad surveyors in 1893. Topographically the peak is the culmination of the Wilmans Peak crestline; the broad arcuate basin between the latter and Columbia is occupied by the '76 Glacier (limits between about 6700 ft and 5700 ft). Columbia is a jagged and rugged rock peak composed of volcanic breccia beds which dip gently eastward; the contact with granodiorite near the base of the Columbia Glacier is quite visible. This significant small valley glacier of about 1 mi. length drains into green-tinted Blanca Lake, which occupies the lower portion of the basin between Columbia and Kyes Peak (the main body of glacier ice extends from about 5700 ft to 4700 ft; there are three higher hanging ice patches on Columbia's E face).

The peak has been a popular ascent for several decades, and is worthy of a summit pilgrimage for the view alone. The first ascent was made by a U.S. Geological Survey party: John Charlton, Louis C. Fletcher, Richard U. Goode, and Albert H. Sylvester, who occupied the summit for triangulation in early August 1897. It is also known the climb was repeated by L. Treen, Jr. of the Forest Service, on June 25, 1911. First winter ascent by Fred Beckey, Roger Maier, and John Yaeger on February 20, 1977. Reference: *Mazama*, 1965, pp. 59-60.

WEST SPUR: This rocky spur, a continuation of the divide between Twin Lakes and '76 Gulch, separates Columbia's steep SW and NW faces. Nearly all climbing parties use this route, taking one of several possible approaches. The most expedient of these is to hike to Poodle Dog Pass♦, then take the 2-mi. trail S to the E-W ridge (5300′) of the divide; keep on the ridge N of Twin Lakes and make one short N-slope traverse to avoid a divide hump. Then ascend steep talus to the right of a flattish heather area beneath Columbia's W spur. Ascend talus, heather, or snow NNE up the rounded spur to a steep rock nose (about 100′ high) on the crest at about 6300 ft (the last clump of hemlock stands just beneath it). Bear left briefly (possible snow), then ascend a wide depression (usually has an oblong snowpatch) in line with the summit for an altitude gain of about 400 ft. When this heads at a short steep cliff band, jog right around a blind corner to the Twin Lakes side of the spur, then continue up a slight depression. Where this heads at a smooth face of reddish rock 50 ft beneath the summit, traverse left on a ledge to the N flank, then scramble easy rock to the highest point. Time: 5-6 hours from Poodle Dog Pass.

Note: the ascent is not difficult, but does have some exposure; variations can be made by climbing along the upper spur and making a direct gully approach from the lakes, but these may add unnecessary minor difficulties.

Alternate Approach: Using the trail from Mineral City, leave where it sharply ascends a cliff (est. 2½ mi.) on the left of the creek (est. 3300′). Ascend the N side of the valley (rockslides, brush, heather) to the ridge N of the lakes.

Alternate Approach: Via Wilmans Gap: See Sawhorse Tower for route to the gap from Glacier Basin; a slight descent leads to the '76 Glacier, which is traversed to its SW extremity beneath a broad cliff; on a slightly descending contour round a corner on an inclined bench beyond the glacier margin to meet the wide depression just N of the hemlock clump and rock nose of the W spur. Time: 3-4 hours Glacier Basin to summit. Note: several approaches can be made directly from '76 Gulch but are less to be recommended.

NORTH RIDGE: First ascent by Tom Benedict, Joan Firey, Joe Firey, and a fourth person in 1955; possible variations August 4, 1963 by Anthony Hovey, Gary Rose, and Klindt Vielbig, climbing from Glacier Basin. Ascend to the head of '76 Glacier S of Sawhorse Tower. A snow finger and scrambling lead to the col on Columbia's ridge. Proceed on the E side of the crest to the summit; the midway tower can be turned on either side. A known variation from the col traverses firn on the E beyond the summit, to reach the final S ridge. The ridge has also been reached from the glacier to the dip about midway. Class 4. Time: 6 hours from road.

SOUTH RIDGE: This is a long, high ridge of rock extending nearly a mi. above timberline to the summit; rock is somewhat loose. First ascent by Kenn Carpenter and Ursula Wiener on September 12, 1965.

Climb E from the southern Twin Lake (see West Spur route) via a W buttress of the S ridge. At 5600 ft is an apparent impasse; go N to get access to a heather bench about 20 ft long; then a vertical tree climb up a 30-ft bluff. Hamburg Pass (5880′) is then easily reached (it is wide and sandy). Continue E to ridge crest at its S end near 6400 ft, or plan route to reach it at near 6640 ft (about ½ mi. from summit). The initial party followed the ridge, except at two places where time saved by passing sheer spots on the E side. Class 3 and 4. Time: 7 hours. Reference: *A.A.J.*, 1966, pp. 130-131.

Variation: From northern Twin Lake, ascend due E to saddle (est. 6640′) about ½ mi. from summit. Cross ridge to E side, where a fine, straightforward contour can be made, often on snow/ice patches that allow fast travel. Folds in rock form weathered ledges and allow good movement. At the last notch one can climb to the ridge and find some scrambling to the top. This variation avoids the looser portions of the true crest.

COLUMBIA PEAK from west
HERMANN F. ULRICHS COLLECTION, University of Washington Library

MONTE CRISTO and KYES PEAK from west
JEFF COLEHOUR

MONTE CRISTO PEAK 7136′/2175 m

From most vantages, Monte Cristo Peak is identified by its pyramidal shape. It is located at the head of Glacier Basin, between Columbia and Cadet Peaks. Early miners called Monte Cristo and the first of The Cadets "Twin Bear Peaks". *The Mountaineer* of 1918 (p. 21) terms it a "huge pile of red rock" (volcanic breccia). It is significant to note that in the past other summits in the area, including the 5404-ft point N of Silver Lake, have been called "Monte Cristo Peak." A group from The Mountaineers finally settled the confusion by applying the name to the peak described above (*Mountaineer*, 1918, p. 29—wrong picture. Also see p. 85.).

The longest rock faces are on the S and W. There is a lower summit about 400 ft S of the summit, and it is broken into two small crags. Snow and ice reach to within 350 ft of its summit on the NE flank all summer. The Pride Glacier (above Pride Basin) on the NE has its main body between 5600 and 4600 ft, with segments and ice couloirs higher. The Columbia Glacier on the SW reaches to 5600 ft at the base of the peak, with an isolated segment remaining in the cirque between the upper southeastern portion of the peak and Kyes Peak. As a climb Monte Cristo has achieved popularity because of short access. The first ascent was made by James M. Kyes and W. Zerum in 1923. The first winter ascent was made by Fred Beckey and Mike Borghoff in March, 1965 (*A.A.J.*, 1966, p. 130).

NORTH COL ROUTE: The N col, a U-shaped notch (6760′+) is at the margin of firn ice that extends to the E atop a high shoulder. The col, easily identified by a flat-topped crag just N, is roughly midway between the U-notch at The Cadets and the summit. Several routes can be used to reach the col, and from there a wall reaches to the summit.

From Glacier Basin♦ at 4100 ft pass left of the last trees on Ray's Knoll, then ascend a talus cone to an obvious gully break in the first cliff (in line with summit). Ascend through a gully in the break and continue slightly left on snow or talus to the col (in late season hard snow may require crampons).

Now either (1) traverse E on névé about 300 ft to a moat crossing to rock (can be a problem in late season). A short steep pitch has an initial 20-ft chimney; then easy heather-rock ledges lead W to the summit. Or (2) climb directly upward steeply to the summit. Either route averages class 3 and some class 4. Time: 5½ hours from road.

Variation: From Glacier Basin♦ ascend to the U-notch (6440′+) adjacent to The Cadets (class 2). Contour and angle up perennial snow until below the summit rock structure (E of the N col); 5 hours road to summit.

Variation: Pride Glacier: From Curry Gap♦ (see also Kyes Peak, Northeast Ridge) follow the ridge about 1½ mi. to where it begins to rise (est. 5500′). Traverse the N side of the ridge (perennial snow) onto the glacier at its flat, lower portion. Here two routes appear quite reasonable, but are not documented: a central snow/ice gully (bergschrund at base) leads to the Kyes-Monte Cristo Peak col; the next snow gully slanting W leads directly to firn ice between the U-notch and N col. Either gully leads to the high firn area on the NE shoulder of the summit.

SOUTHEAST RIDGE: First ascent by Michael Heath on September 14, 1967. From Blanca Lake♦ ascend the Columbia Glacier, then NE via the pocket glacier segment (see South Face) nearly to the Monte Cristo-Kyes Peak col. Then ascend the SE ridge, really a buttress feature on the peak. The climb was rated class 3 and 4, with one short 5.4 pitch. Time: 4 hours from lake.

SOUTH FACE AND SOUTHWEST RIDGE: The Columbia Glacier extends to about 5600 ft at the base of the S face; the pocket segment NE connects narrowly and continues to the ridge col adjacent Kyes Peak. The SW ridge, which begins at Monte Cristo Pass, rises in steps and crags to the peak's summit, and is flanked on the glacier side by the wide face. Due to the confusion of route features and incomplete climbing history, route priorities are uncertain; Joe Halwax and party did a route in this area in the 1930s. Rock has the reputation of being loose, but this may be unwarranted (most of the rock on this peak is quite firm). From the head of Glacier Basin♦ SE of Ray's Knoll ascend the central gully beneath the peak through the lower cliff band, then make an oblique southward ascent (snow) in a depression to cross above an obvious craggy tree-covered rock spur. Continue on an oblique snow ascent SW to Monte Cristo Pass (6000′+); 3 hours from road.

Traverse several hundred ft SE (usually snow) and enter a distinct steep gully sytem with cliffs on its right. Ascend the gully to its intersection with the prominent snow band about two-thirds distance from pass to summit (the last portion of the gully merges into an irregular rock ridge and may be class 4). Above the band ascend the SW crest, which has minor route complexities (keep right (S) of small crags and lower summit just before the true summit). Class 3 and 4. Time: 6 hours from Monte Cristo. Note: the approach to the route or the variation given below can be made from Blanca Lake♦.

Variation: From Monte Cristo Pass descend S below the cliff toe, then follow the glacier slope to the pocket segment. Climb E, then ascend left on a snow band to center face. More direct variations appear feasible, including a prominent more central depression which is filled with snow in early season.

WEST FACE: This face extends just above the snow and talus on the Glacier Basin flank of the peak. The route has become reasonably popular; there is considerable loose rock (advise small party).

Climb to the foot of the reddish face at about 6400 ft, directly beneath the main summit (see North Col route). Then follow a major right-slanting shelf to the red gully that separates the summit formation from the lower S crags; only stay in the gully rock a short distance, then angle right, possibly staying on steep snow, to the gap S of the main summit (loose rock danger in gully). Work around via a ledge to the opposite side, then up an exposed crack for a scramble to the summit. Class 3. Time: 5 hours from road.

NORTHWEST FACE: Several routes appear to have been done on this minor face between the W face and the N col. One report describes the ascent of the snow couloir SW of the N col; by climbing rock on its right, either a hard traverse or a rappel higher gains a steep chimney above the couloir. Some looseness is encountered on the climb to the small skyline notch; easy ledge scrambling leads to the summit (reported 5.5).

The spur right of the snow couloir offers a nearly direct summit route (Dick Gilbert and Linda Jeffcoat, July 1966). Follow the class 3-4 spur to a loose gully; ascend it to slabs, then bear up and right to a belay at the top of slabs. Climb 20 ft right, then left up the corner (class 5, crux) toward the summit; in another 30 ft reach a deep corner cleft on the right. Step across to a hidden ledge, walk right, then climb to a broad ledge above which is a 5-ft vertical step (piton used); above bear up and left on good rock to above the cleft. Continue up, then right to join the top of the S ridge; some of climb is loose rock (Reference: *Mountaineer*, 1966, p. 204).

KYES PEAK 7280′+/2219 m

This important massif, once mapped as Goblin Peak, and earlier referred to as "Mt. Michigan" by miners and the Forest Service, is located closely NNE of Blanca Lake and is ⅝ mi. SE of Monte Cristo Peak; a snow col at about 6700 ft separates the two peaks.

From the N Kyes has a bulky, snowy shape, with a large glacier (the Pride) on the slope above Pride Basin. The glacier extends from 7000 ft on the NE face to 4550 ft (1.8 km long). S of the summit of Kyes there is a nearly level ridge extending about ¼ mi. From the W Kyes is almost a perfect low-angled, symmetrical pyramid with a triangular small ice remnant pocketing under the summit, mimicking its shape. In a basin 1 mi. E of the peak, there is a small unnamed glacier above Goblin Lake (4200′; at head of Goblin Creek). Although rock on Kyes is composed of volcanic breccias, it is generally sound.

In an unusual instance for the Cascades, the peak is now known by the family name of a member of the

KYES PK.
N.W. Ridge
COLUMBIA PK.
MONTE CRISTO PK.
Wilmans Peaks
north col
The Cadets
U-notch
N.E. Ridge
PRIDE GLACIER
rom Curry Gap

first climbing party, and honors James Ellsworth Kyes, who made the climb via the S ridge with Reginald Bacheldor on August 15, 1920, when they were members of the Everett Boy Scouts.

SOUTH RIDGE: This is the gentlest ridge on the peak and has been the popular route. It extends nearly 1 mi. at a high level; an E shoulder of the ridge drops off to a lower steep wall.

Take the Blanca Lake Trail♦ to the divide. The general plan is to follow the lengthy ridge or its upper W slope to the summit, first along an irregular subalpine tree, bush and meadow zone, then up long open talus (snow) slope to aim for the red chute between the high rock band on left and three crags on the right. This break allows easy passage to the ridge crest. Take the crest to Point 7025 (benchmark), then continue on the crest or glacier margin on its E. The final rock crest sweeps conveniently to the highest point. Class 2. Time: 4 hours from trail.

Approach Variation: West Slope: Use route to Monte Cristo Pass per Monte Cristo Peak—South Face, then descend rock ledges and steep snow to the flats of Columbia Glacier at 5400 ft. An alternate approach is from Blanca Lake. Cross the glacier at a 132° bearing to the slope of Kyes. Ascend moderate snow through a break in cliffs fringing the glacier and bear to a W-trending minor ridge spur. Round a heather/rock knob at 6500 ft and then traverse E about 1000 ft to notch in rock ridge to meet normal route. One could vary the final portion by keeping N of the spur and completing as per Northwest route. Time: 5 hours from Monte Cristo.

Northwest Route: Approach per above from either Monte Cristo Pass or Blanca Lake. Ascend to the pocket glacier segment adjacent Monte Cristo Peak nearly to the level of the col (about 6600′). A narrow obvious bench traverses S beneath the upper cliffs of Kyes to the small isolated glacier on the W face. From near the right edge of this glacier climb to the obvious notch in the S ridge rim; follow the ridge to the summit. This is a good route for late spring and early summer. Time: 6 hours from Monte Cristo. Note: this route was completed via a traverse of Monte Cristo Peak (Mike Killien, Dallas Kloke, Jack Newcomer, June 18, 1963).

NORTHWEST RIDGE: This is the jagged crest on the Pride Glacier's N rim; it connects by notches and a col to Monte Cristo Peak. First ascent by David A. Collins, Kenn Carpenter, and Tom Williams on June 8, 1958.

Use the route for Monte Cristo Peak—North Col to the high small glacier. Continue S on a 200-ft descent to the col (est. 6700′) at the beginning of the NW ridge of Kyes.

Note: alternate approach is per Monte Cristo Peak—Southeast Ridge.

Climb snow slopes on the NW ridge for 300 ft to a level rock crest with a sharp, rotten notch below on the right. To bypass a steep step descend 100 ft, staying on the left side of the ridge to where an easy ledge cuts right into a gully. Traverse the gully and ascend 200 ft of very steep snow in a couloir to easy rock and snow slopes (left) leading to the ridge. Follow the level section to just beneath the lower NW summit and ascend 70 ft of rock (class 3) to its crest. Follow the friable ridge toward the main summit, traversing off the right and around a gendarme to a point just under the steep NW face of the main summit. The prominent 50-ft open vertical chimney on the face required four aid pitons on initial ascent. A short scramble leads to the summit. Grade II or III. Class 5 and aid. Time: 10 hours from Monte Cristo. Reference: *Mountaineer*, 1959, pp. 110-111.

NORTHEAST RIDGE: Because of recent road extensions, this route is now the most direct approach to the summit. The Pride Glacier extends high on the NE face and reaches to a margin on the NE ridge. First ascent by Michael Heath on September 14, 1967.

From Curry Gap♦ (est. 4000′) travel SW through timber and along the gentle open ridge to the base of the peak at about 6000 ft (2½ mi.). Continue along sections of snow and glacier ice to where the ridge begins as a feature on the peak. Ascend firn or rock on the left margin of the glacier; the final portion is rock climbing on the east corner. Class 3 and 4. Time: 5 hours. Reference: *A.A.J.*, 1968, p. 136.

PRIDE OF THE MOUNTAINS RANGE

During the mining era the long subrange from Cadet Peak to Sheep Mountain was known as Pride of the Mountains Range (Bailey Willis Photo album, pictures 19, 22, 23, 33, 34, U.S. Geological Survey). Addison Ridge (or Addison Mountain) was popular usage for that portion of the range opposite Monte Cristo, from Sentinal Gap to and including Gemini Peaks.

CADET PEAK 7186′/2190 m (7197′/2194 m)

Cadet is the climax of the NE rim of Glacier Basin, just 2 mi. E of Monte Cristo. Maps and the summit register identify the name with the S summit (7186′/2190 m); an almost level ridge bears N about ⅜ mi. to the N summit, the highest point (7197′/2194 m). Farther W on the ridge is the NW summit (7073′).

The N face of the N and NW summits holds small ice patches of the New York Glacier at several levels. The lowest, just S of Goat Lake, is largely formed by avalanched snow (unusually low, with a base of est. 3400′). This patch of over 0.1 km² is the lowest such measured in the North Cascades S of Mt. Shuksan. Cadet and The Cadets have numerous ice patches and the Mayflower Glacier on the steep E and NE flank (main body extends from 5600′ to 4250′). This glacier, which drains to Cadet Creek, is smaller than the Pride, but descends lower.

MONTE CRISTO AREA from northeast
BOB and IRA SPRING

KYES PK.
COLUMBIA PK.
CADET PK.
FOGGY PK.
Osceola Pass
North Face
Ida Pass
SOUTH GEMINI PK.
Sentinel Gap
NEW YORK GLACIER
Foggy Mine
Cadet Lake
MACKINTOSH GLACIER
GEMINI GLACIER
Goat Lake
Clear Lake
trail
old buildings
Elliott Creek Valley

There is a craggy connecting ridge with Monte Cristo Peak, "The Cadets," which was the name given by pioneers. In mining times the present summit of Cadet was called "Foggy."[80] During mapping the names were changed and the subject is now of only historic interest (the name Cadet was applied in 1896).

Just who made the first climb of Cadet is unknown, but it certainly must have been climbed in early prospecting times (when the first women climbed the peak in July 1907 the altitude was estimated at 8000 ft). The NW summit was apparently visited by the U.S. Geological Survey about 1897-1898. The Cadet lode was high on the peak; some claims such as the Pica, Eureka, and Galore were virtually atop the S and W slopes. The 89 Mine is located on Cadet's SW slope (5200′); it is on the same vein as the Pride of the Mountains, but higher and farther S. The Webster Brown claim location map (Hodges, 1897) clearly shows the position of the Penn Mine on the N slope, with the Aurora and Wyoming claims beneath it. This mine (4600′) is in a notch blasted from the cliff, and still contains the ruins of buildings.

SOUTH SLOPE: From beyond the house-sized boulder in Glacier Basin♦ where basin widens (4400′) keep E of rugged lower flanking cliffs. Ascend N on talus fans and an easy talus and rock slope (with sparse tree cover) to a NE-trending heather spur directed to the "Cadet" summit. Follow the gentlest gradient just N of this spur. One can zigzag through easy rock and heather bands toward the summit or bear left to a long narrow gully; an obstructing rock step in the gully may require a left detour. At the final slope, angle right (no difficulties). Time: 3 hours. Reference: *Mountaineer*, 1918, p. 21.

Note: the summit ridge on the other two summits can be readily followed; the saddle separating the N and "Cadet" summits is about 6920 ft.

Variation: The approach for Foggy Peak (or from Foggy's S slope) can be used to work directly to either the NW or N summit of Cadet. Continue on the connecting ridge to the "Cadet" summit; at the final rock pyramid keep to the W side of the first rocks.

NORTH FACE: From the low snow accumulation beyond Goat Lake♦ ascend the snow or old mine path (on left) to the Foggy (Penn) minesite. Here an obvious break in the cliffs allows an easy rightward traverse to the first snowfield which spreads above the cliffs (it is also possible to ascend talus beyond the lake and take an easy snow gully to right of waterfalls—the gully is nearly invisible from a distance). Then work up on snow and segments of the New York Glacier. Climb through rock bands and a final firn ice slope to the obvious crest W of the N summit.

NORTHEAST SHOULDER: This shoulder drops NE from the N summit to a low point of 5520 ft at ¾ mi. The shoulder is rocky, alpine, and the upper part has some snow/ice sections.

Use approach to Penn minesite (see North Face). Then angle left up major gully and later right to the ridge at est. 5500 ft. Turn SW and ascend the crest over broken rock and some steep snow and ice sections.

NORTHEAST FACE: A route to the "Cadet" summit could be made from the Cadet Creek valley, but an approach from the low base would be very rough. A route via a portion of this face, then up the NE shoulder, was done by Michael Heath in August 1968; other climbing history is unknown.

A study of the perspective indicates a feasible start using the Pride Glacier variation for Monte Cristo Peak, then a traverse farther NW to ascend one of several snow/ice corridors. A system of generally permanent snow from the glacier directly beneath the summit appears to offer a logical and interesting route to the final upper rocks; here a band leads right to the ridge between the two Cadet summits.

THE CADETS

This rocky row of crags trends NW-SE for ½ mi., with the first summit (est. 6880′/2097 m) ¼ mi. from Cadet Peak. The other significant high points of the row are 7040 ft/2146 m, 6880 ft/2097 m (followed by the lowest notch), 6880 ft/2097 m and 6800 ft/2073 m (estimated altitudes). This final summit (with a U-shaped notch adjoining Monte Cristo Peak) was one of the "Twin Bear" summits of mining times. These crags resembled a line of cadets to miners desiring a name for the formation.

Specific information is missing on the ascents, but there is no reason to believe the approach and any climbs from Glacier Basin are more than uphill hikes and mild scrambles; obvious gullies lead to the notches. If a traverse is done, it appears best to keep slightly on the SW side of the crest. Any routes from the Cadet Creek face would involve steep alpine problems. Of the various notches, the one between Monte Cristo Peak and the "Twin Bear" summit would be easiest to reach.

FOGGY PEAK 6810′/2076 m

Foggy is located on the N rim of Glacier Basin 1½ mi. from Monte Cristo, on the Elliott Creek divide. From the S, the summit is an unmistakable thimble shape. Sentinel Gap (5960′+) and another notch (est. 6200′) incise the ridge W of Foggy. At about ¼ mi. SE of the summit is the true Ida Pass (6040′+); NE of the pass is a segment of the New York Glacier (Goat Lake drainage). Foggy has a rocky divide trending N and remaining high to Point 5725 (opposite the S end of Goat Lake). Rock is generally sound for climbing. J.E. Spurr described the "granite face" of the mountain W of Goat Lake as "profoundly fissured."

The peak's name owes its origin to an error in application. A photograph in *The Mountaineer*, 1918,

GOAT LAKE AREA
ROBERT J. DeWITZ, U.S. FOREST SERVICE

FOGGY PK.
N.W. Summit
North Summit
CADET PK.
The Cadets
Ida Pass
Pride of the Mountains
Glacier Basin
Tramway Station
Mystery Hill
Mystery 1
Mystery 2
Mystery 3
Golden Cord
trail
Justice Mine
Glacier Creek

identifies the peak at the head of Goat Lake as "Foggy" and labels the lowest gap above the snowfield "Ida Pass" (see pp. 14-15), confirming the nomenclature of mining times. This earlier "Foggy" is now known as Cadet Peak's northern summits and the name applied to the peak described above. Unfortunately there is no record of Foggy's first climb. Occasional parties combine the ascent with that of Cadet, whose NW summit is ⅝ mi. to the SE.

SOUTH ROUTE: Leave Glacier Basin trail (see Glacier Basin♦) about 200 ft above the first falls, where a way trail descends a brush-free spot. Ford the creek, then proceed diagonally left to a timber strip (begins est. 4200′). A faint path leads to just below rock outcropping in timber 700 ft higher. Turn left for a short bush push and traverse to the light-colored talus slope. Ascend leftward toward the main gully below Foggy's S face (gully begins 700 ft below summit, slightly right of top). Ascend the broad, steep gully (diagonals slightly left toward W side of summit block). A short narrow couloir leads to a tiny ridge notch (loose rock; suggest hard hats). Climb sounder rock (class 3) on the NW side of the summit. Time: 5 hours from road.

Approach Variation: Leave the trail near the end of the old roadway (about 3200′), cross the creek and ascend to the obvious narrow virgin timber belt bearing NE. Ascend this belt and the scrubby higher tree zone to the alp slope beneath Foggy.

Approach Variation: It is possible to reach the S base of Foggy from below Sentinel Gap; this involves about ½ mi. of eastward traverse, mainly on talus. Do not follow the rock crest from the pass, but keep below cliffs.

Approach Variation: One could come from the area of the Penn minesite (see Cadet Peak—North Face); a rising traverse southward is made across snowfields to Ida Pass. Then contour W to beneath the summit. A traverse is also feasible from Cadet's S slope; keep along the top portion of the heather band but beneath all upper cliffs.

SOUTHEAST RIDGE: From Ida Pass traverse the ridge via several crags, then descend 300 ft (rappels) to the base of a wide gully. Continue to the summit via moderately steep rock climbing. Reported class 4 (Roland Amundson party); 10 hours from Monte Cristo.

ADDISON RIDGE

The extremely rugged massif on the South Fork Sauk River—Elliott Creek divide between Foggy Peak and Sheep Mountain has never been given specific summit nomenclature. There are three rocky summits worthy of a name and several more moderate, yet significant crags. Both the S and N flanks have a high gradient and are well spotted with imposing cliffs which force approaches into a few useful lines; perhaps because of unknown access and high local relief the massif has not attracted many climbers. Without question, goats know the intricacies of the ridge best, and what the prospectors knew is largely forgotten.

Monte Cristo miners used the name "Addison Mountain," but it is not certain if the name was generic or applied to an individual summit.[81] The two glaciers on the NW flank were not charted on the most recent topographic maps; the "Mackintosh" and "Gemini" glaciers each cover 0.3 km² (the 0.8 km higher "Gemini" reaches to about 6300 ft; the 1.3 km "Mackintosh" is a narrow cirque glacier that descends to 3900 ft).

Approaches: (largely suggested from reconnaissance) (1) To reach Mackintosh Glacier from Elliott Creek Trail: at first creek before Goat Lake♦ (est. ½ mi. before; 2600′) ascend brushy creek S (keep on its left). Where it splits into a basin (3700′) take a right fork SW past Ida Lake (the Brown map's "Clear Lake"). Ascend moraine to the Mackintosh Glacier.

(2) From Glacier Creek an old trail once switched up the burnt spur toward Sentinel Gap, but this slope is now thickly brushed. The best approach now is to ascend the alluvial cone at 0.2 mi. E of Monte Cristo resort spur road to the two giant "sentinel trees" (about 1000 ft upslope); take the first gully right here and work right again into the last gully right. Ascend this to the burnt spur and stay high (avoid dropping on the right slope—deep ravine there); make an ascending traverse right along the talus patches to the gap.

(3) From the "sentinel trees" a feasible route leads to the Addison crest at about ¼ mi. W of Sentinel Gap. Work into a thin minor gully left of talus gully above trees (this gully remains about 100 ft distant from the parent). Stay on spur left of the parent (which becomes a deep ravine) and ascend to the saddle just E of Pirate Peak, or directly to its upper rocks.

(4) Another possible approach from the S is by the stream at 0.3 mi. (at 2630′) W of Monte Cristo road spur. Except for thick alder at the bottom, the approach appears straightforward; a logical way to reach the low point (est. 6400′) between Gemini South Peak and Pirate Peak.

(5) It seems possible to ascend along the stream at ½ mi. W of Monte Cristo road spur (moderately brushy). When the stream ravine narrows it appears safest and more feasible to stay on the slope right; this leads beneath the E side of the precipitous Addison Spur and into the steep rocky basin S and beneath Gemini South Peak.

(6) Pearsall Pass (5000′+) at the W end of the Addison massif can be reached from the S by following the stream which crosses the Monte Cristo Road at ¾ mi. W of the resort spur. Expect some brush on lower forest slopes; higher, a long narrow gully leads to the pass. From its S flank traverse SE to a basin with a tarn (5400′). This broad basin retains snow cover under the Gemini Peaks. Talus, snow, and easy

CADET PEAK from west
JOHN V.A.F. NEAL

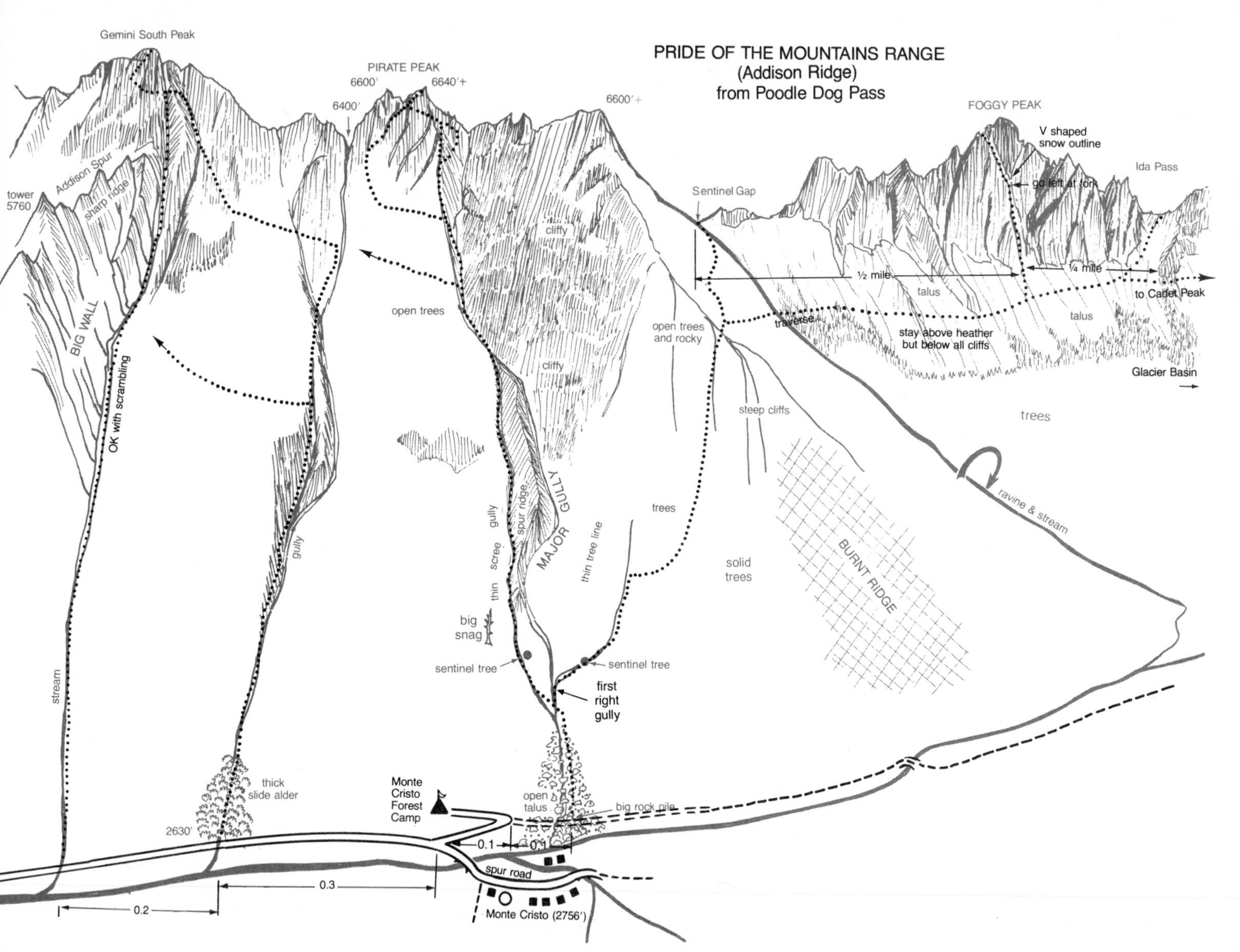
PRIDE OF THE MOUNTAINS RANGE
(Addison Ridge)
from Poodle Dog Pass
Gemini South Peak
PIRATE PEAK
6600′
6640′+
6400′
6600′+
FOGGY PEAK
V shaped snow outline
go left at fork
Ida Pass
Sentinel Gap
tower 5760
Addison Spur
sharp ridge
BIG WALL
OK with scrambling
cliffy
½ mile
¼ mile
talus
to Cadet Peak
open trees
open trees and rocky
traverse
stay above heather but below all cliffs
Glacier Basin
trees
steep cliffs
ravine & stream
gully
spur ridge
MAJOR GULLY
scree
thin
thin tree line
solid trees
BURNT RIDGE
big snag
sentinel tree
first right gully
stream
thick slide alder
Monte Cristo Forest Camp
open talus
big rock pile
2630′
0.1
spur road
0.3
0.2
Monte Cristo (2756′)

broken rock lead eastward to the central saddle (6480′+).

The basin could be reached using approach (4), but this would require a long scrambling traverse to the upper crest of Addison Spur, then an unproven short descent to the W.

(7) To reach Pearsall Pass from the N drop off Elliott Creek Road♦ at about 3 mi. (est. 2600′) and cross the creek (est. 2280′); ascend Pearsall Creek, an old prospector route; some brush now to at least 3600 ft before an easy talus corridor rises to the pass (est. 2½ mi. from Elliott Creek).

PIRATE PEAK 6640′+/2024 m

This is the highest summit between Gemini South Peak and Foggy Peak, and is about midway between Gemini South Peak and Sentinel Gap. It was called Peak 6600 in the A.A.C. Guide. Pirate has a thumb-like summit tower, and like the other summits on Addison Ridge, is hard to single out from Monte Cristo. The N face makes a steep drop into the basin containing the Mackintosh Glacier.

SOUTH SIDE: Reach from approach (3) via the long talus gully. The 20-ft summit block (class 4) is left of the gully. The last short pitch is on the W. Approach it from the lower left side of the S face, or cross the upper S face from the notch on the E.

There is an unnamed, gentler and pointed peak (6600′+) immediately E of Pirate. The ascent is simple from the connecting saddle or from Sentinel Gap (more scrambling).

GEMINI PEAKS

The two peaks, from one aspect nearly twins, are the highest summits on Addison Ridge and are connected by a high saddle (6480′+); the peaks are about ⅜ mi. apart, on a N-S trend. Both peaks are solid, hard, black Darrington Phyllite.

NORTH PEAK 6738′/2054 m

The peak is ⅜ mi. E of Pearsall Pass, and is quite precipitous on this W flank; N of the summit there is a prow that is sheer for about 400 ft. A continuing spur northward ends in ½ mi. (at Point 6092). No early climbing history has been found; probably the first ascent was made by Michael Heath on a traverse from the South Peak, September 23, 1967.

SOUTH RIDGE: Descend (rappels) from the summit of the South Peak, then make the rock climb from the central saddle (class 3). There appear to be several approaches directly to the saddle; from the area of Pearsall Pass, approaches (6) or (7). Another way to the Gemini saddle could be to use approach (1) to Ida Lake, then ascend westward on a long slope to Gemini Glacier under the North Peak, then up the glacier; there seems a system of snowpatches and ledges which lead up-left to the saddle.

SOUTH PEAK 6799′ / 2072 m

The peak is about 1½ mi. N of Monte Cristo and ¾ mi. NW of Sentinel Gap. The entire crest between this peak and Pirate Peak remains high. There does not appear to be a route easier than class 4 from any position. First ascent by Robert W. Craig and Wayne Swift in May 1940 via the S face (referred to previously as Peak 6700).

ROUTES: Approaches (3) or (4) are advised to high on the S slope. Various traverses at different levels have been made left, across gullies and ribs (leftward). The route of the original climb was across the extension of Addison Spur, then W of the spur to the final 100-ft slabby S face. Ascend a large slab (reported as 75° split by a large crack (left of the hornlike summit). Class 4. Time: 6 hours from road.

The route has also been reported as climbing the lower S face and angling up to the W ridge about 300 ft below the summit.

The route can apparently be reached via approach (6), and using the basin closely W of Addison Spur. From this approach a NW completion to the climb appears feasible from near Pearsall Pass, using the route descended to the North Peak (probably more difficult); this NW ridge has a steep step on its crest and here the flanking upper W face may be the solution.

ADDISON SPUR

This rocky mid-altitude spur juts out on the South Peak's S flank, just W of the stream at ½ mi. W of the resort spur road; see approach (5). The spur has a long sheer SE wall above this stream; there is a small but impressive tower at est. 5760 ft. The crest and the tower seem best reached from the Pearsall Pass approach and the tarn—approach (6).

SHEEP MOUNTAIN 6166′/1879 m

Sheep Mountain rises from the South Fork of Sauk River 1¼ mi. E of Barlow Pass. The N side slopes into the footings of Elliott Creek. Although Sheep is not a prominent massif, it rises with much local relief everywhere except at the SE ridge, which connects to Pearsall Pass and Addison Ridge.

WEST SIDE ROUTES: From Monte Cristo Road♦ at 2.1 mi. SE of Barlow Pass a branch road branches N about 1 mi. Either the timbered SW or W ridges may be taken. Some care is needed in route planning to detour short cliffs; generally ascend E or NE up steep timber to meadows. The W ridge reaches the main crest just S of the rocky summit. The SW ridge reaches the crest ½ mi. farther S; follow the ridge crest or heather slopes on its W side over alpine terrain to the summit. Time: 5-6 hours.

SLOAN PK.
MT. PUGH
BEDAL PK.
S.E. Peak
upper shelf
SLOAN GLACIER
west face
lower shelf
east arm

SOUTHEAST RIDGE: There is no problem in a route from Pearsall Pass; see Addison Ridge, approaches (6) and (7). Stay on traverse along talus bowls on the NE side of the ridge, just above timberline. At the final bowl, climb directly to the summit area (or follow ridge crest); most of the route is hiking. If desired, the open alpine ridge can be taken all the way from the pass (keep W of ridge humps).

Other routes: the long wooded N ridge has been used, beginning from Monte Cristo Lake; a long cliffy route, not recommended.

SLOAN PEAK 7835′/2388 m

Picturesque Sloan could be called the "Matterhorn of the Cascades." The highest summit W of Glacier Peak, and standing in splendid isolation, Sloan is a large gneissose granitic mass with a curious form: the W and SW faces are long, with a convex domelike shape; the E face above Sloan Glacier is shorter but nearly vertical. A passage in *The Mountaineer* (1918, p. 22) captures the peak's mood: "craggy lopsided Sloan . . . a challenging puzzle." Oblique master joints determine the principal sculptural features, such as the shelves on the S face.[82]

Located 5 mi. SE of the forks of the Sauk River, the slopes of Sloan drain into Bedal, Sloan, and Elliott Creeks and the North Fork of the Sauk. Sloan supports an apron-shaped glacier on its E flank; its apex is at the SE corner of the peak (7300′) and it terminates at about 5800 ft. A unique eastern rock arm cradles the S rim of the glacier; this arm has several towers—remnants from quarrying. The S face of the arm presents a wide rampart, which on the E reaches to a high point (6439′) at ½ mi. A 6600-ft pass S of Sloan divides it from the long ridge leading toward Cadet Peak.

While Bedal Creek once was the popular approach, the trail from the Sauk to beneath the W face was a gruelling 4-mi. trek; the directness of the Cougar Creek approach made it superior, but now a new logging road makes the Bedal route more attractive. As a climb Sloan has achieved popularity. The peak deserves this recognition, for the scenery, with a combination of evergreens, heather, ice, and firm rock, coupled with a marvelous summit vantage, is hard to surpass. Most routes can be done from the road in one day, although an intermediate camp makes the climb more relaxing.

The peak was locally named for a prospector of the 1890s, James Sloan, but the practical men of the mining era had no inclination to accept the challenge of a difficult appearing "Matterhorn." Even at the time of the 1918 Mountaineer outing, the mountain was still an enigma. After the first ascent by Harry Bedal and Nels Skaar July 30, 1921, via the now-normal route from the glacier,[83] the opportunities for new routes were not exploited until the late 1940s. By 1932 Sloan had been climbed seven or eight times, then its popularity expanded. The first winter ascent was made by Fred Beckey, Mike Borghoff, and Anthony Hovey in February 1963 (*Summit,* May 1963, pp. 26-27). References: *Mazama* 55, No. 13 (1973), pp. 31-32; *Mazama* 56, No. 13 (1974), pp. 31-32.

SLOAN PEAK from south
PHILIP LEATHERMAN

SOUTH FACE and UPPER WEST FACE (Corkscrew Route): The S face, which is actually quite sheer, is marked by two left-slanting shelves that almost converge at its western end. Both shelves offer a feasible route across and up the face to more broken rock where the face turns into the upper W face. The higher shelf begins at the upper corner of the glacier and the lower, converging shelf begins at the southeastern base of the peak, near the steep wall below the eastern arm.

Approach from the Sloan Peak Trail♦. From meadows below and N of the glacier, ascend gully (usually snow), then bear right to just right of prominent skyline rock. Climb onto the glacier and make a traversing ascent to its far upper end; a few crevasses may force detours (take ice axes; crampons optional). Exit from the glacier at the high corner, then follow the broad shelf of broken rock and heather that traverses the S face to a gully at its western side (not far below the prominent notch between the upper SW face and a protruding crag). A short rock pitch reaches this notch. Here cross from 100 to 200 ft W, following the most broken rock, and continue in a rightward arc to the summit. Class 3. Time: 7 hours from road.

Variation: Lower South Face Shelf: Follow Bedal Creek Trail♦ to where it heads near 4800 ft in timber (2-3 mi.), then follow a prominent open stream gully to heather slopes below the W face. Work SE to cross the sharp ridge (est. 5600′) leading W of Sloan, above timberline. Make an oblique traverse E for ½ mi. on the S slope to the ridge crest (est. 6550′) leading S from Sloan.

Traverse broken rock (or snow) a short distance to the SE base of the peak, to reach the lower of the angling shelves. Follow it up and left (a 60′ chimney can be climbed to intersect the shelf; solid, class 4); when the shelf begins to disappear ascend steep heathery rock to the upper shelf, just beneath the prominent notch. The notch can be reached by climbing a gully or by following an extension of the high shelf, then bearing left to the outside of the crag; then a steep scramble up its crest.

Alternate Approach: Leave Elliott Creek Trail (see Goat Lake♦) just pass the creek crossing at the SE end of clearcut (est. 2700′). Climb NE to the saddle (5240′+ NW of Point 5752); could camp on its N. Climb E to the saddle (5800′+) between it and Sloan; cross and climb heather to southern saddle between Sloan and Point 6619. Cross the saddle and make a traverse of snowfields in a NE direction to the lower S face shelf.

SLOAN PK.
North Ridge
?
standard
notch
S.W. Face
variation
West Face
variations

SOUTHWEST FACE: This long face is the western extension of the S face, W of the two angling shelves, and ending at the spur crag S of the prominent notch. The face is very steep for the first 600 ft; it begins just W of a corner at the lowest area on the S facade (est. 6800′). First ascent by Fred Beckey and Jack Schawabland on July 28, 1948.

Heather scrambling is followed by steep but well-jointed rock (dips E) for three leads (class 4). Bear left to a heather patch, and above it traverse on a grassy ledge; beyond a corner an airy ledge overlooks the exposed W face; worm around a blind corner to the crest of narrow arete. The following 100-ft pitch is the crux (probably class 5); more moderate pitches then lead to the easy broken rock on the upper W face. Grade II; class 4 (possibly some class 5). Time: 9 hours from road. References: *Mountaineer*, 1948, p. 53; *A.A.J.*, January 1949, p. 219.

WEST FACE: The broad and convex W face emerging out of upper Bedal Creek is Sloan's longest. While it is both steep and broad, the jointing is so complete that ledges can neatly be used to circumvent the sheer portions; difficult climbing is generally feasible with little protection. Jointing of ledge systems dips N. The face begins abruptly from heather slopes, an indication of its solid character. First ascent by Fred Beckey and Ronald Niccoli on September 7, 1958.

From the end of the Bedal Creek Trail♦ ascend to the top of meadows at the S end of the slope (against the lower W face, est. 6200′). Ascend a right-slanting gully against the right edge of the face for several hundred ft; cut left up a rock chimney and bear sharply left on a sloping ledge (wall steepens). Do two steep good pitches and then walk left 200 ft on an easy grassy ledge. A steep wall (120′) climbs to a ledge (in this area short left and right traverses can be made to find the best cracks; pitons or chocks may or may not be needed for belays and protection). Walk right one lead and then climb a steep (exposed) slab several leads. The upper third of the face is well broken and eventually leads to scrambling. Grade II or III; class 5.4 (generally class 4 with some class 5 in middle section). Time: 9 hours from road. Reference: *Mountaineer*, 1959, pp. 109-110.

Variations: By Eric Cheney, Mike Heath, and Ian Lange on September 21, 1966 (second ascent). This ascent probably followed a line similar to the original, but certainly made some variations. From near the small notch W of the face the climb uses a left-trending ramp, then in the central section of about 500 ft features ledges separated by short steep rock (class 4 and easy 5).

Another variation (by John Hart and Bryce Simon in September 1975) takes a long heather ramp leftward to just before two large caves, ascends one lead, curves left, then climbs a two-pitch exposed wall beginning with a steep dihedral; class 5.7.

NORTH RIDGE: This long ridge extends for over a mi. from the broad saddle at 5330 ft between Bedal Peak and Sloan, to form a divide between upper Bedal Creek and the Sloan Glacier. The average gradient of the ridge is low, but it has a jagged beginning, with shattered rock along fracture zone gaps; there is a notch with a short step about 1000 ft from the summit. Unfortunately the data concerning the first ascent has been lost.

Use either trail for approach (see South Face). Bypass the first portion of the ridge on the W, then apparently bear up and right to the little notch and following step (incomplete information); the step can probably be passed on the W. An account indicates one party climbed from the saddle to the upper notch where the ridge steepens; then contour over easy shattered rock on the E face of the ridge, climbing into several prominent notches along the ridge. About one-third of the way up, a short but difficult notch must be crossed. Climb left out of this notch cutting back to the right until a belay point is reached directly above the beginning of this move. Follow the ridge line along the easier ground until another prominent notch approximately three-fourths of the way along the ridge is reached. Here climb out on the E face a short distance on firm but steep rock for two pitches until the ridge is again gained. From this position proceed to the summit. Class 3 and 4. Another report indicated the ridge required about three roped pitches with some 5th class.

EAST FACE DIRECT: This is the 600-ft perpendicular wall above the Sloan Glacier. The face is wide, tapering down to the N; it remains steep to the SE corner, where the vertical angle breaks down. The face has few clean-appearing crack lines and has massive sections (gneiss). The route taken follows the most obvious system to the tiny notch just S of the summit. First ascent by Gary Glenn and Michael Heath on August 27, 1967.

The start is from the moat 250 ft N of the glacier's S edge (by a slightly overhanging bong crack). Work right up a smooth block (two bolts, rurps) to a cramped, dirty ledge. A hanging belay is found 20 ft higher. Climb directly up and find reasonable aid cracks (one bolt), passing under a small overhang with a left step-across (5.8), then up on knifeblades and a bolt to a prominent downsloping ledge. The original party made a hammock bivouac here (a better ledge can be found at the end of two additional leads). Traverse along the ledge to its N end, then up a large rotten chimney for 100 ft until a crumbly left traverse (5.8) reaches the end of a large level ledge. Climb right on the face above (aid) to a wide sloping platform that leads N to a left-leaning dihedral. Climb 130 ft of class 5 on its left wall to a rubble heap. Traverse left, then up for two class 4 to 5 leads to the summit crest.

Grade IV; class 5.8 and A4. The original climb used 75 pitons and four bolts (hangers on). Knifeblades and rurps are necessary; on the first pitch one 4-inch and two smaller bongs or chocks are needed. Piton list: two rurps, six KB, twelve horizontals, ten angles (⅜″ to 2″), one-2½″, one-3″, one-4″. Time: original ascent took 18 climbing hours. Reference: *A.A.J.*, 1968, pp. 136-137.

EAST FACE, SOUTH CORNER: The E face corners at the glacier head to form a steep profile at the S end of the vertical section. The route is on the S side of the profile, a totally independent line from the Southeast Face route; rock is su-

SLOAN PEAK, West Face
DAVID POWELL

perb. First ascent by Fred Beckey and Jerry Fuller on July 19, 1965.

Start at the highest tip of the glacier to make a difficult traversing rightward climb to a crack system (one pitch; class 5.5 to 5.7). The next two pitches (class 5) are upward, following mainly cracks and chimneys, and keeping as far right as feasible without getting onto the sheer section. The final two pitches are class 4 and lead directly to the summit. Grade II; class 5.7. References: *A.A.J.*, 1966, p. 131; *Mountaineer*, 1966, p. 202.

SOUTHEAST FACE: This triangular shape is marked with several prominent ledges; the face is S and above the upper corner of the glacier. First ascent by Paul Dix and Jack Miller in July 1965.

From the glacier tip climb N along a narrow downsloping ledge a short distance, then directly up a crack for 70 ft (class 4 and 5). The next section of crack (40′) becomes an open book (harder class 5). Then climb N on a big ledge, then back S above the open book on a narrow ledge just under an overhang (involves a belly crawl). Continue 20 ft farther S and 10 ft up on small ledges that go to a series of cracks which are followed for 130 ft (class 5). The route bypasses an overhanging nose on its S; climb for 250 ft (class 3) to the summit ridge, which is reached 250 ft S of the summit. Grade II; class 5. Time: 3-4 hours. References: *Mountaineer*, 1966, p. 202 (cites route incorrectly as W face); *A.A.J.*, 1966, p. 131.

BEDAL PEAK 6554′/1998 m

Located 2 mi. NNW of Sloan; the summit is at the NW end of the craggy granitic gneiss of the Bedal crest (the Bedal Orthogneiss is a meta-igneous rock). Bedal has three distinct summits on a NW-SE crest, all within 0.3 mi. The Southeast Peak (6360′+/1938 m) is 0.6 mi. from the Sloan-Bedal saddle; to its W is the central summit (6400′+/1951 m); the main summit (NW) has steep S and E faces which form a wall about ¼ mi. wide. The slopes N of the summit are easiest and the gradient on the NW is only 20°; the entire upper N side of the Bedal summits consists of a short but extensive wall. The proximity of Sloan distorts the real nature of the peak.

The name honors James Bedal, who settled by the Sauk forks with his Indian wife about 1892, a place which later had a wagon-road post office and became known as "Orient." Bedal's son Harry had a trapper's cabin in upper Bedal Creek and thoroughly explored the high country in all seasons; during one of these excursions he scaled the peak, probably alone (about 1921, probably by the NW shoulder).

NORTHWEST SHOULDER: Follow the Sloan Peak Trail♦ about 3½ mi. to the first meadow (with steep slash at

SLOAN PEAK from southeast
ROBERT J. DeWITZ, U.S. FOREST SERVICE

SLOAN PEAK from east
AUSTIN POST, U.S. GEOLOGICAL SURVEY

SLOAN PK.
SHEEP MTN.
south corner
North Ridge
MACKINTOSH GLACIER
East Face
Corkscrew Route
East Arm
SLOAN GLACIER

opposite end); cross the small creek and travel NW, angling upslope through scrub trees and heather to a large rockslide. From the Sloan-Bedal saddle (est. 5330′) make a long traverse NW on the S slope (steep meadows; stay well below the two eastern summits), then traverse beneath the S wall of the main peak. Work around the W end when feasible (about ¼ mi. from summit, at end of trees—est. 5900′), then ascend the solid rock of the NW shoulder (some large boulders and steep heather). Class 3. Time: 6 or more hours from road.

Note: N slopes below the rock area are moderate, but a direct approach is not very practical.

Alternate Approach (1): Use approach for Sloan Peak via Bedal Creek. Leave trail at a rockslide left of Sloan's W face. Cross alpine terrain to the Sloan-Bedal saddle area.

Alternate Approach (2): From Bedal Creek Trail♦ (at est. ⅓ mi. where an obvious slide descends) climb E up wooded slopes (E of slide) to a large boulderfield at the foot of a great wide cliff. Enter a fault at its left end; the route leads up and right 400 ft (class 3) to a steep heather slope near the NW shoulder.

SOUTHEAST RIDGE: When traversing below the S wall of the main summit, ascend to the gap adjacent the central summit. Then climb enjoyable rock to the summit (oral communication, party names missing); class 3. A longer approach to this completion has been done from the Bedal-Sloan saddle using a traverse, then a climb to the central-SE summit gap (a 30-ft pitch to the gap is about class 4). Climb easy class 5 on the ridge to the central summit, then rappel to the last gap.

CENTRAL PEAK

The easiest route appears to be on the SW side, then a completion on the NW. See variation for Southeast Ridge, main summit.

SOUTHEAST PEAK

The easiest route is via the S side and a final steep 75-ft section on the W.

SOUTHEAST FACE: First ascent by Bruce Garrett and Bill Powell in August 1969. This 600-ft face is shaped as a tilted triangle (visible from Sloan Peak Trail♦). Leave the trail as per Northwest Shoulder, but keep N of the saddle.

Begin at midface—at a right-leaving open book just opposite the lower end of a reddish gneiss outcrop. Climb 140 ft directly up to a heather pedestal (5.4). Now zigzag about 80 ft past two bulges (5.7), then left up a ramp to a pedestal directly above the initial one. Third lead (60′) ascends a layback to a long ledge (5.5—used three runners on horns). Traverse left 300 ft along a ledge and easy slabs until beneath the summit block. Then climb 300 ft (class 3-5); there is a short hard crack just under the summit. Grade II; class 5.7 (bring selection KB to 2″). Time: 4 hours on rock. Reference: *Mountaineer*, 1970, p. 105.

Note: the left and right edges of the face have subsequently been done.

GOBLIN MOUNTAIN 5606′/1709 m

Located 1¾ mi. SW of Curry Gap. For a period of time prior to 1946 this name was on maps for the summit that is now Kyes Peak.

ROUTE: From Curry Gap♦ take the currently unmaintained trail S ½ mi. leave the trail and proceed W across a series of meadows for ½ mi. Climb directly up the timbered ridge to the S; follow this ridge crest SSE, then S, then SW to the prominent summit pinnacle. Two large steps on the SE corner lead to a ledge, from which the final few yards become a bouldering problem. Time: 3 hours from the Gap.

BALD EAGLE MOUNTAIN 5680′+/1731 m

This minor peak is located 2½ mi. SE of Curry Gap.

ROUTE: Walk to the summit from Bald Eagle Trail on the N side at about 5200 ft. See Curry Gap♦.

LONG JOHN MOUNTAIN 5697′/1736 m

Another minor peak, 2 mi. E of Curry Gap.

ROUTE: Walk to the summit from Bald Eagle Trail on the S slope at about 5250 ft. See Curry Gap♦.

JUNE MOUNTAIN 5946′/1812 m

This peak is located on the Sloan Creek-North Fork Skykomish River divide about 4½ mi. E of Curry Gap.

ROUTE: Bald Eagle Trail almost tops the peak on the N. See Curry Gap♦.

JOHNSON MOUNTAIN 6721′/2049 m

Johnson is a high, domelike mountain 2½ mi. W of the Cascade crest at Indian Pass; it is between Sloan Creek and North Fork Sauk River. The name is for Mackinaw Johnson, who had prospects and a cabin on the mountain.

ROUTE: Reach via summit trail. See Pilot Ridge Trail♦.

WHITE MOUNTAIN 7031′/2143 m

White is a gentle, extensive uplift on the NW side of White Pass, only about ½ mi. distant. The summit has been a favorite with topographical surveyors and photographers, and warrants its reputation as a marvelous viewpoint for Glacier Peak and the Monte Cristo peaks.

ROUTES: The ascent is quite feasible on any side. The most common way is from White Pass (see Section II—White River Trail♦ and Crest Trail♦); ascend directly to the summit (under 2 hours). Slopes are heather, talus, and possible snow. A similar way is to hike the flowery crest of the W ridge, beginning about ½ mi. from Red Pass. Reference: *Mountaineer*, 1937, p. 30.

WHITE MOUNTAIN from west
U.S. FOREST SERVICE

PORTAL PEAK 6999′/2133 m

Portal seems diminutive compared to Black Mountain, but it is the highest summit on the ridge connecting to Red Pass.

ROUTE: See Black Mountain, Southwest Ridge.

SKULLCAP PEAK 6562′/2000 m

The peak is located on the ridge between Red Pass and Black Mountain, W of the upper White Chuck River. Forest ranger Nels Bruseth named both this summit and Portal Peak in 1917, for appearance and location.

ROUTE: See Black Mountain, Southwest Ridge.

BLACK MOUNTAIN 7242′/2207 m

Black is located W of the White Chuck River, 5 mi. SW of Glacier Peak. Its height adds to its character, although it offers little technical difficulty. The Black Peak pluton (gneiss) is of Paleocene age. The mountain is steepest on its upper E, where there are short cliffs and snow/ice patches; there is a small glacier on the NE. Black was named by A.H. Dubor, T.G. Gerdine, and Sam Strom during surveying about 1897; they probably made the first climb.

SOUTHWEST RIDGE: From Red Pass (see North Fork Sauk River Trail♦ and Crest Trail♦) hike over or skirt Portal Peak and along to Point 6910. Drop into Red Creek to avoid W-side cliffs and traverse to regain the crest; follow up easy slopes of Skullcap Peak; descend ridge N and over a minor 6350-ft saddle. Continue to the basin on the S side of Black at about 5750 ft and ascend the SW shoulder at 6600 ft. Keep right of a 6803-ft knob; then ascend SW ridge to top (one can scramble along parts of ridge or keep largely on snow or talus). Distance from Red Pass is about 3 mi., not allowing for detours. Time: est. 5 hours.

NORTH ROUTE: Hike around the E side of Lake Byrne (see Lost Creek Ridge Trail♦, then up the meadowed hump; from the saddle S of the lake traverse across a wide E-facing talus/snow basin. At its far end rise to the divide (est. 6100′), then descend SW to about 5600 ft in the basin of Lost Creek (camping) to skirt a cliffy spur, then ascend S to 6000 ft on moderate alp slopes. Completion details are not fully documented for the climb of the sloping NW face of Black (some snow), but a rising traverse to the SW ridge is known; est. class 2, 5 hours. The upper NE slope holds a low-gradient ice patch which appears to offer no problem.

RED MOUNTAIN (Painted Mountain) 6975′/2126 m

This prosaic name was supposedly applied by Sam Strom and a prospecting party. Nels Bruseth recorded the Indian name "Ska-hala-bats," meaning "Painted Mountain,"[84] which would be preferable. The location is 4.6 mi. NE of Sloan Peak. Likely it was climbed by members of the U.S. Geological Survey about 1897.

SOUTHWEST SHOULDER: From the old lookout point (est. 2800′)—see Red Mountain Trail♦—continue on a path to a rocky area. Ascend this, then follow path which starts a left traverse and slowly fades. At a gully head upslope on its right (steep dirt), then atop a steep densely forested ridge to high meadows. Veer N toward the summit (skirt false summit to right) on easy heather and scree. Time: 5 hours.

Approaches from the E or N have no advantage because of long traverses and intervening ridges.

BRECCIA PEAK 6487′/1977 m

Flanking Round Lake (Lost Creek Ridge) is a ridge which consists of breccia filling an ancient volcanic vent. The high points are 6487 ft (0.3 mi. NE of the lake), 6461 ft (0.7 mi. NW of the lake), and two summits (6440′+).

In July 1970 Steve Moore and Joe Vance traversed the ridge and the high points (class 3). The highest summit can be reached from the Lost Creek Ridge Trail♦ by ascending heather slopes, or by ascending directly from the lake.

MT. PUGH 7224′/2202 m

Pugh is strategically located in the converging angle of the White Chuck and Sauk Rivers. Popular usage is Mt. Pugh, but maps refer to it as Pugh Mountain. The Indian name for it was Da Klagwats. Pugh is bulky and lofty with deep footings everywhere. The summit, E flank, and S ridge are gneissose quartz diorite, while the upper W flank is greenschist (Vance). The great Straight Creek Fault which separates these rocks is well exposed on the trail; it forms the depression for the narrow glacier (1.3 km) which trends northward, draining to Stujack Creek. Mine prospects were once made about 1 mi. NW of the summit.

The summit lookout is no longer in existence, but with good trail most of the ascent Pugh affords a popular, easy climb to a high vantage. The name is for John Pugh, who settled at the base in 1891. Nels Bruseth apparently made the first ascent in 1916, and for several years he maintained a summit tent as lookout station; during one period of his summit service he carried on a courtship at Bedal by running down the mountain after hours and returning by morning. As an aid to climb on steep snow and heather he used a cut-down garden rake. On at least one occasion when lightning struck the tent, it caused canned juices to leak. Harry Bedal and Nels Skaar did most of the blasting and difficult trail construction on the solid rock above Stujack Pass so a lookout station could be built on the summit (this Forest Service project was completed in September 1919). Two cable trams with A-frames were used on the upper rock ridge to hoist lumber and supplies nearly to the summit; in 1927 the lower tram was replaced by a horse trail. In 1948 the summit trail was reconstructed; a fixed rope on the rock staircase is now removed.[85]

NORTHWEST RIDGE: Take Pugh Mountain Road♦ 1 mi. to trail (no. 644 at 1920′) which begins just past the second hairpin. Reach Metan Lake (3180′) in 1½ mi., and Stujack Pass (5720′) on the NW ridge in 4½ mi. (can camp at timberline below pass). The final mi. is a marked scramble up the heathery rock ridge (class 2). The route climbs to a narrow rock ridge, then works along cliffs above the trough and small glacier (6360′). In early summer this area will contain steep snow. It would seem remarkably unlikely to become lost here, but some parties have strayed left to encounter cliffs and steep snow. Time: 5 hours. Reference: *101 Hikes*.

Variation: Upper Northeast Face: By Otto Trott and Dwight Watson on August 6, 1939. From the snow bowl a narrow rock face was climbed for at least several hundred ft, this leading to the summit.

GLACIER PEAK 10,541′/3213 m

Glacier Peak was not named by Quimper in 1790 or Vancouver in 1792, for it is not dominating from tidewater, but we may assume they saw it. Captain Vancouver zealously mapped and explored the shores of Puget Sound, charting both Mt. Rainier and Mt. Baker, so it is logical he sighted Glacier Peak as part of the "Eastern Snowy Range."[86] The high, glacierized and eroded volcanic cone, unchallenged by any neighbor, is prominently etched into the Cascade skyline as the highest elevation from Mt. Rainier to the Skagit River, the only remaining wilderness volcano in Washington State.

In any event tidewater exploration did not amount to an effective discovery or a definite naming of the mountain. Indians once called it Great Parent (DaKobed—with various spellings[87]) and noted its cloud caps as weather prophecies, but the Gerdine and Russell surveys mapped it simply Glacier Peak.[88]

Professor William D. Lyman, in an eloquent passage, captured the volcano's magnificent image: "It can be seen in all its snowy vastness, ten thousand feet high, and bearing upon its broad shoulders miles and miles of rivers of ice, the most beautiful and significant of all the poems of nature."[89] Lyman, however, apparently did not then understand how the master stream, the Suiattle, separates the stratovolcano from the Cascade crestline, for he wrote that at Railroad

Creek "we are at the outlet of the glaciers of Glacier Peak."[90]

Glacier Peak is the second northernmost of the large Quaternary stratovolcanoes of the Cascade Range of northern California, Oregon, and Washington, and one of five towering above the average crestline of the range in Washington. It represents another epic in the complex interplay of eruption and erosion in Cascade volcanoes. The summit rises 7,000 ft above the Suiattle Valley some 5 mi. to the E. The many-hued tuffs and deep-colored rhyolites give it a richness of tone, adding to the quite striking contrast between young eruptive materials forming the cinder cone and the ancient rocks of the serrated crest peaks. The early Cascade explorer, Professor Israel C. Russell, identified its andesite rock and called Glacier Peak a cinder cone, younger than the plateau upon which it stands.[91]

It is a much-eroded, steep-sided composite lava cone composed of andesite and dacite, flanked by huge fans of volcaniclastic debris, and perched on a high bedrock ridge of once-molten schists and gneisses (and partly atop a relatively young granitic intrusion). Overlying these structures are what is known as the Gamma Ridge volcanic rocks; the aggregate thickness of lava flows do not exceed 2500 feet.[92] The pre-Gamma Ridge landscape was dominated by NW-trending valleys and ridges parallel to the bedrock grain, a trend well established in the Washington Cascades as early as the Oligocene.[93]

Glacier Peak was formed in latest Pleistocene time, when widespread volcanism gave way to a long period of activity from the central conduit. All flows were erupted within the past 700,000 years, and the latest flows within the past 17,000 years, after alpine glaciers had retreated.[94] The oldest flows are those that cap ridgetops, often eroded into isolated caps (Vista Ridge is an old flow isolated by erosion from Glacier Peak; the adjacent valleys are glacier-carved). Lava was spilled down the basement rocks and batholith as the cone was gradually built on the east side of Lime Ridge. The longest lava flows were to the N and E (the ridge capping flows radiate from the present summit area of the volcano and extend nearly to the Suiattle River). Continued eruption of dacite built the high central dome and summit crater.

The next phase of the volcano's activity (some time prior to 10,000 years ago) culminated with enormous explosions of basaltic-andesite. Molten rock from the volcanic center was ejected to collect in thick layers of tuff and breccia. When Glacier Peak lavas spilled out over earlier rocks the lava flowed down radial valleys cut into the flanks of the volcano and continued for more than 11 mi. down the Suiattle River valley.[95] Late in the life of the stratovolcano a dome was extruded near the summit of Disappointment Peak, to ooze down the smooth declevity of the main cone's S slope.[96] About 13,500 years ago, after major glacial retreat, a dacite dome rose on the E side of the volcano. The cone crumbled as it rose, and generated mudflows to build up great debris onto the fan that filled Suiattle River valley. Growth of the fill in the just-deglaciated valley forced the river farther E and created Chocolate Creek by diverting it from ancestral Dusty Creek.[97]

An explosive eruption about 12,000 years ago ejected a large volume of ash and pumice;[98] successive showers of air-fall pumice included molten blobs which cooled in flight. Immense blankets of volcanic ash drifted E and NE, spread by prevailing winds. Glacier Peak tephra made an eastward swath that blew pumice extending into Montana, Alberta, and Saskatchewan.[99] Yellow pumice accumulated at distances E of the vent, including the Entiat Mountains, although most pumice remnants are concentrated near the summit or on broad ridges E of the volcano.

No evidence has been found of eruptions more recent than of this time, although there probably have been volcanic emanations. During or soon after the big eruption, mudflows and streams on the W side partly filled the recently deglaciated White Chuck Valley with detritus from the volcano, forming the White Chuck fill and forcing the river to its western bank. Since the central vent of Glacier Peak became dormant, eruptions have occurred nearby. During this last phase basaltic cinder cones grew; now the only indication of lingering heat are three hot springs near the base of the cone.

Erosion is rapidly removing the high-standing cone. An old crater with a worn-down rim remains; its southwestern part is the true summit. The crater itself is obscured by erosion and filled with snow and ice. The N crater rim rises to a sub-summit (10,307′ / 3142 m); farther N are a narrow saddle and remnants of a larger summit cone capped by the eroded lava pinnacles known as the "Rabbit Ears" (10,140′/3090 m). A radial system of steep-sided canyons has been cut into flanks of Glacier Peak but the interstream areas are scarcely modified by erosion.

Glacier Peak probably has been ice-mantled ever since it emerged, owing to the northern latitude and high snowfall volume. Ice on the volcano has been estimated at 21.8 km^2 (of this, 6 km^2 is contained on the peripheral Suiattle and White Chuck Glaciers, the two largest).[100] The volcano is thoroughly eroded by glaciers on its W, N, and E flanks, and its principal crater has been breached. Some glaciers have advanced almost continuously while nearby glaciers have been in retreat; the remarkable feature of these ice masses is their diversity of activity.

The major flow of summit ice is the Chocolate, which breaches E from the crater; the breach on the W rim forms the saddle at the head of the Scimitar Glacier. While glacier cover does not equal the volume of Mt. Rainier or Mt. Baker, there are sizeable glaciers. The most notable is the Chocolate, which has shown an advance in the early 1950s and since has stabilized at 5400 ft.[101] The Cool Glacier divides from the Chocolate and flows SE (to about 6400 ft) to drain into the northern terminal fork of the Suiattle River.[102]

The Suiattle Glacier terminates at 5800 ft, but it is known that in 1906 the glacier ended near the stream from Cool Glacier, evidence of vast recession in this area. With a surface of 2.9 km² it lies mainly on the highland S of the volcano (to 8100′) and is the head of the Suiattle River. The White Chuck is the largest glacier (3.1 km² and 2.1 km long) but only tenuous connections make it a part of the Glacier Peak system.[103]

The small Sitkum Glacier drains into Sitkum and Baekos Creeks on the W flank (9700′ to 6500′). On the NW flank are the Scimitar (2.6 km) and Kennedy (2.4 km) Glaciers (descending to est. 5700′ and 5900′); both are narrow ice streams flowing NW from N of the summit (they advanced moderately in the 1950s). The Ptarmigan Glacier (once known as Milk Creek Glacier) is relatively small, but reaches farthest NW to drain into Milk Creek's W fork at about 6100 ft. The small Milk Lake Glacier is an isolated ice body in the Milk Creek drainage SE of Fire Creek Pass. The beautiful Vista, Ermine, Dusty, and North Guardian Glaciers mantle the volcano's NE flank.[104]

The first ascent of Glacier Peak was made in August 1898 by Thomas G. Gerdine of the U.S. Geological Survey, Sam Strom, and three other party members, whose object was to place a survey monument with a flag.[105] In August 1906 Claude E. Rusk and A.L. Cool explored the E side of the volcano, hiking from Buck Creek Pass to make the first climb on that flank. Rusk named the Chocolate and Cool Glaciers.[106] In 1910 L.A. Nelson and two companions climbed by a ridge due E of the summit; during the Mountaineer outing of that year 57 persons made the ascent of the volcano, the first of many club outings and mass ascents. On August 6, 1921 there was a Mountaineer ascent of 67 persons. The first ski ascent was made in 1938 by Sigurd Hall and Dwight Watson (see note 108).

References of special interest include:

Mazama 4, no. 1 (1912): 6-9; 6, no. 2 (1921): 47-50; 8, no. 12 (1926): 31-47, 50-59; 20, no. 12 (1938): 13-17; 31, no. 13 (1949): 45-48; 33, no. 13 (1951): 44-48.

Mountaineer, 1910, pp. 25-40; 1921, pp. 9-23.

Sierra Club Bulletin 8, no. 3 (1912): 174-184.

Bruseth, Nels. "Tall, Little-Known Glacier Peak." *Seattle Times*, magazine section, 18 May 1947, pp. 1-2.

Crowder, D.F. and Tabor, R.W. *Routes and Rocks: Hiker's Guide to the North Cascades from Glacier Peak to Lake Chelan*, pp. 39-45, 53-59, 77-80. Seattle, 1965.

Fryxell, Ronald, "Mazama and Glacier Peak Volcanic Ash Layers—Relative Ages," *Science* 147, no. 3663 (1965): 1288-1290.

Hazard, Joseph T. "Glacier Peak." In *Snow Sentinels of the Pacific Northwest*, pp. 115-127. Seattle, 1932.

Manning, Harvey. *Wild Cascades: Forgotten Parkland.* San Francisco, 1965.

Manning, Harvey and Spring, Ira. *101 Hikes in the North Cascades*, Seattle, 1970.

Miller, Tom. *The North Cascades*. Seattle, 1964.

Rusk, Claude E. "Regal Glacier Peak, Ice-King of the Northern Cascades." In *Tales of a Western Mountaineer*, pp. 152-176. Boston, 1924.

SITKUM GLACIER: Because of the extension of the White Chuck Road approach this route has assumed the popularity of the White Chuck Glacier and Disappointment Peak route. The Sitkum Glacier is nearly divided into three sections by a cliff band and cleaver. These areas are small and much of the ascent is done on snowfields or pumice; numerous variations are possible.

From the junction of White Chuck River Trail♦ and the Crest Trail♦ follow the latter ½ mi. N to the Sitkum Ridge path (at 4100′; also called Glacier Trail). The path follows the steep and rough wooded ridge S of Sitkum Creek (blazes) which finally veers slightly S to timberline at 5500 ft. Here is a boulder basin; ideal camp on heather ridge across the creek, S.

Continue upslope SE to where a ridge forms with a cliff on the left; work onto ridge and turn slightly left over its brow into a snow bowl at about 7600 ft (top is a level area); alternatively one can keep left of the ridge and work up lower bowl of the glacier (a few small crevasses). Traverse slightly right on a snowfield, then ascend a corridor just left of the cleaver that divides the glacier's S segment. Follow the glacier toward the snow saddle in the W summit ridge (immediately above Sitkum Spire). Ascend toward the summit, then bear several hundred yds E to a large chute, keeping right of sum-

GLACIER PEAK from west
NATIONAL PARK SERVICE

GLACIER PEAK
Rabbit Ears
Pt. 10381
Disappointment Pk.
Frostbite Ridge
TENPEAK MTN.
LUAHNA PK.
CLARK MTN.
ennedy Pk.
VISTA GLACIER
Kennedy Ridge
saddle
Northwest Ridge
SUIATTLE GLACIER
KENNEDY GLACIER
SITKUM GLACIER
Boulder Basin
Baekos Creek
Kennedy Creek
Sitkum Creek
Sitkum Ridge
Crest
Trail
acier Creek
White Chuck
River Valley
Kennedy Ridge
Lake Byrne

GLACIER PEAK summit area from west
AUSTIN POST, U.S. GEOLOGICAL SURVEY

mit rocks. The summit is an ice-covered crest of about 100 ft by 500 ft; at the SW end a rock jumble forms the highest point. Time: 4-6 hours from high camp. Reference: *Mountaineer*, 1948, p. 54 (ski).

Variation: From the snow saddle ascend the pumice ridge to the summit rock slope, then bear left on the upper edge of Scimitar Glacier to reach the summit crest.

Variation: From the level area leading to rock outcrop, contour S to the S segment of the glacier. Ascend left to meet normal route left and above the "index finger" of rock which points N. Longer variations include the long gully adjacent to Disappointment Spur or the SW slopes to the Disappointment Peak saddle.

SCIMITAR GLACIER: This narrow glacier, flowing in a canyon between Kennedy and the Northwest (Sitkum) Ridges, emanates from the crater breach saddle (10,100′+) closely N of the summit. First ascent by Roland Emetaz, Don Fager, Tom Lyon, and Bill Prater on September 1, 1957.

Use the Sitkum approach to the basin above timberline, then climb left to cross Northwest Ridge (est. 7200′); from here a traverse on the obvious slope can be made (left) to the Scimitar Glacier. In late season the glacier may be extremely broken; the left side is exposed to rockfall and the surface may be laden with some serac debris. There are two crevassed step-gradients on the glacier; the first is about 500 ft in height (about 8000′) and the other about 9000 ft. These may present problems and icy conditions, depending on season and snow cover. (The original party in late season took 12 hours and called it "some ice climb"). The route ascends to the saddle, then bears right to the summit. Grade II; bring ice screws. Time: 6 hours or more from camp. References: *A.A.J.*, 1960, p. 121; *Cascadian*, 1957, pp. 48-49.

KENNEDY RIDGE-KENNEDY GLACIER: The gaudy-hued andesite cliffs of Kennedy Ridge lie between the Scimitar and Kennedy Glaciers; the Scimitar side is quite steep and should be avoided.

Take White Chuck River♦ and Kennedy Ridge trails, following the latter to the head of a boulder-filled basin (best camping). Work right around its head: first keep on N side of Kennedy Creek and then traverse under Kennedy Glacier to the base of Kennedy Ridge (est. 5700′). Ascend pumice and snow to 7200 ft where there is a cliff in the ridge (and a S arm of the glacier). Ascend this glacier arm; stay right at 8500 ft where a major rock island splits the glacier. Then bear S, following the rim to the saddle N of the summit.

Variation: The steep route, to be used only if conditions allow, continues up the S portion of the glacier and climbs a steep section (possibly rock) to the crater rim at Point 10,381 (about ¼ mi. N of the summit). It is not certain if this variation has been done.

KENNEDY GLACIER: The first recorded climb was by Lavelle Cooper, Marion Marts, and Ralph Shumm on August 26, 1935. They approached via the Ptarmigan-Vista route, then descended onto the Kennedy Glacier from the slope of Frostbite Ridge (11 hours Milk Creek Ridge to summit).[107] The route on the upper glacier simply ascends the main portion to its head between the rock points on the crater rim. Crevasses are about the only problem, and are usually quite negotiable.

One can approach via Kennedy Ridge or via the Vista-Kennedy saddle; reach readily via Glacier Ridge (see Frostbite Ridge) or Milk Creek Ridge (see Milk Creek route). Using the Vista-Kennedy saddle avoids the entire lower portion of the glacier.

FROSTBITE RIDGE (Pumice Ridge) (North Cleaver): This prominent crest leads from Kennedy Peak SSE between the Kennedy and Ermine Glaciers. Its appearance is generally rounded, more a spur than a crest, and at times it becomes indistinct because of surface snow and overlapping glacier ice. Kennedy Peak is a large rock eminence on this flank of the volcano.

Take White Chuck River Trail♦ and Glacier Ridge Trail; cross the Crest Trail♦, then continue up Glacier Ridge (campsites in ½ mi.). At about 7100 ft the ridge turns SE. Follow it to Kennedy Peak (alternative is to pass latter by traverse on north—via Ptarmigan Glacier and to the E side of the Vista-Kennedy saddle. Then ascend the Kennedy Glacier SE or the cleaver on its left. In about ½ mi. the cleaver smoothes and merges into the W edge of Dusty Glacier. Here bear E around the N cleaver; shortly beyond, the ridge curves S and becomes pronounced again. Near the top of the ridge, the snow steepens. Leave the glacier (at 9500′ or lower) and ascend pumice right of the cleaver. After rising about 400 ft return to steep snow (via 30′ of rock) and climb through the rock Rabbit Ears, then down rock to the saddle adjacent Point 10,307 (N crater rim). Note: a traverse rightward around the Rabbit Ears is reasonable but inconvenient.

Now climb 150 ft of very steep snow to the rim and bear W—but bypass closely E of the top horn of rim—and descend into the crater, then rise S to the summit (nearly ¼ mi. from crater). Time: 5 hours from high camp.

Approach Variation: Leave Glacier Ridge at about 6500 ft and traverse S to the lower portion of Kennedy Glacier. Climb its northern margin to reach the Vista-Kennedy saddle.

Approach Variation: One can camp above the apex of Kennedy Ridge Trail by hiking up the lateral moraine to a picturesque meadow (5800′). Then ascend the Kennedy Glacier ESE and bear around the N cleaver.

MILK CREEK ROUTE (Ptarmigan, Vista, and Ermine Glaciers): This is an attractive N-side route with scenic vistas. As a route it is really just a northern approach to Frostbite Ridge or the upper Kennedy Glacier. Scarcity of early climbing records make it uncertain if the route was followed before the ascent of July 5, 1935 by Philip Dickert, Perry Dodson, and Bob Dwyer who apparently used a version of this route via the Vista Glacier and Frostbite Ridge.[108]

From Milk Creek Ridge (see Milk Creek Trail♦ and Crest Trail♦) ascend southward to the last scrub trees, then contour the E slope near 6500 ft to bypass the rocky first buttress (Point 6957) on the ridge. Turn right to a saddle (6700′+) beyond. Traverse SSW on W (Milk Creek) side of divide and then ascend the low-gradient of Ptarmigan Glacier. Work S past the rock spur on the glacier's E side until it is possible to cross left over a minor (7900′+) saddle (est. 1 mi. from first saddle). Gradually ascend SE beneath Kennedy Peak on upper Vista slopes. These lead to the Ermine's margin through the Vista-Kennedy saddle (8300′+). Ascend S on the Ermine as per Frostbite Ridge; some parties here have chosen an ascent SE using the Kennedy Glacier. Time: 5-7 hours from camp at Milk Creek Meadows or Ridge.

Approach Variations: (1) From the Crest Trail♦ at Pumice Creek (est. 5850′) hike up Pumice Creek to the Milk Creek divide (saddle at 6600′+). Travel SE to the Ptarmigan and Vista Glaciers.

(2) From Fire Creek Pass (see Crest Trail♦) travel SE cross-country about 2 mi. to the Ptarmigan Glacier. From the pass first keep on the N slope and cross a 6500-ft+ saddle to Milk Lake Glacier. Continue SE to cross a gradual ridge, then continue along easy slopes to the Ptarmigan.

(3) From Vista Ridge (see Crest Trail♦) W of Vista Creek traverse S at about 6000 ft to the head of the creek, and onto the lower Vista Glacier; ascend it directly to the Ermine.

DUSTY GLACIER (Gamma Ridge): Dusty Glacier merges with the upper Ermine Glacier on the volcano's NE slopes; below 8800 ft they are separated by cleavers. North

Following page: GLACIER PEAK from northeast
AUSTIN POST, U.S. GEOLOGICAL SURVEY

GLACIER PEAK
RAINIER
Pt. 10,381
Rabbit Ears
Sitkum Ridge
CADET PK.
FOGGY PK.
North Guardian Rock
uth Guardian Rock
KENNEDY GLACIER
CHOCOLATE GLACIER
Frostbite Ridge
KENNEDY PK.
to Kennedy Glacier
NORTH GUARDIAN GLACIER
PTARMIGAN GLACIER
DUSTY GLACIER
Pt. 7,717
ERMINE GLACIER
Recession Rock
VISTA GLACIER
Vista Creek

Pt. 10,381
Pt. 10,307
Rabbit Ears
SITKUM GLACIER
Sitkum Spire
saddle
DUSTY GLACIER
UCK MTN.
North Guardian Rock
Frostbite Ridge
Kennedy Ridge
RMINE GLACIER
VISTA GLACIER
KENNEDY GLACIER
SCIMITAR GLACIER

Guardian Rock, about 9200-9500 ft, between Chocolate and Dusty Glaciers, is S of the glacier's head. The Dusty Glacier ends in Recession Basin in two severely crevassed tongues that divide near Recession Rock, a rugged dacite cleaver of ridge-capping lava. The history of climbing on this glacier is incomplete, but it is known that in 1937 a Yakima party led by Curtis Gilbert ascended here to the saddle N of the summit.

Approach by Gamma Ridge Trail♦ and continue SW closely S of Gamma Peak (campsites near 6000′) to the saddle beyond. Reach the N side of the Dusty Glacier at about 7000 ft, then ascend the glacier and upper Ermine Glacier SW to the NE summit (Rabbit Ears, 10,140′/3090 m). The final slopes steepen and have some large crevasses. Then continue as per Frostbite Ridge.

Note: if the N lobe is heavily crevassed it may be necessary to continue by a spur N of the glacier to about 7600 ft before entering; in late summer crevasses become wide and frequent, even above this point.

Approach Variations: (1) Since these glaciers are only of moderate gradient and offer many route opportunities, variations are possible. One could use the Vista (Crest) Trail and "Dolly Dusty" high route (see *Routes and Rocks*) to about 1 mi. W of Gamma Peak, then ascend S on snowfields and cleavers to the Dusty.

(2)From the end of Dusty Creek Trail♦ (near 6000′) ascend the alp slope SW to its head at a pointed moraine at 7000 ft between the Chocolate and North Guardian Glaciers. Then ascend the latter (see Variation 2).

Variation 1: From Gamma Ridge traverse S across the head of Recession Basin below the N lobe. Then ascend the S lobe to left (S) of Recession Rock (best in early season).

Variation 2: Keep farther S in Recession Basin and ascend the North Guardian Glacier to its head, then work right at North Guardian Rock to meet the Dusty Glacier.

CHOCOLATE GLACIER: This important glacier on the volcano's E slope forms at the summit crater breach and terminates in a deep canyon; its crevasses form interesting patterns, and in part form an echelon system trending S 15° to 30°. The glacier may have been climbed before the solo ascent of Hermann F. Ulrichs in August 3, 1936, but no documentation appears.[109]

One could use the approach for Dusty Glacier, variation (2), to reach the N edge of the Chocolate Glacier at about 7000 ft. The other approach is by the Chocolate Creek route (see Upper Suiattle River Trail♦) S of the glacier canyon. Ascend to the apex of two ridges (7135′) above Rusk Basin and follow Streamline Ridge crest W. The ascent of the glacier involves routefinding through crevasses. Between North and South Guardian Rocks it is generally best to stay N and head for the section of glacier between the thin isolated rock outcrop and the NE summit. If climbing left of the outcrop, keep left above a crevassed area at about 9000-9500 ft, then bear toward the summit saddle; a final crevasse may pose a problem.

CHOCOLATE-COOL CLEAVER: This seldom used route was a notable early climb, made in just 4 hours from timberline by Melvin A. Krows, P.M. McGregor, and Lorenz A. Nelson on August 1, 1910. The ascent is more practical in early season, when loose volcanic rock is snow-covered; the original party reported the cleaver to be steep and narrow.

Use the approach to Chocolate Glacier via Streamline Ridge. Follow the crest to its end at 8300 ft where it merges into the Cool Glacier just S of South Guardian Rock (between Chocolate and Cool Glaciers, 8917′). Ascend NE on the Cool Glacier to the cleaver which runs due E of the summit. Reference: *Mountaineer*, 1910, pp. 27-28.

COOL GLACIER: This glacier is heavily crevassed on its lower and steeper areas (below 8000′); its apex is between the Chocolate-Cool cleaver and Disappointment Peak. The first ascent was made by A.L. Cool and Claude E. Rusk on August 26, 1906; they reported their climb being by the Chocolate Glacier as first named by Rusk (the name was later changed).

The best approach is by Streamline Ridge, S of Chocolate Creek (see Upper Suiattle River Trail♦). Continue W to the Cool Glacier and ascend it to the Disappointment Peak saddle (9600′+); turn N and ascend the pumice ridge to the summit. Time: 8 hours from Suiattle River. Reaching the glacier directly involves traveling the overgrown Upper Suiattle River Trail, then another 2½ brushy mi. to the snout. References: *Tales of a Western Mountaineer*, pp. 164-166; *Mountaineer*, 1910, p. 26.

Alternate Approach: From the N side of the Kololo Peaks (Section II) traverse the Suiattle Glacier and moraine basin W of the glacier terminus. Then bear N on a gradually traversing ascent along the E side of Gerdine Glacier toward the S edge of the Cool Glacier.

DISAPPOINTMENT PEAK CLEAVER (Gerdine Ridge) (White Chuck-Suiattle Glacier): The cleaver is the dark-hued spur ending atop the S false summit, the route of the first ascent. Disappointment Peak (9755′/2975 m) is the dome welled out on the upper S flank of the volcano. It may be one of the youngest eruptive features, and its dome truncates many thin flows of the summit cone. Early climbers learned to their dismay that this was not the true summit. The long straight snow gully on its W flank marks the unconformity with basal older flows. It would be possible to make the ascent along the cleaver virtually eliminating snow and ice, but extensive pumice slopes make early season ascents more pleasant. This traditional and easy route is often done by keeping to the E of the cleaver, using the slope of Gerdine Glacier and the cleaver to the upper edge of Cool Glacier.

For approach see White Chuck River Trail♦. From the N side of the meltwater lake bear upslope to the gentle White Chuck Glacier. Rise on a NE crossing (1½ mi.) and ascend the snow chute to Glacier Gap (7200′+). Follow the gentle pumice divide N to a hump where the Suiattle Glacier slope (on E) reaches high; traverse this slope N above the rock island (one can also rise over the hump and follow the divide, but some altitude is lost). Ascend N along the cleaver (divide) to Disappointment Peak. Descend into the little saddle and then directly upslope to the summit.

Preceding page: GLACIER PEAK from northwest
AUSTIN POST, U.S. GEOLOGICAL SURVEY

GLACIER PEAK from east
AUSTIN POST, U.S. GEOLOGICAL SURVEY

Disappointment Pk.
Rabbit Ears
Frostbite Ridge
North Guardian Rock
South Guardian Rock
COOL GLACIER
CHOCOLATE GLACIER
NORTH GUARDIAN GLACIER
DUSTY GLACIER
Recession Rock
Recession Basin
Dusty Wedge
treamline Ridge
Rusk Basin

GLACIER PEAK from south
LARRY IKENBERRY CASCADE PHOTOGRAPHICS

E of the cleaver on the upper edge of the Gerdine Glacier, an ascending corridor leads closely E of Disappointment Peak. The final pumice (or snow) slopes lead directly to the summit. Time: 7 hours (5½-7 hours noted from Glacier Peak Meadows and 5¼ hours noted from White Pass in good conditions).

Approach Variations: (1) From the trail near 5000 ft (est. 6.2 mi. from Kennedy Hot Springs) bear E cross-country to the river; cross on logs and climb steeply NE into the basin NE of the 6800-ft plug. Keep below the glacier tongue, pass the tarn in the basin, then head ½ mi. to a notch (est. 6650′). Cross the upper White Chuck Glacier eastward to Glacier Gap; this approach is shorter but steeper than the normal route.

(2) From the 6650-ft notch (above) ascend to the broad saddle (est. 7050′) at the NW margin of the glacier. Descend slabs E of a small glacier to reach a tarn and moraine at the head of Baekos Creek (est. 6200′; good camping just W). Keep lower on bench near 6000 ft and make a traverse N below cliffs to the northern fork of the creek (est. ½ mi.). Ascend ENE toward the cleaver.

(3) From the White Pass area on the Crest Trail♦ hike 1 mi. NE to the saddle (6500′+) E of White Mountain. Continue along the gentle upper eastern basin of the White Chuck River another mi., then rise gradually to the glacier at about 6800 ft (advise good visibility).

(4) Reach Glacier Gap from the area of the Kololo Peaks (Section II).

KENNEDY PEAK 8384′/2555 m

Kennedy is prominent on the NW spur of Glacier Peak, 1½ mi. from the summit of the volcano. From most vantages it has a pryamidal, rocky shape.

ROUTE: See Glacier Peak, Frostbite Ridge. The summit is just a scramble from the glacier.

SITKUM SPIRE 9355′/2851 m

This is the small but striking spire on the Sitkum-

WHITE CHUCK GLACIER from southwest
AUSTIN POST, U.S. GEOLOGICAL SURVEY

Scimitar cleaver; first ascent by Dwight F. Crowder and Rowland W. Tabor in 1961. Ascend the 50-ft spire by a difficult chimney on the NW (reach from Sitkum Glacier route); the summit block has an exposed mantle.

The highest of the several spires on this cleaver ("Glacier Post Spire"—est. 9500′) was climbed using cracks and flakes on the SW face (August 1974); 60 ft of class 4.

KOPEETAH DIVIDE 7723′/2354 m

This is the prominent remnant ridge between the Honeycomb Glacier on the S and the Suiattle Glacier on the W, 3 mi. SE of Glacier Peak. It was once known as "Glacier Ridge" (U.S. Forest Service photographic records, 1929). Kopeetah Divide spans about ⅜ mi. E to W; the N slopes, which contain ice segments, pitch steeply into the headwaters of the Suiattle. A mountaineering group noticed the divide decades ago: "An immense reservoir of ice is found directly to the S of Glacier Peak. . . . A very large rock island is located on its lower portion, where it separates."[110] (The entire divide is dark-colored biotite-hornblende diorite and tonalite.)

LIME RIDGE
U.S. GEOLOGICAL SURVEY

The W summit is probably the highest, although compilations have calculated the E summit at both 7726 ft and 7676 ft. The central (flat-topped) summit is 7591 ft.

ROUTES: All three summits are simple bedrock, scree, and snow ascents from the S (via the Honeycomb Glacier; see Kololo Peaks, Section II); in late season crevasses may prove frustrating. The W summit is easy from the SW, where there is a spur emanating from the Suiattle-Honeycomb Glacier divide. The E summit is quite feasible by easy scree from the col adjacent the middle summit. A traverse of the summits (not documented) appears to offer no special problems, but some rock scrambling should be anticipated between the W and central summits. It should be possible to traverse the N slopes (more alpine and some ice segments) by coming from the W (Suiattle Glacier—see Glacier Peak); one could keep N of the upper rock cliffs of the middle summit and remain on moderate snow or glacier slopes to the E peak.

LIME MOUNTAIN 6772′/2064 m

This is the highest point of Lime Ridge, a NW-trending ancient spur. During Pleistocene time Glacier Peak (8½ mi. distant) grew to overtop Lime Ridge and sent lava flows westward into tributaries of the White Chuck River; the ridge itself is schist.

Lime Lake Approach: See Crest Trail♦ for route to N side of Mica Lake. Ascend W over humps, rise through a notch (est. 5950′), then descend below cliffs before taking a NW

MT. PUGH and WHITE CHUCK MOUNTAIN from north
PHILIP LEATHERMAN

bearing across benchland to the E end of Lime Lake (est. 5550′). Rise N through a saddle, N past a small lake, then hike diagonally down to between the two Milk Lakes; ascend to a saddle N of the larger lake, then down to lower Twin Lake. Work NE over a spur (est. 5600′), then W down a ramp to Rivord Lake (5300′+). Ascend W to Upper Rivord Lake (est. 6150′), closely beneath Lime Mountain. The ascent is a mere hike from either side of the lake.

Milk Creek Approach: From Milk Creek Trail♦ just S of the Suiattle bridge ascend a wooded spur cross-country (blazes) WSW to Box Mountain Lakes (est. 5000′; 3 hours). Lime Mountain is closely S and an easy ascent.

FIRE MOUNTAIN 6591′/2009 m

This small peak is located 5 mi. NW of Glacier Peak, on the divide between Fire and Lime Creeks. There is a small glacier on the N side of the mountain. A higher unnamed summit, Point 6702, stands 0.7 mi. to the NE, along an easy ridge (really a portion of Lime Ridge). The name comes from a major fire in 1915, fought by 60 men under Harry Grey.

ROUTE: The summit is reached by leaving the Meadow Mountain Trail♦ about ½ mi. W of the summit (est. 5500′). See White Chuck River Trail♦. The ascent can be a scenic tour and be used as a trek to the benchland of Lime Ridge and Rivord Lakes.

MEADOW MOUNTAIN 6324′/1928 m

This summit is located on the Suiattle River-White Chuck River divide 8½ mi. NW of Glacier Peak.

ROUTE: Leave Meadow Mountain Trail♦ near where it crosses the spur ridge at 5800 ft SW of the summit. Hike N along the spur, then bear NE to the first summit. Reference: *Trips and Trails 1*.

CIRCLE PEAK 5983′/1824 m

Circle is a small pointed summit 2½ mi. S of Suiattle River between White Chuck Mountain and Lime Mountain. The former lookout building (1935-1967) is gone, but a path can still be taken to the summit.

ROUTE: Take Straight Creek Road♦ and branch no. 3128. Hike the gated fork (B) about 2 mi. along Crystal Creek. Where the road reaches its second switchback (est. ¾ mi. before Crystal Lake) a path bears upslope NW to the ridge, then traverses the upper basin of Circle Creek NE to the ridge closely SE of the summit (about 1½ mi. trail). An unmaintained trail can also be taken from Circle Creek Road to meet this route.

WHITE CHUCK MOUNTAIN 6989′/2130 m

This outstanding peak, N of the White Chuck River and E of the Sauk, is a solitary craggy massif (greenschist rock) with a steep S face and a lower NW summit (about ⅜ mi. distant, connected by a narrow ridge). A northern cirque is occupied by a small triangular-shaped glacier perched on a slab bed at the head of Black Creek. There is an active crevassed glacier directly beneath the steep E face; Thornton Lake (4403′) lies in a subalpine cirque ½ mi. SE of the summit.

The name is a combination of English and Chinook for "glacial (white) water;" the Indian name for the peak is said to be Hi Khaed, meaning "reaching high, or long neck" (Bruseth, *op. cit.*, 2d. ed., p. 35). The first ascent was made by a U.S. Geological Survey party, including Thomas G. Gerdine, Sam Strom, and Albert H. Sylvester on July 28, 1897, when the summit was used for triangulation.

NORTHWEST ROUTE: Approach from Conn Creek Road No. 3226B (see Dan Creek Road♦). At about 4200 ft a short spur ends in a logged area between Conn and Blackoak Creeks. Head ESE up the gentle wooded ridge between the creeks and climb through brush along upper Blackoak Creek and its watercourse to the talus basin W of the peak. Ascend the gully leading to the saddle (6080′+) between the two summits; just below it, leave the gully for heather shelf slopes up and right. Continue on sloping shelves closely right of the crest until beyond a short vertical step (on crest) to reach a final small notch (note: some parties elect to reach the crest near the saddle, follow the ridge a distance, then drop W down a short gully and traverse about 400 ft on slabs to the final notch). Then work E via a steep heather slope to climb the 50-ft summit point. Note: the gully and shelf system are snow-covered in early season; exposure prompts use of ice axe and rope. Time: 4-5 hours. Reference: *Mazama*, 49, no. 13 (1967); pp. 60-61.

Alternate Approach: Take Dan-Blackoak Creek Road (about 2 mi. along Blackoak Road to 4000-ft level). Ascend NW to a wooded ridge and follow its crest (markers) to where it levels. Continue a short distance to where an easy down traverse left leads into a small basin (Blackoak Creek drainage).

EAST FACE: The route takes the deep cleft starting on the right of the summit pyramid; best in late summer when the couloir is dry. First ascent by Ben Guydelkon and Ron Miller on September 10, 1970.

One can approach from Straight Creek Road♦ (at pass) through cliffy timbered slopes (brushy area about 1 hour from road just below the cliff bands) and open meadows; however another route has proven easier (see East Face—South Side route). A steep snow slope leads to the base of the narrow couloir which splits the E face from right to left. There are 10 leads, all with some difficulty; protection is scarce but adequate (hard hat recommended). Grade III; class 5.8. Reference: *A.A.J.*, 1971, p. 345.

EAST FACE—SOUTH SIDE: First ascent by Ben Guydelkon and Ron Miller on September 2, 1973. Use a western approach (see Southwest Face) and traverse past the pond to a chair-shaped tower on the S ridge. An easy ramp down offers access to the E face. From the base of the ramp traverse 200 ft across snow to the route beginning; here climb to the first of a series of ramps (moderate). Climb up and left (heather) to an overhang. Traverse directly under it (two 5.7 moves) and continue for several leads to the summit (class 3 and 4). Grade II; class 5.7.

SOUTHWEST FACE: This narrow face, the steep portion of which is about 800 ft, is of solid greenschist. First ascent by Michael Heath, Joe Vance, and Ted Carpenter on August 31, 1967.

From the Dan-Blackoak Creek Road (see Northwest Route) at about 4000 ft hike up through timber to the basin on the W side of the peak. Climb rockslides below the SW face to just opposite a 5840-ft pond. The face lies between two steep rock couloirs in a direct line between the pond and the summit. Route begins in gully through lower cliffs. Scrambling for 200 ft leads to the base. Follow the left side of

chairlike tower
from West
ramp
East Face South Side
East Face
snow
trees
from Rat Trap Pass

WHITE CHUCK MT.
East Face

WHITE CHUCK MOUNTAIN from west
JOHN V.A.F. NEAL

SAUK-STILLAGUAMISH PEAKS from west
U.S. GEOLOGICAL SURVEY

the face, taking a series of chimneys interrupted by short ledges, to within 60 ft of the summit. A heather ledge leads right to the S ridge. Continuous class 4 with several class 5 pitches, including two difficult chimney exits (5.6); six jam nuts and two pitons used. Time: 7 hours from road (4½ hours on face). Reference: *A.A.J.*, 1968, p. 137.

Other Routes: It appears possible with a bushy approach to climb the N glacier directly to the summit. A new logging road up Black Creek comes within a mi. of the glacier. Approaches from the Straight Creek Road have no trail.

NORTHWEST PEAK 6445′/1964 m

From the central saddle this is a short scramble via E side ledges (class 3).

WEST FACE: This route is clearly visible from the parking area as a series of steep chimneys in a direct line to the summit. It is best done in late season. First ascent by Dave Hutchinson and Ron Miller September 2, 1974.

Ascend scree to its highest point on the W side. Traverse right on a ledge to the start of chimneys. The first three pitches are very obvious; on the fourth the chimney splits three ways (take the left). Rock is down-sloping except for top of fourth pitch. Above, several hundred ft (class 3) lead to summit chimney (two or three leads). Grade III; class 5.7. Take a nut selection. Time: 4 hours on rock.

TWIN PEAKS 5840′+/1780 m

The Indian name "Toko-bulks," meaning pheasant's heads, is an appropriate description for this cleft peak 1½ mi. E of Mt. Dickerman. The higher W peak has a small but rocky summit formation, sheer on most aspects; the E peak (5836′/1779 m) is closely nearby. First ascent by William Herston, Melvin Marcus, Richard Merritt, and Keith Rankin on June 9, 1946.

ROUTE: From the Perry Creek Trail♦ at 2 mi. (3300′), where it turns from the creek, continue upstream (dry after June) into basin; then follow timbered ridge E up the left side of the terminal fork to the base of cliffs (est. 5000′). Contour S, rising to the saddle (est. 5650′) between the Twin Peaks summits (either snow or talus).

Climb the W peak frontally for 60 ft on rock, then traverse beneath the overhanging S face on a ledge and into a shallow loose rock gully (est. 100 yds); climb steeply to a narrow notch which cleaves the final summit. A short slabby pitch followed by a steep exposed lead allows single visits to the summit flake (W). Class 4. Time: 4-5 hours. Reference: *Mountaineer*, 1946, p. 28.

The E peak is an easy scramble from the central saddle.

Variation: Traverse route: From Mt. Dickerman make an

alpine traverse on moderate S slopes around the head of Buck Creek to about 4800 ft (some light brush). Then work around spur S of Twin Peaks to the S side of the W peak to meet the normal route.

EAST RIDGE: Cross the South Fork of Sauk River on a bridge just S of Bedal campground to summer cabins. Take the ¼-mi. road to Swift Creek. Ascend through brush and second growth, cross the creek and to the wooded E ridge; follow it directly to the E peak. The route is long, with some brush, but not difficult.

CHOKWICH PEAK 5662′/1726 m

Chokwich is the tentative name for the flat-topped rock peak 4/5 mi. NE of the East Peak of Twin Peaks; the top is at the N end of the summit area. The peak is cliffy on the N.

ROUTE: The peak is easiest on the S. Approach as per Twin Peaks to Perry Creek's valley head. Traverse left under cliffs to meet the N-trending ridge at a point where it forks, about ½ mi. N of Twin Peaks. Descend along the crest heading NE toward Chokwich; its lowest dip is 5200 ft—then continue easily to the summit area.

MT. FORGOTTEN 6005′/1830 m

A small but outstanding peak with a rocky summit 2½ mi. W of the Sauk River forks; the middle of three summit points is highest, and there is a short summit cliff on the SW. Surface rock is predominantly loose volcanic breccia cut by dikes. Early settlers thought the peak resembled a hooded woman and called it "Lady of the Mountains;" maps once termed it "Castle Peak."

ROUTE: Take Perry Creek Trail♦ 3½ mi. to the 4880-ft ridge above Shake Creek (the summit is ⅞ mi. NE). Follow meadows, first E, then N, dropping to a col (5120′+) (keep right of 5396′ point). Pass through col and contour N at 5200 ft under W slopes of Forgotten. Climb gradually NE to the saddle (5500′+) which is NE of the summit, then bear left to the top. Class 2 and 3. Time: 5 hours from road.

Variation: From the 5120-ft col contour NE near timberline until E of the summit. Follow the E spur (class 2); this is a simple route, but with more bush.

NORTHEAST SLOPE: From Mt. Forgotten Road No. 3113B (see Falls Creek Road♦) end at clearcut (est. 2900′; top of Section 7) contour cross-country S to bushy creek basin, cross creek to trees and ascend (keep right of major rocky hump and left of rugged peaklets). Continue on talus and heather slopes SW to the pointed summit. Either ascend directly or keep slightly left near the top. This route is direct, but has some brush and is more taxing than the normal way; rope advised.

STILLAGUAMISH PEAK 5683′/1732 m

A secondary peak on the Perry-South Fork of Falls Creek divide, it is of limited interest, but a good viewpoint. The true summit is the third W, directly overlooking South Lake.

ROUTE: Take Perry Creek Trail♦ to where it switchbacks NE (est. 4300′; 2.8 mi.). Hike NW through open timber to ridge crest. Follow the ridge westerly on S side below minor rock bumps. Where rock steepens, one may scramble 200 ft up S side of E ridge of summit; an easier alternative is to make a descending traverse from the final U-notch at 200 yds E of the summit. Work over into the S basin, then an easy climb via a break in the summit slope. Time: 4½ hours from road.

Alternate Approach: Take the trail to about 4800 ft, just below the 4880-ft ridge. An obscure branch trail leads left through woods below the rocky ridge to open meadows.

Note: one could ascend the S side of the peak at almost any place, but lower slopes involve steeper terrain and brush.

MT. DICKERMAN 5732′/1747 m

Mt. Dickerman, Twin Peaks, Stillaguamish Peak, and Mt. Forgotten are part of the Barlow Pass volcanics (a well-exposed series of rocks with local interbeds of sedimentary rock). Reached by summit trail, the mountain honors Alton L. Dickerman, a mining engineer who in the fall of 1891 examined the Monte Cristo mines on a mission for the investment syndicate. From the magnificent summit vantage one can see from Summit Chief Mountain on the S to American Border Peak on the N, and from Bonanza Peak on the E to the Olympic Mountains.

ROUTE: The 4-mi. trail leaves Mountain Loop Hwy♦ (est. 2000′) 16.4 mi. from Verlot R.S. (28½ mi. from Granite Falls). Reference: *101 Hikes.*

NORTHEAST PEAK 5623′/1714 m

There is a rocky connecting ridge to this lower peak, 0.6 mi. distant.

NORTH FACE: First ascent by Dallas Kloke and David Seman on August 21, 1970. Take Perry Creek Trail♦ for 2 mi.; at creek crossing (3200′) climb S through brush and talus to the base of a gully (3600′). This 35° gully (possibly snow) ends at 4600 ft; here entrance is made into a rock gully where one short class 4 pitch is met. A blocking wall forces a broad ledge ascent right to easier rock. In about 500 ft reach the NW ridge at a 5520-ft point; follow to the summit. Class 3 and 4. Time: 4 hours. Reference: *A.A.J.*, 1971, pp. 343-344.

DEVILS PEAK 5455′/1663 m

Devils is a small but attractive hornlike peak N of the South Fork Stillaguamish River. Consisting of sandstone and conglomerate, it is part of a 2-mi. belt of the Swauk Formation (Helena to Jumbo). Devils is steepest on the NW; a row of small pinnacles S of the summit offer additional climbing opportunities.

THREE FINGERS and WHITEHORSE MOUNTAIN from south
NATIONAL PARK SERVICE

THREE FINGERS
South
North Peaks
Camp Saddle
WHITEHORSE MTN.
SALISH PK.
4950
BIG BEAR MTN.
Squire Creek Wall
Squire Creek Valley
LIBERTY MTN.
Copper Creek

SOUTHEAST ROUTE: From about ½ mi. up Deer Creek Road♦ take Coal Creek branch to logged area where road bears farthest N (est. 3200′); here near Coal Creek's W fork follow a rough trail 1 mi. to a basin with several small lakes (est. 3800′). Ascend NW through brush, timber, and meadows into the open basin just under the summit, then to the small notch immediately S of the summit. A steep 35-ft pitch (class 4) and an overhanging ledge slanting right lead to a brushy summit gully. Time: 4 hours.

Note: on descent make a 90-ft rappel from summit.

Note: approach from Deer Creek Road is unpleasant; there is a steep chute of loose rock at the top.

SOUTH RIDGE: First ascent by Orville Dorsett and John Pollock (party of 10) on May 11, 1968. From the 3800-ft basin (see above) ascend directly W to the prominent 5100-ft rock peak (the final pitches on the SE and S may be done on steep snow in late spring). Follow the exposed ridge N, working over and around numerous small pinnacles; the two more northerly may require protection (can contour via short rappels on their E sides). Class 4. Time: 3-4 hours from basin.

NORTH FACE: First ascent by Al Clairmont and Ray Pruiett in 1962. The route ascends a large 100-ft chimney and steep, mossy friable rock (unsuitable for pitons, class 4). Reference: *A.A.J.*, 1970, p. 120.

Note: Richard Berge and party may have done a route on the N face or NW ridge in the 1950s.

EAST FACE: The 250-ft face can be climbed in three leads over fairly solid rock. First ascent by Mike Killien, Dallas Kloke, and Dick Nelson on July 13, 1963. The first lead is over a slab—small holds to mossy ledges. The crux pitch is a crack and short traverse just below the summit. Once on the NE ridge ascend a short wall and then an easy summit scramble. Grade I; class 5.5 (five pitons). Reference: *A.A.J.*, 1970, p. 120.

Note: the entire NE ridge could be taken to the summit (est. class 4—about four leads).

DEVILS THUMB 5170′/1576 m

This is a brownish, pointed rock pyramid composed of peridotite rock 1 mi. NE of Devils Peak. Its steep N and E sides are clearly seen from Darrington. From Clear Creek it resembles a closed fist with thumb up.

ROUTES: Use Devils Peak—Southeast Side to the 3800-ft basin. Climb to the pass at the head of the West Fork Coal Creek basin, then ascend NE up exposed, solid rock to the higher N summit; class 3.

There is a lower summit ½ mi. S. It is possible to traverse the exposed connecting ridge.

The peak can be approached from the E side using Independence Lake Trail♦. This is a longer but very feasible approach. From the lake bear W, upslope, to the long S ridge; follow it about ½ mi. to the summit.

LONG MOUNTAIN 5111′/1558 m

Long is 1½ mi. NW of Silverton, an extended NE-trending ridge. The climb is best done in early season on snow; final 800 ft to summit ridge crest subject to avalanches. Distance: 2¼ mi.; elevation gain: 2600 ft.

ROUTE: Take Deer Creek Road♦ 3 mi. to the basin on the mountain's N side (to approximately ½ mi. beyond Deer Creek's forks). Travel ¾ mi. SW up the gently sloping basin floor to the short, NW-trending spur ridge which rises E of Deer Creek's S fork. Climb the crest of this ridge to about 4200 ft. Traverse W about ⅓ mi. until below the summit. Climb to ridge crest just W of summit, cross the sharp rotten crest and complete the climb just below it on the S side. The crest and summit rocks are very unstable. Time: 4-5 hours.

VIKING HORNS est. 4800′ / 1463 m

Two rock summits, E and W, are located on the ridge just E of Long Mountain. First known ascent by Dallas Kloke and party, May 1969.

ROUTE: From about 3 mi. on Deer Creek Road♦ cross a basin below Bald Mountain to a wooded ridge which leads to the N base of the E horn. The rocky ridge above can be attained by bearing either left or right, then both summits can be reached from the S (class 3).

The N face of the E horn was climbed by Scott Masonholder and Dallas Kloke June 13, 1970; rock reported poor; four leads—class 3 to 5. Reference: *A.A.J.*, 1971, p. 343.

INDEPENDENCE PEAK (North Lake Peak) 5445′/1660 m

This secondary peak is about 1¼ mi. E of Devils Thumb.

WEST RIDGE: From the end of Coal Creek Road (the road now goes W of Pass Lake to over 3600 ft—see Deer Creek Road♦) cross a logged area on spurs N to a stream, then continue N into the open basin below the southern cliffs of the peak. Hike W to a scrub-cedar 200-ft chimney; climb this (class 4) to the W ridge, which is taken some 200 yds to the summit (class 3) Time: 3 hours.

Variation: The ridge can also be approached from the trail to North Lake.

NORTHEAST RIDGE: By Kenn Carpenter, Alta Miller, and Clem Pera on June 8, 1963. From the outlet of Pass Lake ascend right to the NE ridge, then to the rocky summit (class 3).

INDEPENDENCE LAKE BUTTRESS: First ascent by Dave Dixon and Dallas Kloke on June 20, 1970. East of Independence Lake♦ climb an 800-ft rock buttress (class 2 to 5.1), staying to right of a sheer face. From its top follow a class 3 wooded ridge to the W side of the peak; ascend a gully 150 ft to the W summit ridge. Reference: *A.A.J.*, 1971, p. 343.

HELENA PEAK 5401′/1646 m

Helena is a small rugged peak typical of this region. The summit area is a reddish outcrop with a rocky northern shoulder. The Swauk Formation sandstone is

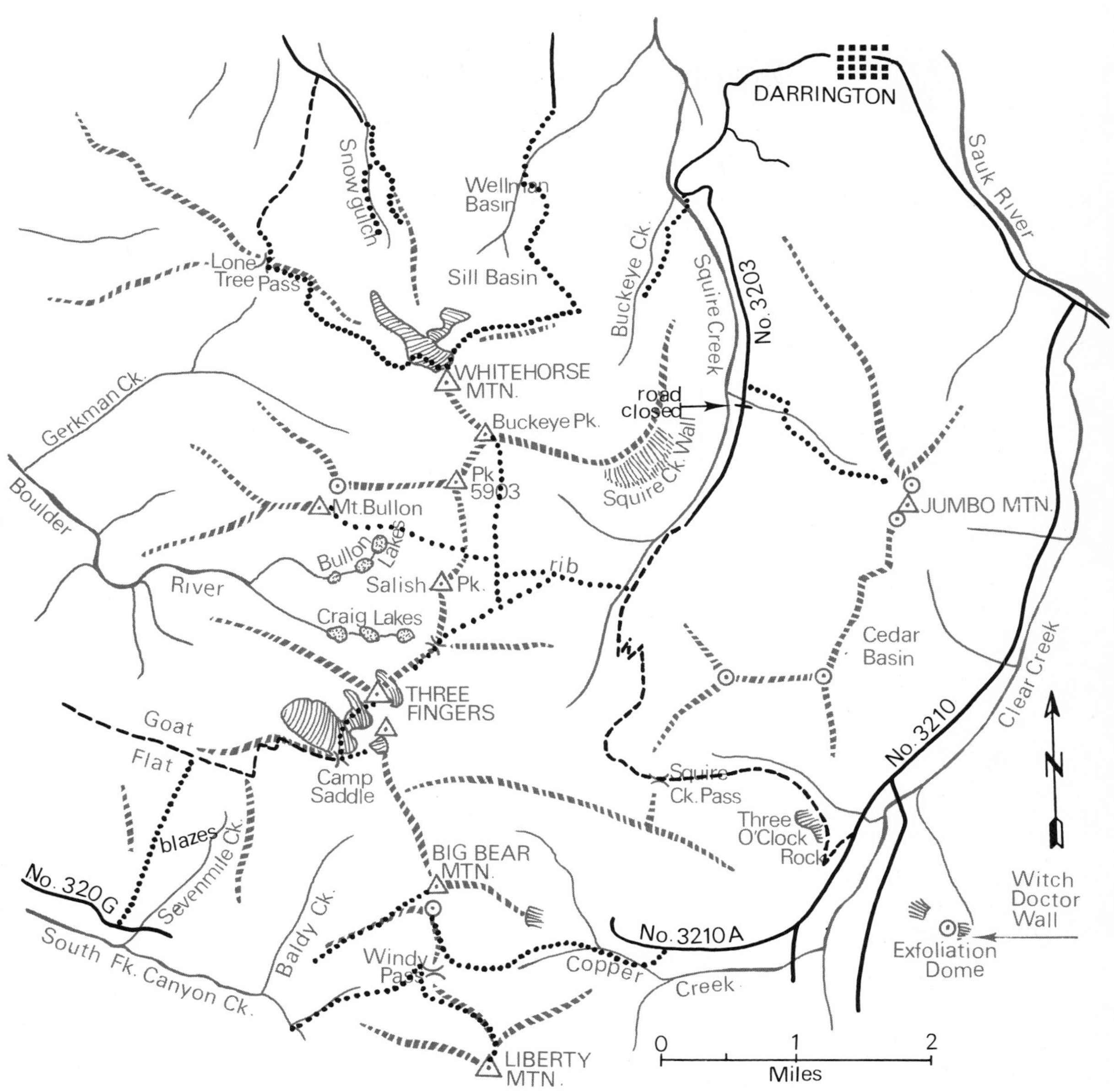

WHITEHORSE-THREE FINGERS AREA

intruded by Squire Creek granodiorite on the W side and on a northern spur (Exfoliation Dome). Located 3½ mi. N of Silverton, the peak was named for the Helena claims, discovered in 1894 by Montana prospectors on the divide between Clear and Deer Creeks. Soon there was a trail from near Lake Kelcema over the pass N and to the upper W slopes of the peak. At one time Helena and Devils Thumb exchanged names.

WEST FACE: From Deer Creek Road♦ find the old trail just N of creek crossing below Lake Kelcema. Take it to Deer Creek Pass (est. 3700′); here take a right-forking path and climb NE 1 mi. to the ridge crest at 5000 ft. Continue N ¼ mi. along the ridge, descending slightly to beneath the W face. Ascend E on talus and a steep 400-ft rock gully to the summit (class 3). Time: 4 hours.

SOUTH RIDGE: From the same approach follow the entire S ridge to the summit. Several steep segments can be avoided by minor descents on the E; class 3. Time: 4 hours.

PEAK 5193 5193′ / 1583 m

Located 1½ mi. N of Helena Peak between Clear and Helena Creeks. First ascent by Ronald Race and Joseph Vance in 1968 via the brushy NE flank from Helena Creek; a shorter but steeper approach would be from the W.

LIBERTY MOUNTAIN 5688′/1733 m

Liberty is 3 mi. S of Three Fingers; much the lesser peak, it is still prominent because of deep surrounding valleys. The E and N faces are steepest and the upper W face has large slabs.

SOUTHWEST RIDGE: From 1 mi. on Canyon Creek Road♦ take Green Mountain Road No. 318, which forks at Canyon Lake. At first turn (est. ½ mi.) beyond the lake descend 800 ft NE through heavy timber to the S fork and cross on logs where creek forks. Ascend bush, then open timber to treeline. Follow the SW ridge directly to easy summit rocks (long green slope); in early season the first tower can be bypassed by easy snow on left. Class 2 and 3. Time: 6-7 hours.

NORTH RIDGE: The upper part of this sharp ridge has a high step with scrub trees. First ascent of route and N peak by Kenn Carpenter and Ron Miller on June 1, 1969. See Big Bear Mountain for routes to Windy Pass.

Head S, then SE, on the divide to the N ridge. The first 200 ft is mixed shrubs and rock (class 4); then a level 20-ft rock bench. The next lead is 100 ft of poor rock (class 5; 20′ of this is vertical). Third lead is 100 ft exposed (class 4). Soon reach N peak. Follow loose ridge (class 4) for 300 ft to main summit. Descent can be made by NW ridge. Grade II. Class 5.6. Reference: *A.A.J.*, 1970, pp. 119-120.

SOUTHEAST RIDGE: This is a longer and more taxing route; because of brush, early season is advised. Take Marten Creek Trail♦ to Granite Pass; descend 500 ft on the NW slope (½ mi.), then rise N to a timbered ridge which runs W to join the S slope of Liberty at about 4800 ft. Here climb easy rock and heather 1 mi. NW on the crest to a 20-ft rock gully leading to the summit. Time: 7 hours.

Alternate Approach: From Copper Creek Road (see Clear Creek Road♦) on the E. This approach would involve fording the creek and a brushy ascent to the heather slopes E of the summit, unless done early. It appears best to stay right in the basin or next to the grey slab-spur to treeline, then angle up-left to the S shoulder.

CANYON PEAK 5274′ / 1608 m

This is the unofficial name for the highest and southern of three jagged subalpine peaks on the ridge which extends SE of Liberty (on South Fork Copper—upper Canyon Creek divide).

ROUTE: Canyon Peak is an easy but brushy trek from Canyon Lake (2.1 mi. direct distance). Reach the lake via roads no. 318 or 3032, branching E off Canyon Creek Road♦. Begin just S of the lake and follow the long wooded ridge E. The other summits could be reached by traversing the divide northward, possibly continuing to Liberty (an uninviting prospect).

BIG BEAR MOUNTAIN 5620′+/1713 m

Big Bear is between Liberty and Three Fingers, really a secondary peak in the area. The N summit is higher; it is flattish, with a sharp central break from the S summit.

ROUTES: From the end of Copper Creek Road (see Clear Creek Road♦) an old miners trail (now bushy) led to Windy Pass (3550′); this trail was in existence in 1913 (1931 maps show a cabin near the head of Copper Creek). The western route is from Canyon Creek Road♦. About ½ mi. before crossing Canyon Creek take fork no. 310 slightly uphill; in about 2 mi. fork left to Canyon Creek (est. 2 mi.; opposite Windy Pass drainage). Ascend cross-country to the pass (camping).

Ascend the wooded S ridge, then low-angle rock and heather to the S summit; one can keep just E of the crest. To reach the notch and N summit a 50-ft rope can be fixed on the 50° slab of the exposed N ridge for the return.

It is reported practical to ascend the SW ridge directly from Canyon Creek (less brush). Bear left near the S summit and ascend a draw to the notch at the final summit.

JUMBO MOUNTAIN 5840′+/1780 m

Jumbo is not a high regional peak, but is bulky and occupies a strategic position about 4 mi. S of Darrington, with low footings on both Clear and Squire Creeks. The middle peak is highest, with the N and S peaks about 80 ft lower; all three are grouped on a crest within a space of ⅜ mi., but the Jumbo massif extends N and S much farther.

In 1890 considerable mineral discoveries were made on Jumbo; prospector Knute Neste and others named

THREE FINGERS and WHITEHORSE MOUNTAIN from southeast
ROBERT J. DeWITZ, U.S. FOREST SERVICE

MT. HIGGINS
THREE FINGERS
WHITEHORSE MTN.
MT. BULLON
JUMBO MTN.
South
North Summits
Squire Creek Pass
EXFOLIATION DOME
DARRINGTON
Pt. 5193
3 O'Clock Rock
Clear Creek
Helena Creek
Pt. 5306
North
Lake

THREE FINGERS
North
Middle
South
SLOAN PK.
DEVILS PK.
DEL CAMPO PK.
LIBERTY MTN.
EXFOLIATION DOME
West
ridge
Camp Saddle
Northeast
Buttress
THREE
FINGERS
GLACIER
to Goat
Flat
saddle
Craig Lakes

the mountain because poor mining claims made it a white elephant. The Queen Anne Mine and a trail were on the N slope. The rock on Jumbo is folded shale and sandstone strata intruded by peridotite dikes. A rock profile, "Old Man Jumbo," about 80 ft from shoulder to top of the head, faces S at the N end of the ridge above Cedar Basin. It seems logical that prospectors made the first climb. In 1916 the Forest Service had a lookout and tent on the summit (one season), the second lookout in the Darrington district, and a useful one for spotting fires; communication was by phone with insulated wire.

WEST SIDE: From Squire Creek Road♦ at 4.8 mi. from Darrington (est. 1600′) and ⅓ mi. N of (before) a major gully up which the summit ridge can be seen, find an old miner trail about 100 ft N of the stream (it flows through mossy rocks to a clearcut). Ascend timber parallel the creek (flagged) about 800 ft to an old shack; cross the creek and ascend creek bed several hundred ft, then find trail again in alder on S side (can gain a total of about 2000 ft on trail). Drop into stream gully on left; this heads into the large basin NW of the summit. In early season this gully is snow-filled and bears directly to the summit. Climb to upper snow bowl, then snow slope to left of middle peak to North-Middle Peak col (snow is steep above the basin until July when it is melted); the final sharp summit ridge is easy rock.

It is also feasible to reach the middle peak from the S ridge crest; there is one short steep scramble. Time: 4-5 hours.

NORTH SUMMIT

The best route is to climb from the col adjacent to the middle summit (class 2). Another way is to climb by crossing over the N summit's N ridge from timber slopes, circle, then ascend on the upper E slope (snow here if early); the alternative approach leaves Squire Creek Road♦ 4.5 mi. from Darrington and is well suited for this finish.

SOUTH SUMMIT

The ascent is easy, since this is the gentlest of the three peaks; keep W under the last rocks of the middle summit where there is extensive talus, then ascend the shoulder.

THREE FINGERS est. 6870′/2094 m

Three Fingers is on the Boulder River-Squire Creek divide 7 mi. SW of Darrington, and consists of contact metamorphosed sandstones and slates intruded on the E by granodiorite. Well-named, its three peaks and western glacier are an unmistakable sight from the Puget Sound Basin. The mountain is unique in that it can be seen from many North Cascade summits, and from diverse locations as Sultan and Victoria—certainly it must have been a landmark to early navigators, surveyors, and settlers. To the Indians the peak was Queest Alb. The Three Fingers Glacier drains NW into Boulder River, which flows through one of the last virgin timbered valleys in this section. From the ridge saddle E of the three Craig Lakes, a face and buttress rise steeply to the glacier segment that hangs horizontally at about 450 ft beneath the North Peak. The South Peak's S slope holds a high perennial triangular snowfield. The E face of Three Fingers is a 2000-ft sheer wall of evil appearanace that has not attracted climbers. The consensus is that the South Peak was the highest by several ft before about 15 ft of its crown was blasted in 1931 to make space for the lookout cabin; the Middle Peak is slightly lower and of less interest.

Both Three Fingers and Whitehorse were first shown on the Forest Service map of 1913. The near-first ascent of the South Peak was made by Harry Bedal and Harold Engles September 24, 1929.[111] The trail via Goat Flat was completed in 1931 and the lookout cabin, reached by a series of ladders, the next year. The North Peak was first climbed by Forest Farr, Norval Grigg, John Lehmann, and Art Winder on July 4, 1931, using tennis shoes on the rock; the ascent was made in 12 hours from French Creek Road. The party saw over 40 goats at Goat Flat, and the atmosphere was so clear that they could see a battleship in the Sound and fireworks in Everett. The Middle Peak was climbed by Grigg the same day (he found a jar with about 12 names on the summit). The first winter climb of the South Peak was made by Fred Beckey and Henryk Mather in January, 1963.

SOUTH PEAK 6854′/2089 m

From Goat Flat♦ follow the trail, which bears E along the ridge, then contours across the S slope and rounds a corner (est. 1½ mi.) into a basin; when nearly to a cliff it switchbacks to a minor saddle with flanking rock outcrops (Camp Pass—5640′+). The last water is about 100 ft off trail to the right where the switchbacks begin, about ¼ mi. below the pass. Tin Can Gap is farther W (Tin Can Ridge) and has no trail. At the snowfield edging the pass, the lookout can be seen. The trail continues E up the ridge; if and where it is snow-covered keep quite high on the N and then W side of the ridge. Some steep snow is encountered even in late season—take an ice axe (fatal slip, July 1940). A final few yards of ladders (rebuilt 1973) and scrambling on the SW side lead to the restored lookout cabin. Time: 5 hours from road; 2½ hours from Goat Flat. Reference: *Mountaineer,* 1940, p. 26.

NORTH PEAK

WEST ROUTE: From Camp Pass make a traversing descent NNE on the glacier to below the South Peak's rock toe. Ascend a narrow glacier segment until below the Middle Peak, then left and up again on a glacier section to closely below the Middle-North Peak col. Ascend broken rock leftward below the ridge to a wide ledge leading across the W face. Follow this ledge, angling up to a narrow, curving and somewhat rotten chimney. Begin up it, then climb left into

THREE FINGERS from northwest
NATIONAL PARK SERVICE

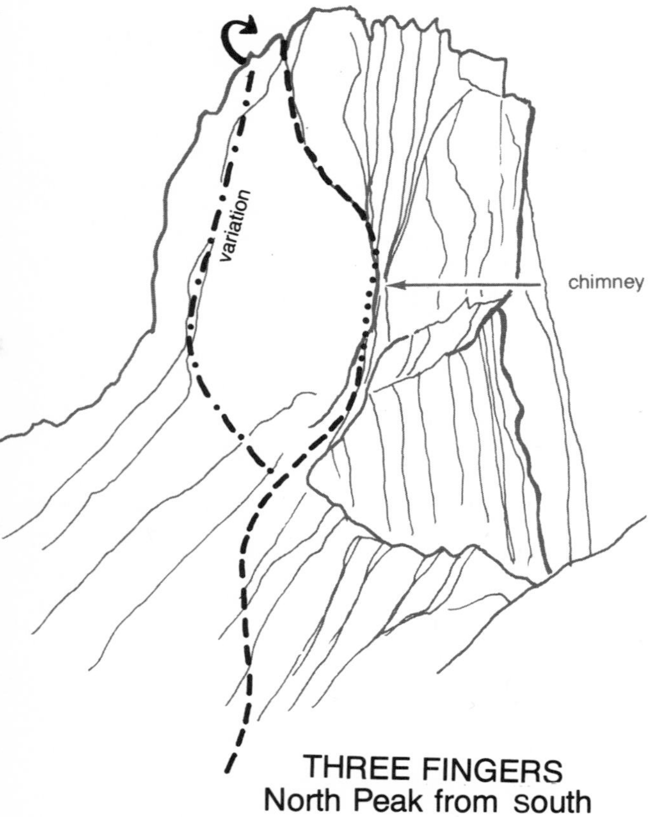

THREE FINGERS
North Peak from south

the upper part of second chimney, then to the thin summit ridge. Class 4. Time: 3 hours from trail. Reference: *Mountaineer*, 1931, pp. 51-52.

Note: crampons advisable in late season.

Variation: Upper West Face: By Ted Carpenter and Jim Stoddard on August 16, 1966. From just below the col traverse a narrow ledge N about 250 ft (past normal chimney), rounding the corner to a vertical flaring chimney which connects with the heather ledge above the normal chimney. Rock friable; hardest part is moving out of chimney—5.4

NORTHWEST RIDGE: First ascent by Paul Bergman, Bob Briggs, Kenn Carpenter, and Don Johnson on July 25, 1965. From Goat Flat♦ make a long N slope traverse about timberline, then cross a firn ice area down the glacier. Make a rising traverse on snow/scree below cliffs to the NW ridge. The original party climbed the ridge to a short level step, then found rotten rock on a near-vertical nose lead of about 150 ft (class 5). Above, follow the ridge to the summit (loose and exposed, but easy); Grade II; 4 hours from step. Reference: *A.A.J.*, 1966, pp. 134-135.

Variation: West Face and Northwest Ridge: By Joan Firey, Joe Firey, Irene Muelemans and John Muelemans on September 17, 1967. Use normal North Peak approach, then traverse across the middle portion of the glacier. Ascend the ridge to below the nose. Traverse S across the SW face and ledges near a yellow patch of rock, then ascend face and gain the ridge above its nose (class 4 to easy 5; three pitons).

NORTHEAST BUTTRESS: This combination face and buttress, which rounds from N to NE, is steep on its lower portion, then slopes to hold ice at a shelf under the narrowly towering summit of the N peak. The route provides an interesting mixed climb in a primitive setting. First ascent by Kenn Carpenter, Jerry Cate, and Ron Muecke on July 20, 1958.

From Squire Creek Road♦ at the clearcut about 6.2 mi. from Darrington (est. 2000′) continue about ½ mi. to opposite a timbered rib on the W valley wall (new trail planned to overgrown creekside trail). The rib is just S of a slide area about ¼ mi. in width, well S of Squire Creek Wall.

Ford the creek and ascend open timber and a creek bed at the slide area edge; work onto the rib (timber and brush) and ascend to talus and heather slopes (est. 4800′). Descend slightly S and traverse ¼ mi. to a saddle (4560′+) on the divide above Craig Lakes (camping here or at upper lake); 5 hours. Ascend and follow the ridge S to a rock knoll (est. 5000′) which is a steep brush climb on its E. Cross snow toward the face, then angle up rightward to a grassy ledge (est. 5250′) where a grass and rock gully, followed by mossy, steep slab (running water) leads to heather and a snow bench at 5700 ft. Climb up and left of the rock tower tip below the glacier and skirt the sheer gully top (which is on left); the traverse around the tower is delicate (poor belaying). Cross firn of the glacier to a prominent rock rib (in line with tower) protruding above the snow. Climb the rib to the E face of the summit tower, then directly up; later spiral slightly right, then left. This final section of about 400 ft is sound rock (class 4). Grade II or III; mostly class 4, but lack of cracks for class 5. Time: 8 hours from saddle. Reference: *Mountaineer*, 1959, p. 109.

Variation: The summit face can be bypassed by keeping left of the rock rib on snow; then ascend 50 ft of rock to the Middle-North Peak col to meet the normal route; this of course is an escape route since it avoids the final sector.

Descent note: it is practical to diagonal N down to the timbered rib directly from the saddle area, for the route is visible.

EAST FACE COULOIR: This long 40° snow couloir rises diagonally N, beginning at the head of talus slopes just under the South Peak, to emerge on the ice at the NE corner of the Middle Peak. There is no mistaking it. Bring crampons. First ascent by Ted Carpenter, Jim Stoddard, and Joe Vance on August 16, 1966.

Reach the area below the sheer E face by ascending out of Squire Creek as per Northeast Buttress route, then traversing S 1 mi. along alp slopes and talus. An alternative approach is to make the circular traverse from Squire Creek Pass. Climb to the upper end of the couloir. Cross the firn ice to the Middle-North Peak col to meet the normal route (class 3). Reference: *A.A.J.*, 1967, p. 350.

Note: a timberline camp is advisable. A feasible descent can be made off the rib of the NW ridge, then a circling return via Craig Lakes.

MIDDLE PEAK est. 6600′/2012 m
The usual way is to traverse onto the NW spur from beneath the Middle-North Peak col, then ascend the rock spur; class 2-3. An equally easy way is from the col.

MT. BULLON 5974′/1821 m

"I felt as if we had joined Sisyphus and his rock in Hell"

HERMANN F. ULRICHS
First ascent of Mt. Bullon

Bullon is less noticeable than Three Fingers or Whitehorse, but equally rocky and rough, and less accessible. Its N face is the steepest; here there is a precipitous lower summit. The Boulder River, with Gerkman Creek (N branch) splits around the peak; at the head of the Boulder are the three hidden Bullon Lakes (est. 4000′). The name is for Chauncy Bullen, killed in a timbering accident at Darrington in 1919. Three Fingers and White Horse (sic) were labeled on the 1899 Stillaguamish quadrangle but Bullon had only a spot elevation (5940′). The first ascent was made by Hermann F. Ulrichs and Sydney Schmerling in June 1932 on an exhausting, wet, bushy trek during which they saw a herd of 22 goats; this was Ulrichs' first contribution to alpine history in the Cascades. The next ascent was made by Charles Kirschner and Will F. Thompson in 1937 or 1938.

SOUTHEAST RIDGE: Ascend the timbered rib from Squire Creek (see Three Fingers-Northeast Buttress). Continue directly up to a 5200-ft notch on the ridge crest (keep N of Salish Peak); descend northerly on the W slope so that a rock gully can be descended 1000 ft into the basin to a position upstream from Bullon Lakes. Ascend heather slopes and broken rock on Bullon's SE slope (class 2) and stay well left of E ridge. Summit is at the SW corner. Time: 10 hours.

Note: campsites can be found above timber E of the ridge notch and in the basin.

Approach Variation: This was the first ascent route, an arduous undertaking; the approach up the trackless Boulder River would be primitive. Use the Boulder River Trail♦, then the river valley to beyond the crossing of Gerkman Creek (est. 1600′). Hike the forest slope E about 1¼ mi. to the long W ridge of Bullon. Follow the ridge to rocky gendarmes (est. 5200′), then drop onto the S face and traverse to the SE slope.

Traverses: One can readily traverse the talus and meadow slopes high on the Squire Creek side of the divide, from the saddle N of Three Fingers to the S side of Whitehorse, to permit combining other climbs with Bullon.

SALISH PEAK 5645′/1721 m

This is the pointed small rock summit with a short steep E face; it is gentle on the W. The location is about ¼ mi. N of Craig Lakes, on the Squire Creek-Boulder River divide.

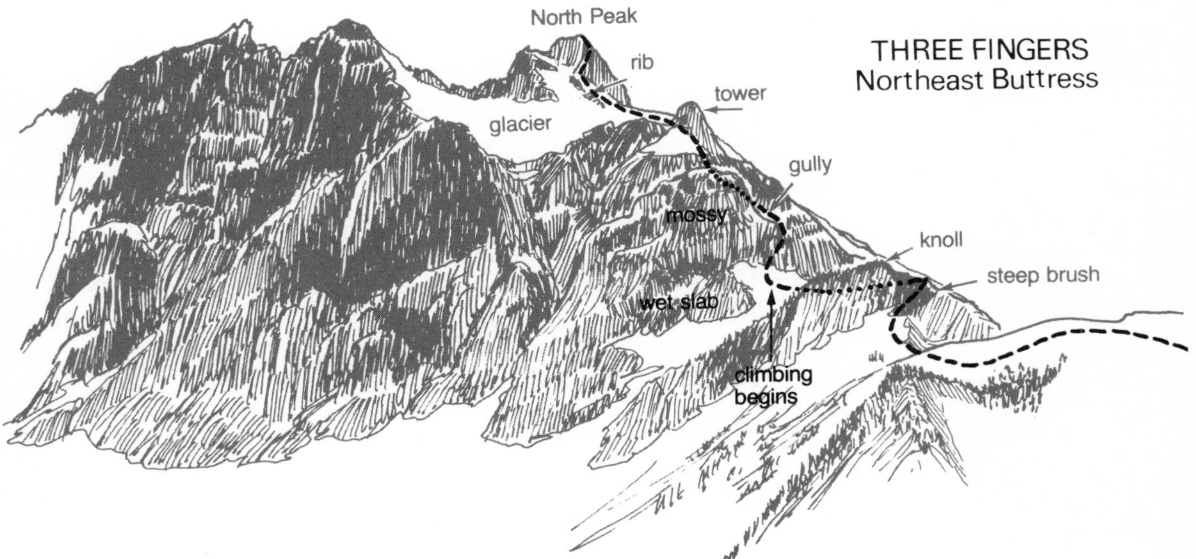

ROUTE: Use approach as for Three Fingers—Northeast Buttress. The climb is easy from the 5200-ft notch on the N or from Craig Lakes to the S.

SOUTHEAST FACE: This is an attractive granite face, about 600 ft high. The route is on the right side of the face for four leads, then takes the E crest five leads to the summit. First ascent by Jeff Dial, Don Williamson, and Greg Rice in July 1971. See topo for route. Grade III. Class 5.7. Time: 5 hours for approach; 7 hours for climb.

A midface variation by Williamson and Dial ascends two pitches, then traverses right to the route at end of third pitch (5.6 and A2).

SQUIRE CREEK WALL

On the W valley wall of Squire Creek, opposite the 5½-mi. point on the road. One of the largest granitic exposures in the area (part of the Squire Creek diorite), it offers potential for hard rock routes (polished, low-angle); the approach is not effortless: ford the creek and struggle with the alders. Reference: Fred Beckey, *Darrington and Index: Rock Climbing Guide,* Seattle, 1976.

BUCKEYE PEAK 5840′+/1780 m

This is a small rock peak above the ridgeline about ½ mi. SE of Whitehorse Mountain (and about ½ mi. NE of Point 5903). The rocky ridge that runs SE of the peak divides Squire Creek from Buckeye Creek. First ascent by Joe Vance and Don Wilde in 1952.

ROUTE: Use Three Fingers—Northeast Buttress approach to about 4500 ft on the rib. A high camp can be made near timberline about a mi. S of the peak. Traverse N for 1 mi.; climb to the peak's E ridge and gain it about 100 ft from the top via a chimney (class 4). Expect about 200 ft of rock climbing. Reference: *A.A.J.*, 1970, p. 120.

POINT 5903′ 5903′/1799 m

Climbing information has not been received. The peak appears easiest on the S.

WHITEHORSE MOUNTAIN 6852′/2088 m

Because Whitehorse rises over 6000 vertical ft in just 3 mi. from Darrington, it has become one of the most notable alpine images in the Cascades. With low footings on all flanks, Whitehorse is indeed a high, massive bulk, and with its distinguished shape capped by ice, is easily recognized from long distances. There are long rock walls on the W and E, and these rise from precipitous forest and brush slopes so characteristic of the North Cascades. Ridges of Whitehorse bristle with crags—many show distinctive varying tones. The N slope of the mountain consists of greenish lava flows giving way to contact metamorphosed sediments on the NW-SE trending summit ridge. The Whitehorse Glacier (1.8 km) is unusual in that it nearly tables the summit area like a miniature ice cap (up to 6700′), then breaks in two sections as a (hanging) slope glacier to descend to 4490 ft on the N frontage. Ice exists above and below large cliffs, but is now barely connected. Avalanche accumulation has built up to form glacier-like characteristics (below 1000-ft altitude) in Snow Gulch, which penetrates into the N face.

To the Indians the mountain warned of rain storms by throwing tufts of fog. They knew it as So-bahli-ahli, the loftly lady from the E (Bruseth, *op. cit.,* 2d ed., p. 31). The name "Whitehorse" evolved when pioneer Fred Olds' white horse ran away. During the search a neighbor noted the image of a horse in the form of a snowpatch on the mountain, and pointed out in jest, "there it is above us."[112] The name, founded in humor, is a good one. The wild Buckeye Creek basin was the scene of claim staking in the 1890s; the Buckeye Ledge (silver) was only 2500 ft under the summit. This activity continued to high on the N flank of the mountain, where Charles Wellman discovered gold; many hikers and climbers have passed the Niederprum claim and cabin of about 1900 at 4200 ft, below Lone Tree Pass (the trail and cabin—now gone—was built by Mat Niederprum). Early prospectors and such foresters as Nels Bruseth explored the high flanks and ridges of Whitehorse, but apparently did not reach the summit. Trails pioneers built were quickly swallowed by brush once mining activity subsided. The first ascent was made by Sidney V. Bryant, Will Doph, and Guy Ford on May 31, 1913, on a climb requiring 7 hours from their camp at Blue Bird Mine; they climbed via High Pass, then termed "Goat's Pass," discovered the first "pinnacle" a false summit, then found "a narrow snow strip" of 50° which made the final 30 ft possible. References: *Mountaineer Bull.,* July 1913; *Mountaineer,* 1913, pp. 69-70; 1923, p. 59. The first winter ascent was made by Pete Schoening and one or two companions in February 1953 via the Whitehorse Glacier.

NORTHWEST SHOULDER: At 5 mi. W of Darrington♦ (Whitehorse Store) take 387 Ave. NE S for 1½ mi. (to about 0.4 mi. from road end). Take Whitehorse Trail No. 653 to Niederprum Spring campspot in 2 mi. (rise from 800′ to 4200′ altitude). The trail ends at a 700-ft high slide path usually snow-covered until June. Follow markers via the timbered ridge on right to meadows below Lone Tree Pass (the tree is below the pass). Hike left (E) to the pass (4720′+), traversing above the alder (at 4 mi.).

Now turn left and follow the ridge crest over rocky outcrops eastward to steep rock walls that block passage. Drop 350 ft SE (right), next to cliffs, to the 4525-ft level above a small lake. Here start back up toward cliffs and traverse about ½ mi. to below High Pass (just NW of this pass is a

WHITEHORSE MOUNTAIN and THREE FINGERS from northeast
PHILIP LEATHERMAN

South Peak
THREE FINGERS
WHITEHORSE MTN.
High Pass
Lone Tree Pass
WHITEHORSE GLACIER
Buckeye Creek Basin
Squire Creek
Sill Basin
right side
Glacier route
Snow Gulch
DARRINGTON

large rocky hump (6357′) at the edge of the upper glacier). Climb the prominent snow finger in a wide gully through the pass (6032′) and onto the glacier. The true summit is SE and is reached by crossing the névé and ascending a steep snow finger directly to the summit. In late season it may be necessary to leave the finger for rocks to the left and traverse ledges on the E face around and up to the summit. Time: 7 hours from road.

Variation: From Lone Tree Pass descend about 500 ft to Bear Lake and then traverse SE to the snow finger leading to High Pass.

WHITEHORSE GLACIER: This is a more direct route than the normal way, but with greater complexities; it is advised only before about June 1 when brush is snow-covered. Then the route is moderate, although the snow becomes fairly steep near the top. Be alert for slide danger from flanking ridges. There are two basins on the N side of the mountain, split by the rock hump N of High Pass; both basins are fed by the summit glacier. The glacier route normally ascends the basin of Snow Gulch. The apparent first ascent was made May 17, 1936 by Joe Halwax, Granville Jensen, George MacGowan, and Marion Marts, who stayed right of the main lower gully.

From the end of 387th Ave. NE (Snow Gulch) follow gravel terraces about ¼ mi. upstream (the stream bed is brushy; keep left and take the left branch). Find old miner path E of creek; it generally climbs upslope well left of the main drainage, then skirts under cliffs. (Some slide alder may be encountered to reach it). Portions of trail may be washed away, but it may be followed to a position above the main cliff band that crosses the basin. Pass cliffs on left. One can follow a central ridge between falls to a ruined cabin, then up a gully in cliff break, starting 250 ft up and right of the cabin (leads to upper glacier). Note: the lower glacier to right is dangerous—avoid it. Gradually angle right on the ascent until the route from High Pass is met. Time: 6 hours with good snow; otherwise add 2 hours to negotiate brush.

Approach Variation: Some parties elect to follow the gulch from beyond the road, especially if it is snow-filled. But it is important to leave gulch at 1600 ft and ascend E (steep bush) to cliff base, then contour right to re-enter at 2500 ft (avoids slabs and waterfalls). Note: a lower basin, right-side variation is reported as satisfactory in early season if solidly snow covered (approximate 1936 route).

EAST RIDGE: First ascent by Ron Miller and Ben Guydelkon on June 2, 1970. From about 3½ mi. W of Darrington drive about 4 mi. up an old logging road that begins on the W side of Squire Creek; walk on to a logged area. Ascend the cut area E to a wooded ridge, then up it about 1000 ft. Traverse SE into brushy basin on the left (when basin broadens). Ascend a gully to the base of the E ridge. Keep close to the crest (brush and snow), then a long rock ridge (class 3 and 4). Drop to the summit glacier and continue S to the top. Grade II; class 5.6 (slings and jam nuts useful). Time: 11 hours. Reference: *A.A.J.*, 1971, p. 344.

SOUTHEAST RIDGE: This is the prominent arete seen from Darrington as a long ragged spur rising above a reddish eastern wall. Recommended time for climbing is May or early June. First ascent by Kenn Carpenter, David Collins, and Tom Williams on May 24, 1956.

From Squire Creek Road♦ reach Buckeye Creek by: (1) Leaving road at 2.4 mi. where it makes a steep uphill switch left; find old trail alongside creek and follow it several hundred yds to opposite Buckeye Creek, then ford Squire Creek. (2) Ascend the brushy Buckeye Creek valley to the hanging basin at 3000 ft; timberline here is about 4000 ft. At the upper end (brushy) climb to névé slopes, then to the lowest notch of the SE ridge (est. 5500′); once could bivouac about 100 ft above notch. The route onward lies generally on left of ridge (class 3 with some class 4). Time: 10 hours minimum.

MT. HIGGINS 5142′/1567 m

Higgins is 8 mi. NW of Darrington; metamorphosed sandstone shale has formed prominent SW-dipping beds, prominent from the highway in the valley of the North Fork Stillaguamish River. Indians called the mountain Ska-dulvas, but settlers named it for Walter D. Higgins who in 1887 homesteaded at Hazel. The first climb was made in 1888 by Al Baker, John Higgins, and Frank Lawrence, who left a flag on the summit.

A trail extends to the former lookout built in 1926 on the 4849-ft W peak (cabin demolished by snowfall in 1965). The middle peak (4960′+/1512 m) is ¾ mi. E, with its upper N side nearly vertical. The true summit is ¾ mi. farther E. A short but steep southern wall extends as a band below the W to middle peak.

EAST RIDGE: Use approach as for Round Mountain, but continue around it in open woods to the E ridge. The short but steep upper ridge may be climbed directly to the summit; or bypass on S side traverse. Time: 3-4 hours.

Alternate Approach: New logging roads just N of Swedeheaven offer a more direct way to the E ridge.

WEST ROUTE: From State Hwy 530 at 17.6 mi. E of Arlington (1.1 mi. W of Hazel Road), take Seapost Road (SL 05500) N for 0.4 mi., cross river bridge and continue to the 1800-ft level (est. 3½ mi.) just before first switchback. Trail No. 640 reaches the W peak in 4 mi. (2½ hours). To climb the middle peak, use the W ridge (scramble above the smooth slabs). To reach the true summit descend and bypass the middle peak on its N, then follow the crest.

ROUND MOUNTAIN 5320′+/1622 m

This tree-dotted massif is between the North Fork of the Stillaguamish River and Deer Creek's S fork. It is more notable as a viewpoint than as a climb.

SOUTHEAST ROUTE: At 5 mi. W of Darrington♦ take Swedeheaven Road 1½ mi. N, then follow road no. 3403 for 12.3 mi. to Segelson Pass. Turn left 0.6 mi. on Coney Pass Road (spur E) and park at creek.

WHITEHORSE MOUNTAIN from west
ROBERT J. DeWITZ, U.S. FOREST SERVICE

Hike along left side of creek (WSW) to a meadow, then W to ridge saddle. Follow ridge S (faint path) to Coney Pass (3960′+), and continue WSW just S of crest; path improves as it crosses two rockslides and breaks into the open basin (about 4500 ft) in ½ mi. Proceed NW over a massive rockslide, toward the summit, taking either the S or E ridge to the top (easy scrambling—mostly heather). Time: 3 hours.

FINNEY PEAK 5083′/1549 m

Finney is a moderate summit, but is the highest elevation N of Round Mountain and W of the lower Sauk River. Its position is 11 mi. NW of Darrington, and offers a good vantage of the North Cascades; the old lookout cabin of 1933 is now gone.

ROUTE: From Concrete take the bridge S to South Skagit Road, then E 8 mi. to Finney-Cumberland Road No. 353. Follow this to road no. 3407 and go 6½ mi. to former road end (3000′); logging has altered the roads here and the summit trail (no. 616) is now no more than 2 mi.

The road approach can be made from the Darrington-Rockport Road (27½ mi. to trailhead) or via Segelson Pass Road (est. 29 mi.). Reference: *101 Hikes.*

MT. HIGGINS from west
HERMANN F. ULRICHS

GLACIER PEAK
MT. PUGH
MT. FORGOTTEN
WHITEHORSE MTN.
JUMBO MTN.
MT. BULLON
THREE FINGERS
EXFOLIATION DOME
BUCKEYE PK.
High Pass
SALISH PK.
BIG BEAR MTN.
Craig Lakes
Lone Tree Pass
Bullon Lakes
Windy Pass
Gerkman Creek
Sevenmile Creek
Goat Flat
Saddle Lake
Boulder River Valley

"On May 1, 1909 I was appointed as a Forest Guard on the Mount Baker National Forest. The Forest Supervisor fitted me out with a badge, the "Use Book" and a marking hatchet. He told me to go to Finney Creek and establish headquarters at the Finney Guard Station. Sixteen miles of trail from Sauk City, the end of rail transportation, to the guard station had been built the previous year and the winter storms made it impassible except on foot. The one major bridge at Gee Creek was out and in many places the trail was obliterated by slides.

"I arrived at old Sauk City at night. The next morning with a pack of beans and bacon on my back, I set out for the Finney Guard Station 16 miles away.

"The Finney G.S. was an old log cabin on an abandoned homestead claim. Never before or since have I seen so many mice. They were as thick as flies around a honey pot.

"As soon as I had fixed something to eat I started killing mice with a stick of stove wood, but headway was slow. So I took a 5 gallon oil tin and cut the top out. Next I got a piece of wire and strung a milk can on the wire and laid it across the opening in the oil can. I put about 4 inches of water in it, and placed a small rock in the water so that just a small portion of the rock extended above the water line.

"Then I was ready to bait the trap by tying two pieces of bacon on opposite sides of the milk can. Then, with a flat stick leaning from the floor to the top of the oil tin, I was ready for business.

"In a few minutes a mouse ran up the stick and not being able to reach the bait, he jumped the few inches necessary to get the bacon. When he lit, the can rolled on the wire axis and Mr. Mouse was in the drink. Soon another went after the bacon and he too went into the drink. Then the war was on. The rock extending above the water was only big enough to accommodate one mouse and a battle started to see who should have the perch. Their squeals attracted others and soon a procession was moving up the stick, some jumping for the bait and others just diving in to see what the commotion was all about.

"Twice that night I emptied the can of dead mice. My first count was 62 and at least as many more on the second count. Business tapered off then for even a mouse will get smart. I spread my bedroll on the old bough bunk and crawled in. In a few minutes mice were in bed with me, that I couldn't take so I moved outside. Mice were even nesting in my boots by morning. The season was pretty well over by the time I got them thinned out enough so I could be comfortable in the cabin."

REMINISCENCES OF C.C. McGUIRE, 1960

APPROACHES

Roads and trails described in this section are noted in the text by the symbol♦.

ROADS

Barclay Creek Road No. 278 branches from U.S. Hwy No. 2♦ at Baring (19 mi. E of Sultan); cross tracks N and follow main road on S side of Barclay Creek; considerable logging. The trail leaves on the downhill side 4.4 mi. before road end.

Beckler River Road No. 280 turns N from U.S. Hwy No. 2♦ 0.8 mi. E of Skykomish to connect with road no. 290 via Jack Pass (12½ mi.); total of 15.1 mi.

Eagle Creek Road No. 2632 extends up Eagle Creek over 5 mi. (leaves Beckler Road to the W at about 1 mi.).

Johnson Ridge Road No. 273 exits Beckler River road at 6.6 mi.; as road no. 2730 it extends into the Sunrise Mountain area (currently logging traffic). ATP can be driven to about 4400 ft. Cat tracks lead E through logging slash to the trail.

Rapid River Road No. 270 exits Beckler River road at 6.7 mi. and extends E about 7½ mi.

Evergreen Mountain Road No. 285 exits East Beckler River road at 12 mi.; it traverses to the low W side of Evergreen Mountain.

Boulder-South Fork Canyon Creek Road No. 320 leaves State Hwy No. 530 (see Darrington♦) 19.8 mi. E of Arlington, then extends 3.8 mi. to Boulder River.

Canyon Creek Road No. 320 leaves Mountain Loop Hwy♦ 7½ mi. E of Granite Falls and extends to the area of Tupso Pass in 17½ mi.

Canyon Lake Road (no. 318 and 3032) branches E in about 1 mi. and extends to endings beyond Canyon Lake.

Branch road no. 310 extends S of Canyon Creek 7.9 mi. (0.7 mi. before bridge) to Section 6, but does not connect with Canyon Lake.

Branch road 320 G exits E at about 9 mi. (at 0.2 mi. past bridge crossing South Fork Canyon Creek).

Clear Creek Road No. 3210 turns from Sauk County Road 2.7 mi. S of Darrington♦. In 4.9 mi. it forks left and extends 4.4 mi. toward Deer Creek Pass (ends ¼ mi. from pass); as late as 1939 the entire valley of Clear Creek was marked only by trail instead of the havoc of logging roads and clearcuts.

Copper Creek Road No. 3210A forks right at the 4.9 mi. division and extends some 3 mi. along Copper Creek.

Coal Lake Road No. 3006 leaves Mountain Loop Hwy♦ 26.9 mi. E of Granite Falls, then ends near Coal Lake at 4.8 mi. (lake is at 4.4 mi.).

WHITEHORSE MOUNTAIN and THREE FINGERS from west
ROBERT J. DeWITZ, U.S. FOREST SERVICE

Dan Creek Road No. 324 leaves Mountain Loop Hwy♦ 7 mi. from the Sauk bridge (Darrington); in 3.3 mi. a right fork (Blackoak Creek Road No. 3118) extends 3 mi. The other fork (324) extends for 2 mi.; here Upper Decline Road No. 3200 extends NW.

Darrington is 30 mi. from Arlington (off I-5) via State Hwy No. 530, or 27 mi. from Concrete via Sauk Hwy (State No. 17A). The East Sauk Road from Rockport (on State Hwy No. 20) connects with the Sauk Hwy 10.8 mi. N of Darrington.

Deer Creek Road No. 3016 leaves Mountain Loop Hwy♦ 24.1 mi. E of Granite Falls, following a pre-1900 wagon road route, and ends in 4.4 mi. near Lake Kelcema. In 1¼ mi. Coal Creek branch road exits, then climbs to 3200 ft.

Elliott Creek Road No. 309 leaves Mountain Loop Hwy♦ 3.6 mi. N of Barlow Pass. Closed to motor vehicles beyond 1.4 mi. Where trails and a wagon road led up this magnificently timbered valley a mile-wide clearcut blights the landscape. Bedal Creek Road No. 309A is closed by same gate.

Falls Creek Road No. 3113 leaves Mountain Loop Hwy♦ 11.2 mi. from Sauk bridge (Darrington♦), crosses the Sauk and extends 6.7 mi. (now closed 2 mi. closer).

Monte Cristo Road No. 2963 leaves Mountain Loop Hwy♦ at Barlow Pass. Generally open to Monte Cristo by June, depending on snowcover. The road reaches the townsite exit at 4.2 mi. (here a short spur crosses bridge to resort and some trails—parking fee); public parking available in lot on left spur. Mine-to-market road (hiking only) continues 1 mi.

Mountain Loop Highway, one of the most scenic of Cascade roads, follows in part the old railroad track. The loop road was completed after the section from Silverton to Barlow Pass was constructed for autos in 1949. Begins at Granite Falls (State Hwy No. 92, becomes Forest Road No. 322; reach in 19 mi. from I-5 at Everett). The loop road reaches Silverton in 23 mi. (winter closure here) and Barlow Pass in 31.6 mi. Distance here to Darrington♦ is 27 mi. on the other loop.

Mt. Pilchuck State Park Road No. 3014 leaves Mountain Loop Hwy♦ 12.4 mi. from Granite Falls (7 mi. to the ski area).

North Fork Skykomish River Road No. 290 leaves U.S. Hwy No. 2♦ at Index junction (13.3 mi. from Sultan) and continues about 18 mi. (1½ mi. past Quartz Creek); there is a loop connection over Jack Pass with Beckler River Road♦.

At Galena junction (9 mi.) a narrow road (no. 291) leads 4.2 mi. to Mineral City. Road is frequently closed to public use during the week. A newer road leaves the trunk at the main river crossing, then extends about 2 mi. up the E side of Silver Creek.

Perry Creek Road No. 3010 leaves Mountain Loop Hwy♦ 27.2 mi. beyond Granite Falls and extends 1 mi.

Pilchuck River Road. From Granite Falls drive SE on Monroe Road 5 mi. to Lake Alyson Road (about 18 mi. from Snohomish on opposite loop). At 200 ft S of this junction bear E on Scott Paper Road SL-P-SP-500, which follows N side of Pilchuck River; crosses to S side about 3 mi. beyond Wilson Creek, then many spurs continue.

Pugh Mountain Road No. 3131 leaves Mountain Loop Hwy♦ 14 mi. from Darrington♦ (Sauk bridge), then reaches the trailhead in 1 mi.

Schweitzer Creek Road No. 3015 leaves Mountain Loop Hwy♦ 16.3 mi. from Granite Falls; it extends S to Lake Evan, then turns W. At 2.6 mi. there is a W branch (B) which goes 3 mi. to the N side of Bear Lake. Total distance to Lake Evan—Boardman Trail is 4.8 mi.

Sloan Creek Road No. 308 (North Fork Sauk) exits from Mountain Loop Hwy♦ 18½ mi. from Sauk bridge (Darrington♦). The road's total length is 15.7 mi., extending into Cadet Creek.

Cadet Creek Road (A) branches S at 9.6 mi. (ending in 2.8 mi.).

June Mountain Road (C) exits at 12.4 mi. (ends 1½ mi. E).

Squire Creek Road No. 3203 can be driven about 5 mi. from Darrington♦ (mileage Red Top Tavern to stream crossing; blocked here but roadbed continues nearly ½ mi.); begin by following Darrington Ave. W and take left fork in 1.4 mi.

Straight Creek Road No. 327 (Rat Trap Pass Road) branches N from White Chuck Road♦ at 6.1 mi. (reaches Rat Trap Pass in 4.3 mi. and Suiattle River Road♦ in 14 mi.). At 2.4 mi. Meadow Mountain Road (no. 3128) forks E; this road is currently closed by a slide ¼ mi. from the fork and probably will remain gated there.

Suiattle River Road No. 345 leaves the Sauk Highway at 6½ mi. N of Darrington (11 mi. S of Rockport) and extends 24 mi. to Sulphur Creek; Milk Creek Trail branches right past Sulphur Creek work center.

Sultan Basin Road is a combination of county, Forest Service, and D.N.R. roads, with some private mining spurs. The system begins ½ mi. E of Sultan (U.S. Hwy No. 2♦) and extends about 26.7 mi. to Florence Rea Mine via road no. 292. No overnight camping allowed on F.S. lands within one mile of lake shore in Sultan Basin (free camp before basin at about 9 mi.); camping allowed only at remote sites away from roads. Sanitary regulations enforced in the basin drainage because water diverted for municipal use. (Culmbach Dam completed in 1965 by Everett and Snohomish County).

At Olney Pass (13 mi.) keep right and downhill; pass Spada Reservoir; junction with Williamson Creek Road at 19 mi. (main road keep ahead). At 19.9 mi. keep left; at 24.7 mi. meet Vesper Creek mine road; at 25.8 mi. reach final bridge on Sultan River; road end at E end of mine property.

Williamson Creek Road forks N to below the 45 Mine, but can only be driven about 4½ mi.; possible pickup travel an additional 2 mi. (road rough beyond 2.8 mi.). Note: confusing branches (stay left at 2.4 mi. and right at 2.8 mi.); no camping allowed. This is an old mining road, following the route of a puncheon road; in 1912 a car could be driven to the foot of the switchbacks. Road accesses private land; posted and gated at boundary of private land.

Kromona Mine Road exits from the main system uphill and right at Olney Pass; it extends SE along the Sultan River's S fork to the Kromona millsite (est. 4½ mi., 2400'); the mine and camp are E of the middle fork (3200'-3300'); gate before mill.

Sunrise Mine Road No. 3012 leaves Mountain Loop Hwy♦ 29.6 mi. E of Granite Falls and extends 2.3 mi. to the trailhead.

U.S. Hwy No. 2 is the basic approach to the S perimeter of this section. Reach from I-5 or I-405 (34 mi. Seattle to Sultan).

Wallace River Road No. 2800 can be driven about 4½ mi. from Gold Bar (U.S. Hwy No. 2♦) to a washout (1500'). Road deteriorating; generally passible only by 4-wheel drive vehicles or motor bikes. Early maps showed the Wallace River by its Indian name—Kakuilla Creek.

White Chuck River Road No. 314 leaves Mountain Loop Hwy♦ 10½ mi. from Sauk Bridge (Darrington) and extends 10½ mi.

Williamson Creek Road. See Sultan Basin Road♦.

TRAIL AND ALPINE HIKING APPROACHES

Use Regulations within the Glacier Peak Wilderness:

The Glacier Peak Wilderness is managed by the U.S. Forest Service; regulations pertaining to use differ from those for North Cascades National Park and National Recreation Areas.

A written Wilderness Permit is required prior to entry for any overnight use. Permits can be obtained in person, by telephone request, or by mail (allow 10 days for mailing) at the Outdoor Information Center in Seattle and at Forest Headquarters, Wenatchee, and at peripheral Ranger Stations (Chelan, Concrete, Darrington, Verlot, etc.). For the most current information on trails, snow, etc., call the appropriate Ranger Station.

A group larger than 12 persons and 15 horses is not permitted to travel and camp as a unit. The use of motorized equipment is prohibited. Some areas have special camping restrictions, e.g., camping is not permitted within ¼ mi. of Image Lake, or within 200 ft of Holden Lake's shoreline.

Observe the following rules when traveling or camping in the subalpine and alpine zones:

Camp in wooded or moraine areas rather than meadows, and always more than 100 ft from a lake shore. Where campfires are permitted use existing fire spots rather than creating new fire scars; preferably, use a camp stove. Do not cut boughs for beds or any green trees for any purpose. Pack out all litter (aluminum foil does not burn). Keep all water pure for drinking; do not wash in streams or lakes. Keep all toilet use at least 300 ft from water and camp areas; cover after digging hole as water saturation from snow melt can contaminate slopes beneath.

Do not mark cross-country routes with ribbon, markers, or blazes. Remove markers left by others. Do not shortcut on trail switchbacks.

No pack or saddle animal is permitted within 200 ft of a lake shoreline, or stream, except for through travel on established routes, loading, or watering; loose herding of stock is not permitted. Dogs are not permitted to annoy or menace visitors or wildlife, and must be kept under control at all times. Hunting and fishing are allowed in the Wilderness consistent with seasons and license requirements set by State law. Non-game wildlife species, including marmots, squirrels, chipmunks, and birds, are protected by law.

Report all injured or missing persons to the nearest Forest Service Station or the County Sheriff.

Whatever the temptation to think or act as if individual violations are unimportant, users should not carelessly and adversely affect the enjoyment of others. It is absolutely essential that the purity of fragile mountain lakes and the unspoiled nature of the parklands be preserved. A degree of elitism is warranted to set the leadership needed to protect our dwindling resources.

Bald Eagle Trail No. 650 reaches Curry Gap♦ 1.3 mi. from the end of Sloan Creek Road♦. The trail continues E to reach the Crest Trail♦ (Dishpan Gap) at 9.5 mi., almost passing over Bald Eagle, Long John, and June Mountains. From Curry Gap reach Spring Camp at 4 mi. and Blue Lake at 7 mi. (side trail). Reference: *101 Hikes.*

Bald Mountain Ridge Trail, new trail about 9 mi. in length, reached from Williamson Creek Road (see Sultan Basin Road♦). At 2.8 mi. on the road, go left, cross bridge over Williamson Creek, and continue up for about 2½ mi. Trail begins at road end and connects with road 3015B (trail is D.N.R. constructed).

Barclay Lake Trail No. 1055 now begins from Barclay Creek Road♦ and reaches the lake (2442') in slightly over 1½ mi. The trail continues 2 mi. to Eagle Lake (3888'), but is currently obscure; ascend forest and talus from behind garbage pit, then contour meadows left. The trail along Barclay Creek is an old one; there was considerable prospecting in early times. Reference: *101 Hikes.*

Bear Lake and *Pinnacle Lake* are reached in 0.2 and 1.7 mi. from road no. 3015B (see Schweitzer Creek Road♦), with trail start about 6 mi. from Mountain Loop Hwy♦. Boardman Lake (3370') is 1 mi. from road no. 3015; a cross-country trek can be made to Mt. Pilchuck. See Bald Mountain Ridge Trail♦ for new trail connection to Sultan Basin. Reference: *Trips and Trails 1.* A scramble route leads from

Pinnacle Lake SW to Twenty Lakes Basin near the E end of Mt. Pilchuck.

Bedal Creek Trail No. 648 no longer maintained; brushy and hard to follow after ½ mi. Must walk 3-3½ mi. on closed Elliott Creek Road♦ to find old trailhead. The trail fades near 4400 ft (just over 2 mi.) but at about 5000 ft a path bears right on a contour into meadows of Bedal Basin. If trail lost stay on side with heaviest timber (the old trail stayed on N side). Reference: *101 Hikes.* James Bedal had a cabin and asbestos claim in the upper valley. The area was called "Goat Pasture." Indians commonly used snares to trap goats, whose wool and hides were in demand.

Big Four Ice Caves are 1 mi. from the Big Four Picnic Ground (spur exit 26.4 mi. from Granite Falls on Mountain Loop Hwy♦); follow boardwalk and new bridge crossing of the river. The glacier accumulation remnant below the mountain wall is perhaps the lowest in elevation of its type in the Cascades.

Big Greider Lake is reached by a new 2 mi. trail (via Little Greider Lake), built by the Department of Natural Resources. Leave the Sultan Basin Road♦ at 20.4 mi.

Blanca Lake Trail No. 1052 climbs steeply from North Fork Skykomish Road♦ at 15 mi. (1900′) to the Troublesome Creek divide (4600′) in 3 mi. (camping and water at pond on divide). The trail diagonals steeply down to Blanca Lake (3972′) in ½ mi. (campsites at E and W ends of lake). The rock-rimmed granitic basin containing Blanca Lake and Columbia Glacier is one of the most magnificent settings in the Cascade Range. Reference: *101 Hikes.*

To circle the lake cross the outlet on a log jam, then continue a cross-country obstacle course route around the S side. Then an open route over talus, old ground moraine, or snow can be taken to Columbia Glacier and Monte Cristo Pass.

Troublesome Mountain (5430′/1655 m) is a good viewpoint SW of the lake but involves a fairly arduous cross-country trek of over 2 mi. Leave the trail at the divide, then follow bumpy subalpine terrain.

Boulder Lake Trail: At 19.9 mi. on Sultan Basin Road♦ go right about 1 mi. (do not cross Elk Creek bridge). Take only spur right and uphill 1 mi. from trunk road for about ½ mi. to end. New D.N.R. trail to Boulder Lake about 2 mi. away.

Boulder River Trail No. 743 extends along the E side of the deep valley, but is not maintained between the river ford and Tupso Pass (see Boulder-South Fork Canyon Creek Road♦). The valley trail, begun in 1926, was built to Three Fingers in 1930; a branch, shown on 1939 maps, was built up the fork N of Mt. Bullon. In the primeval forest, a sanctuary that should be preserved, trees rise out of the ruins of tangled remnants of broken trunks deep in moss and sodden with water.

Copper Lake was noted by Silverton miners from Marble Pass—an emerald green lake between Big Four and Vesper's rocky heights. "One is impressed with its distinct green color and peculiar mineral flavor. The lake is fed by a glacier, which is apparently half a mile long." (W.F. Brown, *Everett Herald,* 27 October 1892) The lake is now reached by a rough trail from Williamson Creek Road♦ (about 5-mi. point) which begins from far side of lake's outlet stream (est. 2000′). Beyond a fork cross a deep gully and use a miner's ladder on opposite cliff, then zigzag steeply up the left side of the canyon to the 3100-ft lake (2 hours). Copper Lake is nearly ½ mi. long; its waters reflect a deep green-blue tint derived from glacial drainage. A series of cascades tumble from the narrow outlet. The slopes of Little Chief Mountain, S and W of the lake, were the scene of much early claim activity. Steep talus extends from cliffs to the water. References: *Mountaineer,* 1918, p. 11.

Crest Trail: Pacific Crest National Trail No. 2000 from Stevens Pass to White Pass (35½ mi.) and E of Suiattle River covered in Section II. Coverage here is from White Pass to Suiattle River.

Gentle and flowered meadow slopes lead to Red Pass (est. 6450′) in 1.8 mi. (*101 Hikes*); a short path leads to *Portal Peak* (6999′/2133 m). At 2½ mi. the trail nears White Chuck cinder cone (6000′), built by ejections of pyroclastic materials; the 75-ft cone and nearby black lava cliffs are younger than Glacier Peak (*Routes and Rocks,* p. 47).

Reach Glacier Peak Meadows (5400′-5500′) at 3½ mi. (camping). Reach Sitkum Creek (3852′) and a meadow camp at 8.3 mi. (junction with White Chuck Trail♦—W). Reach Glacier Creek (campsite) at 11½ mi., Glacier Ridge Trail (6090′) at 12½ mi., Pumice Creek (campsite) in ½ mi. more, and Gray Bear camp (5250′) at 15 mi. Reach Fire Creek Pass (est. 6350′) at 16½ mi.; Fire Mountain high route begins just N of the pass (see Fire Mountain). Closely SE of the pass is Point 6914, an easy tour to an excellent viewpoint. The ridge here can be followed N and E around Milk Lake Glacier; an easy hike can be made E along barrens and then on or near the divide to Ptarmigan Glacier and Glacier Peak.

Mica Lake (est. 5450′), named for the presence of mica flakes (from mica-rich schist—a foliated rock with thin mineral particles, commonly with tiny sheets of mica) along its shores, is reached at 17½ mi. (best camping ½ mi. E in basin). Reach Milk Creek Trail♦ junction (est. 4000′) in 3.9 additional mi.; the Suiattle River Road♦ is 6.2 mi. distant from here—a total of 28 mi. from White Pass.

From the Milk Creek junction the Crest Trail (No. 2052) climbs to nearly 6100 ft on Milk Creek Ridge (est. 4 mi.), then rounds the scenic upper basin of Milk Creek's E fork. On the divide to Dolly Creek a pleasant tour can be made along the rolling ridge to Grassy Point (E summit, 6596′). From the trail at Dolly Creek meadows (est. 5500′, 6½ mi. from Milk Creek) a tour can be made S across Vista Creek, then SE to Ermine Glacier and Harmony Park.

The trail descends to Vista Creek crossing in 4 mi. (campsite) and reaches Skyline Bridge in about 2¼ more mi. A new trail section (Miners Creek) makes a 4.3 mi. link from the bridge E to the trail between Glacier Peak Mines and Buck Creek Pass. For continuation and connections, see Suiattle Trail♦ (Section II).

Curry Gap (est. 4000′) can be reached in 4 mi. via Quartz Creek Trail No. 1050; leave North Fork Skykomish Road♦ at about 17 mi. The name honors a miner who hiked through it on weekends from Goat Lake to Skykomish to court a girl friend. See Bald Eagle Trail♦ for northern and eastern approach.

Deer Creek Pass (3700′) is ½ mi. from near end of Deer Creek Road♦ (trail no. 717) and was once used as a trail route to Clear Creek. Reach from Kelcema Lake Trail at 4.2 mi. on the road. A short northern approach to the pass is from Clear Creek Road♦. The old route to Bonanza Mine used the valley of Deer Creek; a complex of trails led to many mining sites.

Dusty Creek Trail No. 786 leaves the Upper Suiattle River Trail♦ at a new start, about 14 mi. from the road, opposite Triad Creek Trail junction (est. 3900′). It is an old trail (shown on 1931 maps) and receives minimal maintenance. The trail follows a ramp to a sharp crest (Dusty Wedge) at 2½ mi., then soon fades. It is simple to continue to timberline and the broad alp slope of the Great Fill between Dusty and Chocolate Canyons on the E side of Glacier Peak; the highest trees are at about 6200 ft.

To the N is Multicolor Canyon, so-named for the dust clouds arising from constant bank erosion. The ragged cleaver at the head of Dusty Creek consists of Glacier Peak lava that rests on older yellow layers of volcanic ash and breccia (*Routes and Rocks,* p. 34). Higher, one can hike along the apex of Dusty Wedge, traverse N beneath tongues of the North Guardian and Dusty Glaciers in Recession Basin (est. 6100′) at the head of Dusty Creek, then make a rising traverse to the 6650-ft saddle of Gamma Ridge.

From Dusty Wedge S cross the Chocolate Glacier at about 7000 ft, then to a bedrock ridge and timberline meadows of Streamline Ridge. Do not enter Chocolate Canyon (dangerous stream and gravel gorge).

Gamma Ridge. The trail leaves the Upper Suiattle River Trail♦ about 1 mi. beyond Skyline Bridge, then climbs to about 6000 ft (some overgrowth). Gamma Ridge, between Gamma and Dusty Creeks, is an easy hike and can be continued to the N flank of Dusty Glacier. At 4½-5 mi. reach a saddle (est. 6450′) 0.4 mi. E of Gamma Peak; a faded path continues (meadow camping). One can skirt the S side of Gamma Peak (*Routes and Rocks,* pp. 33-36), then regain the ridge SW to reach a broad saddle (est. 6650′; 5.7 mi.). One can readily continue a high route through the meadows of Harmony Peak at the eastern head of Vista Creek, below the Ermine Glacier.

Gamma Peak (7009′/2136 m) is a cap of Glacier Peak lava which offers a magnificent viewpoint. It can be reached via meadows and an open grassy ridge, then an easy tour on its final E slope (avoid the N and W sides). The tuff and breccia of Gamma Ridge are highlighted by the lava columns that top the peak (*ibid,* p. 35).

Glacier Basin is reached in 1.6 mi. from the end of the mine roadway spur (total of 2.6 mi. hiking from Monte Cristo Road♦), a popular trek on a steep, rocky trail. The roadway passes the old collector station, near where the Rainy Mine bores into Addison Ridge. References: *101 Hikes,* p. 136; *Summit,* Oct. 1966, pp. 24-25. In the 1900 era Glacier Basin was called Glacier Gulch, and the trail was known as "Headhouse Trail."

The charms of the basin were known to the Monte Cristo miners: a Swiss miner reported that Edelweiss grew and was in blossom at the upper end of the glacier moraine (*Everett Herald,* 30 August 1894). It is possible to see a wide spectrum of sedimentary and metamorphic formations, the site of mineralized zones. On the Cadet Peak slope at 4400 ft are remains of the famed Pride of the Mountains Mine; one of several adits ends in the middle of a stope. Caution: a 310-ft vertical shaft drops to the lower Mystery Mine.

Mystery Ridge, on the western perimeter of Glacier Basin, has fascinating relics. The Mystery Mines on its W flank are connected by a 3000-ft main tunnel to the lower mine, beneath the basin and into Cadet Peak (and a connecting vertical shaft). The upper Mystery Mine is a yawning cavern; the middle mine bores completely through the ridge into the basin, where it is known as Pride of the Woods (4560′). Ruins down-valley remain from the cookhouse which served some 80 men; just above it, atop the ridge, remain ruins of the anchorage tramway station. This was a waypoint for ore arriving by cable from the 89 and Pride of the Mountains mines across the basin in a single 1400-ft span, then descending to the valley collector (a separate 3700-ft tram carried ore from the lower Mystery Mine to the collector).

The Justice and Golden Cord Mines on the N flank of the Wilmans Spires (W of Mystery Ridge) can be reached by an old but suitable path. After crossing Glacier Creek on the Glacier Basin roadway, turn right through the concentrator ruins. Keep right of the clearing, to re-enter the forest on an old road. In about 200 ft a major street junction is reached. The trail is the second left and climbs steeply ¾ mi. to the mine area at 4000 ft.

Goat Flat: ATP 7 mi. by trail via temporarily reopened portion of Old Meadow Mtn. Trail, reachable by Canyon Creek Road♦. (The Tupso Pass spur road was gated in 1977 due to logging operations. It will likely be closed for two or more years. The Forest Service has reopened the old Meadow Mountain Trail [5+ miles to Saddle Lake] which leaves the Canyon Creek Rd near Saddle Creek.) Original Three Fingers trail closed from Tupso Pass. There is a shelter in the meadows (est. 5000′), constructed when the trail was built to Three Fingers in 1932 (also shelter at Saddle Lake, at 5 mi. ATP). The trail continues below Tin Can Ridge to beyond Tin Can Gap (5760′+). Reference: *101 Hikes.*

A once-popular, steep blazed route begins atop a clearcut 100 yds W of Sevenmile Creek (spur G of road, 1 mi.) and ascends the wooded spur NNE to 4000 ft, then bears N (3 hrs to Goat Flat).

Goat Lake (3161′) soon had the status of a mining hub after its discovery in 1891.[113] Miners reported the upper valley of Elliott Creek is one "vast field of flowers," and that the "whole of the little valley (Goat Lake) is streaked with ore" (*Everett Herald,* 24 September 1896). The name is derived from the many goats which frequented the basin, often providing meat for miners. Numerous old buildings and cabins near the lake outlet were destroyed by fire; abandoned cabins remain here and at the site of the Penn Mine headquarters (⅜ mi. W), S of the creek on the old puncheon road. An 8-mi. wagon road was built in 1896 from Barlow Pass, and a railroad was even contemplated. In 1928 the mining company took sheet metal in to the lake for a building which was never finished.

Now the popular lake is reached by a 3-mi. trail following the old miners' road for much of its length, starting at 1.4 mi. on the Elliott Creek Road♦. Reference: *101 Hikes.* At the lake's W end the campsite is above the trail. A cut path leads around to the S end of the lake, keeping high across the large brush patch on a bearing for the low perennial snow/ice in Ida Gulch. Many relics in the basin bear evidence of the enterprise and hardship undergone by miners.

To reach the headquarters site and the valley of Clear (Ida on map) Lake, leave the trail where the wagon road crosses the creek.

In the claim-patterned basin of Goat Lake the Foggy Ledge and Mine (Penn Mining Co. workings) was the best known. Supplies and ore were rafted across the lake by scow; wagons on a puncheon road carried lumber and ore between the lake and the snow/ice slope in the gulch. Here a donkey engine pulled loads on a wooden sled along the 2500 ft snow surface and cliff to the minesite, located on Cadet Peak's steep flanks at about 4600 ft.[114]

Osceola Pass (5520′+) is above the mine on the divide to Pride Basin. An old trail existed from the S end of the lake directly to the pass, then descended S to mine tunnels and a building (now gone) at the N edge of the Mayflower Glacier; the trail was shown on the Glacier Peak topographic map of 1899.

Cadet Lake can be reached from Goat Lake; a good route can be taken through open forest, bearing right to a heather area at 5500 ft. Hike E to the notch on the divide, then descend to Cadet Lake. Indians long have picked berries on and near the Goat Lake—Cadet Creek divide.

Ida Pass is an alpine route to Monte Cristo, much used by miners during the mining boom; the name is thought to relate to a dance hall girl visited by crossing the pass. From the Penn minesite take the long ledge right of the ravine onto snowfields of the New York Glacier (bearing 254° true) and make a traversing rise of 0.9 mi. to the pass. For the approach from Monte Cristo see Foggy Peak, South Route or second approach variation; or Addison Ridge, Approach (2), to beneath Sentinel Gap to begin a rising traverse.

Heather Lake (2410′) is reached in 2 mi. via trail no. 701 from 1½ mi. up Mt. Pilchuck State Park Road♦. See *Trips and Trails 1.* The lake is similar to Lake 22 in that both are set in rocky talus basins and cliff-ringed. The lake is a possible approach to the northern cliffs of Mt. Pilchuck.

Howard Creek occupies a deep canyon between Iron and Spire Mountains, the scene of much mining activity from 1897 to 1902. The Co-op Mine at 3500 ft was on a good horse trail to Howard Lake; located by Charles R. Howard. For existing route see Spire Peak.

Independence Lake (est. 3700′) is 0.8 mi. from the end of Coal Lake Road♦ (trail no. 712); North Lake is 3½ mi. Pass Lake is 0.3 mi., using trail no. 645. The camp area is located at the far end of the lake (North Lake Trail departs here).

Johnson Ridge Trail No. 1067 follows a scenic crest featuring *Scorpion Mountain* (5540′/1689 m) and *Sunrise Mountain* (5056′/1541 m), then passes Joan Lake (est. 5000′) just E of Scorpion. The trail drops off Johnson Ridge to Kelley Creek and Martin Creek (not maintained). To reach this trail from the S take U.S. Hwy No. 2♦ for 6½ mi. E of Skykomish, then turn N on road no. 2607 along the N side of Tye River. In 2 mi. turn N again on Martin Creek Road No. 2604, then follow nearly 4 mi. to the end. Hike out along a road survey trail to the E bank of Kelley Creek to cross trail no. 1067 (now overgrown).

To reach the N end of the trail follow Johnson Ridge Road No. 273 about 5 mi. to the trail (see Beckler River Road♦).

Lake Twenty Two (2435′) is a 2.2-mi. hike via trail no. 702 (leave Mountain Loop Hwy♦ at 1.8 mi. E of Verlot R.S.). The lake, beneath spectacular waterfalls, and set in a deep cirque on the NE flank of Mt. Pilchuck, is in a Research Area. Camping and campfires are prohibited. Cross-country hiking opportunities toward Mt. Pilchuck.

Lime Lakes. Start on the N side of Mica Lake (see Crest Trail♦) for hiking opportunities. See Lime Mountain, also *Routes and Rocks,* pp. 36-38. These unique highland lakes occupy small basins carved by ice in the schist of the Milk Creek flank of the ridge. Vistas of Glacier Peak and the North Cascades. Several lake basins show scars of excessive camping adjacent to the lakes. Camp more than 100 ft. from lake shores.

Lost Creek Ridge Trail No. 646 extends from the Sloan Creek Road♦ at 3.2 mi. (1849′) and ascends to Bingley Gap (est. 4400′) at 3 mi., then traverses E above Lost Creek. There are six small ice patches on the N slope of Lost Creek Ridge, the largest being N of Round Lake and Point 6472. Round Lake (5040′+), surrounded by colorful volcanic cliffs, is reached by a short spur path; leave the trail about 1 mi. E of Bingley Gap and descend N from the 5600-ft saddle to the lake. The water fills a large breccia pipe and volcanic conduit. References: *Routes and Rocks,* p. 86; *101 Hikes.* To reach *Spring Mountain* (5770′/1759 m) from Bingley Gap (3 mi.; 4400′) follow the crest WSW (avoid a brushy rock point 0.15 mi. W of the gap by a S-side dirt slope traverse). Reach the broad heather slopes of the upper ridge, which curve NW to the small summit (4 hours from road).

The main trail (discontinuous 1 mi., but path) extends to Camp Lake, Sunup Lake, Lake Byrne (11½ mi.) and Kennedy Hot Springs (14 mi.). The trail along the ridge was built in the late 1920s by a Forest Service crew under Nels Skaar. The lakes portray exquisite beauty on a rolling timberline benchland.

Marble Pass (4176′) is reached by an overgrown mine trail from near the 45 Mine. Continue beyond the driveable portion of Williamson Creek Road (see Sultan Basin Road♦). The mine had a sawmill (2581′) to cut cedar, fir, and hemlock timbers.

Marble Gulch Trail, quite overgrown, is the northern approach. Cross the bridge at Silverton (23.1 mi. E of Granite Falls), hike a spur W, then walk down to locate the trail (extends ¾ mi. along river; alternate log crossing 250 yds W of Silverton). The historic trail switchbacks 2½ mi. to Marble Pass, keeping well E of Marble Gulch; if tread lost, ascend right to old traces near the pass.

Marten Creek Trail No. 713 begins 21.3 mi. E of Granite Falls (Mountain Loop Hwy♦) and reaches Granite Pass (1800-ft rise) in 4½ mi.; the final mi. is overgrown.

Meadow Creek Trail No. 1057 extends 9½ mi. to the Crest Trail♦ at 1 mi. NW of Pear Lake, near Fortune Ponds (jewels of water with blossoming heather and blueberries). Begin about 5 mi. up Rapid River Road (Beckler River Road♦).

Meadow Mountain Trail No. 657 spans an attractive ridge highland N of the White Chuck River. The contrast between the formerly ice-protected alp slopes and forested depths of the river-eroded lower valley is magnificent. Use Straight Creek Road♦ and hike the gated Meadow Mountain Road (no. 3128); keep right at fork. Reach the trail at about 5 mi. Reference: *101 Hikes.*

Meadow Mountain (6324′/1928 m) is a short hike from the trail on its S (est. 5400′) at about 4 mi. (campsites on trail).

Emerald Lake (5135′) is reached from about 4½ mi. on the trail; use a gap (est. 5800′), then descend to the lake. Diamond Lake (est. 5250′) is reached by descending a 1-mi. path from about 5¼ mi. on the trail; one can readily hike between the lakes.

Reach good campsites in 7½ and 9 mi., Fire Creek crossing in 10 mi., and White Chuck River Trail♦ in 12.2 mi.

Milk Creek Trail No. 790 is an old one (shown on 1913 maps); the creek's name is from the Suiattle Indians' name for its turbid color. Approach via Suiattle River Road♦; Crest Trail♦ (4000′+) is reached in 6.2 mi.

Mt. Dickerman Trail No. 710. See Mt. Dickerman.

North Fork Sauk River Trail No. 649 begins from inside Sloan Creek campground (¼ mi. spur from Sloan Creek Road♦ at 7.1 mi.; 2070′). The trail follows the river through great cedar forests and climbs to meet the Crest Trail♦ on a meadow highland in 8½ mi. (5900′+) at 0.6 mi. W of White Pass; camp spots at 1.7 mi., 5.0 mi. (shelter), and just W of White Pass. Red Pass is ½ mi. W of the Crest Trail junction.

North Fork Skykomish River Trail No. 1051 extends 9½ mi. from end of North Fork Skykomish Road♦ to connect with the Crest Trail♦ at Dishpan Gap. Pass Creek Trail No. 1053 branches S to meet the Crest Trail in about 4 mi. near Cady Pass.

Pacific Crest National Scenic Trail No. 2000: see Crest Trail♦.

Perry Creek Trail. This is an old trail—built in 1928. From the end of Perry Creek Road♦ to Stillaguamish Meadows (3 mi.; est. 5200′) where the trail fades; steep meadows continue toward Mt. Forgotten. Reference: *101 Hikes.*

Pilot Ridge Trail No. 652 (Blue Lake Trail) leaves the North Fork Sauk River Trail♦ at 1.7 mi. and climbs to Pilot Ridge in 62 switchbacks. Reach Johnson Mountain junction in 8 mi. from North Fork Sauk trail. Here a spur path (est. 1 mi.) leads atop *Johnson Mountain* (6721′ / 2049 m); a lookout cabin was built on the summit in 1938.

From the junction the trail forks again in ½ mi.; the E fork leads 250 yds to the upper lake's outlet (5625′). The W fork reaches lower Blue Lake (5194′) in 0.4 mi.; the trail continues S to Bald Eagle Trail♦ 2.4 mi. from Dishpan Gap, or 0.7 mi. by cross-country path. Reference: *101 Hikes,* pp. 116-117.

Poodle Dog Pass (4530′) is reached from the S side of the bridge and spur into Monte Cristo townsite (trail no. 708; 1.8 mi.); possible fee or restrictions if parking on private land, but public has legal right to trail entry. Silver Lake (4260′), a gem hidden beneath Silver Tip Peak, is 300 yds across the pass (*101 Hikes*). It is interesting to note jointing to the NW of the lake. Terraces up to 20 ft above the lake indicate the former level before water cut the lower outlet. An aerial tramway once lowered ore from the O & B Mine on the E side of Toad Mountain; one of its tunnels is rumored to bore 3500 ft, beneath Silver Lake. The nearby Boston-American Mine (3000′) was a later attempt to reach the mother lode of gold in the district. A single adit was bored in the 1920s to a depth of 2400 ft into Toad Mountain. The tunnel encountered a major fault, losing all traces of the lead.

From Poodle Dog Pass a 3-mi. spur trail extends along a scenic parkland ridge, past Wilmans Pass, and down into the basin of Twin Lakes. These unique jewels of water are in a subalpine basin (4600′) nestled beneath the palisades of Columbia Peak. Reference: *Mountaineer,* 1918, pp. 18-19.

Silver Lake can also be reached in 3½ mi. from a hiking road spur ¾ mi. NE of Mineral City (see North Fork Skykomish Road♦). The trail begins at the first switchback end (est. 2800′), then contours NE to cross Silver Creek in 0.4 mi. (uncertain maintenance; possible relocation); an earlier, more direct trail from Mineral City to the lake is abandoned.

Troublesome Pass (est. 4500′), dividing Troublesome and Silver Creeks (0.7 mi. W of Twin Lakes), can be reached cross-country from the S fork of Silver Creek or from Twin Lakes.

The route from Index to Poodle Dog Pass was once the main trail to Monte Cristo; the mining camp of Galena, a settlement at the junction of Silver Creek and the North Fork of Skykomish River and a local base for supplies, is now deserted. In 1874 there was a stampede to Mineral City, after Hans Hansen located his Norwegian Mine and in 1890 Fred and J.M. Wilmans financed the first packhorse trail up Silver Creek and across "Poodledog", an important stimulus to the boom. The colorful word for the pass is from a prospector's name for marmots.

Red Mountain Trail No. 651 (1 mi. to former lookout) starts at Sloan Creek campground (Sloan Creek Road♦ at 7.1 mi.).

'Seventy Six Creek Trail. This is an old trail of historic interest from the Monte Cristo townsite across the divide between '76 Gulch and Silver Creek. Frank Peabody, one of the original discoverers of the Monte Cristo riches, began the Peabody Mine along '76 Creek—a single tunnel bores into the slopes of Wilmans Spires; higher (est. 4000') is the '76 Mine, where talus meets the rock wall. The non-maintained trail crossing of the divide (4820'+) to Mineral City was once called "Willmann Pass."[115] The correct name is Wilmans Pass: it was the original packtrail route from the Skykomish drainage, and was used as the approach to Monte Cristo for the first three years of development.

This route offers an approach to Columbia Peak.

Sloan Peak Trail No. 648 (Cougar Creek) begins from Sloan Creek Road♦ (at 5.3 mi.); here a dirt spur leads S to the river (1897'). Cross a footlog and follow logjam flagging to markers on left where trail takes bank to old railroad grade. Follow this right about ½ mi. to where trail bears left off the grade and shortly picks it up again on a switchback; follow the grade about ¼ mi. to where it climbs out as a trail to the wooded spur W of Cougar Creek (good campspots at 2 and 3½ mi.—where meadow forms near 3500 ft). Timberline is about 4700 ft—reach from SW corner of meadow by steep path.

Cougar Lake (4602') lies in a pocket ½ mi. E of Bedal Peak; leave the trail where it crosses the creek (est. 3040') and ascend the W fork cross-country (1½ mi. trail to lake).

Squire Creek Trail No. 654 (begun in 1927) starts from the end of Squire Creek Road♦ (est. 2000'); the rise to Squire Creek Pass (est. 4000') is about 3½ mi.; at about ¾ mi. before the pass it is simplest to bear directly upslope to the pass.

A striking feature of the Squire Creek valley is the beauty and frequency of waterfalls in lateral gorges; the glacially sculptured valley is cut in batholith, whose dominant exposed feature is the polished Squire Creek Wall. The name is for Squire Stewart, a pioneer of 1890. (The Indian name was Ke-kepalitch, meaning "shining trout").

Sultan River Trail goes up the E side of the N fork from Sultan Basin Road♦ (begin at final bridge) to Sultan King property W of Crested Buttes (condition uncertain). Maps dated 1922 show the trail marked to the head of the N fork. Old cabins existed W of Sheep Gap at 3600 ft and at the head of Elk Creek at 2900 ft; both the Jones and Marvel properties are near the head of the latter, W of Hard Pass.

South Fork Sultan River: An old trail went up the stream to the Golden Eagle property, NE of Kromona mine. Trails in the Sultan drainage not shown on current maps are mostly vanished.

Sunrise Mine Trail to Headlee Pass, originally built by miners, now begins at the end of Sunrise Mine Road♦. Manley's Cabin (2320') is reached in 0.4 mi.; the fading trail soon climbs through boulder-strewn Wirtz Basin to the pass (2 mi., 4600'+). The Sunrise Mine, near the head of Vesper Creek, operated during the early mining era. Packers made the trek across Headlee Pass with its 37 switchbacks renowned. New operators currently threaten the wilderness resource of the area and have already caused considerable destruction in the Vesper Creek drainage (see Vesper Creek Trail♦).

The location of Headlee Pass (named for prospector F.M. Headlee) is incorrect as marked on current Forest Service maps; it is shown correctly on Brown's 1897 claim location maps and on the state 1909 G.L.O. map, but not on the Skykomish quadrangle of 1905. Its position is defined correctly in *Mountaineer,* 1916 (p. 65 photo) and 1918, pp. 12-14. The trail was first marked over the pass on the 1926 Forest Service map, but without naming. Reference: *Off Belay,* April 1975, p. 45.

Trout Creek Trail. The rough road from North Fork Skykomish River Road♦ (at est. 6 mi.) begins on the N side of the creek (gate may be locked); if passable, roadbed is rough. Hike past the Sunset Mine (est. 1 mi., 1400') to junction with S fork (est. 2200'). Former mine trails in the valley may be overgrown; a 1912 map shows a trail to the Merchant group of claims at 3000 ft on the NE slope of Gunn Peak. Numerous cabins were built in the area as bases for prospecting and mining. Discoveries began in 1897 but the height of copper mining did not come until 1918-1920.

Trout, Howard, and Barclay Creek all show pronounced effect of glaciation. Trout Creek is about 8 mi. long; at 5 mi. it divides into branches, each of which is fed by a small rock-rimmed lake set in an amphitheatre (Lake Simms and Sunset Lake). Water from the lakes drains through narrow outlets into a series of cascades.

Upper Suiattle River Trail No. 798 extends from Crest Trail♦ to Chocolate Creek. See Suiattle Trail♦ (Section II) for approach via Suiattle River Road♦ and Skyline Bridge. At 0.7 mi. upstream from the bridge the Crest Trail forks W, and in about ¼ mi. more Gamma Ridge Trail bears uphill. Reach Triad Creek Trail (E) at about 14 mi. from the road; this is also new start for Dusty Creek Trail♦ (W).

Lavas and gravels have forced the Suiattle River to flow in a large arc around the flanks of Glacier Peak. The river, which now features terraces of river gravels, along with Dusty and Chocolate Creeks, has cut deeply into debris termed the Great Fill; there is desolation from recent floods, with stands of dead timber drowned in gravels at the edge of Chocolate Creek gorge. Both Chocolate and Dusty Creeks have dumped outburst floods into the Suiattle valley; these could become hazardous on rampage.

The trail continues about 2 mi., along the broad pumice-covered valley floor, which produces a primeval forest of Douglas fir, cedar, and hemlock, but is impossible to follow after ⅓ mi. beyond Chocolate Creek; a cross-country route can be taken to Suiattle Glacier, about 4 mi. from Chocolate Creek.

Chocolate Creek Route. Once the Glacier Peak Trail S of Chocolate Creek was in good condition to glacier level (1939 map shows trail crossing from N to S side of the creek; then bearing SW). Ascend easy timbered slopes S of the creek; the broad lower spur narrows at about 4400 ft. Stay S of the spur at about 5650 ft to regain a saddle at est. 6150 ft (*Routes and Rocks,* p. 58). One can camp ideally in Rusk Basin (est. 6150′) S of the saddle; heather on a sloping bench (S of the Chocolate Glacier) screened by alpine firs and hemlocks, with stream water. This is the location of Camp Nelson, a little hollow just beneath timberline; the camp was used and named on the 1910 Mountaineer outing (*Mountaineer,* 1910, p. 27; *Mazama* 8, no. 12, 1926: pp. 37-39). One can continue hiking easily up Streamline Ridge to the glacier or make a traverse S to the Cool Glacier.

Vesper Creek Trail to Headlee Pass (est. 2 mi.) begins from the Century Explorations Co. road that extends up the W side of Vesper Creek for about 2 mi. from Sultan Basin Road♦ at 24.7 mi.; road may be rough. A cat road extends 1 mi. to 4200 ft; there is also a trail, up-bank to right of mine; follow for 900 ft altitude, cross to right side of Vesper Creek and skirt a waterfall, then continue to the basin with the small lake (est. 5000′) between Vesper and Sperry Peaks (2 mi.).

Weden Creek Trail No. 724 (Gothic Basin) is a classic improved miner's trail beginning at Monte Cristo Road♦ 1.6 mi. E of Barlow Pass. It is the original pack trail from Weeden station on the railroad to the Del Campo Mine of 1912; the trail led to a tunnel in Gothic Basin. The name is derived from an upper Sauk homesteader, O.N. Weedin, who killed three settlers during a land feud.

From the road (est. 2300′) follow a dry channel 200 ft downstream, turn left, and cross a river footlog. At about 200 ft before a mine cabin (est. 3 mi.—5000′) turn sharply uphill, right, and use a path on the right side of the stream (or a rib 300 ft higher); a rise W over a little ridge leads to Crater (Foggy) Lake in Gothic Basin (good campsites N side of lake). The mineralized zone and ice-polished rocks are evident.

An alternate route continues beyond 3 mi. and uses a path to the lake from the SE. Tin Cup Lake is an old name for the tarn NE of Crater Lake. Weden Lake (4280′+) is lower in the basin. Reference: *101 Hikes.*

West Cady Ridge Trail No. 1054 leaves North Fork Skykomish River Road♦ at Quartz Creek (est. 17 mi.; 2500′), crosses a bridge to climb SE to West Cady Ridge. *Benchmark Mountain* (5816′/1773 m) is nearly topped at 6½ mi., then the crest Trail♦ is met in about 1 mi., est. ½ mi. S of Cady Pass.

White Chuck River Trail No. 643 extends from the end of the White Chuck River Road♦ (2300′) to meet the Crest Trail♦ at Sitkum Creek (7.1 mi.). The trail was located by Harry Grey in 1914, who set a trap line to the Kennedy area. The trail originally was built in a rush by 60 men under Grey in the summer of 1916 to get horses to a lightning fire on Fire Mountain. During a rainstorm many tenderfoot helpers stampeded back down the trail; only eight veterans continued the project, reaching Fire Creek to find 700 acres burned. The trail to the head of the White Chuck was built in the 1920s, and the trail to Lake Byrne followed the general line of a steep goat path.

Deposits in the White Chuck Valley show that a large lake once formed here because of ice lobe damming from Puget Sound Basin. Meltwater forming the White Chuck carries a considerable quantity of sediment. The name is derived from a combination of English and Chinook, "glacial stream" and "white water."

Kennedy Hot Springs (3275′) is reached in 5¼ mi. from the road. The popular spring was discovered by William Kennedy, who had a cabin there in 1915.

Continuing S on the Crest Trail♦ reach Baekos Creek at about 9 mi. (total); at 12 mi. reach the open, subalpine basin of Glacier Peak Meadows (5400′+; campsites). Another 1.7 mi. via a rocky basin leads SW to Red Pass (est. 6450′).

Meadow Mountain Trail♦ junction is 1.4 mi. up the White Chuck Trail; it passes W of Fire Mountain in 4½ mi. and leads to the slopes of Meadow Mountain.

Glacier Ridge Trail No. 658 leaves the White Chuck Trail at 4½ mi. (est. 3400′), then connects with the Crest Trail♦ in 3.2 mi. Trail abandoned since 1972-; choked with windfalls.

Kennedy Ridge Trail No. 639 (incorrectly marked on some maps) begins at Kennedy Creek, (5.0 mi.) just W of the hot springs. It joins the Crest Trail in 1.5 mi. (est. 4150′); a path which once went steeply E about 1 mi. still can be followed. Reference: *101 Hikes.*

An alternate route to the upper ridge is from the Crest Trail junction with Glacier Creek (est. 5650′); open subalpine forest on the old moraine can be taken SE to the ridge (completely open in ½ mi.).

White Chuck Glacier Route. From Glacier Peak Meadows on the Crest Trail hike E into the flat basin on the S branch of the river; cross on rocks in rapids or on snow bridges in upper basin. Easy terrain leads around the valley corner eastward. Continue up the N side of the stream to the higher basin and ascend the prominent gully N to the basin with the terminal moraine and small meltwater streams to reach the lake (est. 6350′) at the SW toe of White Chuck Glacier. Skirt the lake on the W via ponds, boulders, and pumice. Reference: *101 Hikes.*

There is a larger lake (est. 6250′) beneath a northern tongue of the glacier. This lake's drainage forms cascades on slabs; one can cross below these at 5700 ft and climb N to the lake and its drainage basin.

An alternate more direct route to the gap N of the 6800-ft plug (route to northern tongue) is to leave the main trail about ½ mi. N of Glacier Peak Meadows. Hike E over humps to the river; cross on logs and climb NE up steep slopes to the river fork that comes from the gap.

NOTES

[1]Russell, *op. cit.*

[2]Forty-three small glaciers not in the Glacier Peak complex, clustered in two distinct groups, lie significantly W of the range crest between the North Fork of the Skykomish River and the North Fork of the Stillaguamish; seven of these, covering some 2.3 km^2, lie within the drainage basin of the North Fork of the Sauk River. The Sloan Glacier, which is the largest, has an area of 0.9 km^2, whereas the smallest glacier in the group has an area of only 0.1 km^2.

A northern group of five small glaciers is concentrated about Three Fingers and Whitehorse Mountains, an isolated subrange which has a N-S orientation. The glaciers lie within an altitude range of 2040 m to 1370 m and have a mean altitude of 1767 m (data from Inventory of Glaciers).

[3]J.E. Spurr, "The Ore Deposits of Monte Cristo, Washington," *22nd Annual Report U.S. Geol. Survey, 1900-1901,* pt. 2 (Washington, 1901), p. 787. Commenting on the steep valleys of the region (in particular the North Fork of the Sauk) railroad explorer Albert B. Rogers in 1887 stated there was more avalanche hazard here than in the Selkirk Range (Diary, p. 98).

[4]The Humid Transition Life Zone is generally not considered to extend above 1500 ft in the western Cascade foothills. The Canadian Life Zone occupies an ill-defined area at elevations between 3000 and 5000 ft and may extend lower (Howard E. McMinn and Evelyn Maino, *An Illustrated Manual of Pacific Coast Trees,* Berkeley (1946), p. 19). The Hudsonian Life Zone extends from about 5000 to 7000 ft, and is the highest zone in which trees are found. The Arctic-Alpine Zone is above timberline. (These biological life zones are based on the system devised by C. Hart Merriam in 1894.) More recently Franklin and Dyrness (1969) established new vegetation zonations for western Washington based on a single climax species, and these zones approximately match the old zones: coastal Sitka spruce, western hemlock, silver fir, and subalpine mountain hemlock.

The first zone relates to the narrow coast belt and mountain foothills (mostly below 150 m); soils are formed on glacial drift. There are many coniferous species, but the dominant ones are Sitka spruce, Douglas fir, western hemlock, and western red cedar. The western hemlock zone ranges from sea level to 600 or 700 m in Washington; major forest trees are western hemlock, Douglas fir, grand fir, and western white pine. The silver fir zone occurs along the W side from 600 to 1300 m; here the climate is cooler and more precipitation comes in the form of snow. The principal trees are noble fir, western hemlock, western white pine, Douglas fir, and western red cedar. The mountain hemlock zone extends from 1300 to 1700 m. The dominant trees are mountain hemlock, Alaska yellow cedar, and subalpine fir; present but less important are noble fir, Englemann spruce, and white bark pine (J.F. Franklin and C.T. Dyrness, 1969, Vegetation of Oregon and Washington: *U.S. Forest Service Research Paper PNW-80,* 216 p., cited *in* Barbara Spross Hansen and Don J. Easterbrook, 1974, "Stratigraphy and Palynology of Late Quaternary Sediments in the Puget Lowland, Washington," *Geol. Soc. Am. Bull.* 85:589-590).

[5]Gibbs, *op. cit.,* p. 492—see footnote 46.

[6]J.A. Vance, "The Geology of the Sauk River Area in the Northern Cascades of Washington," Univ. of Washington, Ph.D. diss., 1957. Fills show the Sauk once discharged westward at Darrington during this time. Ash fill terraces can be seen along the Sauk, White Chuck, and Suiattle from the cataclysmic explosion of Glacier Peak; there are remnant terraces of pumice fills near Darrington and at Sauk Prairie. Stream gravels along the Stillaguamish contain evidence of Glacier Peak lava.

[7]*Ibid.*

[8]Valley glacier complexes formed repeatedly in upper river drainage basins during the Pleistocene. During glacial maxima individual valley glaciers merged to form long confluent ice streams (certainly over 25 mi. long). Glaciers that flowed W past the abrupt western range margins may have spread out as broad piedmont lobes along the eastern part of the Puget Lowland when the Puget Lobe was not present (Stephen C. Porter, "Quaternary Glaciation in the Southern Part of the North Cascade Range," *Geol. Soc. America Bull.* (1975), p. 6, 120, preliminary paging).

[9]Dwight R. Crandell, "The Glacial History of Western Washington and Oregon," *in* Wright, H.E., Jr., and Frey, D.G., (eds), *The Quaternary of the United States,* Princeton, N.J., 1965, p. 346. Mackin (1941) and Vance (1957, pp. 292-299) demonstrated that alpine glaciers in the western Cascades dwindled or disappeared prior to arrival of the Puget Lobe. Fraser Glaciation in Late Pleistocene time began with development of alpine glaciers in the western Cascades. These glaciers were out of phase with the Puget Lobe and began to retreat from maximum stands before 15,000 yrs ago, but the Cordilleran Ice Sheet continued to grow (Crandell, p. 345).

[10]Porter, *op. cit.,* p. 89. See also pp. 91 and 97.

[11]J.H. Mackin, "Glacial Geology of the Snoqualmie-Cedar Area, Washington," *Jour. of Geology* 49 (1941): 449-481.

[12]*Ibid.* The existence of a Pleistocene valley glacier system in the Pilchuck area, separate from the Cascade icefield, was first noted by Mackin in 1941.

[13]*Ibid.*

[14]Ward Carithers and A.K. Guard, "Geology and Ore Deposits of the Sultan Basin, Snohomish County, Washington," *Washington Division of Mines and Geology,* Bull. 36 (1945), pp. 11-13.

[15]Vance, written commun., 1973.

[16]The N-trending Cascade rocks rest with angular unconformity on a deeply eroded pre-Eocene basement. Just as N of the Skagit River, there is a general NW trend of foliation, fold axes, and lithologic units in this region, an alignment with earlier regional structural grain. Folding and various periods of faulting have helped shape drainages. The N-trending Straight Creek Fault separates the Shuksan Metamorphic Suite (low-grade meta basalts and phyllites) and the Skagit Metamorphic Suite to the E. This fault is a major dislocation zone—a tectonic boundary between the two pre-Jurassic suites. The Straight Creek Fault, extending N from the Beckler River, through Monte Cristo and N into British Columbia, separates schists and gneisses on the E from unmetamorphosed and weakly metamorphosed rocks on the W. It is a major geologic boundary and structural feature of the North Cascades. The fault trends N-S at about 122°30′ longitude and separates two geologic terranes of quite different pre-Tertiary rocks. The western terrane consists of low-grade metamorphic rocks known as the Easton schist or Shuksan Suite (the latter can be traced S as discontinuous inliers). This unit consists of two members, the Darrington phyllite and the Shuksan greenschist, which have been thrust to the W over unmetamorphosed Paleozoic and Mesozoic sedimentary and volcanic rocks.

E of the Straight Creek Fault is the Skagit Suite, a heterogeneous series of schists and migmatites which extends S to the Mt. Stuart uplift (Grant, p. 38). The migmatitic Skagit gneiss is the most prominent metamorphic unit in this zone. Pre-Tertiary igneous granitic rocks, largely quartz diorite, intruding rocks of the Skagit Suite, are widespread E of the fault.

[17]An important episode of Cenozoic igneous activity was the intrusion of Cloudy Pass batholith; potassium-argon dating places it at 22 million yrs ago. (R.W. Tabor and D.F. Crowder, "On Batholiths and Volcanoes," *U.S. Geological Survey Prof. Paper No. 604* (1969), p. 1). Much of this batholith in the Glacier Peak area lies under a relatively thin roof of older regionally metamorphosed rocks. Volcanism which may be related to the Cloudy Pass batholith is recorded by the volcanic breccias and tuffs of Gamma Ridge, which were extruded between early Miocene and Pleistocene time (p. 19). These volcanic rocks lie on the batholith on the E side of Glacier Peak and may belong to the same episode of igneous activity as the batholith.

[18]The strike of the beds is fairly consistent. The conglomerate-argillite series (Swauk formation) of the eastern rim of Sultan Basin is composed of beds of quartzitic conglomerate, quartzitic sandstone, and argillite. These beds trend N-NW along the peaks and ridges that form the eastern rim of Sultan Basin from Hard Pass through Crested Butte, Gothic, and to Sperry Peak. On Crested Butte the beds dip eastward but become progressively steeper northward until at Headlee Pass they are nearly vertical. Exposures of granodiorite in this area are probably outliers of the Index batholith which underlies Sultan Basin and adjacent areas.

[19]The types of mineral deposits are veins, disseminated sulfides, and placers. Mineralization often occurs along contacts, and is related to granitic intrusions. Commonly iron oxide-stained zones are present in the general area of lode claims (many claims are not found now because of dense vegetation and lack of workings). Zones of disseminated sulfides are found in many places. Tiny grains of sulfide minerals scattered through the country rock are a common occurrence. Sulfides commonly weather to brown iron oxides and the stained rock stands out from the adjacent unaltered rock.

[20]On the divide between Barclay and Lewis Creek the metamorphic quartzite and schists stand out in bold, craggy fashion and at elevation 3000 ft are in contact with the underlying granodiorite. The Gunn Peak formation, extensively metamorphosed, consists of quartzites, schists, slates, limestones, and cherts, with interbedded lava flows.

[21]Alan Robert Grant, "Chemical and Physical Controls for Base Metal Deposition in the Cascade Range of Washington," *Washington Div. Mines and Geology,* Bull. 58 (1969), pp. 74-75.

[22]Vance, *op. cit.* Cascade intrusive rocks are predominantly granodiorite in composition, although they range from quartz diorite to quartz monzonite in composition. The Squire Creek stock is a 30-sq. mi. belt of 5000-ft relief. The general elevation of the peaks within the stock is less than that of their neighbors; the others, including Three Fingers and Whitehorse form a ring of high summits outside the contact. Also see Grant, p. 75. A new study has given potassium-argon ages of granitic intrusions in the Index-Monte Cristo-Stillaguamish area. These batholiths consists of several types of granitic rocks which were intruded at different times in the Tertiary, now shown to be older than the previously dated Snoqualmie and Tatoosh plutons of the central Cascade Range (Robert S. Yeats and Joan C. Engels, "Potassium-Argon Dates of Plutons in the Skykomish-Stillaguamish Areas, North Cascades, Washington," *U.S. Geol. Survey Prof. Paper 750-D* (1971), pp. D 34-D 38). The results indicate that the Index batholith is not a northern extension of the Snoqualmie. Radiometric dating yields an intrusion span of about 24 to 48 million yrs for Granite Falls, Mt. Pilchuck, Squire Creek, and Monte Cristo stocks, and the Index and Grotto batholiths (pp. D34 and D 36). The view that acidic intrusion added material to the core of the North Cascades throughout a considerable part of Cenozoic time is thus supported.

[23]Jointing is a striking structural feature in this area, for it cuts all types and ages of rock; the erosion of joint planes has often caused development of deep gorges.

[24]The Glacier Peak transverse structural belt is an E-W zone of echelon sheeting and jointing. On the W the country rock is Mesozoic-Tertiary sediments and volcanics and Tertiary granitic rocks. The exposed western end passes through

the Sultan Basin district, then the belt cuts through to upper Silver Creek and the Monte Cristo district (Grant, p. 45); in 1901 the geologist J.E. Spurr noted the parallelism of the joint system and principal sulfide veins.

The system strikes NE across the Straight Creek Fault to later cut the Cloudy Pass pluton, being best exposed in the Miners Ridge area. The copper deposits of this area are localized along this zone (Grant, p. 45); the structure passes through the Holden Mine area.

[25]L.K. Hodges states that Joseph Pearsall was on Hubbart's Peak when he sighted rich ore veins high on Wilmans Peak; another report states Pearsall and Frank Peabody made the discovery from the divide near Silver Tip Peak. It is speculated the time was near July 4, since the first claims bore patriotic names, but there is less agreement on how the name "Monte Cristo" became generic to the district. One wonders whether Pearsall had witnessed the gold rush in California and now recalled that impressive event or whether one of them was merely inspired by the recollections of a classical myth to recognize in this mountain terrain a deposit of vast wealth. Pearsall and Peabody met with John MacDonald Wilmans in Seattle, then the three hiked to the divide to verify the discoveries. Peabody may have exclaimed "There is enough gold here to make the Count of Monte Cristo look like a pauper" (Wilkie, *A Broad Ledge of Gold,* p. 9). It is recorded that Wilmans chose the name because of his fondness for the Dumas book (Wilmans diary, John MacDonald Wilmans Papers, University of Washington Library). Another source says that one evening in 1890 prospectors were discussing the name for the town around a campfire; Fred Wilmans suggested "to name this Wonderful place Monte Cristo after the Place named in the Novel." All agreed. (Sam Strom, Memories of pioneer days of Upper Sauk River 1893-1936. Sam Strom Papers, University of Washington Library, p. 7). Soon the two Wilmans brothers funded development and moved to Monte Cristo.

[26]By the summer of 1890 miners built a trail from Silver Creek to Monte Cristo; supplies were then taken in by pony pack train. Galena received its name from deposits of silver-lead ore; as prospecting developed, large bodies of copper and iron-carrying gold were found. Claims are said to have been made as early as 1874, when silver was located (Carithers and Guard, *op. cit.*, p. 36), but until the trail was cut little development was done; Amos Gunn, a pioneer who built Gunn's Hotel at Index in 1891, built the wagon road in 1894. John Scott opened a hotel at Galena, where a branch railroad line and smelter were planned; the length of the entire route caused very high transportation costs. The most notable property of the many in the Silver Creek district was that of Bonanza Mining and Smelting, 1 mi. above Mineral City (Hodges, *op. cit.*, pp. 26-33; see also *20th Annual Report U.S. Geological Survey*, pt. 1, p. 495). Names of claims in the district smack of the pioneer: Jim Dandy, Silver Tip, King Bee, Wild Welshman, Nest Egg, Lucky Monday, Hard Pann.

[27]Sam Strom, *op. cit.,* pp. 13-15. Machinery for sawmill was hauled in as the road progressed. A freight crew using four- and six-horse teams took in heavy machinery weighing tons; along with mules and oxen, they moved like a large caravan behind timber fallers and road builders.

[28]*Ibid.,* pp. 17-19. The apparent first discovery of the pass was in 1891 by F.M. Headlee and Fred Anderson, while prospecting along the Sauk River. But in the capricious communication of the day Barlow Pass was discovered again in 1892 and named. This "little Spring of Water Changed the Whole plan. The Sauk River project was abandoned though the Pioneer Trail was built at great cost" (*ibid,* p. 19). Attention became centered on this pass as best for a railroad because of the discovery and influenced by ore prospects near Silverton. Soon a wagon road was built by the Neste brothers and others across this route. In 1892 Barlow had 30 surveyors under him, and it was estimated 1800 men worked on the railroad simultaneously.

[29]A Pennsylvania syndicate purchased the claims of Mackintosh and others June 2, 1896. The new wagon road enabled 30 men to work at the Foggy Mine all summer, and a crew worked through the winter. The ledge was traced to cut through the divide E, and a tunnel on two levels was dug at a depth of 800 ft. This active company planned a tunnel directly to Monte Cristo to place them in a better shipping position. In addition to the headquarters building and cabins below Goat Lake the company later built a warehouse and office at Barlow Pass—a fire destroyed their irreplaceable records.

[30]Gray, *The Gold of Monte Cristo,* p. 4. An 1892 newspaper source stated that Eastern capital invested over $300,000 in various prospects which had cost only $20,000 in development; another account states that by the end of 1891 $300,000 had been spent in five mining districts.

[31]A 300-ton Fraser and Chalmers concentrator (from Chicago) enabled the company to convert the lower grade ores into a compact article easier to transport to the Puget Sound Reduction Co. lead smelter at Everett. The Mystery Mine had about 4000 ft of underground workings. During a 6-month period this mine produced 32,500 tons of ore (L.K. Hodges, *Seattle Post Intelligencer,* 27 July 1896, p. 1). A large tunnel (1400′) was built in 1896 between the Pride of the Mountains and Mystery Mines. One of the most interesting mines was the Rainy, next to Glacier Creek across from the collector station, with an 800-ft adit which bored into Pride of the Mountains Range. This was the only mine able to operate in the winter; its ore was delivered by a covered mule-drawn tram. But it was the Wilmans tramway, about 4000 ft in length, serving the Comet and Monte Cristo Mines, which was the first in the area, operating (1893) before the Golden Cord and Pride of the Mountains tramways (*Everett Herald,* 17 August 1893). For notes on the Comet Mine, see footnote 79.

In general character the ores of Monte Cristo are constituted of galena and iron pyrite, the latter carrying gold; ore values ran from $4 to $50 in gold. Lode deposits are the most common type of mineral occurrence in the Cascade Range. Most periods of base metal deposition are genetically related to Late Cretaceous-Tertiary intrusive episodes; much of the mineralization is associated with a series of underlying igneous intrusions and extrusions. The minerals were deposited in veins after magmatics were forced into openings when upthrust fractures occurred in the crust. Various other metals such as zinc, gold, lead, silver, and nickel occur in lesser quantities and often are associated with the predominant copper mineralization (A. Robert Grant, "Chemical and Physical Controls for Base Metal Deposition in the Cascade Range of Washington," *Washington Division of Mines and Geology,* Bull. 58 (1969) 107 p.). The Cascades can be considered primarily a copper province and most values in ledges came from copper minerals. The principal occurrences seem to be along transverse structural zones. Josiah E. Spurr, who examined mineral deposits in the Monte Cristo area in the summer of 1900 for the U.S. Geological Survey, said the veins were easily followed, regular in shape and strike. Early mining activity was directed to exploration and development of these high-grade veins. Most discoveries and resultant early production in the Cascades are credited to hard work of early prospectors, rather than to conscious use of geologic principles. The most prominent vein was known as the Monte Cristo. Though it was one continuous vein, its ownership became divided between the Monte Cristo Mining Co. and the Pride of the Mountains Mining Co. The eventual mining disappointment resulted because ore was profitable only for a short distance from the surface. The rough terrain and transportation problems precluded economic consideration of lower grade deposits.

[32]The Trenton Iron Co. designed and constructed the Bleichert System tramway terminals (Monte Cristo Mining Co. Records, vol. 1, p. 256, University of Washington Library). The loading terminal was at the Pride of Mountains tunnel and the anchorage-tension station was located atop Mystery Hill. The system used patent locked wire rope. A separate 3700-ft line took ore from some Mystery tunnels to the common discharge terminal.

[33]Many avalanches were recorded between 1894 and 1897: in November 1894 a snowslide hit the cabin at Pride of the Mountains Mine and buried a man; in December 1895 a man was killed by a slide onto the railroad bed; on February 20, 1896 a great slide caused the men at the Mystery tram to flee for their lives—the mine had to close because a wheel in the head house was broken; in the winter of 1897 an avalanche carried a man over a cliff above Goat Lake; in spring 1897 two were killed by an avalanche below the Mystery Mine. That men adapted to the deep winter snows is shown that snowshoes and skis were used to haul supplies at Silverton and Monte Cristo (1892-1893); skis here introduced from Scandinavia may have been the first ever used in the Cascades.

[34]The puzzle of Ida Pass revolves about sparse documentation, but it is here concluded that topographic maps have not placed the historic name at the correct location. The authentic claim location map of mining engineer Webster Brown (in Hodges, *op. cit.*) shows Ida Pass at 1.4 mi. SSW of the upper end of Goat Lake (SE of Foggy Peak); there is a claim marked Ida en route. The claim (also shown on the Kroll map, 1960) lies in the contact zone (schist, granite) in Ida Gulch; the claim was staked on the ore vein (patent applications dated 8 March 1898 identify Ida Gulch and New York Glacier as being behind Goat Lake and on the NE flank of Cadet Peak).

The pass (6040′+) was apparently a popular route for early miners crossing from Goat Lake and the Foggy Mine to Monte Cristo, the reasons including a desire to visit a girl named Ida. A photo caption from the outing of The Mountaineers in 1918 additionally corroborates the proper location: "Foggy Mountain and Ida Pass seemed to overhang the southern end of the lake" (*Mountaineer,* 1918, p. 14; see also p. 15; see also p. 31—refers to a 6000-ft pass to Glacier Basin and Monte Cristo); see also *Mountaineer,* 1917, p. 68. Also verbal confirmation (Edith Bedal interview, 4 November, 1975). The evidence does not support the location marked as Ida Pass (5960′+) on the Monte Cristo quadrangle (1965) and Glacier Peak quadrangle (1901), which is between the western spur of Foggy Peak and Addison Ridge. Spurr's journal suggests that miners called this pass Sentinel Gap, and he noted: "Head of Goat Lake, below mine, above foot Ida Gulch. Ida Gulch contact of granite and schist" (Notebook no. 2, Monte Cristo District, J.E. Spurr Papers, National Archives). Spurr mentioned the New York Glacier, Mayflower Glacier, and Osceola Pass. Photographic and handwritten caption proof of proper locations of Ida Pass and Sentinel Gap, Mayflower Glacier and Osceola Pass is given in photography by Spurr (Josiah E. Spurr Collection, Western History Research Center, University of Wyoming). The New York Glacier, on the NE slope of Cadet Peak, was partially crossed en route to Ida Pass. (Spurr noted that it had receded 250 ft in 2 yrs.) The first pass N of Cadet Peak (Elliott-Cadet Creek divide) was termed Osceola Pass and the slope on the E holds the Mayflower Glacier (*The Northwest Magazine,* February 1895, p. 2 photo). The lake marked Ida Lake (1.1 mi. W of Goat Lake) is incorrectly marked on current maps; the Brown map shows it as Clear Lake.

[35]Monte Cristo was incorporated May 2, 1893 with Charles L. Colby as president. Everything in the town, ranging from the market to horse barns, the saloons to the church, was built closely together, mostly along Dumas Street. The lure of employment and wealth brought in miners from many states and nations. Though it became known as a "Hell Roaring Mining Camp" (Strom, *op. cit.*, p. 44), and had its share of fights, shootings, and accidental explosions, the miners had a strong regard for fair play and during work every man was on hand to help others. When a miner shot and robbed a jewelry peddler in July 1896, purportedly to gain the favors of a dance hall girl, a posse relentlessly hunted him. The lure

of money is again noted when a girl of 15 was taken into custody after running away from home "with the purpose of entering upon a life of shame" at Monte Cristo (*Everett Herald,* 26 October 1893).

Wildlife did not fare well when venturing into the sight of mining camps; men shot at bear, goat, and deer on sight. During morning coffee in a cabin, a miner heard a grunting sound, then looked outside for an easy shot at a 400-lb. bear. It is on record that a goat of about 400 lb. hung itself from a pole in a freak accident at Marble Pass.

[36]L.K. Hodges, "Monte Cristo Mines," *Seattle Post Intelligencer,* 27 July 1896, p. 8.

[37]The railroad, which ended at a unique turntable W of the townsite, was ready for business on September 19; a special early train carried 156 persons. Construction of the track was a project that Hodges called a triumph of engineering skill. In 1894 two carloads of concentrate were daily sent to the smelter; one day in June 1895 50 tons of ore from the Mystery Mine went on train cars. In 1901, after vast reconstruction, trains revived their glory—one day featuring a brass band and 500 excursionists.

[38]The cable tram to the 89 and Pride of Mountains mines was not completed until July 26, 1894, being much delayed by railroad completion. The tram of the Wilmans brothers to the Comet Mine was actually in operation sooner than the one from the syndicate.

[39]By 1897 the lyric mood of hope began to change into uncertainty. Though it was a bonanza year, prosperity was interrupted by silver price decreases, broken cables, and a repeat of the 1896 track washouts, all contributing to mine shutdowns. When the devastating fall 1897 rains and floods destroyed the railroad bed, miners fled to desert the townsite for 3 years; some of them hiked over Indian Pass or Cascade Pass to seek their fortunes in the Methow and Okanogan region. In 1905 the Wilmans brothers re-opened the Comet Mine and purchased numerous holdings in the district in a new episode of activity.

[40]There was a boom in Silverton in 1893; in that year the Hoodoo Mine was the most promising. Bonanza Queen Mine, reached by wagon road up Deer Creek (N of Silverton) and the St. Louis Mine were active producers. Many claims ran across the summit to Clear Creek; cliffs along the divide showed red stain. At the high altitude of 5000 ft the Helena No. 2 shipped 80 tons of ore in 1896. There were many claims near Marble Pass, on the flanks of Hall Peak, and on the E flank of Long Mountain.

The November floods are not uncommon during drenching W-slope Cascade precipitation in late autumn, and their devastating effects were probably not comprehended by railroad engineers. While on the lighter side "a kitchen at Robe sailed away on the roaring river," a report of November 26, 1897 (*Everett Herald*) stated that the bridge over the Sauk was gone and half of the Robe bridge, as well as much of the railroad bed in the canyon, had been torn away. This calamity stifled Silverton until March 25, 1900 when track rebuilding brought new trains; this event produced a second boom in 1900-1901 at the town and nearby mines.

[41]An interesting sidelight was the three-story Big Four Hotel, built by the Rucker brothers in 1922, which for some time was the leading resort in the Pacific Northwest but was destroyed by fire in 1949. The vista became famed and was termed as a rival in beauty to the Alps.

[42]R.S. Yeats, "Geology of the Skykomish Area in the Cascade Mountains of Washington," Ph.D. diss., University of Washington, 1958. See also Hodges, *op. cit.,* pp. 33-35; and Carithers and Guard, *op. cit.* Weaver, who made a geologic map of the district in 1910, said the ore bodies are chiefly enclosed in granodiorite. This Mesozoic igneous body intrudes the Gunn Peak metamorphic series; both of these units are overlain by Tertiary volcanic and sedimentary formations; Charles E. Weaver, "Geology and Ore Deposits of the Index Mining District," *Washington Geol. Survey,* Bull. No. 7 (Olympic, 1912).

[43]In 1892 Andrew Merchant discovered ledges in upper Trout Creek. The property of 12 claims became the Merchant Mine, at 3100 ft; a trail was built up the creek and W to the claims. The Sunset claims (36) were located in June 1897. For years the Sunset copper mine was the most consistently producing property in the Cascades. A surface tram ran from Index to Trout Creek, then two trams went to the mine. In 1918 a 125-ton concentrator mill was completed. The Non-Pareil Mine was located on the E side of Trout Creek, above the Sunset group at 2200 ft. The Uncle Sam Mine on the N side of Barclay Creek (est. 3200′) was reached by trail from Baring, an earlier trail than the one up Barclay Creek. The Howard Creek prospects (copper and silver ore) had the Co-operative group—at 3500 ft and higher (there were seven mines in the basin by 1891). The claim pattern and trail led to Howard Lake. Opposite the river from Trout Creek a gravity tramway led to the Ethel Mine. The Copper Bell group (1897), SW of Lake Isabell, had a narrow guage surface tram; the name was later changed to Bunker Hill Mining and Smelting Co. In 1912 the Index-Galena Lumber Co. built track from the Great Northern up the North Fork of Skykomish River to get timber, with the definite intention to extend the line.

[44]By 1891 high-grade copper was found and there were 300 locations in Sultan Basin. In 1892 a 4½-mi. trail was built from Silverton to the headquarters camp of the 45 Consolidated Mining Co.; this was once a good trail with bridges and puncheon, and a shelter cabin. It was often used by pack trains (Alec Jones' 45 pack animals—see *Everett Herald,* 18 August 1897).

Fissure veins contained in complex shear zones were the most important ore deposits. The veins in Sultan Basin rarely fill sample fissures, so conditions for prospecting and mining were not easy.

Trails went up Sultan River's N fork to Sheep Gap and a

long trail went over Hard Pass to Mineral City. The Sultan King property (recorded in 1892 as Sultan Queen) was reached by trails from both the Sultan and Silver Creek. A wagon road of 27 mi. was eventually built up the valley. In 1920, 24 tons of ore were shipped from tunnels of this property. Four mines (the 45, Iowa, Florence Rae, Sultan King) had produced 4016 tons of ore by 1923 (Ward Carithers and A.K. Guard, Geologic map and sections of the Sultan Basin, Snohomish County, Washington, in *State of Washington Div. Mines and Geology,* Bull. 36 (1945): 37; see pp. 36-78 for Sultan Basin properties). At the head of Vesper Creek the Sunrise prospect was recorded in 1897 (F.M. and T.E. Headlee and G.E. Humes, later owned by Sunrise Mining Co.). Various prospects in the Elk Creek area, such as the Jones and Marvel, and a cabin 5 mi. up the creek, are obliterated. The Golden Eagle (ten claims), near the head of the Sultan's S fork were reached by trail. The Kromona (nine claims) in the S fork drainage were prospected about 1900.

On the N side of Red Mountain claims of the Sultan Basin Mining Co. run across the ridge that projects NW from the mountain. Trails lead to three groups of workings (Calumet claim at 5000 ft—the third group of workings 0.7 mi. W of Iowa Camp) on the ridge summit. Not much was done until 1914 when the property became the Iowa Mining Co., with a mine camp near the river and trams from workings to the bunker (ibid., pp. 62-68). The 14 claims of the Florence Rae property (staked 1908-1911) are very complex. The mine is at the head of the talus slope at the cliff base on the rough E face of Red Mountain. The higher wall rock is the old metamorphic series and is intruded by peridotite and both these rocks are intruded by a quartz diorite mass lower and several dikes and complicated faulting. Most copper in crude ore was produced in 1918-1919 and 1938-1941.

[45]Carithers and Guard, *op. cit.,* p. 39. In early days some 3185 tons of ore were shipped. During the few years this mine operated (1896-1902?) it accounted for 75 percent of the basin's volume. The 45 Consolidated Mining Co. was formed (1897) from earlier companies which did preliminary work. The mining establishment had 25 patented claims on steep slopes at the head of Williamson Creek, with the main camp buildings at 2500 ft; the workings were N of camp at about 4000 ft (the "Hard to Beat" tunnel at 4500 ft and the Deu Pree were the main ones). Ore was transported by a steep 3700-ft tram (completed November 1897) to camp and the bunker. After sorting, the best was packed by horses and wagons (the first shipments—1896—were packed to the railroad at Silverton). In 1898 the 13,000-ft tram over Marble Pass to Silverton was nearly completed, but the railroad washout ruined plans; at the time there were nearly 5000 tons of ore ready to ship. Plans shifted to the Sultan Basin, considering first pack train, then puncheon road, and even railroad transportation. The tramway to Silverton was not completed until 1901; during this period the company built the puncheon road (6 mi. from Sultan Basin), a project that placed them in debt from which they never recovered (ibid., pp. 40-46). The subsequent final disaster came in February 1913, when an avalanche swept the camp buildings to the foot of the mountainside.

At one time there were railroad survey plans to Copper Lake. This rugged area had claims on the SW side of the lake and on Little Chief Mountain. Here seven patented claims and two millsites were on the steep mountain slopes. The Milwaukee group (eight claims) N of the trail to the lake and the Silver Horseshoe group (ten claims) N of the lake were staked in 1940 (pp. 47-49).

[46]Another map (U.S. North West Boundary Survey, Map of Western Section, 1866; Records relating to the United States-Canadian border, Record Group 76, item 188, National Archives) shows "Reported Trail" trending SE along a river course, which is probably the North Fork of the Sauk, but could be the Suiattle or White Chuck. A connecting trail is shown from the North Fork Skykomish River going NE to the Sauk, and also a trail to Lake Wenatchee. The map vaguely defines a trail up either the Suiattle or Cascade River to Lake Chelan (however, Sketch No. 4 in the Edwin F. Johnson report marks "Trail to Lake Chelan" up the "Suiatl River"). The reconnaissance report of Gibbs indicates he believed the Skywhamish was "probably interlocking with the sources of Chelann lake, and the Wenatshapam" (Report of George Gibbs on a reconnaissance of the country lying upon Shoalwater bay and Puget's sound, Olympia, W.T., March 1, 1854; 33rd Cong., 1st sess., *House Ex. Doc. No. 129* (Washington, 1854), serial 736, p. 491); Gibbs knew of an Indian route over Cady Pass from the last northern fork of the Skykomish River (Quaiquoss Creek). There was an Indian trail N from Snohomish City via Lake Stevens on to Lake Whatcom (Indian trails near foothills are shown on Map of Western Part of Washington Territory, Gibbs, 1856, in Carl I. Wheat, *Mapping the Transmississippi West, 1540-1861,* vol. 4: From the Pacific Railroad Survey to the Onset of the Civil War, 1855 to 1860, San Francisco, 1960, p. 44). This correlates well with the lateral valley near the western base of the range, mentioned by Gibbs. The Indians stated they had a short canoe portage from the Skywhamish across the South Fork Stoluckwamish and then another from its N fork to Sah-kee-me-hu branch of the Skagit (Gibbs, *op. cit.,* p. 492); he learned of this portage to the Sauk while traveling northward in the first months of 1854. Gibbs felt that the route appeared to continue N by way of Whatcom Lake to Frazer's River (1866 map) and that horses had been taken all the way. See also Leo Braun, "History of Sauk-Suiattle Tribe," *Concrete Herald* 50:6. As late as 1887 Indians were portaging canoes to the Sauk River at the location of Darrington (A.B. Rogers, Diary, p. 92).

Gibbs (1854-1858) learned that Sauk valley trails went to the Stillaguamish and E to Lake Chelan. It is known Chelan (Tsilads) and Wenatchee Indians crossed to hunt and trade on the W side; potatoes were traded for hides and wool (Nels Bruseth, "Indian Stories and Legends of the Stillaguamish, Sauks, and Allied Tribes," Arlington Times Press, 2d ed., 1950, p. 13; Bruseth also portrays various Indian terminology and spelling).

[47]"Report of Edwin F. Johnson, Engineer-in-Chief, to the Board of Directors, April, 1869, and Report of Surveys, executed in 1867, by Gen. Ira Spaulding and Gen. James Tilton," *Northern Pacific Railroad,* Hartford, 1869, pp. 18-19.

[48]Gibbs, *op. cit.* See footnote 46.

[49]The river was labeled "Stolokwhamish" on Map of Washington Territory, 1856, and Province of British Columbia, J.W. Trutch, 1871. The similar spelling "Stolokwhamisk" is given on New Map of British Columbia, R.T. Williams, 1884. The earlier map, The Provinces of British Columbia and Vancouver Island, John Arrowsmith, 1859, titles the river "Stoluchwamish," but Map of a Part of Washington Territory, James Tilton (Sept. 1, 1859) shows the river in two forks, named "Stalukahamish."

Dr. Charles Buchanan discussed the name Stillaguamish as the earlier true name "Stoh-luk-whahmpsh," meaning "river tribe" (Edmond S. Meany, *Origin of Washington Geographic Names,* Seattle, 1923, p. 290); Gibbs identifies them as the Stoluchquamish, and his map uses Stoluchwhamich (Map of the Western District Washington Territory Showing the position of the Indian Tribes and the Lands Ceded by Treaty, George Gibbs, 1855, in Wheat, *op. cit.,* p. 36). Various spellings ultimately evolved to Stiliguamish (Map by General W.T. Sherman, Route from Fort Ellis Montana to Fort Hope, British Columbia traveled by General Sherman July and August, 1883; Report of Secretary of War, 48th Cong., 1st sess. (Washington, 1883), serial 2182, pp. 203-252), then Stilaguamish ("Report of W.W. De Lacy to Lt. G.H. Mendell, *Roads in Washington Territory,* Report of Secretary of War, 1858, 35th Cong., 2d sess., *Senate Ex. Doc. No. 1,* serial 998, p. 1222). No doubt the many variances are because Salish Indian words are difficult to spell and pronounce with the English alphabet.

[50]*Map,* 1855, Wheat, *op. cit.* To the N tribes were shown as the Kwehtlamamish, Stoluchwhamish, Nooknachamish, and Sakumehu. Sky-wha-mish as the river spelling is shown on Maps of Surveyor General, Washington Territory, James Tilton, 1856, 1860, and 1870. Variants of the name include Tuxpam (Wilkes map, 1841). After 1870 the word Skykomish became into general use.

[51]"Red-water, a mountain stream which takes its rise in the Cascades." Report of De Lacy, *op. cit.,* p. 1221. It was also called Tuli-Dachub (Bruseth, *op. cit.,* 1st ed., p. 17).

[52]Sherman map, 1883, *op. cit.* Yet the name was shown "Sauk" on the June-July 1883 map by Goethals and Downing (Map of Reconnaissance Showing trails followed by Lieutenant George W. Goethals—Corps of Engineers; Record Group 77, W 402-2, National Archives.

[53]Report, *op. cit.,* pp. 72-73. See also pp. 12-26, 65-77 for reports on surveys executed in 1867. Carlton descended SE and found a lower summit at 5117 ft between the main South Fork Skykomish and the Wenatchee. He thought a "sharp backbone" (p. 73) of 1200 ft above the real summit would need a 3-mi. railroad tunnel; he did not examine the S fork, but estimated it barely practical. There is an element of ambiguity in the recorded position of "Cady's Pass" (not today's Cady Pass). Sketch No. 3 in the Johnson report shows the survey running up the North Fork Skykomish and Quaiquoss Creek, probably West Cady Creek, to the trail summit at 6146 ft to apparently meet closely with the "Sawk" route.

[54]Map of the country from Lake Superior to the Pacific Ocean from the latest Explorations and Surveys, to accompany "Report of Edwin F. Johnson, Engr-in-Chief, to the Board of Directors, November 1867," *Northern Pacific Rail Road Company,* Hartford, 1867 (Bancroft Library). The map shows the Saak and Sto lu qua mah (Stillaguamish) Rivers.

[55]Walker to Thomas A. Canfield, General Agent N.P.R.R., Olympia, W.T., 16 October 1867. Northern Pacific Railroad, Secretary Series, Lake Superior and Puget Sound Company. Minnesota Historical Society.

The Carlton party had no tent and in heavy rain could not examine the Wenatchee drainage; but they went down several miles and believed the course was direct. Carlton reported that the South Fork "Sky-wamish" rises in a lake on the summit and the Wenatchee at the same place, a little to the S. Possibly this refers to Rapid River, Pear Lake, and Lake Creek.

[56]Report, *op. cit.,* pp. 74-76. See also Tilton to Canfield, 19 October 1867, Northern Pacific Railroad, *op. cit.* Treadway reported winter had set in and feared all would perish in snows unless a retreat was made. On October 8 in rainy weather the river rose rapidly, but they took a canoe 10 mi. farther (probably reaching along the Sauk to a position between the White Chuck and North Fork Sauk). When the river rose 3 ft in 12 hrs, his six Indians forecast trouble on fords beyond. Tilton felt no pass as favorable as Cowlitz or Snoqualmie existed in the area.

[57]Report, *ibid,* November 1867, p. 31. See also pp. 18-19. Sketch No. 4 in the Johnson report indicates a trail up "Suiatl R" with the legend "Trail to Lake Chelan."

To complete Treadway's reconnaissance Edwin F. Johnson in June 1870 assigned a field party composed of D.C. Linsley, John A. Tennant, H.C. Hale, and Frank Wilkinson. The party with Indians went from Chief Whometkan's (Wawetkin's) camp on the Sauk River on June 16, and in two weeks reached Indian Pass (Tennant was the first white man to reach this pass; he had crossed to the E side to meet Indians with horses). To the N Tennant and Linsley located and named Linsley Pass (now White Pass), which they believed was a shorter route for a railroad. They descended to the Columbia River and guided by Chief Wawetkin travelled up Lake Chelan and Agnes Creek. See D.C. Linsley, "Pioneering in the Cascade Country," *Civil Engineering,* No. 6 (June 1932), pp. 342-343. Linsley estimated $13 million for the cost of a railroad via the Skagit, Sauk, and Wenatchee Rivers; a shortcut up the Stillaguamish would reduce the route by 10 mi. Treadway had previously noted the 3-mi. portage between the "Steilaquamish" and "Sawk" (Report, *op. cit.*, p. 75 and Sketch No. 4).

In 1872 the Thomas P. Morris party covered the Sauk and other routes (Morris to Milnor Roberts, 26 July 1872, Northern Pacific Railroad, *op. cit.*). During surveying for the Great Northern Railroad in September 1887 Albert B. Rogers traveled the Sauk to Indian Pass and found survey evidence (Diary, pp. 94-95, Albert B. Rogers Papers, University of Washington). He noted that there was a fear of the upper Sauk among Indians and only four knew the route (p. 91); he felt Indian Pass was the only Skagit to Wenatchee route, but that it was not as good as the Skykomish.

[58]I.C. Russell, "A Preliminary Paper on the Geology of the Cascade Mountains in Northern Washington," *20th Annual Report U.S. Geol. Survey, 1898-1899,* pt. 2 (Washington, 1899), pl. 18.

[59]*Ibid,* p. 192. He added, "fifty glaciers are in view within a radius of about 30 miles" (p. 193). Russell mentioned a few glaciers existed on somewhat detached peaks, some of them 10-20 mi. W of the crest of the range. The most numerous are "at the heads of high-grade valleys in the granitic peaks about Monte Cristo." These glaciers had also been observed earlier by Bailey Willis.

[60]*Everett Herald,* 19 September 1895.

[61]*20th Annual Report, U.S. Geol. Survey, 1898-1899,* pt. 1 (Washington, 1899), pp. 122-123.

[62]H.B. Ayres, "The Washington Forest Reserve," *19th Annual Report U.S. Geol. Survey, 1897-1898,* pt. 5 (Washington, 1899), p. 285 and pl. 81.

[63]*Ibid.*, p. 286.

[64]Mt. Baker National Forest files, Federal Records Center, Seattle. Most trails were built by the Forest Service between 1920 and 1940 as part of their fire prevention program. Numerous lookout cabins were built at strategic positions, to provide comprehensive visual coverage; telephone lines were strung along trails to these lookouts. Among the problems crews had with rains and horses, there were occasional attacks from grizzly bears, once a nuisance to sheep and herders. Such men as Nels Skaar, Harry Bedal, and Nels Bruseth were crew chiefs in the late 1920s and early 1930s, and did much of the trail planning and construction; among their efforts were Lost Creek Ridge, Pugh Creek, Rat Trap Pass, Crystal Creek, and Three Fingers.

[65]William Whitfield, *History of Snohomish County, Washington,* vol. 1, Chicago, 1926, p. 216.

[66]*Ibid.* See also *Index News,* 13 October 1910, p. 1.

[67]*Index News,* 9 October 1913, p. 1.

[68]Stevens had helped the Canadian Pacific Railroad locate their line across the Rocky Mountains; he had also located the lowest pass in Montana for the Great Northern. In the Cascades his explorations included the Entiat River,Icicle Creek, Methow River, and under pressure from Bellingham parties he went by rowboat up Lake Chelan and over Cascade Pass, examining valleys along the route. He then followed the Wenatchee River to Lake Wenatchee, and "on up the summits of several small valleys which debouched in the lake . . . From Indian Pass I followed the crest of the Cascade Mountains clear through to Snoqualmie Pass." (John F. Stevens, "Great Northern Railway," *Wash. Hist. Quarterly* 20 (1929): 112.) After his return to the summit of the range Stevens sent Mr. Haskell, his assistant, to proceed up Nason Creek and down the Skykomish River valley to survey.

[69]Charles R. Wood, *Lines West,* Seattle, 1967, p. 26; see also pp. 22-33.

[70]*Ibid,* pp. 113-130, 134-135, 144-150. The avalanches which caused the disaster at Wellington March 1, 1910 were caused by late season snowfall, as much as 1 ft per hr (in 6 days some 11 ft accumulated); the eventual slide, nearly ½ mi. in width, swept down barren, burnt avalanche-prone slopes into Tye Canyon. Various slides stalled the train for 5 days on a siding 400 yds W of Wellington (a few escaped by hiking to Scenic on February 28, using ropes and the help of the train crew). Ironically the train at one time could have backed into the tunnel, but the superintendant feared smoke and lack of ventilation. The total death toll was 101, with only 17 from the train saved; the disaster cost the railroad $81 million.

[71]H.A. Annen Collection, University of Washington.

[72]The property includes two cabins at 3500 ft and workings 1000 ft higher, about ½ mi. NE of Red's summit. The 4500-ft tramway connects the mine (4450′) with the road bunker. Claims are located as high as 5000 ft under the summit. Another tramway, about ½ mi. N, runs to Iowa Mine at 3000 ft.

[73]*Everett Herald,* 27 October 1892.

[74]The Forest Service map of 1931 showed Lewis Peak at Del Campo's location. But the U.S. Surveyor General Office map of November 25, 1922 showed Lewis at the position of Morning Star and Flag at Del Campo's place. Flag Peak again was at the Del Campo location on 1922 and 1926 Forest Service maps.

[75]U.S. Surveyor General Office map, November 25, 1922.

[76]L.K. Hodges, *Mining in the Pacific Northwest,* Seattle, 1897. Another portrayal is given: "two great canyons, parted by a towering ridge which terminates in Wilmans mountain. It is along the back of this big mountain porcupine that the great glacier lies" (*Everett Herald,* 1 September 1892).

[77]The name Wilmans Peak was affixed to the mountain just E of Monte Cristo by some of Mr. Wilmans' friends near the turn of the century (John MacDonald Wilmans Papers,

University of Washington Library). The Wilmans peaks and spires have had various confusing names, successively or simultaneously. The earliest name probably generalized for the entire group of spires and peaks, but a review of the literature indicates that the popular usage in mining times applied to the spires seen from the townsite. But J.E. Spurr's Geological Sketch Map of the Vicinity of Monte Cristo, Washington (Spurr, *op. cit.,* plate 80) calls the higher peak *Wilman Peak* and the spires *Needle Peaks* (see also photo, plate 81).

The forestry report of H.B. Ayres titled the spires "The Needles," (H.B. Ayres, "Washington Forest Reserve," *19th Annual Report U.S. Geological Survey 1897-1898,* pt. 5 (Washington, 1899), pl. 95) and a photo in *The Coast* (1904) titles them "The Sentinels." Both the terms Needles and Sentinels obviously are due to appearance. But Wilmans Peak continued to be the usual name for many years until spelling was altered.

The term "Wilman Peaks" for "Two sharp peaks one mile southeast of the town of Monte Cristo" was an official name proposal of The Mountaineers in 1917 (*Mountaineer,* 1917, p. 92); this would refer to the North and West Spires.

The southern flank of the Spires, sloping into '76 Gulch, was highly prospected and mined during boom times. This name was given by Joseph Pearsall, who first located the claim "Independence of 1776"; now the entire ledge, gulch, and creek go by the abbreviation.

[78]Spurr, *op. cit.,* caption facing p. 802. Spurr says of the spires, "pinnacles produced by erosion along fault zones."

[79]This highest mine in the area became the property of the Wilmans brothers. It consists of a single adit which bores through the Spires to emerge 1500 ft above Glacier Basin; a collapsed tunnel permits passage of only 600 ft of the original 3000 ft. A railroad track for tram cars was dug across a steep slope from the tunnel entrance to the bunker, which stood from 1899 to its collapse in 1958. A cook shack and bunkhouse stood on a nearby cliff edge.

An aerial tramway lowered the ore from the bunker, on the brink of a rock protrusion, to the "Count" in a single span, and then on to the townsite concentrator. Until the winter of 1970-71, one of the original four cables from the bunker to the "Count" was still spanning the gully; the cable parted that winter.

The Hopeful Mine (at 5150') is now largely collapsed. It was one of the older mines in the area. The rails were made of wood with steel straps spiked atop for a running surface. The '76 Mine is on the SW side of the Spires at 4000 ft, where the rock wall meets the talus.

The highest minesite on the NW side of the Spires is the Golden Cord (4400')—actually the upper levels of the Justice Mine. The nearby Justice (3700') consists of an extensive adit tunnel and a main stope to connect with the Golden Cord. The 6800-ft main tunnel bores beneath Mystery Ridge to terminate directly beneath the entrance of the lower Mystery Mine.

[80]The Penn Mine "lying far up on Foggy Mountain" (*Mountaineer,* 1918, p. 14).

[81]Rosemary Wilkie, *A Broad Ledge of Gold,* Seattle, Shorey Bookstore, 1958, map and p. 39.

[82]L.K. Hodges (Hodges, *op. cit.,* 1896) called Sloan "a square block with another of triangular form set upon it." Matthes (1906) pointed out that blocks quarried by glaciers are first loosened by frost. Massive rock seldom allows breaking and dislodging by glacial processes, but where joint fractures are closely spaced, quarrying will proceed with more ease, as on Sloan's E face (see F.E. Matthes, The Geologic History of the Yosemite Valley," *U.S. Geol. Survey Prof. Paper 160* (1930), pp. 89-91.

[83]A party of four Mountaineers in 1923 saw the names Bedal and Skaar carved on summit rock, relating to the first ascent. It is interesting that a challenging alpine peak such as Sloan, which frustrated club-affiliated climbers of experience at least three times, would be first scaled by seasoned woodsmen with no technical background; it is also a reflection of the times, and the lack of communication, that this ascent was never properly documented. In late September 1929 Bedal and Skaar returned with Harold Engles to find a fire lookout site. They first tried a route from the NW, then traversed around on the E to what Bedal had termed the "corkscrew" route (they used calked boots on the glacier, with no ice axes). Several interviews with Engles (1972, 1973) indicates that on this ascent they found a tin can with names below the summit, probably from an earlier attempt.

[84]Bruseth, *op. cit.,* 2d. ed., p. 35.

[85]Historical notations, Harold Engles, personal commun., 1975.

[86]George Vancouver, *A Voyage of Discovery to the North Pacific Ocean,* 1 (London, 1798): 235. On May 2, 1792 Vancouver was near New Dungeness. His entry reads: "The land which interrupted the horizon . . . between the N.W. and the northern quarters, seemed, as already mentioned, to be much broken; from . . . its eastern extent round to the S.E. was bounded by a ridge of snowy mountains, appearing to lie nearly in a north and south direction, on which mount Baker rose conspicuously; remarkable for its height, and the snowy mountains that stretch from its base to the north and south" (p. 227).

[87]Nels Bruseth Papers, University of Washington Library (*Tribes,* 2d ed., pp. 31, 35); also papers, Mt. Baker National Forest files (Tech. Center; Sedro Woolley); see also *Mountaineer,* 1954, p. 49.

[88]This name was probably applied by the Gerdine survey party from contemporary usage of prospectors and railroad surveyors. The earliest appearance on maps, so far as known, is the geological sketch map of I.C. Russell (1898); see footnote 58, pl. 18; also named on Map of Washington Forest Reserve (1898), 19th Annual Report U.S. Geol. Survey,

1897-1898, pt. 5 (Washington, 1899), pl. 74. This interesting map shows a northern fork of White Chuck River curving N of Glacier Peak, occupying the turbulent stream known as the Suiattle. The name Great Glacier Peak is shown on the 1874 map, Asher and Adams' Washington (Washington State Library, Olympia).

[89]W.D. Lyman, "Lake Chelan, the Leman of the West," *Overland Monthly* 33 (March, 1899): 199.

[90]*Ibid.*

[91]Russell, *op. cit.*, pp. 99-100.

[92]R.W. Tabor and D.F. Crowder, "On Batholiths and Volcanoes—Intrusion and Eruption of Late Cenozoic Magmas in the Glacier Peak Area, North Cascades, Washington," *U.S. Geological Survey Prof. Paper 604* (Washington, 1969), p. 24.

Although lavas of Glacier Peak display textures more typical of andesites, chemically they are dacites. Recent studies indicate the normative composition of the volcanic rocks of Cascade volcanoes is dacite, but the name andesite has lingered from earlier field investigations (andesite, the extrusive equivalent of diorite, is widely characteristic of mountain-making processes around the borders of the Pacific Ocean; it is a grey or red quartz-free rock, less fluid and relatively high in silicates compared to basalts).

[93]*Ibid,* p. 55. In early Miocene time Cloudy Pass batholith intruded the metamorphic rocks between Lake Chelan and Glacier Peak, guided by the regional foliation and compositional layering in the host rocks. Other granitic stocks are the Sitkum, E of the White Chuck River and the Cool, on the SE side. Between early Miocene and Pleistocene time thick andesite lava and tuff extruded on and near the exposed batholith; these Gamma Ridge rocks were erupted W of the Cascade crest onto a mountanous terrain. The conspicuous loop of the upper Suiattle River is due to diversion around the eruptive center of growing, extrusive rocks of Gamma Ridge, prior to earliest Glacier Peak time. Below Milk Creek the river flows in a northwesterly course parallel to the crest of Lime Ridge and the bedrock structural trend.

[94]*Ibid*, pp. 1, 27, 28. Studies indicate that the area covered by flows from the volcano was never significantly larger than that covered today. The broad, high area S of Glacier Peak shows no lava outliers; it represents a highland that probably prevented flows from traveling beyond (p. 59). The broad base of the volcano merges with the summit plateau of the Cascades only on the S; it rises some 4000 ft above this plateau and covers an extent of about 22 mi.^{2}

[95]Eruptions consisted mostly of dacitic lava, without much basaltic flow and pyroclastic debris. Compared to similar volcanos, little pyroclastic material is interbedded with the flows. The younger flows, barely dissected, descended into valleys, where they remain on the bottoms or cling to slopes. Large debris flows in the Suiattle and White Chuck Valleys attest to a period of violent volcanic activity at this time.

[96]*Ibid,* p. 24. This flow of dacite is uniform in slope, appearance, and lithology. Dome cones of dacite erupted in viscous masses partly cooled into irregular heaps and blocks.

[97]Chocolate Creek was forced to spill over a confining lava ridge, then cut a gorge. When volcanic activity waned, streams began deeply incising the fractured lavas and unconsolidated valley fill, which was more easily eroded than the surrounding ridges of metamorphic and granitoid rocks. Continued floods of debris from today's Chocolate and Dusty Creeks, which have carved deeply into this extensive outwash plain, keep the Suiattle River pinned to its eastern bank.

[98]*Ibid,* p. 45.

[99]J.A. Westgate, et al., "Late Quaternary Tephra Layers in Southwestern Canada," in *Early Man and his Environments in Northwest North America,* The University of Calgary Archeological Association, University of Calgary, 1970, pp. 15-16 and fig. 4.

Distinctive tephra layers are identified in late Quaternary deposits. There appear to be two closely spaced eruptions; the broad swath is over 600 mi. long and 400 mi. wide at the eastern extremity.

[100]The 1901 Glacier Peak quadrangle shows four named glaciers: Honeycomb, White River, White Chuck, and Suiattle. The latter has also been termed "Cashmere Glacier," shown adjacent to Glacier Gap (U.S. Forest Service records, Portland, Aug. 1929 photo). Russell in 1898 estimated the confluent névé fields on and near Glacier Peak covered an area of some 10 mi.^{2} in extent (Russell, *op. cit.,* p. 193).

[101]The Chocolate measures 4.2 km along its longitudinal axis. Its area is 2.5 km^2 and its mean altitude is 7900 ft. This very active glacier gained an estimated 400 m between 1950 and 1955 (Austin Post, et al., "Inventory of Glaciers in the North Cascades, Washington," *U.S. Geological Survey Prof. Paper 705-A* (Washington, 1971), p. A20 and pl. 3).

The adjacent, less active, North Guardian began advancing in 1956, with small gains until 1968 and length increment of 140 m. Its area is 1.1 km^2, length 2.1 km and its mean altitude is 7500 ft. Now nearly in equilibrium, the glacier trends ENE to the head of Dusty Creek.

[102]The Cool Glacier advanced in the 1950s; it has 1.6 km^2 area and an 8500-ft mean altitude. Small glaciers are located on the SE side of Glacier Peak N and higher than the Suiattle Glacier and W of the Cool; these drain into the Suiattle. The largest is the Gerdine (8900′ to 7400′).

[103]At the glacier's high point (Glacier Gap, 7200′+) on the volcano, the divide to the Suiattle Glacier is now barely spanned by an ice patch, where it was well merged when maps were first compiled. The highest mutual location of the glaciers is a point at 7829 ft on the northern slope of the Kololo Peaks. The White Chuck, however, rises as high as 8000 ft on the broad uplift W of these peaks. Its principal ending is at about 6450 ft, just above a lake located in a broad, moraine-filled basin of low relief. The several ter-

minations drain to the White Chuck River. Russell was intrigued by this glacier at the "head of White Chuck Creek" (Russell, *op. cit.*, p. 192) with its expansive terminus and radial crevasses. Toward the snout, longitudinal compression gives rise to a typical splaying crevasse pattern. The glacier has retreated 430 m between 1949 and 1967 partly due to its relatively low mean altitude of 6850 ft and now has become nearly stagnant ("Inventory of Glaciers", pl. 3). The 18th century trimline shows clearly on the N valley wall.

Evidence of a rapid retreat of the glacier following constant recession is characterized by stagnation and downwasting of an extensive ice area producing chaotic hummocky topography consisting of an irregular ground moraine with numerous small closed ponds and depressions. The upper valley of White Chuck River is associated with glacial erosional topography. There are surficial deposits resulting from mass-wasting, fluvial and volcanic processes, pyroclastic debris, mudflow sediments, and alluvium. Glacial deposits show drifts of different ages. Younger deposits near the glacier are characterized by sharp moraine crests, abundant micro-topography, and poorly integrated drainages. Older deposits have more gentle slopes, rounded moraine crests, and integrated drainages.

[104]The Vista (2.7 km) heads on the E side of Kennedy Peak and trends NE between the Ermine and Ptarmigan Glaciers to Vista Creek at about 6100 ft. The Ermine is 2.6 km long and terminates at 5600 ft. The Dusty (2.6 km) ends at about 6150 ft, but with a mean of 7800 ft is higher than the Vista or Ermine. The name "Pumice Glacier" was once proposed for the largest glacier on this flank (*Mountaineer,* 1917, p. 93).

[105]L.A. Nelson, "Record of Ascents of Glacier Peak," *Mountaineer,* 1910, p. 25; see also *Snow Sentinels,* p. 118. Party members have not been positively identified, but it is known some of Gerdine's survey groups at this time included Darcy Bard, Sam Strom, A.H. Dubor (cook) and Rufus Stebbin (packer). They traveled from the White Chuck Valley via the White Chuck-Suiattle divide, a hard trip since they packed poles. The sub-summit later called Disappointment Peak provided an illusion that almost discouraged continuation to the summit dome. The next ascent was made later in 1898 by I.C. Russell, using about the same route but beginning at White Pass.

[106]Rusk was clearly near the snout of the Cool Glacier (27 August 1906) when he commented "we found issuing streams of Chocolate-colored water" (*Tales,* p. 169). He named this glacier Chocolate Glacier; earlier (p. 160) Rusk named the present Chocolate Glacier the Cool for his companion, confirming his text regarding the route used on the climb. The names were apparently exchanged some time prior to 1910.

[107]They found no record of a N-side ascent and in the summit register jotted "steep intricate crevasse system." On July 23, 1936 Norman Bright and Homer S. Smith used the "glacier on the NW side" probably repeating a similar route. The 1935 party descended Frostbite Ridge.

[108]The party used the approximate descent route of the August 1935 party. Sigurd Hall and Dwight Watson climbed Glacier Peak on skis July 4, 1938, beginning from Mica Lake and using a route N of Kennedy Peak, then the Vista Glacier. They ascended steep snow and a bergschrund onto the high arm of Dusty Glacier to the level shoulder above North Guardian Rock and E of Rabbit Ears. Drifted snow along the steep rock wall on the S flank permitted a narrow ledge traverse along the cliff to the margin of the upper Chocolate; this led to the middle peak's summit rim. On the descent they skied W of the Rabbit Ears via the Kennedy Glacier.

[109]The climb was made from camp near the Dusty Glacier. Ulrichs first attempted a route near its headwall, but was frustrated by crevasses, then made an intricate passage of the icefall to the Chocolate Glacier; its left portion was ascended to the summit (5½ hours from camp).

[110]Fred Stadter, "Glaciation in the Glacier Peak Region," *Mazama* 8, no. 12 (1926): 58.

[111]Bedal and Engles left a trail crew camp below Tupso Pass in the morning to search for a lookout site on Three Fingers. Slick rock during a snowstorm made the crossing of a 6-ft gap about 20 ft from the summit of the South Peak unduly perilous (the route here used a chute and a face to the gap; a crack in the gap comes out on the S face). They then continued to the Three Fingers-Big Bear saddle and descended Squire Creek in the rain and dark to Darrington in a 1-day marathon. With a favorable report on the summit as a lookout cabin site, approval and a budget were secured during the winter. The next summer they went to the summit to begin blasting (12 boxes of dynamite were eventually used); a piece of drill steel and a ladder were placed across the gap. Meanwhile a crew built a trail across the rocky slope from Goat Flat to "saddle camp" (Camp Pass), used as a construction base; tent sites can still be seen. A telephone line was strung along the trail. A 650-ft tram with winch was used to haul material for the 14-ft x 14-ft building, which was completed in 1932. Source: Harold Engles, personal commun., 1973 and 1975.

[112]Nels Bruseth Papers, University of Washington Library; also in Mt. Baker National Forest files, Seattle.

[113]Newspaper reports concerning its discovery in 1891 are in conflict with other sources that indicate William Mackintosh located a number of claims in the basin in 1890.

[114]The Foggy Mine has been described as an "eyrie perch, perfectly secure from snowslide" (*Everett Herald,* 22 October 1896). The mine area consists of a notch blasted from the cliff, which still contains the building ruins. Here is the site of the Foggy No. 1 tunnel. A single adit tunnel bored completely through the ridge N of Cadet Peak and emerged just

above Mayflower Glacier. Maps and Spurr's journal show these workings and contemporary names. He wrote, "Below the tunnel for probably 700-800 ft is a great snowslide, broken from the front of New York Glacier, which itself is half a glacier and does much of the work of one" (J.E. Spurr journal, 11 September 1900, National Archives).

[115] *19th Annual Report U.S. Geol. Survey, 1897-1898,* pt. 5 (Washington, 1899), pl. 76, 77, p. 373.

"The Mule was Undisturbed:

The Monte Cristo Mountaineer says: A mule belonging to the geological survey pack train and heavily loaded with kitchen utensils, missed his footing and fell 105 feet down the mountainside above Sunday Creek Falls. The fall spilled the hard tack in every direction, sent the jams and jelly tins bowling merrily down into 76 creek, and knocked sixteen kinds of Skandinavian milk tickets out of the cook stove, but the mule arose as if from a pleasant dream and ambled along with the rest of the pack train down Sauk valley apparently uninjured."

EVERETT HERALD
19 September 1895

"There is nothing that appeals to the mind of man so strongly as the chance of finding gold and silver ore"
A Monte Cristo observation
EVERETT HERALD
April 7, 1892

SECTION II

East Side of Cascade Crest:

STEVENS PASS AND WENATCHEE RIVER TO SUIATTLE PASS AND RAILROAD CREEK

". . . clear-cut, white and blue, against the azure sky, a hundred miles away, a chain of snowy peaks, bold and serrated even in the far distance. These peaks are the cradle of the lake."

WILLIAM D. LYMAN, 1899

The length of the Cascade crest, which intervenes between W- and E-flowing streams, is some 25 mi. between Stevens Pass and Glacier Peak. The N-trending crest maintains consistent altitude and is punctuated only by peaks of moderate importance until it reaches Glacier Peak, a magnificent Quaternary stratovolcano, and the fifth highest mountain in Washington State, which marks what has long been considered the beginning of the semi-explored North Cascades heartland. Because the Suiattle River arcs about the E and N slopes of the volcano, positioning it W of the crest, Glacier Peak is described in Section I.

This section includes the Cascade crest from Stevens Pass to the head of the Suiattle, then all terrain E of the river to Suiattle Pass. The NW limit of this section is the narrowest span in the great pincer of the Suiattle, where the White Chuck and Suiattle Glaciers meet 2½ mi. S of the volcano's summit.

Just S of Glacier Peak the axial trend bows E, extending along the DaKobed Range, then veering N to Buck Creek Pass. This eastward deviation in the crest from a northerly course across an upland may have been caused by doming over the Cloudy Pass batholith in early Miocene time.[1] The broad glacier-blanketed area S of Glacier Peak "is anomalously high and might be considered to have been once protected by a lava apron." Lacking lava outliers, this area probably represents a highland that hindered southward-traveling flows.[2]

The NW-SE structural trend of the Cascades, which was inherited from early folding, is best displayed here by orientation of master valleys such as the Wenatchee, Chiwawa, Entiat, and Lake Chelan. Between these trenches, high continuous ridges which can be defined as subranges E of the Cascade crest exist because of resistance to erosional forces. These—the Chiwawa, Entiat, and Chelan Mountains—are the alpine climax of this section. These parallel uplifts oblique to the main axis of the range, anticlines which average 33 mi. in length, are characterized by a rolling, subdued aspect in their southern portions, but increase in height and alpine complexity northward. They display a well developed series of cirques, glaciated valleys, and surficial deposits; major valleys have large tracts of morainal topography. Cirques, aretes, U-shaped hanging troughs, and gently sloping glacial valley floors are characteristic of alpine glaciation. Except for the dominance of Glacier Peak, the general level of the higher peaks, which are strikingly accordant when viewed from a distant perspective, is about 8200 ft. The subrange crests, which are decidedly asymmetrical, descend quite regularly to form an accordance sloping eastward.

The first of the NW-trending subranges, the Chiwawa Mountains, is defined by the Chiwawa River and the White-Napeequa drainage. The principal summits, Fortress, Chiwawa, and Buck, provide sharp angular outlines—high bare mountains that reveal their structure. The pioneer scientific observer here, Professor Israel C. Russell (1898), was first to carefully study the span of high peaks from the Cascade crest to the mouth of Chelan River, a distance of 65 mi. His geographic report concluded, "the country is exceedingly mountainous."[3] Later, a club outing report summarized, "it is a place of colossal architecture, peaks, canyons, and glaciers all of majestic scale."[4]

The Entiat Mountains, uplifted after faulting, bordered by the Chiwawa and Entiat Rivers, climax in Mt. Maude, Seven Fingered Jack, Mt. Fernow, and Copper Peak; about two dozen peaks in the upper part of the Entiat River drainage basin rise to altitudes in excess of 8000 ft. These monumental gneissic summits generally exhibit poor rock quality, a feature apparent from the absence of massive cliff faces without a great number and close spacing of couloirs, and the volume of talus largely swept down by avalanche. Competing cirque glaciers have produced ragged aretes through the plucking process. These mountains have been aptly described as "a network of glacier-torn peaks."[5] The middle portion of the Entiat Mountains is a ridge some 5 mi. wide, much of it glaciated upland averaging 6000 ft in altitude, with domelike mountains and nearly accordant summits forming the crest; valleys between the summits are shallowly U-shaped. This eastward-reaching spur was first described by Bailey Willis as the "Entiat Surface," which can be seen on the main ridge extensions as a high level erosion surface extending to Icicle Ridge, and conspicuous because of its topographic contrast regionally.[6]

Lake Chelan and the Entiat River border the Chelan Mountains, which climax at Cardinal Peak and Pinnacle Mountain, and maintain a continuity of ridgeline from Stormy Mountain to Mt. Fernow, where they meet the Entiat Mountains. The range remains consistently rugged only because of its geologic youth. The present topography was dismembered by vigorous erosion from more even-crested ridges. Here, as in the Entiat Mountains, intense jointing exists at alpine levels and incisive glacial cirques which often coalesce have formed narrow crests; these tend to be asymmetric in form, their steep northerly slopes having been intensively glaciated, and their southerly slopes much less so, or non-glaciated. Great alpine climatic energy is expressed by glacial erosion, riving, avalanching, and solifluction. Remnant ridges deeply gullied by erosion and surface stripped of mantle result in an irregular upland surface. The presence of nearby serrate crests now isolated from the main divide strongly suggests that these (such as Cloudcomb Ridge and Devils Divide) are associated with the accordance. The glacial trough of Black Bear Creek is typical of several such on the steep eastern slope of the Chelan Mountains, where local relief is as much as 7500 ft. Flanks descend to Lake Chelan in a series of steep-sided canyons separated by sharp-crested ridges and broad irregular slopes; some timber extends to 7200 ft, but where avalanches and heavy creeping snow inhibit growth, trees are usually absent.

Other dominant high peaks not associated with the three subranges, such as the ones on the DaKobed Range, are located on or near the Cascade crest. Many of the formations in this section are gneissic granite or schists, with some intrusive granite.[7] Extrusive volcanic rocks are largely limited to the area of Glacier Peak. The most recent eruptions of Glacier Peak (about 12,000 yrs ago) sowed ash and pumice over a vast area, thinning markedly eastward.[8] Pyroclastic debris blankets some upland; on the DaKobed Range thin pumice deposits are seen covering granite. Above High Pass pumice is deposited at ridge saddles, and on surfaces in the Ice Creek basin.

In contrast to the crystalline rocks of the mountain ridges is the basalt which can be seen along the escarpment of the Columbia River. Columbia Plateau basalts (Miocene and early Pliocene), which once pushed the river against Cascade foothills, are 3000 ft thick and in places over 10,000 ft thick.

Alpine glaciers in this section once excavated cirques and modified former stream valleys into deep U-shaped cross-profiles. These troughs maintain nearly flat tracts from the interior of the range for over 20 mi., and they are deeply filled with gravel deposit from glaciers which once occupied them; this weathered glacial drift includes thick dissected outwash. Surficial deposit, generally continuous in low gradient valley bottoms such as White River, is mostly alluvium and subdued moraines of various ages. At higher levels deposits include talus and pyroclastic materials.

The erosional abilities of the Pleistocene glaciers left many accessory features in the form of hanging tributary valleys, usually a few hundred to over 2000 ft above larger trough floors. A splendid example is Indian Creek, with a gradient so low that its trough is ponded by fallen timber and vegetation to form marshes. It exhibits a common feature of many Cascade valleys, where rapids plunge in a precipitous descent at the mouth of a low-grade lateral valley to reach the bottom of a larger one which formerly held a trunk glacier.[9]

During the Ice Age the eastern Cascade valleys were

invaded at least three times by trunk glaciers, formed along most of their lengths by the junction of many tributary glaciers that came from the highest regions (William A. Long, 1975, personal commun.). The erosive action of these successive glacial advances transformed the valleys of the Wenatchee and Little Wenatchee, White, Chiwawa and Entiat Rivers and Railroad Creek (a hanging valley) from winding V-shaped river canyons to relatively straight U-shaped glacier valleys. Beyond the easternmost limit of the trunk glaciers, the rivers in their powerful lower courses are deeply incised in bedrock canyons with side drainage spur ridges reaching almost to the rivers which zigzag sharply, probably relating to the bedrock control.

Above the glacier limits the flat valleys, troughs with a semi-circular cross-section without interlocking ridge spurs, tend to be far out of relation to their respective streams, which tend to meander. One of the longest depressions, the Chiwawa Valley, is occupied by a relatively small stream. The moderate valley gradient does not steepen much until 3500 ft, then it rises abruptly to its headwaters. The downvalley limits of U-shaped cross-valley profiles, truncated spurs, and hanging tributaries approximately delineate the former extent of trunk valley glaciers. Tributary glaciers ended their confluence with trunks at varying positions downvalley.

Later episodes of alpine glaciation in the Pleistocene, which produced glaciers less extensive than those preceding, show moraine-building readvances. The terminal position of the glaciers (and former ice margins) is usually marked by a conspicuous ridgelike pile of morainal debris; the moraines farthest from the valley heads are the oldest and those nearest the heads are the youngest. The crests of the moraines appear more subdued with increasing age, presumably a result of the progressively longer time available for modification by weathering, mass-wasting, and erosion. Most of the moraines that lie beyond the thresholds of cirques were built by glaciers during the final Plesitocene episode (William A Long). The youthful moraines which show periods of Neoglacial fluctuation tend to be sharp-crested, unstable, and bare of vegetation, indicative of greater ice volume in the recent past.

As examples of glacial action since the Pleistocene, steep walls of younger cirques are carved in the flanks of the larger Ice Age cirques. Most cirque floors are mantled with talus, frost-wedged blocks, irregular patches of till, and small recessional moraines. High gradients above alp slopes and cirques cause wastes from erosion processes to be rapidly carried downslope. The more recent secondary cirques have accumulated debris, talus cones, and other material which was deprived of a means for transport downvalley. Volume and depth of taluses, often extensive and thick below steeper valley walls, give an indication of Neoglacial disintigration. Lichen cover, differential weathering along cracks, and development of weathering pits give an indication of surface erosion. Snow chutes formed from deep erosion gullying because of minimal depth of permafrost tends to form talus cones.

The greatest testimony to the work of the Ice Age glaciers in this region is the trough of Lake Chelan, where the adjacent Chelan and Methow Mountains rise from water's edge to more than 8000 ft. The 50-mi. lake and 20-mi. Stehekin River lie in a canyon of granitic and gneissoid rocks sculptured by a Pleistocene glacier at least 70 mi. long. Russell considered the lake one of North America's scenic marvels: the lake "resembles in many of its features the far-famed lakes of northern Italy . . . "The bare serrate spires above are white with snow long after the spring flowers have faded in the lower vales."[10]

Russell (1898) was the first to recognize the extent of valley ice which descended the Chelan trough. He estimated the ancient glacier as some 75 mi. long, 1-2 mi. wide, and 2500-3000 ft thick centrally. He states (p. 162) it received several "tributaries in the rugged regions west of the head of Lake Chelan, and an important branch through what is termed Railroad Canyon."[11] Russell believed the Chelan Glacier was prolonged some 40 mi. farther SE than the "Wenache" and Methow Glaciers of this time due to the influence of the region of bold mountains,[12] and that the ice body which occupied Chelan Valley became thicker than the Methow ice because it was sheltered by more precipitous mountain walls which tended to retain ice and delay melting.[13] But the more obvious reason for the thicker Chelan ice is the narrow valley width and consequent higher altitude of ice containment resulting in a very large accumulation area. The Methow, however, was completely ice-covered during the Okanogan lobe expansion so that Russell's argument has some drawbacks (Austin Post, 1974, personal commun.).

Alpine glaciers ranged from small, independent steep tributaries to long and gentle-gradient trunk glaciers in the main valleys. Pleistocene valley glaciers terminated as far as 35 mi. beyond the Cascade crest (nearly as far as the upper end of Tumwater Canyon). Russell examined the geology, glacial geology, and the evidence of multiple glaciations in the range. The ancient

"Wenache" Glacier had two main branches which united at the W end of the site of Lake Wenatchee; after the union the trunk flowed eastward, to leave moraines on the valley sides (between 1700 and 1800 ft in altitude) above the lake.[14] The glacier, some 3 mi. wide here, broadened after uniting with the "Chiwahwah" (itself some 30 mi. in length) in the vicinity of Fish Lake; the combined ice body extended some 5-6 mi. down the Wenatchee Valley.[15]

During the earliest glacial advance a glacier network occupied the Entiat River drainage basin, when nearly every cirque and tributary valley contained glaciers connected with a 35-mi.-long trunk glacier in the main valley. During subsequent advances a long valley glacier failed to develop (William A. Long, 1975 written commun.). In the Entiat Valley, hanging glacier valleys exist 300 ft to 1500 ft above the valley floor; the valley of Ice Creek is the only accordant tributary. High ridges and peaks cut by steep cirques of widely ranging size on the N and E faces are in striking topographic contrast to smoother and gentle S-facing divides and peaks (Maude, Buck, and Fortress offer examples). On the E flank of Chiwawa Ridge ice once formed picturesque consecutive bowl-shaped basins. The upper Entiat Valley vividly displays the natural phenomena associated with valley glaciation; ice transported erratics as boulder trains, and moraines formed by several advances during these glaciations are well represented. A moraine formed at the distal place, marking the termination of each glacial advance. In general the moraines in the Entiat Valley nearest the head are the youngest and those farthest out the oldest (W.A. Long). Successive Pleistocene glaciers, which were more extensive on N and NE flanks, reformed to enlarge pre-existing cirques by headward erosion, and to sculpture new ones.[16] Modern glaciers commonly lie above high-level cirque floors in sheltered recesses beneath steep N- or E-facing walls, or occupy gentle summit slopes at high altitudes.

Glaciers on the highlands E of the Cascade divide lack the grandeur of those on nearby Glacier Peak, but the Honeycomb stands as the longest glacier not on a volcano in the North Cascades. This small valley glacier which drains to the Suiattle measures some 4.7 km along its axis.[17] Reports of early exploration described this glacier as "A perfect Alpine type, which descended from the highest summit downward in curving lines, between precipitous cliffs."[18] There is an icefield system of contiguous glaciers about the Kololo Peaks (the upper Honeycomb-Suiattle-White Chuck Glaciers).[19] The ice system sends glaciers like fingers of a hand, flowing around peaks on both sides of the main divide, down to the region of green coniferous forests, finally thrusting their snouts into the intricate river systems.[20]

Significant glaciers, mostly nourished by direct snowfall, occupy cirques in the DaKobed Range, the most impressive being the Butterfly, Moth, Richardson, and Walrus; all lie on N or E exposures.[21] S slope glacier remnants here are in unfavorable positions because of slope brevity despite high mean altitudes. Lyman Glacier on Chiwawa Mountain (0.21 mi.^{2}) is one of the largest of the new generation of glaciers, but has been diminishing in recent years; melting has separated the remnant glacier into a textbook example of recession, with an upper heavily crevassed portion and a lower, rapidly thinning area of stagnation.[22]

Some 25 glaciers, clustered in a distinct E-W orientation, lie along or close to the range crest between White and Suiattle Passes. A total of 15.4 km^2 ice is concentrated along a sector of the crest and a nearby subrange. An eastern group of 26 small glaciers (6.7 km^2) lie within the drainage basin of Entiat River and Railroad Creek. Several of the remaining glaciers lie on the E slopes of the Chelan Mountains.

Numerous small pocket and hanging glaciers exist, notably on Mt. Maude, Mt. Fernow, Copper Peak, Indian Head Peak, Seven Fingered Jack, Fortress Mountain, and Buck Mountain. Small ice pockets remain in some of the higher and most sheltered cirque basins (generally 0.1 km^2 or less), such as on Dumbell, Tinpan, Pinnacle, Cardinal, Brahma, Napeequa, Cirque, and Ice Creek Ridge. They are nourished largely by prevailing SW winds that eddy winter snow over crests onto leeward basins. In the Entiat and Chiwawa Mountains the mean altitudes of existing glaciers is approximately at the local altitudes of the present orographic snowline (W.A. Long); this is the line joining the lowest edges of perennial snowfields, and it progressively rises eastward. In these mountains this snowline at present lies between 7000 and 7500 ft.

While some glaciers present unique contrasts in their activity, most of them have made only small area changes in the past two decades and are considered to be in balance with recent climatic conditions. Little terrestrial observation was done in the past due to the remote nature of these mountains; glacier study methods have been based almost entirely on aerial photography, with extensive government mapping photography covering glacierized areas beginning in 1947. By coincidence, this was near the time of rejuvenation of glacier activity in the region. The unexpected change from a period of major retreat was determined to be due to a cooler, wetter climate (Austin Post, 1975, written commun.).

Although this region is not as widely pocketed with lakes as that S of the Wenatchee River, Lyman Lake and Ice Lakes, which occupy glacial cirques, are known as scenic marvels of the range. Many tarns occupy ice-gouged basins on cirque floors; Dole, Fern and Choral Lakes are among those blocked by Neoglacial moraines.

E of the range crest there is an increasingly continental climate; mean summer temperatures increase sharply and mean annual precipitation progressively decreases eastward to a minimum of 12 in. annually in the driest locations. Climatic landscape diversity results in marked vegetation contrasts. While dense rain forest and lush undergrowth swath the pumice-rich upper Suiattle River valley, the lower portion of the valley of Lake Chelan has a barren, rocky appearance with light and scattered tree cover. Beneath Pyramid Peak, which in 3.1 mi. thrusts over 7100 vertical ft from the lake, several life zones tier one continuous slope, with several floras in close span.

The Chiwawa and Entiat River valleys therefore exhibit drier characteristics than the White and Little Wenatchee. Lower valley slopes are densely forested, but the rocky crests, which rise to over 8000 ft, are snow-clad through June. Progressive changes are noted eastward: the drier valleys show an increase in meadow openings at the higher levels of the subalpine forest, the shorter trees are generally widely scattered, bedrock crops out in the subalpine forest, there is more talus and felsenmeer, and S-facing slopes are more sharply folded into gullies and ribs. Alp slopes are less continuous, but there tend to be a succession of charming basins. Along upper reaches of the U-shaped Entiat River valley, avalanche swaths have formed a series of parallel openings; in winter and spring slides spread debris over the meadows. Valleys do not have extensive brush, but dense thickets can be found on slopes, especially in avalanche tracks. On some slopes extensive tracts of grass and bush have replaced forest where subjected to avalanches or recent fires. Undergrowth is dominated by beargrass, huckleberry, rustyleaf and azalea. In the subalpine zone forests differ considerably on either side of a line drawn just E of the Cascade divide. On the E subalpine fir, Englemann spruce, and ponderosa pine form the conspicuous coniferous stands. Following fire or logging the first-generation forests are typically lodgepole, whitebark, and western white pine, and western larch. The medium altitudes show a decrease in density of ground flora, with grass cover and meadow openings between clumps and widely spaced specimens of subalpine fir, lovely fir, mountain hemlock, and Englemann spruce. At higher parkland levels amid broad benches, heather hollows, and glaciated knobs, the alpine larch and multi-trunked white bark pine conclude a sparse, sturdy cover. Many specimens of the rare Lyall's larch may be seen above 5500 ft, in particular near Lyman Lake and on high ridges along Buck Creek, the Napeequa and Chiwawa Rivers, and on the Chelan Mountains. This stunted, long-lived timberline tree which grows in the rockiest soil with firmly anchored roots to stand the rigors of wind and snow, remains erect while its associates in this belt are wind-cripples. Its ethereal light-bluish-green springtime foliage turns bright orange-gold in autumn, and is readily detected on distant slopes. The variety of floral communities reflects micro-climatic conditions of the Hudsonian Zone. Displays reach brilliance, particularly in the famed meadows of White Pass, Meander Meadow, and Buck Creek Pass—where the blue lupine, paintbrush, and red columbine abound. In this zone intense biological activity occurs during the short summer when there is massive flowering and intense pollenator activity.

The seaward gradient of timberline is evident in the orographic shelter on the E flank of the Cascade Range. Timberline averages about 2100 m (6900′), in contrast to its westward decline to 1500 m (5000′) because of heavier snow accumulation and lower summer temperatures. Regionally, timberline is closely controlled by climate. The accordance rises eastward across the range as maritime climatic influences diminish. Erosion of mass wasting, much more vigorous above than below timberline, has formed extensive alp slopes at timberline; many subalpine slopes are too gentle to contrast sharply with alp slopes at this level.

The upper Napeequa Valley is an interesting study in timberline basins; ice still remains on high slopes and plateaus, and there are many mid-level cliffs where glacier gorges remain from ancient scouring. Almost all the timber exists on the shadow slope, with bushes, meadows, and only occasional timber fingers on S-facing slopes.

In rocky terrain the process of soil formation is very slow. Shallow soils combined with cold temperatures above 7000 ft result in conditions that are inhospitable to plant life other than mosses, heather, and lichen. This paucity of vegetation coupled with the rigorous climate and the many rock faces discourages large mammals from occupying the higher terrain. Consequently the only large animals here are a few goat, black bear, and deer. Boulder heaps in and above the forest areas form refuge for a variety of animals, the hoary marmot (measuring up to 3 ft long) being the most common. Smaller animals such as pikas, as well as hawks, find adequate food and protection to survive in the austere habitat. The pika and ground squirrel provide animation for the mountain traveler, and can often be observed collecting bouquets and shrilling warnings at their burrows.

The protection of the forest is most important for water conservation. The more mountainous the area and drier the climate, the more serious the damage from cutting, fires, and human impact. The great Entiat fire of 1970, which burned more than 43,000 acres, was caused by lightning, a constant summer threat (the upper White River valley was plagued by fires 1924-1929). In early times, herders and settlers set fires deliberately. Martin Gorman, after the first study of the forest reserve, penned words that ring a timeless wisdom: "It is only necessary . . . to examine a forest in which a band of these 'hoofed locusts' have grazed and their careless herder with his numerous camp fires has dwelt for a season . . . to become thoroughly convinced that the need of forest protection and supervision is imperative."[23]

The principal streams in this section are the Suiattle, Wenatchee, Little Wenatchee, White, Chiwawa, and Entiat Rivers, and Railroad Creek. Both the Little Wenatchee and White Rivers rise at the Cascade crest and flow into Lake Wenatchee, which is held behind a moraine dam. The Wenatchee River issues from the lake, and is shortly joined by the Chiwawa River. Wenatchee Valley represents part of an ancient block (graben) that fractured and slipped along a fault line during regional crustal uplift. The Entiat River flows through a deep, narrow valley cut in crystalline rock. Its valley has fewer and smaller tributaries than the Wenatchee and Methow Rivers, which are developed mainly in softer sedimentary rocks.

The most interesting valley is the secluded Napeequa, whose upper portions, floored by deep glacial deposits and alluvial fans which lie at the mouths of gullies, may be a filled-in lake basin. The river's discharge through a canyon cut into the glaciated valley floor subsequent to the Pliocene Epoch appears to be captured from an earlier course through Twin Lakes and Big Meadow Creek. Although the lakes are separated by a morainal ridge, waters of both drain to the Napeequa. The widened valley is quite out of proportion with Big Meadow Creek, which has a large swamp in its upper end. The Napeequa River valley, like all glaciated valleys in the Cascade Range, was developed by Pleistocene glacial deepening and widening into a relatively straight, open U-shaped trough from a pre-existing V-shaped stream valley having steep gradient and overlapping mountain spurs. The Neoglacial outwash and modern fluvial deposits which cover the valley floor are distinguished by a dense vegetation cover and an integrated river drainage system, an indication of the time which has elapsed since the valley was ice-filled. The tributaries that enter from the N are short and steep, and head in cirques whose floors range in altitude from 6000 ft to 6600 ft. These higher valley floors are covered by relatively unweathered moraines and glacial drift that retains much of its original form.

In the gentle gradient of the upper 6 mi. the river meanders across the nearly flat valley floor but near Twin Lakes leaves its glaciated SE-trending valley and turns abruptly W to cascade down a narrow and precipitous valley cut in gneiss, through the 6500-ft ridge lying between the Napeequa and White River valleys. It is not known why the river was diverted from its former valley (W.A. Long). An extensive lake may have been ponded in the valley postdating ice retreat (when glaciers pulled back from moraine barriers). Saturation of sediments by percolating lake waters could have generated massive sliding of bordering mountain slopes.

Indians were first to roam these valleys. Alexander Ross recorded that tribes from the Okanogan nation in this region were the Pisscows, Intié took, Incomeecanetook, and Tsillane.[24] The Lewis and Clark journal (1805) mentions unseen tribes to include the "Wahnaachee"[25] and George Gibbs stated that a tribe called the En-te-at-kwu lived on a small river.[26] The junction of the Entiat and Columbia was a popular Indian rendezvous; a trail led along the Columbia, up Knapp Coulee, along the S side of Lake Chelan and on to the Methow (Bailey Willis map—1887). An Indian trail sufficiently good for horses led from the Columbia to Stormy Mountain, a high point of the Chelan Mountains, then continued on to cross the Entiat and Chiwawa Mountains. The implication of the term Indian Pass is in the historic usage by Indians for passage from the White River to the North Fork of Sauk River.

Many names are derived from the Indian: the Columbia was Ump-qua (meaning "big river"), Entiat River was Entiat-qua (grassy water), Wenatchee River meant "great opening out of the mountains."[27] The Ross map titles the river "Piss Cows."[28] The establishment of Wenatchee, no doubt the approximate location which David Thompson, then Ross, saw, derived its location and name from the local tribe. Thus when

Ross passed here August 23, 1811 he speaks of "a beautiful green spot near a small Indian camp we put ashore."[29] When Governor George Simpson descended the Columbia River in 1824 in what was the contested Oregon Country he referred to the "Piscahouse River."[30]

Derivations from the Indians are common. White River was their Na-pé-qua (white water); fortunately this attractive name has been preserved for the N fork.[31] Lake Wenatchee was Tah-kwt on the Gibbs map.[32] White River was termed Teh-ko, appended with words "reported trail," and the Chiwawa River was Zu-wash Creek on the very similar Northwest Boundary Survey manuscript map.[33] Chiwawa is a shortening of "Chi-wah-wah," meaning "last canyon next to mountains."[34]

The famed explorer and map-maker David Thompson, who descended the Columbia in July 1811, made the first maps to reasonably depict the Columbia Basin and show Lake Chelan in outline,[35] although it is not known how he learned of the lake's size and shape. On the Ross map the span of the Columbia above the confluence with Lewis' River is shown as Clarke's River, representing the distance between the Snake and an imprecise ending.[36]

Lake Chelan's name is derived from an Indian phrase meaning "clear water." The first recorded reference to the lake is from Ross on August 27, 1811 when he noted the stream "Tsill-ane" . . . "Indians told us it took rise in a lake not far distant."[37] The route of Capt. George B. McClellan's party in 1853 led past the S shore.[38] McClellan reported the lake "is some thirty miles long, and is shut in by high mountains, which leave no passage along its margins."[39] (Today's concerned environmentalists may take surreptitious pleasure in that of McClellan's oft-criticized geographic opinions, this one was understated.) Indians told him that they paddled to the lake's end, then used a steep, poor trail to the summit and the Skagit River.[40] D.C. Linsley ascended Lake Chelan by Indian canoe between July 15-19, 1870, the first white man to travel this route.

The first Army exploration up Lake Chelan, some 24 mi. by canoe in 1879, by Lt. Thomas Symons, Lt.-Col. Henry C. Merriam and three Indians concluded "The water is of diamond-like clearness and yet in places no sight can penetrate to the bottom of its liquid depths."[41] The steep slopes of the lake's valley are noted for the presence of mountain goats; in former times they frequented the lower valleys as well. Below the Chelan River Alexander Ross in 1811 saw "the ibex, the white musk goat."[42]

McClellan, in his search for a railroad pass, only saw the "rough mountains" toward the head of Wenatchee drainages from the Yakima-Wenatchee divide E of Blewett. In spite of the fact he did not ascend the Wenatchee or its branches, he reported "it appears certain that there can be no pass at its head for a road."[43] The resulting map intimates the limits of information.[44] This historic map, of course, in its details is inaccurate, but goes to fill a significant gap in knowledge. George Gibbs, the expedition geologist, in his own report and map, shows he had additional information about the Wenatchee drainage, for he wrote "The Pisquouse is a large and bold stream rising in the main divide of the Cascades, and interlocking with one of those running into the Sound. It passes through a lake, reported by the Indians to be larger than either of those on the Yakima."[45]

Fur traders were the first white men in this region, arriving either from Astoria or Canada. It is known that Hudson's Bay Company trappers were familiar with the Little Wenatchee River between 1814 and 1840. They used an old blazed trail,[46] following an Indian route over Cady Pass to the Skykomish drainage.[47] A well known Indian campsite was at Chikamin (Money) Creek on the Chiwawa, a location good for both huckleberries and trade with trappers.

During the 1800s most relationships with Indians were cordial, probably due to independent trading enlistment.[48] The only expeditions of United States troops in this area during the Yakima Indian War were to search for hostile Indians who had attacked a group of miners. Two parties were sent up the Wenatchee River and branches by Major R.S. Garnett in August, 1858.[49] A party of 60 under Lt. George Crook followed hostiles up the main branch into the mountains. A party of 60 under Lt. Camp and Capt. Frazier then followed rough mountain trails, possibly between the Wenatchee and Yakima Rivers.

Tumwater Canyon was apparently first explored in 1860 by E.T. Cady and E.C. Ferguson, who came via the North Fork Skykomish and Wenatchee Rivers. A historic crossing of White Pass and descent of White River, the first by white men, was on July 5, 1870, by railroad explorers D.C. Linsley and John A. Tennant.

The first settlers in the Wenatchee Valley arrived about 1870, and soon forest areas were used for grazing. Leavenworth prospectors pushed into the mountain valleys and made many discoveries in the upper basins of Phelps Creek, Chiwawa River, and Railroad Creek. The first important discoveries, in 1893, came as a result of red stains of oxidized iron high on Red Hill (this was the zone of greatest mineralization and galena ledges).[50] By 1896 a trail led from near Leavenworth to Phelps and Chiwawa Basins, 38 mi. from the roadhead. Two companies formed, the Red Hill and Red Mountain Mining Companies, located on nearby claim acquisitions. The Royal Development Co. later bought existing properties and built a large mill at Trinity to carry out most of the mining in the district. The Trinity Mine operated on low-grade copper ore in the 1930s, then went out of business after limited production.

The only two mines in this region which ever produced volumes or ore are the Holden Mine on Railroad Creek and the Trinity Mine. The now-dormant Holden Mine was the largest producer of copper in the history of Washington State during the 20 yrs it was in operation (production about 106,000 tons; Vhay and Weissenborn, 1966, pp. 72, 74). In addition about 600,000 oz. of gold was recovered.

The highly mineralized outcrops (copper sulphate ore) were noted by Albert B. Rogers in 1887 on a railroad survey and apparently explored in 1892 by James H. Holden.

A large deposit of gold and copper-bearing ore was claimed near Railroad Creek by Holden on July 20, 1896 (this ore ran through Copper and "Irene" Mountains; see footnote 7). In 1891 the Lake Chelan Railroad and Navigation Co. was organized, with development plans that included narrow gauge tracks between properties and the lake, plans that never materialized (except for the cablecar system to the wagon road), even after the acquisition of the lease to the Holden claims in 1900. After the Howe Sound Co. purchased the properties and began production in 1938 to pursue mining until operations suspended June 1957, the site became the largest producer in the Cascades, with $66.5 million in metal extraction recorded. In 1939 the 2000-ton mill employed 350 men and Holden was called the "Model Mine town" (*Wenatchee Daily World,* 26 April, 1939). But this land-rape operation took their profits and left the valley with a massive blight of unsightly yellowish residue. The poisonous tailings and subsurface waste chemicals are a threat to water quality and an unsolved ecological disaster of magnitude, a prime example of the need for tough impact regulations.

Engineer Edwin F. Johnson was one of the original promoters of a northern transcontinental railroad route, having made proposals even prior to the Governor Isaac I. Stevens exploration. Johnson produced maps in 1853 and 1867, perhaps as an expression of faith, and drew heavily on the material of Lt. J.K. Warren, George Gibbs, and the Northwest Boundary Survey.[51] Johnson's field surveys began in 1867 under James Tilton, who was in charge of Cascade mountain pass exploration. The surveys of the "Wenatchee Passes" were undertaken by W.H. Carlton, who reported two eligible passes for a railroad line: Wenatchee River to Skykomish River, S fork; Wenatchee River to Sawk branch of Skagit River.[52] Additional funding allowed further surveys to be done in 1869 N of the Wenatchee River, but the railroad provided no subsequent construction funds.

James J. Hill, the railroad magnate, placed survey parties in the field in 1890 to continue the search for the ideal northern cross-Cascade route. He chose engineer John F. Stevens to head this exploration. While surveying in the Cascades one of his first entries was the Entiat Valley. He then ventured through Tumwater Canyon to Lake Wenatchee and on to Indian Pass.[53]

When his probing favored the valley now known as Nason Creek, Stevens sent one of his engineers across the divide on a preliminary study (this short span of divide is the nearest a low gradient E-side valley in this region comes to Puget Sound). Later Stevens conducted several surveys across the pass which was to bear his name.[54] To cross the summit Stevens had to plan a series of switchbacks or a 2½-mi. tunnel; these zigzags on the original railroad grade, completed in 1893, took the line over the summit and hampered operations for 7 yrs until Cascade Tunnel opened in 1900 at a cost of $25 million. Before the construction of the new Cascade Tunnel in 1926 Mill Creek and Berne were large camps for workers and engineers. The new 8-mi. tunnel, and a new line through Chumstick Valley greatly improved railroad service. The line on the N side of Tumwater Canyon was abandoned in 1929 to make way for the present highway (and parking for Castle Rock climbers). The highway over Stevens Pass was completed in 1924-1925, following the original railroad grade. Surveyors, scientists, and geologists made pioneering history before the turn of the century. Bailey Willis climbed Stormy Mountain during a reconnaissance. Geological Survey parties climbed Stormy, Dirtyface, and Pyramid in 1897-1899 for triangulation. I.C. Russell traveled up the Little Wenatchee, explored into the Napeequa and White Rivers, ascended Indian Creek, then followed the highland to Glacier Peak in 1898.

Many names in this region came from sheepmen, prospectors, surveyors, and forestry personnel. Whistling Pig Creek was named by herders for the mountain marmot. Shoofly Mountain was named by a trail crew frustrated by deer flies. Albert H. Sylvester, surveyor and forest supervisor, applied many names, some unfortunately capricious, during mapping from 1897 into three decades of the 1900s: examples are Helmet Butte, Liberty Cap, Flower Dome, Mt. David, the "American Poet" peaks, Kodak Peak (lost camera), Lake Valhalla, Dishpan Gap, Mt. Maude, Fortress, Cardinal, Pinnacle and Clark Mountains, Triad Creek, High Pass, Lightning and Thunder Creeks (many natural fires began here). Klone Peak's name was after Sylvester's dog "Klone Pesitkim," whose original purchase price of $3 was but a fraction of the total cost after he invaded a neighbor's chicken yard. Many names were derived from Chinook jargon, mostly applied by the Forest Service from 1910 to 1940; this dialect is incongruous here since it was a coastal Indian trade language. Sheep herders came into the area about 1900 and made some trails. The Forest Service trails came later, and then to provide fire surveillance lookout houses were built. Such trails as the Pyramid Mountain route from Baldy and Stormy Mountains were built before 1916, but most of the trails were built between 1916 and 1925.

Early outdoor club outings approached Glacier Peak and crossed the divide to the Suiattle from the E, either by Buck Creek Pass or by Stehekin and Suiattle Pass (Mazama outing of 1911).[55] The Mazama outing of 1926 found that the few existing trails in the Chiwawa to Chelan region were old, marked first by game and domestic sheep, and with little regard for contour (trails "wander willy-nilly, up and down, steep as a chalet roof"). The outing found that a mountain journey in this region is not easy because of the rugged nature of travel.[56]

The Glacier Peak Wilderness Area (464,741 acres), which includes in a jagged outline most of the region from the "American Poet" peaks to the Middle Cascade River, from Kennedy Hot Springs to Holden (about 35 by 20 mi.) was established September 6, 1960 by the Secretary of Agriculture, and designated by Congress in 1964 as part of the National Wilderness Preservation system; enlarged in 1968 as part of the North Cascades Act, it is managed by the U.S. Forest Service. A flaw in the Wilderness Act of 1964 permits prospecting even in dedicated Wilderness Areas until 1984; patented lands and other valid claims are not affected by that date. Additional territory should and probably will be placed within this urgently needed protection. Among current restrictions, no motorized travel is allowed, visitor impact must be carefully controlled, and *overnight users must obtain a Wilderness Permit* (obtain from ranger stations in person, by telephone or by mail).

Virtually all the uplands are now reached by a good trail network. Because of the fragility of meadows and high altitude soils such human impact as off-trail trampling, waste disposal, and campfire locations must be carefully minimized. Visitation to this magnificent region is increasing as interest is stimulated by its fascinating features, and requires all users to practice the philosophy of "minimum impact."

Contact forest headquarters or ranger stations for current list of packers holding permits and special requirements.

High lakes have a short summer season, but there is a considerable amount of good fishing. Most lakes are stocked, and by July 1 are open. State of Washington game laws apply and designate open seasons for deer, black bear, grouse, and mountain goat. Specific fishing and hunting regulations are available at sport shops (or write Washington State Department of Game, 600 No. Capitol Way; Olympia, WA 98504). The hunting season in September in many areas is open to deer, bear, grouse, and a few special goat permits. Early buck areas in specific open lands include the Glacier Peak Wilderness. Hikers and climbers will be wise to wear bright clothing, or avoid the hunting areas in the Chelan and Entiat Mountains during hunting seasons. The general hunting season (bear, deer) which begins in October covers a wider range.

GLACIER PEAK WILDERNESS AREA

For information and use regulations see Trail and Alpine Hiking Approaches, Section I.

CAMPGROUNDS

There are numerous campgrounds on the forest roads in this section. For locations see Wenatchee and Mt. Baker-Snoqualmie National Forest maps or National Forest Campground Directory, which also lists facilities and usage fees. For specific information write to District Ranger Stations.

RANGER STATIONS

District Ranger Stations

Leavenworth; Leavenworth, WA 98826
Lake Wenatchee; Star Route, Leavenworth, WA 98826
Entiat; Entiat, WA 98822
Chelan; Chelan, WA 98816
Darrington; Darrington, WA 98241
Skykomish; Skykomish, WA 98288

Forest Service Stations (summer only)

Lucerne
Twenty Five Mile Creek
Silver Falls (Entiat Road)
Cottonwood (Entiat Road)
Rock Creek (Chiwawa Road)

FOREST HEADQUARTERS

Wenatchee National Forest
301 Yakima Street
Wenatchee, WA 98801

Mt. Baker-Snoqualmie National Forest
1601 Second Ave.
Seattle, WA 98101
(206) 442-5400

National Park Service-Forest Service Information Center
Room 110, 915 Second Ave.
Seattle, WA 98174
(206) 442-0170 or 442-5542

Wilderness permits issued at Ranger stations, Forest headquarters and the Information Center.

MAPS

U.S. Geological Survey Topographic

Holden (1944)	1:62,500
Glacier Peak (1950)	1:62,500
Lucerne (1944)	1:62,500
Wenatchee Lake (1965)	1:62,500
Labyrinth Mountain (1965)	1:24,000
Poe Mountain (1965)	1:24,000
Benchmark Mountain (1965)	1:24,000
Captain Point (1965)	1:24,000
Stormy Mountain (1968)	1:24,000
South Navarre Peak (1968)	1:24,000
Silver Falls (1968)	1:24,000
Plain (1968)	1:24,000
Sugarloaf Peak (1968)	1:24,000
Tyee Mountain (1968)	1:24,000
Brief (1968)	1:24,000
Chikamin Creek (1968)	1:24,000
Baldy Mountain (1968)	1:24,000
Big Goat Mountain (1968)	1:24,000

U.S. Forest Service

Wenatchee National Forest Recreation map (½ in. = 1 mi. scale)
Glacier Peak Wilderness (topographic)

LABYRINTH MOUNTAIN 6376′/1944 m

Located several mi. E of the Cascade crest and 7½ mi. N of Stevens Pass, Labyrinth is a modest but bulky peak named by A.H. Sylvester for its puzzling map contours. It makes up ridges between Little Wenatchee River, and Lake and Rainy Creeks. Minotaur and Theseus Lakes are exceptional tarns occupying glacial cirques near the summit.

ROUTES: The climb presents no real problem. The simplest approach is the SE side from Lake Minotaur♦; complete the climb by the S ridge via the saddle (5900′+) just W of the lake (1½ hrs). The NW shoulder could be climbed readily from 2600 ft on the Lake Creek Road♦—a longer ascent.

ROCK MOUNTAIN 6852′/2088 m

This is the second highest summit on Nason Ridge, the short E-W subrange between Nason Creek and Lake Wenatchee-Little Wenatchee River. The summit is about 1 mi. SW of Mt. Howard.

ROUTE: See Nason Ridge Trail♦.

MT. HOWARD 7063′/2153 m

This highpoint of Nason Ridge, about halfway between Stevens Pass and Lake Wenatchee, offers an easy ascent and excellent 360° viewpoint. Its upper NE slope holds snow in the shape of a large triangle much of the summer. The name was apparently applied by an early survey party, and appeared in print as early as 1887.

ROUTE: The most direct is the S slope; ascend from Nason Ridge Trail♦ at Crescent Lake (5440′)—about 2 mi. E of Rock Mountain (2 hrs). A direct approach from Merritt Lake Trail♦ to meet the ridge trail near Merritt Lake (5003′) could be used; from here it would be possible to travel NW toward Mt. Mastiff (traverse under its S side) to reach the saddle (6300′+) between Mastiff and Howard.

MT. MASTIFF 6741′/2055 m

This peak is 1 mi. ENE of Mt. Howard, on Nason Ridge. It was named by A.H. Sylvester because its outline as seen from Lake Wenatchee resembles a dog's head.

ROUTE: Hike N from Nason Ridge Trail♦ and reach the SE ridge at about 6200 ft. See also Mt. Howard; an easy walk can be made along the ridge from this summit.

POE MOUNTAIN 6015′/1833 m

Poe is the best known of the "American Poet" peaks, as named by A.H. Sylvester. It is located 12 mi. NW of Lake Wenatchee, on Wenatchee Ridge.

ROUTE: See Poe Mountain Trail♦.

WHITTIER PEAK from Mt. David
HERMANN F. ULRICHS

LONGFELLOW MOUNTAIN 6577′/2005 m

Longfellow, about 2 mi. N of Poe, is on Wenatchee Ridge.

ROUTE: See Poe Mountain Trail♦.

WHITTIER PEAK 7281′/2219 m

The highest of the "American Poet" group on the ridge N of Little Wenatchee River, on the divide between Indian and Cougar Creek 4½ mi. W of White River. It is a striking though barren peak with distinctive connecting ridges. The N side of the David-Whittier massif has an extensive alp slope but little incised by glacial action; small ice patches remain between high rock spurs separating shallow basins.

ROUTE: The gentle connecting ridges make the peak merely an alpine hike. The simplest approach would be the Poe Mountain Trail♦ (then Wenatchee Ridge Trail) to Longfellow Peak's near N side (est. 6400′), then walk the divide E toward Whittier—some 2 mi. distant. Another route would be the traverse from Mt. David (keep on crest or high on S slope).

MT. DAVID 7420′/2262 m

The ascent of this outstanding mountain, which offers such a unique vista of both flanks of the Cascades, is simplified by a summit trail. The summit pyramid is a gentle rock mass. Anticipate snow until July at the higher levels. The summit area was blasted to provide space for the lookout building, begun in 1933, 2 yrs after the trail was built. Frequent summer lightning storms frightened lookout personnel, sometimes with good reason. The building was removed later. David, Jonathan, and Saul were named for Biblical figures by A.H. Sylvester.

WHITE RIVER VALLEY, view south
U.S. GEOLOGICAL SURVEY

ROUTE: From the end of the White River Road♦ (2200′) cross the river bridge, then fork downstream on Panther Creek Trail No. 1522 about 1½ mi.; then bear right via the Mt. David Trail (8 mi. road to summit). Time: 5 hours.

MT. JONATHAN 7195′/2193 m

This is a secondary summit connected to and ½ mi. W of Mt. David.

ROUTE: The summit can readily be reached by a ridge traverse. First keep on the ridge to the saddle, then on the S to avoid a cliff. Finish on the long easy crest. See Mt. David.

BRYANT PEAK 6401′/1951 m

Bryant is the northern of the "poet" peaks, on Wenatchee Ridge NW of Longfellow.

ROUTE: See Poe Mountain Trail♦.

MT. SAUL 7311′/2228 m

Saul stands out on the Indian Creek-White River divide 3½ mi. E of Indian Head Peak. There is a long alpine connecting ridge from the eastern summit of Indian Head; the remainder of Saul has much local relief. Its long rocky S slopes are deeply gullied; its upper N side is a rock wall above extensive talus. A.H. Sylvester gave the granitic peak this name because of its gloomy appearance.

ROUTE: Leave the Indian Creek Trail♦ at about 3.8 mi., then hike up the E side of the stream draining Airplane Lake (5300′+). From the saddle N of the cliff-ringed lake (est. 5750′) hike W to Saul's summit. Another way is to follow the long divide from Indian Head; this involves minor gains and losses, but all in the category of cross-country hiking. Reference: *101 Hikes*.

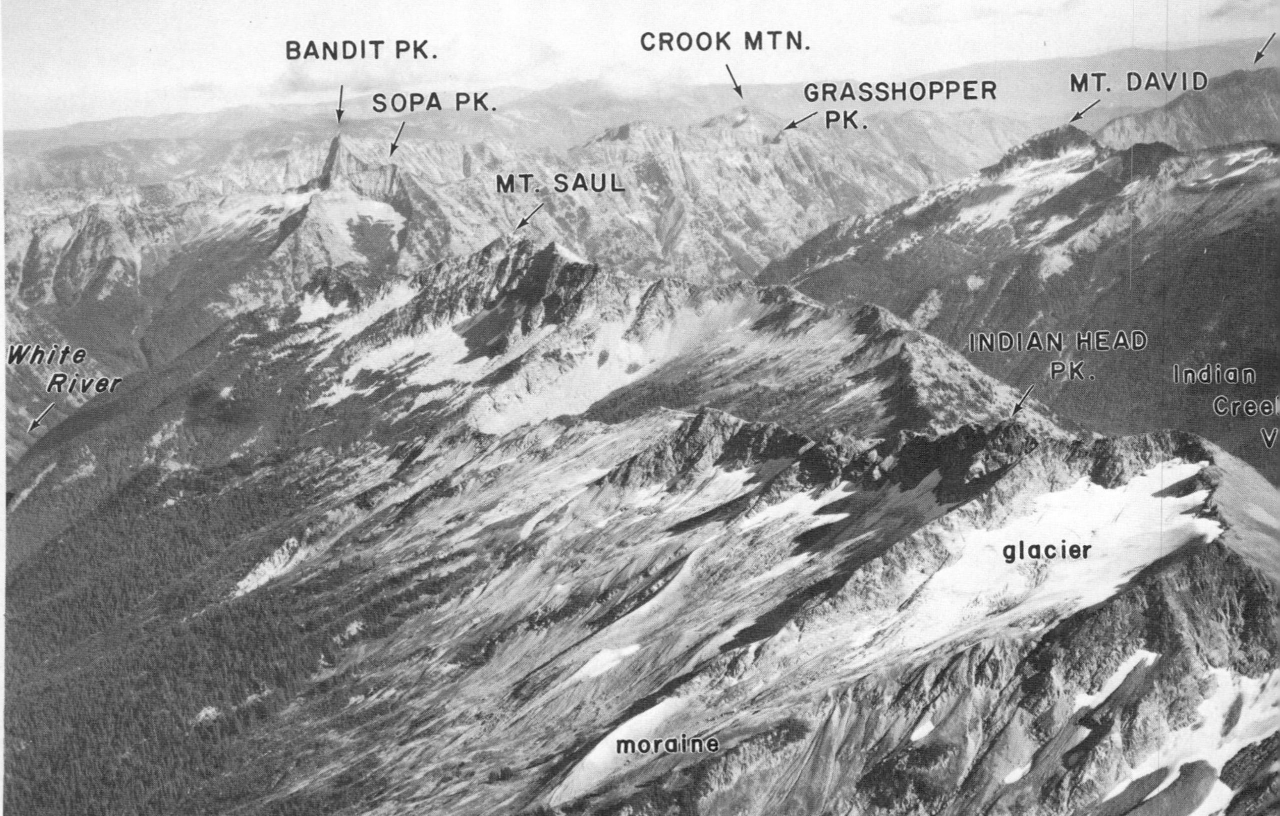

INDIAN HEAD PEAK from northwest
U.S. GEOLOGICAL SURVEY

INDIAN HEAD PEAK 7442′/2268 m

This high, gentle and massive peak on the White River-Indian Creek divide, 1 mi. NE of Indian Pass, was so named by Sylvester because from the pass it bears a resemblance to an Indian head-dress. Its southern slopes are uniquely broad, open, and grassy. There are a small slope glacier NW of the summit, and additional ice patches in the high cirques eastward beneath the summit crest (schist rock). The first ascent was made by D.C. Linsley and John A. Tennant on July 2, 1870 during the survey for a railroad pass.

ROUTES: From Indian Pass (Indian Creek Trail♦ and Crest Trail♦) continue N ¼ mi. beyond a stream (5200′) where there is a spur. Ascend it to treeline, then traverse up and E across vast, steepish meadows. Cross a rocky shoulder 100 ft below its junction with the main ridge; around the corner and E is the summit (no difficulties; 3 hours).

There is a cross-country route from the top of Mt. Saul; scrambling and a detour at a notch (est. 7000′) and adjacent crag. When nearing the summit, stay along the easy S side of the divide. Reference: *Routes and Rocks,* pp. 115-119.

DIRTYFACE PEAK 6240′+/1902 m

Two summits about ½ mi. apart peak above an extensive uplift, prominent N of the W end of Lake Wenatchee. The NW summit is higher; the SE is triangulated at 6223 ft. Railroad explorer Albert B. Rogers hiked up to some elevation on the uplift on August 2, 1887. A U.S. Geological survey party, including A.H. Sylvester, made the ascent for triangulation, probably in 1898.

ROUTE: See Dirtyface Peak Trail♦.

McCALL MOUNTAIN 5765′/1757 m

A semi-wooded point on the ridge between Twin Lakes

and Raging Creek, 5 mi. N of the upper end of Lake Wenatchee. The original name was Huckleberry, for the area was a berry picking site of local Indians. The present name was applied for Lt. James McCall, involved in the mission against hostile Indians in 1858.

ROUTE: Raging Creek Trail♦ passes high on the NE slope at est. 4 mi. Then hike up.

CROOK MOUNTAIN 6930′/2112 m

Crook is nearly the last massif of importance in the southern portion of the Chiwawa Mountains. Various Forest Service maps, dating from 1925 when the summit was titled Goat Mountain, and the revised 1901 Chiwaukum quadrangle, show the correct location 2 mi. N of the larger of Twin Lakes and 1.4 mi. S of Schaefer Lake. The Wenatchee Lake quadrangle (1965) positions the name incorrectly at 3.7 mi. N of Dirtyface Peak and lists the elevation as 5999 ft. The more recent name is for Lt. George Crook, who was involved in the 1858 Yakima Indian campaign.

ROUTE: Approach by Raging Creek Trail♦ to the divide (5¼ or more mi.), then continue NW to the summit (est. 2 mi. of hiking).

MT. SYLVESTER 6913′/2107 m

This is the massif immediately S of Schaefer Lake in the southern portion of the Chiwawa Mountains. The southern slope is gentle, but there is a rock cliff on the N and W. The name is for Albert H. Sylvester, surveyor, explorer, and forest supervisor.

ROUTE: Use trail to Schaefer Lake♦. It appears best to cross the exit stream of the lake and ascend the NE slope, then the E ridge to the summit. A route from the NW appears possible, but is certainly steeper.

BANDIT PEAK 7625′/2324 m

Bandit is the name proposed for the attractive peak on Napeequa Ridge (Chiwawa Mountains) 1 mi. E of the Napeequa Valley and about 4 mi. S of Little Giant Pass; the W summit is the higher of twin rocky horns (the E summit is at least 65 ft lower). The entire upper E side of the summit crest is cliffy, with perennial snow patches, steep alp slopes, and brushy subalpine basins set above glacial troughs. Dividing spur ridges which separate these troughs feature a series of steep rock outcrops. At Bandit's western base the valley is only 2800 ft in altitude; a long slope of rock and scrub timber steepens to a moderately impressive rock slope.

ROUTES: From Schaefer Lake♦ ascend W to the main divide (est. 6160′); traverse the W slope and keep W to two high points at 6931 and 7270 ft; the rough terrain may make a ridge traverse more practicable. No report is on hand, but moderate rock work should be anticipated to reach either the E or W summit.

Approaches directly from the Chiwawa Valley are long and timbered. Choose a spur dividing one of the troughs, since the valleys tend to be brushy; watch for the position of cliffs on these spurs.

GRASSHOPPER PEAK 6950′/2118 m

This is the obvious rocky peak at the southern end of the divide from Sopa Peak, about 2 mi. N of the Napeequa terminus and 1½ mi. E of White River Falls. The peak's N flank is moderately steep rock.

ROUTE: A study of photographs suggests the easiest way is to hike uphill from Grasshopper Meadows campground (White River Road♦) to the upper S ridge for a final scramble.

SOPA PEAK 7235′2205 m

The high point on the White-Napeequa divide S of Clark Mountain (about 3½ mi. S of Boulder Pass and just NW of Lake Elsey). From flanking vantages the peak is quite distinctive; there is a small face on the upper NW. The proposed name "Sopa" is for the Indian chief who befriended the Pacific Fur Company party in 1811.

ROUTE: This appraisal is speculative: the W side appears to be a moderate though long ascent from the White River Trail♦ at about 2½ mi. Bear upslope to reach the main ridge S of the summit.

DAKOBED RANGE

DaKobed is proposed as a name for the important rugged 11-mi. subrange which forms a crescent-shaped topographic outline from Kololo Peaks to Boulder Pass between the White River on the S and the Suiattle-Napeequa Rivers on the N and E. The western side of the subrange is composed of garnet-biotite schist. E of Lightning Creek and to the E of the Butterfly Glacier is the Tenpeak pluton (Pre-Tertiary); this body is largely light-colored hornblende-biotite granodiorite and quartz diorite gneiss. The contact between the pluton and the schist and quartzite of the Napeequa River area is about 1 mi. E of Tenpeak Mountain.[57]

The name "DaKobed," meaning "Great Parent," is applied to preserve the Indian word for Glacier Peak.[58] Exploring climbers have described these mountains as "literally curtained with glaciers"[59] and rhapsodized that "scores of cliff glaciers hung to the shattered remnants of ancient peaks."[60]

DIRTYFACE PK.
MT. STUART
MT. HOWARD
Pt. 6263
GRASSHOPPER PK.
Nason Ridge
lookout
CROOK MTN
MT. SYLVESTER
BANDIT PK.
Raging Creek
Pt. 7270
Schaefer Lake
(hidden)
Pt. 6764
D Lake
Schaefer Creek
Chiwawa Ridge
Y Creek
Chiwawa
River
Valley

Despite brevity, this distinctive watershed crest meets the definition of a small range by its compactness and continuity of summit levels; the range is continuously high, with no pass lower than 7000 ft. A portion of the DaKobed Range forms the eastward deviation of the Cascade crest from its general N-S axis. Typical of the region, the entire subrange is far steeper on the N and E than on the S, a consequence of intense alpine glaciation. Some rock is of sound quality, especially the quartz diorite of the Tenpeak pluton.

The summit marked Tenpeak Mountain is the most striking to the eye, but is surpassed in height by Clark and three of the unofficially named peaks. The title "Tenpeak Range" has had informal association with these peaks, but the principal historic reference is the name "White River Range," applied by the Mazama outing of 1911.[61]

The complexity of this subrange requires analysis: at the eastern end is the highest and bulkiest mass, Clark Mountain, 8576 ft (2614 m). Wholly on the White-Napeequa River divide, it is about 8 mi. SE of Glacier Peak. Clark's distinctively carved rock summit (schist) can be seen from long range; no better description has been seen than the one penned during a Mazama outing: "It is a ponderous wedge of rock, tilted to the sky with glacier cloaking of voluminous drapery."[62] On the E white granite stock is in contact beneath older dark-colored schists.

Clark has a prominent SE summit (8373′/2552 m) 0.7 mi. from the summit. The Napeequa facade of Clark is clad with severely crevassed slope glaciers extending a nearly continual 2 mi. in width. The largest is the Richardson (1.9 km long and 1.4 km^2) which extends from 8200 ft to 5900 ft in two major arms on the N slope. Stadter described it as a "mass of tumbling ice bergs as they coursed down the badly worn cirque to the brink of the precipice which drops down into the canyon of White River" (i.e. Napeequa).[65]

The Walrus (Clark) Glacier (1.9 km wide and .31 mi^2), E of the summit, extends to a spur—Point 7242. Ice extends from 8200 ft to 5800 ft. The Walrus appears to be favorably situated for stability or growth; the period 1947-1967 showed an 1100-ft advance. The glacier contrasted with meadows and scattered tree groves in the parklands provides one of the most esthetic scenes in the Cascade Range.

The next peak from Clark (1.1 mi. NW) is also next in stature (est. 8450′/2576 m). Given the Indian name Luahna, it has a pyramidal shape, with a long rock spur extending down and E. The Pilz Glacier, which slopes 1.8 km. E into the Napeequa, lies on the N side, and heads between Luahna and Chalangin Peak, the next one W (it ranges from 8000′ to 6500′). The W arm of the Richardson Glacier borders the S of the E spur of Luahna.

Chalangin Peak (est. 8350′/2545 m) is ½ mi. W of Luahna, and is the third highest summit in the subrange; it has a rocky, craggy alpine summit area (schist). Its NW side is covered by a portion of the 1½ mi.-wide Butterfly-Moth Glacier ice mass. The Butterfly (1.4 km. long and 1.4 km^2) drains into the Napeequa, and is an extensive, crevassed glacier with a mean altitude of 7200 ft; it is in a general state of retreat. Its westward continuation, the Moth Glacier (est. ¾ mi. wide, 0.5 km^2), drains to the Suiattle from its foot at 7080 ft. The 1926 Forest Service map showed a "Cashmere Glacier" at these locations, but this name, applied by Sylvester, was deleted on the next edition.

There are no other outstanding summits on the crest until Tenpeak Mountain, but at the western extremity of the Moth a diminutive crag (at ½ mi. E of Tenpeak), Neyah Point (8175′/2492 m; name means "good spirit" in Algonquin chinook) crowns the divide.

Tenpeak Mountain is made prominent by a 300-ft summit tower protruding from the granitic crest, which on the N and NW forms an alpine wall some 2000 ft in height. The three sections of the Tenpeak Glaciers are remnant ice on the N face of Tenpeak and Neyah Point; the ice descends to about 6100 ft. A rock buttress divides the two largest portions; the western one consists of a narrow corridor leading to the divide crest at the saddle E of Tenpeak's summit.

The West Peak of Tenpeak is an important separate point ¾ mi. SW of Tenpeak's summit. It has a long S rock spur separating Thunder and Lightning Creek drainages; uniquely, the peak's SW face is its longest and steepest (below the summit on the SE there is a permanent snowpatch). Continuing W, there is a 7000-ft saddle touching the Honeycomb Glacier, and ¼ mi. beyond is a final summit (7600′+ on contours; 7697′ compilation) with the glacier high on its N.

The highland S of Glacier Peak (Kololo Peaks and associated summits) can logically be called part of the DaKobed Range.

Aside from the summits of Clark, Luahna, Tenpeak, and the Kololo Peaks, climbing history is vague. At last one party has traversed from Tenpeak along the crest to Clark, but the subrange still has the fascination of discovery.

CHIWAWA RIDGE from north
U.S. GEOLOGICAL SURVEY

DAKOBED RANGE from south
HERMANN F. ULRICHS COLLECTION, University of Washington Library

CLARK MOUNTAIN 8576′/2614 m

SOUTHEAST ROUTE: The southern slopes of Clark are generally moderate, but are long and avalanche swept, mostly clear of forest. The distinctive features are the S rib leading to the main summit, and a S spur S of the SE summit.

Take Boulder Pass Trail♦ to meadows (est. 5000′), then hike W up brushy talus, then a herder path (can camp in meadow at 5700′). Ascend on talus W (snow in early season), then NW to the obvious "step" at 7000 ft on the S spur of the SE summit. Descend a couloir of 250 ft (class 3) into the SE cirque of the main summit, then angle up snowfields directly to the summit. This is a very direct route in early summer with ample snow cover. One could vary the route by passing over or near the SE summit. Time: 3 hours from camp.

Approach Variation: Leave White River Trail♦ at 6.8 mi. on an old sheep path; follow about 1 mi. to the main S rib. A more westerly route could ascend the SW slope and a continuing rib.

SOUTH RIB: From camp at 5700 ft (Southeast Route) hike W and cross the meadow and brushy areas of the two basins; this involves a descent of about 700 ft after crossing the first spur. Rise obliquely to the high SE cirque of the main summit, then angle directly to the summit—or climb the S rib on the left; here is a short section of broken rock near the top—class 2. Time: 4 hours from trail. Reference: *Mazama* 54, no. 13 (1972), p. 24.

RICHARDSON GLACIER: The glacier is named for J.B. Richardson, a Chelan area settler who roamed these mountains.

Follow the Napeequa River Trail♦ upstream about 2½ mi. from the ford to the upper end of a large meadow (opposite where timber forms on S side); leave the trail before bush begins and follow to extreme end of meadow and cross the river. Hike NW through open timber a short distance to the Richardson-Pilz meltwater stream; follow up, then left on the fork toward the Richardson to reach a small lake (est. 5700′) near a meadow S of Butterfly Butte (good camp; lake is ½ mi. N of ice snout). Traverse S to the glacier; here two routes are apparent: ascend either the E or W arm (arms divided by a rock island between 6600′ and 7100′). Bypass lower ice cliffs on the right; it appears the E arm offers a good route to where it meets the SE ridge about ¼ mi. from the summit, then follow the ridge onward. It appears the W arm can be climbed to high and NW under the summit, then a traverse made E to the upper E ridge, or ascend the steeper, short W ridge.

WALRUS GLACIER: First ascent by Neil Bostick, Clifford Hopson, and Rowland Tabor in August 1954. From about 1 mi. up Napeequa River Trail♦ (from trail junction) cross the river (may find log) and ascend into a small bushy basin. Scramble up heather, slabs, and moraine to snow banks leading up to a saddle (est. 7350′) on the E ridge and below the S flank of the Walrus Glacier. Ascend the glacier westward

(crevasses) to the saddle just SE of the main summit (est. 8100′); cross to the S side and walk to the summit. Crampons advisable.

The route can also be approached from near Boulder Pass (6200′+) by climbing to the E ridge (*Cascadian*, 1964, pp. 50-53). A satisfactory approach from the pass is to ascend NW easy snow to the E end of the glacier, then bear W upglacier toward the summit saddle.

LUAHNA PEAK est. 8450′/2576 m

This is the "White River Mountain" climbed on August 13, 1911 by Rodney L. Glisan, H.H. Prouty, Winthrop E. Stone, and C.W. Whittlesey, members of the Mazama outing, on an extensive trek from Buck Creek Pass (Glisan, *op. cit.*, note 61). From their report it appears they ascended from the Napeequa Valley up a portion of the Pilz Glacier, then climbed a "backbone with the rock so thin in places that the elements had carved a hole or tunnel through which the mountain goats had made a trail" (note 61, ref. p. 8). This would be the final eastern spur of the peak; rock is schist.

ROUTES: The Richardson Glacier's W arm is an apparent route (see Clark Mountain) to its head at about 7500 ft; it appears one could ascend to the W on snow/ice to the easy summit rock. The N side of the peak has been climbed by the Pilz Glacier (see above); use an approach from the Napeequa River Trail♦ and then upstream to the main glacier terminus (6500′). The Pilz heads at a minor saddle on the final eastern spur (est. 8000′); climb rock to the summit. A more pleasant approach is to hike via Butterfly Butte, then traverse easy open slopes to the lower portion of the glacier.

From Thunder Creek the S slope could be ascended; the route appears to be simple and involve nothing more than scrambling. Approach from the White River Trail♦ and the E side of Thunder Creek.

CHALANGIN PEAK est. 8350′/2545 m

From the S, approach from Thunder Creek (see Luahna Peak). From the E, use the Pilz Glacier. From the N, the approach and ascent are more difficult; from the Napeequa River Trail♦ (see Neyah Point) hike upstream to the Butterfly Glacier, then ascend it S to the upper rock area (scrambling).

NEYAH POINT 8175′/2492 m

From the S, approach as for Luahna Peak, or reach from the head of Thunder Creek (see Tenpeak Mountain). The summit is a crag and will require scrambling (details not available ATP).

From the E, leave the Napeequa River Trail♦ where it runs

CLARK MOUNTAIN *and* DAKOBED RANGE *from east*

CLARK MOUNTAIN and upper Napeequa Valley
AUSTIN POST, U.S. GEOLOGICAL SURVEY

CLARK MOUNTAIN from High Pass area
JOHN V. A. F. NEAL

WHITE and NAPEEQUA RIVER VALLEYS

WALLACE C. GUY, U.S. FOREST SERVICE

BANDIT PK.
CLARK MTN.
GRASSHOPPER PK.
DIRTYFACE PK.
SOPA PK.
LUAHNA PK.
CHALANGIN PK.
Butterfly Horn
RICHARDSON
GLACIER
'apeequa
River
Saddle 7750
To Thunder Basin
BUTTERFLY GLACIER
Neyah Pt.
MOTH
GLACIER
Saddle 6750
Moth
Lake
TENPEAK
GLACIERS
Honeycomb
High Route

out on the meadow (5250′), then continue up moraines to the valley head (keep N of stream); scramble up outcrops near the Butterfly's ice to gentler slabs above. Bear W, ascend slabs and snow to logically head for the snow saddle (est. 7750′) on the divide; then travel W to the summit crest. An alternate is to ascend the Moth Glacier and make a traversing ascent to the summit ridge.

A N and NW approach is possible from the Suiattle River Trail♦ using the approach route for Moth Lake, just to the E of the Tenpeak Glaciers. Ascend S to the 6750-ft saddle on the Napeequa divide, then to the upper Moth Glacier and on to the summit ridge.

TENPEAK MOUNTAIN 8281′/2524 m

The first ascent was made by Lloyd Anderson and Tom Campbell on September 21, 1940.

ROUTE: From the N end of upper Thunder Basin (see White River Trail♦) ascend N (some gullies and minor cliffs), then rise leftward (talus, heather, snow) to the base of the summit area. A snowfield steepens to a finger that leads to the E summit col, closely under the summit block. Climb a short loose rock gully left of the col, then solid rock in the face above for 60 ft (face climbing leads to a broken chimney with a good jam crack). Take the obvious ledge left about 30 ft, then broken rock and cracks to the summit. Grade I; class 5.0. Time: 4 hours from basin. References: *Mountaineer,* 1940, pp. 37-38; *Mazama* 54, no. 13 (1972), p. 25.

Descent note: there is a fixed rappel piton 50 ft from the summit on the N corner.

Variations: At least two variations have been done. The first ascent party followed a gully with much loose material to a ridge crack 150 ft below the summit; once on solid rock they took a high angle pitch (one aid and one safety piton), then went up a shallow crack along the N face, and a steep pitch lead to easier rock.

The lower E face was climbed by Harold Deery and Craig Nyce on July 17, 1970; this may be more nearly a new route than a variation. Begin from snow on the S face about 200 ft W of the snow finger. Angle up and right along the left margin to broken rock of the upper E face (class 5.0).

Approach Variation: From Thunder Basin a reasonable route takes a bushy gully adjacent to waterfalls on the W side of the basin; this leads to a passage to high benches with two tarns. Then cross snow below the peak to the route.

WEST RIDGE: First ascent by Dwight F. Crowder, Lesley Tabor, and Rowland W. Tabor, June 12, 1960. Approach from Thunder Basin NW to the open ridge; there is a prominent saddle (7450′) W of the main summit pyramid. Then follow the ridge (some scrambling) to the summit pyramid. Climb the broken ridge (some large loose blocks); class 4 to 5.0. Time: 5 hours from basin.

NORTHWEST FACE: First ascent by Fred Beckey, William Nicolai, and Peter K. Williamson on September 22, 1971.

Start up the snow tongue above the Honeycomb Glacier (see Kololo Peaks), then after some scrambling left, make a right traverse (on or below snowfield) to a heathery rock area. Ascend this and later bear left into a long steep rock depression that leads directly to the summit. Grade II; last pitch is class 5—otherwise class 3 and 4. Reference: *A.A.J.*, 1972, p. 115.

NORTHWEST COULOIR: This long snow/ice couloir of about 35° is a striking feature of the N portion of the Northwest Face. Information about a possible ascent has not been received.

NORTH BUTTRESS: First ascent by Philip Leatherman and Gregory Markov on August 19, 1973. Approach from Honeycomb snout toward Moth Lake, or make a 1500-ft descent via the Moth Glacier from the saddle to Thunder Basin, then contour to the base of the buttress (done on original climb). Follow the crest for 1800 ft (largely class 3 and 4, with a few class 5 pitches). Grade II or III; class 5.7. Reference: *A.A.J.*, 1974, p. 142.

WEST PEAK 7900′+/2408 m

First ascent by Lloyd Anderson and Tom Campbell on September 1, 1940.

ROUTE: The original party climbed a very steep couloir near the eastern head of Lightning Creek to the crest of a spur (this position can also be reached from the western part of Thunder Basin). This spur ridge circles to a high point; the route follows along the knifed crest. Near the high point two pitches of solid rock lead to the summit (class 4). References: *Mountaineer,* 1940, p. 137.

KOLOLO PEAKS 8200′+/2500 m

These are the small rock peaks (almost nunataks) cresting the icy highland S of Glacier Peak, and nearly enveloped by an extensive *mer de glace.* The highland (over 8000′) extends more than 1 mi. E-W and ⅞ mi. N-S (a schist area). The source of three contiguous glaciers, drainage flows to the White, Suiattle, and White Chuck Rivers. The highest points are the crest of E-W crags that divide the Honeycomb from the White River Glacier: the two western crags are barely over 8200 ft and the one to the E is charted at 8197 ft.

Glaciers here are situated so that accumulation zones extend over large areas at high elevations, while lower valley ablation surfaces are relatively narrow. These glaciers therefore tend to remain healthy under present climatic conditions. The declevity of the highland area indicates that from the ice divide the Suiattle and Honeycomb Glaciers flow slowly toward the N and E; these two valley glaciers actually extend outward as distributory tongues from this small icefield.[64]

SOUTH SLOPE: From the White River Trail♦ at about 9.7 mi. ascend by the Lightning Creek High Route to about 5000 ft on the W side of Lightning Creek (good camping);

DAKOBED RANGE and Butterfly Glacier
AUSTIN POST, U.S. GEOLOGICAL SURVEY

TENPEAK MOUNTAIN from southwest
AUSTIN POST, U.S. GEOLOGICAL SURVEY

TENPEAK MOUNTAIN from north
AUSTIN POST, U.S. GEOLOGICAL SURVEY

TENPEAK MTN.
Neyah Pt.
West Peak
MOTH GLACIER
HONEYCOMB GLACIER
Suiattle River

KOLOLO PEAKS and White River Glacier
AUSTIN POST, U.S. GEOLOGICAL SURVEY

TENPEAK MOUNTAIN and Honeycomb Glacier from east
AUSTIN POST, U.S. GEOLOGICAL SURVEY

WHITE MTN.
Pt. 7529
BLACK MTN.
KOLOLO PK.
Pt. 8018
SUIATTLE
GLACIER
West Summit
Pk.7697
HONEYCOMB
GLACIER
West Peak
Saddle
7000
TENPEAK
MTN.
Suiattle
River
Kopeetah
Divide
Thunder
Basin
ice
North
Buttress
Neyah
Point
TENPEAK
GLACIERS
tarn 5600
MOTH
GLACIER

then W to the 7000-ft level—here traverse W ¾ mi. to the moraine at the foot of the White River Glacier. Ascend the moderate E side of the glacier to its upper half, then angle left to an easy hanging section above a thin rock wedge. Ascend to the left tip of this section and onto the rock. Scramble to either of the highest points (very short). There are several similar crags aligned on the crest, just W, easy to reach by traverses; the glaciers touch close to all summit points.

Note: one could ascend through the gap (7800′+) at the head of White River Glacier to reach the head of the Honeycomb, then traverse glacier slopes to the desired summit (the crags are steeper on the N). The terrain here offers wide latitude.

EAST and NORTH SLOPE: From Honeycomb Glacier tarn (see Suiattle River Trail♦) continue S up moraine slopes to about 6000 ft, and then cross the last flat bedrock W onto the ice (crossing below the snout may be dangerous because of high meltwater stream). In early season it is simple to follow near the N margin some 2 mi. to the 7400-ft divide to the Suiattle Glacier (crevassed area just E of divide may cause delays in late season); then ascend SW on the Honeycomb aiming for the windcrest where the two glaciers meet again. Travel W onto the Suiattle—bear around N side of crags and climb to ridge N of western summit (class 2 to summits).

Generally it is simpler to head up the left-center of the Honeycomb (stay left of the center nunatak) all the way to the windcrest. Note: the Kololo Peaks can also be reached from the high southern segments of the White Chuck Glacier (see Glacier Peak for approach).

BRAHMA PEAK 8078′/2462 m

This peak is a high summit on Napeequa Ridge, not named on maps, 2 mi. S of Buck Mountain. Above Napeequa Valley the peak exhibits a long sweep of lavender-colored schist cliffs. The N face forms a steep rock wall spanning almost 1½-mi. and up to 1000 ft in height, with the bedding dipping sharply E; the wall rises abruptly from a wide, shallow glacier (0.3 km²) that drains into Alpine Creek and the Chiwawa River. The narrow E-trending ridge of the wall features a spire with a reddish S face. There are ice segments on the SE side of the spur, at the head of James Creek.

ROUTES: Technically, the easiest way to gain the summit seems to be a long ascent due N from Napeequa River Trail♦ (near Boulder Pass Trail junction—4200′+—to the summit crest closely E of the top). The scenic rewards could be compensation for an easy but long ascent.

It appears possible to reach the upper S side of the W ridge from Louis Creek at about 6000 ft (hike from Napeequa River). This approach involves ascent at about 1¼ mi. of steep mountainside and some scrambling with careful route-finding.

BUCK MOUNTAIN 8573′/2613 m

Buck, one of the two highest peaks in the Chiwawa Mountains, dominates the divide between the upper Napeequa and Chiwawa Rivers about 9 mi. E of Glacier Peak. Buck has a long W ridge leading to a W summit at 8254 ft (2516 m); the S side of this ridge is gentle and the N extremely precipitous. There is a gentle 8300-ft (2530 m) summit 1 mi. S of the true summit. The upper S slope of the summit area is largely filled by perennial snow of an elliptical shape.

The northern facade of Buck is formidable black schist. The 1½-mi.-wide face is notable for a near-vertical step resembling a shoe-horn; granite here was intruded between schist layers. The description from the Mazama party is appropriate: "Buck Mountain unfolded into three rakish pinnacles of sensational aspect, with walls that descended thousands of feet."[65] The account also commented on three places on the walls where isolated glaciers clung to sharply pitched shelves. Immediately W of the step is a long, sheer and dangerous N wall with a small pocket ice patch resting on basal slabs (its foot at 5600-ft is low for an E-side glacier). A steep but shorter NE face features two rocky arms which cradle the hanging King Glacier (7600′ to 6500′); it drains to King Lake, then waterfalls cascade through brush and cliffs to Buck Creek.

WEST SHOULDER: Follow Buck Creek Trail♦ 10 minutes past the 4-mi. mark, to the large slide track (good camp by stream just below trail beyond track). Cross Buck Creek and hike through heavy timber straight toward Mt. Berge. Round the E-facing timber shoulder to talus farther into the basin of the S fork; ascend talus or snow until above all brush, then traverse left under cliffs and climb to the pass (6700′+) above Louis Creek on easy terrain (the low point between Buck and Berge, with a thin fence of larch). Now the ascent is a long, gentle snow hike up the W shoulder to the summit. Keep just S of the W summit; at the top there is a bit of scrambling (class 2); Time: 6 hours from trail.

Approach Variation: From the Napeequa River Trail♦ hike to the head of Louis Creek at about 6500 ft. One can follow the W shoulder to the summit or take the low-gradient SW slope almost anywhere.

NORTHEAST FACE: A relatively open, easy route can be taken to King Lake (5900′+), but poor planning will lead into thick brush. Take Buck Creek Trail♦ about ¼ mi. beyond Chiwawa River footbridge (3450′), where on the left some trees have been cut (to verify, sheep trail right of foot trail climbs to extensive rock outcrop in 150 yds). Hike W

UPPER CHIWAWA RIVER AREA
WALLACE C. GUY, U.S. FOREST SERVICE

slightly downstream toward Buck Creek. Locate an obvious rocky stretch where the stream narrows between large boulders and forms two successive small falls; cross at boulders or 100 yds upstream (danger when high water). About 60 ft downstream of falls is a deer trail, near where timber meets slide alder area on S side of King Lake watercourse; follow this until it fades, but obvious brush-free areas can be taken, gradually working closer to the descending ridge. At about 4600 ft the last open area closes in with huckleberry bushes; begin bearing slightly right, then more sharply right until a stream bed at 5000 ft is reached. Follow bed to the lake (best camp is on knoll N of exit). Time: 5 hours from road.

From the lake's N side ascend debris and a rockslide. When snow is reached, angle left toward the ice front (watch for falling debris when beneath icefall), then round the corner and gain rock rib. Several hundred ft of scrambling (to about 7450′) passes crevasses; then bear up and left. Climb the upper lobe of the glacier to about 7950 ft, then the route becomes a very steep snow chute at its head. One report states from the top of the chute 100 ft of class 4 rock leads to the summit crest. Another report indicates the glacier is left near the chute's base, then easy rock on a ridge is followed to the N face; a corner is turned right to a solid chute (class 5) which leads to the NE summit ridge. Travel W to the base of the summit tower. Grade II; take crampons. Time: 5 hours from lake.

Note: The N wall was climed by Cal Folsom and Mark Moore in September 1976. The wall proved to be extremely loose and dangerous—the party warns they recommend others avoid this climb.

SOUTHEAST ROUTE: Can be seen from Trinity. From King Lake (see Northeast Face) contour and rise on a rockslide to a small notch (est. 6700′) to the SW. Descend slightly into a small E-facing basin, then climb easy heather and scree to a low notch on a subsidiary ridge descending from Buck (its southern slope is quite gentle). Follow rockslides to a snowfield leading to the high saddle between the S and main summits. The W side of the summit pinnacle is easily climbed over loose rock (class 2). Time: 5 hours from lake.

MT. BERGE 7953′/2424 m

This granitic peak is located between Buck Mountain and High Pass; bedrock is High Pass pluton. The name is in memory of Richard Berge, who met tragedy on Mt. Baring. The eastern of two summits is higher (W summit surveyed at 7923′); the N wall is precipitous, and there is a residual glacier on the peak's NW. The S and W slopes are more moderate; there is a long ridge, rocky and alpine, extending SW nearly at summit level, then trending S. The first climb was apparently made by the 1926 Mazama party which called the peak Granite Mountain and circled the southwestern cliffs from the barren basin at the head of the Napeequa's N fork; however, their chronicle does not describe the summit rock climb. The summit was definitely reached by a Seattle Mountaineer group in the late 1950s on a traverse from Buck Mountain.

ROUTES: From the Napeequa River Trail♦ and basin 1 mi. S of High Pass (about 6700′) ascend SE, keeping S of the spur from the W summit. A high open basin on the S of the true summit offers the best route to the small hornlike summit. This is a short exposed rock climb (class 4). Reference: *Mazama* 8, no. 12 (1926): 56.[66]

The summit approach is feasible from the pass (6700′+) between Louis Creek and Buck Creek's S fork (see Buck Mountain—West Shoulder). Ascend snow and alpine slopes W to the rocky ridge extending S of the W peak, then follow it toward the W summit until practical to bear right into the open basin.

NAPEEQUA PEAK 8073′/2461 m

This pyramidal granodiorite peak stands 1 mi. SW of High Pass, on the divide between the Napeequa and Suiattle Rivers. The solid rock is fractured into generally large blocks on the summit horn; in the high cirque facing N and E there is perennial snow, while the W slope is largely rocky. Members of the 1926 Mazama outing refer to this cirque, but it is not apparent that they made the summit ascent. Reference: *Mazama* 49, no. 13 (1967):27.

ROUTE: The Napeequa River Trail♦ passes about ¾ mi. E of the summit on the ascent to High Pass. An exit in the basin at about 6400 ft would allow a traversing ascent. On the final pyramid, climb to the top of the snow, then bear left onto good rock (class 3 to summit). Time: 2 hours from pass.

CIRQUE MOUNTAIN 7966′/2428 m

The name given by the Mazama outing should prevail, though the massif could really be considered an extension of Napeequa Peak. The outing personnel were inspired by the impressive sight of Triad Lake at the glacier's foot in the northern cirque, and the masses of white granite (High Pass pluton). They wrote that the precipitous crest of the mountain "extends for nearly a mile to the highest point, and finally juts down into the canyon of the Suiattle River. There are no less than five or six fair-sized cliff glaciers perched on its eastern slopes. It presents a terribly shattered appearance."[67]

ROUTE: Photographic study indicates the same approach as Napeequa Peak should suffice, then with a moderate ascent of the S or E slope to the highest point; climbing history is incomplete. It appears that the N face would offer interesting alpine climbing.

MT. CLEATOR 7630′/2326 m

This small but alpine peak, N of Mt. Berge and NE of High Pass, has precipitous walls on the Buck Creek (N) drainage, and an isolated tower beneath the N summit rim. The tentative name is for Fred Cleator of the Forest Service who is known to have explored the glaciers and high country between the Napeequa and upper White Chuck Rivers in 1929. The first ascent was possibly done by a party from The Mountaineers on August 3, 1921.[68]

ROUTE: Nothing is documented, but the SW spur from High Pass appears straightforward. The summit trek would be combined with the ascent of Berge.

BUCK MOUNTAIN from northwest
JOHN V.A.F. NEAL

RAMPART MTN.
OLD GIB MTN
GARLAND PK.
Horn
BUCK MTN
Middle summit
Tower
MT. CLEATOR
MT. BERGE
Buck Creek Valley

Pt. 7529
CIRQUE MTN.
GLACIER PEAK
Streamline Ridge
Chocolate
Creek canyon
pocket glaciers
Triad Creek
Triad Lake

LIBERTY CAP 6700′+/2042 m

This is a prominent crag of black schist, flanked by steep grassy slopes, 1 mi. SW of Buck Creek Pass.

ROUTE: See Buck Creek Trail♦.

HELMET BUTTE 7366′/2245 m

With its helmet of white granitic gneiss on the northern summit edge, this well chronicled formation stands about ½ mi. NE of Buck Creek Pass. It has been described as "a steep pyramid of green vesture and . . . craggy crest."[69]

ROUTES: The ascent is a steep hike on the W of SW. Another way is from the heather shoulder on the N; near the top bear left of the rock cap to the step on its S; a short class 3 scramble on the W side puts one atop.

FORTRESS MOUNTAIN 8674′/2644 m

Fortress, the highest and northern termination of the Chiwawa Mountains, is about 2 mi. NE of Buck Creek Pass at the head of the Chiwawa River; the N and W slopes drain into branches of the Suiattle. An apt description is taken from the Mazama outing of 1911, "A frowning crest surmounted by what appeared to be a lava spout with perpendicular walls, unscalable from any angle."[70] Recent studies indicate quartz diorites of the Cloudy Pass pluton here are in contact with roof pendant metamorphic rocks; surface rock is gneiss.

Fortress has a S-protruding spur, with a short, steep E face. In a complex arrangement, there is a very rugged, rocky NW ridge extending some 1¼ mi. with high points (notably at 8386′ and 8197′) The wide, alpine, 2000-ft NE face of this ridge falls steeply into the head of Miners Creek, with the Fortress Glacier and a terminal lake. The quite suitable name "Fortress" has long appeared at the correct location, except in 1926 when the Forest Service map interchanged names and position with Chiwawa Mountain.

SOUTHWEST ROUTE: From Buck Creek Pass (see Buck Creek Trail♦) follow the path contouring the SE slopes of Helmet Butte; when it bears S, leave and ascend the gentle lower SW slopes of Fortress; a broad heather belt leads to a wide snow-patched basin under the rocky summit slopes. Take the principal snowfield to its apex, and the continuing wide finger to the high SW ridge. Turn left and scramble readily to the summit (class 2). Time: 4 hours. References: *Mazama* 49, no. 13 (1967):26; *Routes and Rocks,* Massie Lake High Route.

SOUTHEAST ROUTE: Traverse Chiwawa basin W at the 6500-ft level (see Red Mountain Trail♦) until beneath the SE side of Fortress (1½ mi.). Ascend directly on easy slopes toward the summit into a shallow basin (scree or snow); keep right of the steep SE rock spur, then continue to the depression (wide gully) which reaches to the E ridge near the summit. Ascend the depression to the level area on the ridge, then scramble the final ridge SW (est. 400 vertical ft). This is a slightly harder route than the SW one; class 3 max.

An approach variation from Pass No Pass traverses around the S flank of the upper cliffs, then bears closely beneath the E face, bearing to the upper E ridge.

Approach Variation: From the head of Miners Creek and the forested basin NE of the mountain, ascend creek bed, talus, moraine, then a long snow slope to the 7200-ft col about 1 mi. E of the summit. A variation using the E ridge from this col was reported by John Prochnau and Clark Stockwell, September 1962 (*Mountaineer,* 1963, p. 94). There is considerable loose rock—keep a practical distance S of the crest to minimize scrambling.

CHIWAWA MOUNTAIN 8459′/2578 m

Because of its association with Lyman Glacier on the NE slope, Chiwawa is better known than Fortress Mountain. The smaller Hanging Glacier nests in a cirque on the E face of the mountain's northern spur. Chiwawa also has a long rocky eastern arm, peaking at 8000 ft 1 mi. E of the summit, close to Spider Pass. A large party from the 1921 Mountaineer outing led by Lorenz A. Nelson climbed the mountain, but it is hard to imagine that prospectors did not precede them. The N spur, rising from Cloudy Pass, was visited by a Mazama group in 1926, but loose rock stopped them and a succeeding party. Rock on Chiwawa is biotite gneiss, intensely migmatized on the S flank (Crowder, p. 833). References: *Mountaineer,* 1921, p. 24; *Mazama* 8, no. 12 (1926): 21-23; vol. 20, no. 12 (1938), pp. 20-21; vol. 6, no. 2 (1921), p. 49.

LYMAN GLACIER: From Upper Lyman Lake (see Railroad Creek Trail♦) ascend to the SW corner of the glacier terminus. Ascend moderately steep névé (bare rock in late season) around the N of the central rock island to the glacier's upper portion; if conditions are icy, one can keep to right on slabs. Ascend to the extreme S tip of the glacier where it joins the summit ridge. A short scramble W (class 2) completes the climb. Grade I or II. Time: 5 hours.

SOUTHEAST SLOPE: From Chiwawa basin at about 6400 ft (see Red Mountain Trail♦) ascend moderate slopes on an ascending traverse into the basin SE of the mountain. Bear toward the snowfield under the short, steep SE face, then work up to the final E ridge a few hundred yds E of the summit (final rock scramble; difficulties not documented).

SOUTHWEST ROUTE: Approach as for Fortress Mountain, Southeast Route. Bear toward the Fortress-Chiwawa saddle; just before the saddle ascend NE on snow slopes (these lead into the low-angle face between the W ridge and a rock spur on the right). At the upper end of the snow exit on the right and follow easy talus and brownish rock slopes to the summit (class 2). Time: 2½ hours from Chiwawa basin.

CIRQUE MOUNTAIN from High Pass area
JOHN V.A.F. NEAL

FORTRESS and CHIWAWA MOUNTAINS from southwest
JOHN V.A.F. NEAL

CHIWAWA MOUNTAIN and Lyman Lake
L.D. LINDSLEY PHOTOGRAPHIC COLLECTION, University of Washington

(Below) DUMBELL MOUNTAIN from Cloudy Pass Meadows
ROBERT J. DE WITZ, U.S. FOREST SERVICE

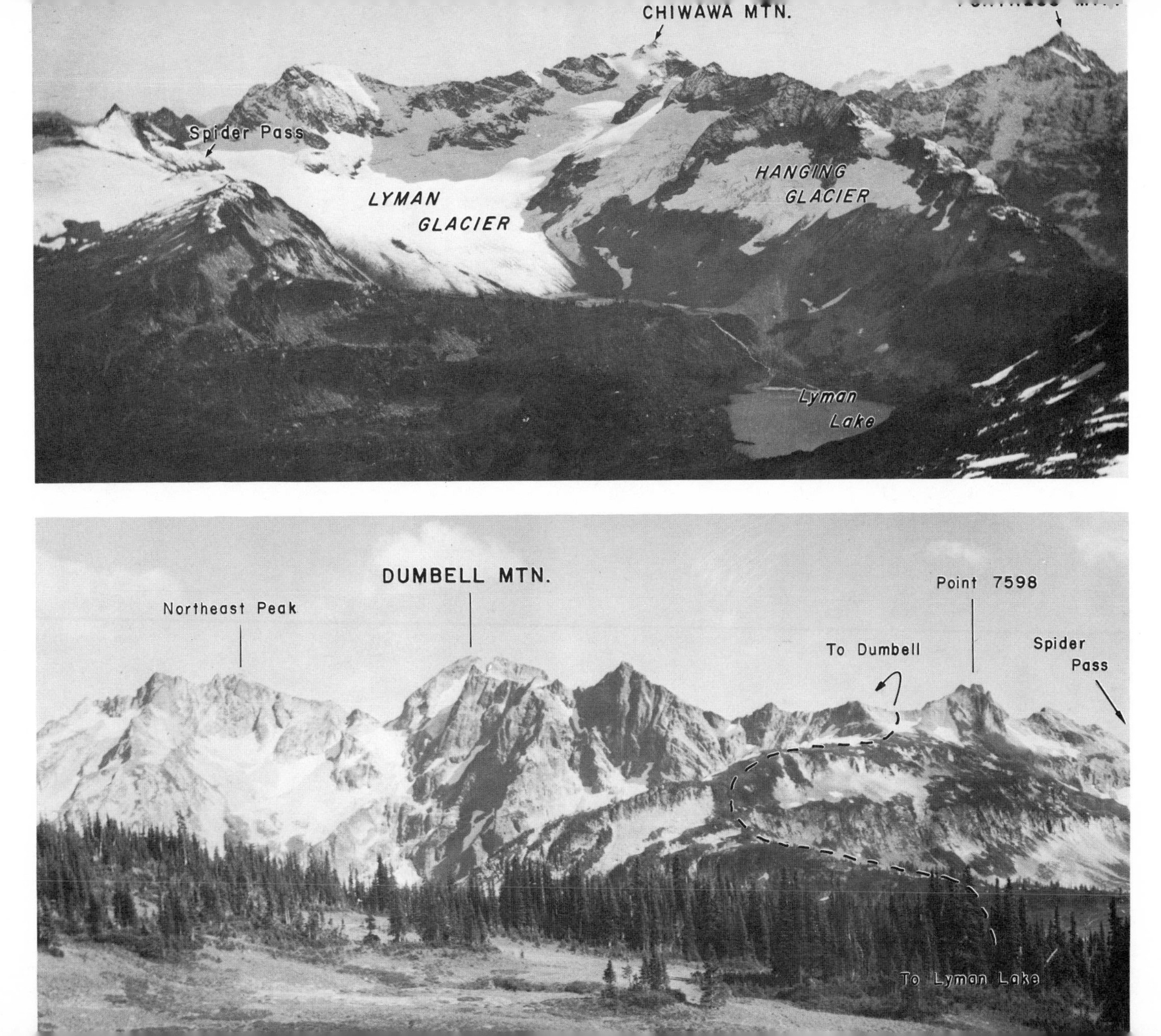
CHIWAWA MTN.
Spider Pass
LYMAN GLACIER
HANGING GLACIER
Lyman Lake
DUMBELL MTN.
Northeast Peak
Point 7598
To Dumbell
Spider Pass
To Lyman Lake

Using this route, the ascent can be made from Buck Creek Pass and return in one day.

Other routes: no history on completion of the N ridge is known; once the high crest is gained, scrambling onward appears feasible.

DUMBELL MOUNTAIN 8421′/2567 m

Dumbell is a strategic massif on the Phelps-Railroad Creek divide, approximately 2½ mi. SE of Lyman Lake. An early description of the mountain referred to it as "a ponderous gendarme in regal isolation and reaching to a dizzy height" (McNeil, op. cit., p. 23). The summit marked Dumbell (named by Sylvester) is the SW peak of the alpine massif, and from the N it could fit this exalted description. From the S the peak resembles a rocking chair, with the highest portion on the E, and a permanent snowpatch cradled beneath the summit rock (gneiss).

The NE peak (marked at 8415′, but apparently higher at the northern tip), ½ mi. distant on the divide between Big Creek and Hart Lake, is actually more bulky and could be considered a separate mountain. Its N flanks are steep and alpine, and to the N and E is a rugged area of sub-summits and steep crests holding three small cirque glaciers. S of both peaks, in a high pocket at the western head of Big Creek, is attractive "Dumbell Lake" (6500′).

Dumbell may have been climbed in the era of prospecting; it was definitely climbed by Richard Alt and George Fahey in August 1932 from Phelps Creek.[71] A climbing report from the Mazama party (Lee Darling, Ed Hughes, Curtis Ijames, and Don Woods—August 15, 1938) credited two Holden miners with the climb in 1937. Reference: *Mazama* 20, no. 12 (December 1938); 18-19.

SOUTHWEST ROUTE: From Lyman Lake (see Railroad Creek Trail♦) take the hiker route to the crest E of the lake. Follow a path east, then bear SE across the basin of Rubin Creek to the shallow ridge depression immediately E of the double-summited rock peak (Point 7598/2316 m); then drop several hundred ft on the Phelps Creek slope (big blocks here). Cross a cirque eastward (est. 1 mi.), then ascend easy, solid slabs toward a false summit (W part of "rocking chair"). Work around its S about 300 ft before the top, cross onto the cradled snowpatch, then climb to the saddle W of the true summit. Class 3; time: 5 hours.

From the false summit it is feasible to make a ridge traverse to the summit (possible short rappel at start).

SOUTH SLOPE: From upper Phelps Creek Trail♦ in Spider Meadow (est. 5200′) ascend N, then NE directly toward the summit to reach the snowpatch.

Other routes: The N side of Dumbell appears feasible from the NE, but involves moderately steep mixed alpine terrain. From Big Creek and Dumbell Lake it seems possible to simply ascend scree and rocky slopes to the snowpatch.

There is an unnamed tower on the W ridge of Dumbell which may offer a rock climb. The dominant crag to the W is Point 7598.

POINT 7598 7598′/2316 m

This small but noticeable sharp rock point, between the Dumbell massif and Spider Pass, was climbed by Ed Johann on August 16, 1972 from the Phelps Creek face; the ascent and descent were done unroped (class 3 or 4). A rusty miner's axe and old piece of rope were found at the base.

NORTHEAST PEAK

Routes seem feasible from Holden, but are not documented. Follow Big Creek to about 4500 ft, then ascend due W. Use a broad shallow drainage basin: its lower portion is rocky, with brush and small timber patches. Above is a long talus slope, then snow and a glacier under the summit rim. A short rock climb can lead to the summit. An alternative would be to make the ascent from the lake, farther up Big Creek.

RED MOUNTAIN 7600′+/2316 m

Red is a lesser summit of primarily historic interest; early miners dubbed it "Red Hill" and such pioneers as "Red Mountain Ole" had claims on its slopes near the Spider Glacier.[72] Here along the S contact of Cloudy Pass pluton the iron sulphide deposited by gases promoted weathering of breccia, lava, and granite to a rusty color.[73] About 1½ mi. SE of Chiwawa Mountain on the divide of Phelps Creek, Red has a snowcap on the summit's N side well into summer. The flanking Spider Glacier is a very narrow ice defile (0.1 km^2) at the terminal W fork of Phelps Creek, and lying against the S side of Entiat Ridge. The actual ice is not really on Red's slopes, but in a hanging valley branch of upper Phelps Creek.

SOUTHWEST SLOPE: The 40° reddish slope forms a quite regular profile. Take Red Mountain♦ and Phelps Ridge trails to 6000 ft SW of the summit. Ascend NE directly from meadows, along the easy slope. A variation would be to exit from the trail, S of the summit or on Phelps Ridge SE of the peak; simple ways can be used to ascend along or W of the ridge crest.

NORTH SIDE: From Spider Glacier or Spider Pass (see Phelps Creek Trail♦) ascend S over rubble and snow to the north saddle (7200′+). Two small teeth N of the summit, can be bypassed; the N saddle can also be reached by ascending NE from the end of the Chiwawa River Trail (see Red Mountain Trail♦).

COUGAR MOUNTAIN 6701′/2042 m

This is a prominent domelike summit on the crest of the Entiat Mountains, about 5 mi. NE of Fish Lake; trails reach to the summit from the SE.

DUMBELL MOUNTAIN from Southeast
JOHN V.A.F. NEAL

BONANZA PK.
tentative route
Big Creek
Northeast Peak
ice
NORTH STAR MTN.
DOME PK.
DUMBELL MTN.
Dumbell Lake

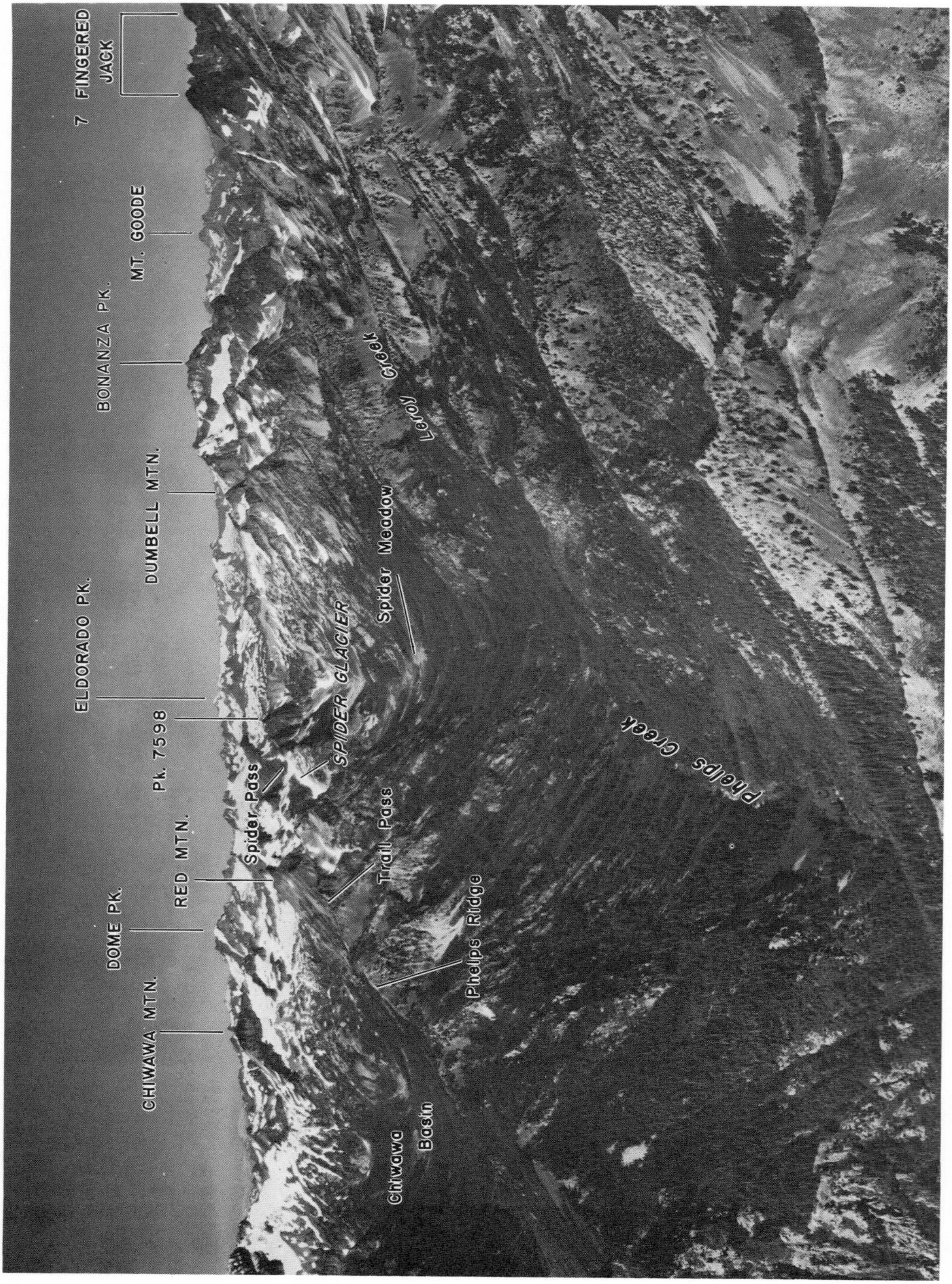

PHELPS CREEK BASIN
WALLACE C. GUY. U.S. FOREST SERVICE

ROUTE: From Entiat River Road♦ and Tommy Creek Road♦ take South Tommy Creek Trail No. 1423. It is about 7 mi. to the summit area. Another route is to use Mad River Trail and branch up Jimmy Creek to S of the summit. Approach via road no. 2924 (see Klone Peak Trail♦).

SIGNAL PEAK 6920′+/2109 m

Another prominent domelike summit on the crest of the Entiat Mountains, about 7 mi. NE of Fish Lake. Of the two summits, the SW is higher; the peak is rocky on the N and E.

ROUTE: From Brief on the Entiat River Road♦ take trails W to Tyee Ridge Trail No. 1415, which leads close to the summit on the SW (est. 8 mi.). One could also use South Tommy Creek Trail (per Cougar Mountain) and then hike SE on Tyee Ridge Trail (est. 8 mi. total).

KLONE PEAK 6820′/2079 m

Klone is a largely forested summit between the middle portions of the Entiat and Chiwawa Rivers. A trail reaches the summit, which was once used for a lookout station (the summit area has humps on the E and W); the Forest Service lists summit altitude at 6834 ft.

ROUTES: See Klone Peak Trail♦. The approach can be made from Tommy Creek Road♦, or from the NE via Three Creek. Mad River Trail is another approach.

KELLY MOUNTAIN (6760′+/2060 m) is about 1 mi. SE of Klone. Reach by hiking along the slope SE into the saddle, then onto Kelly.

BASALT PEAK 6004′/1830 m

This moderate summit is 2.3 mi. NE of Chiwawa River and Rock Creek in the Entiat Mountains. A trail leads over the summit.

ROUTE: Take Rock Creek Trail♦ about 3 mi., then E on trail no. 1530, then S to cross the peak (est. 7 mi. total). One could also approach from the end of Minnow Creek Road No. 2924, which branches off Chiwawa River Road♦ (est. 4 mi. total).

GARLAND PEAK 7535′/2296 m

The first summit of note in the S portion of the Entiat Mountains, the peak has a rock wall on the N of nearly 1000 ft at one place; however, it is probably not of unique climbing interest.

ROUTE: From the Shetipo-Garland Trail♦ exit at about the 7½-mi. point, near 7000 ft on the SW side of the summit; an easy scramble leads to the top. The ascent could also be done from the saddle W of the summit (at about 9 mi.).

DEVILS SMOKESTACK 7600′+/2316 m

This is a prominent rocky summit of the Entiat Mountains. The peak is actually an eastward-bearing crag spur rising off the main ridge crest at about 1 mi. NW of Garland. Its rocky S slope is characterized by a sequence of gullies above an immense scree/talus basin. The peak's E corner and broad N face are composed of steep but well broken rock. The first ascent was made by Michael Hane, Robert Grant, and Duane LaViolet in 1951.

ROUTE: WEST SLOPE: At about the 10-mi. point (see Garland Peak) the trail traverses about ½ mi. W of the summit. The route follows gullies and broken rock (class 2).

NORTH FACE: First ascent Bruce Garrett and Donn Heller in July 1970. Hike the Entiat River Trail♦ 2½ mi. to Anthem Creek, ford the Entiat, then ascend forested slopes 2500 ft (party bivouacked among blocks under NE side). Begin the 1500 ft face on the E edge, traversing right on ledges, then up loose ribs for 500 ft. A water-polished gully at the 700-ft level provides solid class 5. Complete the ascent on ribs (class 3 and 4); used four shrub runners. Time: 5 hours on face. References: *Mountaineer,* 1970-1971, pp. 81-82.

RAMPART MOUNTAIN 7693′/2345 m

Rampart is about 1½ mi. NW of Garland. Its upper slopes are gentle, especially the S, which resembles a tilted erosion plateau. There is a massive rock cliff on the NE side above Cow Creek Meadows (6000 to 7000′).

ROUTE: An easy climb from the trail (see Garland Peak) at about 10½ mi., where the S side is reached about 7000 ft.

FIFTH OF JULY MOUNTAIN 7696′/2346 m

About 2½ mi. NW of Garland this peak is slightly more distinctive than its neighbors. From its summit N to Ice Creek Ridge, the main crest becomes lower and without specific interest.

ROUTE: The trail (see Garland Peak) passes high (est. 7000′) on the mountain's SE side at Cow Creek Pass—est. 13 mi. A shorter approach from the road is to use the Cow Creek Meadows Trail♦ connection from Entiat River Trail♦. The ascent appears to merely be an alpine hike.

OLD GIB MOUNTAIN 7081′/2158 m

This is a volcanic neck featuring vertical columns and joints which formed when molten lava cooled and shrank. The neck is located nearly 3 mi. SE of Trinity between Chiwawa River and Rock Creek.

ROUTE: One can readily hike the S ridge. See Estes Butte Trail♦.

CARNE MOUNTAIN 7085′/2160 m

Carne is a gentle summit in the Entiat Mountains, only 1¼ mi. E of Phelps Creek.

ROUTE: A short path from the main trail junction leads to the summit lookout from the S. See Rock Creek Trail♦ and Leroy Creek—Carne Mountain Trail♦.

ICE CREEK RIDGE 8109′/2472 m

An NW-trending alpine ridge of over 3 mi. which extends from the saddle 1 mi. S of Mt. Maude to Pomas Pass. Although the western slopes and basins of the ridge are moderate, the E scarp is rocky and rugged, with a number of small glaciers and ice patches tucked beneath the crest.

The highest peak is about 1½ mi. S of upper Ice Lake, and features a broad, steep 2000-ft wall dropping into Ice Creek. The second highest peak (8033′/2448 m) is less than ½ mi. S of the 7600-ft saddle adjacent to Maude. The ridge is crowned with a number of minor though rocky points.

ROUTES: The easiest approach is to use the Leroy-Carne Mountain Trail♦ which traverses below the W side of Ice Creek Ridge (reach ridge slope at 3 mi. from Leroy Creek basin). This position can also be reached by taking the 3½-mi Carne Mountain Trail (see Phelps Creek Trail♦), then hiking the above trail N. The high points of Ice Creek Ridge can be reached by ascending the W slope from the trail. An alternate route is to travel S from the 7600-ft saddle (keep on W side of crest).

The Ice Lakes Trail♦ can be used to reach the E side of the ridge, but climbing routes will be more difficult and alpine here; there is a 3000-ft altitude differential from the trail.

SPECTACLE BUTTES 8392′/2558 m

Two craggy rock peaks (gneiss) 2 mi. E of Mt. Maude between the upper bight of the Entiat River and Ice Creek. The higher summit (1¼ mi. SE of lower Ice Lake) is pyramid-shaped, with a large talus basin on the W. A col (7200′) separates it from the NW summit (8070′/2460 m), which has a crown of shattered blocks; both summits are steepest on the E.

WEST ROUTE: From Ice Lakes Trail♦ contour E from the lower lake to the central col, from where either summit is an easy hike and scramble. The higher summit is also moderate on its W; easy to reach directly from the trail.

NORTH ROUTE: From near the 14-mi. point on the Entiat River Trail♦ ford the river and ascend S through a draw to a basin near the 7000-ft level. To reach the lower summit ascend talus to a broad ridge crest (7450′) that leads SE; easy from here. To reach the higher summit travel through the central col and work S to the western slopes.

MT. MAUDE 9082′/2768 m

Maude, one of the two highest peaks in the Entiat Mountains, is among the few Cascade non-volcanic peaks above 9000 ft. Maude is a dominating hulk with a magnificent position, connected with the Seven Fingered Jack and Fernow massifs. Maude's southern and western slopes are moderate, but the South Entiat Glacier on the steep N face is the most spectacular in this region of the Cascades. The peak was named by A.H. Sylvester.[74] Despite their prominence, both Maude and Fernow were unusually late in being listed on Forest Service maps. First ascent by John Burnett and Hermann F. Ulrichs in July 1932 (via a couloir on the WNW); this was one of Ulrichs' first contributions to alpine history in the Cascades. Reference: *A.A.J.*, 1936, p. 468.

SOUTH SHOULDER: From meadows and campsite at 6000 ft in the basin (Leroy Creek Trail♦) traverse SE and ascend a scree/talus-covered slope to the S shoulder at about 8000 ft. The route from here to the summit is moderately angled scree. Time: 4 hours.

Approach Variation: From Ice Lakes reach the shoulder from the 7600-ft saddle SW of the upper lake. The scramble from the lake to the saddle involves a bit of broken rock and possibly snow patches.

WEST SLOPE: Using the Leroy Creek approach make an ascending traverse SE above the right fork of the creek, then ascend a straightforward 2000-ft couloir on the W slope. The entire slope is a corrugation of minor rock waves and scree gullies, low-angled and slabby, with much climbing latitude. The rock is generally swept clean, climbing is firm. The first ascent was made on the N portion of the W slope (class 3).

NORTH FACE: This is the 3000-ft face of the South Entiat Glacier, the largest of the Entiat Glaciers (est. 3000 ft wide and 2000 ft downslope). It has a N orientation on a steep irregular slope and is broken and hanging in character, above steep slabs that continue W to the cirque headwall. First ascent by Fred Beckey, Don Gordon, John Rupley, and Herb Staley June 16, 1957.

From upper Ice Lake (via Phelps Creek Trail♦ or Ice Creek Trail♦) cross the ridge N through a 7600-ft saddle to the glacier's E section. Make a descending traverse W (moderately steep snow) to bypass a rock arm, then slightly upward and across a glacier to the snow/ice depression on the central/W portion of the face. Ascend this 2000 ft to the summit (40° to 50°); crampons advised. Grade III. Time: 5 hours. Reference: *A.A.J.*, 1958, pp. 82-83; *Mountaineer,* 1958, pp. 102-103; *Climbing,* July-August 1975, pp. 24-26.

The ice depression could also be reached from upper Entiat Meadows by a direct climb to the glacier. Note: in late-season the ice may be discontinuous. In early season it is easy to mistake a couloir E for the route.

Variation: Crawling Rat Rib: By Tim Benedict and Gary Jones, July 23, 1971. From Entiat basin take the main snow chute right of the South Entiat Glacier, or use rock outcrops, to beneath the main upper depression. Then traverse left (crossing the depression/gully) over mixed snow and rock to the prominent rib which forms its left flank. The rib is

ENTIAT MOUNTAINS from northeast
WILL F. THOMPSON

DEVILS SMOKESTACK
FIFTH OF JULY MTN.
MT. DAVID
RAMPART MTN.
MT. SYLVESTER
GARLAND PK.
BANDIT PK.
DUNCAN HILL
SASKA PK.
CHORAL PK.
Pomas Pass
Cow Creek Meadow
PINNACLE MTN.
Larch Lakes
Pinnacles
7638
Milham Pass
Peak 7942
Peak 7738
Emerald Park
Tumble
Creek
Valley

UPPER ENTIAT RIVER VALLEY from east
WALLACE C. GUY, U.S. FOREST SERVICE

climbed (some loose rock). In a gully near the summit (loose rock and snow) work right out of gully and reach a narrow ledge under a small roof which requires a belly-crawl. Grade II. Class 3 and 4 with a few moves of 5. Time: 7 hours. References: *Mountaineer,* 1970-1971, p. 82.

NORTH FACE—ENTIAT ICEFALL: This is the icefall high on the E side of the face. First ascent by Fred Dunham and James Wickwire on August 24, 1967.

From Entiat Meadows climb scree and water-polished slabs to the belt of ice cliffs forming the hanging glacier. Ascend a steep snow finger between ice blocks (possible danger). In the upper icefall (nine pitches) ice pitons were used; slopes run to 55° but belay platforms available. A 20-ft ice pillar in a crevasse required aid. Easy rock bypasses a schrund and leads to the ridge crest E of the summit; scramble up the E spur. Grade III. Reference: *A.A.J.*, 1968, p. 133.

MARMOT PYRAMID 8500′+/2591 m

The pyramid is a subsidiary summit located ⅜ mi. E of Maude and connected by a snow col. First ascent by Charles

MT. MAUDE and SEVEN FINGERED JACK from Mt. Fernow
HERMANN F. ULRICHS

Franklin, Don Moody, and Verl Rogers in 1951. The Pyramid can be reached from upper Ice Lake or Entiat Meadows. Climb a rock gully at the eastern corner to the E ridge. Class 3.

NORTH TOWER OF MAUDE 8600′+/2621 m

The tower, located on the crest about ½ mi. NW of Maude's summit, first appears in climbing history when John Burnett and Hermann Ulrichs (July 1932) mistook it for the route to the summit of the main peak and climbed it to find the route barred by a pronounced gap.

The approach is from Leroy Creek basin; the original route took the S face. Ribs and gullies allow route flexibility. The climb is reported as steep scrambling, somewhat loose and exposed (class 3 and 4).

The tower was climbed from the W side by Dick McGowan and Ralph Pratt in September 1954, by probably at least partially a new route (class 3-4). References: *Mountaineer,* 1954, p. 64.

SEVEN FINGERED JACK 9077′/2767 m

Here is a descriptive name appropriate for a rugged formation of steep gneissic crags once called "Entiat Needles" by miners.[75] On roughly a 1-mi. N-S axis between Maude and Fernow, the highest summit is almost exactly 1 mi. NW of Maude's summit. Most of the "Jack" crags lie N of the high point: of these only two really stand out, with the second peak being pointed and third craggy and flat-topped. The crags S are slightly lower, but more jumbled and rugged.

The spectacular, steep alpine wall on the E of the massif forms part of the vast headwall cirque of the Entiat Valley. Two sections of the Entiat Glaciers (0.3 km^2) exist here, one section (largely avalanche snow) is directly E of "Jack's" summit and the other lies on the rock apron at the N end of the formation. Parallel concave snow chutes, separated by a series of minor rock ribs, feed these glacier ice remnants above the cirque floor. The Entiat Glaciers reached Neoglacial maximum in the 16th century and subsequently built moraines in the 19th and 20th centuries during several post Ice-Age fluctuations. During the recent past, ice has receded from massive, sharp-crested and fresh moraines nearly to the headwall.

There are a small glacier (not shown on topographic map) and several permanent snowpatches on the NW flank of the true summit, at the head of the E fork of Big Creek. Rock on the entire massif has a warranted reputation for insecurity. First ascent (main

MT. MAUDE from northwest
AUSTIN POST, U.S. GEOLOGICAL SURVEY

SEVEN FINGERED JACK from Leroy Creek Basin
JOHN V.A.F. NEAL

summit) by Richard Alt and a companion in 1932; priorities on the crags may never be known. Reference: *A.A.J.*, 1936, p. 468.

SOUTHWEST SLOPE: From Leroy Creek Trail♦ in the meadowy floral basin near 6000 ft, ascent the prominent gully NE toward the Maude-"Jack" col. At the large bench (7800′) traverse N up the talus (keep just S of the long, thin, left-slanting snow gully) toward the summit, which is the northernmost point seen from the basin. The final ascent is largely scree, with a bit of scrambling at the top (class 2). Miniature gardens of fleabane and phacelia have been reported high on the route. Time: 3 hours.

ENTIAT FACE: This steep face appears to have possible gully routes, but nothing is documented. A variation to the normal route from this approach would be to ascend the ice remnant of the Entiat, then climb the narrow gully system (mainly snow) that curves left to the Maude-"Jack" col, then traverse to the W slope.

SOUTH CRAGS

Three minor crags, S of the true summit, can be climbed by gullies on the W face (probably class 3 and 4).

NORTH CRAGS

These crags appear feasible from the W; here they form a steep parapet above snow patches at the head of the E fork of Big Creek. Gullies offer routes to notches between summits: some rock climbing appears probable, especially to the summits. The N end of the formation can be reached via the permanent snowfield that reaches the high ridge (8700′) between this position and Mt. Fernow.

MT. FERNOW 9249′/2819 m

Fernow is the highest of the Entiat Mountains and nearly a rival of Bonanza Peak as the supreme summit W of Lake Chelan. Fernow is 2 mi. N of Mt. Maude, at the northwestern head of the vast Entiat cirque. Rock is gneissic granite, friable as related to climbing. The magnitude of ice erosion can be seen on Fernow's steep, alpine N and NW flanks, not yet fully explored. The largest glacier (Fernow—0.8 km. length) lies E of the minor 9000-ft E summit in a slabby cirque on the Copper Creek drainage. There is a steep ice finger on Fernow's N face, really the upper portion of an "L"-

shaped glacier which narrows to a point below the summit crest; an isolated section of ice to the W lies in a pocket slightly lower than the main body.

The mountain was named for Bernhard E. Fernow, first Chief of Division of Forestry (1886). First ascent by Oscar Pennington and Hermann F. Ulrichs in August 1932 from the SW.

EAST RIDGE: From Holden use Copper Creek High Route (Railroad Creek Trail♦). From the outlet of Copper basin there is no trail but the terrain is open and not difficult. Proceed S and SW to gain the ridge (est. 7200′) either 1.1 or 1.3 mi. E of Fernow, using a steep, loose gully to get through a lower band of minor cliffs. Once on the ridge follow the easy S side past two minor false summits. The last 0.2 mi. traverse to get below Fernow is best done a little below the ridge crest on the S side. The route is across a semi-obvious ledge system. Immediately below the summit is a major funnel-shaped chute which is climbed up the center and then by working left on the rock above the chute. The SSW ridge is gained about 50 ft from the summit. The entire SE side of the summit involves up to class 3 scrambling over loose rock. A rope is not recommended because it would seriously increase rockfall. Note: it is not known if the Fernow Glacier has been climbed as an alternative to the ridge.

SOUTHEAST SLOPE and EAST RIDGE: From moraines beyond Entiat Meadows (Entiat River Trail♦) climb rocky slopes NW to about 7500 ft. Here continue up snow and scree in a shallow sloping basin to reach just beyond the step at 8900 ft immediately E of the summit. One could vary the route by reaching the E ridge lower. The completion to the summit is per East Ridge or one of several minor variations. Only the final 300 ft is considered class 3.

Descent: One can drop down the E ridge 75 ft, take a gully and scree to a SE notch, then descend to snow S of the mountain.

SOUTHWEST ROUTES: From Leroy Creek Basin (Leroy Creek♦) at 6000 ft climb the left fork of the creek NNE to a 7700-ft col W of Seven Fingered Jack. From 200 ft W either descend gully or shifting rock/scree (class 2) on a descending traverse to the top of "Gloomy Glacier," NW of "Jack", at the head of Big Creek (some 500-700-ft loss from col); glacier is badly broken in late summer. Cross to a rockslide gully or snow finger, then ascend to a large diagonal bench above the glacier. Contour N on heather and loose rock for ¾ mi. to a deep gully which is climbed on its right to the high perennial snowfield between "Jack" and Fernow. Ledges, gullies, and chimneys lead NE to the W summit ridge. Follow the shattered skyline to the true summit; time: 6 hours. Note: the report of the first ascent party indicates that they kept high around the N flank of "Jack."

Variation: Descend the glacier additionally (up to 500′) to rock ledges on its margin, then bear E to Fernow along a watercourse; this is easier though longer. Another approach to this position would be from Holden and Big Creek (see North Face).

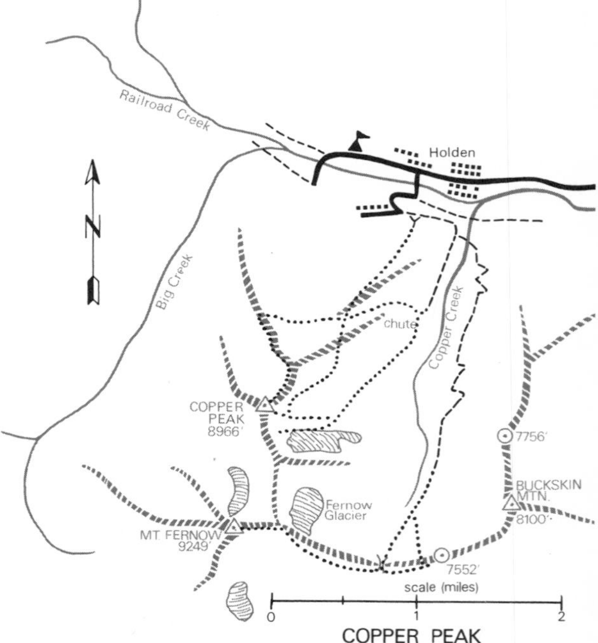

COPPER PEAK

Variation: From the high snowfield, climb E diagonally up a loose gully, then cross the sharp S ridge (est. 8700′) to minor ups-and-downs on the E side; here a shallow, broken rock gully leads leftward to the summit.

NORTH FACE: First ascent by Fred Dunham, Bill Prater, Gene Prater, and James Wickwire on September 17, 1961.

From Holden (see Lake Chelan♦) take the trail 1½ mi. W; leave to cross Railroad Creek, then take a miner's trail upslope on Dumbell Mountain (est. 1000′ rise), then traverse S into Big Creek. Follow game trails high on its E side to where the stream draining the cirque and ice finger between Copper and Fernow enters from the E (est. 2 mi.); poor camping at a gully below moraine near last alder (est. 5500′). Follow the creek to above timberline (or use a rockslide to north), then ascend broken snow sections and talus to the glacier. The final 1000 ft of the ice finger is steep (up to 45°). Icy conditions on the original climb required ice pitons at belays and some step cutting. A rightward traverse was taken at about 500 ft above the last rock island in the ice to the prominent rock buttress W; the final 500 ft leads to the summit ridge (fractured, class 3). Four leads (unroped) E along the ridge continue to the summit. Grade II or III; class 3 and 4. Take crampons and ice screws. Time: 6 hours from timberline. References: *Mountaineer,* 1962, pp. 103-104; *A.A.J.,* 1962, pp. 207-208; *Cascadian,* 1961, pp. 28-29.

Note: descent was made via rock bordering ice finger on W, then a descending traverse across 40° ice to the highest rock island.

MT. FERNOW from Mt. Maude
JOHN V.A.F. NEAL

SEVEN FINGERED JACK
MT. GOODE
MT. FERNOW
Southwest routes
col
East ridge
var.
TUPSHIN PK.
var.
ENTIAT GLACIERS
(north section)
moraine

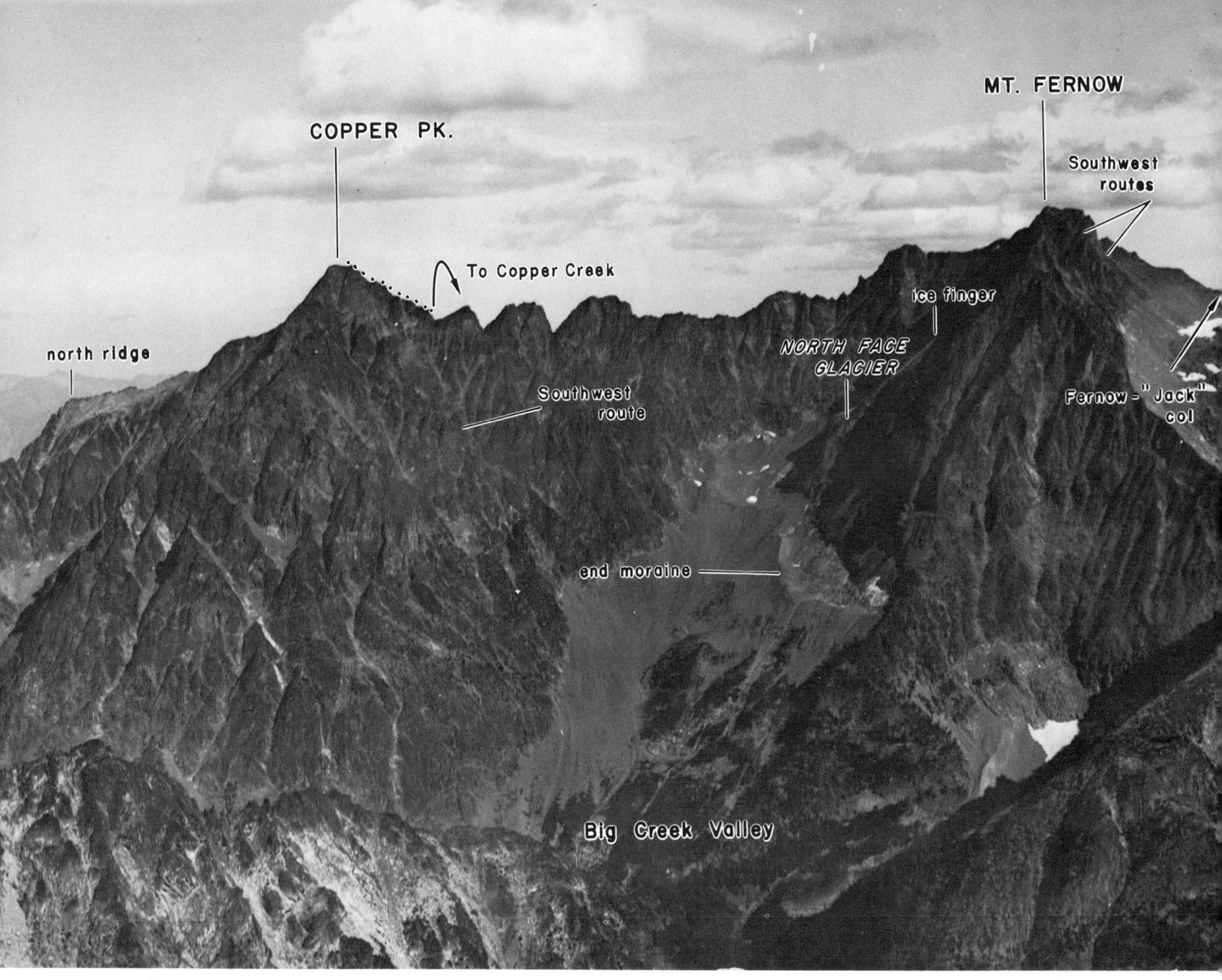

COPPER PK.
To Copper Creek
MT. FERNOW
Southwest routes
north ridge
ice finger
NORTH FACE GLACIER
Southwest route
Fernow - "Jack" col
end moraine
Big Creek Valley

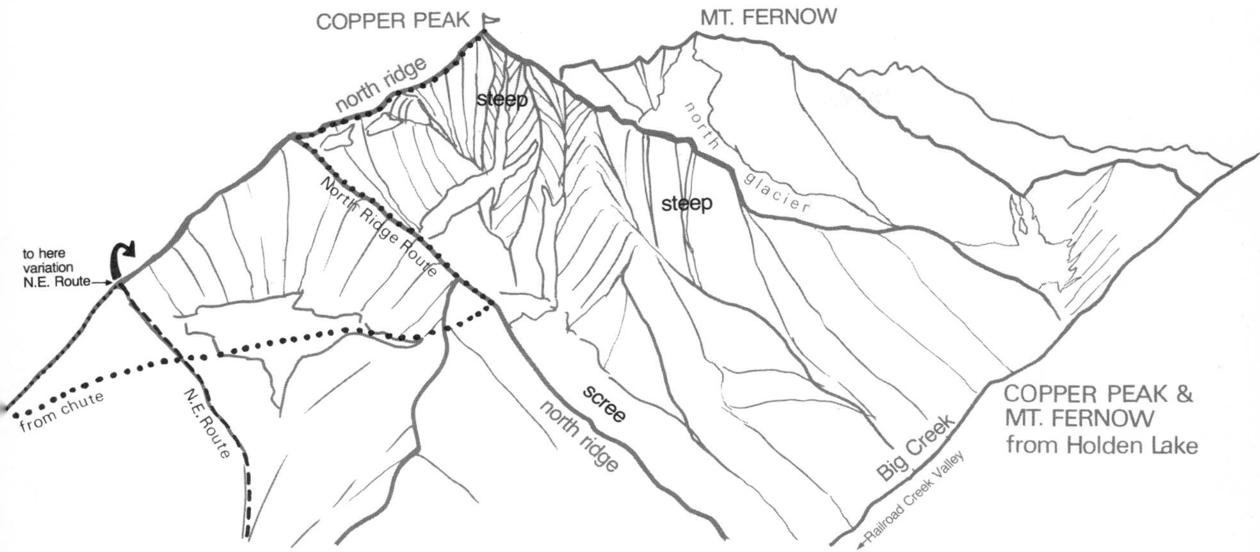

COPPER PEAK 8966′/2733 m

Copper is an imposing pyramidal peak, formed of gneiss, entirely within the Railroad Creek drainage, and with a rough rocky ridge connecting to Mt. Fernow on the S. Copper rises with a 5600-ft relief on the N, featuring a long, curved alpine ridge. Headward erosion of ice has produced steep E and N-facing rock walls; there is an unnamed glacier remnant SE of the summit. First ascent by G. Franklin Bennet, Edgar Courtwright, and Toivo Hagman in August, 1937 (via E face).

EAST FACE: From Holden (see Lake Chelan♦) cross Railroad Creek on a road spur to old mine buildings; take the first fork down, near tailings. Ascend a cat road, then a game trail along the W side of Copper Creek to alder patches. Ascend to the old mine trail, follow it a short distance, then bear upslope (some bush) SW to the basin at 5000 ft. Make a rising traverse, then ascend heather, snow, and rock on the E face. Class 3. Time: 6 hours from Holden.

Note: a variation using the SE glacier and a continuing gully toward the last notch S of the summit is not documented, but appears to be of about the same difficulty.

NORTHEAST ROUTE: First ascent by Ward Carithers and J. Kerr in 1939. From Holden take the old road above the mine to the first and lowest of upper mine dumps. Climb SW on brush and rock, keeping well to the right of the NE ridge. Cross the ridge at 7400 ft, ascending rock ledges, and snow and heather slopes on the upper E face to the final 400 ft of summit rock. Class 3. Time: 7 hours.

NORTH RIDGE: This is a long moderate route with considerable exposure. First ascent by two miners, names unknown.

Take Copper Creek route (see East Face) to the alder (est. 4500′) then ascend a chute W (often snow) to a spur at 6700 ft. Cross the slope to the N ridge at about 6500 ft, then ascent the ridge; expect sustained scrambling.

BUCKSKIN MOUNTAIN est. 8100′/2469 m

Dwarfed by the Fernow massif, Buckskin is of minor interest; it is 2 mi. S of Holden on the Entiat River divide. The name comes from the Buckskin claim, located between Wilson and Copper Creeks.

SOUTHWEST RIDGE: Start at Holden (Railroad Creek Trail♦ and Copper Creek High Route). From meadows in Copper basin turn SE and ascend gullies and talus to the ridge saddle (est. 7250′) at the SE valley head SW of Buckskin's summit. The remainder is simple. Time: 5 hours.

Buckskin's SW ridge can also be reached from Entiat Meadows (about 14½ mi.; see Entiat River Trail♦) Reference: *Routes and Rocks,* pp. 191-92.

Other routes: the ascent appears easy anywhere on the SE. A long scree gully from Entiat Meadows (about 13 mi., above McKensie Camp in the second of double meadows) offers access to the easy little basin under the summit. The gentle E ridge is another variation.

TINPAN MOUNTAIN 7422′/2262 m

A small peak on the Railroad Creek-Entiat River di-

COPPER PEAK and MT. FERNOW from west
WILLIAM A. LONG

vide 3½ mi. SE of Holden (named after Tinpan claim). A high summit ridge extends to the E summit, another 0.6 mi. The divide above the loop of the Entiat continues SE from Tinpan, reaching Point 7437 (2267 m; a more rugged formation than Tinpan) and later, Pinnacle Mtn.

ROUTES: From the Entiat River Trail♦ at 12 mi., ascend N to just E of the summit at about 7070 ft to the connecting ridge between the two Tinpan summits (hiking from here).

Another approach from the Entiat is to ascend the SW slopes from the 6500-ft saddle W of Tinpan.

The position ¼ mi. E of the summit could be reached from Holden. Old mine roads cross Copper Creek to the old Railroad Creek trail on the S side; follow it across Dole Creek, then ascend the E side—keeping away from the creek. Keep W of lower Dole Lake, then ascend to the saddle nearest Tinpan. Reference: *Routes and Rocks,* pp. 192-93.

PINNACLE MOUNTAIN 8402′/2561 m

Pinnacle is a twisting row of granitic rock points, the highest about 1¼ mi. NW of Milham Pass. An important summit in the Chelan Mountains, Pinnacle is an impressive formation with steep supporting ridge spurs (rock is part of the Cardinal Peak pluton). Cirques quarried by glaciers have here enroached on each other until separate ridges became narrow knife edges. The map roughly outlines a giant "S"; the W and S sides of the outline are relatively gentle. The two highest summits are at the top (NW end) of the "S" (the southern of these is the true summit). The eastern and northern slopes of Pinnacle's twisting crestline have interesting deep cirques, rocky spur ridges, and two N-facing remnants of glacier ice. The largest (0.5 km length) nests in the cirque of a small hanging branch valley at the head of a branch of Tumble Creek; below the glacier is a conspicuous fresh lateral moraine and arcuate end moraines which overlap talus. These were produced during fluctuations of small cirque glaciers developed during intervals of colder climate. Assignment of a Neoglacial age of deposits is justified because they are inferred to reflect a period of cooler climate accompanied by rebirth and growth of glaciers following the last Pleistocene deglaciation.

Pinnacle is topographically complicated by four important outlying ridges: Borealis Ridge to the SW; Chelan Mountain crestline to the NW; the Klone-Tumble divide with the bulky mass of Peak 7942 (2421 m) to the N; and the rocky divide between Emerald Park and Tumble Creeks to the NE. The name probably comes from the four prominent pinnacles (bottom of the "S" outline) just NW of Milham Pass; these rise just above the pine and larch scrub that represents the extreme limit of the evergreens. The earliest ascent is unknown; the mountain was definitely climbed in September 1948 from Milham Pass by Ken Fleming and Dwight Watson.

SOUTH ROUTE: Take the Entiat River Trail♦ 8.1 mi. to the 45-mi. Sheep Driveway Trail (4250′). Beyond the crossing of Pinnacle Creek (3.3 mi.) ascend to a basin (est. 7200′), then climb NE up a rocky draw and talus on the S side of Pinnacle where a notch (est. 7850′) on the main divide crosses to Tumble Creek. From here the ascent is easy scrambling. Using an alternate start, the climb could be begun almost anywhere on the W side from the Entiat Valley.

Other routes: it is possible to make an ascending traverse to the W from Milham Pass (Emerald Park Creek♦), keeping SW of high points on the ridge, to reach the 7850-ft notch (this is about 1¼ linear mi. from the pass).

The valley of Tumble Creek (trail only from Lucerne to base of creek) offers an open cross-country route of 4 mi. via Mirror Lake. Make the final ascent via described high cirque (some snow and ice) and ascend snow (or loose scree) gully to the 7850-ft notch. More direct lines certainly could be taken; one could follow the deep couloir to the notch between the two highest summits.

Pinnacle's four pinnacles near Milham Pass offer rock climbing opportunities.

BEARCAT PEAK 8035′/2449 m

A proposed name for the culmination of the long, rocky Bearcat Ridge. The peak is 1½ mi. NE of Milham Pass, between Emerald Park and Black Bear Creeks.

ROUTE: Ascent from the W seems most sensible, leaving the Emerald Park Trail♦ between 5500 and 6000 ft in the Park (about 1 mi. E of Milham Pass). Ascend talus and snow E to the main ridge S of the peak (est. 7300′). Follow N to first summit; one can then probably cross along ridge NE to the highest point.

SASKA PEAK 8404′/2562 m

Saska is less than a mi. S of Milham Pass, a rugged peak that stands out ½ mi. SW of the Chelan Mountain crest into the drainage of Snow Brushy Creek and the North Fork of the Entiat. There is a steep cliff on its NW flank. A.H. Sylvester applied the name for a chief of the Entiat tribe.

SOUTH ROUTES: Leave the Pyramid Mountain Trail♦ at 7400 ft, just S of the summit (this is about 2 mi. E of its junction with Snow Brushy Creek Trail♦), and make the ascent. Several obvious gullies on the S and SE sides appear feasible, and one could readily reach the 7700-ft saddle NE of the summit to meet the N route. The SW side of Saska is a long, moderate slope, and offers an alternative.

NORTH ROUTE: From the S side of Milham Pass ascend E to the head of Snow Brushy Creek, past a small lake

PINNACLE MOUNTAIN, view southwest
AUSTIN POST, U.S. GEOLOGICAL SURVEY

BANDIT PK.
MT. DAVID
MT. JONATHAN
INDIAN HEAD PK.
BRAHMA PK.
Pt. 8109
Little Giant Pass
OLD GIB MTN.
Pt. 7968
Pt. 7811
Chiwawa River Valley
Ice Creek Ridge
Pomas Pass
Borealis Ridge
Pomas Creek
Ice Creek
PINNACLE MTN.
Entiat River Valley
North summit
Pt. 8111
ice
Tumble Creek

Cow Creek Pass
FIFTH OF JULY MTN.
DEVIL'S SMOKESTACK
RAMPART MTN.
GARLAND PK.
Larch Lakes
Pt. 7936
CHORAL PK.
Cow Creek Meadows
Pt. 7909
GOPHER MTN.
Pt. 7725
Entiat River Valley
SASKA PK.
trail pass
North Fork Entiat Valley
Snow Brushy Creek
EMERALD PK.
Saddle 7700

(7700′) NE of the summit. From here ascend the rocky ridge to the summit. One could make the climb more alpine from the lake by ascending the body of névé/ice on the N face to a high ridge position just NW of the summit.

GOPHER MOUNTAIN 8001′/2439 m

Gopher rises on the divide 1⅓ mi. SW of Saska Peak. Leave Pyramid Mountain Trail♦ where it crosses the saddle between Saska and Gopher (7300′). A gentle ridge rises to the summit. Rock is biotite quartz schist.

CHORAL PEAK 7900′+/2408 m

Choral, the high point 1 mi. S of Gopher, resembles a mini-Matterhorn from the N (part of Duncan Hill pluton). It is between the heads of Anthem and Choral Creeks; final slopes are gentlest on the S and E. The talus and meadow basins and larch groves in the vicinity of this seldom visited peak are unusually lovely. Several small peaks with rocky contours and small high talus slopes stand between Choral and Duncan Hill.

ROUTES: One could reach Choral from the head of Anthem Creek (see Duncan Hill Trail♦) from the Entiat River Trail or the trail up Choral Creek (branch off Snow Brushy Creek). Then hike to Choral Lake (7100′+) and the upper E slope.

Another approach is from the North Fork Entiat River Trail♦ where it leaves the valley floor (est. 5700′). Ascend W to the pass (7400′+) above Choral Lake, then traverse above the lake to the upper E slope.

DUNCAN HILL 7819′/2383 m

This is a massive rounded summit between Entiat River and its N fork, just over 2 mi. N of the Entiat River roadhead.

ROUTE: See Duncan Hill Trail♦.

EMERALD PEAK 8422′/2567 m

Emerald is a major Chelan Mountain summit located midway between Cardinal Peak and Milham Pass. It is a rocky peak (Cardinal Peak pluton), with an alpine N rock face laced with snow patches until late summer. First ascent by William A. Long in 1937.

SOUTH SLOPE: From the North Fork Entiat Trail♦ at about 1¼ mi. N of Pyramid Mountain Trail junction (near 6900′), where trail curves at valley head, ascend readily to summit. The slope is easy to moderate.

SOUTHWEST ROUTE: From the S side of Milham Pass (see Emerald Park Trail♦) ascend the valley E to a glacial lake at its head, then ascend to the 7700-ft saddle E of Saska Peak. Turn NE, then E, to follow the ridge to the summit. Also on the upper SW slopes is an easy corridor that veers up and right to just S of the summit.

SASKA PEAK and Entiat Mountains
AUSTIN POST, U.S. GEOLOGICAL SURVEY

NORTH FACE: First ascent route, 1937. From Emerald Park. The route is rocky and steep, but reported as only moderately difficult (est. class 3).

Note: nothing is documented about the N or NW ridges, but routes appear satisfactory.

CARDINAL PEAK 8595′/2620 m

Cardinal, situated only 6½ mi. S of Lucerne on Lake Chelan, is one of the lords of the Chelan Mountains. The peak is a large massif, quarried to craggy gendarmes atop a NE-SW spine, with a gentle spur emerging from Skidgravel Point. The upper western facade is the steepest, but the eastern appears more alpine because of perennial snow and small ice bodies.

The summit formation consists of three significant rock points: the wedge-shaped middle one appears highest by a slight margin; 400 ft SW is the jagged S summit; the N summit stands on an extended spur (est. 800 ft from middle summit).

Cardinal has three small hanging glaciers, which remain above a vast deposit of fresh bouldery material. The "Goatrax" is largest (0.2 km^2) and is high, directly E of the middle and N summits (8400′ to 6985′). The "Glissade" is situated E of the S and middle summits; Glissade Lake (est. 7800′), with its summer ice floes, is located in a deep rockbound cirque between Glissade and Skidgravel Glaciers. The narrow "Skidgravel" (0.8 km. length) is located on the N flank of Skidgravel Point.

Indications are that the middle and N summits were climbed long ago; a very old giant cairn stands on the N summit ridge. Austin Post climbed the middle summit in 1941 and 1942, approaching from over Skidgravel Point and descended to the W through the notch between the middle and N peaks. A party in June 1960 composed of Don Avery, W.A. Gilbaugh, and Burr Singleton claimed Cardinal's first ascent, though it was the lower S summit they reached (*A.A.J.*, 1961, p. 368; *Cascadian,* 1960, pp. 5-6.

WEST ROUTE: Use North Fork Entiat River Trail♦ to opposite the middle summit (est. 10 mi., 6600′). Then ascend through open forest and the wide talus slope and continuing gully to the ridge notch between the middle and N summits. One can easily follow the ridge S to the middle summit. Another approach to this position is from an old survey cairn located on the NE buttress. To reach the N summit from the notch, follow the spur out northward, keeping a bit E of the crest. An alternate route is directly up the E side from Goatrax Glacier. These routes are presumably more difficult than the S and central peaks; no record of ascents is known.

EAST ROUTE: From the scree shoulder on the S, traverse

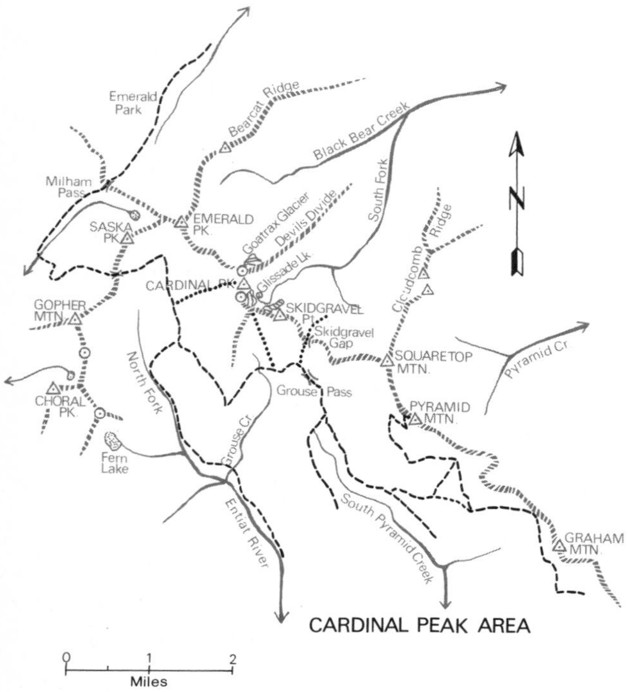

N across the upper part of the Glissade Glacier (keep below upper cliffs), then up shattered cliff to the middle summit rocks (Post's route). Rather than striking directly for the rocky summit, it is simpler to aim for either N or S ridge nearby (not difficult).

SOUTH RIDGE: This is the route of the 1960 party. The long narrow summit structure features four gendarmes (the third from the S is highest) from 20 to 50 ft in height, nearly vertical and fragmented.

From the basin of Grouse Creek ascend a gently sloping meadow from the Pyramid Mountain Trail♦ to the saddle W of Skidgravel Point. A broad ridge bears NW to become a scree shoulder. At about 1000 linear ft before reaching the S summit the shattered crest becomes narrow, with the first gendarme blocking; holds are good for a 20-ft descent into the cut that separates the ridge from the gendarme. From the floor of the cut follow a steep talus gully which drops W, then continue and pass E of the second gendarme. Continue 300 ft on a broad ledge to the base of the summit gendarme. The ascent reported a traverse (class 5) to a vertical chimney, a steep 25-ft rock pitch, and a narrow summit edge straddle; class 4 and 5.

Note: one can continue to the middle summit (scrambling) by following scree and rocky ledges E of the crest.

SKIDGRAVEL POINT 8339′/2542 m

This is the rounded, almost conical junior summit of Cardinal Peak, ½ mi. to its SE. The scree which makes a fast descent route is the source of the name. Skidgravel Gap (7190′), which separates Grouse Creek and the South Fork of Black Bear Creek, is immediately SE. The small Skidgravel Glacier on the N makes a picturesque corridor to the summit.

ROUTES: The entire S, SW and E slopes are moderate; there is an easy basin on the SW. A useful route is from the Pyramid Mountain Trail♦ about ⅓ mi. after it descends N from Grouse Pass: ascend N through pleasant meadows to Skidgravel Gap, then struggle in the loose scree NW to the summit.

Another route is from the saddle adjacent Cardinal; the summit is merely a hike.

DEVILS DIVIDE 7925′/2416 m

This 2-mi. rocky divide forms a descending axis NE of Cardinal Peak, between Goatrax Creek and Black Bear's S fork. The divide has a very rocky S slope that provides rock climbing opportunities. There is a spectacular overhanging notch in the ridge, formed by the collapse of a dike of less resistant rock. The divide can be reached from South Fork Black Bear Creek and from the S by way of Skidgravel Gap (see Skidgravel Point).

SQUARETOP MOUNTAIN 8189′/2496 m

Between Pyramid Mountain and Skidgravel Point. The summit is flat with a minor horn on the N; the peak presents a ridgelike appearance from the W, with a high scree basin. The N side rises steeply from the deep cirque heading Black Bear Creek's S fork. First recorded ascent by Austin Post in 1940, via SW side.

ROUTE: Traverse the ridge from Pyramid Mountain. Or approach from Pyramid Mountain Trail♦ just S of Grouse Pass by ascending E to the head of the E terminal fork of South Pyramid Creek. The upper SW and W slopes are moderate, offering numerous ways to the top.

CLOUDCOMB PEAKS 8085′/2464 m

Cloudcomb Ridge is the informal name for the serrate ridge which extends about 3 mi. NE of Squaretop Mountain as a divide between Pyramid Creek and Black Bear Creek's S fork. There are four significant sharp rock summits on the uniform portion of the ridge; the third from Squaretop is highest (2 mi. N of Pyramid Mountain) and the fourth next highest. Rock is friable and shattered gneiss; the flanks of the peaks have steep rock walls, with considerable couloir dissection and resultant talus. First ascent of highest summit

CARDINAL PEAK from west
WILLIAM A. LONG

orth summit
CARDINAL PEAK
middle summit
south summit
south ridge
North Fork
Entiat River
Trail

by Fred Beckey and Philip Leatherman in September 1973.

ROUTE: Approach as for Squaretop Mountain, but cross the divide S of the summit. Descend steep dirt and snow to where the upper basin flattens; here it is feasible to begin a long traverse of the steep, loose gully systems on the S flank of the ridge. To reach the highest summit, climb the rock gully and chimney leading to a minor notch just W of the top; there is some class 3 scrambling.

A descent and scrambling would appear to lead to the fourth (NE) summit. However, a more direct way would be via Skidgravel Gap and a descent to where gully routes appear on the W summit flank.

PYRAMID MOUNTAIN 8245′/2513 m

This massive summit in the Chelan Mountains rises about 7145 ft directly from the W shore of Lake Chelan, about 30 mi. from the SE end of the lake. Here is a nearly completely felsenmeer-mantled, graded summit upland. The N face of the mountain contains ice pockets. In 1897 a U.S. Geological Survey team built a 7-ft cairn during triangulation; impressed with the view and vantage, they termed Pyramid "a high, bare, round-topped mountain on the west side of Lake Chelan."[76]

ROUTE: See Pyramid Mountain Trail♦.

STORMY MOUNTAIN 7198′/2194 m

This prominent uplift, near the SE termination of the Chelan Mountains, is 12 mi. NW of the Columbia River. The U.S. Geological Survey used Stormy for triangulation about 1899, noting it as the highest timbered peak between Entiat River and Lake Chelan.

ROUTE: This magnificent viewpoint is traversed by trail—2 mi. from near the end of Slide Ridge Road at 5850 ft (see Shady Pass Road♦).

APPROACHES

Roads and trails described in this section are noted in the text by the symbol♦.

ROADS

Chiwawa River Road No. 311 extends 23½ mi. to Trinity (road closed at private property). From U.S. Hwy No. 2♦ take the Lake Wenatchee Road♦ 4½ mi. to a major triangle; then go E on county road no. 22 for 1.4 mi. just beyond the Midway store to reach the Chiwawa Road (or arrive at this point in 18 mi. from Leavenworth via State Hwy No. 209).

Phelps Creek Road No. 3000 bears uphill just before Trinity (22.8-mi. point) and continues 3 mi. to the end of permitted driving. A wagon road made one of the deepest penetrations into the Cascade Range here in early mining times (shown to valley head on the 1913 Forest Service map). Trinity has been an active copper mining venture employing over 275 miners, with a concentrator mill and a long tunnel into Phelps Ridge; the Royal Development Mine now is a scene of derelict buildings and equipment. However, copper ore bedrock drilling is now being conducted beyond the road end. Reference: *Trips and Trails 1.*

Entiat River Road No. 317 leaves U.S. Hwy No. 97 at Entiat, then extends 38 mi. to road's end at Cottonwood Camp.

Tommy Creek Road No. 2900 branches W at about 30½ mi. and extends 6.3 mi.

North Fork Entiat River Road No. 317B branches E at about 32½ mi., and extends about 5½ mi.

Lake Chelan. From Chelan road distance to Twenty Five Mile Creek is 20 mi.; if driving from the S, the Navarre Coulee cutoff from U.S. Hwy No. 97 saves distance. There is boat service from Chelan and Twenty Five Mile Creek to Lucerne: from May 15 to September 30 daily, northbound run leaves Chelan at 8:30 A.M. and Twenty Five Mile Creek at 10 A.M., southbound trip leaves Lucerne at 2:20 P.M.; from October 1 to May 14 northbound runs leave Chelan at 8:30 A.M. on Monday, Wednesday, Friday and Sunday, leaving Twenty Five Mile Creek at 9:45 A.M. and returning from Lucerne at 12:30 P.M. For specific information write or call Lake Chelan Boat Co., Box 186, Chelan, WA 98816 (phone 509/682-2224). Lucerne offers a store, resort, and campground.

Railroad Creek Road No. 3100 extends 13 mi. Lucerne to Holden. Bus and taxi connecting with boat schedules subject to space availability; packer and stock at trailhead. The abandoned mining camp at Holden (3262′) is now used as a summer church center. Immense tailing piles left from deep mine workings indicate the vast quantity of rock removed.

Lake Creek Road No. 2801 is reached from Little Wenatchee River Road♦ at left fork no. 2714 (6 mile point); follow the latter ½ mi., then Labyrinth Mountain Road No. 2713 for 5 mi. Lake Creek Road extends 2.3 mi. beyond.

Lake Wenatchee Road (State Hwy. No. 207) extends from U.S. Hwy No. 2♦ at Cole's Corner (20.3 mi. E of Stevens Pass). Branches extend to the Little Wenatchee, White, and Chiwawa Rivers.

Little Wenatchee River Road No. 283 exits from the Lake Wenatchee Road♦ in 11 mi. and continues 16 miles.

Phelps Creek Road. See Chiwawa River Road♦.

Rainy Creek Road No. 2728 branches from the Little Wenatchee River Road♦ at 6 mi.; links with Smithbrook Road.

Shady Pass Road No. 298 crosses the Chelan Mountains via Junior Point (6600 ft) in a 28-mi. connection from 25 Mile Creek on Lake Chelan♦ to the Entiat River Road♦ at its 29-mi. point. A branch from Shady Pass extends 1½ mi. to Big Hill Lookout.

Slide Ridge Road No. 2805 branches at Ramona Park and continues 10 mi. to closely E of Stormy Mountain.

Smithbrook Road No. 2714 exits from U.S. Hwy No. 2♦ 4.2 mi. E of Stevens Pass, then extends to a trail connection to the Cascade Crest and Nason Ridge; links with Rainy Creek Road♦.

Suiattle River Road No. 345 leaves the Sauk River Road 6½

mi. N of Darrington (11 mi. S of Rockport) to end in 23 mi. (Sulphur Creek).

Tommy Creek Road No. 2900 is slated for extension, so has no current trailhead. There is a connection to North Tommy Creek Trail No. 1425; see Klone Peak Trail♦.

U.S. Hwy No. 2 between Stevens Pass and Leavenworth defines the southern boundary of this section.

White River Road No. 293 branches from the Lake Wenatchee Road♦ in 10 mi., then extends 11 mi.

TRAILS AND ALPINE HIKING APPROACHES

For use regulations within the Glacier Peak Wilderness, see Trails and Alpine Hiking Approaches, Section I.

Anthem Creek Trail No. 1435 leaves Entiat River Trail♦ at 2½ mi. (3500′) and reaches a junction with Duncan Hill Trail (5900′) in 3½ mi.; the Duncan Hill Trail No. 1434 crosses Anthem Creek and a saddle N to Choral Creek, then descends to meet Snow Brushy Creek Trail♦.

Boulder Pass Trail leaves from the White River Trail♦ at the 4-mi. point (2400′) and reaches Boulder Pass (6250′) in 6.7 mi.; good camping just W of pass. The trail descends 3.7 mi. to Napeequa Valley (4300′); at the river stay left for horse ford. The Little Giant Trail continues E over Little Giant Pass♦ and to the Chiwawa River. Clark Mountain High Route begins at 5000 ft en route to Boulder Pass at 3.2 mi., at an old herder trail; see *Routes and Rocks,* pp. 107-110; *101 Hikes.*

Buck Creek Trail No. 1513 extends from Trinity (2772′; see Chiwawa River Road♦) to Buck Creek Pass (5796′) in 8.7 mi.; begin by following the old roadway through private property. Good campsites at the Chiwawa footbridge (2.6 mi.), at 5½ mi., at 7 Mile Camp, and on the E side of the pass. Buck Creek Pass, an old trail crossing from the Chiwawa to the Suiattle River, was surveyed in 1907 for a trans-Cascade road. It was also once heavily used by herders; in 1912 some 2500 sheep grazed the area from the pass to Miners Ridge. Before the grazing declined in 1930s there was severe meadow damage. Because of heavy use at Buck Creek pass, overnight campers should continue west to Middle Ridge camp below Fortress Mountain. Trail no. 789 connects N with the new Crest Trail section in 5 mi.

The Buck Creek Pass area is famed for its vistas of Glacier Peak. *Liberty Cap* (6700′+/2042 m), SW of the pass, has a broad trail along its N ridge and W slope. It was observed that this "rock crowned green hill"[77] had a goat trail along its backbone, part of it through a mat of alpine fir. A hiker route of 1½ mi. leads around the E side of *Helmet Butte* toward Pass No Pass (6400′+), the wide grassy saddle between Helmet and Fortress Mountain. *Flower Dome* (6300′+/1920 m) can be readily reached from the trail ½ mi. N of Buck Creek Pass; hike W along a meadowed spur to the rounded summit. These marvellous scenic points are clad with scattered clumps of hemlock and alpine fir (timberline about 6500′) amid meadows that display an incredible range of flora variety.

Cady Creek Trail No. 1501 meets the Crest Trail♦ at Cady Pass (4300′+) 5.1 mi. from the end of Little Wenatchee River Road♦. Shortly up-trail is an alternative route, *Cady Ridge Trail No. 1532,* which reaches the Crest Trail in 6 mi., at a point farther N.

Carne Mountain Trail No. 1509. See Rock Creek Trail♦.

Cow Creek Meadows Trail No. 1404 leaves Entiat River Trail♦ at about 4 mi. The trail reaches Myrtle Lake (3700′) in ½ mi., Cow Creek Meadows (5100′) in 2½ mi., and Garland Peak trail junction (6500′) in 4½ mi. Cow Creek Pass (Fifth of July Pass) at 7000 ft is a mi. S.

Crest Trail: See Pacific Crest National Scenic Trail♦.

Dirtyface Peak Trail No. 1500 starts directly behind Lake Wenatchee R.S. (county road no. 207); the 4-mi. trail climbs from 1900 ft to Dirtyface Point and former lookout (5989′). Reference: *101 Hikes.*

Dirtyface Peak (6240′+/1902 m) is about 1.8 mi. NW of the Point, and can readily be reached leaving Dirtyface Trail at the lowest point on the ridge and crossing over the ridge to the valley on the N side. This route also provides access to a small pond, Dirtyface Lake. The U.S. Geological Survey occupied Dirtyface and built a 7-ft. cairn, in 1897 or 1898. In their times a wagon road was used from Leavenworth to "Wenache Lake," then a "foot-climb of 5000 feet, very steep and rocky."[78]

Duncan Hill Trail No. 1434 leaves Anthem Creek Trail♦ to reach the summit area in 3½ mi., with a spur to the lookout. This scenic high point (7819′) offers an excellent panorama of the surrounding ranges. An alternate route is the longer trail leaving the Entiat River Road♦ shortly beyond the North Fork road junction (2600′); the spur to the lookout leaves at 9 mi. (7400′).

Emerald Park Trail No. 1230 (Snow Brushy Creek) leaves the Entiat River Trail♦ at 6.4 mi. (3944′) and reaches beautiful Milham Pass (6663′) in 6½ mi. The pass is colored by Lyall's larch, and among prominent natural features are a protalus rampart and nearby granitic pinnacles. Reference: *101 Hikes.* Emerald Park Trail No. 1230 extends from Lucerne (see Lake Chelan♦) to Emerald Park (8 mi., 5400′) and Milham Pass (10 mi., 6663′; named for George Milham, Chelan Forest supervisor). The trail is an old one—shown on 1916 maps. The large meadow at Emerald Park was once a lake, then it filled as the topography matured; a description pictures it as 50 acres of flat terrain that in late July is "a sea of shoulder-high blue bell bloom." The park's name is from a trapper in the 1890s; a fire devastated the valley in this decade. Near the narrow pass the slope consists of talus blocks and larches.

Mirror Lake and Tumble Creek are reached cross-country from the lower end of the park NW through a 6700-ft saddle, then an easy descent (2 hours).

Entiat River Trail No. 1400 begins from the end of the Entiat River Road♦ (3144′). Reach Anthem Creek Trail (N) in

2½ mi., Cow Creek Meadows Trail (W) in 4 mi.; Larch Lakes Trail (W) in 5 mi.; Snow Brushy camp (shelter) in 5½ mi.; Snow Brushy Creek Trail (E) in 6.5 mi.; Ice Lakes Trail (W) in 8½ mi.; Copper Creek High Route (N) in 14½ mi.; Entiat Meadows (5500′) between 14 and 15 mi. (prepared campsites are at 11.3, 12.8, 13.2, and 14.1 mi.) This is an old trail, shown extending to the meadows on 1916 maps.

At trail's end there is a hiker camp in a setting of low willow bushes, alpine larch, and large angular blocks; the floor is composed of fresh bouldery debris of a recent ice advance, spread in a 2500-ft-long moraine belt. The moraines are composed of rubble and coarse blocks—some to 30 ft high.

The head of Entiat Valley is a large broad-floored valley-head cirque whose walls are cut by smaller secondary cirques, some of which contain small bodies of glacier ice which collectively constitute the Entiat Glaciers. High protective mountain shelter is a significant reason for the relatively low altitude of the principal mass of these glaciers, whose central section terminates at 6100 ft. During the relatively recent past the ice bodies were considerably larger and united to form a glacier about 2 mi. long. This larger glacier descended to an altitude of 5200 ft and deposited a well defined end moraine at Grouse Camp. The three youngest ice advances in the upper valley date from early Neoglaciation. Moraines reinforce the impression of a newly altered land. The outermost older Neoglacial moraine (5500′) is some 1½ mi. from the cirque headwall. At the head of the barren Mt. Maude moraines overlap an older moraine belt, where a large closed moraine ("Y" horseshoe—5800′) rises 200 ft and encloses glacier ice (W.A. Long, oral commun., 1975). Here is a belt of chaotic mounds and ridges over ½ mi. in width; the sharp crests, favored by goats for travel, are very unstable (est. age 300 yrs).

Rusk suggests what is apparent, that man will always be impressed with the great Entiat Cirque . . . "the awe-inspiring spectacle that marks the head of the Entiat River . . . the wildly broken masses of snow and ice, at the upper end, cling with precarious tenacity to a thousand-foot precipice rim."[79]

Forty Five Mile Sheep Driveway No. 1432 begins from the Entiat Trail on the S side of Aurora Creek (8.1 mi.). One can approach this way to cross the Pinnacle Mountain massif S of the summit (7700′+), then descend to Mirror Lake.

Dole Lakes. From Entiat Meadows cross the ridge between the two summits of Tinpan Mountain, then descend to the W side of the lakes (2-3 hrs).

Estes Butte Trail No. 1527 leaves Chiwawa River Road♦ at the 15.2-mi. point, just N of the bridge at Rock Creek; it climbs steeply about 2900 ft to the former lookout site (5397′) in 2½ mi. and continues to Estes Butte (5942′). Continuing N, an old fire trail (Gold Gib Trail No. 1528) passes closely W of *Old Gib Mountain* (7081′/2158 m) then continues to the Carne Mountain Trail♦ junction (6500′) (total 12½ mi. from road).

Garland Peak Trail No. 1408. See Shetipo-Garland Trail♦.

Heather Lake Trail No. 1526 begins from Lake Creek Road♦. The subalpine lake (3½ mi.) on the E side of the Cascade divide is the largest between Stevens Pass and White Pass.

High Pass. See Napeequa River Trail♦.

Ice Creek Trail No. 1405. The valley of Ice Creek is the only one entering Entiat Valley at accordance. The 4½ mi. trail leaves the Entiat River Trail♦ at 8½ mi. 4300 ft. To reach the lakes ascend rocky meadows along the E bank of Ice Creek's E fork; good camping at the outlet of the lower lake (est. 6800′, 6 mi.); reach the upper lake (7150′) in ½ mi. by hiking SW from the SW end of the lower lake. Fires are prohibited within ½ mi. of Ice Lakes; bring stoves. In Rusk's words, "a wonderful mountain basin wherein lay two lake gems of rare beauty . . . only a few hardy dwarfed trees appearing here and there; while the shores were margined by grassy swards . . . " (Rusk, *op. cit.,* p. 174).

Above the bedrock barriers that contain the lakes in large hollows, the terrain becomes barren, with perennial snowfields. Glaciated rock and deep yellowish pumice from Glacier Peak eruptions provides additional contrast. An easy high cross-country route can be made from the upper lake across boulders and snow to the saddle (7600′+) S of Mt. Maude to the head of Chipmunk Creek and the Leroy Creek Trail♦. From lower Ice Lake one can readily ascend ½ mi. NE, bearing E of Point 7746, then descend N to Entiat Meadows (see *Routes and Rocks,* pp. 162-66; *101 Hikes*).

Indian Creek Trail No. 1502 extends from the end of the White River Road♦ to Indian Pass, a 2800-ft rise in 11 mi. The pass was a favorite cross-mountain route of the Sauk and Wenatchee Indians and an early trail route; the Forest Reserve map of 1898 shows the trail as the only culture mark between the Great Northern Railroad and the trail across Cascade Pass. Indian Pass cinder cone is a circular mound on the S slope of Indian Head Peak, reduced by erosion.

Klone Peak Trail No. 1427 almost reaches the summit of Klone Peak; there is temporary access to the existing North Tommy Creek Trail No. 1425 from Tommy Creek Road♦ until a final connection is built (use this to Klone Peak). A southern approach is via the Mad River Trail and Two Little Lakes: drive to Plain (Hwy No. 209), then to roads 2616 and 2924 to reach the trail.

Lake Minotaur Trail extends from the Rainy Creek Road♦ (branch B)—6 mi. from Little Wenatchee River Road♦—and reaches the 5550-ft lake in 4 mi. (follow North Fork Rainy Creek Trail No. 1516 for 2 mi., then Minotaur Trail No. 1517 steeply for 2 mi.); a short steep path descends east to Theseus Lake (5060′), set in a small bowl near timberline. Reference: *101 Hikes.*

Larch Lakes Trail No. 1430. Begin 5 mi. on Entiat River Trail♦ (3800′). Reach the lower lake (5650′) in 2.2 mi. the upper lake in ½ mi. Here Pomas Creek Trail♦ climbs 700 ft to Larch Lakes Pass, then continues to Pomas Pass and at 6 mi. reaches the Ice Lakes Trail♦.

From upper Larch Lake cross meadows and in 2 mi. reach a junction with the Cow Creek Trail (6600′) and Garland Peak Trail; it is an additional mi. to Cow Creek Pass (Fifth of July Pass)—7000 ft. Reference: *101 Hikes.*

Leroy Creek—Carne Mountain Trail No. 1512 leaves Phelps Creek Trail♦ on the N side of Leroy Creek (3.2 mi., 4200′) and closely follows Leroy Creek to Leroy basin at 2 mi. (5200′), then veers E; to reach higher campsites in the flat basin, leave the trail and ascend along the stream to timberline meadows at 6000 ft.

Ice Lakes can be reached best from the trail where it reaches the 6800-ft level near the saddle between Leroy and Chipmunk Creek; a simple cross-country route crosses the saddle (7600′+) S of Mt. Maude, then descends névé and boulders to the lakes. Rusk and Cool crossed here with horses on August 30, 1906 (Rusk, *op. cit.*, pp. 173-174).

The main trail (an old sheep driveway) makes a high traverse S (many meadows and camps), then bypasses Carne Mountain to a junction with Rock Creek Trail♦ (9 mi.).

Little Giant Pass (6409′, 6 mi.) and Napeequa Valley (4300′, 8 mi.) can be reached by trail no. 1518 from Maple Creek Campground at 19.8 mi. on Chiwawa River Road♦ at 2600′; the Chiwawa River must be forded, since bridge to the campground is gone. The Little Giant claim was located in 1893 by George N. Watson, an active early prospector. The steep trail, used by sheep herders early in the century, was so rough that horses were lost annually.

Little Wenatchee River Trail No. 1525 leaves the end of the Little Wenatchee River Road♦ and meets the Crest Trail♦ in 7.3 mi. at Sauk Pass; good campsites at 4 and 6 mi. Reference: *101 Hikes.*

Lyman Lake Trail to upper Lyman Lake and Lyman Glacier leaves the Railroad Creek Trail♦ at 7.8 mi.; cross Railroad Creek on logs at the lake outlet and take the trail around the E shore. Continue on this side, then follow the inlet stream SE upslope to the upper lake, then stroll around its E onto the relatively flat glacier, which begins at about 6000 ft. Camping prohibited within 200 ft horizontally of Lyman Lake; do not burn wood—take stoves. There is a trail along the W shore to a campsite.

Greenish with glacial silt, the lake reflects a color that intensifies with the advance of summer and makes an even more striking contrast with the mountains in fall when the brilliant foliage of deciduous shrubs contrast with the water, glacier, and Chiwawa Mountain. Lyman Lake, named for William D. Lyman, professor of history at Whitman College and one of the early explorers of the region between Lake Chelan and Glacier Peak, has undergone a series of name changes. Brown's mining claim map shows the names Red Lake, Green Lake, and Rodgers (for Lyman) Lake.[80] The Aurelia Crown Co., which staked claims in 1906, designated Lyman Lake as "Aurelia Lake," and the upper lake as "Glacier Lake;" the glaciers were known as "Aurelia" and "Crown Point." Cabins and a powder house were built at Crown Point, where the glacial rounding of bedrock by ancient ice is evident; one can see the adits near Crown Point Falls, driven in quartz veins that contain molybdenum. The trail to Cloudy Pass crossed the Crown Point claims, which were protested in proceedings (1922) and disallowed because of their non-mineral nature and other allegations; of dubious sincerity was a plan by the company to build a railroad to Lyman Lake. In summer 1935 Everett Darr, on a climbing venture to Bonanza Peak, found a man's body in the Washington Water Power cabin near the S end of the lake. When this was reported to the post office at Lucerne, a woman exclaimed, "That's my husband. We've been looking for him for two years."

Spider Pass Route: (Phelps Pass) Take a path to the broad crest 300 ft above and E from midway around Lyman Lake, then bear SE through meadows to the edge of upper Railroad Creek basin. The path parallels the old moraine (camping), then up the more recent moraine; the route crosses a rock spur, then the prominent snowfield to the pass (est. 7050′). An old mining path across a cliff and steep talus barrens leads E, above the glacier's edge, to the alpine parkland of the upper basin; this offers a route variation to the pass. Members of the 1926 Mazama outing were surprised to find a mine building with heavy machinery on this precipitous path. Reference: *Mazama* 8, no. 12 (1926): 23-24. In 1936 Dwight Watson noted that this tin-roofed building (Galena King Mine) contained a Ford gasoline engine. The Alaska number 1 and 2 claims are on a 25-ft ledge that is mineralized across to "Red Lake" (L.K. Hodges, 1896). The area of Spider Pass ("Red Mountain Pass" in early usage), where the rock is weathered to a rusty red, and its flanking basins, is patterned with relics and claims. The 1931 Forest Service map showed a trail from Lyman Lake to upper Phelps Creek, but it was only a rudimentary miner's trail partially across snow.

Mad River Trail. See Klone Peak Trail♦.

Merritt Lake Trail No. 1588. Begin on U.S. Hwy No. 2♦ 12½ mi. E of Stevens Pass (at 2640′) to reach the lake (5003′) in 2.7 mi. From above the lake Nason Ridge Trail♦ can be taken E to *Alpine Lookout* (6237′/1901 m; 3 mi.). At 1¼ mi. W of this trail junction, a path crosses the ridge and drops steeply to Lost Lake on the N slope.

Miners Ridge Trail No. 785 connects Suiattle Trail♦ at 9.3 mi. (2900′) and Crest Trail♦ at Glacier Peak Mines (17.9 mi. from road or 14.4 mi. if using Miners Cabin trail connection).

The trail climbs to a fork at Sunnybrook Corner in 3.9 mi., then on to Miners Ridge in 1.8 mi. (est. 6150′). Here Bear Creek Mining Co. has patented claims and prospected intensively. Brown gneiss lies over granite; the mineral zone is along the contact (*Routes and Rocks,* p. 52). Closely W a branch leads to the lookout tower (6210′; manned only during high fire hazard). The trail traverses E 1 mi. to Image Lake (6050′), famed for its views and mirrored reflections of Glacier Peak. Camping allowed only in a small area downhill from outlet; regulations limit camping and fires within ¼ mi. of lakeshore. Use established campsites (no fires; use stoves). No swimming or dishwashing in lake. One can hike to Point 6758 N of the lake for views.

E of Image Lake the trail crosses meadow slopes to Lady Camp in 1.3 mi. (horses permitted) and in another 1.5 mi. joins the Crest Trail♦ at Glacier Peak Mines (est. 5550′). Trails to the pass area were first shown on maps as from the E, the trail from the Suiattle Valley not being built until after 1916. This locality of low-grade copper has been extensively explored since claims were staked in 1900 by the Glacier Peak Mining and Smelting Co. Subsequently claims were leased to various firms for prospecting and development.

Present mining laws take precedence in wilderness areas such as this one in the concept of multiple use, allowing a persistent threat of Kennecott subsidiaries to conduct open-pit operations on the company's patented lands on the SW slope of Miners Ridge; there are about 350 acres of patented lands and 2560 acres of claims. The greatest value of this unique area is its superlative scenic and recreational treasure. References: *Mountaineer,* 1967, pp. 8-25; *101 Hikes.*

Miners Cabin Trail No. 795 is a lower-level, shorter connection between Sunnybrook Corner and Glacier Peak Mines (2.1 mi.).

The continuation from Glacier Peak Mines on Crest Trail♦ to Suiattle Pass (5983′) is about 2¼ mi. (campsites en route include those at 5700′ and 5810′—about 0. 2mi. W of pass in meadow). Total distance from road to Suiattle Pass is either 16.6 mi. or 20.1 mi. A cutoff path extends through the lowest part of the pass to save distance. Suiattle Pass, known to both Indians and early explorers, was named on the Washington Forest Reserve Map of 1898. The pass has been called "a high green place, cut deep with streams and guarded by scarred peaks and ruined forest" (*Mountaineer,* 1921, p. 19).

The new Crest Trail♦ (No. 2052—Miners Creek Section) of 4.0 mi. connects Skyline Bridge on Suiattle River to the junction of Buck Creek Pass Trail at ¼ mi. S of upper Miners Creek (from the junction it is 2¼ mi. N to G.P. Mines and 5 mi. to Buck Creek Pass). A higher hiker variation to the latter crosses Middle Ridge at 6300-ft. Richardson Pass (named by the Mazamas in 1926), a high, nearly-barren meadow; one can traverse to Pass No Pass for several high route opportunities.

Mt. David Trail No. 1521. See Mt. David.

Napeequa River Trail No. 1562. The Napeequa River, a laterally swinging postglacial stream, flows in a deeply incised and secluded valley with a nearly-level floor of some 6 mi. (see Boulder Pass Trail♦ and Little Giant Pass♦). The meanders in the flat valley tend to come against confining bedrock canyon walls. The area is part of the central schist belt (Pre-Tertiary).

The river has cut a precipitous canyon through the gneissoid bedrock, the excavation probably dating subsequent to the Pliocene. S of the river's sharp westward slice through the canyon to the White River the wider valley continues past Twin Lakes. Access to this superlative glaciated valley is only by effort, with a long climb and descent. The sequence of avalanche swaths is notable, a sharp reminder of the dangers of winter and springtime travel. The narrow valley abounds in game; this is marmot and mountain goat territory.

The trail into the valley, first shown on the 1926 Forest Service map, was made by herders and sheep in the decade of 1910; herds were driven over Boulder and Little Giant Pass. Until 1942 maps carried the mundane legend "North Fork White River." Early climber-explorers termed the valley "White River Cañon" (*Sierra Club Bull.* 8, no. 3 (1912): 177). References: *101 Hikes; Cascadian,* 1957, pp. 39-41.

The upper portion of the N fork valley leading to High Pass is composed mostly of white biotite granite (*Routes and Rocks,* p. 113); conspicuous beds of white marble streak the dark schist on the E wall of the valley's lower portion and along the trail where it climbs from the river.

Leave the river trail W of the N fork (4880′+) at an old path; keep near the stream bank, then in the upper barrens of the hanging valley there is space for mobility. Ice from the large cirque S of High Pass once discharged both to the Napeequa and Suiattle Rivers. The polished bedrock, remnant glacier, and surficial deposits, including "enormous granite shafts" on the cirque floor fascinated early observers.[81] A small glacier extends to near the floor; the lower edge of the cirque has rounded, ice-planed, striated rock and the surrounding walls glisten whitely.

Hike slightly E and above the northernmost saddle at High Pass (6876′) and drop via a steep gully to snow and talus. Closely below is the ice basin that contains secluded Triad Lake (6500′+); the deep narrow lake is iced over much of the summer (not advisable to descend to the lake and follow a lower course). The stream issuing from the lake is largely hidden under rock blocks before it cascades down steep canyon walls (the valley was once called the Little Suiattle). To continue N hike up to the ridge (est. 7150′) dividing Triad's basin from the Buck Creek drainage; a new trail section crosses the E slope, then follows on or closely W of the ridge to the saddle just S of Liberty Cap and on to Buck Creek Pass. Distance from Louis Creek in Napeequa Valley to High Pass is 4½ mi.; then 4.8 mi. to Buck Creek Pass (20 mi. from White River Trail).

Louis Creek offers a simple cross-country route; ascend a steep meadow beyond the creek and pass spectacular falls. The upper basin is an interesting pumice desert of light brown color, material blown from Glacier Peak. The ridges above are dotted with larch.

Butterfly Butte. Cross the Napeequa in the meadow about 2.6 mi. from the trail ford (4700′), then ascend timber to the open meadows of the Butte. Scenic hiking opportunities abound.

Tenpeak High Route. Where the river trail ends on a meadow (est. 5 mi. from the ford at 5200′) hike the moraine to the valley head. Continue up outcrops near Butterfly Glacier to slabs above. Bear W up snow and slabs toward the broad saddle (est. 7750′) of the glacier; this saddle is the logical place to hike across the divide to Thunder Basin.

Honeycomb High Route. From the trail's end in the river bottom, angle upward to the crest, then S ½ mi. to the saddle (6750′) S of Moth Lake. One can descend to connect with the Honeycomb Glacier or Suiattle River (see *Routes and Rocks,* p. 59-61).

Nason Ridge Trail No. 1583 begins from Smithbrook Road♦ at 2.1 mi. and passes near the top of *Rock Mountain* (6852′/2088 m) in 7 mi., Merritt Lake in 12½ mi., and on to Alpine Lookout and Round Mountain. The complete trail covers 26 mi. from Union Gap on the Crest Trail to Nason Creek Campground. The western 3 mi. from Rainy Pass to Snowy Creek is a hiker route at present.

Rock Mountain Trail No. 1587 from 9 mi. E of Stevens Pass connects with the ridge trail in 4 mi. Rock Lake (5800′+) is ½ mi. E and below this junction.

Alpine Lookout (6237′/1901 m) can be reached more directly via *Round Mountain* (5700′/1737 m), then taking the ridge trail W. This area appears to be a favorite of goats. Use Butcher Creek Road No. 2717 (about 3 mi. W of Lake Wenatchee Road junction) and then Round Mountain Trail No. 1529 (1.6 mi. to ridge trail).

Snowy Creek Trail No. 1531 has the least altitude gain in reaching Nason Ridge. Begin on Rainy Creek Road♦ (branch C) at 3.9 mi.; in 2.2 mi. reach the ridge trail. The junction to the former lookout station on Rock Mountain is met in 7 mi.; one can bypass the summit, or pass over with a 300-ft gain. Rock Mountain Trail is ¾ mi. E at 6200 ft. For Nason Ridge see also Merritt Lake Trail♦; references: *101 Hikes; Trips and Trails 1.*

North Fork Entiat River Trail No. 1437 leaves the North Fork Entiat Road (see Entiat River Road♦) at the 4-mi. point, then extends 8 mi. to a junction with Pyramid Mountain Trail♦ (6500′) near Cardinal Peak.

Fern Lake (6800′) can be reached by a hiker path no. 1436 from the trail at about 6.3 mi. (5200′); cross the river opposite the outlet creek and hike up the N side of the stream.

Where the trail leaves the river near the valley head begin a cross-country ascent W to the high pass above Choral Lake; this charming lake is dammed by an interesting Neoglacial moraine. A loop hike can be made to Choral Creek and Snow Brushy Creek Trail.♦

Pacific Crest National Scenic Trail No. 2000: Stevens Pass to White Pass. The significant highlights, viewpoints, trail and cross-country junctions are briefly noted, with mileages from Stevens Pass (4061′); deduct 6½ mi. if starting from Smithbrook Trail.♦

The first of nature's jewels is 4830-ft Lake Valhalla at 5½ mi. (best campsite W of lake). Closely across the lake is the rocky formation of *Lichtenberg Mountain* (5844′/1781 m).

Reach Union Gap (4680′) in 7 mi.; junction with Smithbrook Trail♦—E. *Union Peak* (5696′/1736 m) is a hike closely NE of the gap; the term "Union" was used because this is the junction of the Cascade crest and Nason Ridge. Reach Lake Janus (4146′) in 9½ mi. (campsite, forage, shelter); A.H. Sylvester named the lake for the two-faced Roman god of beginnings. The west slope of *Jove Peak* (6007′/1831 m)—named after the Roman god Jupiter—is an attractive walk of about 1 mi. Glasses Lake (4626′), set amid subalpine conifers, is below the trail leading toward Grizzly Pass (reach via spur path).

Reach Grizzly Meadows (5500′) in 14½ mi., then the trail bears over *Grizzly Peak* (5593′/1705 m). At 16½ mi. the forested depression of Wenatchee Pass (4240′), studied by railroad surveyors before the turn of the century, is reached (campsite, forage). Top Lake Trail No. 1506 forks E at ½ mi. N of the pass; the 4600-ft lake is ½ mi. away—camping W of lake. The trail reaches high on the S slope of *Fall Mountain* (5594′/1705 m) before descending to Little Wenatchee River valley.

The Crest Trail from Wenatchee Pass reaches pear-shaped Pear Lake (4809′) in 1½ mi. (campsite), then passes Fortune Ponds; the route climbs about 400 ft through Frozen Finger Gap, then reaches Meadow Creek Trail♦ (see Section I) (W) in 19 mi. (campsite). Reach West Cady Ridge Trail♦ (W) at 23 mi. (campsite, 4920′); from here an easy hike leads to *Benchmark Mountain* (5816′/1773 m). The main trail passes through Saddle Gap (5040′) on Benchmark's E slope, makes a juncture with Pass Creek Trail No. 1053 (camping), then touches Cady Pass (4280′) at 24½ mi. (meets Cady Creek Trail♦) (E). Reach Lake Sally Ann (5479′) at 27 mi. (no camping) and Ward's Pass (5690′) ¾ mi. beyond. The pass honors an 1872 railroad surveyor who traveled along and across the divide in this area. Reach North Fork Skykomish Trail♦ (see Section I) (W) at 28.7 mi. and Bald Eagle Trail♦ (see Section I) (W) at Dishpan Gap (5560′+, 29 mi.—best camping W of trail).

Reach Sauk Pass (5500′) and Meander Meadow in 30 mi. (Little Wenatchee Trail♦—E). The Crest Trail now crosses the lush grass slopes of *Kodak Peak* (6121′/1866 m; short walk to the summit). At Kodak Ridge meet the way trail to Wenatchee Ridge. At 31½ mi. a grassy meadow amid timber is the scene of Indian Pass (4960′, campsite, forage; junction with Indian Creek Trail♦—E).

Little White Pass (5378′) and White River Trail♦ (E) are at 33 mi. (camping on meadow ridge). Pass Reflection Pond, then reach White Pass (5904′) at 35 mi. (shelter, forage at 0.2 mi. W). The pass area is truly a Garden of Eden with flower-strewn meadows and green hills. Reference: *101 Hikes.*

For coverage of Crest Trail N of White Pass, see Section I, Trails, and Miners Ridge Trail No. 785, Section II.

Phelps Creek Trail No. 1511. From the end of Phelps Creek Road♦ (3500′) the trail meets Carne Mountain Trail No. 1508 (E) in just 0.1 mi.; reach campsites in 2½ and 2.8 mi., and Leroy Creek camp (4100′) in 3.2 mi. Leroy Creek Trail♦ (E) departs just beyond.

Phelps Ridge Trail No. 1514 bears W at 3½ mi.; this old sheep trail winds steeply to the ridge in 3 mi. (6650′), then bears N across the slope to Red Mountain Trail♦.

Phelps Creek is named after an Englishman who lost his life fording it. There are many mining claim locations on Phelps Ridge and near the head of Phelps Creek basin; the cabin of the Red Hill Mining Co. had annual avalanche problems. In 1896 the owners of the Alaska and Harvey group extended claims from the Red Hill group to the head of the basin. Claude E. Rusk wrote that here "towered the red and black peaks about the head of Lyman Glacier with a pass leading through to the snowfields of the glacier." (Rusk, *op. cit.*, p. 173).

Spider Meadow camp (est. 4750′) is reached in 4.8 mi.; the trail becomes a path, then fades at about 6.7 mi. (6200′) near the snout of Spider Glacier (use stoves for camping). L.K. Hodges described "the great meadow at the head of the canyon in the basin in which Phelps creek takes its rise . . . flowers of every tint . . . of every form and texture, grow in profusion . . . The horses gorge themselves on green . . . There are the heather, buttercup, wild bean or lupin, larkspur, deer's tongue, which shoots its leaves through the snow" (Hodges, 1896, *op. cit.*). The valley here is truly the domain of flowers, subalpine fir, marmot and pika.

Spider Pass (Phelps Creek Pass), est. 7050 ft, between a long eastern arm of Chiwawa Mountain and a rocky eminence to the E, can be reached easily in about 1 mi. by a short hike to a low spur on the E, then heading NW to the pass (see Lyman Lake Trail♦—Spider Pass route). References: *101 Hikes; Routes and Rocks*, pp. 131-32, 197-99.

Poe Mountain Trail No. 1520 begins at 0.1 mi. on Little Wenatchee River Trail♦ then extends 2½ mi. to the summit of *Poe;* there is a 3000-ft gain to the summit (6015′/1833 m). Devil's Club Road (No. 2817) from about 3 mi. before the end of the Little Wenatchee Road works 4 mi. up Poe's S slopes (est. 4100′). Cockeye Creek Trail No. 1545 (from road 2817C) leads NW to the ridge in 2½ mi., then a hiker route (Little Wenatchee Ridge Trail No. 1543) continues to Poe. *Irving Peak* (5862′/1787 m), 2½ mi. SE of Poe, can be reached by this approach and a ridge traverse hike. The ridge trail takes a lovely high route NW from Poe, virtually climbing over other "American Poet" peaks *Longfellow* and *Bryant* to meet the Crest Trail♦ at a 5630-ft saddle above Meander Meadow. Some of this scenic 8-mi. highland route is cross-country, but paths appear; generally stay on the crest or its S slope.

Pomas Creek Trail No. 1453 leaves the Ice Creek Trail♦ at about 2 mi. and connects with Pomas Pass and Larch Lakes Trail♦ (6 mi. to upper Larch Lake). Pomas was a Forest Service mispelling of pumice.

Pyramid Mountain Trail No. 1433. The S end begins at the last road grade at Big Hill Lookout (Shady Pass Road♦), then passes closely W of *Crow Hill* (7366′/2245 m) in 2 mi., high on *Graham Mountain* (7297′/2224 m), and *Albicaulis Mountain* (7200′+/2195 m). The 2.3-mi. spur to the summit of *Pyramid* (meadows and camping) leaves at 6.7 mi. (6800′) and winds to the summit (8245′/2513 m).

The main trail continues N to join the South Pyramid Creek Trail♦ (at 7½ mi.), then passes Buck Camp (in 2 mi.) and winds through Grouse Pass on Pugh Ridge (7200′+) to meet the North Fork Entiat Trail♦ (6500′-12.6 mi.) near the W side of Cardinal Peak in a broad meadow and larch area. The trail rises along meadows under Saska and Emerald Peaks, then crosses the divide (est. 7400′) to Snow Brushy Creek Trail♦ (est. 5700′).

Raging Creek Trail No. 1541 extends from Brush Creek Road No. 2923A at 9.2 mi. from Chiwawa River Road (3100′; reach from Fish Lake; start as per Chiwawa River Road♦). The trail extends for 5 or 6 mi. to the ridge on the divide between Twin Lakes and Raging Creek N of McCall Mountain; trail not maintained.

Railroad Creek Trail No. 1256 extends from the road end campground (3450′) at Holden (see Lake Chelan♦) to the Crest (Agnes Creek) Trail♦ in 10.2 mi.; 1 mi. more to Suiattle Pass. Campsites are at Hart Lake above the trail (3.2 mi.), at 4.2 mi., Lyman Lake (N end, in trees); reach Cloudy Pass (6438′—8.8 mi.) with good camping in North Star Park's meadows E of the pass. In 1936 at Cloudy Pass a signpost read "Lucerne—22 miles, Stehekin—29 miles, Sauk R.S.—49 miles." References: *101 Hikes; Mountaineer*, 1967, pp. 108-11; *Mazama* 20, no. 5 (1938): 5-12.

Railroad Creek valley is abundant with meadows and stands of Douglas fir and yellow pine. The name emanates from the Great Northern Railroad explorations.[82]

Copper Creek High Route. From Holden cross Railroad Creek on a road spur to mine buildings. A new trail start leaves from top of tailings pile about 200 ft W of Copper Creek. An alternative is to take the road up from the top level of the mill building to the old water intake for the mill, where the trail joins the road. Cross Copper Creek by the bridge at the water intake and proceed by good new trail to meet the old one at about 3700 ft (see *Routes and Rocks*, p. 191; old path begins at roadcut tread in forest thicket across Copper Creek). The path ascends steeply to about 4800 ft, then traverses the slope at the bush fringe of Copper Creek basin (camping, about 5600′). From the end of meadows go SE up gullies to talus, then S to the ridge saddle (7200′+) SW of Buckskin Mountain. Cross to Grouse Camp on the Entiat.

Dole Lakes High Route. Take the old Railroad Creek Trail (on S bank) to Dole Creek, then ascend the E side of the stream. The two lakes are at about 6150 and 6550 ft. One can cross to Entiat Meadows using the saddle (7070′) near the summit of Tinpan Mtn. Reference: *Routes and Rocks*, p. 192.

Red Mountain Trail No. 1550 (Chiwawa River Trail): Leaves Buck Creek Trail♦ at about 1½ mi., following old prospecting roadway and continues about 7 mi. to closely below Red Mountain Pass; the upper trailway crosses meadows blighted by mining. Here at the upper E fork of Chiwawa basin one can readily hike N of Red Mountain to the Spider Glacier area.

To reach Phelps Ridge Trail No. 1514 take the prospecting road ½ mi. S; leave the old road at the first bend—the trail crosses open meadows to the ridge.

Chiwawa Basin Trail No. 1505 makes a 3-mi. loop through meadows; it forks from the main trail about 1 mi. below Chiwawa basin, then connects again on Red's lower slopes. Early prospectors crossing the pass N of Red commented on the basin. "Where 28 streams pour over the rim into a gorgeous meadow . . . its eternal snow feeding twenty cascades which combine to form the Chewah river" (L.K. Hodges, 1896).

Massie Lake (5900′+) is on an old 6-mi. sheep trail to Buck Creek Pass (see *Routes and Rocks,* pp. 138-40). The lake trail (no. 1504) branches from the basin trail at about 1 mi. on a faintly marked trail.

Fortress High Route bears W from the trail in Chiwawa basin. There are suitable traverses at several levels, but a start at 6400 ft is suggested (see *Routes and Rocks,* pp. 134-35). The smooth outcrops and grassy benches of the basin offer supreme camping. Rise to cross the main S spur of Chiwawa Mountain at 6700 ft, cross the spur dividing the upper stream forks at 6600 ft and then contour to a passage in the cliffs around the S ridge of Fortress Mountain and toward Buck Creek Pass.

Rock Creek Trail No. 1509 leaves the Chiwawa River Road♦ at Rock Creek (15.1 mi.) and meets the Basalt Pass Trail in 2 mi. and the Carne Mountain junction in 11 mi. The trail makes a direct connection with Phelps Creek Road♦ (0.1 mi. along Phelps Creek Trail). It is possible to make a loop trip from the Carne Mountain junction by hiking S on the primitive Old Gib Trail #1528, and Estes Butte Trail #1527 to Rock Creek crossing. Carry drinking water on the ridge route.

Schaefer Lake (5131′) is reached in 4½ mi. via trail no. 1519 from the Chiwawa River Road♦ (13.4 mi., 2500′). The lake, nearly a mi. in length, nests in a deep glacial cirque high on the Chiwawa Mountains.

There is an attractive viewpoint atop *Mt. Sylvester* (6913′/2107 m) SW of the lake; this summit is an easy hike via the E ridge from the lake outlet. Another viewpoint is a 6931-ft summit NW of the lake—ascend its SE slope readily.

From Schaefer Lake a cross-country hike can be made NW to "D" Lake.

Shetipo-Garland Trail No. 1429 leaves from Cottonwood Camp (3075′) near the end of the Entiat River Road♦. In 4½ mi. merge with Garland Peak Trail NO. 1408, which rises to the 7000-ft level closely W of Garland Peak in 4 mi., continues W of Rampart Mountain and climbs through 7000-ft Cow Creek Pass; the trail lowers to Larch Lakes, then continues over Pomas Pass as Pomas Creek Trail♦ (distance from Shetipo trail junction to Larch Lakes is 11.1 mi.). The detour W of Rampart Mountain can be avoided by hiking over the top of Rampart or via the notch (7400′) on the upper W shoulder to join the trail at Cow Creek Pass.

Basalt Ridge Trail No. 1515 is a connection to the Garland Peak Trail from the W; distance is 8½ mi. from Rock Creek G.S.

Smithbrook Trail No. 1590 leaves the Smithbrook Road♦ (at 3¼ mi., 3800′) and connects with the Crest Trail♦ in 0.9 mi. at Union Gap (4680′); Lake Valhalla is only 1½ mi. S. From the Smithbrook Road, Cady Pass is 18 mi., White Pass is 28½ mi.

Snow Brushy Creek Trail: see Emerald Park Trail♦.

South Pyramid Creek Trail No. 1439 branches from the North Fork Entiat Trail♦ at 1¼ mi. (est. 4000′) and joins the Pyramid Mountain Trail♦ in 4 mi. (est. 5800′) for continuation to Grouse Pass at the valley head; the upper basin is outstanding for its white pines and immense stands of western larch.

Suiattle Trail No. 784 extends from the Suiattle River Road♦ end (1600′) to Crest Trail♦ at Skyline Bridge (10.6 mi.). Reach Canyon Creek shelter at 6.5 mi. and Miners Ridge Trail♦ to Suiattle Pass at 9.3 mi. (shelter 1 more mi.); distances given from new road closure at Sulphur Creek.

Suiattle River Trail No. 798. See Upper Suiattle River Trail♦.

Top Lake Trail No. 1506 extends from Fall Creek Road No. 2713A (reach from Little Wenatchee River Road♦) to Wenatchee Pass (5.3 mi.) on the Crest Trail♦.

Triad Creek Trail No. 792. See Upper Suiattle River Trail♦. Extends 5 mi. to Buck Creek Pass. The Mazamas in 1911 called the creek "Little Suiattle" but Sylvester errantly chose "Triad" for three supposed branches.

Upper Suiattle River Trail No. 798 leaves Crest Trail W of Skyline Bridge and extends to Chocolate Creek. Also reach via Suiattle Trail♦. From the Suiattle River Road♦ reach Triad Creek Trail♦ (E) at about 14 mi. The trail continues along the W side of the valley about 2.2 mi. to an area ⅓ mi. beyond Chocolate Creek, where the old trail is swallowed by forest growth. Cross-country hiking is flat, with only light bush for another 2 mi. where logs abound for a river crossing and a route to the eastern foot of the Honeycomb Glacier.

Honeycomb High Route: Hike SE through timber to a gravel crossing of the Honeycomb's meltwater stream. Ascend SE to the base of a timbered spur (est. 4500′), then climb SW, keeping E of any cliffs on the glacier stream side, to arrive at a tarn on a bared moraine (est. 5600′) just E of the ice snout; wood and camping at end spur end N of tarn. One can continue E about 1½ mi. to Moth Lake (est. 6450′), crossing barren unstable moraine slopes (good camping N of lake). Continuations can be made to the saddle S (meadows) of the lake to Napeequa Valley, or from the saddle S via the Moth Glacier to the 7750-ft saddle and Thunder Basin. Reference: *Routes and Rocks,* pp. 59-61. One of the first traverses of this area was made September 10-17, 1938 by Paul Flint and Dwight Watson, on a trek from Napeequa Valley and the Honeycomb Glacier to White Mountain.

Wenatchee Ridge Trail No. 1524E. See Poe Mountain Trail♦.

White River Trail No. 1507 extends from the end of the White River Road♦ (2300′) to meet the Crest Trail♦ at Little White Pass (14.2 mi.). The trail reaches Thunder Creek at 6.2 mi., Lightning Creek high route at 9.7 mi. (good camps at 4, 6.2, 9.4 and 10.9 mi.). This is an old trail begun in 1924.

Clark Mountain High Route can be hiked up Thunder Creek, then E across basins on the SW and S flank of Clark to Boulder Pass Trail♦. The 1939 Forest Service map showed a connecting trail from Thunder Creek across the S slope of Clark to Boulder Creek, but this herder path has almost entirely vanished; the beginning is W of the bridge at Thunder Creek (2750′). Start up a switchback path through an old burn, then a path bears to the creek (est. 3650′); the route continues up a brushy area and on toward the slopes of Clark (see *Routes and Rocks,* pp. 107-110).

Thunder Creek. Beyond the burn (above) a path takes open woods on the spur between Thunder Creek and the White (leave path before it crosses Thunder Creek). Follow open semi-forest on the shoulder; cross talus, then woods and brush parallel to Thunder Creek to reach the W fork (est. 4200′); stay well over on the W side of the lower basin (4100′-4300′). Cross flat meadows, and climb a steep rocky meadow to reach dense brush at the lip of the upper basin. Beyond the brush a grassy draw leads over; cross to the minor ridge W of the creek. The flat floor (5200′-5500′) of Thunder basin offers good camping, with a setting of meadow and huge boulders.

An impressive high route can be taken to the Butterfly Glacier and Napeequa Valley. Go to the N end of the basin and work up through lower cliffs then climb diagonally eastward, to reach a poorly defined arete S of the main band of cliffs on the E wall of the basin. Climb easy rock which levels off to snow at about 7000 ft. Ascend NE to reach the saddle (est. 7750′) overlooking the head of the Napeequa. See also Napeequa River Trail♦ and *Routes and Rocks,* pp. 109-110.

From Thunder Basin there is a good high route NW (pass the tarns at est. 6200′ and 6400′) to the ridge crest and pass W of Tenpeak Mountain.

Lightning Creek: This ice-carved hanging valley offers a number of hiking possibilities, including a crossing to the Suiattle River drainage. One can start up the W side of the creek from the trail (3180′) and climb N up timber; after crossing a spur bear NE and across a NW tributary, then up a wooded spur between Lightning Creek and the tributary. From the flat floor of the upper creek the best way is the W side near the stream; good camping in meadows. One can go over moraine and polished rock surfaces. The edge of the Honeycomb Glacier (7200′) is reached by bearing NW.

One can hike the Lightning High Route by generally traversing westward at about 7000 ft to the foot of White River Glacier. *Rocks and Routes* advises continuing up the spur between the NW tributary and Lightning Creek to timberline, then W into the basin of the tributary. Later a rising ascent is made to over 7000 ft. One can go up NW onto the White River Glacier or drop to its eastern snout. It is feasible to ascend the gentle glacier for alpine routes, or traverse SW to White Pass (see pp. 119-21).

There is a good route to White Chuck Glacier from the W terminus of White River Glacier (at 6850′). Ascend NW on scree to the saddle (7500′+) on the crest above the White Chuck. Then descend snow NW on the glacier edge. One can drop W to the lake at the foot of the glacier or keep high and traverse to White Mountain and White Pass.

NOTES

[1]R.W. Tabor and D.F. Crowder, "On Batholiths and Volcanoes—Intrusion and Eruption of Late Cenozoic Magmas in the Glacier Peak Area, North Cascades, Washington," *U.S. Geological Survey Prof. Paper No. 604* (Washington, 1969), p. 55.

[2]*Ibid,* p. 59.

[3]I.C. Russell, "A Preliminary Paper on the Geology of the Cascade Mountains in Northern Washington," *20th Annual Report U.S. Geological Survey, 1898-1899,* pt. 2 (Washington, 1900), p. 161.

[4]Fred H. McNeil, "In the Glacier Peak Region, 1926," *Mazama* 8, no. 12 (1926): 7.

[5]Fred Stadter, "Glaciation in the Glacier Peak Region," *Mazama* 8, no. 12 (1926): 53.

[6]Bailey Willis, "Physiography and Deformation of the Wenatchee-Chelan District, Cascade Range," *U.S. Geological Survey Prof. Paper No. 19* (Washington, 1903), pp. 41-101; ref. p. 64. See also p. 78, 79, pl. 8. Willis explored and made terrain studies in the Entiat Mountains and in the Lake Chelan area between 1895 and 1900. He observed, "Restoring what the (Columbia) river has cut away," the topographic continuity of Badger Mountain and the Entiat Mountains is apparent (p. 64).

[7]The oldest rocks in the Miners Ridge area consist of a magmatic gneiss complex. Following extensive and complex metamorphism, a pocket of rock deep in the crust melted and intruded the older and more rigid surrounding rock units. This Tertiary plutonic body (the Cloudy Pass, Miocene age), which took millions of yrs to cool, is a composite batholith (A. Robert Grant, "Bedrock Geology of the Dome Peak Area: Chelan, Skagit, and Snohomish Counties, Northern Cascades, Washington," Ph.D. dissertation, Univ. of Washington, 1966, p. 73).

The gross structural features in the Miners Ridge-Holden area involve intersection of NW-trending structures and the transverse Cloudy Pass structural belt (p. 73). Transverse tectonic belts have been shown to be important controlling structures in erratic distribution patterns of sulfide deposits. This fact is evident at Miners Ridge, where copper deposits are confined to parts of a transverse structural zone within a largely similar geologic environment (p. 46).

Here the main sulfide deposits occur at the intersectional point of E-W echelon sheeting in the batholithic rocks and the axial projection of a series of overturned anticlines in the roof pendant metamorphic rocks (p. 73). At Holden the ore deposition appears to have occurred prior to Cloudy Pass pluton intrusion and seems related to the Cascade metamorphism cycle. The Holden mine is situated within predominantly amphibolite and biotite schist terrain (pp. 73-74).

The extensive pre-Tertiary central schist belt (mostly garnet-biotite schist) extends SW and NW of Glacier Peak. The pre-Tertiary gneissic granite Tenpeak pluton outcrops E of Lightning Creek, but the rocks surrounding Clark Mountain, those E of Napeequa, and those in the upper Chiwawa valley, are mostly schists and gneisses. The SE-trending Entiat Mountains are in part a fault-block range whose core is composed of a tabular shaped quartz diorite complex believed to have been formed principally by the granitization of hornblende schists and biotite gneisses which occur in broad belts on both sides of the complex (Crowder, p. 828); dikes that cut all rocks of the complex are widespread (p. 865). The Entiat fault, which forms the western contact of the quartz diorite complex is a narrow linear depression that can be traced along the western side of the Chiwawa valley to the vicinity of Leavenworth (p. 830). Small patches of Eocene sedimentary rocks unconformably overlie the basement gneisses throughout the range. In the NW part of the Holden quadrangle the younger batholith of massive granodiorite (Cloudy Pass) cuts off both the Entiat fault and the basement gneiss of the Entiat Mountains. The Cretaceous biotite granodiorite High Pass pluton is centered between the Suiattle River and Buck Creek.

The Entiat and Seven Fingered Jack plutons are massive to gneissic. The Eocene-aged Rampart Mountain pluton of biotite quartz monzonite is exposed on Rampart and Fifth of July Mountain as well as farther N. The similar Larch Lakes pluton outcrops W of Larch Lakes. Plutons of about the age of stocks near Mt. Pilchuck include granodiorite and quartz diorite of the Duncan Hill pluton (45 m. y. old) and granodiorite and quartz monzonite of the Railroad Creek pluton. A long NW-trending belt of schist on the side of Chelan Mountains lies between the Duncan Hill pluton and Holden. The crest and E side of the Chelan Mountains are composed mostly of gneissic granite with subordinate amounts of schist. The Cardinal Peak pluton extends from the Tinpan Mountain-Dole Lakes area along the Chelan Mountains to Graham Mountain. This Upper Cretaceous body is largely granodiorite and biotite quartz diorite. Various gneisses outcrop on the middle and lower E flank of the Chelan Mountains; the Bearcat Ridge plutons are largely gneissic and are exposed on and near Bearcat Ridge and W of Emerald Park Creek.

References: *Routes and Rocks* (geologic map, facing p. 11); Cater, F.W. and Crowder, D.F., 1967, Geologic map of the Holden quadrangle, Snohomish and Chelan Counties, Washington: U.S. Geol. Survey Quad. Map GQ-646. Scale 1:62,500; Cater, F.W. and Wright, T.L., 1967, Geologic map of the Lucerne quadrangle, Chelan County, Washington: U.S. Geol. Survey Quad. Map GQ-647, scale 1:62,-500; Crowder, D.F., 1959, "Granitization, migmatization, and fusion in the northern Entiat Mountains, Washington," *Geol. Soc. Amer. Bull.* 70, no. 7, pp. 827-877; Crowder, D.F., Tabor, R.W. and Ford, A.B., 1966, Geologic map of the Glacier Peak quadrangle, Snohomish and Chelan Counties, Washington: U.S. Geol. Quad. Map GQ-473, scale 1:62,500; Morrison, M.E., 1954, "The petrology of the Phelps Ridge-Red Mountain Area, Chelan County, Washington," MS thesis, Univ. of Washington.

[8]Tabor and Crowder, *op. cit.*, pp. 41, 45.

[9]Russell, *op. cit.*, pp. 160-161. Russell commented that geographer H.H. Gannett renewed the suggestion that the differences in the elevation between the bottoms of lateral and main valleys to which they are tributary are due to the deeper corrasion performed by the larger ice streams as compared with the similar work done by tributaries.

[10]I.C. Russell, *North America,* New York, 1904, pp. 157-158.

[11]Russell, *op. cit.,* footnote 3. See also Henry Gannett, "Lake Chelan," *National Geographic Magazine,* vol. 9 (1898).

[12]*Ibid,* p. 161. Recent studies indicate an Okanogan lobe of Canadian ice which descended the Columbia River valley entered lower Chelan Trough, probably pushed in at least 10 mi. (Richard B. Waitt, Jr., "Geomorphology and Glacial Geology of the Methow Drainage Basin, Eastern North Cascade Range, Washington," Ph.D. dissert., Univ. of Washington, 1972, p. 1). The relationships between the alpine and Ice Sheet glaciation overlap is obscure and awaits further study.

The Okanogan Lobe of Cordilleran Ice Sheet invaded lower Chelan Valley, and constituted the 400-ft morainal embankment that impounds Lake Chelan (Waites, p. 64; citing A.C. Waters, "Terraces and Coulees along the Columbia River near Lake Chelan, Washington;" *Geol. Soc. Am. Bull. 44* (1933): 783-820).

The contemporaneous ice tongue descended Chelan Trough, a tongue of the ice sheet, and not locally derived alpine ice (Waites, p. 108), possibly to Wapato Point. Overflow of cordilleran ice from Chelan tributaries into the Methow tributaries reveals that the ice sheet innundated the Chelan Trough (pp. 79 and 106). This ice sheet dwindled without a rebirth of alpine glaciers.

Chelan Trough is flat only because it is deeply filled—a topographic similarlity of the flat floor of Methow and Yosemite Valleys. The submerged bedrock floor of the upper trough is parabolic; however, where Stehekin River sediment has filled in the head of the trough to a depth of 1200 ft, the valley floor is flat (p. 31).

[13]*Ibid.,* p. 163. The gravel-filling task of the Chelan Glacier was greater and time available less than in similar valleys. A process of gravel-filling is still underway; the deposit is the delta, which is being prolonged into the lake. Russell noted terraces show the lake level had been lowered about 275 ft; he found the surface of the lake 408 ft above the adjacent portion of the Columbia River. The rushing torrent of the 4-mi. Chelan River would cut a channel in any ordinary moraine, but the overflow stream met solid rock on the S side of the old valley and resistance "in corrading its channel." A

former outlet of Lake Chelan, Knapp Coulee, is a canyon carved by water when a Pleistocene Glacier blocked the present outlet.

[14]*Ibid,* p. 160. There were two important feeder ice streams, "one in each of the deep canyon-like valleys now occupied by the North and West forks, respectively, of White Creek."

[15]*Ibid,* p. 159. Russell did not travel either the Chiwawa or Entiat River valleys; curiously his map on Pleistocene glaciation shows no ancient ice in the Entiat River valley. He was likely misled by the narrow river valley, which hardly suggests a drainage of extensive former glaciation.

[16]There is an eastward rise across the Cascade Range of both Pleistocene cirque floors and of modern glaciers, owing presumably to orographic effects of moisture-bearing Pacific air masses (Stephen C. Porter, "Composite Pleistocene Snowline of Olympic Mountains and Cascade Range, Washington," *Geol. Soc. America Bull.* 75, pt. 5 (1964): 477-481). In the southern Cascades the mean altitude of existing glaciers was shown to be about 1500 ft higher than cirque floors, with a similar E-rising trend.

Cirque floors in the Monte Cristo area average about 4600 ft, but near the eastern limit of glaciation they appear to average about 5700 ft. The Entiat-Railroad Creek and Monte Cristo areas have about the same amount of ice today, though separated by 28 mi. In the Entiat and Lyman Lake area mean altitude of glaciers is about 7000 ft and at Cardinal Peak about 8000 ft; in the Clark Mountain-Butterfly Glacier area to the W it is about 7500 ft. A comparison shows the Entiat-area glaciers lie within an altitude range of 2620 m to 1860 m, and have a mean altitude of about 2185 m. In the Monte Cristo area a compilation for 27 glaciers shows a mean altitude of 1768 m (base data from Inventory of Glaciers). Valleys tend to less gradient on the E side of the Cascade crest than on the W side. The altitude of 2000 ft on the Suiattle River is reached in 7½ mi. from Suiattle Pass; about the same distance E reaches to Holden, at about 3300 ft. The distance on the North Fork of Skykomish River from the 2000-ft level to the main divide is about 7½ mi.; the altitude at this distance on the E slope is about 2600 ft.

[17]Austin Post, et al., "Inventory of Glaciers in the North Cascades, Washington," *U.S. Geol. Survey Prof. Paper 705-A* (Washington, 1971), p. A 20. The Honeycomb Glacier totals 1.44 mi.^{2} with a mean altitude of 6750 ft. Barren zones and other evidence shows rapid retreat after the turn of the century (est. 4750′ retreat since most recent downvalley maximum about 1890, determined from positions of forest trimline, lateral and terminal moraines, as evidence of dwindling from advanced Neoglacial position; 1270′ est. retreat 1949 to 1973). Austin Post, personal commun., 1974. The lower glacier is flanked by barren, unstable recent moraine slopes.

[18]Stadter, *op. cit.*, p. 57.

[19]*Ibid,* p. 58. "Immense glaciers likewise reach the summit of the ridge . . . leaving a long series of nunataks protruding through the ice."

[20]Russell, *op. cit.,* footnote 3, p. 193. Russell emphasized that "the broadest névé fields and most numerous glaciers occur on Glacier Peak and the rugged mountains surrounding it. The snow fields in this region cover a rugged area some 10 square miles in extent, and are confluent, and from this gathering ground there flow several short ice streams." The surfaces of these névé fields "are undulating and show the broader inequalities in the rocks, which they cover as a blanket . . . These glaciers on melting, supply the West Fork of White Creek, which flows east, and both the south and north forks of Whitechuck Creek, which flows west."

[21]Stadter, *op. cit.,* p. 57. "There is an almost continuous stretch of ice field for nine miles . . . It extends to the very summit of the ridge for nearly its entire length."

[22]*Ibid,* pp. 58-59. O.W. Freeman measured the recession and found it to be 1748 ft during the 40-yr period ending in 1941. The glacier has separated into two parts; the upper is crevassed and the lower is thinning (William A. Long, "Ancient Cirques and Modern Glaciers in the North Cascades," *Summit,* May 1964, pp. 2-7).

L.D. Lindsley's measurements showed that the ice front had retreated an average of 40 ft annually between 1915 and 1930 (photo 16106, Oct. 2, 1930, Special Collections, University of Washington).

[23]Martin W. Gorman, "Eastern Part of Washington Forest Reserve," *19th Annual Report U.S. Geological Survey, 1897-1898,* pt. 5 (Washington, 1899), p. 349. Near the head of Twenty Five Mile Creek Gorman studied a lodgepole pine and subalpine fir tract which fires and sheep had desolated.

[24]Alexander Ross, *Adventures of the First Settlers on the Oregon or Columbia River,* ed. Milo M. Moore, London, 1849, p. 289. Ross at this time was in the David Stuart party traveling up the Columbia to establish trading posts for John Jacob Astor's Pacific Fur Company.

[25]When Lewis and Clark heard of the Wenatchee River and the Indians living along its banks in October 1805 they recorded both under this name (Elliott Coues (ed.), *History of the Lewis and Clark Expedition,* vol. 3 (New York, 1893), p. 973, 1255). However, the spelling is broken in the Thwaites edition of the journals: "Cuts-sâh-nim Nation reside on both Sides of the Columbia Above the Sokulks & on the Northerly branches of the Tapteel river and also on the Wah-na-a-chee river (Reuben Gold Thwaites (ed.), *Original Journals of the Lewis and Clark Expedition 1804-1806,* vol. 6, pt. 1 (New York, 1905), p. 119); on the map (vol. 3, pt. 2, p. 184) the form is "Wah-na-â-chee."

Edmond S. Meany (*Origin of Washington Geographic Names,* Seattle, 1923, p. 342) states the word is from Yakima language, meaning "river issuing from a canyon." Another early use of the name is in the treaty of June 9, 1855 by Isaac I. Stevens, referring to the river as "Pisquouse or Wenatshapam" (p. 345); the latter also used in Pacific Railroad Reports. Lt. Thomas W. Symons wrote that the river was called "Piscous" on the War Department Map of 1838 and cites Commander Wilkes calling it "Pischous" but mentioning that some Indians called it "Wainape" (Report of Lieutenant Thomas W. Symons, Corps of Engineers, *Columbia River,* 47th Cong., 1st sess., Senate Ex. Doc. No. 186 (Washington, 1882), serial 1991, vol. 6, p. 133). Symons mentioned that none of the early writers called it the Wenatchee.

[26]Journal of George Gibbs (1854-1856). Records relating to the United States-Canadian border. Record Group 76; item 198. National Archives. Variants of the name Entiat River include "Intyclook" (Ross), "Entiyatcoom" (Wilkes map, 1841), "Ente-at-hwa" (Johnson map, 1867), "En-ti-at-kwu" (U.S. Northwest Boundary Survey, Map of Western Section, 1866), "Entiatqua" (Washington Forest Reserve map, 1898).

[27]William C. Brown, "Old Fort Okanogan and the Okanogan Trail," *Oregon Hist. Society Quarterly* 15 (1914): 12. The river is also referred to as the Pisquowsh. The Pacific Railroad Reports gave the similar name "Pisquouse or Wenatshapam" of the Yakima language. The Lewis and Clark map of 1814 designated the river "Wah-na-a-cha" and the David Thompson map of 1814 labels it "Piskowish." Gibbs titles it "Winitsha" (the 1860 manuscript map of George Gibbs; Records relating to the United States-Canadian border. Record Group 76; Item 215. National Archives). Commander Wilkes called the river "Pischous," but added that some Indians termed it the "Wainape." General James Tilton, during the Northern Pacific Railroad Surveys used "We-na-chee." (Tilton letter to Thomas Canfield; 12 September 1867, Secretary Series, Records of Lake Superior and Puget Sound Company; Minnesota Historical Society).

[28]Carl I. Wheat, *Mapping the Transmississippi West 1540-1861,* vol. 2: *from Lewis and Clark to Fremont, 1804 to 1845,* San Francisco, 1958, p. 106. The Ross map of 1821, now in the British Museum.

[29]Ross, *op. cit.,* Lakeside edition, p. 149. The next morning they reached the Pisscows, "a beautiful stream, which empties itself into the Columbia . . . here the Indians met us in great numbers . . . Sopa, the chief made us a present of two horses."

[30]Frederick Merk (ed.), *Fur Trade and Empire, George Simpson's Journal* (Harvard University, 1931), p. 52. Simpson was governor of the Northern Department of Rupert's Land. He also refers to the "Intatook" and "Tsillani" Rivers. The journal (p. 52) credits the name from a "Tribe who inhabit the banks in the interior." Simpson injects an interesting trade route across the Cascades with this comment: "from the sources of these Rivers there is a communication formed by small lakes narrows and Portages to Puget's Sound the distance not exceeding Six or Eight Days March with small canoes," but this probably was meant for the crossing using the Yakima River drainage and lakes. An interesting cartographic appendage—the Washington Forest Reserve map (1898) depicts the main course of the Wenatchee as the stream now called the Little Wenatchee and through Lake Wenatchee. See also footnote 45.

[31]This term is conjectured to indicate the milky color (from glacier flour) of the river, but this opacity would seem to be too common to have attracted aboriginal or early attention as a name-giving characteristic.

[32]Footnote 27, *op. cit.*

[33]The map clearly shows "Teh-ko Creek." U.S. North West Boundary Survey, Map of Western Section, 1866. Records relating to the United States-Canadian border. Record Group 76; item 188. National Archives. The General Land Office map of Washington Territory (1887) confirms the Indian names of this and the Gibbs map, with slight spelling variance. Albert B. Rogers wrote "Tekho." Other river names include Sat-chaal for Twentyfive Mile Creek and Natapoc for Nason Creek. White River valley has long been a favorite hunting ground for Indians because of the plentiful deer, beaver, goat, small game, and huckleberries; much of the valley bottom is "beaver dam" land. Old burns were caused by Indians (Fred G. Plummer, "Forest Conditions in the Cascade Range, Washington," *Professional Paper No. 6,* U.S. Geological Survey (Washington, 1902), p. 29).

[34]The spelling in Russell's Geological sketch map of the Cascade Mountains in Northern Washington, pl. 9. *Op. cit.,* footnote 3. Also G.L.O. map of 1887. Earlier Rogers had termed the river "Chewaw" (Diary, p. 65).

[35]Thompson's 1814 "Map of the North-West Territory of the Province of Canada" was made for the North West Company. Thompson's 1818 map "The Oregon Territory from Actual Survey" is in the British Museum (Wheat, *op. cit.,* p. 105). Thompson made frequent stops to confer with Indians, make observations, and examine the country. However, no journal entry indicates he saw Lake Chelan. With its remarkable detail, the 1818 map shows Puget Sound and three Cascade volcanoes, yet the position of the Columbia narrows the main chain to a ridge (N-S apex) Lake Chelan is marked quite correctly, with perhaps a guess exaggerating its width. The Wilkes map (1841) overlooked the lake.

[36]Wheat, *op. cit.,* p. 106. Ross correctly represents the Columbia's main western branches, but gives no indication of Lake Chelan, although a stream of some length entering from the mountains at about its location is titled "Tsillane River." Ross correctly stated that the Columbia's tributaries are de-

rived from the mountains to the W. Thompson here corroborates Ross, for on his 1814 map the "Piskowish" is exaggerated in length, to originate well N of Lake Chelan. Yet the maps differ irreconcilably on the width of the Cascade Range and the subjects of Puget Sound and Lake Chelan.

[37]*Ibid.*, p. 139.

[38]The map published (Preliminary Sketch of the Northern Pacific Rail Road Exploration and Survey from the Rocky Mountains to Puget Sound, by Isaac I. Stevens, Governor of Washington Territory, 1853-4; map drawn by John Lambert, topographer of McClellan exploration, and Lt. Johnson K. Duncan, U.S. Army-topographer, western division. *Reports of explorations and surveys to ascertain the most practicable and economic route for a railroad from the Mississippi River to the Pacific Ocean;* 33rd Cong., 2d sess.; House Ex. Doc. 91, vol. 11, map no. 3 (Washington, 1855); (also in Wheat, vol. 4, opp. p. 12) and the Edwin F. Johnson map (1867) depict the lake outline reasonably.

The Gibbs map (1860) has the legend "L Chelann." The Arrowsmith map of 1859 "The Provinces of British Columbia and Vancouver Island" (Bancroft Library) has the legends "Clear Water or Chelan R and L," and toward the SW, "Snow in April." Yet on the otherwise generally accurate General Land Office map of the United States and Territories (1885) the lake is omitted (the Map of a part of Washington Territory—1860—Surveyor General's Office; Olympia, W.T., September 20, 1860 shows the lake and name). McClellan and his party were the first white men to actually see the lake.

[39]"General report of Captain George B. McClellan," *Reports, op. cit.*, vol. 1, pt. 2, serial 758, p. 196. Gibbs measured the lake at 474 ft above the Columbia. "Its length seems, from Indian account, to be thirty-five or forty miles." Gibbs, *op. cit.*, footnote 45, p. 507.

[40]Philip H. Overmeyer, "George B. McClellan and the Pacific Northwest," *Pacific Northwest Quarterly* 32 (1941): 41. McClellan had his problems in the narrow Columbia valley when en route to Fort Okanogan; at 3 mi. past the "Enteat kwu" two mules fell to death from a trail precipice.

[41]"Report of Lieutenant Thomas W. Symons Corps of Engineers, for the fiscal year ending June 30, 1880," *Report of the Chief of Engineers, U.S. Army;* 46th Cong., 3d sess., House Ex. Doc. No. 1, pt. 2 (Washington, 1881), serial 1955, vol. 5, p. 2552. Symons concluded Lake Chelan "is the most grandly beautiful lake that I have ever seen" (p. 2553). Symons did not then understand the lake's sources, for he wrote "It is supplied from mountain-springs and from the melting snows of the mass of snow-capped mountains lying about Mount Baker" (pp. 2552-53). Symons also noted "the shores are in places exceedingly steep, the granite walls rising smooth and shiny, without a tree or a blade of grass, for a thousand feet or more from the water's edge." (Report of Lieutenant Thomas W. Symons, Corps of Engineers, *Columbia River,* 47th Cong., 1st sess., Senate Ex. Doc. No. 186 (Washington, 1882),serial 1991, vol. 6, p. 40). In 1880 Chelan was briefly the site of Camp Chelan, established by Lt. Henry C. Merriam; the location was also the site of the Indian village Chelann. Merriam canoed to the head of the lake, admired the scenery, and noted the Indian petroglyphs.

[42]Ross, *op. cit.*, Lakeside edition, p. 150. When Lt. Samuel Rodman canoed up Lake Chelan in August, 1883 he reported "the mountain goat, unsuspicious of danger, browses on the slopes. We landed several times and stole upon them, bringing down several fine specimens. They are snow white, slightly larger than the tame goat . . . The meat is strong and gamey." (Samuel Rodman, Jr., "Explorations in the Upper Columbia Country," *Overland Monthly,* 2d series, vol. 7 (London, 1886), p. 265). Goat herds have been seen many times between the lake and Glacier Peak. A Mazama club group in 1911 in descending to the upper Napeequa River saw a herd of 18. Contemporary periodicals give many accounts of goat hunting in the Lake Chelan basin during the 1890s and early 1900s.

[43]*Reports, op. cit.*, footnote 39.

[44]*Op. cit.*, footnote 38. The principal course of the Wenatchee and branches (titled "Pisquouse or Wenatshapam") is suggested to be N of the outline of what was probably meant for Lake Wenatchee; the lake is shown too far S. Near the river headquarters the main crest of the Cascades divides, with a second axis diverging NE beyond the head of Lake Chelan (this artistic device of dual crests was emulated by a number of maps). The regions both SW and NE of unnamed Lake Chelan are titled "mountainous country covered with pine forest."

[45]"Report of George Gibbs upon the Geology of the Central Portion of Washington Territory," *Reports, op. cit.*, p. 481. The Gibbs 1855 map (Washington Territory showing the position of the Indian Tribes); Wheat, Vol. 4, p. 36; marks the lake "Pisquouse L", uniquely far S for Lake Wenatchee, but certainly meant for it. His 1856 map (p. 44) gives the legend "Pisquouse or Wenatsha R."

So far as is known, the 1866 Northwest Boundary Survey Map marks the first appearance of today's name in cartographic history, using the legend "Tah-kwt or Wenatchee L." The 1867 map of Edwin F. Johnson places the legend "Wenathee (sic) Mines" in the blank space N of the lake, but the river is titled "Wenache." The Goethals-Downing Army map of 1883 drawn to show the route traveled by General William T. Sherman from Fort Ellis, Montana to Fort Hope, British Columbia also spells "Wenatchee Lake" and adds the title "Klaklin Lake" for the position of Fish Lake (Report of Secretary of War, 48th Cong.—1st sess., vol 1). The John Arrowsmith map, British North America, dated 1824, also April 25, 1840, depicts the lake in outline with the legend "Piscous R" to the SE; this indicates Hudson's Bay trappers knew of the lake. The generally exaggerated distances reported by the first explorers, who were unable to correct their estimates by precise observations, distort those parts of early maps based on their reports.

[46]Albert H. Sylvester estimated blazes across Cady Pass were made between 1830 and 1850. See Lindley M. Hull, *A History of Central Washington,* (Spokane, 1929), p. 17. In August 1887 Albert B. Rogers noted what he believed were Hudson's Bay cuttings here and in the lower valley of White River. (Albert B. Rogers Papers, University of Washington, Diary, p. 68). On August 6, traveling up Sanders Creek (Little Wenatchee) he noted occasional signs of a blazed trail. He estimated that old cuttings near Lake Wenatchee were probably 50 yrs old (p. 67).

[47]*Op. cit.,* footnote 27. The Gibbs map shows a trail connecting to the North Fork Skykomish River (probably via Cady Pass), one extending to the Stillaguamish, and one to the Sauk (probably via Indian Pass). The Map of Washington Forest Reserve, 1898 (*19th Annual Report, U.S. Geological Survey, 1897-1898,* pt. 5 (Washington, 1899), pl. 74) marks the name Cady Pass, but shows no trail. The only cross-Cascade routes shown on this map are the trail from Wenatchee Lake to Indian Pass and the North Fork of the Sauk, and the Great Northern Railroad track up Nason Creek to Cascade Summit. The enigma of Indian crossings of the Cascades is given further perspective by noting that in 1887 A.B. Rogers learned that only two Indians knew the mountains in the region of his survey and not one had crossed that year (Diary, p. 64—see note 46).

[48]*Op. cit.,* footnote 29. Ross met friendly Indians at his camp near the Wenatchee's mouth. In another report Indians near Rock Island Rapids in the summer of 1880 found and helped Alfred Downing from a near drowning ("Report of Lieutenant Thomas W. Symons, Corps of Engineers, for the fiscal year ending June 30, 1881," *Report of the Chief of Engineers, U.S. Army;* 47th Cong., 1st sess., House Ex. Doc. No. 1, serial 2013 (Washington, 1882), vol. 5, p. 2866).

[49]Major R.S. Garnett (Wenatcha River, W.T.) to Major W.W. Mackall (Fort Vancouver, W.T.), 30 August, 1858, *Report of the Secretary of War, 1858,* 35th Cong., 2d sess., Senate Ex. Doc. No. 1 (Washington, 1859), serial 975, pp. 379-380. See also Andrew J. Splawn, *Ka-mi-akin: the Last Hero of the Yakimas,* Portland, 1917, pp. 102-103. Sylvester states that Major Garnett divided troops under Lts. Crook and James K. McCall and sent them over Blewett Pass to intercept Indians. These troops overtook the Indians probably near Leavenworth (August 22-23), captured and executed five who were murderers; it is unclear if there were further skirmishes. There is a tradition that Lt . Crook chased Indians into the mountains northward. Hull, *op. cit.,* footnote 26, pp. 15-16. This may have resulted in a stand near the head of Raging Creek; however this is disputed in a letter from Army War College to Sylvester which states the only Indians killed under Crook and Lt. Thomas E. Turner were in connection with the execution (A.H. Sylvester Papers, University of Washington Library).

[50]L.K. Hodges, *Mining in the Pacific Northwest,* Seattle, 1897. See also L.K. Hodges "Mines in the Cascades—The Chewah District," *Seattle Post Intelligencer,* 16 August 1896, p. 20. Hodges (1896) relates that in 1893 pioneer prospector George N. Watson was told by a trapper he was at the head of "Chewah" River 25 yrs earlier and "saw a great copper mountain." This may have been Moses Splawn, who in about 1868 went as far as Phelps Creek and brought back samples. Here on Phelps Ridge the intrusive breccias are altered and mineralized with sulfides; prospectors found mineral to be white quartz and diorite heavily charged with sulphide of iron carrying gold and silver. Hodges wrote, "A single glance suffices to satisfy a man that Red hill, which stretches away to the left from the upper rim, contains mineral . . . red stains of oxidized iron all along the line of cliffs . . . shining red in the sunlight."

Prospectors soon arrived in number; they hiked along the Entiat divide, where they found free gold, and made claims in Rock Creek, in Maple Creek, W of Mad River, and S of Whistling Pig Mountain. In addition there were placer locations along the Chiwawa and Entiat Rivers to locate free gold. In the fall of 1901 prospectors crossed Buck Creek Pass to find the copper deposits on Miners Ridge. The Forest Service map of 1916 shows a trail constructed to Buck Creek Pass and on to Suiattle Pass. The Red Mountain Mining Co. bought up many claims and along with the Red Hill Mining Co. vied for supremacy ("Red hill may rival B.C.'s Red Mountain"). At one time over 200 men worked in the district. A tunnel was bored nearly 2 mi. under Phelps Ridge; by 1916 a road was shown on maps up Phelps Creek beyond Red Mountain. While a large quantity of ore was mined, it turned out mostly low grade.

There are many relics in upper Phelps Creek and Railroad Creek basins, including an old cabin near the Lyman Glacier's terminal moraine. "Red Mountain Ole" (Johann Smeds) had a cabin up Phelps Creek (opposite Leroy Creek); the cabin across Spider Pass may also have been his. Miners of his genre toiled hard, braved winter weather and avalanches, but seldom had much to show for their effort. While Trinity is a "ghost town" now, higher prices and demand for copper may revive mining in this district.

[51]Map of the Country from Lake Superior to the Pacific Ocean from the latest Explorations and Surveys to accompany the report of Edwin F. Johnson Ch[f] Eng[r] Northern Pacific R.R., November 1867, in *Northern Pacific Railroad Company* (Hartford, 1867), in Carl I. Wheat, *Mapping the Transmississippi West 1540-1861,* vol 5: *From the Civil War to the Geological Survey,* pt. 1, pp. 205-208; pt. 2, pp. 408-409, San Francisco, 1963.

[52]Records of Lake Superior and Puget Sound Company; N.P./Secretary Series, Minnesota Historical Society. See also Eugene V. Smalley, *History of the Northern Pacific Railroad,* New York, 1883, p. 152.

In 1879 surveyor Ward explored what is probably Wenatchee Pass and called the location Chusalle Pass (A.H.

Sylvester applied the current name in 1912); but Chusalle Pass could be the Rapid River-Lake Janus-Lake Creek route. The Asher and Adams' Washington map (1874) identifies "Index Mt., Monument Pk., Chusalle Pass, Chusalle Lake, Cadys Pass, Wards Pass, Indian Pass and Linseys Pass." When Albert B. Rogers was engaged in field surveys of the Wenatchee Passes in 1887 he found evidence of earlier explorations, such as blazes at various positions, including Indian Pass and probably Little White Pass, and two other passes that he felt were not as good as Cady and Wenatchee Passes. Rogers may have gone up Lake Creek's N fork to Wenatchee Pass on August 16; he mentions (p. 73) survey evidence on what appears to be this stream and its S fork to the divide (later he crossed near Wenatchee Pass en route to Skykomish). Rogers made a 13-day trip up "Sanders Creek" (p. 67) on foot due to brush and windfall (Little Wenatchee River; also Te-Te-ak-um). In noting the general incorrectness of existing maps he felt the pass he reached (Cady, August 11) might be the mythical Ward's Pass. Rogers climbed Benchmark Mountain for a view. Later he traveled up White River to the divide, but concluded Cady Pass was best and the Skykomish route the shortest. Diary, Albert B. Rogers Papers, University of Washington Library.

[53]Records indicate Stevens then made a high reconnaissance S to Snoqualmie Pass in search of the optimum railroad pass; unfortunately his journal on this exploration has not been located. Stevens had helped the Canadian Pacific locate their line through the Canadian Rockies and employed by Hill, he located the lowest pass in the Montana Rockies for the Great Northern in December, 1889. Under the presidency of Theodore Roosevelt, Stevens became Chief Engineer at the Panama Canal.

[54]John F. Stevens, "Great Northern Railway," *Washington Hist. Quarterly* 20, no. 2 (1929): 111-112. This pass was apparently missed by earlier surveyors Ward and Rogers.

[55]Comprehensive documentation on this area and outings is given in: *Mountaineer,* 1910, pp. 29-40; 1928, pp. 7-19; 1958, pp. 7-15, 28-39; *Mazama* 4, no. 1 (1912): 6-9; vol. 8, no. 12 (1926), pp. 7-30, 50-59; vol. 20, no. 12 (1938), pp. 5-12, 20-21. See also *101 Hikes.*

[56]Fred H. McNeil, "In the Glacier Peak Region, 1926," *Mazama* 8, no. 12 (1926): 7-30.

[57]See Footnote 7.

[58]DaKobed, Dakobad, or Dahkobed, a variation of Takobud. Nels Bruseth Papers, Manuscripts, University of Washington Library. Also see Nels Bruseth, "Indian Stories and Legends of the Stillaguamish, Sauks, and Allied Tribes," 2d ed., 1950, Arlington Times Press, pp. 31, 35.

[59]R.L. Glisan, "Glacier Peak Outing of the Mazama Club," *Mazama* 4, no. 1 (1912): 13. Rusk during his Glacier Peak exploration in 1906 referred to "the spires and precipices of the range of rock-peaks" (p. 169) and regretted not having time to explore "these remarkable glaciers and the adjacent peaks" (p. 170); Rusk, *op. cit.* (see Glacier Peak references).

[60]Fred Stadter, "Glaciation in the Glacier Peak Region," *Mazama 8,* no. 12 (1926): 57.

[61]Glisan, *op. cit.,* photo caption opp. p. 1; see also pp. 7-8, and caption opp. p. 32. See also *Sierra Club Bull.* 8, no. 3 (1912): 177. The first to show Tenpeak Mountain was the 1931 Forest Service map. The name Clark, which first appeared on the 1925 map, was applied by A.H. Sylvester for a distant relative of a friend. A recent publication erroneously attributes its ascent to the Mazama party of 1911.

[62]McNeil, *op. cit.,* p. 14.

[63]Stadter, *op. cit.,* p. 56.

[64]The Honeycomb Glacier extends from the summit crags eastward, descending to the 5400-ft level. The White River Glacier (1.2 km^2) exists on the S side of the highland between 7700 ft and 6800 ft; there are two other ice patches to its E, on the same slope. The divide between the Honeycomb and Suiattle Glaciers lies in a line from the summit crags to an 8018-ft outcrop, then descends to 7400 ft at the upper saddle of Kopeetah Divide. At this ice divide there is a longitudinal windcrest of several hundred yds, trending NE, one of the most striking such formations in the Cascades. The White Chuck Glacier covers much of the W side of the highland, recession having reduced area and thickness; there is now just a trace of ice crossing to the Suiattle (Forest Service records indicate this place was called "Glacier Gap" in the summer of 1929).

Professor I.C. Russell apparently made the first climbs on a traverse of this highland in August 1898; it is uncertain which summits he climbed (Russell, *op. cit.,* Geological sketch map of the Cascade Mountains in northern Washington, plate 9, opp. p. 90).

[65]McNeil, *op. cit.,* p. 11. Buck Mountain was shown on the 1916 Forest Service map.

[66]Stadter, *op. cit.,* pp. 53, 54, 56. See also *Mazama* 49, no. 13 (1967).

[67]*Mazama* 8, no. 12 (1926): 55.

[68]Glen Bremerman, H.E.D. Brown, J.M. Gleason, E.B. Horning, Lars Loveseth, Ben Mooers, and Charles Simmons. The *Mountaineer,* 1921 (p. 13) mentions the climb of "Dummy Dummy" (an unnamed peak) S of Buck Creek Pass. In 1910 a party explored unnamed peaks between 6000 ft and 7800 ft in this local area, but no specific climb is given (*Mountaineer,* 1910, p. 33).

This peak is also probably the "Goat Mountain" of the 1926 Mazama outing; from the summit they referred to sheer walls descending into Buck Creek canyon (Stadter, *op. cit.,* p. 53).

[69]*Mazama* 4, No. 1 (October 1912): 11.

[70]*Ibid.,* p. 18.

[71]Hermann F. Ulrichs, interview, 28 December 1972. The miners were Lynn Bennett and a companion, who found a cairn (source: Larry Penberthy).

[72]Hodges, *op. cit.,* footnote 50.

[73]Tabor and Crowder, *op. cit.,* p. 134.

[74]The perpetration of this name, for General Frederick Stanley Maude of British Mesopotamian troops in World War I, is both unfortunate and incongruous here in the Cascade Range.

[75]L.K. Hodges (1896), "the summit of this ridge is split into pointed crags called the Entiat Needles." The present name was given by A.H. Sylvester.

[76]*Op. cit.,* footnote 78, p. 363.

[77]*Sierra Club. Bull.* 8, no. 3 (1912): 177. This issue describes the steep heather slopes above the pass, the thick carpet of white cassiope rising to the crests; on Flower Hill are masses of aster and purple lupine, paintbrush, valerian, gentian, and anemone. See also *Mazama* 8, no. 12 (1926): 13-14. This issue describes the scenic glories of the area and the sheep camps. See also *Mazama* 49, no. 13 (1967): 24-27; *Mountaineer,* 1928, pp. 7-8; 1946, pp. 9-15 (place names); 1958, pp. 28-39 (plant life); *101 Hikes.*

[78]*U.S. Geological Survey 21st Ann. Report,* part 1 (Washington, 1900), p. 366.

[79]Rusk, *op. cit.,* p. 175.

[80]Hodges, *op cit.*

[81]Stadter, *op. cit.,* p. 54.

[82]The name first appeared on the 1898 Washington Forest Reserve Map, but no trail was shown. Prospectors improved Indian routes. In July 1887 railroad explorer Albert B. Rogers went up the valley to about Cloudy Pass, calling the stream "Stehekin Creek" (Diary, pp. 48-50, Albert B. Rogers Papers, University of Washington Library). He noted extensive slides in the valley had swept away acres of large trees; on July 13 he sighted a grizzly at Lyman Lake. The valley has been prone to avalanche problems: in 1916 the Oscar Getty cabin was swept into Hart Lake. In 1902-1903 the Chelan Transportation and Smelting Co. built a grade for a railroad from Lucerne, but used it only as a pack trail despite railroad plans and promises; when machinery was taken to the Holden claims in 1906 the bed was finished into a wagon road by the Crown Point prospectors.

Before World War I the Crown Point molybdenum mine was operating adjacent to Railroad Creek. There was a mule haulage way with wooden rails on the hillside 300 ft above Hart Lake Falls. The ore had been sent to Germany, but the mine shut down during the war and never re-opened. A cog railroad on a cable once ran from the lake for 1500 ft upslope to the wagon road; in 1937 a Model T operated here. Some time prior to 1921 the Forest Service rebuilt the trail to Suiattle Pass.

"The many water courses have been burrowed by the mountain beaver, which feeds on the grass and weeds and lays them up in neat sheaves to dry and then stows the hay away in his hole for winter consumption. Among the rocks the whistling marmot burrows his holes, from which he comes to feed and sit on the rocks, where he gazes around and emits his melancholy whistle. He is shaped like a small pig, with gray fur stripped with brown and is nimble as a cricket and shy of human society. Instead of being no better than dog meat, as I was led to say in writing about the whistlers of Horseshoe basin, his flesh is sweet and tender as that of a rabbit and is a favorite article of diet up Phelps creek. I . . . feasted off the boiled whistler at Mr. Harvey's cabin in the Phelps basin and found it sumptuous fare."

L.K. HODGES, 1896
Phelps Creek Basin

source:

"Mines in the Cascades"
Seattle Post Intelligencer, 16 August 1896, p. 20

SECTION III

Cascade Crest Region:

SUIATTLE RIVER TO SKAGIT RIVER (WEST SIDE) AND LAKE CHELAN TO GRANITE CREEK (EAST SIDE)

"Of all the mountain climbing I have ever done, the switchback up to Doubtful Lake is the worst. We were hours doing it. There were places where it seemed no horse could possibly make the climb. Back and forth, up and up, along that narrow rock-filled trail, which was lost here in a snow-bank, there in a jungle of evergreen that hung out from the mountainside, we were obliged to go. There was no going back. We could not have turned a horse around, nor could we have reversed the pack-outfit without losing some of the horses.

"As a matter of fact, we dropped two horses on that switchback. With infinite labor the packers got them back to the trail, rolling, tumbling, and roping them down to the ledge below, and there salvaging them. It was heart-breaking, nerve-racking work. Near the top was an ice-patch across a brawling waterfall. To slip on that ice-patch meant a drop of incredible distance. From broken places in the crust it was possible to see the stream below. Yet over the ice it was necessary to take ourselves and the pack."

MARY ROBERTS RINEHART
"A Pack-Train in the Cascades"
Cosmopolitan 63, (Oct. 1917), p. 32.

GEOGRAPHY

The North Cascades between Suiattle Pass and the Skagit River are aptly described as "The Snowy Range," the name applied by Captain George Vancouver in 1792, for even in midsummer they are considerably cloaked by a mantle of snow and ice. Dazzling glaciers proclaim the alpine character of the terrain above the green pedestal of forest vegetation, and even on the inland eastern slope the Cascades are a partly glacierized, rugged range. One of the most distinctive features of the range is the abundance of slope (hanging) glaciers lying on moderated alp slopes. The contrast between the formerly ice-protected alp slopes and the forest-clad depths of the torrent-eroded lower valleys is dramatic.

Between the latitudes of Suiattle Pass and the Skagit River the Cascades are 60 to 90 km wide and begin to reach maximum width. Great peaks stand solitary or in compact, isolated groups. An individual aloofness adds much to the impressiveness of a vast, wild, icy beauty, and contrasts them sharply with the jumbled rivalry of smaller summit clusters. When haze and smoke shroud the lower levels in winter, these peaks, high in the crystal clear atmosphere above foothills, appear as a line of magnificent icebergs floating on the denser air. In the Cascades N of Snoqualmie Pass 77 peaks rise with 6000-ft relief in 3 mi., compared to 38 peaks in the Sierra Nevada. A description of the area N of Glacier Peak, where Dome Peak stands conspicuously above the general summit level, seems fitting: "Scores of peaks soared in vast array, blackly silhouetted against the darkening sky. There were flat-topped mountains with minarets on the corners; smooth, round domes; monsters whose domes had been scooped into great basins by the glaciers bursting down their sides; aiguilles, gendarmes, cones and pyramids; knife-edged crests and dumpy knolls."[1] The North Cascades Study Team, which much later analyzed the region for its status as a national park, concluded that here is "a matchless complex in an untouched land of silent glaciers, unique geologic exhibits, and important ecological communities."

The hydrologic boundary formed by the Cascade divide is so obscure that it is hard to recognize. Few of the higher peaks are on the watershed, but they are randomly placed near it. While such dominant peaks as Dome, Buckner, Logan, and Black rise along the erratic divide, equally important summits such as Eldorado, Goode, and Bonanza do not. The Western Chelan (Bonanza) cluster of peaks and the Buckindy-Snowking group can be considered distinct subranges. But precise structural control of topography is lacking in comparison to the Entiat and Chiwawa Mountains.

The alluvium-buried valleys of lowest elevation, such as the Skagit, Sauk, Suiattle, and Cascade, are surrounded by dense forests of fir, hemlock, and cedar, with a lush, thick understory, a combined forest mantle that makes the range additionally difficult to decipher. At one time "The entire land area from tide water . . . is clothed with a splendid forest of giant trees . . . Its grandeur in an artistic sense is beyond description."[2] The heavily forested valley floors and foothills of the seaward slope are clad with a mixed lowland temperate forest (Douglas fir and western hemlock are the most abundant species, and Pacific silver fir is common). Above about 2000 ft in altitude this forest merges with the montane coniferous forest, and higher lies the subalpine zone, where natural forest openings become scattered meadows. The timberline of this forest averages 5000 ft to 5500 ft, and is characterized by subalpine fir and mountain hemlock. The lower and middle slopes are generally clad with a dense understory that includes red alder, vine maple, black cottonwood, devil's club, and salmonberry. This vegetation often covers avalanche scars that extend up valley walls. As has often been noted, "A climate more favorable to the growth of underbrush or to the starting of young trees would be hard to find."[3]

The subalpine forest soils often lie on glacial trough walls which retain much of the steepness they acquired during periods of massive valley glaciation; the result is some dramatic forest localities. Forests and brush provide nature's protective vegetal cover—erosion and siltation results from removal of cover and soil loosening by logging and road building. Fortunately the 702 sq. mi. Glacier Peak Wilderness will preserve a portion of this forest from such destruction.

Vegetation on the east slopes extends high and only the snow/ice-covered areas and craggy peaks are barren.[4] Engelmann spruce, Alaska cedar, and whitebark pine are commonly found at higher levels. Many factors limit tree growth, usually at elevations from 5500 to 7000 ft.

Approaching timberline the ground flora decreases in density with mainly heather cover between groves of alpine trees. Tarns, the glorious results of vanished glaciers—as John Muir pointed out—often occupy ice-gouged basins on cirque floors. Disintegration of rocks through physical and chemical change provides the source and foundation of soils; living organisms and the product of their decay help build alpine soils. These have shallow profiles with a high percentage of gravel and undecomposed organic material. This is especially noticeable in the upper courses of some valleys, where ground moraines have only stubbornly yielded to the growth of new vegetation. Alpine travelers sometimes will find snow surfaces alive with myriad insects; red snow, caused by the presence of *protococcus nivalis,* is of frequent occurrence. Mosquitoes are usually at their worst in the few weeks immediately after snow melt.

Herbaceous plant communities provide summer wildflower pageants in a zone from roughly 4500 ft to 7000 ft. There is often a rich profusion of flowers on ridges and the older portions of glacier moraines. Common varieties include the paintbrush, anemone, penstemon, pussytoes, cow parsnip, lupine, monkey-flower, saxifrage, fleabane, moss campion, phacelia, phlox, and cinquefoil. The process of mineral soil formation is extremely slow at the higher altitudes. Shallow soils combined with cold temperatures above 6500 ft result in conditions that are inhospitable to plant life other than mosses, heather, and lichen. This lack of vegetation coupled with the rigorous climate and precipitous glacierized terrain discourages most large mammals from the alpine habitat. Consequently the only large mammals that inhabit this zone are a few mountain goat and bear. Smaller animals such as marmots, pikas, mice, as well as hawks and eagles find adequate protection and food to survive the austere terrain. The upper Skagit and lower Sauk River valleys harbor 35-80 bald eagles during the winter season.

The diverse regional ecosystems provide an important sanctuary for animals, including the blacktail deer, mule deer, black bear, weasel, otter, mink, beaver, marten, fox, coyote, cougar, and mountain goat. Conspicuous mammals include the marmots, who love to bask in the sun on meadow boulders; porcupines and packrats enjoy such delicacies as the food and boot leather of hikers. Black bears are fond of the root of yellow arum, the western skunk cabbage, found in moist valley bottoms (few hikers will care to compete with them for this roughage). But the more open slopes are commonly clothed with the luxuriant growth of huckleberry bushes; during fruiting season these may be a favorite haunt of both hikers and bears.

The Skagit River, named for an Indian tribe of the region, has captured the dominant drainage W of the Cascades. It is similar to rivers of the British Columbia Coast Mountains which rise in the interior plateau region and follow broad valleys, and upon piercing the main range flow in precipitous canyons. The united waters of the Skagit's western tributaries combine with Ruby Creek, Granite Creek, Thunder Creek, Cascade River, Suiattle River, and Sauk River to flow into Puget Sound. The Seattle City Light Power Project embraces Gorge Dam near Newhalem, Diablo Dam 9 mi. E of Newhalem, and Ross Dam at the end of Skagit Arm of Diablo Lake. Maximum water level of the reservoir at Gorge Dam is 878 ft, of Diablo Lake 1206 ft, and of Ross Lake 1602.5 ft. Diablo Lake and Ross Lake (24 mi. long and 2 mi. maximum width) are the two great reservoirs of the Skagit, which once flowed freely through a deep S-trending valley and then elbowed into a steep-gradient narrow rock canyon toward its lower course. The peculiar form of Diablo Lake is due to the dilation of the Skagit River and Thunder Creek. The mouth of the latter at Thunder Arm is about 48°41′ N latitude, this stream being the next great branch of the Skagit above the Cascade River, which enters opposite Marblemount. The S fork of the latter heads in South Cascade Glacier, in close relationship with the Agnes Creek drainages. From here the stream runs N with little trend, in a deeply incised valley to the N fork; in this course it is reinforced by numerous tributaries from both sides, the principal one being the middle fork.

The principal axial stream E of the Cascade divide in this section is the Stehekin, whose northern tributaries are Bridge and Park Creeks. The Stehekin River system is the principal hydrologic feeder to 55-mi. Lake Chelan. The upper valleys of these various streams display the natural phenomena associated with valley glaciation. Some rivers have cut deep canyons below the glacial carvings (examples are the canyons of the Skagit River, Bridge Creek, and Agnes Creek). Typical of the North Cascades, there is a difference in elevation between lateral and main valleys due to the deeper corrasion by larger ice streams. A striking feature of such valleys as the Stehekin, West Fork of Agnes, and North Fork Cascade is the beauty and frequency of the waterfalls in lateral gorges. Professor I.C. Russell noted in 1898 that the Cascade River's N fork, after a sluggish course, forms rapids and falls to a larger lower valley. Similar examples of cut-off valleys and precipitous descents were noted along the Stehekin River by Henry H. Gannett, who had come to regard the hanging side valleys as characteristic accessory features of deeply glaciated canyons (most tributary glaciers were generally not large enough to erode to valley depth; therefore tributaries are now left hanging, and water reaches bottoms by falls and cascades).

GLACIAL HISTORY

Glacial activity has had a continuous series of effects through the Pleistocene Epoch and in post-Ice Age time. During each major glacial episode ice overrode much of the region and undoubtably overflowed most present topographic divides to feed the deep outlet valleys. Steep slopes accelerated the headward and downward cutting, so that by the time Wisconsin stage ice began to disappear, the glaciers had cut themselves into deep valleys and away from accumulation sources. Thick ice and rapid runoff was highly effective in carving major valleys to base level, a process begun by the mature dissection of stream erosion.[5]

During the Pleistocene glacial ages the northern part of the region was invaded by the Cordilleran Ice Sheet, which covered most of the Skagit and Methow drainages.[6] The last major episode obliterated most evidence of earlier episodes. Though deeply scalloped by glacial cirques, much of the Cascade crest still bears remnants of its pre-glacial topography (showing the range was never completely domed over by ice). After the withdrawal of the regional icecap, large valley glaciers aligned and straightened trenches by the truncation of projecting spurs and cut off hanging valleys. The absence of Skagit and Chelan Valley moraines is evidence that the ice sheet postdated the most significant alpine phase. Where alpine glaciers have largely disappeared, small lakes often occupy cirque depressions, and some lakes are held behind massive morainal embankment.

The worldwide return to colder climatological conditions (Neoglaciation), after nearly complete retreat of glaciers in middle-latitude areas of Earth is also reflected here in the North Cascades. Little Ice Age fluctuations, which began about five centuries ago, began a worldwide expansion of glaciers. Maximum post-Pleistocene glacial advance generally has been less than 1 mi. downvalley from the present terminus. These temperate glaciers reached culminations in the early to mid-18th century and again in the late 19th to mid-20th centuries. After the Little Ice Age terminated in the mid-19th century there has been a general diminution of ice cover, and the majority of low-altitude glaciers have only existed precariously. Recently deglaciated slabs and end moraines devoid of vegetation reflect this recessional trend. Modern glaciers in this region are bordered by extensive belts of moraine and trimline evidence of fluctuation (most of today's moraines are below the level of regional timberline).[8] Most larger glaciers are associated with relatively unweathered moraine that lies several hundred ft to as much as ½ mi. down-valley from present ice margins.

North Cascade glaciers experienced a period of glacier rejuvenation in the decade beginning in 1945, but most glaciers have been stationary since then. A few glaciers afford spectacular contrasts in activity. The terminal regime of glaciers reveals that in adjoining areas the regime may be out of phase.[9] Those glaciers located so that most surface is lower than the summer snowline are wasting most rapidly.[10]

The results of repeated oscillations of glaciers in mountain cirques and over floors of deep outlet valleys is apparent; these have included the effective abrasion, transport, and removal of material. Erosion here is a consequence of glacioclimatological oscillations affecting the growth and retreat of glaciers. Turbid rivers and glacier moraines here are examples of the great eroding power of glaciers; vast quantities of fine rock flour are carried out from beneath glaciers by subglacial drainage streams. Cirque basins often have steplike levels, the result of plucking of smaller glaciers after the Pleistocene; two levels in basins are not uncommon. Headwalls of glacial cirques have been vigorously undercut in Neoglacial time.

Streams such as Downey Creek and Kindy Creek typically lie in straight deep glacial troughs which head in large two-storied cirques with floors from 2500 ft to 4000 ft. Often several higher cirques with floors from 4500 ft to 6000 ft are present above the upper ends of the trough.

In the sequence of cirque erosion, closely spaced cirques have intersected so that the walls at the top often form knifed edges. This convergence of glacial cirque headwalls has been destroying the sharp summits of the high topographic accordance and many peaks are quarried to craggy remnants. Blocks are broken mostly in jointed rock; massive rock seldom allows breaking and dislodging by ice. Minor fractures or joints commonly form both parallel and perpendicular to the bedding; freeze-thaw action along joint planes has caused splitting of blocks. The natural processes of erosion and frost wedging have over-steepened slopes and developed deep cirques with shattered backwalls. As fragments fall off cliffs and become entrained in ice transport, their plucking action becomes a critical tool of erosion along the ice/bedrock interface.[11]

GLACIERS

The Cascade crest in this section is the most heavily glacierized along the axis of the range. The glaciers in this section are a substantial proportion of 317 glaciers within the boundaries of North Cascades National Park, which alone contains about one-third of the glaciers in the 48 contiguous United States (the State of Washington has about 800 glaciers covering 160 sq. mi.). Heavy snow accumulation W of the crest[12] has resulted in a few glaciers situated below the regional timberline (including the South Cascade and McAllister Glaciers). In the Eldorado-Klawatti area are small icefields consisting of contiguous glaciers of varying forms, with several distributary outlets. The South Cascade Glacier is a good example of a small alpine valley glacier: it is about 2¼ mi. in length from its head at 6800 ft, and ranges from 1000 to 3500 ft in width. The terminus is an ice front that calves into a small lake at 5300 ft—this being the source of the South Cascade River.[13] The glacier is the lowest of the nearby large glaciers and its advance about 4900 years ago was the earliest recognized Neoglacial advance in the region. An early advance of the glacier produced a massive moraine half a mi. beyond its present terminus position (Meier, 1964). The South Cascade, Dana, and Le Conte Glaciers reached Neoglacial maxima in the 16th century and subsequently built moraines in the 19th and 20th centuries.[14]

The Chickamin Glacier, which contains nearly 5 sq. mi. of ice, is a composite slope and valley glacier; it can be described as an upper glacier which descends from nearly 8800 ft to about 6600 ft, where a thick and very crevassed apron of ice vigorously feeds a valley tongue, and a lower portion that continues to 5000 ft; the apron showed growth from 1948 to 1958. Toward the snout, longitudinal compression gives rise to a typical splaying crevasse pattern. Forest trimline and the position of lateral and end moraines show evidence of much dwindling from the advanced Neoglacial position in the 13th century; several moraines were built between the 16th and early 20th century.[15]

The lower portion of the McAllister Glacier (5.4 km^2), confined in a narrow valley, acts as the principal distributory for the small icefields in the northern portion of the Eldorado Peak area; the glacier is oriented in a northerly and northwesterly direction, then bends nearly W to its terminus.[16] The contiguous

Inspiration Glacier (5.1 km^2) occupies the large accumulation basin E of Eldorado Peak and drains to the West Fork of Thunder Creek.

Boston Glacier (7 km^2) is the most spectacular in this section and is the largest single glacier in the North Cascades. It displays a crevasse orientation which tends to be perpendicular to the principal extension axis.[17] It is a hanging glacier which occupies a broad cirque between Forbidden Peak and Mt. Buckner. The glacier has a high degree of activity, judging from its relative size and high rates of accumulation and ablation. Both the Boston and Inspiration Glacier showed slight advances in the 1960s.

GEOLOGY

The Skagit Metamorphic Suite, the backbone of the North Cascades, is E of the Straight Creek Fault. The migmatitic Skagit gneiss is the most prominent member of the crystalline rocks in this axial zone. The oldest granitic rocks are Skagit gneisses which underlie a large region. They originated during the time of Mesozoic folding.[18] Pre-Tertiary igneous granitic bodies that intruded the rocks of the Skagit suite and which were later regionally metamorphosed, are widespread E of the fault. Beginning about 90 million years ago the major structural units formed during intense folding, faulting, metamorphism, and igneous activity.

The deeply eroded North Cascades are predominantly plutonic rocks of pre-Tertiary and Tertiary age. Except for local remnants the Tertiary volcanic rocks in this region have been removed by erosion and the pre-Tertiary metamorphic basement is widely exposed.[19] The plutonic intrusive belt of the Cascade Range in Washington State is composed of batholiths and stocks which range in age from pre-Jurassic to early Pliocene; these granitic magmas have invaded the crystalline basement and overlying Tertiary sediments and volcanics.[20]

The Cloudy Pass batholith (quartz diorite) was emplaced in early Miocene time.[21] This intrusive mass occupies an area of about 100 sq. mi.—about one-third of the batholith's exposure is the area of Dome-Spire-Gunsight Peaks and the remainder lies S as far as Glacier Peak and the head of Railroad Creek.[22] This batholith intruded NW-striking pre-Tertiary metamorphic and granitoid rocks and exists mostly beneath a thin roof of the schist and gneiss host rocks;[23] as in most contacts of intrusive masses, this one is sharp.

The Cretaceous Snowking batholith (roughly the same age as Mt. Stuart batholith) covers a large area.[24]

There is a long finger of igneous intrusive rocks pointing NW, to the W of Lake Chelan; this belt includes Pinnacle Mountain and extends through Tupshin Peak. There are three important Meta-Igneous rock belts in this section: the Eldorado Orthogneiss, Marblemount quartz diorite, and Gabriel Peak Orthogneiss.[25] The Eldorado-Snowfield Peak area consists of a great expanse of highly deformed metamorphic rock. The Cascade Pass Tertiary quartz diorite pluton follows a NE-trending fracture system, as determined by Misch (1966). The Hidden Lake stock, a small quartz diorite pluton, is one of several small bodies that became detached from the Chilliwack granodiorite mass and now appear as isolated intrusive stocks. The Cretaceous Black Peak batholith is of earlier origin than the Golden Horn granodiorite, which is to the E (the contact is not preserved with the younger intrusive). The Black Peak granodiorite is at the eastern border of the Skagit gneiss, and on the W these rocks have apparently formed from the gneiss (the granodiorite extends from E of Mt. Goode and Logan to near Rainy Pass; Misch, 1952, pp. 16-17).

HISTORY

Various Indian tribes on both flanks of the Cascades left a rich heritage of nomenclature, but much of their culture and history has vanished. Indians that probably predate all knowledge were acquainted with the land in the North Cascades, and had some trail routes. Certainly the mountains, with their forests, game, fish, and berries, attracted them on a seasonal basis.[26] They personified the natural forces and were in awe of the great peaks: Sahale Tyee was chief of their upper world. Such mountain routes as Cloudy, Suiattle, Cascade, Rainy, and Twisp Pass may have been used for centuries. It is known horses were used by Indians near the mountains in the 18th century.[27] Naturalist George Gibbs, who canoed the Skagit to its canyon exit in 1858, learned of various routes, including the S fork (Sakumihu) of the Skagit, up which was the Indian trail to Lake Chelan and the Columbia River.[28] His 1860 map shows a trail route from the Twisp River via its S fork vaguely toward Cascade Pass.[29] Because of impending conflict with settlers, in summer 1880 Indians were said to have constructed a wide trail across the mountains to obtain aid from a Columbia River tribe.[30] Gibbs had learned that the present Cascade River was "Hukullum," and he discussed various native names, including Scatchet and S' cho-kehn, which ultimately became Skagit and Stehekin. Since native languages do not have established written forms, transcriptions of names to our Roman alphabet is quite varied.

Forces of relentless search for fur treasure which precipitated exploration came from both America and Canada. Leading the search was the North West Company, later merged into the Hudson's Bay Company. This daring and energetic vanguard crossed the continent and reached British Columbia before 1800, then later began to explore waterways and mountain valleys of the eastern flank of the North Cascades during the period of joint occupation and when the dispute over the Oregon country was unsettled. But the expedition to find the River of the West, which was Thomas Jefferson's vision when he sent Lewis and Clark across the land, and the Bonneville and Frémont expeditions, added only to the knowledge of geography E and S of the Cascade Range. Various detailed reports, which enthused traders, stirred inquiry into the mountainous frontier beyond the Columbia.

Defeated in their 19th century search for cross-North Cascade military routes, the Army satisfied themselves with the occupation of posts E and W of the range. They had learned but little of the real secrets, and as the Army era passed, the mountains still remained much of a mystery.

Geographical conceptions of the Cascades are well portrayed by the rendering on the Surveyor General Map of Washington Territory, 1860, which showed an imaginative depiction of spur ranges S of the Skagit River, with little indication of a true knowledge of various important drainages. Large words "Unexplored" were placed between the Skagit River and the artistic chain bearing NE from Lake Chelan.[31] The report of Lt. Thomas Symons, made after he canoed on Lake Chelan, indicates the state of knowledge in 1879: "It is supplied from mountain-springs and from the melting snows of the mass of snow-capped mountains lying about Mount Baker."[32]

The earliest explorer who perhaps crossed the North Cascades was Alexander Ross, a member of John Jacob Astor's Pacific Fur Company, in the summer of 1814. His narrative is a grim testimony to the demoralization which the mountain wilderness can work on the lonely spirit.[33] The July-August 1877 expedition organized by Otto Klement to investigate a gold discovery in the Methow Valley may have been the first non-native crossing of Cascade Pass. Klement, buoyed by strong companionship, was stirred to write "A more enchanting scene our eyes had never before gazed upon. Mountains piled upon mountains, stretching away in every direction." Strangely the prospectors did not note the ore deposits near the pass.[34] In August 1882 the Army expedition of Lt. Henry H. Pierce made the arduous trek from E of the Okanogan River to the Skagit; he followed an Indian route and crossed Cascade Pass on his 22nd day of travel. In the tradition of honoring contemporaries and party members, such names as Pierce River, Agnes Creek, Backus Fork, and Symon's Fork appeared on his map. Pierce noted floating speciments of quartz, rich in gold, W of Cascade Pass, "surely the Eldorado of the old man's dreams."[35]

The obscure early history of the North Cascades is given perspective by an observation made over 50 years ago: "Surveyors of the U.S. Geological Survey go almost everywhere, without making much ado about it." And prospectors for obvious reasons don't leave many records of their work.[36] Eventually the second rush to the Ruby Mines, when adventurous spirits revived the old dream of gold in the North Cascades, provided the stimulus for methodical investigation. Little prospecting was done near Cascade Pass until trails were built in the early 1890s, opening a route for horses. The romance of the more remote areas is derived from mishaps and achievements of miners who explored alpine slopes, where one can still find relics of an unrecorded history.[37] How much of this rugged landscape was covered by prospectors will never be fully known, but L.K. Hodges gives an insight: "The granite formation carrying this galena belt has been traced northeast across Doubtful and Horse Shoe basin . . . between the north forks of Thunder and Bridge Creeks . . . the southwest through the whole watershed of the Cascade's several forks to Mineral Park."[38]

The principal discovery of the Cascade River district was made by George L. Rouse, John C. Rouse, and Gilbert Landre in September 1889, while tracing ledges exposed by the glaciers of Horseshoe Basin and along the rim of Doubtful Basin.[39] They discovered the Boston Ledge cleaving the summit; the Rouses located the Boston claim and Landre the Chicago where a rich galena body was exposed in a cliff. At the time the district was almost inaccessible from the W, the natural route; the wagon road up the Skagit Valley was only completed to Birdsview, 58 mi. from the summit.[40] But in 1890 the Boston Mine had hundreds of tons of silver-lead ore piled up, awaiting transport. It is evident early claims were made high not only in Boston Basin, but toward Eldorado Peak, on Johannesburg Mountain, and far into the Middle Fork of Cascade River.

In the Stehekin district discoveries began at Doubtful Lake, then extended to Horseshoe Basin. In September 1885 the Rouse boys located the Quien Sabe on a galena ledge,[41] and in 1889 the Doubtful Lake veins were traced through to Horseshoe Basin[42] A report from 1892 stated that both water power and timber were plentiful. Pershall became a miner's stop on the State Trail along upper Stehekin River, just W of Basin Creek.[43]

John Russner and two others crossed the glacier in Boston Basin, climbed through the "Sawtooths," and in descending the northerly slope crossed the glacier (i.e. Boston) that forms the head of Thunder Creek. "The trip was a dangerous one, but the men were rewarded by finding a 'good prospect.' "[44] A ledge of green ore near 7500 ft turned out to be rich in silver, stirring a rush to the area in 1892. Skagit Milling and Mining Co. was formed; after obtaining control of claims the company soon shipped several tons to the smelter. Silver returns were good, but transportation costs were punishing.[45] In 1908 an adequate horse trail led from Marblemount, 40 mi. from the planned small city. At Cedar Bar a bridge crossed the Skagit, but it accidentally burned when a miner tried to rid the area of hornets. The Skagit Trail went along Box Canyon (later named Diablo Canyon) and then descended into "Punch Bowl" where Thunder Creek joined the main river. Some gear was packed in from Lake Chelan; M.E. Field took a mill over Park Creek Pass, with one piece weighing 450 lbs. He had 27 horses out in November 1908—nine were killed falling off the wintry trail on the return trip. By 1913 the Thunder Creek mining companies had largely folded.

Contemporaries of early prospectors were railroad explorers. After the surveys made in summer 1867 James Tilton believed there was no practical pass from the Skagit to Lake Chelan or the Okanogan S of 49° latitude.[46] In June 1870 the party of D.C. Linsley, a locating engineer for the Northern Pacific Railroad, set out from the end of canoe travel on the Suiattle by an old Indian hunting trail.[47] Railroad surveyor Albert B. Rogers followed "Pierce River" (the Stehekin) in July 1887 to find a route via Agnes Creek to a branch of the Skagit. But he learned from land surveyors that the NW fork (Bridge Creek) is the one Indians travel when going to the Skagit.[48] John F. Stevens, making examinations for the Great Northern in spring and early summer 1890, was said to have examined every creek from the mountains to Lake Chelan, and found the route over Cascade Pass of no value.[49] In 1891 Northern Pacific men ran surveys in several valleys; it was their hope to build a railroad up Stehekin Valley.[50]

The detailed and laborious mapping by the U.S. Geological Survey, which in 1897 was assigned the surveying and mapping of forests, had a very marked effect on the regional knowledge. Prior to their arrival there had only been the few well documented Army expeditions (but whose reports had been largely retained in government publications, where they remained virtually unknown) and the somewhat secretive and competitive surveying of railroad explorers. The acquired knowledge of the latter, and that of the prospectors, seldom reached the public. Lack of communication, withholding of knowledge, and departmentalization of effort contributed to the shrouding of history, conflicting feature nomenclature, and gaps in the documentation of topographic knowledge.

The Glacier Peak quadrangle, printed in 1899, became the first detailed and accurate map of the complex drainages of the southern Skagit River tributaries.[51] Much of the field work was done in the summer of 1897, under W.T. Griswold, who mapped from Lake Chelan to Cascade Pass.[52]

The U.S. Forest Service later engaged in their own surveying and mapping; little is documented regarding their exploration efforts, but it is known that such district rangers as Tommy Thompson (1913-1924) knew such Skagit branch valleys as the S and middle forks of the Cascade River quite well. This agency built many trails, mostly in the 1920-1930 decades for fire control. Much of the original Cascade Crest Trail was laid out by such men as Nels Bruseth and Hugh Courtney, who hiked into and explored approaches to the rugged high peaks of this region. Lage Wernstedt was the person responsible for detailed mapping of much of the Mt. Baker National Forest. In the mid-1920s he set up a complex triangulation network from numerous mountain summits, some of which were previously unclimbed; he also did the first aerial photography for mapping these regions.[53] New trails shown on the maps of the 1930s identify the era of trail building into the high country, a practice which hopefully has passed its apogee. The Suiattle River Road, built in this era, was the spearhead that fostered trail building into the alpine lands. Many logging branches and other valley trunk roads have vastly altered the surficial appearance of this region from the days of the early prospector.

Seattle City Light, under James D. Ross, received Department of Agriculture permission in December 1917 to construct the Skagit damming project, and in the next year established its Rockport base, at that time only for horses. The original Gorge Creek Dam was completed in 1919 and the railroad to Newhalem finished in 1921. Water usage for hydroelectric power generation began with the establishment of the Gorge power plant on the Skagit River in 1924. Diablo became a small company townsite, and the 389-ft Diablo Dam was completed in 1930 to create a 5-mi. lake. The next project, Ross Dam, was completed in 1949 and built to a height of 540 ft above bedrock. Logging and consequent flooding of the Upper Skagit formed a vast lake which greatly changed the natural environment.

Federal lands in this region originally became part of the public domain in 1846 when the United States established title to the Oregon Territory. Lands remained in that status until the Pacific Forest Reserve was carved out of the lower portions of the North Cascades in 1893 and the Washington Forest Reserve was created February 22, 1897; these reserves came under new administration in 1905 when the old Bureau of Forestry was designated the Forest Service. The Glacier Peak Limited Area was classified as Wilderness in 1960 by the Secretary of Agriculture. Boundaries of the wilderness were later modified to include portions of the White Chuck and Suiattle Valley corridors. There is still considerable adjacent land open to public and private abuse which would best serve the needs of today and the future as classified wilderness.

The North Cascades National Park idea was first proposed by the Mazamas in 1906, and in 1916 the first director of the National Park Service, Stephen Mather, planned an investigation of the regional potential. In 1917 writer Mary Roberts Rinehart endorsed the park theme in a serialized account of a horseback trip made from Lake Chelan. Continuing pressure by the public and outdoor groups prompted the 90th Congress to pass the 1968 North Cascades Act and establish a park from legislative proposals worked out jointly by the Departments of Agriculture and Interior. A two-unit North Cascades National Park (505,000 acres), and the Ross Lake and Lake Chelan National Recreation Areas (170,000 acres) were created. The Glacier Peak Wilderness was slightly enlarged (about 10,000 acres) and the Pasayten Wilderness (500,000 acres) was established by the same act.

From the mountaineering standpoint the North Cascades in this region only recently experienced a revitalization of explorative activity. Except for the early surveyors, who climbed generally only in line with their fieldwork and seldom used mountaineering techniques, climbing developed fairly conventionally. The earliest mountaineering expedition was the Mazama outing of July 1899, from Lake Chelan via Cascade Pass to the Skagit River.[54] While their personnel were most impressed with the complex confusion of rocky wilderness, and great broken glaciers, they and their contemporaries accepted only limited challenges. Surveyors between 1897 and 1926 pioneered the more significant ascents, such as Sahale, Buckner, and Black. Mainly because the identity and labor of such men as Lage Wernstedt were obscure, some important ascents were not chronicled. It was not until 36 years after the Mazama outing that an important climb in the wilderness S of Cascade Pass was successfully made by an independent party, this on Sentinel Peak, an arduous project in a remote area.

Among the first climbers to dramatize the glories of mountaineering possibilities and explore many of the sharp heartland peaks was Hermann Ulrichs, a veteran of the Sierra Nevada, the Alps, and mountains of Canada. His initial venture into the North Cascades was by Thunder Creek in 1932, and here he discovered "the unheralded conglomeration of peaks, glaciers, and deep valleys—probably the most rugged and alpine in the 48 states . . . The Mountaineers ignored the area—having only once gone up the Stehekin and climbed Boston (sic Sahale)."[55]

By 1931 climbers had made successful ventures to the Snowfield Peak group and in the mid-1930s Ulrichs and his partners climbed Corteo, Booker, and nearly scaled Goode and Cutthroat. On one expedition Ulrichs would have accomplished more, but a porcupine ate the leather of partner Dan O'Brien's boots in Park Creek.[56] In 1936 the puzzling Mt. Goode, nemesis of climbers from both Oregon and Washington, was conquered, and the following summer Bonanza Peak, an equally challenging massif, was scaled by a Portland group.[57]

The rugged and glacierized crest from Sulphur Creek to Cascade Pass was traversed in 1938 for the first time by an intrepid foursome from a little-known Seattle climbing club by a basic route now popularized as the Ptarmigan Traverse; Calder Bressler, Ralph Clough, Bill Cox, and Tom Myers have now received the recognition they did not achieve in mountaineering circles of the time. The highlight of their accomplishment was the ascent of Sahale, Boston, and Buckner within one day. Not until 1953 was the alpine crest between Dome Peak and Cascade Pass again traversed in its entirety.

Technical skill and sometimes pure luck has tended to belittle the seriousness of some of the alpine routes in this region and their potential hazards. In past decades the Cascade Pass area has seen an increasing number and variety of accidents, with fatalities occurring on Johannesburg, Sharkfin, Boston, and Forbidden Peak.

On big climbs such as Bonanza, Goode, Forbidden, Eldorado, and Johannesburg it is a questionable tactic to seek out the most difficult rock sections on a specific route. Perhaps the increasing number of successful ascents has contributed to a degree of laxness.

GLACIER PEAK WILDERNESS AREA

For information and use regulations see Trail and Alpine Hiking Approaches, Section I.

NORTH CASCADES NATIONAL PARK

The two-unit National Park, and two National Recreation Areas, were established by an act of the 90th Congress in 1968. Park headquarters are at 311 State St., Sedro Wooley, Wa. (98284).

Ross Lake National Recreation Area includes Gorge, Diablo, and Ross Reservoirs. Campgrounds, lodges, stores, marina, and interpretive facilities are to be developed on Diablo and Ross Lakes. Special boat service is available on Ross Lake to public use areas not accessible by road. Lake Chelan National Recreation Area has lodges, store, marina, visitor center, cross country ski outfitter, and pack horse concession at Stehekin. Shuttle bus transport is available on the Stehekin River Road.

Fishing is allowed in the Park and Recreation Areas. Hunting is allowed in the Recreation Areas, but not in the Park.

Ranger Stations are at Marblemount (1 mi. NW of townsite), Chelan, and Stehekin. Backcountry permits must be obtained for any off-road travel. These are available at ranger stations, (in summer also at Hozomeen and Colonial Creek). Arrangements can be made by phone to have after-hour permits placed in envelopes in a special box near station entrances. Permits may also be obtained from U.S. Forest Service Stations at Twisp, Early Winters, Darrington, and Glacier by visitors entering the Park through Forest Service-administered lands.

Restrictions include maximum group size of 12, no open fires above 4500 ft, no pets on trails or cross-country (leashed dogs permitted in the Recreation Areas and on Crest Trail), no firearms in the Park, no camping in subalpine meadows or passes (no camping at Cascade, Park Creek, and Easy Pass). Wood fires are prohibited anywhere in alpine and subalpine areas, and may be built only at designated campgrounds with steel grates. Trail hikers must camp only in camp areas which are marked with trailside posts. Cross-country camps must be more than ½ mi. from a maintained trail and more than 1 mi. from designated camps.

Administrative units may be further developed on a coordinated basis; considerable National Park and Recreation Area is coterminous with that of the National Forest. The Early Winters and Concrete contact facilities are operated jointly by the Forest Service and National Park Service.

RANGER STATIONS

Baker River R.S. (F.S.)
Concrete, WA 98234

Concrete Information Center (N.P.S.)
Concrete, WA 98234

Darrington R.S. (F.S.)
Darrington, WA 98241

Marblemount R.S. (N.P.S.)
Marblemount, WA 98267

Chelan R.S. (F.S. and N.P.S.)
Chelan, WA 98816

Stehekin R.S. (N.P.S.)
Stehekin, WA 98852

Twisp R.S. (F.S.)
Twisp, WA 98856

Winthrop R.S. (F.S.)
Winthrop, WA 98862

Early Winters Information Center
c/o Winthrop R.S.

In summer season ranger stations are open on weekends. Maps may be for sale, depending on availability.

MAPS

Topographic maps covering 7½ minutes of latitude and longitude are published at the scale of 1:24,000. Quadrangles covering 15 minutes of latitude and longitude are published at the scale of 1:62,500.

Maps can be ordered from:
Distribution Section, U.S. Geological Survey
Federal Center, Bldg. 41
Denver, CO 80225

Requests for advance prints in 7½-minute units which cover published 15-minute units should be sent to: Pacific Region Engineer, U.S. Geological Survey
345 Middlefield Road
Menlo Park, CA 94025

It should be noted that more recent roads and trails may not be shown on topographic maps because revisions can only be made at intervals. Trail relocations and deletions may likewise not be shown. When it is felt there are errors in feature names or in the lettering placement, these will be pointed out in the text and in special area maps.

The following topographic maps apply to the area covered in this section:

North Cascades (1972)	1:250,000
North Cascades National Park (1974)	1:100,000
Holden (1949)	1:62,500
Glacier Peak (1950)	1:62,500
Lucerne (1949)	1:62,500
Marblemount (1953)	1:62,500
Dome Peak (1963)	1:24,000
Agnes Mountain (1963)	1:24,000
Cascade Pass (1963)	1:24,000
Goode Mountain (1963)	1:24,000
Sonny Boy Lakes (1963)	1:24,000
Downey Mountain (1963)	1:24,000
Stehekin (1969)	1:24,000
Mt. Lyall (1963)	1:24,000
McGregor Mountain (1963)	1:24,000
Mt. Arriva (1963)	1:24,000
Mt. Logan (1963)	1:24,000
Forbidden Peak (1963)	1:24,000
Crater Mountain (1963)	1:24,000
Ross Dam (1963)	1:24,000
Diablo Dam (1963)	1:24,000
Eldorado Peak (1963)	1:24,000
Huckleberry Mountain (1966)	1:24,000
Snowking Mountain (1966)	1:24,000
Prairie Mountain (1966)	1:24,000
Rockport (1966)	1:24,000
Illabot Peaks (1966)	1:24,000
McAlester Mountain (1969)	1:24,000

National Forest recreation folder maps are available from Forest Headquarters or district ranger stations. The new Mt. Baker-Snoqualmie National Forest map shows use restrictions; it is printed at ½ in. to the mi. scale (Mt. Baker-Snoqualmie National Forest, 1601 Second Ave. Bldg.; Seattle, WA 98101). Also useful is a Glacier Peak Wilderness topographic map (Forest Service).

Planimetric maps based on aerial photography, with contours superimposed and up-to-date culture, are in 15-minute units, available through: Pacific Northwest Region, U.S. Forest Service; P.O. Box 3623; Portland, OR 97208. Maps relevant to this section are: Glacier Peak (no. 41), Stehekin (no. 40), Stehekin (no. 39), Diablo Lake (no. 20).

SELECTED REFERENCES

Anderson, Ada Woodruff. "Lake Chelan and the American Alps." *Pacific Monthly* 11, no. 5 (May 1904): 300-308.

Beckey, Fred. *Challenge of the North Cascades.* Seattle: The Mountaineers, 1969.

Crandell, Dwight R. "The Glacial History of Western Washington and Oregon." *The Quaternary of the United States,* Review vol. for VII Congress, 1965.

Crowder, D.F. and Tabor, R.W. *Routes and Rocks: Hiker's Guide to the North Cascades from Glacier Peak to Lake Chelan.* Seattle: The Mountaineers, 1965.

Gannett, Henry. "Lake Chelan." *National Geographic* 9, no. 9 (1898): 417-428.

Graves, C. Edward. "The Glacier Peak Wilderness." *National Parks Magazine* (June 1956), pp. 125-170.

Hodges, L.K. *Mining in the Pacific Northwest.* Seattle: Shorey Bookstore, 1897.

Kenney, Nathaniel T. "The Spectacular North Cascades." *National Geographic* 133 (May 1968): 642-667.

Manning, Harvey H. *North Cascades National Park.* Seattle: Superior, 1969.

Manning, Harvey H. *Wild Cascades: Forgotten Parkland.* San Francisco: Sierra Club, 1965.

Miller, Tom. *The North Cascades.* Seattle: The Mountaineers, 1964.

Misch, Peter. "Geology of the Northern Cascades, Washington." *The Mountaineer* 55: 4-22, 1952.

Mitchell, Bruce. "By River, Trail, and Rail." Wenatchee Daily World Supplement, 1968.

Park, Edwards. "Washington Wilderness, The North Cascades." *National Geographic* 119 (March 1961): 335-367.

Pitzer, Paul C. *History of the Upper Skagit Valley 1880-1924.* Seattle: University of Washington M.S. Thesis, 1966.

Post, Austin, et al. "Inventory of Glaciers in the North Cascades, Washington." *U.S. Geological Survey Professional Paper 705-A,* Washington, 1971.

Rinehart, Mary Roberts. "A Pack Train in the Cascades." *Cosmopolitan* 63, no. 3 (1917): 44-49, 122-124; no. 4 (1917): 44-49, 116-120; no. 5 (1917): 32-37, 154-159, 163.

Rinehart, Mary Roberts. *Tenting To-night: A Chronicle of Sport and Adventure in Glacier National Park and the Cascade Mountains.* Boston: Houghton, Mifflin, 1918, pp. 100-188.

Roth, Lottie R. *History of Whatcom County,* vol. 1 Chicago, 1926.

Steel, W.G. "Lake Chelan and the Valley of the Stehekin." *Oregon Native Son,* January, 1900.

Warth, John F. "The Glacier Peak Wilderness." *National Parks Magazine* 30, no. 127 (1956): 173-176. Also pp. 193-194.

Ulrichs, Hermann F. "The Cascade Range in Northern Washington." *Sierra Club Bulletin* 22, no. 1 (1937): 69-79. Also *American Alpine Journal,* 1936, pp. 462-474.

Additional articles of interest are found in the following periodicals:

Living Wilderness 13, no. 26 (Autumn 1948): 9-15
16, no. 39 (Winter 1951-1952): 5-8
22, no. 60 (Spring 1957): 9-16
23, no. 66 (Autumn 1958): 18-24
24, no. 70 (Autumn 1959): 1-24
25, no. 74 (Autumn 1960): 36-40
29, no. 91 (Winter 1965): 32-39
30
39
70 (Autumn 1970)
74

Mazama 2, no. 4 (1905): 185-189
30, no. 13 (1948)
39, no. 13 (1957)
40, no. 13 (1958)
50, no. 13 (1968)

Mountaineer, 1928, pp. 11-13
1934, pp. 11-16
1935, pp. 10-12
1936, pp. 11-13
1946, pp. 17-19
1953, pp. 39-41
1958, pp. 7-87
1964, pp. 27-36, 66-72, 99-107
1967, pp. 8-28
1968, pp. 159-162
1969, pp. 44-48

National Parks Magazine 31 (July-Sept. 1957)
33 (Oct. 1959): 8-11, 145-148

Sierra Club Bulletin 41, no. 10 (Dec. 1956): 24-31
42, no. 6 (June 1957): 13-16
52, no. 9 (Oct. 1967): 40-45

Sunset, June 1965, pp. 84-97

Appalachia 29 (Dec. 1952): 211-216

CLOUDY PEAK 7915′/2412 m

The summit, 0.9 mi. NE of Cloudy Pass, has a rocky top section. A party of 47 from the 1921 Mountaineer outing climbed it; most likely prospectors and surveyors had preceded them. References: *Mountaineer,* 1921, p. 17.

ROUTE: The peak is a mere hike from Cloudy Pass, or from the trail in the meadows just E (see Railroad Creek Trail♦, Section II).

NORTH STAR MOUNTAIN 8068′/2459 m

North Star was climbed by a U.S. Geological Survey party about 1904 and used as a triangulation point. The craggy summit 1.7 mi. NE of Cloudy Pass is an excellent viewpoint and provides a panorama of the Lyman Lake area. The mountain's original name was Bonanza Peak. Rock is granodiorite of Cloudy Pass pluton; the Grant Glacier is on the N slope. A ski ascent was made by Ralph Eskenazi, Sigurd Hall, and Dwight Watson on May 29, 1938 on a tour from Phelps Creek basin.

SOUTH RIDGE: From about 1 mi. E of Cloudy Pass at 6200 ft (see Railroad Creek Trail♦, Section II) hike up meadows and rockslides. Keep E of Cloudy Peak. The ascent is a hike then simple scramble at the top. Time: 2 hours round trip. Note: routes on the W are also simple.

BONANZA PEAK 9511′/2899 m

The majestic peak of Bonanza dominates not only the upper half of Railroad and Company Creek Valleys, but the entire Western Chelan subrange of peaks, for it is the highest non-volcanic mountain in the Cascade Range. On its eastern flank the summit rises 8213 ft from Lake Chelan in 10 mi. The cumulative effect of this spidery web of precipices and dramatic glaciers is one of the highest mountain walls in the range on the N and W flanks. Yet the S and E faces are uniquely large and complex. The greater Bonanza massif—some 4 mi. in extent, not including North Star and Martin Peak, includes seven glaciers and fully ten intersecting ridges radiating from principal and subsidiary peaks. The three highest summits rise on a 9000-ft crest which spans 1 mi., giving an overall impression more of a massif than a single peak. As viewed from a vertical perspective, the complex characteristics of Bonanza resemble a gigantic NW-trending octopus, with two prominent southern ridges 1 mi. apart. The West Peak (sometimes called Point Two) is 100 ft lower and about 600 ft distant from the true summit and separated from it by a most serrated and spectacular ridge. The horn-shaped Southwest Peak (9320′/2841 m) is sometimes termed Point Three.

Although he did not single out Bonanza by description, as a result of his geologic reconnaissance in the summer of 1898 Israel C. Russell mentioned the glaciers E of the Cascade divide on the high granitic peaks overlooking the W portion of Lake Chelan.[58] The largest glacier, and the one least visited or seen, is the Company, on the N flank (2.1 km^2 and 1.3 km long); aprons of its ice extend up to about 9200 ft on the summit ridge; the glacier terminates at 6000 ft. The Mary Green Glacier on the E flank of the true summit owes its name to the Mary Green claim (for the wife of an early prospector; located in 1896).

This spectacular glacier (8500′ to 7000′—0.8 km^2) lies on an immense sloping terrace in the broad cirque above Holden Lake. In late summer the crevasses produce a chaos of ice above bare slabs, and a dramatic contrast with the tamaracks fringing the lower cirque. The pass nearby, at the head of the valley NW of Holden Lake, has been called Mary Green Pass, Horton's Pass, but now usage seems settled on Holden Pass. The Isella Glacier, a small modern glacier lying high on the southern flank of the mountain, occupies part of an ancient Ice Age cirque.[59]

Bonanza is composed of hornblende quartz diorite gneiss of the Dumbell Mountain pluton. The rock is greenish to gray, medium and fine grained in broad zones parallel to foliation; swirled foliation and mafic streaks are common. The contact with Cloudy Pass pluton is W of Isella Glacier. The small Holden Lake pluton is N and E of Mary Green and N of Company Glacier. The mountain was originally known as "North Star" by early miners and the present North Star was "Bonanza."[60] A name interchange was apparently perpetrated by the U.S. Geological Survey in 1904. The surveyors used North Star for triangulation, but during subsequent mapping the names were interchanged, and so were the triangulation station marks.[61] Because of the erroneous assumption that surveyors had ascended Bonanza some aspiring mountaineers did not attempt it in the early 1930s (*Mountaineer,* 1934, p. 16). Certainly the mystique of Bonanza attracted curiosity among the earliest climbers, but the nature of any probes is largely unknown. The 1926 outing of the Mazamas apparently reached Peak 8599 on the NW spur of the mountain, but no details have been found. The 1921 outing of The Mountaineers was held in the area, but it is not known if they made an attempt.

In the mid-1930s Bonanza was one of the most celebrated alpine problems in the Pacific Northwest. But despite an appearance of evil, the mountain has now yielded six routes. Before the first ascent in 1937 various walls and buttresses had been the object of attempts, the first in 1935 by Everett Darr and Joe Leuthold, who hiked via Agnes Creek and Lyman Lake to attempt a route on the cliffs facing North Star; beyond the top of Points Four and Five they found the route too disconnected. The same problem arose in the 1937 attempt by five Oregon climbers, who reached the top of Point Two. They wrote "knifed teeth and vertical walls gave absolute protection" to the true summit.[62] In 1936 Everett and Ida Darr spent 2 weeks in the Holden area. They traversed onto the Company Glacier and attempted the N face, then managed to reach within 300 ft of the top of the Holden Lake face; the momentum of this reconnaissance was the legacy to the successful ascent by the latter route on June 28, 1937 by Curtis Ijames, Barrie James, and Joe Leuthold.[63]

BONANZA PEAK from West Peak
CURTIS IJAMES

BONANZA PK.
West Pk.
S.W. Pk.
Point 5
Point 4
S.E. Ridge
N.E. Ridge
snow thumb
ISELLA GLACIER
MARY GREEN GLACIER

The complexity of the mountain and attendant routefinding problems renders the ascent of Bonanza very questionable in anything but settled weather. Its sheer size and height above the protection of the timberline zone, its treacherous couloirs and snow conditions, make it an ascent of character. There is some danger of stonefall after July, when firn cementing scree in couloirs begins to disappear. Rain or warm temperatures are liable to begin stonefall. In many respects Bonanza has something of the quality of the large peaks in the Alps and Canadian Rockies. Time: 16 hours round trip from the base is common; a very early start is wise. References: *Mazama* 19, no. 12 (1937): 35-38; 43, no. 13 (1961): 50; 52, no. 13 (1970): 61-62; *Mountaineer,* 1950, p. 41; *Summit,* May 1964, pp. 4-5; *A.A.J.,* 1971, p. 346.

MARY GREEN GLACIER ROUTE: Holden Pass offers a better campspot for the climb than the lake (see Holden Lake Trail♦). From the pass turn uphill onto the boulderfield. An obvious game trail ascends diagonally left (W) under a cliff band (one can traverse boulderfield to reach ledge system that crosses center of waterfall cliffs). Beyond the upper heather slope (bench) ascend to the right hand (NE) end of the Mary Green Glacier. After most of the seasonal snow is gone this involves scrambling up several leads of polished slab (some cascading water and gravel); one report states the route here is over broken rock and near cliff base a ledge bears over to bedrock.

Ascend the glacier close to the N edge, under towering cliffs, and make a long nearly flat traverse across the top to the highest (SW) corner; many large crevasses invisible from below may make any other crossing impossible once bridges vanish. The objective is to continue to the glacier headwall's center; usually a central snow bridge crosses the schrund and leads to upper bench—but on far left there is always a large schrund. This crux area is fairly steep. If the bridge is gone traverse N to the far margin. From the upper bench ascend the long firn thumb to right upper edge where it leads into an obvious rock gully (crampons off). Ascend to light-colored band that slopes right, and climb easy rock, keeping well right. Keep right of the ice block, then begin rock climbing for about 800-ft gain. First ascend slabby class 3 rock up and slightly left of the gully (harder when not snow free); the rock here is of lighter color. After reaching the left side of the main gully it is preferable to continue over to next gully left. Beware of snow sliding off slabs here and stonefall. Climb to reach crest of NE summit ridge at the prominent notch about 100 yds from the top (do not choose the second notch). The last few pitches are pure joy and distinctly alpine. Note that the summit horn is at the S end of a series of teeth which require about 300 ft of traversing. Time: 7-8 hours from Holden Lake.

Variation: From the N flank of Holden Lake ascend the large talus cone. Near its tip is a 20-ft pitch (on right) giving easy access to slabs beneath the glacier. (Or from cliff base traverse right 100 ft to another stream; climb cliff, then W on spur est. 200 yds.) Depending on snow cover, ascend glacier directly or travel on via bedrock on long NW diagonal toward upper glacier bench. This variation is shorter but harder than the normal route.

Variation: Another way through the glacier from Holden Pass is to traverse N on bedrock. Climb to the lower ice margin where it is possible to overlook the main portion of glacier. Then bear NW toward the large cliffs on the cirque's N flank.

Variation: Several are possible above the schrund: two can be recommended. (1) A direct line involves apparent class 4 rock for about ½ lead (about 200 ft above schrund). This is easily bypassed by going about 100 ft to the right around the only difficult spot and working back immediately above the rappel bolt; this bypass is not obvious until at the scene. (2) It is possible to make a harder alternate from above the snow block. This variation ascends chimneys etc. up to the ridge crest.

SOUTHEAST RIDGE (Holden Ridge): This is a narrow rock crest with some spectacular steps, between the Mary Green and Isella Glaciers. The climbing route does not follow the peripheral lower extremity, which has several sharp ridge summits. First ascent by James Burrows and David Isles in August, 1956. Follow the Mary Green route almost to the high point on the glacier, then traverse S and climb to the crest of the SE ridge. There can be a schrund problem here, and some steep unconsolidated rock and debris. On the crest climb easy rock to a smooth tower, which is passed on the right by a nearly-horizontal traverse. Then climb a difficult pitch with small holds (class 5). Another ledge permits a traverse to a chimney (quartz crystals); ascend this to the crest. The summit is three leads distant over steep, difficult rock. Anchor pitons used on original climb. Grade III (est.) and class 5. Time: 10-12 hours round trip.

COMPANY HEADWALL—EAST SIDE: The headwall of this route is on a flanking wall above the E portion of the Company Glacier. The headwall actually faces NW, and is on that flank of Bonanza's NE ridge. The route takes several eastern glacier segments and a final ice apron, then finally ends on the upper NE summit ridge. Rock is generally solid but there is a considerable amount of loose surface rock. The route should only be attempted in settled weather and solid snow conditions. First ascent by Hans Altenfelder and Larry Penberthy in late July 1940.

From Holden Pass bear up the meadow to the edge of the Company Glacier. Turn the corner and rappel 200 ft to an easy ledge. Make a moderately steep snow and glacier traverse SW about 0.4 mi. to end atop the promontory (buttress) projecting from the wall about 300 ft above the glacier (between two high ice sections of the headwall); can bivouac atop. Just before the promontory the route crosses a 45° ice slope on a rightward bearing. Now ascend a 50-ft-wide rock face of about 60°; many ledges and holds for a 1200 ft altitude gain. At 60 ft below the NE ridge there is a 3-ft-wide

BONANZA PEAK from east
AUSTIN POST, U.S. GEOLOGICAL SURVEY

N.E.
Ridge
West Peak
N.W.
Buttress
S.W. Peak
Pk. 8599
North Face
promonotory
Company Headwall
East Side
to
Holden Pass
COMPANY GLACIER

ledge: this portion steepens and is difficult (est. class 5.7) but originally done unroped. A short hump is crossed on the ridge to join the Mary Green route (100 ft loose rock). Grade III (est.); class 5.7; take crampons. Time: 8 hours from meadow (2 hours on upper wall). Reference: *Mountaineer,* 1951, pp. 63-64.

NORTHWEST BUTTRESS (Company Glacier Route): The route takes the imposing NW buttress from the Company Glacier to the West Peak. It has been reported as a moderate snow and rock climb, but the original party found it steep and brutal, with avalanche danger. The route climbs about 2000 ft of snow-covered ice tongue; there may be a cornice to cut through. First ascent by Everett Darr, Ida Zacher Darr, Curtis Ijames, Barrie James, and Joe Leuthold on June 25, 1937.

From Holden Pass drop 700 ft to the head of Sable Creek, then rise over 700 ft to the Sable-Company Creek ridge. Drop about 1000 ft to a rocky island amid snow. The circuit has also been done from Holden Pass across heather slopes to a pass at the foot of the NE ridge, then onto the E edge of Company Glacier. The route on the buttress-face begins at the upper W portion of the glacier. Time: original party took 5½ hours on the ice climb; a full day should be allowed for the ascent, and a possible bivouac if continuing to the main summit. Bring crampons, flukes, and some ice screws. References: *Mountaineer,* 1951, p. 63; *Mazama* 19, no. 12 (1937): 36-37.

Alternate Approach: Take Company Creek Trail♦ to Hilgard Creek, then travel SW along the main stream 4-5 mi. to the basin at its head (can camp at timberline).

SOUTH FACE: First ascent by Charles Raymond and Patricia Raymond in September 1971. From Hart Lake reach Isella Glacier (see Isella Glacier Route). Climb the glacier, then ascend a snow tongue of about 100 ft. Climb up and left to the base of an obvious slot. Climb this and then take a rightward branch directly to the summit. The most difficult portion is the upper slot where the chimney overhangs at a chockstone (class 5.5); the remainder of the rock climbing is class 4 (2 hours). Grade II.

ISELLA GLACIER ROUTE: This route should be done only when dry; with much early season snow on ridges, hazards increase. The feeling of insecurity experienced gives the climb a serious air. Certainly it is one of the most unusual routes of its standard in the Cascades, if completed to the true summit. First ascent by Hans Altenfelder and Larry Penberthy July 4-6, 1940.

From the upper end of Hart Lake (see Railroad Creek Trail♦) ascend cliffs to camp at the foot of the Isella moraine. Take the glacier NW to the W ridge by a steep (hidden) 1000-ft snow chute; the chute is on the W side of a buttress descending near the Southwest Peak. Climb to the West Peak (Point Two)—9400′+. The main summit can only be reached by a long traverse of the exposed connecting ridge. The first part traverses the S side of the ridge, then continues on the crest. Midway on the traverse a 40-ft straddle was used. A new ledge on the NW face permits bypassing a gendarme; once beyond, one is 30 ft below it on the N. Then cross an 8-ft wall 80 ft from the summit (class 5). Time: allow 4 hours for the traverse. Reference: *Mountaineer,* 1951, p. 63.

Approach Variation: From Cloudy Pass keep altitude and traverse the slope of Railroad Creek Valley E, then NE (at about 6500′). Turn western of S buttresses, then ascend to the glacier (3 hours).

SOUTHWEST PEAK 9320′/2841 m

The summit is considered an easy climb from the Isella Glacier. It has been suggested that early miners first climbed it because of copper mineral showing on Bonanza (source: Larry Penberthy). The route is via the Isella Glacier.

NORTH FACE OF SOUTHWEST PEAK (Soviet Route): This is a long steep rock buttress with about 2000 ft of technical altitude gain (22 leads). A bivouac should be anticipated. First ascent by Sergei Bershov, Alex Bertulis, Valentin Grakovich, Anatoly Nepomnyashchy, and Vyacheslav Onishchenko on September 12, 1975.

From Hart Lake (see Railroad Creek Trail♦) hike up the rock and heather terraces W of the waterfalls (W of cliffs) to the North Star—Bonanza Pass (7100′+); good campsites; 2½ hours from lake. Descend several hundred ft to the base of the buttress face. About 60 ft above the lowest point gain access onto the N face via a ramp on the W. Begin to climb directly up a chimney, then continue with occasionally delicate face climbing toward the right and up to the underside of a major overhanging headwall. Proceed on its E until a major, nearly-horizontal ramp is reached. Traverse the ramp to the W side, then up on difficult rock: one point involves a hard free move over nearly-vertical and crumbly red rock followed by friction climbing on solid slab. From a deep, cave-like belay ledge, continue straight up and over delicate face terrain and vertical chimneys. From an exposed belay just below the "first step" (at three-fourths of route) face climb up and traverse left to the top of the step. Easy climbing across the knifed connection to the "upper step" brings one to comfortable terraces on the W side (good bivouac). Continue up the crest of the buttress to the base of the overhanging summit headwall. From a broad belay ledge climb left and up over mixed rock and ice to a notch 30 ft E of the summit. Descent: via S face. Grade V (est.); class 5.9. Selection: six knife blades and many chocks used (possible aid climbing if not prepared for hard free). Time: 10½ hours rock climbing. References: *A.A.J.*, 1976, pp. 340-344; *Mountaineer,* 1975, pp. 99-101; *Off Belay,* Feb. 1976, pp. 19-23.

NORTH COULOIR OF SOUTHWEST PEAK (Beowulf Couloir): This 50° couloir of 2200 ft reaches to the crest of the E summit ridge of the Southwest Peak at about 9000 ft. The route actually faces NW (Glacier Creek drainage) and is not generally visible. Avalanches could be a problem at times. First ascent by Alex Bertulis and Mark Fielding on May 31, 1970. From Hart Lake ascend N over the North Star-Bonanza pass, then traverse around the West Buttress. The route climbs directly up the couloir; original party found snow conditions good for step kicking, but some ice (bring protection and crampons). Grade II or III. Time:

BONANZA PEAK from north
AUSTIN POST, U.S. GEOLOGICAL SURVEY

S.W. Peak
West Pk.
BONANZA PK.
S.E. Ridge
1940
1971
ISELLA GLACIER
MARY GREEN GLACIER
to Hart Lake

2 hours in couloir. Descent: via S slope to Isella Glacier.

PEAK 8599 8599′/2621 m

This is a sub-summit of Bonanza, on the NW ridge about 0.7 mi. from the West Peak. Photographic evidence indicates the summit was likely reached on the 1926 Mazama outing.

SOUTHWEST ARETE: First ascent by Michael Helms and James R. Mitchell on September 12, 1975. Make approach as per North Face of Southwest Peak. From the pass drop several hundred ft on the N side, then traverse scree-talus to approach the SW Arete at about 6600 ft. Climb class 3 rock to 7300 ft (original party bivouac). Ascend the arete near its crest to 8000 ft, then walk to the summit. Class 5.4 (much loose rock and poor protection on 12 pitches). Reference: *Mountaineer,* 1975, p. 101.

DARK PEAK 8504′/2592 m

Located 2 mi. SE of Needle Peak between Company Glacier (on E) and Dark Glacier (on N). There is a rugged ridge trending NW along the W margin of the Dark Glacier; the glacier is about 1 mi. long and ranges from 8200 ft to 6400 ft. The peak was probably climbed on the 1926 Mazama outing.

Specific route details are lacking, but the ascent appears simple from the SW. Approach as per Southwest Peak-North Face, Bonanza, and continue traverse of basin of Glacier Creek to the SW flank.

NEEDLE PEAK 7880′+/2402 m

This is a pointed rock peak, located in the converging angle of Agnes and Swamp Creeks. It is quite noticeable from the head of the Agnes valley and the summits to the W. The name is an early one, probably from prospectors of the area, and shown on the first Forest Service map in 1913. First ascent by W.V. Graham Matthews in 1949.

ROUTES: From the old cabin in Swamp Creek (see Agnes Creek Trail♦) the original route ascended the long N ridge. The route is a pleasant scramble, but for a short distance near the summit some exposure is presented (class 3). Other routes have not been confirmed; from Agnes Creek the SW flank of the summit appears feasible.

MT. LYALL 7892′/2405 m

On Swamp-Company Creek divide. Several summits to the NW on the same divide are above 7600 ft (Lyall Ridge); the highest point is 7745 ft. The name is for the eminent British geologist Sir Charles Lyall, 1797-1875.

ROUTE: From Company Creek Trail♦ at Hilgard Creek continue up Company Creek 1½ mi. Then ascend W up rock-slides and an easy slope. The SW ridge looks easy, via a 7300-ft col; reach from upper Company Creek basin.

BONANZA PEAK from south

LARRY IKENBERRY, CASCADE PHOTOGRAPHICS

HEATHER RIDGE 7928′/2406 m

This is a ridge between Pass and Cabin Creeks; the 7928-ft high point is 2.8 mi. N of Mt. Lyall. There are long but easy slopes on the W; reach from Pass Creek.

SISI RIDGE 7444′/2269 m

The long divide between Cabin and Company Creeks; trends NE to Stehekin River valley. The highest summit is SW of Battalion Lake and 2 mi. S of Stehekin River. Three other points rise above 7000 ft.

There is no route information, but the ascent is merely an exercise.

WHITE GOAT MOUNTAIN 7800′+/2377 m

This is a unique thin NW-trending gneissic fin, 0.6 mi. SW of Tupshin Peak. First ascent by Everett Darr, Ida (Zacher) Darr, Joe Leuthold, and Eldon Metzger on September 10, 1940. References: *Mazama* 22, no. 12 (1940): 61; 23, no. 12 (1941): 47.

ROUTE: Approach via Bird Creek (Devore Creek Trail♦). On the SW side of the fin, climb a chimney one pitch to notch at headwall on NE face. Several alternatives seem possible; all begin from a broad ledge and are about 150 ft. The original party climbed this final pitch on the E face on steep broken rock. Keep right of a sharp outside corner and work into a slight depression; then bear left while climbing. Class 5.

Possible Variation: East Side of Northwest Face: By Joseph Vance and party, August 1974. Using the ledge on NE face, follow it around a corner to just beyond the summit. Ascend about 100 ft up the broad shallow portion of the steep face, then traverse left around the corner (class 5.3) to the ridge SE of the summit. Continue to the top on easier rock.

TUPSHIN PEAK 8320′+/2536 m

This striking, ragged peak is on the Devore-Company Creek divide about 4 mi. W of Stehekin. The name means "needle" in Chinook jargon (first shown on 1922 Forest Service maps). Rock is gneiss, sometimes badly shattered. The peak has a broad steep N face, one reported not inviting for a route. It appears there may be a rock glacier at 6400 ft-6000 ft under this face. The climb of Tupshin is intriguing, and in a seldom visited area; by 1974 there had been only five ascents. The traverse of the W face of the pinnacled peak presents both routefinding problems and moderately difficult climbing (the route marked in *Mazama,* 1940 is either in error or much more difficult than done on a later climb). Tupshin was attempted by the Darrs in

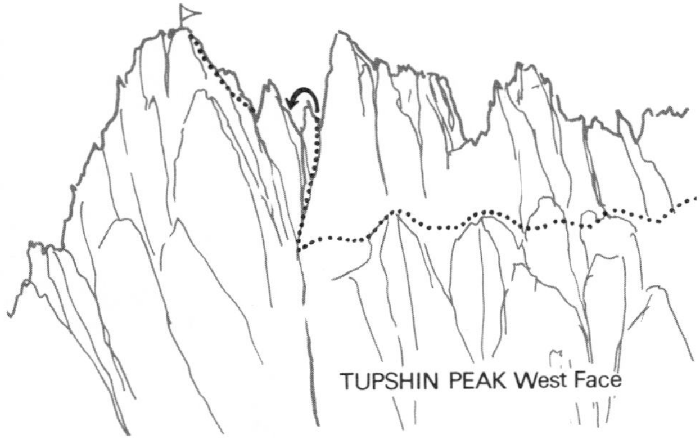

July 1940, then successfully climbed on September 9 together with Joe Leuthold and Eldon Metzger; the ascent took 7½ hours. The next climb was made in August 1941 by Harold Bonebrake, Everett Darr, Larry Ruch and Helen Spalding. Reference: *Mazama* 22, no. 12 (1940): 60-61; 23, no. 12 (1941): 47.

ROUTE: From camp at Bird Creek on Devore Creek Trail♦ (4.5 mi.) or in the 7000-ft alpine lake basin ½ mi. N of Devore Peak at the head of Bird Creek, approach Tupshin over the SW ridge. The route traverses the exposed W face on narrow ledges below the main pinnacles, ascending to the gap between the summit tower and next highest pinnacle.

From a crag on the ridge first traverse downward on scree ledges toward a blank section of face. Climb above the blank section via a narrow overhung ledge, followed by a short chimney with a chockstone (class 5.1) and traverse upward to the steep 200-ft gully/chimney below the ridge gap. Climb the chimney (class 5.3) to reach the ridge in the notch between two needles. Climb around the higher N needle on the E face (steep and loose) to the notch (use narrow ledge) between it and the summit tower. Work upward and right to the summit on easier rock. Grade II; class 5 (take runners). Time: 8 hours from Devore Creek; 5 hours from lake basin.

DEVORE PEAK 8360′+/2548 m

Devore is an important summit of the Western Chelan group, located on the Devore-Hilgard Creek divide 5½ mi. SW of Stehekin. The peak has a steep NE face, where there is a small body of glacier ice. There are several attractive lakes below the glacier, in the tamarack belt, which drain into Bird Creek. The name is for Dan Devore, early packer and Stehekin resident. First ascent by Everett Darr and Ida (Zacher) Darr on September 8, 1940. Reference: *Mazama* 22, no. 12 (1940): 60; 23, no. 12 (1941): 46.

SOUTH RIDGE: The ridge can be approached from Lake Marie (7120′+) or from West Fork Devore Creek. (see Devore Creek Trail♦). Follow the S ridge to the summit (class 2-3); 2 hours from lake.

Variation: From camp in alpine lake basin N of Devore, climb SE, then contour W to the S ridge (2 hours total).

WY'EAST MOUNTAIN 8202′/2500 m

Located 0.7 mi. SSW of Devore Peak on Hilgard-Devore Creek divide. First ascent by Everett Darr, Ida Darr, Joe Leuthold, and Eldon Metzger on September 13, 1940. References: *Mazama* 22, no. 12 (1940): 62-63; 23, no. 12 (1941): 46 (note error on location of Lake Marie).

ROUTE: Approach via Devore Creek Trail♦. Ascend to the N side of the peak (there is a false N summit near the top). The peak was considered a good rock climb. Time: 6 hours. On the second ascent, a N-S traverse party reported some ice climbing.

BLACK TOWER (Oversight Peaks) 8280′+/2524 m

There are three rock peaks on the divide between the basin of Lake Marie and Fourth of July Basin near the head of Devore Creek. The peak at the center of Fourth of July Basin is 8220 ft (2505 m), and the two on the crest SE are each shown as above the altitude of 8280 ft. These peaks were apparently all climbed on an outing of the Mazamas in the second week of August 1941, but were bypassed on the outing of the previous summer. A more recent climbing party thought that perhaps the 1941 group had not climbed one of the peaks, and therefore dubbed it "Oversight." The identity of each summit climbed in 1941 is still open to question, but it appears that the 8220-ft peak was called "Little Joe," the western of the two highest peaks was called "Black Tower," and the eastern was "Johnson's Jonah."

"Little Joe" was climbed by several persons, led by Everett Darr; "Johnson's Jonah" was climbed by a party of about 12, led by Al Gerding (the peak appeared difficult on approach, and Harold Johnson felt it would be too difficult to lead; when it later proved quite easy, the name evolved). "Black Tower" is the most impressive and difficult of the group. The ascent was made by several persons, led by Al Gerding; the rock climbing involved belaying (est. 200 ft of climbing from the ridge adjacent). Reference: *Mazama* 23, no. 12 (1941): 46-47.

ROUTES: The ascents were made from Fourth of July Basin (see Devore Creek Trail♦). "Little Joe" is a scramble; "Johnson's Jonah" is maximum class 3; "Black Tower" is class 3 and 4. Additional detail is not available ATP.

CASTLE ROCK 8197′/2498 m

The distinctive characteristic of Castle Rock is its abruptness from Lake Chelan (7100-ft rise in 2.3 mi.) rather than exceptional height. Its craggy nature stimulated many early visitors. Professor William D. Lyman wrote, "The Stehekin River issues from a narrow defile over which towers the steep cone of Castle Mountain, eight thousand feet high, the grandest single object visible from the water."[64] When the summit was reached by Joe Leuthold and Eldon Metzger on September 11, 1940, there was a cairn with evidence that the climb had been done in 1917; this may have been by surveyors. Early photos taken by Forest Ranger Barney Zell (1910-1920) indicate that he was on or nearly on the summit. References: *Mazama* 22, no. 12 (1940): 62; 23, no. 12 (1941): 46.

ROUTE: See approach to Flora Mountain. Ascend the W flank (mostly scree) from upper Castle Creek basin. The summit can also be reached by traversing around the W side of Flora at the 7000-ft level. Time: 4 hours from Devore Creek.

Note: Flora, Riddle, and Castle can all be climbed in a long 1-day loop from upper Devore Creek.

FLORA MOUNTAIN est. 8320′/2536 m

Flora is on Riddle-Castle Creek divide 3 mi. from Lake Chelan and W of Castle Rock. It is a desolate pile of loose gneiss, on contact of Railroad Creek pluton on the W and S and Swakane biotite gneiss. The S peak is highest. First ascent by Joe Leuthold and Eldon Metzger on September 11, 1940. References: *Mazama* 22, no. 12 (1940): 62; 23, no. 12 (1941): 46.

SOUTHWEST ROUTE: From upper Devore Creek (Devore Creek Trail♦) climb E to the 7400-ft pass leading into the upper Castle Creek valley. Traverse benches to the SW flank of Flora and ascend over loose talus (3½ hours from Devore Creek). If traversing from Riddle Peak one can descend the SE shoulder into upper Riddle Creek, then ascend NE through the pass to Castle Creek.

EAST ROUTE: From the pass (see above) traverse and climb above the head of Castle Creek basin and onto the peak's E ridge. Cross to the N side and ascend easy gullies to the summit.

RIDDLE PEAKS 8232′/2509 m

The Riddle Peaks are shaped in ground outline like a star, with the highest in the center. The rugged mass of black gabbro 2½ mi. N of Railroad Creek and 6 mi. E of Bonanza Peak, forms the northern divide of Railroad Creek. At the highest peak the ridge runs N 1 mi. (E side of Fourth of July Basin) to the North Peak (8000′+/2438 m). The Riddle Peaks pluton is a small body of hornblende gabbro, interlayered with blocks of gneiss and schist, located E of Tenmile Creek. The pluton includes the peaks just N of Fourth of July Basin E to the head of Riddle Creek; farther E and N is the Railroad Creek pluton. First ascent by Everett Darr, Ida Zacher Darr, Joe Leuthold, and Eldon Metzger on September 11, 1940. The Darrs climbed the N peak while the two others did the main summit. References: *Mazama* 22, no. 12 (1940): 62; 23, no. 12 (1941): 44.

WEST RIDGE: From Ten Mile Pass (see Railroad Creek Trail♦ and Devore Creek Trail♦) the summit is in the center of the peaks, about 1 mi. E of the pass. The ascent is by a long easy ridge (class 2 and 3). The N peak was rated a superior climb.

MARTIN PEAK 8511′/2594 m

Martin is the outstanding summit between Bonanza Peak and Lake Chelan. The serrated gneissic summit ridge trends N, with a large face on both flanks. The Tenmile Park Glacier, E of the peak has carved a semicircular trend into the narrow summit arete. First ascent by Ida Zacher Darr in July 1936. An inscription dated 1901 with names, was found etched in slab some distance below the summit. Reference: *Mazama* 18, no. 12 (1936): 6.

SOUTHWEST ROUTE: Begin from near Holden Pass (see Holden Lake Trail♦) or above the lake and ascend to mine tailings near the base of the W ridge. Keep on the S flank, near the crest. Climb up and right through a gully system to the summit.

Variation: While still in forest ½ mi. before the lake ascend avalanche swath to within 150 ft of the SE ridge. Turn left on a white rock band (on W) and follow it ⅓ mi. on an easy traverse; this places one 100-200 ft from the summit on its W face. An easy chute scramble leads to the top.

SOUTHEAST RIDGE: This is the original route. Climb from the S up the serrated arete. About 1000 ft from summit descend to ledge on W and traverse several hundred ft, then return to the arete.

Variation: By Barrie James and Joe Leuthold. The variation follows the arete the entire distance; much rock climbing in gaps and on edges. Time: 4 hours from lake.

SABLE RIDGE 7800′+/2377 m

This is a 2-mi. N-S ridge, trending N from Martin Peak (in the converging angle of Hilgard and Company Creeks). The highest point is 2.9 mi. SE of Mt. Lyall and 1 mi. from Martin Peak. The ascent is easy on the SW.

PLUMMER MOUNTAIN 7870′/2399 m

Located 1½ mi. NW of Suiattle Pass, Plummer and

MARTIN PEAK from west
CURTIS IJAMES

the crest of Miners Ridge are carved in brown gneiss lying over granite. The peak is the gentle culmination of Miners Ridge.

WEST RIDGE: Easy slopes are taken from Miners Ridge. A SE route can also be made from Suiattle Pass: one can hike NW along a ridge (avoid bumps) to a saddle at 0.8 mi. E of the summit; then an easy ascent is made (3 hours).

SITTING BULL MOUNTAIN

7759′/2365 m

On the Canyon-South Fork Agnes Creek divide 2.1 mi. NW of Suiattle Pass. The double summits and long snow gully are obvious from Cloudy Pass. The craggy N summit is highest; close by is the pointed S summit. A high ridge S extends to Point 7509; here are perennial snowpatches on the E flank. First ascent by a large party of The Mountaineers on August 9, 1921. References: *Mountaineer*, 1921, p. 19; 1949, p. 11.

SOUTHWEST ROUTE: Approach via Canyon Lake Trail♦. At Canyon Creek's middle fork (est. 3 mi. from Miners Ridge) ascend the streambed to broad heather slopes, then cross a large snowfield to the col just S of Sitting Bull. A short snow traverse and easy rock scramble on the S face lead to the summit.

SOUTHWEST ROUTE: (original route) This was described as "a comfortable afternoon's climb with little snow work." The approach was a long traverse from Suiattle Pass. One can approach from Agnes Creek Trail♦ 1½-2 mi. N of Suiattle Pass, and ascend into the timberline basin SE of the mountain. Ascend via the long snow gully on the face to the summit notch, then scramble N to the top.

SOUTH PEAK

In 1949 a party of 13 persons described a tricky climb, using two fixed ropes, and claimed the first ascent.

SADDLE BOW MOUNTAIN

7410′/2259 m

This is a pretty double summit 1.7 mi. ENE of Bannock Mountain, an isolated peak W of the deep Agnes Creek valley. The NW peak is higher; there is a SE peak (7280′+/2219 m) at 0.3 mi. from the summit. The mountain has a gentle saddle (6600′+) on the SSW, at the head of Bannock Lakes; this is a good hiking route from the Agnes Creek valley. The Mazama outing of 1926 reported "One can not conceive of a better example of a torn and glacier-rent mountain peak." First ascent by Glen F. Bremerman, H.E.D. Brown, E. Brooks Horning, Frank I. Jones, Lars Loveseth, Ben C. Mooers, and Charles Simmons on August 9, 1921. References: *Mountaineer,* 1921, p. 24; *Mazama* 8, no. 12 (1926): 54.

ROUTE: From Agnes Creek Trail♦ 3 mi. N of Suiattle Pass climb W up the forested lateral valley S of Saddle Bow. One can leave via easy forest slopes any time after ½ mi. from the trail. A gentle spur ridge leads NW to the saddle SSW of the summit. The final ascent is via the gradual SW slope; this is completed via 300 ft of easy rock. Time: 6 hours.

Approach Variation: It is feasible to traverse to the mountain from Suiattle Pass but the route is long and impractical because of the cliffs of Sitting Bull (best to stay low).

BANNOCK MOUNTAIN

7760′+/2365 m

Between the headwaters of Spruce, Canyon, and Sulphur Creeks on a NW-SE crest near the terminal forks of Spruce Creek. Bannock has a very steep NE wall at the head of Spruce Creek, and here has a glacier; the wall is scoured by parallel avalanche gullies. The three secluded Bannock Lakes are in the basin between Bannock and Saddle Bow Mountain. First ascent by Art Johnson, Hermann Ulrichs, and Dwight Watson on July 28, 1936 (two routes).

SOUTHWEST ROUTE: Done on the first ascent by Johnson and Watson. For approach see Canyon Lake Trail♦. From Totem Pass or Canyon Lake the SW slope is an easy route, with a short rock scramble at the top.

SOUTHEAST FACE: Done on the first ascent by Ulrichs. The climb went from the SW to the S ridge, then to the SE face (class 3-4).

DOME and SINISTER PEAKS from south
DWIGHT WATSON

GLACIER PK.
SINISTER PK.
GUNSIGHT PK.
Stonehenge Ridge
Main Pk.
North Pk.
South Pk.
col
7640 +
N.E. Pk.
CHICKAMIN GLACIER
BLUE GLACIER

STONEHENGE RIDGE 7382′/2250 m

This is a distinctive alpine ridge on the Sulphur-Canyon Creek divide. The subrange extends NW from near Totem Pass 2½ mi. to the S valley wall of Sulphur Creek; there are two glaciers on the N slope. The highest peak (7382′) is 1.2 mi. W of Totem Pass, and the next highest (7346′/2240 m) is farther NW. The 7382-ft peak is a small rock crag above the upper part of the western glacier—W of a castle-shaped rock summit; the S slope appears easy. The entire ridge is rugged—of gneissic rock. The appropriate "Stonehenge" name was given by Dwight Watson during the Hanging Gardens traverse in 1936.

ROUTE: From Totem Pass (see Canyon Lake Trail♦) hike W below the ridge crest; it appears best to keep high but under the summits. Beyond the first peak it appears feasible to traverse the two main glaciers on the N flank. Another possible approach is from Totem Pass, using the Bath Lakes High Route: the best average area to traverse the S slope is about 6400 ft.

SINISTER PEAK 8440′+/2573 m

Sinister is 0.9 mi. E of Dome Peak on the Chickamin-Dome Creek divide. It is a very asymetrical peak of granodiorite rock, with steep ice slopes on the N. The S face is relatively short, but quite sheer. There is a ridge of castellated crags to the E. S of Sinister, below the slabs of "Garden Glacier" is a very pronounced lateral moraine. A sharp pinnacled ridge separates the glacier from a similar body of ice to the E.

On early Forest Service maps (1926-1931) the peak was mapped as "Blue Mountain." In July 1936 Hermann F. Ulrichs and Dwight Watson made a 22-hour round trip from near Totem Pass to the U-notch E of the summit (between the eastern crags and the sweep of the E ridge), they probably were within about 400 ft of the summit, but the climb appeared too exposed without a rope. The first ascent was made by Lloyd Anderson, Jim Crooks, and Clint Kelley on May 29, 1939. Reference: *Mountaineer,* 1939, pp. 26-27.

WEST RIDGE: First ascent by Barrie James, Paul Livingston, and Herb Rasor on August 26, 1939 (on second ascent). The ascent was made from an alp camp near the snout of Chickamin Glacier, after the climb of Dome Peak. See Agnes Creek Trail♦ for the brushy approach via the W fork. The approach up the glacier is made as for Dome Peak, with a final ascent of the moderately steep slope (crevasses) to the broad snowfield in the Sinister-Dome col (7640′+); in late season a schrund may make the approach a problem. Traverse to the S side of the ridge on an easy snowfield to reach rock at the first notch below the summit. The rock is class 3 (a 30′ pitch is the steepest portion; a narrow ledge then makes a switchback onto easier rock); the completion is an easy scramble.

Approach Variations: A possible approach is from the ridge due S of Dome Peak. At about 6000 ft descend into Dome Creek basin via a very steep grass gully. Then make a long traversing rise on slabs, rock and snow to the col. Another approach to the col is from Hanging Gardens: traverse into Dome Creek basin, then up moraine slopes and firn.

EAST RIDGE: This is the original route. The approach was made via Sulphur and Dome Creeks. From the ridge S of Sinister ascend to the S face. Keep right (E) of small pinnacles and cross a small glacier ("Garden Glacier"). A steep 300-ft gully slants along the right edge of big slabs to the summit ridge. This steep ridge has snow on the N face; in early season a dangerous cornice may exist here, and if the snow is loose, the climbing could be dangerous. Where the ridge flattens there is a sheer 15-ft step (shoulder stand on original). The upper part of the ridge widens and the route joins the S ridge just under the summit. Time: 4-5 hours from Dome Creek basin.

BLIZZARD PEAK 7880′+/2402 m

This is the double-summit crag at the junction of the Sinister-Gunsight Peak ridge, at the upper eastern edge of the glacier in the Spruce Creek drainage (0.6 mi. E of Sinister Peak). Lower summit is 7875 ft (2400 m). The ascent was made by the 1939 party, by traversing the ridge above Chickamin Glacier from Sinister.

GUNSIGHT PEAK 8198′/2499 m

Gunsight is a remarkable peak of granitic rock, with a light grey tone, 1.8 mi. E of Dome Peak. Its three striking summits form a dramatic wedge between the Chickamin and Blue Glaciers. The Middle Peak is higher than either the North Peak (8160′+/2487 m) or the South Peak (8080′+/2463 m). All three peaks have sheer rock faces above the glaciers; of these the E face of the Middle Peak and W face of the North Peak are the most impressive. The great Chickamin Glacier is described elsewhere; the Blue Glacier extends from about 8000 ft to 6600 ft in the Icy Creek basin.

Maps in 1939 showed "Blue Mountain" at the location of the present Sinister Peak, but because of the name Blue Glacier, the first ascent party affixed this name to the peak. But the party which climbed Sentinel Peak in 1935 had already referred to an "unnamed peak we christened Gunsight because of the twin spires comprising its summit" (*Mazama, op. cit.*). Fortunately a plea to confirm the original name was successful, for the notch formed by the middle and north peaks indeed resembles a gunsight. Probably the first to consider an ascent were Hermann Ulrichs and Dwight Watson when in July 1936 they reached the S

GUNSIGHT and SINISTER PEAKS from east
AUSTIN POST, U.S. GEOLOGICAL SURVEY

GUNSIGHT PEAK from west
DWIGHT WATSON

margin of the Chickamin Glacier. But they "were too pressed for time, too fatigued . . . to cope with the very obvious difficulties ahead. Pitons are in order here" (*Sierra Club. Bull.* 22, no. 1 (1937): 38). The first ascent was made by Lloyd Anderson, Lyman Boyer, and Agnes Dickert on July 3, 1938 on an extended trek from Sulphur Creek. Reference: *Mountaineer,* 1938, pp. 28-29.

MAIN PEAK

The original party crossed the ridge E of Sinister Peak and descended the crevassed Chickamin Glacier, then trversed the glacier flank to the W face beneath the summit. Other approaches are from the Dome Glacier with a traverse over the high col of Dome Peak, from Icy Creek, or from Totem Pass. A good camp is at the Icy-Spruce Pass just N of the lake; to reach the normal route, ascend W over the divide S of Gunsight.

Begin on the rock at the lower left edge of the snow finger between the South and Main Peaks; cross left on slabby rock—a 60-ft pitch of class 4. The schrund here may cause a detour, or a jump across the moat (original party used a piton for aid here). An easy scramble follows up the dike (shallow gully) to the Main-North Peak notch. Make a traverse on the W face 50-100 ft to steep cracks and a chimney system which is taken to the arete just N of the summit (class 5); a good rappel block is found here. Climb around on E face for the completion. Time: 2 hours from glacier.

SOUTHWEST FACE: First ascent by Fred Beckey and Leif-Norman Patterson on June 20, 1967. Climb the S couloir (snow) to near its end, then make an obvious traverse left. Make a half lead (class 4) to steeper slabs and cracks. Climb directly up, keeping slightly left, for one long pitch (5.6) to the SW arete. One pitch (class 4) leads to the summit. Class 5.6 (good rock, 10 pitons used). Time: 2 hours.

NORTH PEAK

First ascent by Fred Beckey, Robert W. Craig, and Will F. Thompson on June 28, 1940 (also second climb of Main Peak); it was estimated that this summit was only about 10 ft lower than the Main Peak. From the Main Peak notch traverse across the W face on a prominent ledge for about 500 ft. Where it corners to the N face there are a series of giant blocks and horns, nearly textbook examples of massive rock fracturing. From the NW corner climb an 80-ft chimney to a notch between blocks; the highest block is some 70 ft to the S. Pass between two large blocks, then by a corner, and make a strenuous finger traverse to a tiny notch 20 ft below the true summit horn. Stem the open gap between the horns, working to the left (highest); class 5.6.

A variation is to begin at a short chimney 40 ft before the end of the ledge. Make a short slab traverse right and use finger holds in a crack to work to the E side around a corner and block; this leads to the open gap at the summit horns.

EAST FACE: First ascent by William Blair, Ron Burgner, and Mike Kennedy in June 1965. The route ends on snow patches just right of the steepest wall; there is about 750 ft of climbing. The route was reconnoitered by the 1940 party but snowpatches appeared loosely adhered to the wall. Contour below the E faces of Gunsight via easy firn. Below the northern part of the Main Peak cross the schrund (possibly difficult). Follow a route alternating on snow and rock to the platform 60 ft below the summit, then complete as per normal route. Grade II; class 5 (solid rock—six pitons placed)

NORTHWEST FACE: This route climbs from the Chickamin Glacier to the N ridge above the notch. First ascent by Fred Beckey and Leif-Norman Patterson on June 19, 1967. From the glacier ascend free and with some aid to a belay. Bear right on the next pitch, which is a tricky slab. The next pitch includes an overhang (aid), then three leads are made along or near the corner to the summit ledge of the normal route; there are some moderately difficult moves along this portion. Grade III; class 5 and A2 (used 35 pitons). References: *A.A.J.*, 1968, pp. 137-138; *Mountaineer,* 1968, p. 202.

SOUTH PEAK

This peak is quite sheer on the W, but well broken on the upper N face. First ascent by Fred Beckey and Robert W. Craig on June 27, 1940. Ascend to the head of the steep snow finger below the Main and South Peaks. Traverse left 50 ft (beneath a cul de sac) and veer back S above this wall (this lead is exposed). Ascend gullies and cracks to the ridge (reach 100 ft from summit); a short smooth wall completes the ascent. Class 4 and 5.

NORTHEAST PEAK 8040′+/2451 m

This summit, extended along the Chickamin Glacier from the three Gunsight Peaks, features large granitic slabs; there is a ridge extending due W at the edge of the glacier (this ridge spur isolates a section of ice on the NNW. First ascent by Gibson Reynolds and Philip Sharpe in September 1951. The approach was made via West Fork Agnes Creek to a camp at the last larch trees on the moraine above the Chickamin Glacier. The route may have first gone to the col (7160′+) at 0.4 mi. N of the summit, but did follow the N ridge. There is a "step" about 400 ft below the summit; class 3 and 4 (est. 2 hours roped climbing). Climbing reported as solid and enjoyable.

AGNES MOUNTAIN 8115′/2473 m

Agnes is an immense Matterhorn-shaped massif, rising from a base of 2200 ft at Yew Creek on the NE and 2400 ft on the West Fork of Agnes Creek. The shortest flank is on the W, yet this rises steeply from 5400 ft. There is a steep, uneven spur extending NNW, and a main ridge trending S with sub-summits. At ⅝ mi. S of the summit there is a 7458-ft point; here the ridge runs SW toward the pass at the head of Icy Creek. Being in the lee of higher summits, Agnes has no glaciers, but there is an ice finger at the head of Yew Creek.

Agnes was named on the Henry H. Pierce Army expedition of 1882, but not shown on Forest Service maps until 1922. Asa Post explored the mountain in 1909, when he climbed *Mt. Asa* (7060′/2152 m), a sister peak of Agnes, while working on the Agnes Creek trail. Agnes was first climbed by W. Ronald Frazier and Dan O'Brien in summer, 1936; they made the climb from the West Fork valley and reached the summit late, so made a bivouac on the descent. Later they wrote that Agnes "stands up like a forgotten tooth." (*Mazama* 18, no. 12 (1936): 58). On August 4 of that year George Freed and Erick Larson attempted the mountain, but a leg injury prevented the climb's completion. Agnes is seldom climbed, and all approaches are rugged (only four ascents made through 1972). In August 1947 Lawrence E. Nielsen and Austin Post hiked via the Yew-Spruce ridge, and Asa ridge continuation, to cross the rugged pass (6960′+) between Asa and Agnes, to reach the Dome Peak area—un-

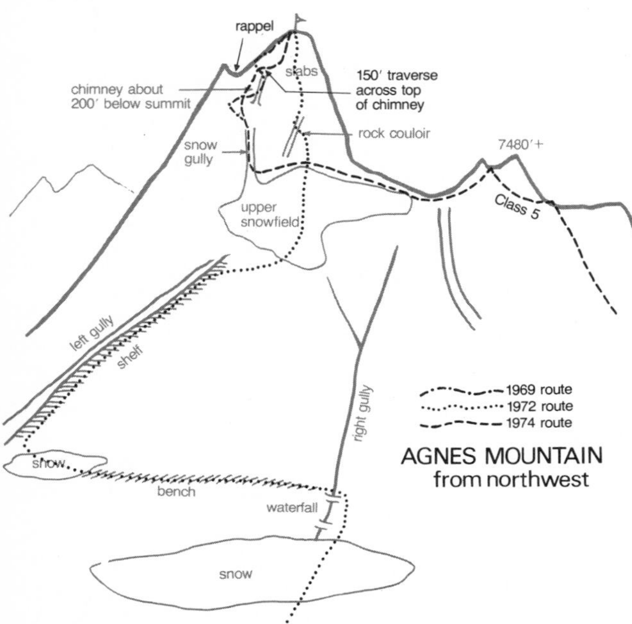

doubtedly the first to use this exploration and approach. Reference: *Appalachia* 29, no. 115 (1952): 213 (photo opp. p. 212).

NORTHEAST ROUTE: This is the route of the first ascent. Leave West Fork Agnes Creek trail (see Agnes Creek Trail♦) just beyond Yew Creek. Ascend SSW up the forest slope, then up an "endless" series of shelving cliffs. Keep E of the NNW arete (which has a minor peak at about 7200′). Ascend a long snow gully close under this peak and arete. At the base of the upper NE face, bear right on an oblique snow finger to the notch at about 8000 ft. The final pitch is steep, with 100 ft of vertical cliff in the ridge center; the summit formation is very thin at the top. Class 4.

SOUTH ROUTE: For approach see Agnes Creek Trail♦—Icy Creek Route. This is a long climbing and traverse route, beginning at the Icy-Spruce Creek Pass (6720′+); the ending is on the NW face of the summit tower. First ascent by Cal Magnusson, Joyce Magnusson, Phil Stern, Gordon Thomas, and Roe (Duke) Watson on July 31, 1969 (second ascent of Agnes).

Follow the ridge crest ⅜ mi. E to the next saddle (6760′+), then make a long climbing traverse (scree and broken rock and gullies) on the W flank of the ridge. Reach the crest again at a small saddle on the highest part of the ridge point S of Agnes (some class 5 climbing involved getting around this point). Make a talus descent of 200 ft to the last saddle (7480′+), then traverse the upper edge of the large W snowfield. Scramble up easy rock on the left of a snow-filled gully (which bears NE) to a wide chimney about 15 ft high (at gully head). Its top is flared and overhangs; climb out on the left face near its top (class 5.7—one piton used). Above, climbing becomes easier; scramble up a shallow gully on loose rock to the summit. Time: 8 hour round trip from first saddle. Reference: *Mountaineer,* 1969, p. 91. Note: a long rappel makes the best chimney descent.

Variation: By Betty Felton, Jon Hall, Frank King, Joan Williams Lennox, Monty Lennox, and Norman Winn in August 1974. The approach was via a nearly-level traverse from the Icy-Spruce Pass; then up a gully to the upper W snowfield. Ascend a loose gully, angle left, and ascend about 150 ft to reach steep rock. A hard 50-ft pitch is done about 100 ft beneath the summit. A 150-ft travese is then made across the top of the chimney, then a slab face. Class 4-5.

Note: the approach to Agnes from the Icy-Spruce Pass is complex and lengthy, and difficult to connect with routes. It is better to begin on Icy Creek to the shelving-ledge route on the W flank.

WEST FACE. First ascent by Greg Ball and Bill Fryberger on August 12, 1972. Begin from Icy Creek about beneath the summit (est. 5200′). The route ascends cliffs between two waterfall streams. Leave the lower snowfields just right of a waterfall at the base of the right-hand gully. Then cross over on an easy bench to the edge of the left gully. Scrambling up and slightly right leads to the base of the upper W snowfield (est. 7200′). Then ascend snow and enter an obvious rock couloir at the top (class 3). Several hundred ft of climbing is done in the couloir; then bear left up well broken but sometimes loose rock to the summit (class 4). Time: 3 hours from lower snowfield.

DOME PEAK 8920′+/2719 m

Dome is a massive Gothic structure, chiseled from a granitic intrusion, the result of weathering and ice erosion. The magnitude of glacier action of the ages is evident, and even a short distance beyond the margin of the Chickamin Glacier are fresh, bouldery unstable moraines indicative of greater ice volume in the recent past. This magnificent fortress of glaciers and monolithic rock forms the centerpiece of the Cascade crest region N of Glacier Peak. Dome has two main summits separated by a narrow crest with Dome Glacier on the NW and a long rock face on the SE. These two summits, the higher Northeast Peak and the slightly lower Southwest Peak, divide the Chickamin from the Dome Glacier, while a series of jagged crags extend 1.1 mi. NW (dividing the Dana and Chickamin Glaciers) to Elephant Head, the prominent ice-sculptured bastion which has great cliffs plunging into the cirque of Agnes Creek's W fork.

The S and SE face of Dome is a formidable recessed wall, a complex facade; at about 7400 ft a master joint forms a large slanting ramp which bisects the main face from the upper wall of the Southwest Peak. E of this ramp the face continues to the Dome-Sinister col. The upper part of the complex Southwest Peak is a steep SE-facing wall, while the narrow, serrated W arete features a cannonhole of about 10 x 20 ft—perhaps the largest such phenomenon in the Cascade Range. Dome's rock is quartz diorite of Miocene Cloudy Pass batholith. Northward and westward from this batholith there is a sequence of gneisses, following the structural trend of the metamorphic-plutonic terrain, continuing to the Skagit River. These rocks vary from pre-Jurassic through Tertiary in age. Various metamorphic and sedimentary formations which abut against the southern, eastern, and western contact of the batholith are in obvious contrast with the light grey tone of the Dome intrusive.

In 1910 summer outing members of The Mountaineers viewed Dome and discussed climbing possibilities, but not until 1921 did an outing list the peak as a potential ascent, which in the field seemed unfeasible because of distance. Explorations in the early 1930s by Hermann Ulrichs and the Farrs again stimulated interest. In May 1935, and again in July, Forest Farr and Norval Grigg attempted to reach Dome; on the latter trip, which was largely spent under a tree in the rain, they climbed to about 8500 ft, where fresh snow on the rock forced a retreat. In 1936 they organized a new party including Don Blair and Bob Hayes, then did the entire climb from Sulphur Creek to the summit of the Southwest Peak on July 5 (Blair, Farr, Grigg). Following snow to the summit structure, they donned tennis shoes to climb the cracks and slabs of the final several hundred ft; the route led through a notch to reach above the glacier on the N, then a chimney near the top corkscrewed nearly to the summit. The party lacked time to continue to the Northeast Peak, of "about the same height." Their priority was vigorously contested by George Freed and Erick Larson, who first climbed the other peak on August 1, and felt it definitely higher. An editorial comment later indicated both parties believed their respective summit higher. Both peaks were climbed again by the Ptarmigan traverse party (first summit traverse) on July 21, 1938.[65] References: *Mountaineer,* 1936, pp. 16-18; 1949, pp. 18-19; 1964, p. 21; 1967, pp. 26-28; *Mazama* 52, no. 13 (1970): 90.

There are four distinct approaches to Dome Peak: Downey Creek Trail♦—Bachelor Creek Route; Agnes Creek Trail♦—West Fork Route; Canyon Lake Trail♦—Chickamin Glacier Route; and Sulphur Creek Trail♦. Some climbs are made during the Ptarmigan Traverse, or some version of same (see Cascade Pass Trail♦).

NORTHEAST PEAK

DOME GLACIER ROUTE: From a camp S of Spire Point (Itswoot Ridge) traverse easily SE under the Spire-Dome ridge to Dome Glacier. Ascend easily to the high col (8560′+) just N of the summit. Follow the snow ridge 300 ft and then climb a rock arete for 500 linear ft to the summit (arete may be snow-covered); class 3. The summit is a curiously perched boulder, seemingly placed by a playful deity. Time: 6 hours from Cub Lake.

Summit Traverse: The rock is excellent: this is a sharp exposed ridge containing several small gendarmes. The traverse can be made in either direction; mostly a ridge scramble—keep close to the crest on the S side (class 4—1 to 2 hours).

CHICKAMIN GLACIER ROUTE: First ascent by original party (11 hours West Fork Agnes to summit). Approach via the West Fork (see Agnes Creek Trail♦). Thickets of vine maple and slide alder exist for 2 mi. beyond Icy Creek (allow one day beyond trail's end to the glacier). The original party used a steep ridge to reach the glacier; there is a timbered hillside that can be taken to the E side of the snout. From the N side of the valley it is possible to cross the creek (about 3800′) and then ascend a steep brushy ridge to the slabs and flat terminal moraine area below the glacier (one party made the creek ford above the falls with a rope pendulum). There is good camping at the larch groves E of the snout. Keep on the E glacier lobe to avoid icefalls and reach the flat area (6800′) beneath Gunsight Peak. Bear W and climb through a wide crevassed area, then ascend to the high col.

Approach Variations: The glacier can be approached from Hanging Gardens and the Spruce-Chickamin ridge; the crossing to the glacier can also be made via the Dome-Sinister Peak col (see Sinister Peak).

Other Routes: The route via the S-face ramp may offer a reasonable way, but uncertain if it has been done (Route 2, of 1961 guide). One could reach this ramp from the upper end of Dome's SW ridge. The crossing into Dome Creek basin is steep and may need rappels. The entrance to the gully at 7000 ft is over moderately steep snow and ice; the right-slanting gully-ramp ends between Point 8788 and the summit.

The 1800-ft S face is not as classic as it might seem at first sight, but could yield hard routes. An incomplete ascent was made by Manuel Gonzalez and Bill Sumner after a descent of the E ridge; rock reported as loose (*A.A.J.,* 1971, p. 346).

SOUTHWEST PEAK 8880′+/2707 m

SOUTHWEST ROUTE: First ascent by original party. From camp on Itswoot Ridge or the SW ridge of Dome ascend the S arm of Dome Glacier to the area of the cannonhole, then bear right on a snow finger. Continue by a series of oblique right-bearing ledges to the crest of the W ridge just below the final summit block. The original party may have completed the climb by a chimney on the N face; the 1938 party apparently crossed the W ridge and completed by the upper N face.

DOME PEAK from southwest
AUSTIN POST, U.S. GEOLOGICAL SURVEY

DOME PEAK from northeast
AUSTIN POST, UNIVERSITY of WASHINGTON

col
Tower
East Spire
Elephant Head
CHICKAMIN GLACIER

ELEPHANT HEAD from northwest
PHILIP LEATHERMAN

SOUTH FACE: First ascent by John Holyoke, Warren Spickard, Pete Taft, and Roe (Duke) Watson in August 1957. Reach from Dome Glacier and its southern segment. Cross the glacier and climb to the moat beneath the center of the face (about 650′ below the summit). The route consists of chimney climbing for 450 ft (2 hours). At the head of this system, work left below an overhang. Cracks and slabs (three pitons safety) lead to a crux: this is a tension traverse across a slab. Easier climbing and a 40-ft layback lead to the summit. Reference: *Mountaineer*, 1958, p. 104.

Variation: By Bruno Fanconi, Curt Johnson, and Mickey Schurr in September 1965. This variation is quite continuous—the first two pitches are hardest. Diverge from the original at an alcove about midway (original route went upright in slanting continuation of the gully). Climb left in a difficult overhanging dihedral; reach a large recession in one-half pitch, then climb up and traverse right across a difficult slab to an outside corner. Two pitches complete the climb; class 5.8.

HYDRAMATIC SPIRE 8400′+/2560 m

This is "a large flaky needle" just W of the cannonhole on the arete W of Dome's Southwest Peak (named on 1949 outing). The rock has excellent vertical jointing. First ascent by

Dale Cole, Robert Grant, Erick Karlsson, Michael Hane, and Tom Miller on September 13, 1953.

The route makes a descending traverse across easy ledges on the N face, leading out and right from the cannonhole. Then directly up across a small snowpatch into the groove leading up to the sharp W-ridge notch (short groove is class 5.5). Climb along the ridge to the blank summit block, then shinny to the top. Class 4 except for groove. Reference: *Mountaineer,* 1953, p. 41.

Descent: done in reverse, and also via E ridge by crossing over the cannonhole bridge.

SNOW DOME 8775′/2675 m

This peak is the second summit from the high Dome-Chickamin Glacier col (0.3 mi. distant). The name is for the aesthetic ice dome appearance on the E; on the Dome Glacier flank the summit has the appearance of a rock pyramid. There is a smaller summit closer to the col ("Flattop"—8720′+/2658 m). The first ascent was made on September 14, 1953 by two routes.

WEST ROUTE: By Dale Cole and Michael Hane. Approach by the Dome Glacier. Climb a slanting ledge system on the S and SW side; the route is largely a long diagonal trough, right to left, and is easier than it appears.

EAST ROUTE: By Robert Grant and Erick Karlsson. The route is from the Chickamin Glacier; a substantial descent is made from the col to reach the prominent snow/ice finger leading up on the E side of the summit. Fairly steep and difficult snow and ice is climbed on the arete to the summit (last 100 ft is 55°). A possible alternative is to bear left to rock (class 4) at 200 ft below the summit.

OVERDRIVE TOWER 8560′+/2609 m

Located closely NW of Snow Dome. First ascent by Dale Cole, Robert Grant, Michael Hane, and Erick Karlsson on September 14, 1953. The route is on the SW—a short rock scramble. Reach from Dome Glacier.

DYNAFLOW TOWER 8080′+/2463 m

This is the thin tooth in the ridge trending toward Dana Glacier, SW of Overdrive Tower. First ascent on August 8, 1947 by Vic Josendal, Tom Miller, Earl Mossberg, Walt Reed, Ray Rigg, and Dick Safely. Reach from the Dome Glacier side. Two routes done: NE ridge by Miller and Safely; SE face via a gully series by rest of party. Both routes are moderate scrambles (class 4).

ELEPHANT HEAD 7990′/2435 m

This glacially rounded endpiece of the Dome Peak massif, between Dana and Chickamin Glaciers, is similar to many such horn shapes in the British Columbia and Alaska Coast Ranges. First ascent by Dick Pratt and Tom Simpkin on July 22, 1958. The route was done by a girdle traverse beginning from the eastern head of Dana Glacier. Cross the ridge col S of Elephant Head, then traverse near the upper edge of the Chickamin, and climb up the edge of the bergschrund to the highest point. Cross the schrund and climb the SE face of the summit horn (steep class 3-4 scramble).

SOUTH FACE: By Fred Beckey, Phil Leatherman, Greg Markov, and Thom Nephew in September 1972. Climb a class 5 slab from the glacier edge, then a gully to the notch at the edge of the Chickamin Glacier. Then climb the S face to the summit (class 4). Reference: *Mountaineer,* 1972, p. 78.

SPIRE POINT 8264′/2519 m

Spire Point is the sharp culmination of the junction of complex ridges, quarried to craggy remnants, between Downey Creek, Sulphur Creek, and the Dana Glacier. The long W ridge, with several secondary summits, is over 1½ mi. long. The NE ridge extends to the Northeast Peak, then continues N nearly to White Rock Lakes. There is a rugged alpine E ridge which forms a wedge between Dana Glacier and Spire Creek (extends 0.8 mi. to a saddle—its high point is 8120′+). The highest summit of Spire is at the junction of the E, N, and W ridges.

Spire Col is the low point on the ridge SE of Spire (at crossing to Dana Glacier). Spire Point is split down the middle by the contact between granite and gneiss; rock is partly gneiss (migmatic complex) and partly an intrusion of the Cloudy Pass pluton (the intrusive contact is at the high col between the Main and West Peaks). The Spire Glacier occupies the wide NW cirque, beneath the impressive NW face; there is a striking lateral moraine beneath the ice. The "West Spire" glacier is a smaller body of ice SW of the peak. Spire Lake is a rock-ringed lake 1.2 mi. W of the main peak.

Spire Peak (not Point) was first shown on the 1922 Forest Service maps (prior to Dome Peak). The first ascent was made on May 29, 1938 by O. Philip Dickert, Dave Lind, and George MacGowan (a scouting trek in 1937 was made by Dickert and Jack Hossack); second ascent by Ptarmigan traverse party on July 21, 1938. Perhaps alone Spire is not of sufficient climbing appeal, but in combination with Dome Peak it makes for a rewarding project. References: *Mountaineer,* 1938, pp. 27-28; 1953, p. 41; 1964, p. 21; 1967, p. 28; *Mazama* 52, no. 13 (1970): 89.

NORTHEAST ROUTE: This is basically the completion of the route used by the original party, who apparently made an eastward traversing approach from the W col below the S face to the E side (via a SE notch), finding various problems that can be avoided by a direct approach. Reach the peak via Cub Lake (Downey Creek Trail♦—Bachelor Creek Route) and ascend to Itswoot Ridge (camping). The approach is then easily done across Spire Col (7760′+) to the Dana Glacier. From the snow col at the head of the glacier make a long easy climbing traverse (wide ledge) on jointed slabs, then a short lead (class 5.2-5.3) which is mainly a 60-ft section in a trough. A 50-ft scramble (over a few large blocks) leads to

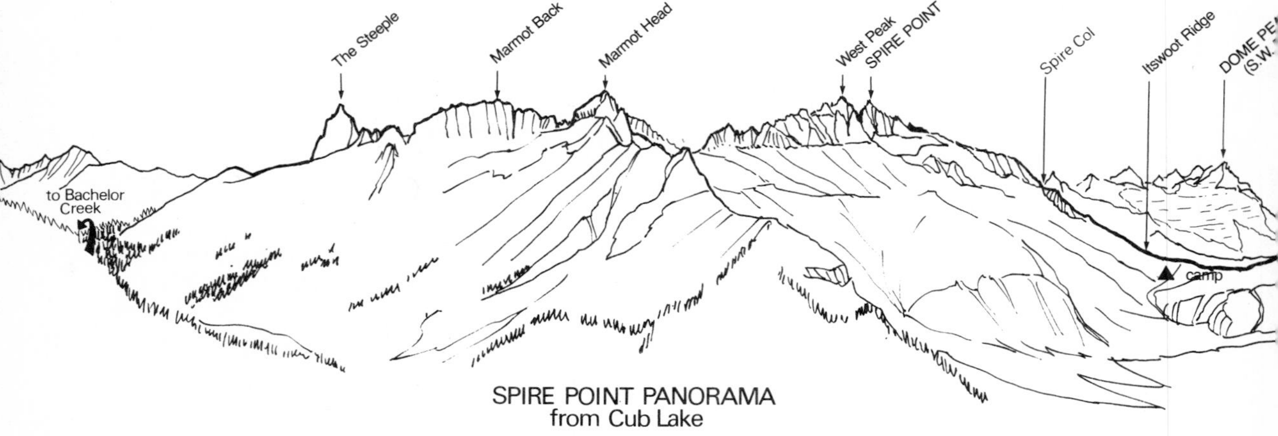

SPIRE POINT PANORAMA
from Cub Lake

the summit. Time: ½ hour from snow, or 4 hours from Itswoot Ridge.

SOUTH FACE: This 400-ft face is good rock; the ascent was done in five pitches. First ascent by Dick Benedict and Paul Karkiainen on September 14, 1967. From snow at the base begin with a low-angle rock skirt. A chimney is climbed W of the main base. The route continues on face and broken slabs (generally middle class 5 except for an easier portion near mid-upper face). Class 5.6. Reference: *A.A.J.*, 1968, p. 138.

WEST RIDGE: First ascent by Fred Beckey, Robert W. Craig, and Will F. Thompson on June 25, 1940. The climb was done from the E at 300 ft beneath the summit by a route that halfway circled the peak. A knife edge was crossed and traversed to a parallel ridge on the W side (hard finger traverse, one piton for safety). A 100-ft pitch was done on solid rock—this featured a strenuous traverse and a chevâl.

Variation: The route can be reached from the glacier S of the W col (directly from Itswoot Ridge); the route is basically several hundred ft of steep but well-broken rock (class 4).

WEST RIDGE AND NORTHWEST FACE: First ascent by Pat Cummings and Tom Miller on July 6, 1952. This climb began at the W col, then followed the ridge about halfway before bearing left onto the face. Class 4.

WEST PEAK 8120′+/2475 m

This summit is .015 mi. W of the Main Peak. The first ascent is unknown, but is certain to have been made long ago from the Main-West Peak col.

SOUTHWEST CORNER: By Brad Bradley, Doug Bradley, James Lucke, Larry Sandstrom, and Russ Maynard on August 19, 1970. From Itswoot Ridge the route kept left of the ridge towers and bore to the moraine and main col. An obvious gully on the SW face leads to a sharp small notch just W of the summit; class 5.

NORTHEAST PEAK 8120′+/2475 m

A cluster of three pinnacles 0.2 mi. NE of the Main Peak; the highest pinnacle is the slim center one, which tilts N. There is a steep wall on the W, above Spire Glacier. Climbing history unknown.

THE TENINO TOWER 7720′+/2353 m

A nunatak rising out of Dana Glacier 0.3 mi. NE of Spire's Main Peak, just downslope from the Northeast Peak. First ascent by Greg Ball and Bill Fryberger in August 1972. This two-pitch climb begins on the S face (class 4) and works to the E (final part is class 5).

MARMOT HEAD 7665′/2336 m

This summit is 0.7 mi. W of Spire's Main Peak (at lower SW corner of Spire Glacier). It has been described as a "giant rock monolith which resembled a giant marmot" (*Mazama* 52, no. 13 (1970): 90-91). The first ascent, in 1962, was made from Marmot Back (NW and W route).

SOUTHEAST FACE: By Doug Bradley, Harold Deery, John V.A.F. Neal, Vinita Neal, Larry Sandstrom, and Joe Throop on August 20, 1970. Most of the route follows a gully-chimney with a few chockstones (some class 4), with a beginning on the "West Spire" glacier. Higher, break out of the gully and bear left (slabs—a class 4 pitch to summit ridge). A scramble is made along a sharp exposed ridge to the summit (one class 4 pitch on this section).

MARMOT BACK 7560′+/2304 m

This rock formation is 0.2 mi. WNW of Marmot Head (has been described as "a rocky pile"). The first ascent is unknown; the route appears most feasible from the flat vale near the head of Bachelor Creek, then up the center (slight grassy depression) from the alp slope.

SPIRE POINT from north
AUSTIN POST, U.S. GEOLOGICAL SURVEY

N.E. Peak
FORTRESS MTN.
SPIRE
POINT
West Pk.
Pk. 7021
Bath Lake Peaks
SPIRE
GLACIER

N.E. Spire Point
SENTINEL PK.
OLD GUARD
Pt. 7940

GERMAN HELMET from north-northwest
DWIGHT WATSON

THE STEEPLE 6960′+/2121 m

The first ascent of this heather-toned rock steeple NW of Spire Lake (on the same ridge as Marmot Head and Marmot Back) was made in 1962 by an unknown party. From Bachelor Creek climb from Mule Lake upslope to Spire Lake, then up on the SE slope to the summit. The route (uphill side from the notch) is rocky, but more feasible than the first impression (class 3 or 4). Reference: *Mazama* 52, no. 13 (1970): 91.

PILOT PEAK 7088′/2160 m

Pilot Peak is the unofficial name for the high point on the Downey-Sulphur Creek ridge 1 mi. E of Downey Lake (4.9 mi. from the Downey-Suiattle River junction). A possible first ascent was made in August 1970 by Gordon Fulks, Frank Head, and Jim Lucke. References: *Mazama* 52, no. 13 (1970): 91; *101 Hikes.*

ROUTES: The 1970 party approached from Cub Lake Pass and Talapus Pass and climbed the E ridge. A slanting tricky chimney (class 4) was climbed on the N face to the ridge; the approach and remainder of the climb are not difficult.

From Downey Lake (see Downey Creek Trail♦—Downey Mountain Way Trail) ascend S to the pass at the ridge crest (5960′+). Then simply follow the crest easily NE to the summit—about 1¼ mi.

VIEW NORTHEAST from SPIRE POINT
TOM MILLER

HEATHER SPIRE 6556′/1998 m

This is the high ridge point 0.8 mi. E of Pilot Peak, and 1.3 mi. SW of Cub Lake. A known climb was my a Mazama party led by Ed Engel on August 20, 1970. From Cub Lake Pass follow near the ridge crest, past Talapus Pass, and on to the summit (hiking). Reference: *Mazama* 52, no. 13 (1970): 90-91.

GERMAN HELMET (White Rock Thumb) 7510′/2289 m

The source of the name is the shape of the termination of the ridge N of Spire Point, ½ mi. W of White Rock Lakes. First ascent by John Chichester, Ned Gulbran, and Mike Kennedy in July 1959. Make the approach from White Rock Lakes, via the snow shoulder on the E. The climb is made via the N ridge, or its E flank, and follows a crack system; rock is solid. The climb was done originally in four pitches of 60 ft (class 5.5—some jamming).

THE LIZARD (Lizard Mountain) 7400′+/2256 m

This small two-summited peak is at the SE head of South Cascade Glacier (.075 mi. from Sentinel Peak).

The Lizard is distinguished from the N by W-dipping bedding which makes a form that probably inspired the name. The ascent is often made in connection with the Ptarmigan traverse. It is uncertain who made the first ascent. The route is quite easy via the W slope from the pass (est. 6800′) at the glacier head.

PEAK 7340 7340′/2237 m

A pointed rock summit on the South Cascade Glacier rim 0.8 mi. W of The Lizard and NW of White Rock Lakes. The peak has a moderately steep ice apron reaching virtually to the summit on the N; the S side slopes gently to White Rock Lakes and the W side flanks Downey Creek.

HOCH JOCH SPITZ 7360′+/2243 m

This summit is W of the South Cascade Glacier, 1½ mi. W of Sentinel Peak. An arm of an unnamed glacier rises prettily to the summit on the north. The cross-country route to Downey Creek crosses the notch NW of Hoch Joch.

ROUTE: From South Cascade Glacier ascend the long firn slope westward on the E of the peak. Cross the snow saddle, then bear SW up firn for a very short class 3 scramble at the top.

POST PEAK 7188′/2191 m

A knob-shaped summit, nearly a nunatak, rises NE of Hoch Joch Spitz and ¾ mi. S of South Cascade Lake. The summit is an easy trip and affords a good view. From the snow saddle (see above) ascend the easy W side for a short rock scramble.

SENTINEL PEAK 8261′/2518 m

Sentinel is a prominent peak of this section located on the Cascade divide between Flat, South Cascade, and West Fork Agnes Creeks. The extensive Le Conte Glacier reaches to within 200 ft of the summit on the N; here a bergschrund and ice slope continue to the summit knob. The first ascent was made by Ronald Frazier, Dennison Lawrence, and Dan O'Brien in August, 1935, the day after the ascent of Old Guard, from the Le Conte Glacier. They found "millions" of lady bugs on the summit. On descending the SE arm of the glacier, Lawrence slipped and was saved by O'Brien's diving tackle just before he reached a waterfall cliff. With serious injuries the party got him out in two days, with the help of a trail crew, to where a horse could carry him. The next ascent was made by the Ptarmigan traverse party on July 23, 1938, via what is now the normal route. References: *Mazama* 18, no. 12 (1936): 58-59; *Mazama* 39, no. 13 (1957): 35; *Mountaineer,* 1964, p. 16

SOUTHWEST ROUTE: From the upper portion of South Cascade Glacier (see Ptarmigan Traverse) ascend to the SW slope of Sentinel. The climb is an easy scramble on this slope (snow and easy rock); the route basically ascends, then makes a left traverse, then up again to the top at the W end of the massif. Some parties drop packs on the traverse of Sentinel's W side, then make the climb before continuing.

SOUTHEAST ROUTE: Taken by the original party. Use the same route as for Old Guard to Le Conte Glacier (via West Fork Agnes). On the original climb a bergschrund and an ice bridge led onto the rock; the final climb is not difficult. Crampons should be taken. An approach appears possible from a brushy start in the West Fork Agnes valley, via the long snow gully SE of the peak (from stream fork about ½ mi. beyond Icy Creek); the route would lead directly to rock on the upper S side.

OLD GUARD PEAK 8240′+/2512 m

The eastern summit of the Sentinel Peak massif, .025 mi. E of Sentinel, is very nearly as high as the latter. The Le Conte Glacier reaches to high on the peak's N flank; a SE branch of the glacier descends in a tongue to 7400 ft. There are extensive sections of the glacier NE of Old Guard at the head of Rimrock Ridge. Ronald Frazier, Dennison Lawrence, and Dan O'Brien made the first ascent in August 1935 (via the SE arm of Le Conte Glacier and a rough approach from the valley of West Fork Agnes Creek) and named the peak. Reference: *Mazama* 18, no. 12 (1936): 58-59.

WEST ROUTE: From the upper Le Conte Glacier (can be reached from South Cascade Glacier by crossing the glacier pass N of Sentinel Peak) climb a snow gully and make a rock scramble of about 300 ft to the summit (the final ascent begins from near the Sentinel col). The original party completed the ascent from the W, but approached from the SE. This is a very brushy ascent that climbs cliffs from West Fork Agnes Creek alongside waterfalls (some roped climbing here); a steep valley slope is taken to the SE arm of Le Conte Glacier. The route follows on to the main portion of the glacier.

EAST RIDGE: First ascent by M. Chessler, W. Espenlaub, R. Smith, and Donald M. Wallace in August 1970. The short rock route begins from the glacier; two pitches from the firn—class 5.4.

SOUTH FACE: First ascent by Dale Cole, Michael Hane, and Robert Grant in 1953. The approach is made via Sentinel's summit: descend 200 ft of class 3 rock, rappel into the schrund, then cross the glacier to Old Guard. There are 250 ft of class 3 rock on an open face.

SEVEN SISTERS 7203′/2195 m

The peaks form a high ridge spanning over 3 mi., in a tortuous pattern forming the Flat-West Fork Agnes-Junction Creek divide; the highest peak, 5 mi. NE of Sentinel Peak, is near the center of the group, and has a short steep N face. There is a summit of about 7100 ft just to the E; then the ridge turns N to a higher sum-

SOUTH CASCADE GLACIER
AUSTIN POST, U.S. GEOLOGICAL SURVEY

SENTINEL PK.
SINISTER PK.
The Lizard
LE CONTE GLACIER
PK. 7340
POST PK.
to Downey Creek
SOUTH CASCADE GLACIER
early season route
South Cascade Lake

SENTINEL PK.
OLD GUARD PK.
LE CONTE
S.E.
Ridge
Pt. 7456
LE CONTE
GLACIER
Le Conte
Flat Creek
Yang Yang
Lakes

mit (Big Sister). Climbing history is unknown, but the summits appear to offer no difficulties if one hikes along the crests.

BIG SISTER 7160′+/2182 m

This is the second highest summit on the ridge, at the NW head of Junction Creek. First ascent by Rowland W. Tabor in 1960. Approach via Junction Mountain Trail (see Agnes Creek Trail♦). Follow the trail over the summit of Junction Mountain, then descend to the saddle W (camping). The ridge W to Seven Sisters has many pinnacles (pass on steep and loose S face). One-third the distance up this ridge a steep 200-ft snow gully leads down to talus slopes (camping) at the head of Junction Creek. An alternative is to continue on the ridge and cross a 7000-ft shoulder into the high basin above South Fork Flat Creek. To reach Big Sister continue northward along the ridge; pass over or around Point 6809 on its W. The S side of Big Sister is mostly steep rubble and brush. Time: 12 hours from Agnes Creek.

TOLO MOUNTAIN 6931′/2113 m

Between Tolo Creek, Junction Creek, and 2.2 mi. S of Stehekin River; first ascent unknown.

SOUTHWEST RIDGE: From the base camp for Big Sister (about 6600′) cross over Seven Sisters ridge to the basin (6000′) at the head of Junction Creek. Traverse eastward to reach a flat saddle (5800′+) at the head of Tolo Creek. Ascend the SW ridge to the summit; time: 2½ hours camp to summit.

NORTH RIDGE: First ascent by Rowland W. Tabor in 1960. From the Stehekin River Road♦ just W of Bridge Creek gorge drop down to cross the river on a log jam. The ridge is long and cliffy; the descent route should be well noted. At about 4900 ft, where the ridge levels to a flat shoulder below cliffs, traverse and climb southward on talus slopes forming a lineament along a fault; avoid brush by staying high, close to the cliffs. At a second shoulder overlooking Arrow Creek, ascend directly up steep heather and brush to regain the N ridge (at 6400′) and continue over easy terrain to the summit. Time: 12 hours from road.

RIMROCK RIDGE 7240′+/2207 m

Rimrock Ridge is a high area, generally above 6500 ft, with a zigzagging ground outline. The ridge divides Flat and West Fork Agnes Creeks, and logically extends from Old Guard for some 5 mi. NE. The highest point is 3.2 mi. NE of Sentinel Peak; there is a NE point (7080′+/2158 m), and a summit to the SW (7100′+/2164 m).

Climbing history is incomplete, but it is known Dwight Watson, in summer 1936, hiked along the ridge nearly to Le Conte Lake, but made no ascents. The ascent was E of Hellebore Creek (brushy beginning from West Fork Agnes), then followed easy open slopes on the ridge; the descent was via a high narrow canyon to Rimrock Creek. Watson learned that Nels Bruseth of the Forest Service, during trail surveys, referred to the ridge as "Rock Canyon Mountains," but it is uncertain what exploration he and surveyors did here.

LE CONTE MOUNTAIN 7762′/2366 m

The mountain is a 2-mi.-long NW-trending ridge, the center of intense alpine glaciation, scoured by both the Le Conte and South Cascade glaciers. There are a rugged and prominent S summit (7612′/2320 m), and a middle summit (7456′/2273 m). The mountain is named for the Sierra Nevada geologist Joseph Le Conte. First ascent by Calder T. Bressler, Ralph W. Clough, Bill Cox, and Tom Myers on July 23, 1938. References: *Mountaineer,* 1953, p. 40; 1964, p. 16; *Mazama* 20, no. 13 (1958): 20-21.

ROUTE: For approach see Cascade Pass Trail♦—Ptarmigan Traverse. From Yang Yang Lakes cross the forested ridge high, make a traverse (talus) and cross slide; then bear up path to the ridge near Le Conte Pass. Ascend snow patches to the shoulder SE, then ascend snow to its head on the NE spur of the summit. Climb gradually left to right to a wide ledge; this is followed W (shelves) to the ridge notch 150 ft SW of the summit. Time: 1½ hours from meadow at 6600 ft.

SOUTHEAST RIDGE: First ascent by Dale Cole, Robert Grant, Michael Hane, Erick Karlsson, and Tom Miller on September 9, 1953. This route is reached from the Le Conte Glacier. From firn on the E slope a snow finger (0.3 mi. SE of the summit) leads to the ridge notch; from notch follow the ridge to the summit (class 3). Time: 1 hour from snow.

Note: variations have been done, including an approach to the same ridge notch from the opposite flank. Various gully routes from the South Cascade Glacier have been done to the summit (history unknown); rock tends to be loose on the W flank.

THE DONJON 7200′/2195 m

A curious tower on the S ridge of Le Conte's middle peak—just S of the first deep notch, 0.2 mi. from the middle peak. First ascent by Bob Sprenger and Jim Stuart in July 1964. From South Cascade Glacier bear N and up on slabs to the N notch; from a belay above, climb 100 ft of easy class 5. The descent was made via the E side of the notch.

SPIDER MOUNTAIN 8280′+/2526 m (est. 8300′/2530 m)

Spider is on the main divide between Flat Creek and Middle Fork Cascade River, 4.1 mi. SSE of Cascade Pass. Spider is a large massif, with a very alpine northern flank, containing Spider Glacier, rising steeply above the deep cirque of Flat Creek's W fork. The long SE slopes have a 5000-ft relief from Flat Creek, and

SENTINEL PEAK from north
LEE MANN

MT. FORMIDABLE and SPIDER MOUNTAIN from south
AUSTIN POST, UNIVERSITY of WASHINGTON

the NW ridge of Spider separates Spider Glacier from the Middle Cascade Glacier. The narrow summit crest has several high points; the one nearly central is highest (the E point with a triangulation mark 8286′ is lower). Very reddish rock (E-dipping schists) dirties snowfields and glacier ice on the mountain, which has a reputation for loose rock. The Ptarmigan climbing club group which climbed Spider, Formidable, and Magic all in one day termed the mountain "crumbly arkosic sandstone" and felt there was a distinct danger while climbing. Spider has few great characteristics as a climb, but the setting is in the core of the North Cascade heartland, and its "spidery" steep snow on the N face inspired early mountaineering comment. Uniquely, there has been sufficient rock disintegration at the summit to allow a few miniature flowers, including hulsea algida, timberline phacelia, and moss campion. First ascent by Calder T. Bressler, Ralph W. Clough, Bill Cox, and Tom Myers on July 25, 1938 (from S or SE). Spider had been attempted by Forest Farr and Art Winder on August 4, 1936 via the W ridge, but they were halted at a gendarme, then frustrated by loose rock on the S face. On a climbing outing in 1947 an attempt via the W or NW ridge turned back because of loose rock, yet the second ascent party in 1953 found the correct route on Spider and climbed it in 2 hours from camp over easy scree and rock on the SE slope. References: *Mountaineer,* 1936, p. 12; 1947, p. 46; 1953, p. 40; 1957, pp. 39-40; 1964, p. 15.

SOUTHEAST ROUTE: Probable first ascent by Dale Cole, Erick Karlsson, and Tom Miller on September 8, 1953. There is a possible camp at a heather knob (est. 6400′) S of the Spider-Formidable Col (see Cascade Pass Trail♦—Ptarmigan Traverse). From 500 ft S and beneath the col traverse about ⅓ mi. E under southern cliffs to an easy scree or snow slope. Ascend either of two gravel gullies (possible snow) and some poor rock and dirt to reach the summit ridge near its E end. An easy ridge traverse (loose rock) leads to the center and highest summit.

NORTHWEST RIDGE: This is an easy but potentially dangerous scramble over quite loose rock; on the ridge there is little rockfall danger. From Spider-Formidable Col cross the glacier to the NW ridge (or ascend glacier from a NW approach). Follow the ridge to the W summit, and then continue on. Class 4; time: 3 hours.

Note: a variation using the W ridge from the col would join the NW ridge about midway to the summit; it is uncertain if this variation has been completed.

NORTH FACE (Route 1): First ascent by Dallas Kloke and Reed Tindall on July 21, 1972. From Kool-Aid Lake cross at the saddle between S Mountain and Art's Knoll, then descend and traverse to Spider Glacier. Ascend the glacier to the bergschrund beneath the large obvious hook-shaped snow (firn) finger. A short rock pitch (class 4 or 5) is climbed here.

SPIDER MOUNTAIN, North Face
BOB AND IRA SPRING

Make 11 leads on the 40-45° finger to the summit. Time: 6 hours from Cache Col. Reference: *Mountaineer,* 1972, p. 79.

NORTH FACE (Route 2): First ascent by Fred Beckey, Clark Gerhardt, Greg Markov, and John Yaeger on September 21, 1976. The approach is the same as for Route 1; a bivouac was made at a small alp in West Fork Flat Creek's basin. Climb the crevassed eastern portion of the glacier, then bear rightward toward the western of two obvious similar firnfields on the face. A rock pitch (class 5.5) leads from the lower glacier to a snow gully; the latter and an adjacent rock rib is climbed, then the long, moderately steep firnfield. The route ends near the cornice W of the E summit; Grade II or III. Reference: *A.A.J.*, 1977.

East Ridge
North Ridge
reach ridge
pinnacle
behind
FORMIDABLE GLACIER
MIDDLE CASCADE GLACIER

MT. FORMIDABLE 8325′/2537 m

While not dominant in the array of magnificent peaks in the span between Dome Peak and Cascade Pass, Formidable is certainly one of the most impressive. Its serrated W-trending ridge crest has dramatic towers (E of the summit) and on the northern flanks the Formidable and Middle Cascade Glaciers are significant strongholds of the Ice Age. Formidable is 3.6 mi. S of Cascade Pass; the rock is a gneiss schist complex cut by soft diabasic dikes which have formed staircase gullies (climbing parties have found the rock sound). Hermann Ulrichs, in 1934 one of the first mountaineers to scrutinize the mountain after the early surveyors, suggested the name because of the rugged northern flank: "Immediately west of the divide, is a grand, unclimbed peak, listed on the map as 8350 feet . . . . I suggest the name 'Mount Formidable' as expressing the quality of the peak".[66] First ascent by Calder T. Bressler, Ralph W. Clough, Bill Cox, and Tom Myers on July 25, 1938, who called the mountain "Daiber." References: *Mountaineer,* 1947, p. 45; 1953, p. 40; 1964, p. 15.

SOUTH ROUTE: For approach see Cascade Pass Trail♦—Ptarmigan Traverse. From Yang Yang Lakes or firn slopes 200 ft below the Spider-Formidable Col traverse to the first main rocky rib (main divide). Ascend this to a prominent notch (est. 7050′), then proceed down an obvious narrow gully to a basin (snow here); from the gully base traverse upward (325° bearing) across or below the second snowfield to the second main rib. Cross the rib (keep below cliff) to the large high snowpatch on the left, and then at its top bear rightward onto rock. Climb easy rock (class 3) to the summit. Time: 4-5 hours from lakes.

Variation: From a lower traverse ascend the second rib to the high snowfield. Contour snow and ribs W. Ascend the third gully to the left (keep altitude until below or past the summit); make the final ascent on the SW.

SOUTHWEST RIDGE: This is the long ridge between Drop and Cleve Creeks. First ascent by Bob Briggs, Kenn Carpenter, Gene Mason, and Bill Myers on July 2, 1961. Take the South Fork Cascade River Trail about 3 mi. past the Middle Fork (see Cascade River Area♦). Just beyond Deliverance Creek ascend ESE, E, and NE along the wooded ridge crest. The original party camped at 6500 ft S of an unnamed lake. Traverse right of the first large tower and climb a 400-ft couloir of steep ice. This gains a narrow notch at about 7300 ft on the W end of the summit ridge; a small glacier is on the opposite flank. Then follow the ridge about ¼ mi. to the summit (class 3 and 4); bring crampons. References: *Mountaineer,* 1962, p. 101; *A.A.J.,* 1962, p. 202.

NORTH RIDGE: First ascent by Franz Mohling and a party of nine Mountaineers on Labor Day weekend, 1957. From Red Ledge on the Ptarmigan traverse, cut obliquely down and reach the Middle Cascade Glacier where it is level. Cross to Formidable Glacier on the E flank of the N face, then ascend icefalls of varying complexity. Bear right, traversing and climbing to reach the N ridge at a prominent notch. Then cross the top of the broad snowfield (est. 7100′) to the W of the ridge and climb another very steep snowfield higher (could be some ice). Then climb the N ridge (sometimes loose; all class 3); the final part is a buttress. Grade II; take crampons and a few ice screws and rock pitons. Time: 7 hours from Kool Aid Lake. Reference: *Mountaineer,* 1958, p. 103.

Approach Variation: By Kenn Carpenter, Tom Williams, and one other, May 31, 1958 (entire ridge from its base). Leave the Middle Fork Cascade River Trail 0.5 mi. E of Cleve Creek (2900′). Cross the stream to reach steep forest on spur between Middle Fork and Cleve Creek; climb along the E side of an avalanche scar to where tree cover comes close to latter. Ascend the avalanche-swept channel of creek (wade and avoid bush). Take the eastern branch, but at 4800 ft climb a steep spur to reach basins at about 6200 ft on the N ridge of Formidable (8 hours); there is good camping on knoll where ridge has a flat basin on W. It is simple to gain the ridge route via basins and a small glacier on the W of the ridge.

NORTHEAST GLACIERS AND EAST RIDGE: From beyond Red Ledge descend from heather and scree slopes to Middle Cascade Glacier. Make a rising glacier traverse and cross hanging glacier section (crevasses) to the prominent N buttress. Gain it near large pinnacle which becomes visible as one crosses behind it. Climb up and right (class 4) until more broken rock on edge of a gully is found; this leads up and left. Reach the top of the buttress where it is capped by a sharp snow ridge (which joins Formidable Glacier). Now climb glacier: two pitches of 40° ice or firn to col.

There are two ways to complete the ascent: (1) Cross to the S flank and contour an exposed ridge system for 300 yds (class 3), then climb easy rock to the E ridge, or traverse onward as per normal route. Do a short tricky step and then climb onto the N face on a rising traverse; reach the summit over broken rock. Class 4 and possibly some class 5; bring crampons and several ice screws. Time: 7 hours. (2) Follow the ridge or near it to the summit the entire distance. The rock is sound high on ridge and on its N flank; class 4. Take a few rock pitons for one exposed lead.

Variation: On Middle Cascade Glacier contour below the buttress and ascend on its W side up the glacier to the col; this is probably only feasible in early season because of crevasse problems.

S MOUNTAIN (Hurry Up) 7800′+/2377 m

This peak is on the Cascade divide between Middle Cascade Glacier and Trapper Lake, WSW of the latter and 0.8 mi. S of Magic Mountain. The SE summit point is highest. The S Glacier (0.6 mi. long) heads on the mountain's NE flank and trends NE toward Trap-

MT. FORMIDABLE from north
PHILIP LEATHERMAN

per Lake; it is an irregular hanging glacier, with avalanche tracks usually in evidence. The original name by which it was known to miners 60 years ago was "S", for the S-shaped glacier configuration. The peak first appeared in climbing history when members of an outing mistook the mountain for Trapper, and later called it "Hurry Up"—a name which has subsequently appeared in publications and on maps. It is recommended that the present whimsical name be omitted and the original descriptive one be retained. First ascent by John Robertson and Joe Vance in August 1947 (from W). References: *Mountaineer,* 1947, p. 45; 1953, p. 39; *Mazama* 32, no. 13 (1950): 37; *Appalachia* 29, no. 115 (1952): 215.

WEST ROUTE: Approach the area of Kool-Aid Lake (see Cascade Pass Trail♦—Ptarmigan Traverse) and ascend NW slope over steep but easy heather and rock; an obvious gully leads to the minor NW summit. Then cross an airy ridge SE to the main summit. Class 2-3. Time: 2 hours from lake. Note: a variation ascends the snowfield nearly to the col between the mountain and Art's Knoll; an obvious heather band traverses N to the NW slope.

S GLACIER: First ascent by Dallas Kloke and Don Turnbull on June 16, 1969. From Pelton Basin (E of Cascade Pass) ascend 1800 ft to the Pelton-Magic col via the Yawning Glacier. Descend 1000 ft to reach the S Glacier at 5600 ft. Ascend easy firn slopes to the schrund (6600′); one can pass this by moderate rock (on right) for 100 ft. Continue up loose rock and steep heather to the upper part of the glacier near the base of the summit area; a short scramble up the S side leads to the top. Class 4. Time: 6 hours from Cascade Pass. Reference: *A.A.J.*, 1971, p. 346.

MAGIC MOUNTAIN 7610′/2320 m

Magic is a modest peak in regional altitude, but very impressive from Cascade Pass, with its conspicuous long, curving NW ridge. The entire NW and N flank of Magic is alpine and steep, quite in contrast to the short SW slope. The Yawning Glacier on the NE face heads between Magic and Pelton Peak. As on nearby peaks rock is gneissic. First ascent by Calder T. Bressler, Ralph W. Clough, Bill Cox, and Tom Myers on July 25, 1938. References: *Mazama* 32, no. 13 (1950): 35; *Mazama* 37, no. 13 (1955): 46-47.

SOUTH RIDGE: From Kool-Aid Lake (see Cascade Pass Trail♦—Ptarmigan Traverse) ascend 1000 ft directly up heather and scree to the saddle (est. 7100′) between Magic and S Mountains. Note: if approaching directly from Cache Col descend 400 ft SE (to below prominent rock rib, then contour E to the cirque SW of Magic), and ascend to the saddle. The first third of the S ridge is an easy heather scramble, then possibly snow travel to the false summit (about 300′ SE of the true summit). Then descend about 80 ft to climb the summit tower on the NE face (class 3); time: 1½ hours from lake, or 5 hours from Cascade Pass.

Variation: Some parties have made a more difficult and circuitous summit completion after descending from the false summit, then traversing the N face at the upper edge of steep, narrow snow bands (runners useful on projections) until beneath the summit (four leads), then ascending rock directly (class 3 and 4).

SOUTHWEST CIRQUE: Approach as for South Ridge route to the cirque SW of the summit. Climb any of numerous heathery gullies at the N or NE head of the cirque to gain the summit ridge (class 3-4). Time: 2-3 hours from Cache Col.

NORTHWEST RIDGE: Approach as for South Ridge; ascend easy slopes SW of Magic to its base, then climb steep rock and finally an easy chimney to a notch NW of the summit. Then traverse and climb the short remaining distance to the summit via the NW face; class 4. Time: 4 hours from Cascade Pass.

Variation: Follow the ridge directly from Cache Col, dropping onto the N flank when necessary to avoid loose rock and minor pinnacles.

NORTH FACE: This is a long face, beginning at about 5400 ft, possibly with some rockfall problems; crampons should be taken. First ascent by Art Holben, Dick Merritt, Keith Rankin, and Herb Staley on August 5, 1946.

From Pelton Basin ascend easy slopes, then a steep couloir and Yawning Glacier to the Magic-Pelton col (6480′+). Bear back and cross the head of the glacier to the N face, then climb 600 ft of steep rock to a notch immediately NW of the summit; class 4. Time: 5 hours from Cascade Pass. Reference: *Mountaineer,* 1946, pp. 17-19.

Variation: The face has been done directly from the cirque of Yawning Glacier—a more direct route.

NORTHEAST COULOIR: Use route to Magic-Pelton col (see North Face). Ascend the glacier to the prominent couloir which splits the SE rock face (may be snow-filled). Climb this via rock or snow directly to the summit (class 3); time: 3 hours.

PELTON PEAK 7120′+/2170 m

Pelton is a subsidiary summit ENE of Magic, 1.8 mi. SE of Cascade Pass. The name is for the Pelton wheel, used locally in mining times. The Yawning Glacier (0.6 mi. long) heads between Pelton and Magic, and drains to Pelton Creek; it is conspicuous for a large cave between ice and rock, the source of its name. First ascent by Lawrence E. Nielsen and Walt Price on August 3, 1948. Reference: *Appalachia* 29, no. 115 (1952): 212.

ROUTES: The original route took an easy ridge scramble from the col (see Magic Mountain, N face). The NE ridge was climbed by Martin Ochsner and Florence Wedell on August 7, 1946.

TRAPPER MOUNTAIN 7530′/2295 m

Trapper is a pyramid-shaped rock peak 0.6 mi. SW of

TRAPPER LAKE AREA
NATIONAL PARK SERVICE

TRAPPER MTN.
S MTN.
MAGIC MTN.
PELTON PK.
MIXUP PK.
col
S
GLACIER
Pt. 5973
Trapper
Lake

MAGIC and MIXUP PEAKS from north
HAROLD A. DEERY

Trapper Lake and 1.4 mi. SE of Magic Mountain; the N face is steepest, but Trapper is moderately steep on all flanks (the N face has a prominent slanting ramp, and above the talus of Trapper Lake a narrow gully leads to the V-notch between Trapper and Trapper Annex. On Trapper's NE face is a portion of the S Glacier, and on the W and SW flank is the Trapper Mountain Glacier. First ascent by George Bell, Andrew Griscom, Harry King, and W.V. Graham Matthews on August 24, 1949 (via Southwest route). Reference: *Appalachia* 27, no. 108 (1949): 503.

SOUTHWEST ROUTE: The approach is from Kool-Aid Lake (see Cascade Pass Trail♦—Ptarmigan Traverse). From the prominent col NW of Art's Knoll (6880′+) descend about 350 ft on a long eastward traverse below the cliffs of S Mountain; one zone of relatively easy scrambling around the steep SE arete of S Mountain via broken rock and rubble to reach steep snow and slabs. This leads to the snow bowl of Trapper Mountain Glacier, S of the main saddle between S and Trapper. Complete the climb via the exposed but easy, heather/rock SW face (class 3). Time: 6 hours.

Approach Variation: From Trapper Lake (see Stehekin River Trail♦) climb the avalanche debris cone W of the lake until an easy ascending traverse to the SE leads to the saddle (6340′+) between Trapper and S Mountains (ascend part of the margin of S Glacier). Descend SE about 300 ft and then contour the cliff base until an obvious break leads up broken ledges and a short chimney. Time: 4 hours from lake.

EAST RIDGE: First ascent by Joan Firey, Joe Firey, John Muelemans, Irene Muelemans, and M. Katherine Tarver in July 1960. From Trapper Lake ascend a narrow steep snow couloir (800′) to the col (6320′+) between Trapper and Trapper Annex. Then climb the face above to the summit (class 4).

Variation: A possible variation along the E ridge was done in May 1968 by Dave Dixon and Dallas Kloke.

TRAPPER ANNEX (East Trapper) 6960′+/2121 m

This is the imposing crag ½ mi. E of Trapper; it appears most easily reached via the steep E ridge from a prominent notch S of Trapper Lake. The steep fault couloir leading to the notch can be ascended directly from the lake (bring crampons). The wooded cliffs on the S flank appear reasonable, but the approach via Flat Creek's W fork is not easy.

GLORY MOUNTAIN 7228′/2203 m

Located 0.8 mi. SE of Trapper Lake and 1.3 mi. S of the Stehekin River, Glory is steep and rocky on the N, but wooded and uninspiring on the S slope. There is a jagged ridge between Trapper and Glory; the best summit here is Halleluja. First ascent by Bill Fix and Richard Whitmore, August 3, 1956. (Northwest Route).

NORTHWEST ROUTE: From the E or S side of Trapper Lake (see Stehekin River Trail♦) climb to the col (6600′+) between the main and W peaks of Glory; keep below 6000 ft when rounding cliffs of the W peak. There are some problem slabs beneath the col; part of the route is up the W edge of a small glacier. Then climb E to the summit (class 3-4). Time: 5 hours.

Note: the traverse from Cascade Pass via Trapper Lake makes a very long day, with elevation gains totaling about 7000 ft; a good training program.

NORTH and EAST ROUTE: First ascent by Rowland Tabor on July 7, 1958. From Trapper Lake ascend diagonally E to the prominent spur, then traverse E at about 5900 ft where easy sloping ledges between cliffs lead to a small glacier on the N slope of Glory. Ascend the galcier eastward to a high saddle (6680′+) E of the summit. Traverse onto the E side and climb 100 ft of steep but easy rock to the gentle S side of the summit (class 3-4). Time: 4 hours.

HALLELUJA PEAK (West Glory) 7120′+/2170 m

Stands ½ mi. SE of Trapper Lake. First ascent by Bob Briggs, Kenn Carpenter, Jim Whitcomb, and Ursula Wiener on October 3, 1965. From the W end of the lake traverse the S side ⅓ mi., then ascend a bushy gully to the saddle between Trapper Annex and Halleluja's ridge. Traverse E 0.8 mi., usually on the crest; no difficulties. References: *Mountaineer,* 1967, pp. 130-131; *A.A.J.,* 1967, p. 352.

MIXUP PEAK 7440′+/2268 m

Mixup is a long, narrow asymmetrical wedge 0.9 mi. S of Cascade Pass, on the W flank of Cache Glacier; the summit is on the S extremity, facing the upper basin of the Middle Fork of Cascade River. Rock is gneissic; the E face is a solid gray-colored staircase. On the S and W there is an extensive glacier-carved alp slope with two shallow cirques; the slope continues NW to Johannesburg Mountain. First ascent by Wesley Grande and Jack Kendrick in August, 1947 (via E face). References: *Mountaineer,* 1947, p. 44 (photo), 46; *A.A.J.,* 1961, p. 365.

EAST FACE: This route appears nearly impossible until one begins climbing; then it turns out to be a wide staircase with considerable route flexibility. There are two class 4 sections, one of 30 ft (the most difficult) out of Gunsight Notch, and the final one 70 ft from the summit ridge; between these the climb is often done unroped.

From Cascade Pass traverse to Gunsight Notch (6600′+)—W of and lower than Cache Col. A moat may undercut the glacier ice. The route can begin about 30 ft past the top of the right-hand notch, but an easier beginning is reported about 100 ft down the side-gully. After 30 ft (class 4) climb up and rightward for several hundred ft on the well broken downslab, then over a shoulder. Continue slightly right (class 3) to the break in the summit ridge; then the final pitch to the ridge. The summit is a short scramble to the S. Time: 4 hours. Descent: place sling on knob at last cliff above the notch.

SOUTHEAST RIDGE: The blocky ridge rising directly to the summit from below Gunsight Notch was first ascended by Fred Ayres, Gale Dick, Dave Pearson, and Pat Pearson on September 2, 1950. The route is slightly complex, and possibly meets the E face route at times. The eastern notch, and bypass the intervening pinnacle. Climb a vertical rock face (class 5); overhangs force the route farther left; there are some down-slope traverses. Finally bear right up a shallow couloir, then emerge onto the broad heather shoulder. An easy stairway becomes a steep face. The gendarme high on the ridge forces a northward traverse for several hundred ft. Turn up toward more climbable rock of a black band (gray steps here); climb between the gray and black border (class 5; steeper), then to the small notch in the knifed ridge 50 ft N of the summit. Class 4 and 5. Reference: *Mazama* 32, no. 13 (1950): 37.

WEST FACE: First ascent by Donald (Claunch) Gordon and Winslow Trueblood on August 2, 1959. The approach was made via the traverse as per reaching Johannesburg. Locating the entrance couloir may be a problem. The rock is somewhat loose (class 4 and 5). Note: the 1950 party found a descent from the summit ridge notch to the W easy except for the upper 50 ft; the route followed a U-shaped trough.

NORTH FACE: First ascent by Art Amot and Dave Beckstead on August 2, 1963. From Cascade Pass ascend S on the alp slope route to Cache Glacier until beneath the N face. Climb directly up until steep rock is met. Here begin at the left of a long snow couloir located on the right side of the face. After crossing a schrund, two leads of class 4 were done, then class 3 to the N summit ridge. While on the ridge, it is necessary to descend and climb occasionally to bypass obstacles (mainly keep on W). Class 3 and 4 (may wish to place some leader protection). Time: 6 hours. Reference: *Mountaineer,* 1964, p. 131.

NORTH RIDGE: First ascent by Rowland W. Tabor and William Stark, Jr. in 1957. From the lower slopes of Cache Glacier climb snow NNW to reach a steep rocky spur overlooking Cascade Pass (N) and the glacier (S). Ascend the spur to within 100 ft of the ridgetop, then traverse southward along the exposed E face of the ridge. The climbing is easy, on ledges and broken slabs. Just before the summit tower, cross the ridge through notches to reach easy scrambling on the W side, or continue to join the normal E face route. Class 4. Time: 4 hours.

Variation: By Dean Caldwell and John V.A.F. Neal in 1962; this may have similar portions as above (uncertain). Ascend the ridge midway to Cache Col; from snow turn S for the middle of a rock rib. Ascend until directly below a wide gully on the face. Ascend snow to the gully, then 120 ft up the latter to a wall. Turn left and ascend a chimney with a

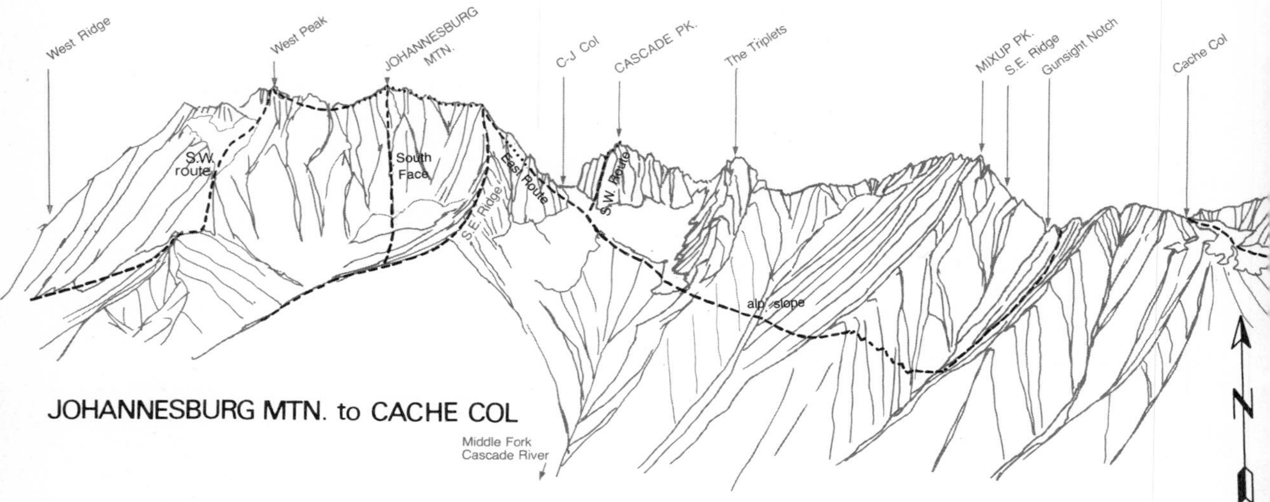

chockstone, then make the high traverse on loose rock and heather patches to solid rock; continue across the face to the N end of the summit tower.

EAST FACE CHIMNEY: First ascent by Larry Baum and Dan Davis on September 11, 1960. Begin up the second large (deep) chimney N of Gunsight Notch; it may have some snow blocks. Possible problem to cross the bergschrund. An easy scramble on loose rock is made up the chimney and barrier chockstones. Make a short pitch (class 5 and several pitons for aid) on the right wall, then climb back into the chimney. Climb one lead out of the chimney (class 5) and onto a ridge to bypass another barrier of chockstones. Continue up the chimney/gully, then leave it and angle left over easy rock to the summit ridge notch; class 5 and aid. References: *Mountaineer,* 1961, p. 101; *A.A.J.,* 1961, p. 365.

THE TRIPLETS 7240′+/2207 m

These three striking pinnacles 0.8 mi. SW on the ridge between Mixup and Cascade Peaks are very prominent from Cascade Pass and the trail. The early geologist Bailey Willis noted the structure of vertical cleavage here, and commented on the inclined joint planes.[67] The SE summit is highest, the central summit next highest, and West Triplet is lowest. The steep rocky N face of the entire formation begins at 5800 ft. Reference: *Mazama* 37, no. 13 (1955): 47-48.

SOUTHEAST PEAK

First ascent by Fred Beckey and Jack Schwabland on October 8, 1945. From Gunsight Notch (see Mixup Peak) descend and contour W about 1 mi. across gullies and steep heather slopes. Here the summit is climbed on the final E side. From Cascade Pass a shorter route (original climb), but a more difficult approach, is to ascend the gully (ice ribbon) between Mixup and The Triplets. Climb to the highest part of the glacier; there is a considerable span of steep rock climbing to the ridge E of the summit.

WEST TRIPLET

First ascent by Michael Hane and Art Maki in August 1954 or 1955. From Cascade Pass traverse under the N face of The Triplets and then ascend directly up the face to the ridgetop W of West Triplet (the climb is easy but exposed to here). The last three leads are continuous and steep (est. class 5.3); time: 5 hours from pass.

CASCADE PEAK 7428′/2264 m

This peak is on the North-Middle Fork Cascade River divide ½ mi. E of Johannesburg. On the N is a long steep alpine face, flanked by the Cascade-Johannesburg couloir; the peak on the S presents a short steep rock formation above an alp slope. First ascent by Fred Beckey, Pete Schoening, and Phil Sharpe on July 23, 1950. References: *Mountaineer,* 1950, p. 41; *A.A.J.,* 1951, pp. 174-175.

SOUTHWEST ROUTE: From Cascade-Johannesburg col (see Johannesburg Mountain) climb the first rock gully E of the peak's SW corner (est. 500′ beneath summit). Reach the crest of the W ridge, then climb grassy rock on the NW side

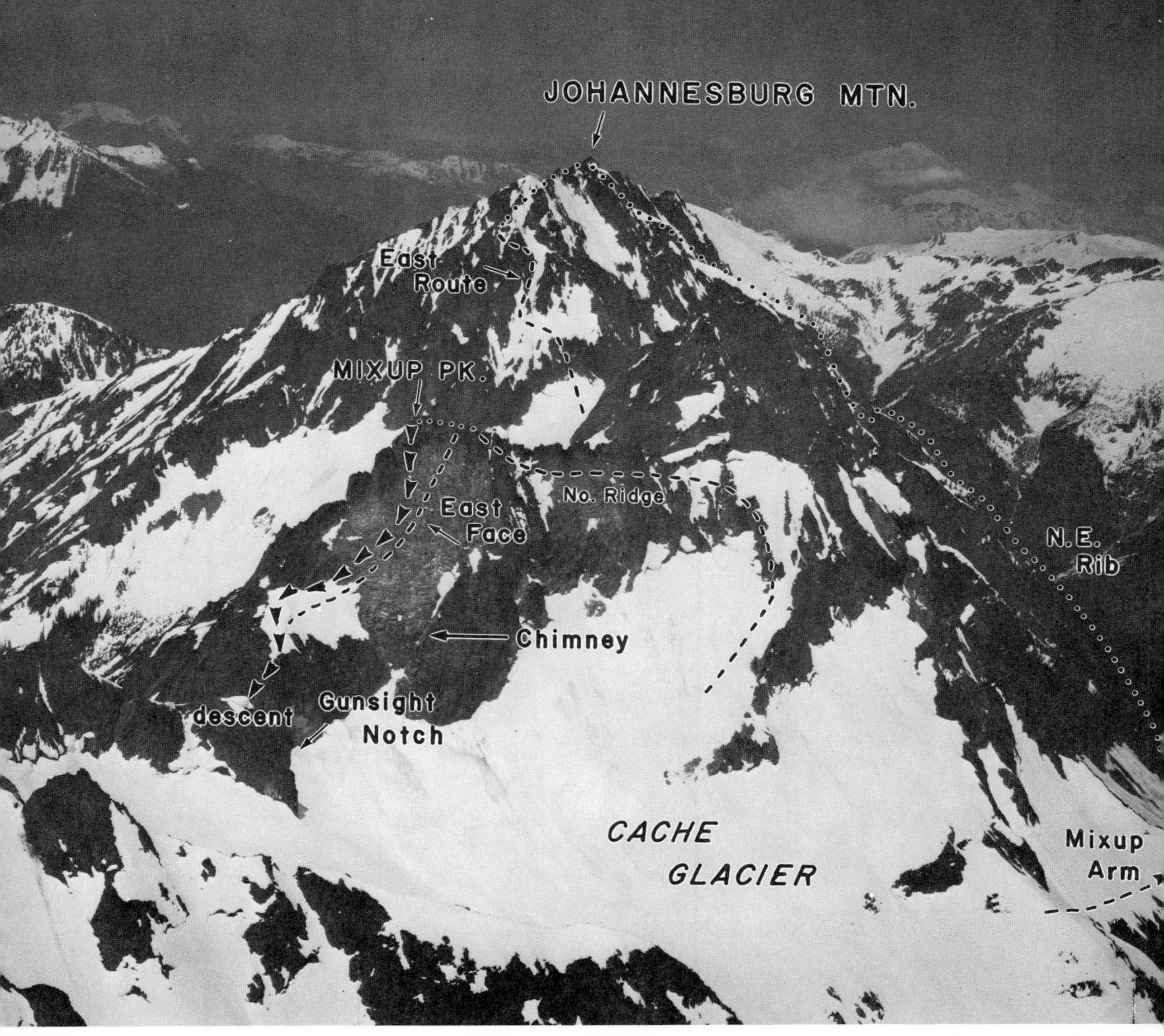

MIXUP PEAK from east
AUSTIN POST, U.S. GEOLOGICAL SURVEY

to the summit; rock is quite friable—class 3-4.

NORTH BUTTRESS: First ascent by Ed Cooper, Glen Denny, and George Whitmore in September 1961. From Cascade Pass traverse or ascend to the lower portion of the Cascade-Johannesburg couloir, then climb to the base of the buttress-wall (est. 5400′). The route uses the prominent N buttress directly from the snowpatch at its base. The first 350 ft are class 3 and 4 slabs; above where the first step recedes (central snowpatch) a chin-up on mossy rock is awkward (class 5). The remaining 1500 ft are only moderately difficult, but with exposure and some loose rock. Grade II; class 5.6. References: *Mountaineer,* 1962, p. 93; *A.A.J.,* 1962, p. 209.

EAST RIDGE: First ascent by Mike Anthony and Larry Nielson in July, 1974. Approach from the alp slope on the S. Rock is reported to be quite crumbly; class 4-5. References: *Mountaineer,* 1974, p. 62; *A.A.J.,* 1975, p. 128.

JOHANNESBURG MOUNTAIN

8200′+/2499 m

No peak in this region of the North Cascades has had more notoriety than Johannesburg, whose immense N and E faces, visible to all who enter the North Fork valley of Cascade River, are a convolution of couloirs and rock ribs, and adorned with steeply pitched, crevassed small hanging glaciers. Much of the mountain's impressiveness is a result of sheer size, despite a modest altitude among some higher nearby peaks: local relief is 6800 ft in 3 mi.—of which 5000 ft are in the final mi. Any one of several areas of glacier ice and steep snowfields may produce stupendous avalanches, but the most apparent is the ice (Sill Glacier) which reaches from Cascade-Johannesburg col (6760′+) to about 3300 ft, an unusually low altitude for the latitude. Here spectacular avalanches frequently occur where ice becomes spilled over an area as large as 0.5 km^2. The Klement prospecting party camped at Cascade Pass in the summer of 1877 described a crashing sound of "thousands of tons of ice" which awoke them from a sound sleep, and caused them to fear "the world was coming to an end."[68]

The mountain trends WNW from the col to the 6000-ft level between the North Fork and Pincer Creek. The true summit is near the E end of the highest crest (Skagit gneiss), which continues in a serrate form past the West Peak (8065′/2458 m). The S flank W of the col is a prominent fault gully; the broad S face is deeply gullied rock.

The mountain acquired a human history early. The name Johannesburg (which first appeared in print in 1934) is incorrectly derived from the Johnsberg claims[69] (discovered on the N face by three men named John). The astounding feats of the early miners can truly be associated with the boldness and risks of later technical climbing. A miner of the early 1890s, Billy Murtagh, drilled holes and put spikes in to reach the ledge high above Gilbert's cabin.[70] The first ascent was made by Calder Bressler, Bill Cox, Ralph Clough, and Tom Myers on July 26, 1938; they called the mountain "Elsbeth." Their route traversed from Cascade Pass under The Triplets and up the Cascade-Johannesburg couloir to the col, beyond which a goat trail led them toward the summit. They bivouacked on the S slope, then completed the return traverse above the valley of the middle fork to beyond Mixup Peak. References: *Mountaineer,* 1934, p. 15; *Mazama* 28, no. 13 (1956): 36; 32; no. 13 (1950): 34-35.

EAST ROUTE: This route may not be the simplest on Johannesburg, but is the easiest to approach, and the most climbed. The final rock climb is rather indirect, on mossy and broken gneiss. The climb does not strictly follow a natural line, but links a series of rock pitches, gullies, ribs, and a final summit ridge. The approach is usually made either by the long traverse from the Cache Glacier or via the Cascade-Johannesburg couloir.

From Cascade Pass climb to Gunsight Notch (E of Cache Col)—see Cascade Pass Trail♦—Ptarmigan Traverse. Descend 600 ft of steep heather, then traverse W below the cliffs of Mixup on a goat path (this rises and descends on the steep sidehill—numerous gullies). A rise is made to flowery alp slopes nearly a mi. wide, then a traverse and rise to the snowpatch on the S side of the Cascade-Johannesburg col. Ascend rock, keeping left of the crest. The route is fairly steep, but broken; it leads toward the highest visible point, then bears left up a trough, bypassing a high tower on the left. From 8000 ft onward follow the crest NW to the summit. Time: 9½ hours.

Variation: Cascade-Johannesburg Couloir: Where the road comes closest to the river (near final fork), traverse to the stream, ford, and ascend the long narrow Sill Glacier. This route is a 3400-ft ascent to the col (6760′+). There are steep slopes at places and possible ice, and sometimes the danger of falling ice debris. In late summer the couloir is a poor descent choice. Time: 5 hours to col; bring crampons.

Variation: via Middle Fork Cascade River: This S slope approach is feasible, but also fairly long and tedious. It is not known when first done (a 1956 entry noted by Edwards, Hovey, Magnusson).

Descent Route: After the ascent of Johannesburg by any of the routes, this is the down-route preferred by many parties. It has its risks, but is generally safer than the couloir, and less tedious than the long return traverse via Gunsight Notch and Cascade Pass; further, it offers the variety of a mountain traverse.

From the Main Peak scramble along the ridge (class 3) to the area of three awkward notches (these are best avoided by a traverse mostly below the crest—on the S), then return to the ridge, and continue to the West Peak (2 hours). Scramble down the S slope from W of the summit (class 3 gullies and solid broken rock on SW slope); then descend and traverse open slopes W. Now it is necessary to gain 600-800 ft to cross a ridge saddle (the final part is a steep slope). Descend timber (path exists, but may be hard to locate) to the area of the road's river crossing. Keep W of slide areas; the route is quite steep forest, but not very brushy. Time: 6 hours. Note: this is essentially the descent route of the 1949 N face party, but they began from the summit rather than the West Peak.

SOUTHEAST ARETE: First ascent by Claude Garrod and Leon Slutsky on August 15, 1971 (also Julian and Eva Ansell to summit ridge). Use the approach as per South Face. From camp gain the ridge/arete. At 7000 ft climb two pitches (class 4) to E of the crest along an outsloping ledge, to reach a notch N of a large gendarme (keep right of latter). Cross to the W through the notch and scramble to the summit ridge (join upper part of East Route). Grade II; class 4.

References: *Mountaineer,* 1972, p. 80; *Summit,* September 1974.

SOUTH FACE: First ascent by Julian Ansell, Claude Garrod, Mickey Schurr, and Leon Slutsky on August 29, 1971. Take the Middle Fork Cascade River Trail to beyond a stream crossing (est. 3000′). Ascend N through timber; there is a burnt brushy area at about 4000 ft (good camp at 6200′). From the basin at timberline climb the western of two tiny pocket glaciers. Begin climbing at an eroded dike: a crack (class 5) leads into a series of shallow basins and narrow dikes (good holds) that bear directly to the summit. Grade II; class 4 and 5. Time: 1½ days from road to summit. Reference: *Mountaineer,* 1972, p. 80.

NORTH FACE (Central Rib): N face routes which begin at low altitudes, such as on the Johannesburg face, tend to have brush and mossy vegetation, even on high-angle rock. Snowpatches and ice seek natural drainages which wet the rock and produce waterfalls at times, and they present objective dangers. This route was the first of the N and NE face technical routes on the mountain. First ascent by David Harrah and Gene Schoeder on August 26, 1949.

Begin from the road near the area of Gilbert's cabin; ford the river below Gilbert Creek. The climbing begins quite promptly. About 1000 ft up a rib it is possible to traverse right into a long, easy polished trough which bears to the lower glacier; this may be bare ice and crevassed in late summer. Climb left and rise to the upper glacier (4 hours to here). Make the glacier exit on the upper right to gain the cliff belt under the West Peak; this section of rock is steep (class 4 and 5). The object is to get into the obvious trough running upward along the left side of the upper central rib. This trough is awkward at one place, but usually easy for 500 ft. Then a ledge system leads to the major difficulty of the route; it appears that the route traverses E somewhat on this portion. Climb a polished shoulder to slabs. Left of a corner is a chimney which is the key: climb 80 ft up the chimney (class 5). There is a final 70-ft pitch on a steep wall (solid rock but small holds; poor cracks for protection). The route leads to the ridge W of West Peak (upper glacier to summit ridge, 5 hours). The original party traversed E on the S flank of the ridge, then ascended again near the true summit. Time: 16 hours plus bivouac on S flank. References: *Mountaineer,* 1949, pp. 35-36; *A.A.J.,* 1952, pp. 346-347.

NORTHEAST RIB (East Rib of North Face): This is the eastern of the two nearly-parallel NE ribs. The route features the elegant snow crest which leads to the summit ridge upon completion of the rock portion. The lower main rib is protected from stonefall by its own projection. First ascent by David Harrah and Tom Miller on July 28-29, 1951 (a bivouac was made about two-thirds up the rib).

Reach the rib from the lower part of the Cascade-Johannesburg glacier couloir (before it narrows). Ascend the face immediately right of the rib (class 3-4) to its intersection with the long narrow snow crest; the original party used three pitons for protection near the top of the rib, at a difficult chimney (it is easier to the W). Follow the snow for several hundred ft, then leave it for rock climbing (class 4) at the foot of the summit pyramid. Time: 9 hours. Reference: *Mountaineer,* 1951, p. 61.

Variation: Western Rib: By Stan Curtis, Ned Gulbran, Michael Hane, and Rowland Tabor on July 13, 1957. From about 1000 ft up the couloir climb onto the western of the parallel ribs. At a steep buttress or rock near the top of the rib, make a short rappel from a piton rightward into a narrow gully. Ascend snow in the gully to the snow/glacier crest. Time: 9 hours. Note: several variations have been made on the brushy, dirty lower portions of both ribs.

Variation: Western Rib Direct: By Arnold Bloomer, Donald (Claunch) Gordon, Jim Richardson, and Winslow Trueblood on August 8-9, 1959. The final buttress is climbed on the rib; this portion is about 300-400 ft of steep rock, with a mixture of climbing from class 3 to 5. Above a bivouac the party climbed 200 ft of dirt and heather to the steep section. A short left traverse led to a class 5 pitch on the left side of the rib; the pitch included a crack and chimney—the final part of the crack is quite steep for about 70 ft with some loose rock, then an immediate leveling to the easy snow crest. Class 5.3.

NORTHEAST FACE (Yellow Flower Route): This 1800-ft route is mainly class 4 and 5; it is difficult to protect, and belay anchors are hard to find. The rock is a mix of good and bad (take hard hats). The name originated because the original party noted small flowers in the face. First ascent by Scott Davis, Al Givler, and Doug McGowan on August 19, 1967.

Begin from the Cascade-Johannesburg couloir and make a right traverse on the hanging glacier arm to beyond where there may be a big block of ice. Rock climbing begins from the highest point of the glacier, near the right edge of ice cliffs (class 5.6 at first). The route follows headwalls, subridges, and gullies N of the long central gully/fault that bisects the face. There is some class 5.4 about midway, but otherwise mostly class 4. The route exits via a funnel-shaped snow finger onto firn below the summit. Grade IV; class 5.6 Time: 10 hours on face (17 hours road to summit—bivouac made). Reference: *Mountaineer,* 1968, p. 203.

NORTHEAST FACE (Route 2): The line of this 23-pitch route was generally the major depression in line with the summit. Rock is friable, but is at its best on the harder pitches (the first pitch was the most solid). The route was considered generally unpleasant and frightening; a bivouac was made in the upper chimney system. First ascent by Dave Anderson, Don Brooks, Julie Brugger, and John Teasdale on July 29-30, 1973.

The route climbs from the ice upward, then works slightly left out of a major chimney into another chimney system. This leads to the highest area of the face, close to the completion of the 1963 route. Grade IV; class 5.8 (all chocks; mostly class 4 and 5); hard to protect in many places, especially in the central slabby area. Reference: *Mountaineer,* 1973, p. 78.

NORTHEAST FACE (Route 3): This face is a good test of one's alpine skills, with about 20 leads of moderate class 5

Summit
West Peak
1951
1957
N.E. Rib
1949

climbing (5.3 to 5.6). The route keeps mostly within a major fault (or gully) which bisects the face about midway between the E ridge and NE rib. First ascent by Hans Baer, Alex Bertulis, Jack Bryan, and Frank Tarver in July, 1965. Ascend the glacier couloir and climb onto the hanging glacier rightward along the base of the face until past the fault. The first and most difficult pitch (class 5.7) starts from flat slabs and ascends diagonally right, and around a sharp corner to reach the fault (described as a 40′ traverse). Continue straight up for over one-third of the face until a small catwalk traverses left; then continue straight up, eventually reaching a friction slab and a diagonal ramp (right) just before the top of the wall. Here a terrace leads toward the right and across a deep gully (snow finger). Then climb up onto the N ridge (at 7800′ the face levels abruptly). A final firn slope of about 35° leads to a notch just E of the summit pyramid. Grade IV; class 5.7 (take protection up to ¾″ angle size; used three-four placements on most leads). Time: 11 hours (16 hours round trip). Reference: *Mountaineer,* 1966, pp. 200-201.

NORTHEAST FACE/RIB (Route 4): This route, the first on the NE face, is mostly on a rib where rock is sound. The climb is alpine and enjoyable; water from high snowfield drainage is available in the lower gully. The hanging glacier approach should be made by sunrise to avoid rockfall (original party kept left to minimize this danger). The route ascends about 2500 ft of the Cascade-Johannesburg couloir, then some 2500 ft of rock climbing (mostly class 4 and 5). No rockfall was encountered, but some loose rock was found on the bottom of the rock climb and on the final five leads there is some brittleness. First ascent by Dave Beckstead, Donald (Claunch) Gordon, and Jim Stuart on August 28, 1963 (a bivouac made 300′ below the summit).

Ascend the lower avalanche fan, then keeping to the left where the couloir narrows, bear right onto the small hanging glacier. The wall ascent begins at a great left-trending fault. Cross the moat where feasible and climb a 150-ft pitch (sustained class 5.2) left of the gully. After another pitch cross the gully and ascend a rounded rib (class 4). Work left into a basin, then back right, ascending many hundreds of ft over broken steps (class 3 to 5.0); rock is quite solid in the basin. A prominent high shoulder on the rib-buttress on the W is met (rib W of high snowfield); some class 4 and 5 on the long climb to rib. Climb on moderate class 5, trending left. The final portion is firm in shallow gullies and on airy faces for several leads until the ridge is met (interesting class 4 and 5 climbing—up to 5.4). The summit pyramid is across a small area of firn. Grade III or IV; class 5.4 (take eight horizontal and small angle sizes. Time: 10 hours; may need bivouac. References: *Mountaineer,* 1964, pp. 130-131; *A.A.J.*, 1965, p. 410.

WEST PEAK 8065′/2458 m

WEST ROUTE (Southwest Route): First ascent by Charles Cehrs, Bill Elfendahl, Dave Lind, Tom Miller, and Jay Todd on July 3, 1949. The route climbs brush, forest, heather, steep snow, and some moderate rock. From near the road's river crossing ascend a snow finger (or old mine path) on the wooded NW flank of the mountain. The best route is in steep wooded slopes W of slide areas and a prominent stream. Cross the saddle on the W ridge and descend a steep slope to snow basin (on S); make a rising traverse on open slopes, then ascend steep snow or broken rock (some gullies) on the SW face of the West Peak (class 3). Several steps lead to the base of the summit rock area, which is done on the SW. See also Descent Route (East Route). Reference: *Mountaineer,* 1950, p. 39.

The first traverse from the West Peak to the Main Peak was done by Rowland W. Tabor and Joe Vance in 1958. This is an exposed traverse but generally not difficult scrambling (class 3); the original party descended three times on the S face to avoid three notches (4 hours round trip.)

JOHANNESBURG MOUNTAIN, North Face
PHILIP LEATHERMAN

BUCKINDY-ILLABOT GROUP

W of the principal Cascade divide for a N-S span of about 20 mi. stands a distinctly separate and important outlier group of peaks. The lateral span is about 16 mi., and the group can be conveniently considered as bounded by the Suiattle River and Downey Creek on the S, and the South Fork Cascade, Cascade, and Skagit Rivers. Important streams which drain the interior of this group are Illabot, Found, Big, Otter, Boulder, Jordan, Kindy, Goat, and Buck Creeks. Much of the area is a pristine wilderness consisting of rich green meadows and alp slopes, dark green coniferous forests, rugged black, grey, and reddish rock peaks, conspicuous and crevassed slope glaciers, and myriad magnificent lakes equal to the larger Alpine Lakes region farther S. Many of the peaks, lakes, and glaciers are but little known and difficult to reach, a situation that hopefully will protect their wilderness integrity. Extensive logging in valleys and lower slopes has blemished the appearrance of the western and northern fringe of the group.

The outstanding peaks are Snowking, Chaval, Buckindy, and Misch, but the eastern and northern periphery of the group contains a number of other attractive peaks, many of them unnamed or recently given provisional names.[71] The reddish color of the Buckindy Ridge summits makes them easily distinguishable from the remainder of the group. The southern breccia contact of the Buckindy unit is exposed on the two major peaks of the ridge; the unit extends nearly to Snowking Mountain, which is distinctly granitic. The largest glaciers are the Snowking, Kindy, and on the eastern flank of Buckindy Ridge; several unnamed glaciers here total 1.1 km^2, of which

MT. BUCKINDY area from northwest
WILL F. THOMPSON

MT. BUCKINDY area from northeast
AUSTIN POST, U.S. GEOLOGICAL SURVEY

the largest ("Goat Creek Glacier") is a vigorous cirque glacier.

The history of the area is brief. The relative inaccessability and little publicity has not encouraged many hiking or climbing groups. Snowking, the dominant massif, was the first important summit to be climbed, probably because it is visible from many vantages. In January 1945, when a Navy crew bailed out over the Buckindy area, two of eight men perished. In the summer of 1953 geologist Bruce Bryant made extensive traverses from Green Mountain to beyond Buckindy, and also spent many weeks trekking the high ridges near Chaval, Snowking, and along the heartland of alpine lakes. Possibly the first mountaineering traverse from Buckindy Ridge to Snowking and Kindy Ridge was done in July 1969 by Allen A. Smith and Robert A. Wilson. The Goat Creek Glaciers and Kindy Glacier were traversed by John Pollock and three others in September 1973. For the extended traverses, one should allow 4-6 days in the area. The principal reference is the *Climber's Guide* of 1961 and Allen A. Smith, "Explorations in the Illabot Range," *Summit,* April 1973, pp. 4-7.

GREEN MOUNTAIN 6500′/1981 m

See Green Mountain Trail♦.

MT. MISCH 7435′/2266 m

This reddish-toned peak is the highest and most prominent in the subrange of Buckindy Ridge, 6 mi. NNE of Suiattle River and Downey Creek and 5.8 mi. SE of Snowking Mountain. The peak has been the subject of some past name confusion. The earliest map to define its position was the Glacier Peak quadrangle of 1899, which placed no name, but marked the figures 7311 as a summit altitude near the head of Buck, Goat, and Big (i.e. Kindy) Creeks.[72] The first map to associate a name with this altitude was the Mt. Baker Forest map of 1931, which letterd "Mt. Buckindy" here. Successive maps continued this association, but generalized lettering and contour placement cast some doubt regarding which peak was meant; no competing name or altitude nearby was indicated for some time. However, from vistas of the area it is apparent that a higher peak, on the Goat-Buck Creek divide (but not Kindy), and 0.7 mi. S of the 7311-ft triangulated altitude, is the distinct one on the subrange. The first ascent party and 1961 guidebook added further contradiction by innocently terming this highest peak "Mt. Buckindy." With the absence of an official name, and in view of the historical confusion about Buckindy, Mt. Misch is proposed as a tribute to the eminent University of Washington geologist Peter Misch, who has contributed so much to the understanding of the complex geology and geologic history of the North Cascades. The first ascent was made by Donald Grimlund, David Nicholson, and Winslow Trueblood August 28, 1955. References: *Mountaineer,* 1955, p. 58; *Summit,* April 1973, pp. 4, 5, 7.

WEST ROUTE: For approach see Green Mountain Trail♦. Begin from the W flank of the mountain at about 7000 ft. Here a southerly traverse below a small snowfield leads to the W rib, which is ascended for about 200 ft, then crossed. A rising traverse on the S side of the rib (now SW of the summit) leads into a couloir which is climbed to the ridge crest 50 ft N of the summit. Class 3-4. Time: 2½-3 hours from camp at 5200 ft in Horse Creek basin.

PEAK 7280 7280′/2219 m

This is the next summit SE of Mt. Misch, also on the crest of Buckindy Ridge. Possible first ascent by Robert A. Wilson, Dean Wilson, and Allen A. Smith on August 12, 1972. Reference: *Summit,* April 1973, p. 6 (peak called "Minas Anor").

SOUTH ROUTE: Use the approach for Mt. Misch. Ascend the cirque on the W slope, and take a snow finger to the col S of the summit. Then follow the S ridge (one pitch of class 5.1).

SOUTHEAST ROUTE: First climbed during traverse of Goat Creek flank by Orville Dorsett, Randy Nowack, John Pollock, and Doug Sanders on September 10, 1973. Approach from the W and cross the main ridge through the notch immediately N of Peak 7185 (2190 m). Contour the glacier northward to the NW corner, then climb through a bottleneck to firn area beneath E rock face. Ascend very loose rock on the left side of the face to the summit ridge (large blocks, class 3).

PEAK 7185 7185′/2190 m

This is the most southern summit of note on Buckindy Ridge, a pointed and conical-appearing small rock peak, 0.6 mi. SE of Mt. Misch. The peak has a long S ridge with several points, including 7160′+, on the nearly level ridge SSW. The summit beyond (6855′/2089 m) is the last pointed one on the ridge. First ascent unknown. Reference: *Summit,* April 1973, p. 6 (peak called "Minas Ithil").

ROUTE: Approach from the edge of the boulderfield on the ridge to the S. Scramble up to the ridge, over several false summits and reach the top.

MT. BUCKINDY 7320′+/2231 m

The summit is the highest of a series of reddish crags

MT. BUCKINDY from west
AUSTIN POST, U.S. GEOLOGICAL SURVEY

on the W-trending ridge on the Kindy and Horse Creek (branch of Buck Creek) divide. This is probably the summit that was shown as 7311 ft for many years on maps, and later linked to the name Buckindy. The suspicion lingers that this name was actually intended for the dominant peak of the main ridge, Mt. Misch, but the name "Buckindy," with its inference of location, is difficult to dispute. The summit is 5.4 mi. SE of Snowking Mountain. There is a large slope (hanging) glacier (Kindy Glacier—0.8 km²) on the N (Kindy

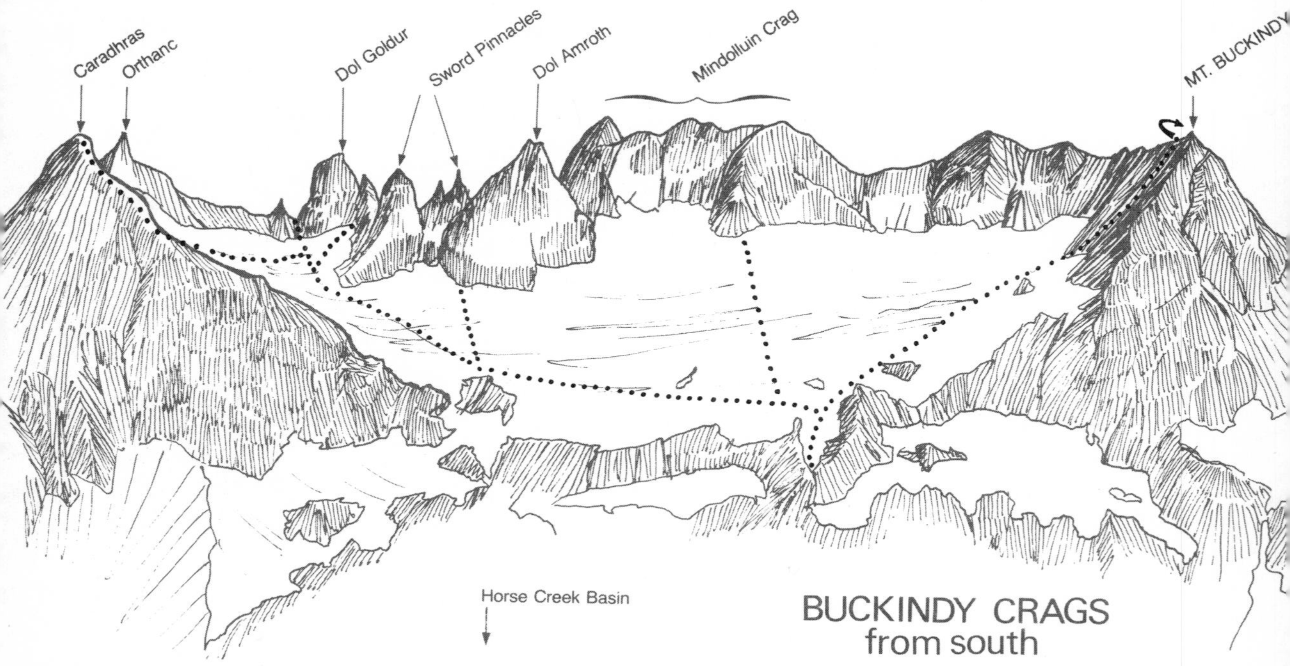

Creek) flank and extensive glacier ice on the Goat Creek flank. Recent moraines are in distinct evidence beneath these glaciers. First ascent by James A. Carlson and Kenneth Carpenter on August 17, 1963. Reference: *Summit,* April 1973, pp. 4-5, 7.

NORTH ROUTE: This is basically the first ascent route. See Green Mountain Trail♦ for approach; then ascend N to a snowfield at 6800 ft to avoid a gully traverse. Contour and rise easily W and N and pass around SW ridge of Buckindy to W flank. Ascend the shallow 40° snow-filled chute on the W face (bare in late summer) which leads to a notch in the N ridge (about 100 ft below the summit). Climb onto the NE and E face, climbing ledges and slabs (second ascent party Allen A. Smith and Robert A. Wilson July 19, 1969 climbed final pitch on the SE) Class 4. Time: 3 hours from Horse Creek basin at 5200 ft.

EAST RIDGE: First ascent by Allen A. Smith and Dean Wilson on August 13, 1972. Cross the main ridge just E of the peak (gully slants to the ridge). The route follows the 55° rock ridge, and works somewhat onto the E face about 200 ft below the summit, then roughly joins the 1963 route. The climb is short but somewhat loose; Class 4 and 5.2.

Other Approaches: A possible approach is via Kindy Creek; use Kindy-Buck Pass (col at 6320′+) and traverse to the basin SW of Buckindy. Or climb Kindy Glacier to the notch E of the summit (crevasses permitting). Another approach is via Snowking area; the long narrow ridge between Buck and Mutchler Creeks is easy to cross. See Green Mountain Trail♦—Snowking Route.

BUCKINDY CRAGS

A castellated ridge of reddish and grey breccia crags and spires extends 1 mi. W from Mt. Buckindy. The 1972 traverse party applied names from *Lord of the Rings:* from E to W are Mindolluin, Dol Amroth, Dol Goldur, Sword Pinnacles, Caradhras, and Orthanc (see *Summit,* April 1973). Rock is quite fractured, with many surface holds loose; leads are difficult to protect. Reach as per Mt. Buckindy.

Mindolluin Crag (7280′+/2219 m) is a thin E-W wedge of rock with three points; steep snow hangs on the N above a cliff. First ascent by Dean Wilson, Robert A. Wilson, and Allen A. Smith on August 13, 1972. The route is from the S to the E peak, then via a traverse along the ridge. The W peak appears slightly the highest. Class 4 to 5.0 (runner protection).

Dol Amroth (est. 7130′/2173 m) is an isolated tower, the next W of Mindolluin, with a sheer S face. First ascent by the same party, on August 13 via the rotten W ridge.

Sword Pinnacles, from E to W: Glamdring, Orcrist, and Anduril, are named after the three great swords in *Lord of the Rings.* The climbs were made by the same party, all from the S; each had one class 5.0 pitch.

Dol Goldur (est. 7110′/2167 m) is an isolated tower of very light grey and loose rock. First ascent by same party, August 12, via chimney on SE (unroped).

Caradhras (7160′/2182 m) is 0.6 mi. W of Buckindy. Apparently the first ascent was by a U.S.G.S. party (date unknown). The SE ridge is a scramble.

Orthanc (7040′+/2146 m) is the chisel-shaped pinnacle of light grey tillite, obvious from its shape and color, 3100 ft W of Mt. Buckindy. The rock is nearly vertical and loose, and the W face overhangs. First ascent by Robert A. Wilson and Dean Wilson on September 10, 1969.

A saddle at its S base is gained from the S by climbing over a broad shoulder and descending a 100-ft gully (class 3; loose). Climb directly up 60 ft to the knife-edged SW ridge at a notch N of a gendarme. Follow the ridge to the summit (150′). Leader protection is poor; climbing rated class 5.5, but may seem harder. Descent: down the SE face to a shoulder, traverse W to ridge crest, down-climb ridge to gendarme, and rappel to base. References: *Mazama* 51, no. 13 (1969): 61; *Summit,* April 1973, pp. 5-6.

PEAK 6720 6720′/2048 m

This is a moderate but somewhat isolated summit on the West Fork Kindy Creek-Buck Creek divide, 1.75 mi. NW of Mt. Buckindy. On the peak's N slope is a remnant of a former glacier whose extent is identified by a recent moraine at 5000 ft. The peak is asymmetrical: the S slopes are barren and moderate. The E summit of the peak is triangulated at 6662 ft (2031 m). Possible first ascent by Orville Dorsett, Randy Nowack, John Pollock, and Doug Sanders on September 12, 1973.

ROUTE: For approach see Green Mtn. Trail♦-Snowking Route. One can camp at Lake 5975 just SW of the Kindy-Buck Pass (6200′+). The route taken ascended the SE ridge of Peak 6662 (loose but not difficult), then traversed W to the summit. A short rappel was made off the N side.

MT. BRUSETH 7220′/2201 m

A strategic peak on the eastern fringe of the outlier group, ½ mi. N of Bench Lake and 0.8 mi. W of Woods Lake. It was identified as "Peak 7000" in the 1961 guidebook, and has also been informally known as "Bench Lake Peak." The provisional name given here is for forest ranger Nels Bruseth of Darrington, who made many explorative treks into the North Cascades from the early 1900s to mid-1950s. There is a glacier of 0.6 km^2 on the peak's N slope and in the N cirque, at the head of the western terminal fork of South Cascade River. There is also a narrow trough of glacier ice in the fault trending ENE to Woods Lake. First ascent by Erick Larson and Dwight Watson on July 4, 1940.

ROUTE: For route to Bench Lake see Downey Creek Trail♦. Circle the lake on its N, then ascend talus and heather behind the lake to the ridge. Ascend, then follow the SE ridge to the summit. No difficulties, but there is some scrambling at the end.

GOAT-KINDY PEAKS

There are three rock peaks (not including Mt. Bruseth) on the NW-trending ridge bordering the NE valley wall of Goat Creek; the opposite drainage is Kindy Creek and the South Fork Cascade River. Peak 7103 (2165 m; 0.4 mi. NW of Bruseth) is at the head of the cirque of Bruseth Glacier and its summit forms the watershed of three drainages. The summit is a small rock horn, with a flanking serrated crest. The first ascent is unknown; possible new route or variation by Fred Beckey on November 6, 1976 from E (class 3). Peak 6680′+ (2036 m) is a flat-top crag to the W, on the Goat-Kindy ridge; the obvious route is a rising traverse from Bench Lake, with the final climb on the SE. Peak 6723 (2049 m) farther W, rises higher off the same ridge, but is more bulky and less attractive; it would be tedious to reach. Peak 7000′+ (2134 m) is a turret-shaped isolated rock summit on the Kindy-South Fork Cascade divide (0.8 mi. N of Bruseth). The obvious route is the SE ridge; from a distance the peak appears to have a cairn. There are other summits on the rugged and seldom visited ridge to the north, including Peak 6840′+ (2084 m).

Rock in this small peak grouping is quite solid (biotite granodiorite). These peaks are somewhat inaccessible; one approach could be from the South Cascade River Trail and the stream to Bruseth Glacier; another way is from Bench Lake with a high traverse over the E flank of Mt. Bruseth, then a descent on the glacier N. From Bench Lake a very feasible approach is a rising traverse on the open W slope of Mt. Bruseth to the col (6640′+) at the head of the glacier. The history of some traverses is known, but climbing history is incomplete.

MUTCHLER PEAK 7160′+/2182 m

This peak is a southeastern appendage of Snowking Mountain at the eastern head of Buck Creek; the summit at the E end of a relatively inaccessible, ragged ridge forms a wedge to divide part of the headwaters of Kindy and Mutchler Creeks. The extensive Mutchler Glacier is located on the northern cirque (at head of Mutchler Creek—7050′ to 5800′). The S slope is barren and light-colored granite and talus. First ascent by Bruce Bryant on July 29, 1952.

ROUTE: The peak can be reached from the Buckindy area-Snowking traverse (see Green Mountain Trail♦-Snowking Route, and Snowking Mountain). The hiking traverse route

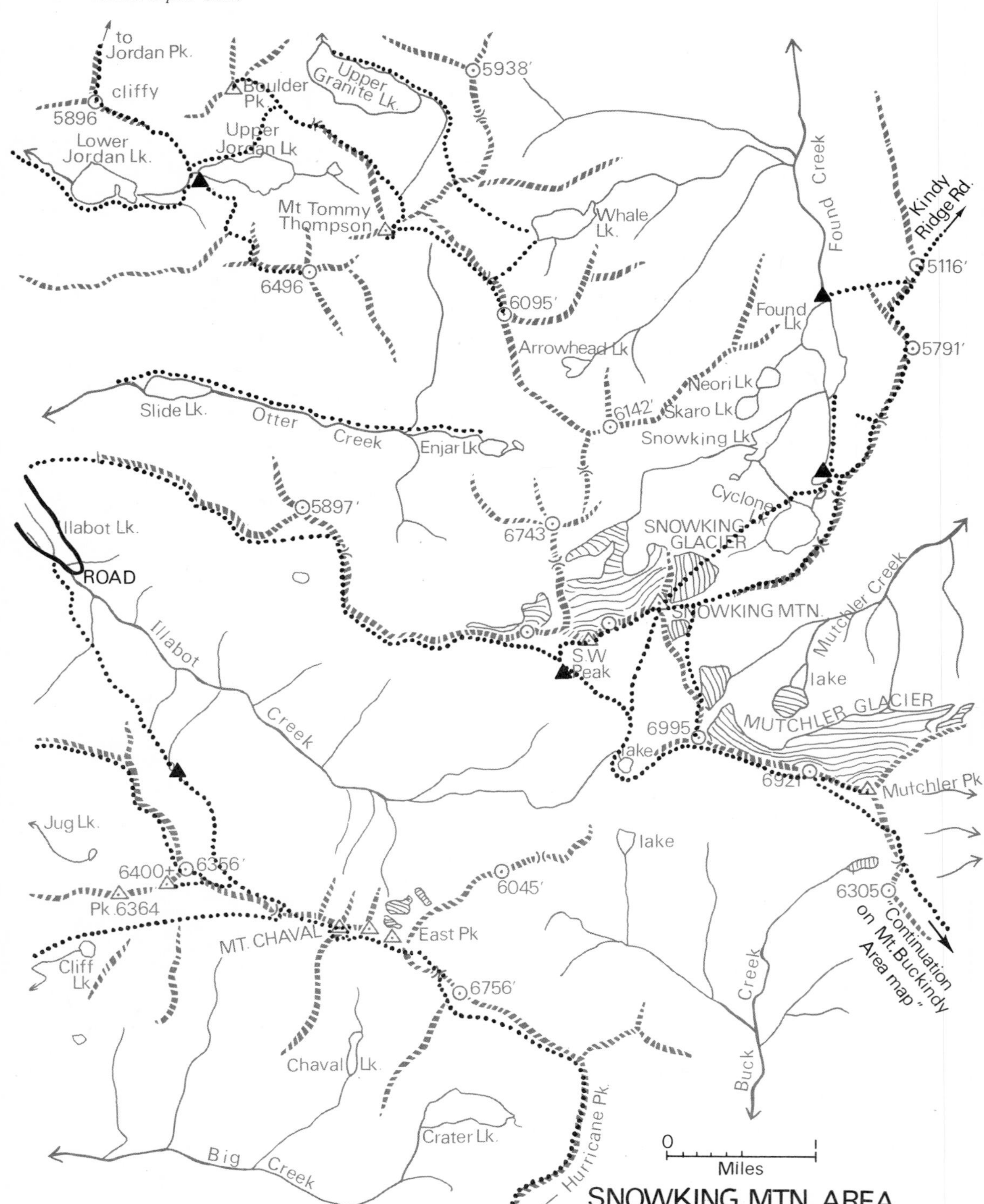
to Jordan Pk.
cliffy
5896
Boulder Pk.
Upper Granite Lk.
5938'
Lower Jordan Lk.
Upper Jordan Lk
Mt Tommy Thompson
Whale Lk.
Found Creek
Kindy Ridge Rd.
6496
6095'
5116'
Found Lk
5791'
Arrowhead Lk
Neori Lk
Slide Lk.
Otter Creek
6142'
Skaro Lk
Snowking Lk
Enjar Lk
Cyclone Lk
5897'
Illabot Lk.
6743
SNOWKING GLACIER
ROAD
SNOWKING MTN.
Mutchler Creek
Illabot Creek
S.W Peak
lake
MUTCHLER GLACIER
6995
lake
6921
Mutchler Pk.
Jug Lk.
lake
6400+
6356'
6045'
Pk.6364
6305
"Continuation on Mt.Buckindy Area map"
MT. CHAVAL
East Pk
Cliff Lk
6756'
Creek
Chaval Lk.
Buck
Hurricane Pk.
Crater Lk.
Big Creek
0
Miles
SNOWKING MTN. AREA

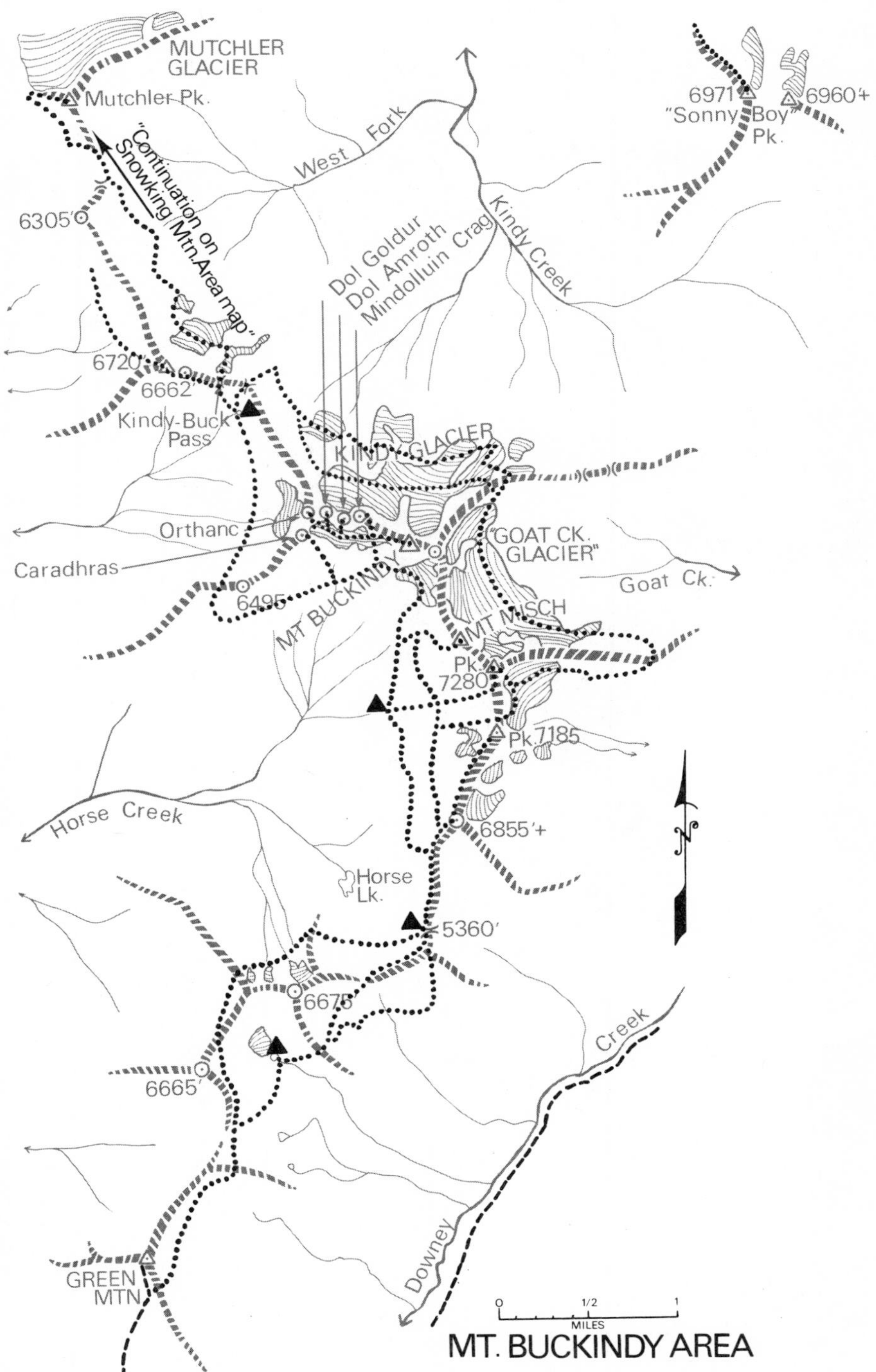

MT. BUCKINDY AREA

MT. BRUSETH
Pk. 7103
Pk. 7000+
SNOWKING MTN.
"Sonny Boy" Pk.
Woods Lake
Downey Creek

reaches high on the open slope SW of the summit. Make a final climb via the slope or the easy W ridge, a minor scramble. If approaching from the NW, small points on the W ridge such as Point 6921 and the knob to the E can be passed on the S beneath the ridge crest.

SNOWKING MOUNTAIN 7433′/2266 m

Snowking, a granitic intrusive, is an extensive gently sloping alpine massif which culminates in three small summits. The highest summit is the NE; a high crest trends to the SW summit (7425′/2263 m). Located at the headwaters of Illabot, Found, and Mutchler Creeks, Snowking forms a long high crest between the drainage of Suiattle and Cascade Rivers. Due to its western position in the outlier group between these rivers, and in the Cascade Range, its bulk and high accumulation area, snowfall is heavy. There is an unusual amount of glacier ice for a peak under 8000 ft in altitude, and in this respect the mountain is similar to Mt. Daniel, Mt. Hinman, Bacon Peak, the Kololo Peaks, and nearby Mt. Buckindy. Direct storm accumulation and the plateau height of Snowking are responsible for glacier sizes: the NW-trending erratic Snowking-Mutchler crest remains above 6000 ft for over 4 mi.[73] The NE slope of the massif is blanketed by the Snowking Glacier (largest sections total 0.8 km^2 and 1.4 km length); the segment draining toward Found Lake descends to 5500 ft. The Mutchler Glacier, in the same local area (head of Mutchler Creek), has an area of 1.3 km^2.

While on the slopes of Boston Basin in 1896, L.K. Hodges noted what must be Snowking: "its broad summit shimmering white with glaciers divided by black rocky ribs. Big Creek, (i.e. Kindy) one of the southern tributaries of the Cascade, having its source there" (Hodges, *op. cit.*). E.C. Barnard apparently surveyed the area for the U.S. Geological Survey in summer 1899, but it is not known what points he reached.

First ascent by Albert Heath and Hermann F. Ulrichs on September 4, 1938 (in 3 days round trip from Seattle, with pure wilderness from Cascade River); route was via entire Found-Kindy ridge to the glacier.[74] Reference: *Summit,* April 1973, p. 5.

NORTHEAST ROUTE: See Kindy-Found Ridge Route♦ for approach. From Cyclone Lake (est. 5350′) the ascent is straightforward; bear SW over heather, gentle rock and gradual snow and firn slopes. Both the true and middle summits involve very short rock scrambles on their E; the crest traverse to the SW peak is a mere hike.

Approach Variation: One can continue along the Found-Mutchler Creek divide to the glacier; this avoids both Found and Cyclone Lakes.

ILLABOT CREEK ROUTE: Climbed via SW peak by Bruce Bryant on July 27, 1952. From Illabot Creek Road♦ (at crossing of Illabot Creek) hike E uphill cross-country to 5400 ft, then along Otter-Illabot Creek ridge. Eventually reach the snow and ice; keep bearing upward and E to gain the upper W ridge of Snowking.

NORTHWEST ROUTE: See Slide Lake Trail♦ for approach. Hike into the open basin at the head of Otter Creek, then ascend SE to the SW summit.

SOUTH ROUTE: See hiking continuation, Green Mountain Trail♦—Snowking Route.

HURRICANE PEAK 6414′/1955 m

ROUTES: See Huckleberry Mountain Trail♦. See Mt. Chaval-South Route. A quicker approach is via a northern spur of Tenas Creek Road♦. Traverse cross-country NE to upper Tanas Creek and reach Boulder Lake (4975′) set in a talus basin beneath Hurricane Peak. From its E end hike upslope to the S ridge of Hurricane. The summit ridge is easily traversed. The entire route is only 2 linear mi.

MT. CHAVAL 7127′/2172 m

Chaval is a striking, craggy rock peak of three summits 3.1 mi. SW of Snowking Mountain. It is on the Illabot-Big Creek divide about 1 mi. NW of Crater Lake, and can be seen from many vantages, including the Sauk River valley. The pointed W peak is clearly highest; the E peak is 7040 ft + (est. 7050′/2149 m) and the small central peak about 50 ft lower. Chaval is a metamorphosed igneous complex (mostly hornblende and quartz dioritic gneiss); there are zones of schist inclusions. There are small bodies of glacier ice on the N and NE cirques, draining to Illabot Creek. On the N side of the E portion of Chaval Ridge are recent moraines (Little Ice Age developments), but all ice is vanished.

Seldom visited for years, Chaval is becoming better known; by 1974 there had been only 13 ascents. First ascent by Richard Merritt, Keith Rankin, and Ruth Rankin on July 20, 1946 (via Hurricane Ridge). Reference: *Mountaineer,* 1946, p. 29.

WEST ROUTE: Done by Bruce Bryant and Ben Carey on September 16, 1954, apparently Chaval's second ascent. The route is long, but scenic and not difficult. Approach via the long ridge between Illabot and Arrow Creek (leave Illabot Creek Road♦ at about 17½ mi.—about ½ mi. past Arrow Creek). It is best to travel off-ridge at several stretches: keep slightly W of the crest at the head of Jug Lake basin, but beyond Point 6356 stay slightly on the N side. Reach the summit via heather and easy rock on the W (class 3).

Variation: Northwest Approach: From Illabot Creek

UPPER DOWNEY-KINDY CREEK AREA
DWIGHT WATSON

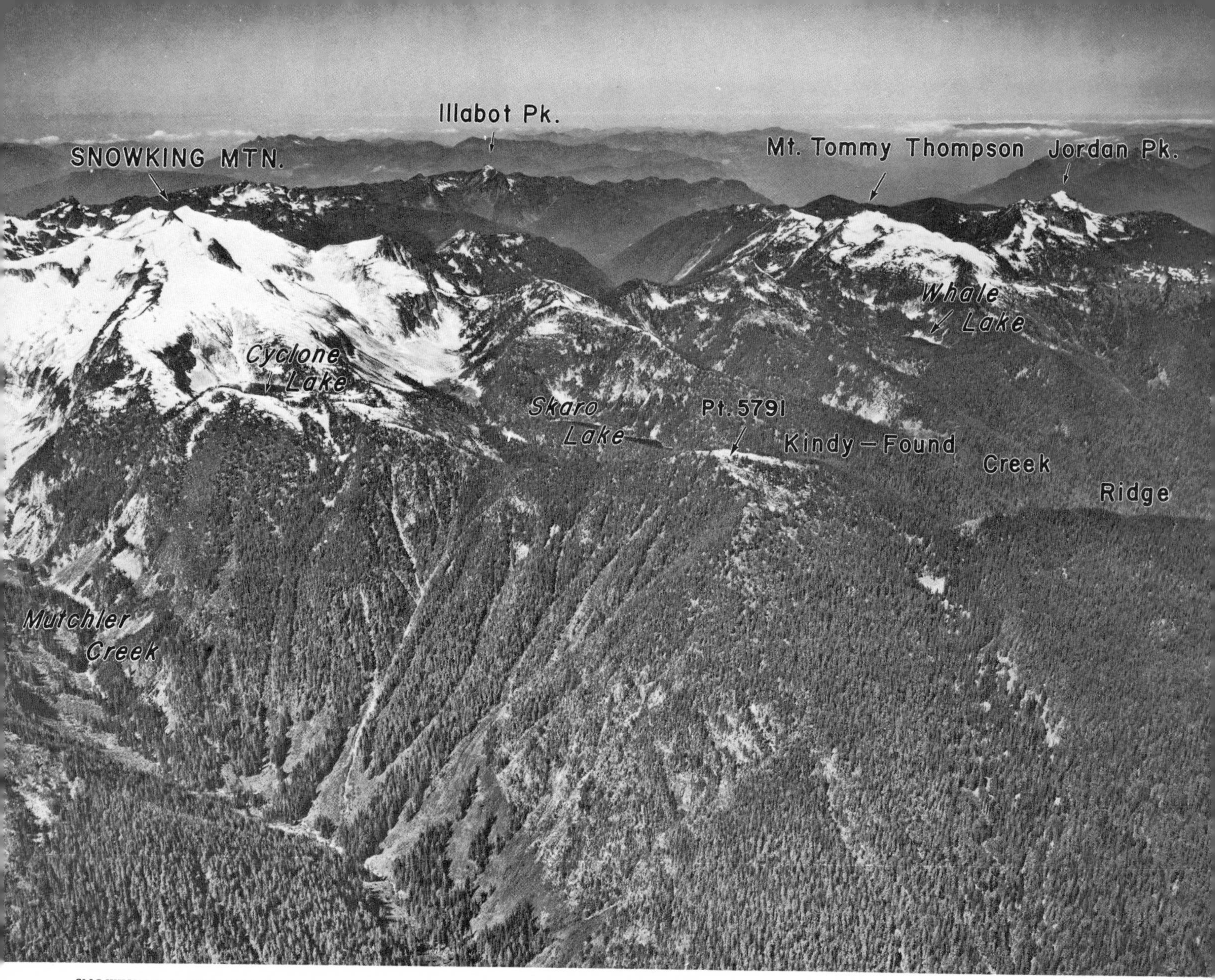

SNOWKING MOUNTAIN from east
U.S. GEOLOGICAL SURVEY

SNOWKING MOUNTAIN from northeast
AUSTIN POST, UNIVERSITY of WASHINGTON

Road♦ ascend slash of last clearcut (above parking area—2400′) to upper left corner. Make a long rising traverse in open timber and cross two brushy basins. Just before where upper valley becomes very brushy, climb S through steep forest to timberline; at the end of the third basin come out of the forest. Here is a tarn (4400′+); good camp—4 hours. Continue SE up a broad snow basin toward Chaval. Time: 4 hours from tarn to summit.

NORTH RIDGE: This is a 1500-ft rock route of solid, well fractured granitic rock. The route is basically a pleasant alpine scramble with two pitches of harder climbing on the steepest part of the ridge; the only disadvantage is some heather on the rock. First ascent by Paula Kregel. Phil Leatherman, Greg Markov, and Jim McCarthy in August 1974.

The approach was made via Bluff and Cliff Lakes (see Jug Lake Route♦). Begin climbing at the ridge toe; the route stays on the crest. The hardest portion is the gendarme about two-thirds distance. Here the first pitch climbs slabs to a ledge; the second pitch follows a jam crack (class 5.7) to a belay directly beneath a small roof on the gendarme crest. Turn the corner to an easier area, then get back on the ridge. The final portion of the ridge is snow. Grade II or III; class 5.7. Selection: small number of medium to large chocks, and runners. References: *Mountaineer,* 1974, p. 62; *A.A.J.,* 1975, p. 125, 128.

SOUTH ROUTE: The way taken by the original climbing party; a long but scenic approach requiring about 2 days. Take route to Hurricane Peak via Huckleberry Mountain Trail♦ (A shorter alternative is to take the Tenas Creek-Boulder Lake route). Follow the long Buck-Big Creek ridge leading NE of Hurricane and reach the low point (5480′+) just E of Crater Lake. Some parties bypass Hurricane's E slope at about 5600 ft (possible snow), or even descend to Lake Toketie, then continue N up to the ridge. Traverse the open, moderate S-facing slope above Crater Lake, crossing to the N side of the ridge at the col W of Point 6756. Drop slightly on the NE flank (snowfields) and ascend NW to a slight col; cross to the S slope again close to Chaval's East Peak. Traverse W, then ascend a steep snow finger to the notch adjacent the West Peak. Cross to a funnel-shaped couloir; a rock scramble leads to a steep snow gully on the N face to conclude the ascent (also possible short rock section). Class 3 or 4. Note: one could vary the summit section by continuing the traverse to the upper W side of the peak (see West Route).

Approach Variation: Via the western slope of the ridge beyond Hurricane Peak. Descend to Crater Lake (4471′); steep timber leads N to open slopes of the ridge SE of Chaval.

Jug Lake-Jug Creek Approach: See Jug Lake Route♦. Most feasible route is via Bluff Lake; if ascending from Jug Lake meet West Route at Peak 6356.

EAST PEAK

First ascent by Bruce Bryant and Richard C. Hubley on July 14, 1952. The climb was done from a camp at Lake Toketie. Beyond the col W of Peak 6756 drop slightly across the ridge and ascend NW to the col just N of the East Peak. The ascent is via the N face; of the final portion of several hundred ft of rock, the last 50 ft are class 4 (one roped pitch).

MT. CHAVAL from Snowking Mtn.
PHILIP LEATHERMAN

MT. CHAVAL from south
WILL F. THOMPSON

MT. BAKER
MT. CHAVAL
Middle Pk.
East Pk.
BIG CREEK

PEAK 6400 6400′+/1951 m

This peak is 1.2 mi. WNW of Mt. Chaval, between Peaks 6364 and 6356. Possible first ascent by Tom Menzel and J. Wilson on June 30, 1974.

ROUTE: See Mt. Chaval-West Route. From the 6100-ft saddle just NE of the peak ascend S to the top of snow, then traverse left in moat at cliff footing. Traverse around to heather slopes on the S side. Then ascend class 4 rock directly to the summit (chocks and runners advisable). Time: 2 hours from saddle.

PEAK 6356 6356′/1937 m

Climbed by Bruce Bryant on traverse from Mt. Chaval on September 16, 1954.

PEAK 6364 6364′/1940 m

Located 1½ mi. WNW of Mt. Chaval. No data. The peak has a sheer N face, and appears to be the most attractive of the several minor peaks here.

PEAK 6103 6103′/1860 m

Between upper Grade Creek and Arrow Creek, SE of Illabot Peaks. First ascent by Bruce Bryant July 6, 1953.

ROUTE: One could use Grade Creek Road♦ from near its end (est. 4000′), then bear easily NE. A divide (wooded ridge) leads to the SE summit ridge, which is then followed. A traverse along the ridge to the E was done by Bryant, traveling over Peak 5955 (1815 m) to Peak 6356 (1937 m).

ILLABOT PEAKS 5944′/1812 m

These moderate but isolated peaks are between White and Illabot Creeks, 8.2 mi. SE of Rockport. Because of their relative proximity to the Skagit River, they offer nice viewpoints. Flanking the central and highest peak are two lower W summits (5600′+/1707 m and 5603′/1708 m) and a lesser NE summit. The first ascent is unknown; all summits climbed by Bruce Bryant on July 3, 1953.

SOUTHEAST ROUTE: Take Grade Creek Road♦, then W branch to about 4300 ft (this is 2 mi. SE of summit on Grade Creek-Suiattle River ridge). Hike NW along the divide to the ridge S of Lake Tupso (was old trail along ridge to lake). A continuing cross-country route leads N, NE, and NW to the 5400-ft point E of Lake Louise. Then follow the ridge to the W Illabot Peak. Turn E and traverse to the summit; the route is mostly a hike with a summit gully (class 2). Time: 4-5 hours.

Approach Variation: Take Illabot Road♦ 6 mi., then drive to end of West Boundary Road (no. 346) at just over 4000 ft (providing road conditions permit). An old path led E 1½ mi. to above Lake Tupso (uncertain condition).

NORTHWEST ROUTE: Take Illabot Road off East Sauk Hwy. At 12 mi. from Rockport take S branch (Illabot Peaks Road No. 3414) to the head of Hilt Creek (end about 4000 ft at 1.8 mi. NW of Illabot Peaks—if passable). From road end contour E to the ridge crest in ½ mi., then follow the ridge spur SE between the heads of Iron and White Creeks; gradually climb to the far western summit—pass over one ridge hump en route. Turn E and traverse ¼ mi. to the summit (see Southeast Route).

Alternate Approach: There is a new logging road in White Creek valley (possibly locked). One could hike E in forest to the peaks.

JORDAN PEAK 6397′/1950 m

A minor peak ½ mi. N of Lower Jordan Lake on the Jordan-Boulder Creek divide. Probable first ascent by Bruce Bryant on August 13, 1953.

ROUTE: From Upper Jordan Lake (see Falls Creek Route♦) ascend NW through forest to Point 5626 (1715 m). On the ridge W at about 0.3 mi. (just before Point 5626) the travel is cliffy; it is difficult to drop off the ridge. The easy S ridge is completed to the summit.

BOULDER PEAK 6377′/1944 m

This peak is ½ mi. W of Upper Granite Lake and ½ mi. N of Upper Jordan Lake. Possible first ascent by Bruce Bryant on August 14, 1953.

ROUTE: From Upper Jordan Lake (see Falls Creek Route♦) ascend to the E slope, then complete on the N ridge (no difficulties).

MT. TOMMY THOMPSON 6780′/2067 m

The principal peak between the Skagit River and Snowking Mountain, 3.2 mi. NW of the latter, between Upper Granite Lake and Otter Creek. Part of the rock unit is related to Snowking, of quartz diorite-biotite granodiorite. The name is unofficial, being proposed for the early Skagit district ranger, who made many explorations into and contributed to the knowledge of the greater region. First ascent by Bruce Bryant on August 14, 1953; the sub-peak (6496′/1980 m) to the W was also climbed, but had a cairn. Reference: Bruce Bryant, Ph.D. dissert., Univ. of Washington, 1955, p. 188.

ROUTE: From Boulder Peak (and Upper Jordan Lake) approach via the NW semi-alpine ridge. At 5800 ft leave the ridge and bear SE upward (snow) in N-facing cirque (talus, moraine, snow-ice patches). Contour top of SE-facing cirque and cross the ridge through small spruce to a heather-filled gully. Here are two summit gullies: the W gully is simpler except at the top; the E gully is easier at the top. Class 3.

PEAK 6559 6559′/1999 m

An obvious mass with a rounded and craggy rock summit 1 mi. E of Upper Granite Lake, on the divide of Boulder, Irene, and Found Creeks. Climbing history unknown.

ROUTE: The best route may be the NW ridge from the sub-peak. The SE slope (Found Creek) is the gentlest. One could reach this from Irene Creek Trail or via Lower Granite Lake.

Sub-peak 6469 (1972 m), ½ mi. to the NE was climbed by Bruce Bryant on July 21, 1953.

RAZORBACK MOUNTAIN 6110′/1862 m

E of Boulder Creek and W of Irene Creek, Razorback is a moderate summit which forms a long ridge trending NW. On the SE flank of the summit a large quantity of rock slid into the valley of upper Irene Creek, leaving a great volume of talus; this recent slide is controlled by the fault plane in granitic rock (Bruce Bryant, Ph.D. dissert., Univ. of Washington, 1955, photo p. 289).

ROUTE: The entire ridge of Razorback is merely a hike from Lower Granite Lake or Boulder Creek.

SONNY BOY PEAK 6960′+/2121 m (est. 6980′/2128 m)

This peak, which has a small but sharp summit cluster, is 3.3 mi. NE of Mt. Buckindy, between Kindy and Milt Creek. Rock is biotite granodiorite. The Sonny Boy quadrangle marks the altitude 6971 ft at the W summit, but the E peak seems slightly higher. The 1961 guidebook designated this summit Peak 7000. First ascent by Bruce Bryant on July 16, 1953.

ROUTE: This original route covers over 6 mi. cross-country, but is probably the quickest route. From just beyond the beginning of Kindy Creek Trail♦ follow the long and dry Kindy-Sonny Boy ridge (possible camp spot E of ridge past Point 6775). The route continues along the ridge; allow 1½ days.

MILT CREEK ROUTE: Take South Fork Cascade River Trail (see Cascade River Area♦) to opposite Milt Creek (est. 3 mi.; identified by huge waterfall). Cross river on logs upstream. Ascend the forest up and rightward, entering a dry creekbed (follow to 3500′); then traverse right for ¼ mi. into upper Milt Creek basin. Rise to the ridge SW between creek branches. Keep left (S) and head for summit ridge at saddle (6400′+; some snow). Easy rock and heather lead WNW to the summit. Note: the route is verified to about 5000 ft., and beyond is proposed from study.

Other approaches: a long but complex traverse route is possible from Bench Lake; one could hike via Woods Lake and Long Gone Lake. A traverse has been made from Downey Creek-Bench Lake to Sonny Boy Ridge.

MT. BUCKNER 9080′+/2768 (est. 9114′/2778 m)

Mt. Buckner, 1.7 mi. WSW of Park Creek Pass, competes with Mt. Goode as the monarch of the area beyond the head of Lake Chelan. Located at the eastern end of the vast cirque that holds the immense Boston Glacier, Buckner is much more of a mountaineer's summit than Booker or Sahale. It is not a difficult climb when done with caution, but some loose rock (Skagit gneiss) is unpleasant.

Buckner has two summits of nearly-equal height: The SW peak is estimated at 2 ft higher than the 9112-ft NE peak. The mountain has four distinct ridges: W, E, SE, and S. The twin Buckner Glaciers are located in the E and SE cirques. The N face features hanging glacier ice with exposed rock ribs. The ice on the face displays a textbook example of a bergschrund where a deep crevasse separates the active Boston Glacier from the steep headwall of its cirque container. The mountain is named after Henry F. Buckner, who was manager of the mining company which located claims and mined in upper Horseshoe Basin in the early 1900s. The first ascent was made by Lewis D. Ryan of Washington State Geological Survey on August 1, 1901; his record was found on the summit by Dan O'Brien and Hermann F. Ulrichs when they made the second ascent on July 24, 1934 (first climb of the NE peak). Buckner was climbed again by Don Blair, Norval Grigg, and Art Winder on July 26, 1934. References: *A.A.J.*, 1936, p. 472; *Mazama* 30, no. 13 (1948): 15; *Mountaineer,* 1934, p. 14; 1964, pp. 126-130; 1971, map p. 42; *Harvard Mountaineering,* no. 6 (1943): 36-37; *Appalachia* 24, no. 93 (June 1942): 42-43; 29 (Dec. 1952): 215; *Summit,* Nov.-Dec. 1971, p. 12.

SOUTHWEST ROUTE: Original route; also variation on third ascent via Booker-Buckner col and traverse across snow at head of Horseshoe Basin. The route consists of much talus (or snow) climbing, a steep snow finger, and then rock scrambling on summit-area rocks. (class 3).

Approach Variation (1): Ascend Sahale Arm up and E to the lower E end of Sahale Glacier (7200′). Cross glacier just above terminus to rock rib of Sahale Peak; drop by this rib 600 ft to a notch with snowfinger leading to it on N. Descend snow 100 ft to upper Horseshoe Basin at about 6400 ft. Make gradually steepening traverse around the basin to Davenport Mine and bear to the S side of Buckner's W ridge. Time: 4 hours from Sahale Arm to summit. Reference: *Mountaineer,* 1966, p. 202.

(2): One can traverse above Doubtful Lake and cross a ragged rock ridge about 6850 ft, then descend 100 ft down a rotten red dike into the basin.

MT. BUCKNER from south
AUSTIN POST, U.S. GEOLOGICAL SURVEY

MT. BOOKER, Northeast Face
DWIGHT WATSON

NORTH FACE: First ascent by Calder T. Bressler, Ralph W. Clough, Bill Cox, and Tom Myers on July 28, 1938. The route ascends the 40-45° firn and snow from Boston Glacier directly below the SW peak; the route steepens at 7800 ft. The original party took 5 hours from Sahale Arm via Sahale and Boston Peak; the route has been done in 1 day from a camp in Boston Basin by crossing the Sahale-Boston col, traversing easy rocks E around Boston Peak, and descending Boston Glacier to the climb's foot. Take crampons, snow flukes, and ice screws. Reference: *Mountaineer,* 1958, p. 58.

NORTH COULOIR: First ascent by Steve Doty and Van Brinkerhoff on November 14, 1976. This 1300-ft snow/ice couloir is a consistent 45-50° from the bergschrund to the summit; some water ice may be encountered (bring ice screws). Grade II. Time: 2½ hours.

EAST RIDGE: This is a long moderate rock climb. Much of the ridge is knife-edged with very loose rock, and dangerous without a rope. The lower part is easiest. First ascent by Abigail D. Avery, Stuart B. Avery, Everett L. Darr, Ida Zacher Darr, Henry S. Hall Jr., Kenneth A. Henderson, Grant McConnell, Jane McConnell, and Paul Parker on August 2, 1940 (on traverse of Buckner; descent via SW). Climb from Park Creek Pass (see Park Creek Trail♦). When the ridge narrows, continue through some snowpatches. When the ridge turns SW toward the summit, some crumbly rock is encountered on the exposed arete. The climb to the NE peak is moderately difficult, but the short traverse to the higher summit is simple. Time: 8 hours. References: *Appalachia* 23 (Dec. 1940): 240; 24, no. 93 (June 1942): 42-43.

SOUTH RIDGE: This is a long crest (1 mi.) from the Booker-Buckner col. From Horseshoe Basin (see Stehekin River Trail♦) steep game trails lead to the col (7080′+); 3 hours. At a tree-covered break about 6500 ft cross a dike N of the col's SW slopes. Then follow the rocky S ridge of Buckner. An alternative is to descend W from the col to avoid the first half of the ridge; the obstacle is the same dike: some parties have made a bypass and descended to an ice patch below a chimney. Then cross snow and ice to easy rock and talus N (the best way is to just climb the prominent chimney which is about 200 ft W of the S ridge; easy if done correctly). The final third of the ridge is quite solid; class 3 or 4. Time: 3 hours from col.

Variation: Park Creek Pass Approach: By third ascent party, 1934, who climbed to S ridge above col's notch. A good camp can be made on the large bench (about 6000′—tarn there), between the pass and head of the creek (est. ¼ mi. SW of pass). Descend some and then contour easily around benches at western basin, then cross the glacier to the SW. There are several hundred ft of steep snow and ice on an arm of Buckner Glacier; crevasses and a bergschrund may be a problem. One can ascend snow and rock slopes to either the col or to the S ridge; of two snow/ice gullies which extend to the ridge the western (highest) is preferable (ends on ridge about 200 yds from col). Time: 2-3 hours to ridge.

MT. BOOKER 8280′+/2524 m

Mt. Booker is 1½ mi. SE of Mt. Buckner between Park Creek and Stehekin River. The NE face is a broad wall some 2800 ft high; the SW slope is cliffy but of moderate angle, with rockslides and brush beneath. Small ice patches punctuate the NE face and SW slope. The name was given by an artist for Booker T. Washington. First ascent by Dan O'Brien and Hermann F. Ulrichs on July 24, 1934. References: *Mazama* 30, no. 13 (1948): 15-16; *Appalachia* 29, no. 115 (1952): 215; *Mountaineer,* 1964, p. 13.

NORTHWEST ROUTE: A narrow gorge forming the col (7080′+) between Booker and Buckner can be reached from Horseshoe Basin or Park Creek (see Mt. Buckner). The ridge to the summit is then quite simple (1¼ hours).

NORTHEAST FACE: First ascent by Dan Davis and John Holland on August 22, 1964. The route takes the prominent central rib of the face to the summit, and is quite spectacular when seen face-on. From Park Creek Trail♦ ascend to the small icefall of the lower glacier (just S of the rib). Climb the icefall to where a ledge leads rightward onto the face. From the glacier climb onto a flake which leads to a tree-covered horizontal ledge. From a large tree at flat on ledge climb to just beneath a loose section, then make a delicate traverse right. Then climb straight up to the rib crest (at the red band traverse left about 150′ and then bear back to the crest). From the major notch about two-thirds of the way climb up about 20 ft, then angle left around a corner, then back to the crest (this is the most difficult section). Grade III; mostly class 4 but one class 5.8 section (used 10 pitons). References: *Mountaineer,* 1965, pp. 83-84; *A.A.J.,* 1965, pp. 410-411.

RIPSAW RIDGE (Horseshoe Minarets)

These striking, closely spaced spires on the long and serrated over-8000-ft ridge between Boston Peak and Mt. Buckner, were called "dark red minarets" by William D. Lyman, who estimated their altitude at 10,000 ft. Thunder Creek miners of 1891 called this Saw Tooth Ridge.[75] A more appropriate name than Rip Saw Ridge, applied by climbers (*Mountaineer,* 1934, p. 11) would be Horseshoe Minarets. W. Ronald Frazier in 1935 discussed the glacial cirque above Horseshoe Basin, "topped by a knife-like arete consisting of spires so symmetrical that I called them minarets" (*Mazama* 18, no. 12 (1936): 58). Martin Gorman, who explored the area in 1897, wrote "one aiguille to the west of Horseshoe Basin, near a mining prospect known as the "Blue Devil," cannot, I think, be surpassed anywhere for acuteness of angle" (Gorman, *op. cit.,* p. 318). Current maps label "Horseshoe Pk." (8440′+) on the ridge; this is fatuous—none of the spires should be called peaks, as they are such obviously subsidiary summits. Names such as Blue Devil, Flamingo, and Black Warrior would be appropriate and of historic association. Climbing history is incomplete and vague; some of the spires certainly have been climbed. The rock is generally unpleasant for steep ascents.

MT. BUCKNER and BOSTON PEAK from north
AUSTIN POST, U.S. GEOLOGICAL SURVEY

MT. BUCKNER
North Face
Ripsaw Ridge
BOSTON PK.
Sharkfin Tower
Sharkfin Col
BOSTON
GLACIER
Skagit Queen Creek

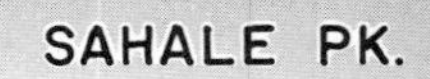

CASCADE PASS to HORSESHOE BASIN
L.D. LINDSLEY PHOTOGRAPHY COLLECTION, University of Washington

BOSTON PEAK 8894′/2711 m

The name was derived from the Boston Mine and glacier. Boston was once the name of the glacier on the W flank, now called the Quien Sabe. The Boston Glacier, which was "Silver Basin Glacier" to early miners, occupies the immense cirque N and E of the peak. The U.S. Geological Survey party of 1897 believed the summit inaccessible and applied the name to the present Sahale.[76] The original climbing party termed Boston a heap of "low grade ore." The peak's color tone is indeed rusty. First ascent by Calder Bressler, Ralph Clough, Bill Cox, and Tom Myers on July 28, 1938 (Southeast Face). Reference: *Mountaineer,* 1958, p 58.

SOUTHEAST FACE: Reach the Sahale-Boston col (8560′+) by a descent from Sahale or direct ascent from the W (see Sahale Peak, West Route). Follow the ridge to the corner of the S face, then climb on an E bearing. Moderately difficult rock, which is steep and loose, is climbed on the SE and E face for 350 ft. Class 4.

Approach Variation: Traverse and ascend Boston Glacier to the E face. The glacier can be reached via Sharkfin Col (see Forbidden Peak, North Ridge).

SOUTH FACE: First ascent by Robert Grant and Richard N. Safely in 1950: Make the ascent directly from the Sahale-Boston col and ridge adjacent; the face is quite exposed and loose. Class 4.

WEST FACE: First ascent by Keith Anderson and John Shonle on September 7, 1956. Approach per Sahale Peak-West Route. Diagonal left up the snow tongue of the col and gain the rock at the lower of two prominent gullies. Begin from gully and climb the W face; easy class 4. Reference: *Sierra Club Bull.* 42, no. 6 (1957): 62.

SAHALE PEAK 8680′/2646 m

Sahale is noted for its panoramic views and easy ascent. The small horn-shaped rock summit is on the same massif as higher Boston Peak, a situation that has been a source of confusion since surveyors placed a benchmark on Sahale's peak with the identification

"Boston." When 30 members of the Mazama outing climbed Sahale on July 17, 1899 they thought the name—meaning "high up" in Indian legends—should honor the great spirit which reared the chain of the Cascades.

In the 1899 outing report H.S. Pattullo wrote that he believed it was possibled to see "400 distinct snow peaks" from the summit. A contemporary report given William D. Lyman by a miner noted that from one of the loftiest summits he had counted 200 distinct snow mountains; this suggests a possible unknown earlier ascent of the peak. John Charlton and Albert H. Sylvester (U.S. Geological Survey) climbed the peak in August 1897, making the apparent first ascent, and wrapped a few yards of white cotton around the summit rock for a survey target; a copper bolt was set in a hole drilled in the rock. Later Sylvester wrote "This was the sharpest peak I was ever on. No necessity for a cairn here." The list of geologist Bailey Willis' panoramic views (1895-1900) includes Boston Mountain, but the date of ascent is not known.

There are three glaciers adjacent to the peak: The Sahale (0.3 mi. wide) high on the S slope and draining to Doubtful Basin; the larger Davenport (0.7 mi. wide) in upper NW Horseshoe Basin (the name stems from the famed Davenport Mine at about 7000′ on the glacier's E edge); the Quien Sabe in the eastern cirque of Boston Basin. References: *Mazama* 2, no. 3 (1903): 141; 30, no. 13 (1948): 17-18; *Mountaineer,* 1928, pp. 12-13; *Summit* Nov.-Dec. 1971, p. 12; William G. Steel, "Lake Chelan and the Valley of the Stehekin," *Oregon Native Son* 1, no. 8 (1900): 412-414.

SOUTH SLOPE: For approach see Cascade Pass Trail♦. Ascend Sahale Arm, then follow the western margin of Sahale Glacier to the final rock slabs; a scramble leads to the sharp summit (class 3). Time: 4 hours from Cascade Pass.

Variation: From Horseshoe Basin a broad talus and snow chute extends to the SE edge of Sahale Glacier.

WEST ROUTE: From Sahale Arm traverse northward onto the Quien Sabe Glacier (or reach glacier from Boston Basin). Ascend around the large rock buttress of Sahale (base at 7600′), then climb the high glacier arm. Pass the large bergschrund (several hundred ft below ridge) on its right; climb one steep snow or ice pitch (45°), then easier gradient to the rock ridge N of the summit. The ridge along the ice edge is usually very corniced. Climb steepening rock (class 3) to the top; the final portion requires care because of exposure and some looseness.

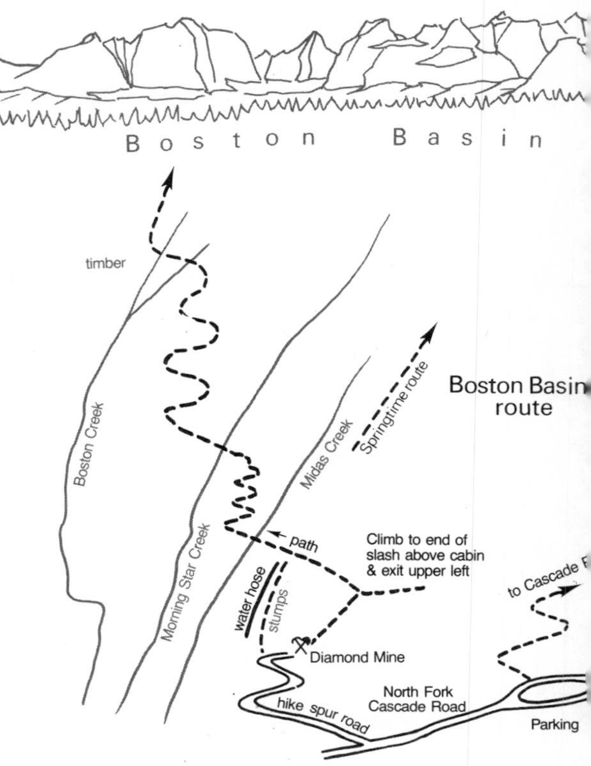

SHARKFIN TOWER 8120′+/2475 m

A prominent tower of excellent climbing rock (quartz diorite) 1.1 mi. SE of Forbidden Peak, on the ridge connecting the latter with Boston Peak. First ascent by Wesley Grande, Jay Todd, and Joseph Vance in August 1947. References: *Mountaineer,* 1947, p. 46; *Summit,* Oct. 1964, pp. 6-7.

EAST FACE: This is a short, enjoyable but exposed rock climb. For approach see Cascade River Area♦—Boston Basin Route. Ascend gully right of the narrow U-notch on the E ridge; the gully leaves from the glacier on the S and extends through the cliff band—class 2 and 3. The first lead is on the N and goes around to the tiny level spot on the ridge; then follow skyline to the top.

SOUTH FACE: First ascent by Cecil Bailey and Ed Cooper on November 7, 1959. Approach as for East Face. This 225-ft route is three leads up the chimney that splits the face and has interesting chockstones. The second pitch is 80° (the crux is a mantle). Class 5.6 (original party used five pitons because of wintry conditions; climb may be class 4); references: *A.A.J.*, 1960, p. 120; *Mountaineer,* 1960, pp. 82-83.

Note: there is another chimney route of 100 ft on the face, to the E; the route has a prominent chockstone; class 5.7.

SOUTHWEST FACE: This route follows the second buttress W of the prominent snow gully beneath the tower. First ascent by Leon Blumer and party on June 20, 1959. Cross snow to the notch W of the tower and up the face toward the SW edge; the route bears to the E of the buttress. References: *Mountaineer,* 1960, p. 83; *A.A.J.* 1960, p. 118.

WEST FACE: First ascent by Les MacDonald and party on June 20, 1959. Begin as per Southwest Face, but the route is W of the buttress. Begin with a pendulum; climb cracks and down-slab to an edge below a shallow scoop; climb around the edge, up an overhang on the edge (aid), then right across a little chimney onto easy ledges; total two leads. Class 5 (four pitons safety) and two pitons for aid. References: same as above.

NORTHWEST FACE: A pleasant mixed ice, snow, and rock climb. First ascent by Michael Heath, Dan Raish, and Woody Savage on July 1, 1967. From N of Sharkfin Col (see Forbidden Peak-North Ridge) make a short traverse E. A steep ice tongue leads up to the NW rib of the tower (three leads of steep firn to crest of arete). Then there is 500 ft of solid rock; all pitches are class 4 except one harder to exit from rib to upper N face. Bring crampons. Time: 7 hours from Boston Basin. Reference: *A.A.J.*, 1968, pp. 138-139.

NORTH FACE: First ascent by Dallas Kloke and David Seman on August 3, 1971. The route begins on the E side of the N face. There are three leads of solid rock to a steep, well broken band. Make a short traverse W over loose blocks and then climb up several ft (hanging belay). The next pitch is the crux: 50 ft of aid goes to a ledge on the rib between the E and N faces; the final lead continues up the rib 60 ft and then diagonal ascent is made to reach the E ridge about 100 ft below the summit. Grade II; class 5.6 and A2. Time: 9 hours from Boston Basin. Reference: *Mountaineer,* 1971, p. 82.

SHARK'S TOOTH

This prominent but small pinnacle is E of Sharkfin Col. First ascent by Ed Cooper and Stuart Ferguson on September 14, 1961. One lead from the E; class 5. Reference: *Mountaineer,* 1961, p. 101.

FORBIDDEN PEAK 8815′/2687 m

Glacial erosion, which tends to produce sharp angular landforms, has created the classic horn formation of

FORBIDDEN PEAK from southeast
PHILIP LEATHERMAN

FORBIDDEN PK.
West Ridge
East Ridge
cross behind
North Ridge
PRIMUS PK.
TRICOUNI PK.
to N.W.
col 7680+
to North Ridge
Sharkfin Tower
BOSTON GLACIER
Shark's Tooth
Sharkfin col
gully
Boston Basin

Summit
dihedral
chimney
traversing up
alcove
East Ridge
1968
right
traverse
2 leads
crossing
West Ridge
Couloir
overhang
2 leads
1950
groove

Forbidden Peak by the merging of several cirques. Three cirques and three aretes culminate in a sharp summit of solid Skagit gneiss which has resisted the plucking of glaciers. The remarkable ridges are so quintessentially perfect, and its setting so grandiose that Forbidden has a special status in the Cascade Pass area. While there is a definite similarity about the ridges, the faces differ noticeably: the S face is slabby and down-sloping, the NE face is a formidable recessed wall, and the NW face is ice-clad with a prominent rock rib. Boston Glacier extends from the eastern cirque of Forbidden to the E and N, the NW cirque holds Forbidden Glacier—draining to Moraine Lake—and on the SW the smaller Taboo Glacier rests on bedrock slabs in the cirque between Forbidden and Mt. Torment; a section of ice reaches to over 7900 ft under Forbidden's S face.

The dramatic peak has been likened to a "great obelisk of rock," and the party which climbed Eldorado Peak in 1933 remarked, "especially prominent was a high unnamed peak, heavily glaciated, directly to the east." Hermann Ulrichs, who was interested in traversing the Boston Glacier in 1932 for an attempt, called the peak "Isosoles," it has also been called "Forgotten." The first attempt on Forbidden was made by Lloyd Anderson, Fred Beckey, and Dwight Watson on April 14, 1940; cornice formations and snow problems on the rock of the W ridge halted this adventure. The first ascent was made by Lloyd Anderson, Fred Beckey, Helmy Beckey, Jim Crooks, and Dave Lind on June 1, 1940 (tricouni nailed boots were used except for tennis shoes on the tower pitch). The next ascent was made by Art Holben, Dick Merritt, and Keith Rankin on August 8, 1946. References: *Mountaineer,* 1940, pp. 35-36; 1946, pp. 18-19; *Accidents in North American Mountaineering,* 1976.

EAST RIDGE: This route now has become the standard. The climb really does not follow the E ridge, but reaches it from the S at a notch at about 8300 ft, then makes a rising traverse on the NE face beneath the crest, where the bedding dip is favorable. Many parties do not rope on some or all of the traverse, but the exposure is relentless; a fatal accident in 1975 resulted from a slip on the traverse. First ascent by George Bell and Harry King in August 1948.

From Boston Basin (see Cascade River Area♦—Boston Basin Route) ascend N up snowfields and a portion of the glacier to the cirque nearly at the foot of the S face. Then ascend a snow couloir between rock buttresses in a NE direction, then bear left on a rock spur. Reach the notch in the E ridge left of the solitary gendarme. Drop slightly on the opposite side and traverse across the NE face. It is best to stay well below the ridge and reach the N ridge about 300 ft beneath the summit, then follow it. Class 3 and 4. Time: 2 hours from notch. Note: original party passed the next ridge gendarme on the S side before crossing to the N (class 4 and 5).

EAST RIDGE DIRECT: This is a route of elegance, seldom done, which merits more attention. First ascent by Fred Beckey, Ed Cooper, Donald (Claunch) Gordon, and Joe Hieb on May 25, 1958. From the notch of the East Ridge route follow the towers. These are either climbed directly or turned at a high level. The first major tower is bypassed on the N and the next one passed on either flank. Grade II or III: class 5.7-5.8. References: *Mountaineer,* 1959, p. 106; *A.A.J.,* 1959, p. 306.

SOUTH FACE DIRECT: This demanding slab route of 8½ leads ascends closer to the center of the face than the 1950 route, but is still somewhat indirect; the route meets the W ridge about 300 ft from the summit. Rock is solid but unfavorably down-slabbed, so no obvious line suggests itself. First ascent by Jim Langdon and Jim McCarthy in August 1968.

Begin near the left margin of the face, on the lowest slabs above the glacier (class 5.4); the second pitch starts from a ledge and involves a low-angle, 30-ft right-facing dihedral (class 5.8) which is below a small roof. Get on a sloping ledge, then traverse 30 ft rightward under a roof; where the roof ends there is a belay recess. The next pitch aids another roof (A3-15′) and then ascends an easy crack to a ledge. The next portion of the route is on a low-angle slab area (numerous possibilities) near the 1950 route, then two class 5 pitches reach a belay alcove under an overhang. A lead traverses somewhat left; cross ramps and overhangs into a prominent dihedral (class 5.7). The final pitch ascends the dihedral to end at an overhang. Layback and stem through to the ridge. Grade IV; class 5.8 and A3 (used about 23 placements including three for aid; route should be good for chocks). Selection: include ample angle sizes to 2″ and KB. Time: allow 8-12 hours on face. Reference: *Mountaineer,* 1970, p. 103.

SOUTH FACE, WEST SIDE: The face in the area of the original climb is about 800 ft in height, with an extreme down-slab character. The route appears deflected for one never climbs the upper wall to the summit area, yet it is a challenging objective. First ascent by Bill Fix and Pete Schoening on July 3, 1950. (The previous day Schoening and Dick Widrig climbed 400 ft, with Fix and Fred Beckey following to the chimney; then Fix and Schoening went into the chimney, and after the ascent made seven rappels to reach the snow at dusk).

Follow the approach for West Ridge to E of the couloir. Begin at the edge of a chimney to pass ice-carved area, then at about the 200-ft level make a rightward climbing traverse (class 5). The route bears toward the 400-ft chimney, which eventually becomes very narrow and leads to the summit ridge. At 60 ft beneath the ridge there is a complex jumble of overhanging cracks and blocks (the lead is belayed from a cave) which may take several hours. Grade III or IV; class 5

FORBIDDEN PEAK, South Face
AUSTIN POST, U.S. GEOLOGICAL SURVEY

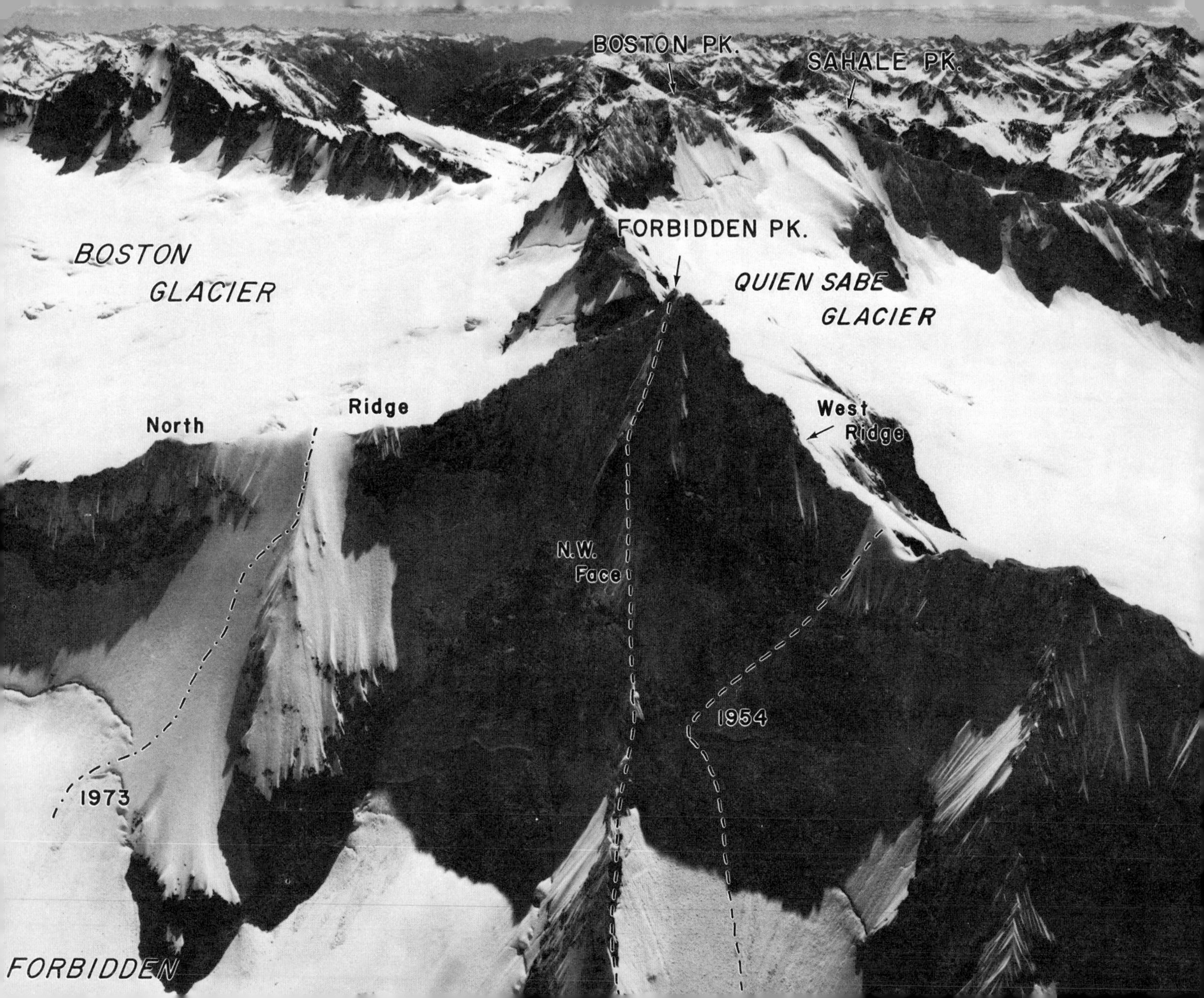

BOSTON PK.
SAHALE PK.
FORBIDDEN PK.
QUIEN SABE
GLACIER
West
Ridge
1954
N.W.
Face
BOSTON
GLACIER
North
Ridge
1973
FORBIDDEN

(35 pitons used on original—eight for aid). References: *A.A.J.*, 1951, pp. 172-173; *Mountaineer,* 1951, p. 35.

WEST RIDGE: This route, the one used on the original climb, is in a magnificent position. The narrow W ridge, whose pitches are pure joy and distinctly alpine, rises 550 ft from the ridge notch in a length of some 1500 ft. From Boston Basin ascend to the cirque beneath the prominent 500-ft couloir W of the S face. This couloir may be snow-filled or very icy, and may be broken by small schrunds and sections of rock, depending on season and conditions (serious accidents have occurred here including a tragedy on August 25, 1958); in late season conditions may force the route to moderately difficult slab on the left flank. On the ridge blocks and small ledges provide good belay stances; some parties bypass problems by N-side traverses. A tower 175 ft below the summit is usually protected by a piton (there is a good rappel point at top); a N-side bypass of the tower is feasible. From the slightly lower W summit drop into a small notch and climb to the E summit. Class 4 and 5. Time: 6 hours from basin; 4 hours descent.

Approach Variation: This variation is the couloir bypass, directly beneath the notch. Begin on slabs W of couloir (several steep class 4 pitches), then enter a steep gully; the latter becomes easier on approaching the ridge notch, but watch loose rock. An alternate is to take the gully partway, then use the rib on its left.

NORTHWEST FACE OF WEST RIDGE: The original party began at Gilbert and pioneered a new glacier approach from Torment Col, then later made a bivouac on the face. The route is very alpine and exposed, but not a direct summit route. First ascent by Donald (Claunch) Gordon, David Harrah, and Brad Sturdevant on July 25, 1954. Ascend to where Forbidden Glacier reaches the rock beneath the round-shaped snowfield on the face. There may be a schrund problem at the base of the rock. A series of steep shelves and slabs with ice and snowpatches follow. Bear up and right on a major shelf (class 5) with a wall on the left; there may be verglas and ice on the rock. The final portion is 200 ft of 50° snowfield and ice, which leads to the W ridge. Grade III; class 5 on face to where bivouac made just beneath snowfield, then mostly class 4 or snow (15 pitons used).

NORTHWEST FACE: An exceptional climb of purity, with enough variety and difficulty to satisfy almost anyone. Its mixed character, requiring some genuine ice climbing, places it in a rather select group of North Cascade climbs requiring flexible alpine skills. First ascent by Fred Beckey and Ed Cooper on July 15, 1959.

Reach the face as per North Ridge and make a piton rappel to the Forbidden Glacier (or cross easily farther N at the lowest col—7680′+). Continue on a descending traverse across the glacier, then ascend through the crevasse system beneath the NW face and climb onto the prominent central rib at its lower right flank (rib begins about 7100′). Follow the rib directly to the summit. Grade IV; class 4 and 5 (about 10 placements). Time: 9 hours from Boston Basin (5 hours on face). References: *Mountaineer,* 1960, p. 82; *A.A.J.*, 1960, pp. 117-118.

NORTH RIDGE: This ridge, with its classic alpine characteristics, is about 0.7 mi. in length, and divides the Boston from Forbidden Glacier. The ridge actually trends NE, but the "N" name is firmly established. First ascent by Fred Beckey, Jack Schwabland, and Don Wilde on June 8, 1952.

The usual approach is from Boston Basin, over Sharkfin Col (7720′+); cross the left side of the col and make a descent to the Boston Glacier (a rotten gully of the col may require a rappel). Descend diagonally about 400 ft NW below a rock buttress, then traverse the glacier to the northern end of the N ridge. Climb to the ridge crest (at est. 7850′) via a high accumulation of glacier and rock on the E face (N of first ridge cornice). The ridge involves two easy glacier segments and some exposed but firm alpine rock climbing. Cornice danger can be avoided by keeping below the crest on the W flank. Note: The upper portion is sometimes avoided by various sorties onto the NE face; a ledge system can be taken for an entry. Grade III; class 3 and 4 (can be class 5 if icy conditions). Time: 8 hours from Boston Basin. References: *Mountaineer,* 1952, p. 79; *Appalachia* 29, (Dec. 1952): 401; *A.A.J.*, 1953, pp. 540-541.

Variation: Northwest Face of North Ridge: This is a very aesthetic route combining an ice climb with the enjoyable rock of the upper N ridge. The ice face (on a N-facing arm of Forbidden Glacier) is composed of two sections divided by a narrow rock area. The upper section ends at the cornice at mid-ridge (est. 8375′). This may be an especially good ice climb in late season, but in early summer will be covered by seasonal snow. First ascent by John Teasdale on August 23, 1973.

The initial bergschrund (est. 7600′) crossing was difficult. Then 900 ft of hard ice was encountered (front pointing); the angle reaches 50° in the upper portion (bring ice screws). Time: 3 hours glacier to summit. References: *A.A.J.*, 1974, p. 143; *Mountaineer,* 1973, p. 79.

NORTHEAST FACE (Route 1): The base of this face varies from about 7600 ft to 7900 ft (ice Boston Glacier reaches to as high as 7950′ at one margin). First ascent by Ed Cooper and Stuart Ferguson on September 15, 1960. Approach over Sharkfin Col (see North Ridge). The line of ascent is on rock just below and left of a large ice patch on the lower face. The original party had to climb down a short ice wall to regain the schrund, then did 300 ft of rock (class 4) to the 50° snowpatch (this about 300′ in height). The remaining 600 ft of the face beneath the summit is steep but favorably bedded. Grade II or III; class 3 and 4. References: *Mountaineer,* 1961, pp. 100-101; *A.A.J.*, 1961, p. 361.

NORTHEAST FACE (Route 2): First ascent by James R. Bedrick and Scott Davis in August, 1967. After the traverse of Boston Glacier to the NE face (see above) climb the ice cliff and lower snowfield in the center of the face directly. Cross the schrund and ascend a left-sloping ramp to its end, then climb up and right to a belay ledge. Traverse right to a

FORBIDDEN PEAK from northwest
AUSTIN POST, U.S. GEOLOGICAL SURVEY

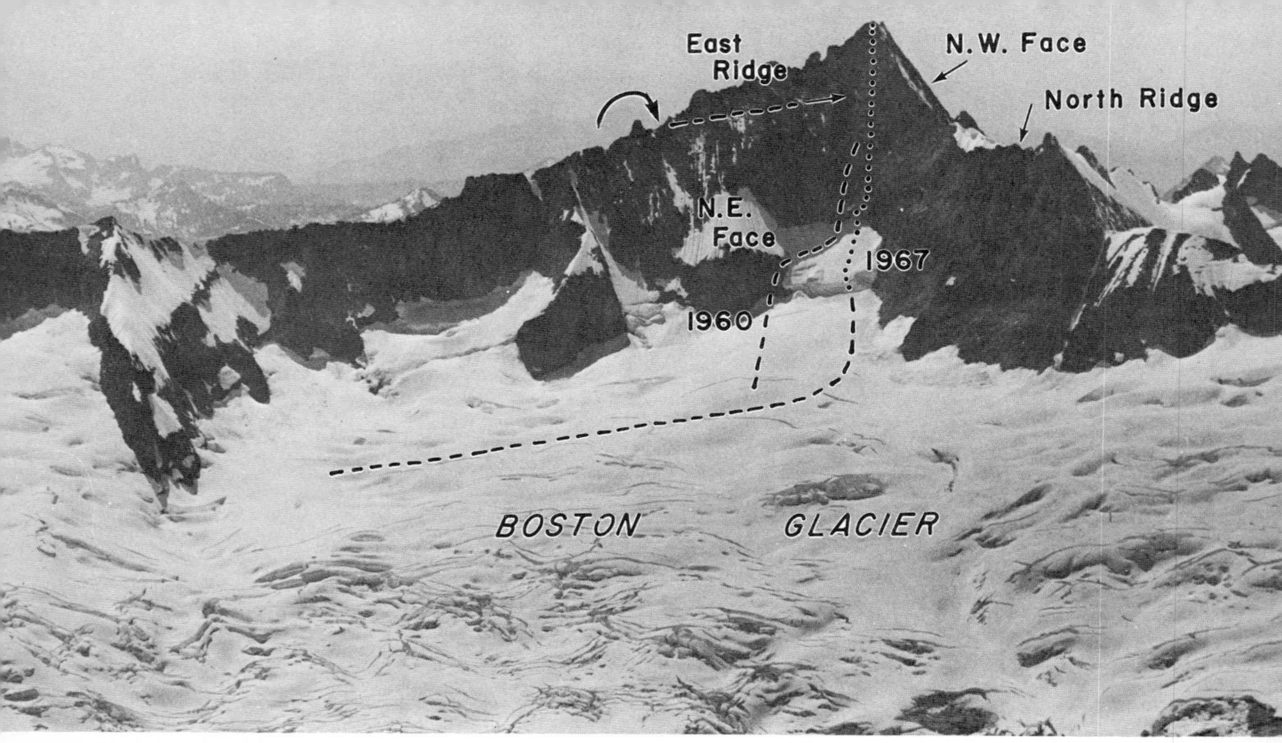

FORBIDDEN PEAK from northeast
PHILIP LEATHERMAN

ledge system which leads to a prominent chimney; from its top bear right and up to the summit. The route merges in this area with the 1960 climb. Grade III; class 5.7 (used 10 pitons including wide angles). Time: 7 hours from Sharkfin Col.

MT. TORMENT 8120′+/2475 m

Torment has diminutive status in comparison to neighboring Forbidden Peak, but has attracted continued climbing interest because of its alpine setting, solid rock, and many feasible routes (eight routes were done during the first eleven ascents). Torment is 0.9 mi. W of Forbidden, on the same W-trending divide; the W peak is highest by a small amount. An arm of Forbidden Glacier reaches nearly to the summit on the NW and another arm on the N face to the eastern col. There are two small glaciers in the SW cirques and Taboo Glacier is the designated name for the ice in the SE cirque. The best approaches are via Boston Basin or Torment Basin Routes (see Cascade River Area♦). The name was originated by the first ascent party because of the torture of a hot day with only one orange for thirst. First ascent by Jack Schwabland and Herb Staley August 23, 1946, via the SW face.

SOUTHEAST FACE: First ascent by Dale Cole and Michael Hane in mid-June 1958 (route descended in 1954 by second ascent party). This is considered the normal route, and presents the most direct way to the summit with route flexibility and steep but generally short leads; rock is slabby but good. The climb is class 3 and 4 except for the problem of the moat on the small glacier at the base; the crossing after July 1 can be difficult (aid has been used in September). The upper portion of the route is broken rock and leads to the cleft between the summits; both are easy from here. Class 4, with possible easy class 5 at times. Time: 9 hours total from road.

Descent: This is a good descent; usually two rappels are made on the lower face.

SOUTH RIDGE: This spur ridge separates the S and SE faces, and is a distinct result of ice scouring in the flanking cirques. First ascent by Ed Cooper and Walter Sellers in the fourth week of July, 1958. Ascend the lower S ridge and keep to its left side until forced to descend to the large snowfield on the W. Ascend snow (can be icy in late summer, forcing movement along its margin) to the narrow notch where the ridge joins the main peak's S face. Climb diagonally left below the crest about 500 ft (about 4½ pitches; class 4 but on third pitch varying 5th class difficulties reported). Cross the ridge through a small high notch to the upper SE face. Ascend here on easy rock for about 200 ft to the cleft between the summits; both summits are an easy scramble from here. Grade II; class 4 to mid-5th (take a few chocks; some fixed pitons on route). Time: 4-5 hours from below the peak. References: *Mountaineer,* 1959, p. 107; *A.A.J.,* 1959, pp. 301-302.

SOUTHWEST FACE: This route takes the center of the face as seen from the road. The Torment Basin approach is best for this route, which was used on the first ascent. Climb from snowfields at the base via the W edge of the S face. The route, which consists of solid but down-slab rock, keeps left of mid-face gendarmes. At about 150 ft from the NW ridge traverse left and ascend chimneys (possibly a gully) to reach the ridge about 200 ft below the summit; there is a giant boulder here. Make a traverse and diagonal ascent on the N face; the original party traversed on to the E peak. Class 4 and 5 (original party used 13 pitons, mostly for belay anchors).

Note: the original descent route was down the glacier moat N of the NW ridge to beyond a notch, up chimneys to the ridge, then down a couloir on the SW to W of the ascent line; one rappel made off the ridge. Later the route traversed W on a ledge, then down-climbing provided a good route.

NORTHWEST RIDGE: This route passes over and around many ridge features, but is mostly on the crest; rock varies from good to poor. First ascent by Tom Miller and Franz Mohling in mid-June 1958.

The route begins near the S of Torment Col (6640′+) then rises E on an easy gravelly sloping ledge system; bypass the first ridge hump on the S to gain the NW ridge at the notch beyond (7360′+). Then one is seldom more than 20-30 ft off the crest. The best rock is on the first portion, the worst in the middle. The first step from the notch is steep class 4. There are several class 5.6 leads and an occasional lead on the S side places one on rotten rock; it is easier if one stays more on the N flank. Make a rappel from the last tower to the snow col before the final summit.

NORTHWEST GLACIER: The route ascends the far western arm of Forbidden Glacier, then there is a short rock climb to either summit or to the notch between them; it is a classic alpine ascent of moderate difficulty. First ascent of upper glacier, via lower NW ridge by Joan Firey, Joe Firey, Anthony Hovey, and Don Keller in June 1961. The complete route involving the lower glacier was first done by Michael Heath, Ran Raish, and Woody Savage on July 3, 1967. The 1961 party ascended the Northwest Ridge route to the first notch, then descended about 400 ft of steep snow on the N flank to the glacier.

Make the approach via Torment Basin to the col (6640′+). Descend glacier firn on the N to about 5800 ft before it is possible to turn E past a buttress (slab problems and 150-ft rappel made here). The glacier ascent is straightforward but crevassed. There is a bergschrund at two-thirds height, then 600 ft of 40° snow and ice to its end at the summit rock. The 1961 party climbed directly to the W summit; the 1967 party did 200 ft of class 4 rock on the N rib of the E summit, then traversed. Grade II or III, class 4; bring crampons and snow flukes. Time: 6 hours from saddle.

NORTH RIDGE: The N ridge is a long spur between the

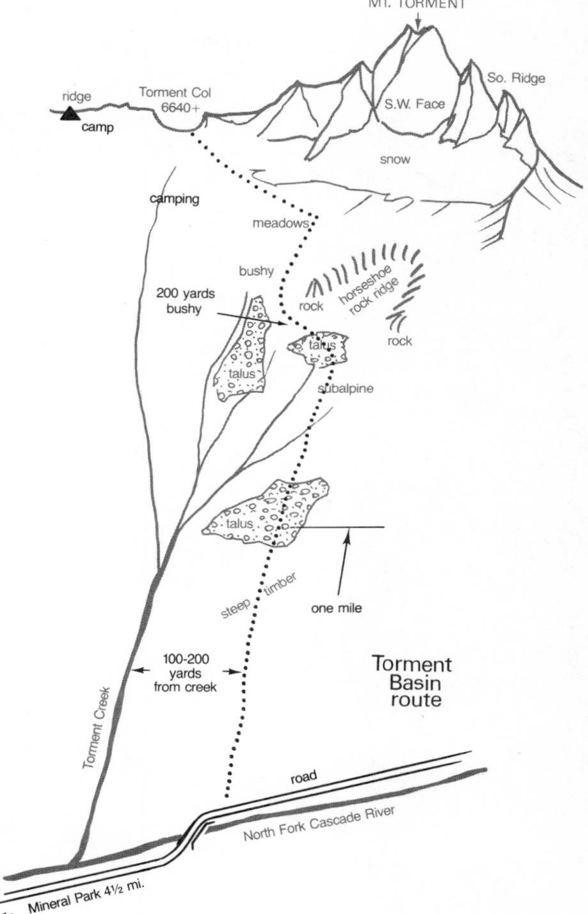

two glacier arms on this aspect of Torment. The ridge is obvious, as it bears left on an ascending curve; rock is clean and granitic. First ascent by Ed Cooper and Jim Kurtz on July 8, 1960. Approach as for Northwest Glacier. Traverse under ice cliff and gain altitude on the E flank of the N ridge. The original party remained on firn until about 300 ft above the end of ridge. A steep narrow snow gully which ends in a short class 4 pitch leads to the crest. Then climb 1000 ft of rock (class 3). Make only one traverse at the ridge top to gain the E summit. Grade II; class 3 and 4; take crampons. References: *Mountaineer,* 1961, p. 100; *A.A.J.,* 1961, pp. 361-362; 1971, p. 347 (repeat of route).

UPPER NORTHEAST FACE: Use the SE snow and ice finger to the E col (see East Ridge), then climb the top several hundred ft of the NE face. With good snow conditions this is not a difficult route; can be icy in late season. First ascent by Richard McGowan and Tom Miller on July 24,

JOHANNESBURG MTN.
MIXUP PK.
MT. TORMENT
East Pk
rappel
N.W. Ridge
West Ridge
East Col
N.E.
Route
North
Ridge
notch
hump
1961
Torment Col
N. W.
Glacier

MT. TORMENT from northwest
AUSTIN POST, UNIVERSITY of WASHINGTON

ELDORADO PEAK and THE TRIAD
DWIGHT WATSON

1954 (second ascent of Torment). Approach from Boston Basin. From the high col (7840′+) traverse onto the face to beneath the E summit, then directly up easy solid rock. Follow the ridge to the higher W summit (class 3 and 4). Take crampons and ice screws. Reference: *Mountaineer,* 1954, p. 64.

EAST RIDGE: A good route but a poor choice when the bergschrund is difficult to cross (see above). First ascent by Michael Borghoff and David Hiser on June 17, 1961. Cross the bergschrund under the SE face on the right and ascend 300 ft on snow slabs (may be dry in late season). Two pitches or rock and ice (class 4) lead to the E col. The hardest problem of the climb is "Torment Tower," the large gendarme just above. Begin it on the NE via cracks (class 5) to an overhang (several pitons for aid). A piton traverse to the right leads to the notch behind the tower; keep N of the ridge to the E summit. Time: 7 hours from Boston Basin; take crampons. References: *Mountaineer,* 1962, p. 89; *A.A.J.,* 1962, pp. 202-203.

TORMENT-FORBIDDEN TRAVERSE. This is a long alpine route with about 1 mi. of scrambling and some rewarding climbing problems. First ascent by Ed Cooper and Walter Sellers in July 1958 (done after South Ridge ascent). From the summit of Torment descend the SE face about 250 ft, then make a gradual ascent E to gain the main ridge. Follow this crest except for an occasional waver on the N. The route joins the West Ridge route on Forbidden. Time: 24 hours. References: *Mountaineer,* 1959, p. 107; *A.A.J.,* 1959, pp. 301-302.

HIDDEN LAKE PEAK 7088′/2160 m

See Hidden Lake Peak Trail♦.

THE TRIAD 7520′+/2292 m (est. 7550′/2301 m)

The Triad is a three-peaked formation crowning the divide between Marble and Roush Creeks, 1.8 mi. SW of the more dominating Eldorado Peak. Visual estimates place the middle peak slightly the highest, followed by the E peak and W peak (the latter at 7440′+). The N (Marble Creek) face of the massif is a long, precipitous rock wall; on the shorter S flank the middle and W peaks are steep crags, while the E peak is sufficiently broken to permit snow to reach near its summit.

The original climbing party, in 1949, climbed first the W peak and then the middle peak. The traverse, made near the summit, was partially along a narrow exposed ridge which consisted of steep rock. This party, three of whom had identical first names, called the formation The Three Dicks, but in the interest of good taste the name later was officially changed. The climb of the W peak was done from the NW in September, 1949 by Dick Iglitzen, Dick Lowery, Dick Scales, and Don Wilde during a traverse of the ridge from Sibley Creek to Eldorado Peak.

ROUTE: To reach The Triad from Sibley Creek Pass (see Hidden Lake Peak Trail♦) ascend to the divide. After the ridge turns E and rises toward The Triad descend slightly (on N) on firn-ice and traverse E. Cross through a col (6720′+) between Points 6840+ and 6804. Descend a steep rock and snow gully (can be treacherous; beware of avalanches in spring) southeastward (200-300′), then round a spur and cross a rock ledge on a traverse of the Hidden Lake Creek slope (some snow) to beneath the middle peak. The remainder is subject to more accurate route reporting: ascend the slope (some snow and ice) toward the E-middle peak notch, but before reaching it climb NW to the middle peak (a descent on the S face was done with two rappels). Snow reaches high on the SE flank of the E peak, and the climb appears to offer no problem.

WEST ROUTE: This is the original route. The 1949 party did not cross through the col, but remained on glacier and snow of the N flank until the rock wall and buttress of the W peak forced them into technical climbing. Rock climbing (est. class 4, exposed) led to the summit on the NW and N face.

From near Sibley Creek Pass hike E and traverse glacier and snow on the N flank of Hidden Lake Peaks ridge (keep N of Point 6804). The original party followed the ridge, then descended onto the glacier. Continue E to a steep gully trending up the N side of the W peak. Here one is forced to ascend the N face to the summit; a short exposed traverse leads to the middle peak. The final portion is steep rock.

NORTH FACE: This 3000-ft face is one of the largest walls in the area, but is less well known because of its position and moderate altitude. The route climbed leads to the W peak. First ascent by Dallas Kloke and Dave Seman on July 26, 1973. Traverse to the col E of Triad (6720′+), then descend Triad Glacier NW to the lower (W) glacier tongue at about 5000 ft. A prominent rock rib ascends directly; to reach its crest cross a narrow moat to an obvious ledge at the base of a wall. From this ledge an 80-ft sustained class 5.6 pitch is climbed to reach the crest (original party bivouac two pitches higher). The remainder of the climb is somewhat loose and dirty. A detour around the W of the rib results in climbing a closed end chute (aid to regain crest). About midway up rib the climbing becomes quite easy with steep heather and scrambling. The route report states that from the W peak the middle peak is hard to reach by a traverse due to a steep rotten notch and smooth slabs. Grade III; class 5.6 and aid. Time: 9-10 hours on face. Reference: *Mountaineer,* 1973, p. 79.

ELDORADO PEAK 8868′/2703 m

Eldorado is one of the great mountains in the North Cascades; its W flank features a dramatic rise of 6400 ft in 2 mi. from Marble Creek. Eldorado is of colossal

McALLISTER GLACIER area from northeast
BOB AND IRA SPRING

ELDORADO PK.
Flower Tower
Oliphant Tower
Bandana Spire
Tyee Crag
Dean's Spire
DORADO NEEDLE
Marble Needle
Praying Mantis
cross
Mc ALLISTER GLACIER
Chaco Spire
Austera Ridge

size and has an individual aloofness above the rivalry of adjacent ridges. If Mt. Buckner is king of the Stehekin Valley, Eldorado, crowned by ice, should have the sobriquet "Queen of the Cascade River." The Inspiration Glacier mantles the peak on the E flank to the capping snow dome, where a sharp arete of firn distinguishes the summit shape. The smaller Eldorado Glacier is on the S, and there are several moderately sized bodies of ice beneath and flanking the W face in Marble Creek drainage (the unnamed glacier in the cirque between Eldorado and Dorado Needle is 0.7 mi. wide). Banded Skagit gneiss is conspicuous on the W face, which is convoluted by ribs and couloirs.[77] The name comes from the Eldorado mining claim group N of Gilbert's cabin. In 1896 L.K. Hodges noted Eldorado from Boston Basin when he referred to a mountain "clothed with an ice cap" (Hodges, *op. cit.*). As a climb its first appearance in history is when on August 27, 1933 Donald Blair, Norval W. Grigg, Arthur T. Wilson, and Art Winder made the ascent from Hidden Lake Pass. The second ascent was made by George Freed, Erick Larson, David Lind, and Walt Hoffman on September 23, 1939.

References: *Mountaineer,* 1933, p. 12; 1937, pp. 28-29; 1969, pp. 44-48; *Mazama* 28, no. 13 (1956): 34-35; *Mazama* 54, no. 13 (1972): 81.

References to Inspiration-McAllister Glacier area: *Mountaineer,* 1953, p. 67; 1966, p. 200; 1971, pp. 42-46; 1973, pp. 79-80; 1974, p. 64.

ELDORADO GLACIER ROUTE: For approach see Cascade River Area♦—Eldorado Glacier Route. One can also make the approach via Torment Basin Route or from Boston Basin via a longer traverse. Depending on the approach used, contour W and cross any spur ridges. Beyond the second spur of the first approach drop slightly and proceed N beneath a rock wall to the Eldorado Glacier. Ascend firn to the saddle SE of the summit (7480′+), bear N on Inspiration Glacier, then ascend W to follow the easy snow ridge to the narrow crest of the summit snow dome; take ice axe and crampons. Time: 3½ hours from camp in Torment Basin.

Variation: South Face: By Brad Fowler, Linda Fowler, and Earl Hamilton in June 1970. Ascend the Inspiration Glacier to its high margin on the S face. Aim for the base of a rib that leads down the summit structure's face. The original party went to the left side of the rib for a start, then climbed up right for a half pitch (class 5.4) to easier rock. Several pitches of class 3 and 4 are followed by a final pitch with several easy class 5 moves to the top of the rib. Ascend steep snow to the summit. Rock is solid; variations appear feasible. Time: 2 hours on rock. Reference: *Mountaineer,* 1971, p. 83.

SOUTHWEST ROUTE: Begin the approach via Hidden Lake Trail♦ and Sibley Creek Pass, then take the route to The Triad. Continue on the snow slope traverse to a minor saddle S of the E peak of The Triad, then make a descending traverse eastward to the southwestern base of Eldorado Glacier (6300′); on the traverse of the snow cirques one can arrive at a bench E of Triad for a campspot. Then bear NE to the flat plateau of the Inspiration Glacier and complete the ascent to the summit.

Note: one could vary the approach by following the trail farther, then following the ridge of Hidden Lake Peaks (camping on W side) and heather benches, then the ridge NE. A variation is to gain altitude beneath the E peak of The Triad and cross a small notch behind a leaning pinnacle; then descend 400 ft and traverse to the glacier.

WEST FACE: The complex western face of Eldorado is distinguished by a long buttress-face, a quite unmistakable W arete which splits the W face, and numerous couloirs, as well as patches of glacier ice in a central couloir depression and along the base of the face. The long SW ridge separates the Marble Creek basin from Eldorado Glacier.

The original climb on this face, August 29, 1951 by Dwight Baker and Pete Schoening, was an aggressive venture on unknown terrain. They reached the base of the face by traversing NE from Sibley Creek Pass to a pass at the head of Sibley Creek's N fork, on the Marble Creek cirque rim. Then it was necessary to make an intimidating 1200-ft descent of a very steep couloir on August 28 to reach a camp about ½ mi. from the face. A more expedient route is the one followed by the 1969 party: from Hidden Lake Trail♦ follow the route for The Triad and Eldorado Peak—Southwest route; allow a full day from the road to the promonotory beyond The Triad. A short climb leads to Triad col (6720′+) near the western margin of Eldorado Glacier. Descend Triad Glacier and slopes beneath about 1000 ft, then begin a traverse of Marble Creek basin under rock walls and the SW buttress of Eldorado.

The 1951 route begins S of the W arete and generally remains N of a rounded rock buttress on the face. The approach was by the moraine bearing toward the W arete, then climbing N of a section of snow and ice. When the rock steepens traverse right across the lower portion of the ice onto the rock of the buttress. Some climbing, then wandering on obvious ledges on the buttress leads toward gullies trending toward the summit. Part of the route may have climbed two small, hanging pocket glaciers (some stepcutting). Follow a series of ledges and gullies for the summit; the route possibly was climbed the final several hundred ft on the SW exposure beneath the summit. Grade III, class 4 (rock was solid); crampons advisable. Time: 4 hours on face. Reference: *Mountaineer,* 1951, p. 49.

Note: an attempt on the long SW ridge-buttress flanking the W face, in 1972, was halted after seven pitches because of insecure and dirty rock, and scarcity of anchor points (*Mountaineer,* 1973, pp. 83-84).

WEST ARETE: This arete leads directly to the summit in about 2800 ft of moderate to serious rock climbing, with 16 leads of class 4 and 5 (some class 5.6 and 5.7), then ends

ELDORADO PEAK from southwest
PHILIP LEATHERMAN

EARLY MORNING SPIRE
Marble Needle
DORADO NEEDLE
Pt. 8386
S. W. Face
West Arete
1969
1951
buttress
Southwest ridge
Marble Creek

with about 800 ft of class 4 approaching the summit. The arete is seldom really difficult but requires constant attention; one is generally forced to keep on the crest. First ascent by Richard Emerson and Walter Gove on August 29, 1969.

For approach see West Face. After traversing past the first W buttress enter the broad gully (some snow) to start up the SW corner of the arete. An open chimney bears up to join the arete (one-two pitches). Several pitches along the edge (class 5.0 to 5.6) take one to the towers. The noteworthy section is the very sharp and deeply serrated portion near the center of the route. Here one climbs two-three pitches in and out, on towers, without an altitude gain. Pass the first tower high on the N; there is some exposed down-climbing which makes it wise to leave piton protection for the last man. Worm through the chimney-notch and pass the next towers on the S. A short rappel was made in getting off the last tower; this is followed by two leads up a "step," keeping slightly right of the crest, then easier climbing onward, bearing slightly left. Grade IV, class 5.7 (bring small selection of 10 pitons up to regular angle; bring runners). Time: 9 hours on arete. Reference: *A.A.J.*, 1971, p. 347.

DORADO NEEDLE 8440′+/2573 m

This pyramidal rock formation, 0.9 mi. NNW of Eldorado Peak, has an extensive SW rock face on the rim of Marble Creek cirque. Rock on the peak is considered to be solid. The McAllister Glacier margin comes high on the E of the peak and adjacent summits NW. The snow-filled col (7600′+) between Dorado Needle and Point 8386, a northern crag of Eldorado Peak, offers a good crossing route from McAllister Glacier to the Marble Creek cirque. First ascent by Lloyd Anderson, Karl Boyer, and Tom Gorton on July 7, 1940; the summit was not reached again for 25 years.

ROUTE: For approach to the 7600-ft col, see Eldorado Peak; see also Eldorado Glacier Route-Cascade River Area♦. It is easy to contour around the E and N flank of Eldorado. The original (normal) route is two pitches: leave the glacier at its high margin NE of the summit, and climb to near the N ridge. Reach the ridge near a place that it is necessary to chevál for 15 ft, then scramble on. Reference: *Mountaineer,* 1940, p. 39.

SOUTHEAST RIDGE: This sharp crest leads from the col E of Dorado Needle toward the summit. First ascent by Joan Firey, Joe Firey, Hans Hoesli, Dave Knudson, and Peter Renz on July 4, 1971. The route involves class 3 to 5 sound granitic rock. Ascend to eastern sub-summit, then rappel into the notch for completion to the summit. Class 5.5 (take chock selection). Reference: *Mountaineer,* 1971, p. 83.

DEAN'S SPIRE 8360′+/2548 m

A small rock crag ¾ mi. NE of Eldorado Peak between the Inspiration and McAllister Glaciers. First ascent by Lawrence E. Nielsen and Walt Price on July 30, 1948. Climb from Inspiration Glacier by a steep snow slope to the final rock pyramid; this is completed on the W. Reference: *Appalachia* 29 (Dec. 1952): 214.

Traverses ranging from several days to over a week have been done in the Eldorado area:

Colonial Creek to Inspiration Glacier (1969 route): Use Colonial Creek Route to Neve Glacier (see Snowfield Peak). Closely W of Snowfield Peak descend off the S end of the glacier via a high snow ridge; make a long descending traverse SW to reach the large brushy rock-walled McAllister Creek cirque. Traverse thickets and talus, and ascend up a brushy stream. To avoid the chaotic E-fork icefall from near the tongue of McAllister Glacier ascend a steep dirt gully in the cliff slope (use rib with steep unstable moraine debris) to reach benches with alpine fir—a goat path leads to meadows. Continue S up McAllister Glacier between Klawatti Peak and Tepeh Towers to the ice divide (est. 7800′), then traverse Inspiration Glacier SSW for 1.9 mi. to the Inspiration-Eldorado Glacier divide. For route entry or continuation see Cascade River Area♦-Eldorado Glacier Route. Reference: *Mountaineer,* 1971, pp. 44-46.

Inspiration Glacier to Newhalem Creek: From the Inspiration Glacier flank of Eldorado Peak an easy glacier traverse leads to the upper SW portion of McAllister Glacier, then through the col at Dorado Needle to the cirque of Marble Creek above timberline. Descend around Early Morning Spire, then make an easy crossing of the cirque at about 5800-6000 ft. Note: a variation of the route is to cross through the high notch (7960′+) between McAllister Glacier and Marble Creek Glacier ½ mi. NW of Dorado Needle (one rappel).

Cross the corner of the Marble-Newhalem Creek ridge at 6300 ft (SW of the Coccyx), then traverse N and W to Stout Lake. See Newhalem Creek route♦. In 1973 a party made the traverse from the NW end of Backbone Ridge to Snowfield Peak. The most difficult section was the northerly descent into the western fork of McAllister Creek. The route ascends to a pass and glacier SW of Wilcox Lakes, then takes a ridge NE toward Isolation Peak; bypass on the S and ascend to the high ridge closely W of Snowfield Peak.

McAllister Creek to Inspiration Glacier: In 1973 a party gained access to the high country via McAllister Creek (brush) and a lateral stream on the S side at 3¼ mi. (drains Austera Lake). Ascend moraine, snow, and glacier slopes E; the head of North Klawatti Glacier is gained via a steep glacier col with a snow finger (NE of Tillie's Towers and 0.4 mi. W of Primus Peak). Traverse to Klawatti Glacier and then make a rising ascent to a 7950-ft. snow col on the SE ridge of Klawatti Peak; the route then leads easily to Inspiration Glacier. Reference: *Mountaineer,* 1974, p. 64.

Note: for the first portion of the route it would be simpler to use the McAllister-Thunder Creek ridge to Borealis Glacier, then traverse W high around the N flank of Primus Peak.

MARBLE NEEDLE 8401′/2561 m

The summit, the crest of a massif N and slightly W of Dorado Needle, was so named on the original climb because it commands a fine view of Marble Creek valley. First ascent by Joan Firey and Joe Firey in September 1964 via Marble Creek slope.

ROUTE: Approach as for Early Morning Spire. From the glacier in the S-facing cirque of Marble Creek slope (W of Dorado Needle) ascend to its SE corner. Then ascend on rock to the summit; about two pitches of class 4, remainder class 3. Note: a route from the margin of McAllister Glacier appears to be easier.

PRAYING MANTIS 8360′+/2548 m

A crag with a peculiar summit block closely N of Marble Needle. First ascent by Fred Beckey and Tom Stewart in September 1971. Approach via Newhalem Creek-Stout Lake Route♦ and Marble Creek cirque, then up the Marble Creek Glacier's upper section to the NW ridge. Two pitches follow the ridge (class 5.0). Reference: *Mountaineer,* 1971, p. 83.

EARLY MORNING SPIRE 8200′+/2499 m

This rock pyramid is a large massif wholly within the Marble Creek drainage, located 0.4 mi. WNW of Marble Needle. Marble Creek Glacier is on its N in a large deep cirque. The best approach is per Eldorado Peak-West Face, then traverse along Marble Creek cirque; or per Eldorado Glacier Route (see Cascade River Area♦) and the col at Dorado Needle. The easiest route appears to be the NW; the distance from the glacier is shortest here.

SOUTHEAST FACE (East Route): First ascent by Dave Anderson and Bruce Carson in July 1972. This five-pitch climb is generally quite enjoyable, but there is some very loose rock. The route begins from the ice segment on the SE flank; start in an obvious chimney of two pitches near the bottom-center of the face. On the third pitch follow ramps and ledges up and right; the next pitch climbs through a band of overhanging and vertical sections of the face. Very loose class 4 leads to the base of a wide, straight-in crack. Climb this and the following loose gully, which bears left and directly to the summit. Grade II; class 5.7 (all chocks). Reference: *Mountaineer,* 1973, p. 83.

SOUTHEAST FACE (West Route): Rock is excellent and climbing enjoyable. First ascent by Steve Barnett and Mark Weigelt in July 1972. The route follows a prominent dihedral/chimney system. The first four pitches are difficult, with the third the crux (this is a steep chimney, possibly wet). The final four pitches are class 4. Grade II; class 5.9 (all chocks except one large angle). Reference: *Mountaineer,* 1973, p. 83.

SOUTHWEST FACE: This interesting steep face is directly in line with the Marble Creek slope. On the original climb a bivouac was made several hundred ft from the finish. About 10 leads up the face a narrow obvious line begins as a crack; near halfway the line reflects itself as a somewhat resistant dike and the final part passes through steeper and less firm rock at a series of short overhangs and chimneys.

First ascent by Richard Emerson and Tom Hornbein in September 1971. Begin from the schrund at the base of the face. The first four leads are the hardest (averaging class 5.5-5.6 with one steep layback of 5.8); rock is solid here. Above the shelf climb aid (Al) up a short overhang. Next several pitches are moderate and up the dike to the final crack system, where the wall steepens. Several short overhangs within the chimney required some aid (loose blocks here). The route continues up the chimney to just beneath the summit. Grade IV; class 5.8 and aid. Time: 14 hours climbing.

Descent: involves two rappels to firn of Marble Creek Glacier on the N; possible crevasse jump.

KLAWATTI PEAK 8485′/2586 m

No other peak in this region is so enveloped by glaciers. Klawatti is actually a nunatak, with glacier ice completely surrounding it. Here the contiguous portions of Inspiration, Klawatti, and McAllister Glaciers form a small icecap unique even in the glacier-borne North Cascades. As late as September the mountain mass of the Eldorado-Klawatti area is still sheathed in dazzling whiteness. It is a scene of incredible brilliance, of a contrast between the blackness of the protruding serrated rock crests and the blinding reflected light. Intense alpine glaciation here has resulted in ragged ridge crests with many gaps and pinnacles, constantly sculptured by the active ice and climatic agents of weathering.

The Klawatti Glacier drains the cirque E of Klawatti Peak. The glacier drains into Klawatti Lake (1.2 mi. E of the peak) which drains via Klawatti Creek to West Fork Thunder Creek.[78] The terminal fork of the latter stream originates at Inspiration Glacier (S of Klawatti Peak) and passes through Moraine Lake (earlier known as "Pea Soup Lake" because of the color derived by suspended silt). The McAllister Glacier reaches to the W slope of Klawatti Peak at 7800 ft. The Austera Glacier is the portion of ice NNW of Klawatti Peak; it joins the lower McAllister near its snout. Klawatti Peak rises only 300 to 700 ft above these glaciers, 1.8 mi. NE of Eldorado Peak, and is one of the two highest elevations between the Eldorado massif and Skagit River. The original climbing party, perhaps not as appreciative of the scenic environment as annoyed at the crumbly rock, dubbed the peak "Sloppy Mountain."[79] First ascent by Lloyd Anderson, Karl Boyer, and Tom Gorton on July 7, 1940; the second

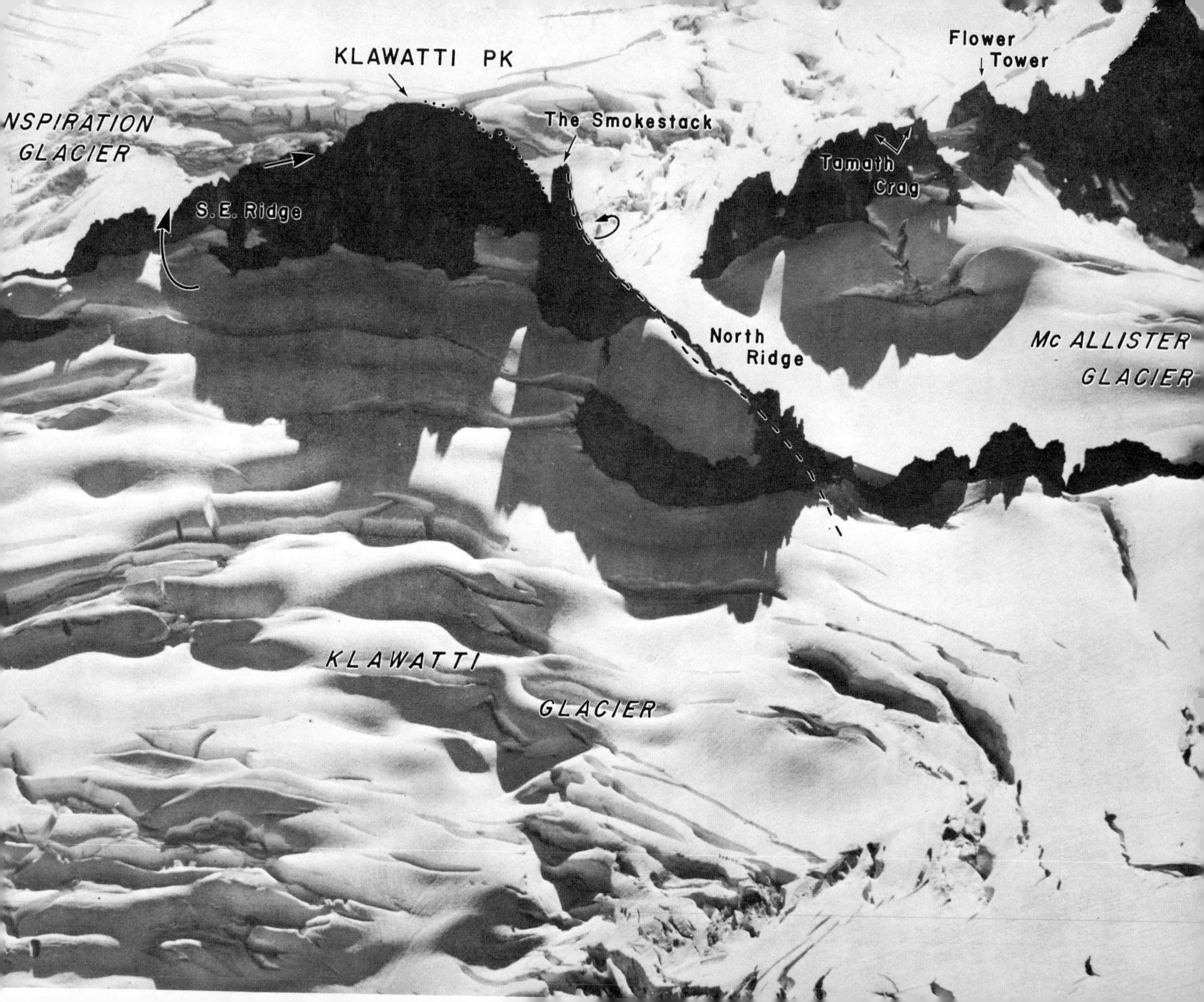

KLAWATTI PK
NSPIRATION GLACIER
The Smokestack
Flower Tower
Tamath Crag
S.E. Ridge
North Ridge
Mc ALLISTER GLACIER
KLAWATTI GLACIER

KLAWATTI PEAK from northeast
AUSTIN POST, UNIVERSITY of WASHINGTON

TEPEH TOWERS from southwest
BOB AND IRA SPRING

ascent was not done until 1965. Reference: *Mountaineer,* 1940, p. 39.

SOUTHWEST ROUTE: This was the original route. For general approach, see Cascade River Area♦-Eldorado Glacier Route. From the E side of Eldorado Peak make an easy traverse across the Inspiration Glacier. In late season it may be difficult to get off the glacier (at about 7800'); class 3.

SOUTHEAST RIDGE: First ascent by Joan Firey, Joe Firey, Anthony Hovey, John Meulemans, and Irene Meulemans on September 18, 1965. From Klawatti Glacier on the N, ascend to the prominent notch in the SE ridge. The route stays fairly close to the ridge until the summit is reached. There are two class 4 pitches on the lower part of the ridge; the remainder is scrambling. Reference: *Mountaineer,* 1966, p. 200.

NORTH RIDGE: This ridge divides the Klawatti and McAllister Glaciers; the route begins at about 8000 ft. First ascent by Bruce Albert, Carla Firey, Joan Firey, Joe Firey, Irene Meulemans, Jim McCarthy, and Peter Renz on July 4, 1973. From Klawatti Glacier ascend to lower portion of the ridge. Ascend the crest to closely beneath The Smokestack, then traverse W beneath it, and ascend the couloir on its S to regain the ridge; class 3.

THE SMOKESTACK est. 8400'/2560 m

This tower is located on Klawatti's N ridge. First ascent by ridge party (except Irene Meulemans), same date. The route ascends about 50 to 80 ft of class 4 rock on the N side; rock is rather loose.

TEPEH TOWERS

The row of needle-like granitic towers 0.6 mi. in length extends WSW from Klawatti Peak (from 0.3 mi. W of Klawatti Peak to 0.7 mi. E of Dorado Needle) between the Inspiration and McAllister Glaciers. Tepeh is from the Chinook jargon, meaning "quills" or "sharp points."

Tamath Crag (8160'+/2487 m) is a serrated crag located closest to Klawatti Peak; there are several summits of almost equal height. First ascent by Joan Firey, Joe Firey, Hans Hoesli, Dave Knudson, and Peter Renz on July 4, 1971. The route was via the W ridge (class 4); it is uncertain if all points on the crag were climbed.

Oliphant Tower (8120'+/2475 m; est. 8150'/2484 m) is the first prominent tower W of Tamath Crag. First ascent unknown; the E ridge was climbed by the Tamath Crag party, same date. Easy class 5.

The first ascent of ***Flower Tower*** (8184'/2494 m) was by Tamath Crag party on July 5, via W ridge (easy class 5).

The NE ridge was first done by Don Dooley, Marilyn Jensen, Stan Jensen, Harry Morgan, Rosemary Purdue, and Joanne Williams on July 31, 1973; this is a pleasant 150-ft scramble (class 3).

Bandana Spire (est. 8100'/2469 m) is the thin spire near the center of the ridge. First ascent by Virginia Mohling Powers via the SE face; August 1958; class 4.

Tyee Crag (8200'+/2499 m) is the name given the western towers; the E of two summits is higher. No climbing information.

KLAWATTI KLAWS 8200'+/2499 m

A row of minor crags on the ridge between Klawatti and McAllister Glaciers, closely N of Klawatti Peak and SW of Austera Peak, the crags are short on the E, but do offer some sound rock of one-three pitches of class 4 and easy class 5. Points 8120+ (2475 m) and 8200+ (2499 m) were climbed in September 1965 by Joan Firey, Joe Firey, Anthony Hovey, John Meulemans, and Irene Meulemans. Other crags were climbed in August 1969 by Carla Firey, Joan Firey, Joe Firey, Dave Knudson, and Frank De Saussure; some points may be unclimbed. Reference: *Mountaineer,* 1971, p. 45.

AUSTERA PEAK 8334'/2540 m

The high point of the Klawatti, North Klawatti, and McAllister Glacier divide, 1.0 mi. N of Klawatti Peak, Austera Peak is shaped like a wedge, the highest point of Austera Ridge. The North Klawatti Glacier lies in the cirque to the N and E. The Austera Glacier branch of McAllister Glacier (1.1 mi. long)—immediately SW of the peak, trends NW from Klawatti Peak. A number of names have evolved for the peak, including "McWatti." First ascent by Joan Firey, Joe Firey, Anthony Hovey, John Meulemans, and Irene Meulemans on September 16, 1965. Reference: *Mountaineer,* 1966, p. 200.

SOUTH ROUTE: The climb is made from the Klawatti Glacier, which reaches to about 8250 ft. There are 100-200 ft of scrambling—a short class 3 climb of loose rock.

AUSTERA TOWERS (Austera Ridge)

The Austera Towers are the 1.4-mi. rugged ridge trending NW from Austera Peak, between the North Klawatti and Austera Glaciers. Austera Ridge continues E 0.3 mi. as the divide between the Klawatti and North Klawatti Glaciers. The serrated arete of Austera Towers has a nearly countless variety of rock profiles. Such aretes are commonly found where narrow ridges are being sculptured by active glacial ice moving along either flank of the bases. The aretes result from a combination of erosion by glaciers and snow slides on steep slopes, with rock weathering at high altitudes, where there is a wide range of diurnal temperature. The name is for austere, barren rock towers consisting of many massive rock blocks and spires.[80] The N flank of the western towers is above an unnamed glacier where there is the steepest wall of the ridge. Beyond the present glacier margins N of the ridge are interesting 18th and 19th century moraine exhibits and a meltwater lake (Austera Lake) with an ice margin and closed end moraine.

TOWER 8200+ 8200'+/2499 m

The first summit W of Austera Peak; the ridge here averages from 8000 ft to over 8200 ft and has a craggy outline; the rock is quite solid. The towers here have a sheer wall on the North Klawatti face. This tower was first climbed by Carla Firey, Joan Firey, Joe Firey, Dave Knudson, and Frank De Saussure in August 1969 from snowfields above the Austera Glacier; reach these via Klawatti Glacier to just S of Austera Peak; then make a steep descent to the W over rock. Class 3-4.

TOWER 8240+ 8240′+/2152 m

This tower, next NW of Tower 8200+, is more of a problem to reach. First ascent by same party, same date. Using the same approach, ascend steep class 4 rock to E ridge of objective; then ascend the ridge, using the N face occasionally to the summit; class 3-4. Reference: *Mountaineer,* 1971, p. 45.

TILLIE'S TOWERS 8260′/2518 m

Two towers are the highest on Austera Ridge, .075 mi. NW of Austera Peak. These are two impressive towers, one being the W and the other E; they are close to the same height. *East Tower:* First ascent by Carla Firey, Joan Firey, Joe Firey, Dave Knudson, and Frank De Saussure in August 1969. From Tower 8240+ continue NW along the ridge (class 3); occasionally use the N flank. There is a short class 4 pitch on the summit block; rock is solid. Reference: *Mountaineer,* 1971, p. 45.

West Tower: First ascent by Bruce Albert, Joan Firey, Dave Knudson, and Peter Renz in July 1973. From the high snowfields above Austera branch of McAllister Glacier traverse across the S face of objective (class 3 ledges) to reach W ridge. Then ascend this to the summit; two class 5 pitches.

PILTDOWN TOWER 8120′+/2475 m

This tower is the next W of Tillie's Towers.

CHACO TOWER 7920′+/2414 m

On the ridge 1 mi. NW of Austera Peak; there are a number of crags and pinnacles remaining to the ridge terminus.

PRIMUS PEAK 8508′/2593 m

Although Primus is a moderately sloping glacier-clad peak offering few technical difficulties, it has an attractive character and the importance of being the highest between Eldorado Peak and the Skagit River. The Borealis Glacier is on the NE slope, the North Klawatti is S of the peak, and a high glacier basin exists on the W and NW. First ascent by Les Carlson, Elwyn Elerding, and Jeanne Elerding in August 1951. Reference: *Mountaineer,* 1952, p. 83; 1953, p. 67.

SOUTH ROUTE: The original party came from the snow col W of Klawatti Peak, then hiked onto Klawatti Glacier and crossed the E spur of Austera Ridge; the route then descended to a base camp (heather) high above the lower North Klawatti Glacier. From here a 500-ft descent was made, then a traverse on firn and steep snow ¼ mi. reached the S flank of Primus. The route takes the broad, snow-patched S slope; no difficulties. Time: 4 hours from camp.

EAST ROUTE: First ascent by Marc Bardsley, Paul Bergman, and two others, 1967. From Thunder Creek Trail♦, cross Thunder Creek via the bridge S of McAllister Creek, then ascend the long ridge SW (brushy and scrub hemlock to timberline); allow full day from road. There is good campspot on the spur E of Borealis Glacier. Ascend the glacier to "Lucky Pass" (adjacent Tricouni Peak), then ascend easily to the summit.

TRICOUNI PEAK 8102′/2469 m

Located on the McAllister-West Fork Thunder Creek divide 0.6 mi. due E of Primus Peak. Tricouni is gentle on the S to W slopes but steep from NW to SE. Borealis Glacier lies in the cirque NW of the peak. First ascent by Les Carlson, Elwyn Elerding, and Jeanne Elerding in August 1951; the party made the ascent of Tricouni by traversing Primus. References: *Mountaineer,* 1952, p. 83; 1953, p. 67.

WEST ROUTE: See Primus Peak for approach. Traverse North Klawatti Glacier and ascend to "Lucky Pass" (7200′+) between Primus and Tricouni. Continue the ascent E, then NE over broken rotten rock and moderately steep gullies to the summit; the high point is left of the snow bowl.

Variation: Descend from the summit of Primus to the pass (original route).

NORTH RIDGE: First ascent by Bob Greisman, Dallas Kloke, Scott Masonholder, John Roper, Mike Theobald, and Reed Tindall on May 29, 1972. For approach, see Primus Peak-East Route. Make an interesting steep snow ascent, then a rock climb via the N face and ridge; this is a moderatley long route. Reference: *Mountaineer,* 1972, p. 83.

TEEBONE RIDGE

Although this high ridge located in the converging angle between Skagit and Cascade Rivers is of only modest altitude, great local relief makes it impressive. The name is derived from the T-shape of the ground outline, with Big Devil at the head of the bone. The long crest extends in an erratic NE- and N-trending pattern from Lookout Mountain to beyond Last Devil. The largest glacier is the Monogram, at the head of Haystack Creek. An impressive waterfall on the slopes of Big Devil, the highest peak, is directed toward the Skagit River. The ridge offers feasible traverses, much of it on alp slopes; the usual way is to reach the area from Lookout Mountain Trail♦, but other routes have been used. From the trail leave at the broad pass to the ridge extending NE, at the head of Lookout Creek basin.

In 1966 Paul Bergman, Bob Briggs, Jim Carlson, Kenn Carpenter, Dave Fluharty, and Ron Miller traversed along or near the crest. Beyond Little Devil a

ELDORADO PK.
KLAWATTI PK.
AUSTERA PK.
Tillies Towers
PRIMUS PK.
KLAWATTI GLACIER
NORTH KLAWATTI GLACIER
TRICOUNI PK.
East Route
BOREALIS GLACIER
North Ridge

traverse was made on the W ridge flank (snow) to reach Baccus (Middle Devil); the route crossed the peak's W ridge and with some trouble descended a steep loose couloir on its N side (steep snow). On the first part of a ½-mi. traverse to meadows, some steep ice was encountered. The route continues to Big Devil and Last Devil; the traverse route was generally found best on the W flank about 100-200 ft below the crest to avoid crags and pinnacles. References: *A.A.J.*, 1967, pp. 352-353; *Mountaineer,* 1967, p. 130.

LOOKOUT MOUNTAIN 5719′/1743 m

Lookout is an E-trending ridge extending from Skagit-Cascade River junction bearing to Teebone Ridge; the high point is 5 mi. NE of Marblemount. Rock here is metamorphosed quartz diorite, some of the oldest known in the North Cascades. See Lookout Mountain Trail♦.

LITTLE DEVIL PEAK 6985′/2129 m

Located 2.25 mi. SW of Big Devil Peak. First ascent by U.S. Geological Survey, date unknown. The trivial subsidiary peaks (6844′/2086 m and 6438′/1962 m) on the ridge to the SW were climbed by the survey party.

ROUTE: The ascent is easy from the SW; class 3.

BACCUS PEAK (Middle Devil) 6960′+/2121 m

This summit is about ½ mi. NNW of Little Devil. Baccus is the name Indians gave the peak at the head of Alma Creek (per Glee Davis) and allegedly means "The Nose" in some dialect. First ascent on September 3, 1966 by full traverse party.

ROUTE: The climb is not difficult from Little Devil—see approach (class 3).

PEAK 6840 (Go to the Devil) 6840′/2085 m

About ½ mi. NE of Baccus. First ascent by Kenn Carpenter and Dave Fluharty on September 4, 1966.

ROUTE: Reach via the traverse from W of Baccus to Big Devil. The route is on the W side; class 4.

BIG DEVIL PEAK 7065′/2153 m

The highest point on the ridge, opposite the terminal West Fork of Newhalem Creek. The first ascent is in question, as there was evidence of a survey party; the 1966 traverse party made the ascent on September 4, 1966.

SOUTHEAST RIDGE: By traverse party. From foot of Peak 6840's summit traverse W on N side and keep high to cross lateral rock ridge, then follow the crest W.

NORTHWEST ROUTE: First ascent by Jay Haggerty and John Roper on September 7, 1963. From North Cascades Hwy♦ at Sky Creek raft across the river. Make the ascent through brush, moderately open timber, then meadows, snowfields, and a short dirt and rock scramble, keeping on the E of the N-flowing creek. Round trip: 2 days.

NORTH RIDGE: First ascent by Dick Hunich and Ken Hunich on September 1, 1964. Take logging road no. 376 SE from Newhalem. Cross Skagit River and at ¾ mi., where the road is closest to Teebone Ridge, hike generally S to a high camp at 5827 ft (keep as far left of Martin Creek as possible and gain height to avoid canyons). Then climb to 10-ft notch at Last Devil. From here the ascent of Big Devil is non-technical, but crampons may be needed. This is a long but sensible route.

LAST DEVIL (The Trapezoid) 6960′+/2121 m

The northernmost summit of importance on Teebone Ridge, 1.2 mi. NE of Big Devil. The peak has a trapezoid crag shape. First ascent by full traverse party, September 4, 1966.

ROUTE: Via broken rock on W face, from notch (class 3). Other summits: the smaller peaks (6960′+/2121 m, 6880′+/2097 m, and 6800′+/2072 m) to the NE of Last Devil are known as the *Maurine Peaks.*

BACKBONE RIDGE

The sharp alpine NW-trending crest of 1.7 mi. separating Marble and McAllister Creek basins was so-named because its seven summits are regularly spaced, resembling a vertebral column; the peaks are neatly separated by snow or talus cols (intervertebral discs). The first summit on the ridge, The Coccyx, and Perdition Peak, the highest on the ridge, were the earliest climbs. The Marble Creek slopes of Backbone Ridge are a magnificent example of Cascade Range alp slopes. The McAllister (NE) slope is almost a continuous glacier 2 mi. in width. Backbone and Perdition Glaciers are unofficial names for the two largest sections. The latter overhangs its wall and dumps ice to lower McAllister Glacier. The name of the ridge and its peaks was applied by John Roper to be in keeping with the physical and spiritual nomenclature of the area. References: *Mountaineer,* 1972, pp. 83-84; *A.A.J.,* 1970, pp. 120-121. The peaks are here listed from NW to SE.

THE COCCYX 7280′+/2219 m

This small rock peak 1½ mi. from Perdition Peak is

TRICOUNI and PRIMUS PEAKS from northeast
AUSTIN POST, U.S. GEOLOGICAL SURVEY

the "tail end" summit, the NW anchor of Backbone Ridge. First ascent by Phil Dahl and John Roper on August 27, 1967.

NORTHEAST RIDGE: See Stout Lake approach, Newhalem Creek-Stout Lake Route♦. The route comes from Newhalem Creek's upper basin via the N ridge; there is a small glacier on the slope, nearly to the ridge. The climb is not difficult.

The Coccyx has also been ascended and descended via the SE ridge; this route is more exposed and steeper.

THE SACRUM 7148′/2179 m

This is the first summit SE of The Coccyx, a lesser point of no known ascent. A steep short pitch is probably involved from either the SE or NW.

LUMBAR PEAK 7040′+/2146 m

First ascent by John Roper, Steve Shelton, and Theresa Smith on July 30, 1972. The ascent is easy from the col at Thoracic Peak; class 3.

THORACIC PEAK 7170′+/2185 m

Located 0.6 mi. SE of The Coccyx. First ascent by Lumbar Peak party, same date. The route is via the slightly exposed NW ridge; class 3. The SE ridge is easier.

CERVICAL PEAK 7360′+/2243 m

A pointed rock peak about midway on the ridge. First ascent by Lumbar Peak party, same date; steep grass and rock from the col at Thoracic Peak; class 3.

IN SPIRIT PEAK 7480′+/2280 m

Located ½ mi. NW of Perdition Peak, with a wall above the Backbone Glacier. First ascent by Lumbar Peak party, July 31. The route is from the SE; class 3.

PERDITION PEAK 7675′/2339 m

This is the highest and rockiest peak on Backbone Ridge, 1.35 mi. NW of Dorado Needle. There is a steep rock face above the Perdition and Backbone Glaciers. First ascent by John Roper on August 27, 1967.

WEST RIDGE: An exposed route via the serrated ridge; generally keep to the N side; class 4.

THE BAT 6475′/1974 m

The bat-shaped rock formation on Newhalem-Marble Creek divide is visible from Newhalem Creek Road. A small but impressive peak, it has a sheer N face 600 to 800 ft above a small glacier. The high point is the E peak, with the W peak (6417′/1956 m) 0.4 mi. distant; there are two minor points between. First ascent by Phil Dahl and John Roper on August 26, 1967. Reference: *A.A.J.*, 1970, pp. 120-121.

ROUTE: From the end of the brushed logging road in Newhalem Creek♦ climb SE to Stout Lake. Then cross S over the ridge to "Purgatory Pond" (5360′+)—about 1 mi. distant; this is a good camp—6 hours. Angle SW and climb to the E ridge which is climbed without difficulty (class 3).

NEWHALEM PEAKS 6920′+/2109 m

Of the three summits, the highest is farthest SE. These peaks are on the Newhalem-East Fork creek divide, just NE of Stout Lake, and can be seen as twin pinnacles from Newhalem; both summits are shown at the same highest contour. First ascent by Jack Roper, John Roper, Reenie Roper, and Steve Shelton on September 18, 1971. Reference: *Mountaineer,* 1971, pp. 83-84.

ROUTE: The SW slope is an easy scramble from Stout Lake.

ISOLATION PEAK 7102′/2165 m

Between East Fork Newhalem Creek and McAllister Creek, in a rather inaccessible position, the peak is 1.85 mi. from Snowfield Peak on a spur ridge extending SW. First ascent by Marilyn Jensen, Stan Jensen, Frank King, and Joanne Williams on August 3, 1973. Reference: *Mountaineer,* 1973, pp. 79-81.

ROUTE: The route is from the traverse between Snowfield Peak and Backbone Ridge (from the col W of Snowfield or NW from McAllister Creek starting at about 2350′ to a small lake at est. 5750′ ENE of the peak). From the lake ascend SSW about 800 ft via moderate slopes to a prominent bench SE of the peak. Reach the ridge which curves W, then N to the summit; class 2.

Note: one could also reach the peak from Stout Lake. Cross the pass to the E, then to the glacier pass SW of Wilcox Lakes, then descend and traverse NE along the ridge above the lakes.

SNOWFIELD PEAK 8347′/2544 m

Snowfield, the highest peak of the subrange SW of Diablo Lake, has a number of high attractive summits and three important glaciers. It is a pyramidally shaped summit massif of Skagit gneiss of sufficient altitude to be a distinct regional landmark. The Neve Glacier (3.0 km²) extends high on the N flank of the peak and on its W resembles a small icefield which borders a rim of small peaks on the Ladder Creek drainage; the glacier is nearly connected with Colonial Glacier on the N. The Ladder Creek Glacier (2.5 km length) drains northwestward from the Neve as a distributary outlet. The first ascent was made by William A. Degenhardt and Herbert V. Strandberg on August 1, 1931; they repeated the climb in 1933. Reference: *Mountaineer,* 1931, p. 36.

ROUTE: For the best approach see Pyramid Peak; high

BACKBONE RIDGE and McAllister Creek Valley
AUSTIN POST, UNIVERSITY of WASHINGTON

BACKBONE RIDGE
LITTLE DEVIL PK.
In Spirit
Lumbar
Coccyx
The Bat
Perdition Pk.
Cervical
Sacrum
Newhalem Peaks
to Stout Lk.
Isolation Pk.
BACKBONE GLACIER
lake
Austera Lake
Mc Allister Creek Valley

PRIMUS PK.
SNOWFIELD PK.
Horseman's Pack
The Horseman
The Needle
NEVE
GLACIER
Cat's Ear
Col 6840+
PAUL BUNYAN'S
STUMP
PINNACLE PK.
COLONIAL
GLACIER
LADDER
CREEK
GLACIER
PYRAMID PK.

camp can be made on the Pyramid Peak ridge. Traverse the slope of Colonial Creek, then make a rising ascent of Colonial Glacier southward to the very gentle Colonial-Neve Glacier col (6840′+), where ice nearly touches both flanks. Descend about 200 ft on gentle firn, then ascend southward to where the glacier reaches the NW ridge of the summit rock pyramid at about 7900 ft. Then climb the narrow W ridge with a notch at 200 ft from the summit; the notch crossing is not very difficult, but does take some caution (class 3); an alternative is to stay out more on the N face; the original party went on this flank above the notch; when glacier conditions are icy or otherwise unfavorable, some parties reach the W ridge at about 800 linear ft from the summit, then follow it the entire way. Time: about 4 hours from high camp.

Approach Variation: Colonial Creek Route: An unmarked 1½-mi. way trail (brushed out by Skagit Alpine Club in 1968) gives the quickest access to the Colonial-Snowfield group of peaks, but its validity depends greatly on current trail condition. When the trail ends in the cirque near the head of the creek climb through scree and brushy wooded cliffs on the N edge to the ridge, then traverse S to Colonial Glacier camp. Begin from the highway (1280′) ½ mi. beyond Thunder Lake, 50 ft S of Colonial Creek; the path takes an uphill line until meeting the creek (less than 1-mi.). Then take the creek bed to the basin meadow waterfalls (path leaves streambed on right for 200-300 yds at one place to bypass difficult sector); 1½ mi. to basin at 3200 ft—2½ hours. Now traverse rightward through maple on rockslide (below rock band). Cross gully which descends from obvious ridge notch and continue on rightward bearing into thick new fir growth to slight ridge right of the gully. Switchback up ridge in dense fir almost to the notch (reach it by long left traverse); 1400-ft gain—3 hours. From notch continue up ridge to base camp (2 hours).

Approach Variation: Ladder Creek Route: From Gorge Dam powerhouse (500′) follow 4-mi. Ladder Creek Trail (not maintained) and continue up streambed. Ladder Creek arm of Neve Glacier descends a steep gorge, which can be avoided by climbing S-side cliffs. A good camp is N of the glacier at meadows (5500′—10 hours). Ascend the ice or its left fringe to the main body of the Neve. Time: 4-5 hours camp to summit. Note: there are deer trails through the cliffs but the lower valley is somewhat brushy.

MANTIS PEAK 7614′/2321 m

An eastern subsidiary summit (1.25 mi. distant) of Snowfield; the peak has a steep N face flanked by the Neve Glacier on the NW, and a small glacier on the NE. The route is not difficult, but long and with considerable route-finding problems. First ascent by Marilyn Jensen and Stan Jensen on August 16, 1973.

From McAllister Creek (see Thunder Creek♦); a log jam was found in about 1 mi. for creek's crossing. Traverse E on burnt slope to the ridge; follow ridge W (original party camped at 6100′). Continue on or near crest to about 6700 ft where it is possible to traverse around the S side of Point 6972 to the saddle adjacent Mantis. Then traverse S to the SE ridge; follow easily to summit (class 2-3). Reference: *Mountaineer,* 1973, p. 81.

THE NEEDLE 8040′+/2451 m

A prominent rock tower on the W margin rock rim of Neve Glacier. The Needle is ⅜ mi. N of The Horseman and is identified by a sharp rock block just N of its summit. The Diablo Dam quadrangle erroneously shows its location at the Horse's Pack. First ascent by William Degenhardt and Herbert Strandberg on August 1, 1931.

Ascend the snow arete to the ridge crest; scramble 100 yds W along the ridge and follow an exposed spur ridge SW to the top (some loose blocks); class 4. Reference: *Mountaineer,* 1931, pp. 36-38.

NORTH FACE: By Greg Lazear and Norman Winn on August 3, 1973. This is a short, solid rock climb (class 4 and easy 5). Reference: *Mountaineer,* 1973, p. 81.

CAT'S EAR 7560′+/2304 m

The most prominent feature of the point at the ridge terminus NNE of The Needle is the 1300-ft NW face. First ascent unknown. The easiest route is on the SE.

THE HAYSTACK 7139′/2176 m

This rounded peak W of the main Snowfield Peak group is ⅜ mi. W of The Needle, on the S flank of Ladder Creek. The peak was climbed on May 8, 1976, by Richard Pellem and John Roper , who saw evidence of a U.S. Geological Survey party's visit in the form of lumber and bailing wire; it is not known if the earlier group arrived by foot or helicopter.

THE HORSEMAN est. 8140′/2481 m

This is a curious rock formation on the W rim of Neve Glacier, W of Snowfield Peak; it resembles a man on horseback; the thin tower is about 50′ x 30′ x 10′—the "Horse" is a lower, thin block closely N. The formation was named by William Degenhardt and Herbert Strandberg when they climbed *Horseman's Pack* (8152′/2485 m), a block just SE, on August 1, 1931. A route on the latter was climbed from the N by Joe Firey and Joan Firey (class 4). Reference: *Mountaineer,* 1931, pp. 36-37.

PYRAMID PEAK 7182′/2189 m

Pyramid makes an outstanding postcard impression from Diablo Lake because of steep N and E rock faces, but unknown to the tourists, on the SW the peak is seen as the final—and minor—point of a ridge between Pyramid and Colonial Creeks. Pyramid Peak is 2.7 mi. SSW of Diablo Dam and rises in outstanding local relief, but the summit is less than 200 ft higher than the SW saddle. First ascent by William Degenhardt and Herbert Strandberg on July 30, 1931; they did the normal route after attempting a chimney on the E face. Reference: *Mountaineer,* 1931, p. 35.

SNOWFIELD PEAK from north
AUSTIN POST, U.S. GEOLOGICAL SURVEY

PAUL BUNYAN'S STUMP
PINNACLE PK.
East Ridge
S.W. Route
to north ridge
PYRAMID PK.
COLONIAL
GLACIER

ROUTE: Follow the trail to Pyramid Lake♦, which lies in the basin N of the peak. Ascend SE to the subalpine ridge bearing NE of Pyramid. There are several small ponds at timberline about ⅛ mi. below the junction of ridge and N face (trees end about 5400′); good campsites; 6 hours. From the highest pond a heather bench descends obliquely to the Colonial Creek basin. Traverse below the NE face of the peak to the Colonial Glacier, then ascend and traverse firn slopes NW to the broad snow saddle (7000′+) between Pinnacle and Pyramid Peaks. Caution should be taken on these slopes because of cliffs beneath. Follow slab or snow on the ridge crest to the summit (est. 800′ distant). Time: 2-3 hours.

Approach Variation: From Thunder Lake ascend due W through open timber to the ridge crest, which is then followed through light underbrush. After 4500 ft keep on the crest or its N, and at about 5400 ft begin to bear S on a traverse. Note: in summer there may be no water en route. Time: 6-8 hours.

Other Routes: The status of the NW buttress is uncertain, but believed to have been done. Ascend via a shallow gully which begins in a large basin N of Pyramid Peak, and leads near the Pinnacle-Pyramid Peak saddle. In early season, when avalanche conditions may exist in the gully, the rock on its left may be the best way (class 3-4; 2-4 hours from basin).

The route via the glaicer arm that leads to the saddle is known to have been done.

PINNACLE PEAK 7360′+/2243 m

This small rock crag is midway between Pyramid Peak and Paul Bunyan's Stump at the high edge of a NW arm of Colonial Glacier.

SOUTHWEST ROUTE: From the col (6920′+) facing Paul Bunyan's Stump traverse W to a gully (snow finger) on Pinnacle's SW corner. Here moderate left-bearing slabs lead to the ridge crest just N of the summit block. This is gained by a 40-ft face—a steep class 4 section (both other routes completed here).

NORTH RIDGE: From the highest snow on the NE bear around N to the N ridge. The first pitch is loose, then two solid pitches follow; the summit is at the far end; class 3-4.

EAST ROUTE: There is a class 3 route to the ridge crest just N of the summit. Begin off the snow near the NE corner.

PAUL BUNYAN'S STUMP 7480′+/2280 m

The "Stump" is a chisel-shaped truncated rock pyramid 0.6 mi. SSW of Pyramid Peak and closely resembling Pinnacle Peak (The Chopping Block) across the Skagit Valley. The Ladder Creek arm of Neve Glacier is on its S and the Colonial Glacier on the NE. At the western head of Colonial Glacier, 0.3 mi. SE of the "Stump", there is a saddle (6520′+) which leads to the Ladder Creek drainage. First ascent by William Degenhardt and Herbert Strandberg on August 2, 1931; they called the peak "What's the Matterhorn." Reference: *Mountaineer,* 1931, p. 38.

PAUL BUNYAN'S STUMP from southeast
WILLIAM A. LONG

SOUTHWEST ROUTE: Take approach for Pyramid Peak and ascend to the SE saddle (about 450′ below the summit). Climb loose rock and talus up the broad S ridge. Just beneath the upper band of cliffs traverse N (left) about 200 ft on the W face to a chimney (or easy gullies) leading to the summit. Care is needed when traversing slabby rock on the very narrow summit ridge; class 3. Time: 3-4 hours from camp.

COLONIAL PEAK 7771′/2369 m

Colonial is a craggy rock peak (Skagit gneiss) between Colonial and Neve Creeks. The summit is at the eastern end of the ridge, 2.1 mi. SW of Thunder Arm. The peak drops abruptly from the SE to E and N faces; 1 mi. from the summit the Neve Creek valley is only 3200 ft in altitude. The Colonial Glacier (0.9 km²) extends from 7000 ft to 5800 ft W of the peak. First ascent by William Degenhardt and Herbert Strandberg on July 31, 1931. A party in 1936 erroneously claimed the honor; the 1931 party clearly reached the true summit on the extreme E edge of the ridge. References: *Mountaineer,* 1931, p. 36; *Appalachia* 21, no. 82 (1936): 268, 272-273; *Summit,* Nov. 1964, pp. 28-30.

WEST RIDGE: Use Pyramid Peak approach to reach Colonial Glacier. Traverse SE to steeper slopes, then ascend into the wide snow finger which leads to the summit ridge. Ascend the finger for half its length, then make a short loose-rock scramble left. Traverse talus and the high firnfield to the notch just W of the summit pyramid. Gain the top via the rock ridge. Time: 3-4 hours from camp on ridge.

Variation: Keep N and below the snow finger and cross to the snowfield by talus slope just below a band of cliff. Ascend steep snow 150 ft and then gentler slopes to the base of summit rocks.

NORTHWEST COULOIR: This route on W side of the N face follows a steep couloir and finally ends on the upper part of the W ridge variation. First ascent by Dallas Kloke and Bryce Simon on June 29, 1973; bivouac was made just below the N face.

From Colonial Creek campground follow the rudimentary trail on the left side of Colonial Creek about 1½ mi. (see Snowfield Peak). Leave the trail before it crosses the creek and follow a dry creek bed S; this leads to a steep brush and forest ascent to the base of the N face. The original party reached the face by a gully and the second ramp to get on the wooded rib on the right (considerable bushwhacking). Traverse the base of N face to its W portion, then ascend easy rock. Here enter an 800-ft couloir of 40 to 45° (hard snow) which terminates with a short class 5.6 rock pitch. The com-

MESAHCHIE PK.
KATSUK PK.
ELDORADO PK.
KIMTAH PK.
COSHO PK.
KIMTAH GLACIER
KATSUK GLACIER
MESAHCHIE GLACIER
Panther Creek

pletion of the climb is up the steep snowfield angling left. Grade II; class 5.6 Time: 8-10 hours from road; 4 hours down. Reference: *Mountaineer,* 1973, p. 82.

NORTHEAST GULLY and EAST RIDGE: First ascent by Dallas Kloke and Scott Masonholder on July 5, 1968. Make approach per Northwest Couloir route. At the base of N face traverse left a few hundred ft, then ascend a 40-45° snow gully for about 1000 ft to the E ridge. The climb on the ridge is class 5.2 to 5.3, avoiding several ridge blocks by passing on the S. Grade II. Time: 9 hours from road. Reference: *A.A.J.*, 1969, p. 388.

RUBY MOUNTAIN 7408′/2258 m

Ruby is a massive mountain E of the South Arm of Diablo Lake 2.8 mi. SE of Ross Dam. Local relief is impressive: it rises 6200 ft above Thunder Arm in 2.4 mi. The summit is on the W end of the mass, with a ridge horseshoe around S and E to the East Peak (7148′/2179 m). There are small glaciers on the NE, but Ruby is very moderate on the S, SW, and SE. Prospectors and goat hunters probably visited its summit in early times; a known ascent was made by Morley Buck in about 1934.

ROUTE: Take Panther Creek♦-Fourth of July Pass Trail for about 2 mi. to the old Ruby Mountain way trail. Then it is 4½ mi. to the summit. One could also reach the pass in about 4½ mi. via the Panther Creek Trail from North Cascades Hwy♦.

BEEBE MOUNTAIN 7416′/2260 m

Beebe is a gentle, moderate but solitary mountain with a long S and NW ridge between Granite and Stillwell Creeks; the N side is steep. The name is for Frank Beebe, early prospector of the area.

ROUTE: The long S ridge is easy. One can reach it from the E, from North Cascades Hwy♦ up bush, or via Panther Creek Trail♦ and hike up Stillwell Creek (cross-country).

ELIJA RIDGE 7739′/2359 m

This is a long NW-trending ridge between Panther and Gabriel Creeks, and Stillwell Creek, to the NW of Gabriel Peak. There are several small glaciers on the N slope. The highest point is flanked by a W peak (7665′/2336 m, 0.7 mi. NW) and an E peak (7521′/2292 m, 0.5 mi. SE).

ROUTE: It is probably best to do the SW slope from the Panther-Gabriel Creek junction; no technical difficulties. It is easily ascended via E ridge from Beebe Mountain.

GABRIEL PEAK 7722′/2354 m

Located in the angle between Panther and Gabriel Creeks, N of Ragged Ridge. The S flank is the most moderate. Gabriel, Elija Ridge, and Mt. Prophet all refer to the mental state of the religious fanatic Tommy Rowland, who came to the upper Skagit in 1895 and then later announced he was the "Prophet Elisha"—after various investments were made on his claims.

ROUTE: The ascent is not difficult on the S slope, but the approach requires considerable cross-country travel. Best route is Panther Creek Trail♦ and up Panther Creek valley.

RAGGED RIDGE from northeast
AUSTIN POST, U.S. GEOLOGICAL SURVEY

RAGGED RIDGE

Ragged Ridge consists of a series of high alpine rock peaks aligned in a general WNW direction between Fisher and Panther Creeks. The five principal peaks span 3½ mi., but the overall length of the ridge is 10 mi. The highest peak, Mesahchie (8975′/2736 m), rises 4400 ft from its flanking valley bottoms. The broad N slope holds three large glaciers and numerous small bodies of ice, and is an impressive face of mixed rock, snow and ice. The S slope is at its most pleasant in early summer, but becomes barren as snow melts. Surveyors, prospectors, and geologists explored parts of the ridge in early to mid-20th century, but left few records, and it is uncertain if any of the principal peaks were climbed. Lage Wernstedt climbed Red Mountain for surveying purposes at least twice (1926) and may have reached other high points. Peter Misch may have climbed some peaks during geological research. Most of the peaks are still relatively unvisited in comparison to similar areas in the range.

A traverse route was done in June 1971 by Alan Firey, Joe Firey, Joan Firey, and Jerry Swanson. The N flank of the ridge offers easy to reasonable travel on connecting glaciers from Red Mountain to Easy Pass. The traverse party crossed the main ridge just SE of Red; the lakes on the N flank 2 mi. E offer good camping. The route led around the S side of Cosho Peak and through the col of Kimtah Glacier, descended it easterly and gained Katsuk Glacier's basin, descended under the cliffs and ice of Mesahchie Peak, then climbed the glacier here to Panther Col (7440′+) at the head of Panther Creek. Mesahchie Pass (5960′+), between Panther and Kitling Creek offers a cross-country route to Granite Creek. References: *Mountaineer,* 1970, pp. 104, 121; 1971, pp. 50-51, map p. 42; 1973, p. 83.

KITLING PEAK 8003′/2439 m

At the E end of the main summits and 1 mi. NW of Easy Pass; the peak has a rugged cliffy area on the N and E, above the basin of Kitling Creek. The name

KATSUK PK.
JACK MTN.
MESAHCHIE PK.
South Rib
rib
1968
Fisher Creek

means "kettle" in Chinook jargon. First ascent by Chris Roper and John Roper on August 24, 1968.

ROUTE: Approach from trail W of Easy Pass♦; make a NW diagonal ascent over mostly an easy rubble slope. Or make the ascent from Fisher Creek Trail♦ at about 5000 ft.

Peak 7690 (2344 m) is ½ mi. NW of Easy Pass. This is merely a point on the ridge, but has easy access for a view. Make the ascent from the W.

New Morning Peak (7230′/2204 m) is a minor summit located N of Easy Pass♦. The W ridge is a hike. Reference: *Mountaineer,* 1973, p. 83.

Cub Peak (7985′/2434 m) is a small peak W of Easy Pass, between Mesahchie Peak and the col, with the glacier on its N. A known ascent was made by John Roper. Approach as for Kitling Peak.

MESAHCHIE PEAK 8975′/2736 m

Mesahchie, the main peak of Ragged Ridge, has a rugged alpine thimble-shaped summit 4.4 mi. NE of Mt. Logan. Most of the southern escarpment is talus and broken, barren rock, but the rocky N face is impressive with its curtain-like mix of rock and steep snow above the mile-wide Mesahchie Glacier. The name is from the Chinook jargon, meaning "wicked." First ascent by Joe Firey, Joan Firey, John Meulemans, and Irene Meulemans on July 5, 1966 (via S rib). References: *Mountaineer,* 1967, p. 128; 1970, p. 104

SOUTH RIB: Begin with a climbing traverse from a position as high as feasible on the trail W of Easy Pass♦. Cross a wide obvious snow gully to gain the central S rib, which leads to the summit. Rock is solid, interesting class 3 (some scrambling on moderately steep snow and rock).

WEST RIDGE: First ascent by Chris Roper and John Roper on August 22, 1968. Begin from Fisher Creek Trail♦ at 5000 ft. Angle NW over open meadows and rock to a flat basin at 6400 ft beneath a knob on the W. Then ascend snow and loose rock to the col (8200′+) between Mesahchie and Katsuk Peaks. Contour to the N side of the ridge and enter into a large winding couloir on the W ridge. Take this to its apex; from here the summit is a short scramble. Time: 4 hours. Reference: *A.A.J.*, 1970, p. 121.

KATSUK PEAK 8680′+/2646 m

The second highest peak on Ragged Ridge, 0.4 mi. W of Mesahchie Peak, and near the center of the ridge. The Katsuk Glacier on the N and NW flank is 1.2 mi. wide, the largest in the area. In early summer the S slope and steep N face feature snowy ribs and couloirs. The name is from the Chinook, meaning "center." First ascent by Chris Roper and John Roper on August 22, 1968. Reference: *Mountaineer,* 1970, p. 104.

EAST RIDGE: From Fisher Creek Trail♦ at 5000 ft ascend NW to a rib which ends in a stumplike knoll extending S from the peak's E shoulder. Ascend this rib directly toward the E summit (8480′+/2585 m). Follow the rib within 200 ft of the main crest, then make a rising traverse W on the S slope. Class 3. Time: 4 hours.

KIMTAH PEAK 8600′+/2621 m

This prominent peak is on the central-western portion of Ragged Ridge, 3.9 mi. NNE of Mt. Logan. The summit is at the E end of the massif; on its S flank are a row of striking towers which have been called "Grotesque Gendarmes." The peak's S flank is a corrugation of ribs and gullies; the Kimtah Glacier on the N and NW slope is about 1 mi. wide. First ascent by John Roper and Jerry Swanson on June 6, 1970. Reference: *Mountaineer,* 1971, p. 87.

SOUTHWEST ROUTE: From about 14 mi. up Thunder/Fisher Creek Trail♦ (¼ mi. downstream from trail crossing of Fisher Creek there is a stream log) follow the hillside creek draining S from Cosho Peak to the 7000-ft level. Here bear E and cross the ridge coming S from Peak 8120+ (large yellow-orange peak). The ascent is then made to the ridge crest. The Grotesque Gendarmes will be close on the right. Continue E to the summit (drop S around false peak) via ledges and snowpatches.

COSHO PEAK (Ragged End) 8332′/2540 m

At the extreme W end of the main section of Ragged Ridge. SE of the summit is a sub-peak (8120′+/2475 m), also on the main crest, ¼ mi. distant. First ascent by John Roper and Jerry Swanson on June 7, 1970. Reference: *Mountaineer,* 1971, p. 87.

EAST RIDGE: Approach as per Kimtah Peak. From the head of the stream bear NE to the low point between Cosho and Peak 8120+. Follow this ridge W (snow and broken rock); keep slightly on the N side over snow and then loose rock to the summit. Time: 6 hours from Fisher Creek.

RED MOUNTAIN 7658′/2334 m

The extensive NW portion of Ragged Ridge that could be called Red Mountain is about 4½ mi. long. The SE summit is highest; 0.8 mi. NW is Point 7598 (2316 m). Lage Wernstedt climbed several of Red's summits in 1926, both in summer and early winter, and likely made the first ascent. The summit is a scenic viewpoint to Logan, Klawatti and other parts of Ragged Ridge.

ROUTE: One can take a bridge across Fisher Creek at Thunder Creek Trail♦ junction. An old miner's trail bears upslope until a semi-brushy area is reached. Higher, slopes are open and easy.

RAGGED RIDGE from south
AUSTIN POST, U.S. GEOLOGICAL SURVEY

SNOWFIELD PK.
RAGGED RIDGE
MT. ARRIVA
PK. 7945
FISHER PK.
GRAY BEARD PK.
Little Tack
S.E. Ridge

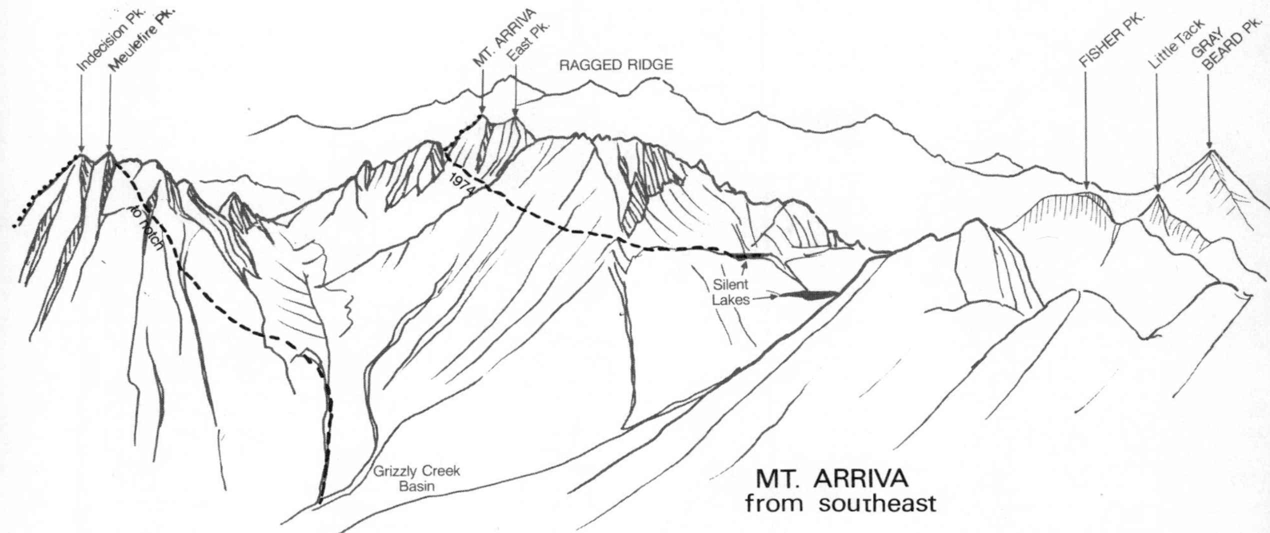

INDECISION PEAK 7945′/2422 m

A double summit 0.9 mi. S of Mt. Arriva, on the divide between Fisher and Grizzly Creeks. The slightly lower NE summit is known as Meulefire; the peak has striking avalance-chute type couloirs on the SE flank. First ascent by Bill Arundell, Marilyn Jensen, Stan Jensen, Frank King, and Joanne Williams on August 2, 1972. References: *Mountaineer,* 1972, p. 81; *A.A.J.,* 1970, p. 121.

SOUTHWEST RIDGE: Approach from Fisher Creek Trail♦ or via Mt. Logan cross-country route (see Mt. Logan). From camp at upper end of SE fork of Fisher Creek (at edge of large snowy flat at 6000′) ascend SE to col (6960′+) on Grizzly Creek divide. Make the ascent via the SW ridge. About midway up from the col ascend a cliff band via a short steep chimney (class 3 and 4). Time: 12 hours from camp.

MEULEFIRE PEAK est. 7930′/2417 m

First ascent by Joe Firey, Joan Firey, John Meulemans, and Irene Meulemans on July 7, 1966.

EAST ROUTE: Approach to Grizzly Creek via North Fork Bridge Creek (see Bridge Creek Trail♦). From basin of Grizzly Creek (large meadow at 4800′) up E flank of peak. The route takes the E ridge system to a notch just NE of the summit (class 5.2 out of notch—rock solid). The traverse from Indecision appears possible, but has not been explored. Reference: *Mountaineer,* 1967, pp. 128-129.

MT. ARRIVA 8215′/2504 m

Arriva is a rugged, rocky mountain, the highest between Black and Logan, on the divide between Fisher and Grizzly Creeks. The W peak (highest) and E peak are connected by a narrow shattered ridge; the mountain's S flank has the least gradient and on the NE there is s small glacier. The first climb was done by Fred Beckey, Jim Crooks, and Ed Kennedy in August, 1940, to reach the summit of the E peak (8160′+-est. 8190′), about 0.2 mi. from the W peak. The first ascent of this was made by Joe Firey, Joan Firey, John Meulemans, and Irene Meulemans on July 6, 1966, on a traverse from the E peak. Reference: *Mountaineer,* 1967, p. 128.

EAST RIDGE: From Grizzly Creek (see Mt. Logan cross-country route) climb directly toward the E peak (S slope). From its summit traverse along the very loose ridge, which has a difficult exposed notch (class 4). The eastern route to the E peak (original ascent) was made from Fisher Creek basin; no difficulties, but some loose rock (class 3).

SOUTH ROUTE: First ascent by Ken Hunich, Gary Mellom, John Roper, and Mike Theobald on July 5, 1974. From Fisher Creek basin (see Fisher Creek Trail♦) hike to Silent Lakes via the pass (6960′+). Cross Arriva's S slope (gullies and ribs) and ascend to the SW notch (7760′+). Ascend a steep gully (class 3) and then scramble to completion on the SE.

ARCHES PEAK (Little Johannesburg) 7945′/2422 m

This is the summit between the terminal forks of Fish-

MT. ARRIVA and RAGGED RIDGE from southeast
AUSTIN POST, U.S. GEOLOGICAL SURVEY

BLACK PK.
South
Slope
Pt. 8395
Indecision Pk.
REPULSE PK.
Wing Lake

er Creek, 0.7 mi. NNE of Mt. Arriva. It has a resemblance to Johannesburg Mountain as seen from Easy Pass; the name was selected by the first ascent party for the patterns on its N face and for the prominent arch on its NE flank. First ascent by Chris Roper and John Roper on August 23, 1968.

ROUTE: From near the head of Fisher Creek basin climb W over a plateau (snow or broken rock) until it ends in a large face 0.2 mi. SE of the summit (bypass face cliffs to a 7200′ col on the main ridge). Cross to the S side, then diagonal up over gullies and ribs to the summit (class 3). Time: 3-4 hours.

GRAYBEARD PEAK 7965′/2428 m

This recently named peak, 1 mi. SE of Easy Pass, it is impressive from Granite Creek, and from any eastern vantage resembles a large rocky pyramid. First ascent by Carl Ben Casey and William A. Long in August 1959.

SOUTHWEST ROUTE: Via Easy Pass♦. Make a rising traverse SE to 7400 ft on the peak's S slope. Then scramble NE on scree to within 200 ft of the summit. A 25-ft notch requires climbing (class 3 or 4). Time: 3 hours.

LITTLE TACK 7400′+/2256 m

Named for its outline; 0.3 mi. S of Graybeard. First ascent by John Roper and Steve Shelton on August 11, 1973.

NORTH RIDGE: A short lead of class 4 or harder. Reference: *Mountaineer,* 1973, p. 83.

FISHER PEAK 8040′+/2451 m

Fisher is a thimble-shaped, dark hued peak of metamorphic rock on the Fisher-Grizzly-Granite Creek divide between Easy Pass and Black Peak. There is a small glacier on the NW. First ascent by Fred Beckey, Jim Crooks, and Ed Kennedy in August 1940 (via NW face). Reference: *Summit,* Nov.-Dec. 1971, pp. 16-17.

NORTHWEST FACE: Approach via Fisher Creek Trail♦. From upper Fisher Creek basin (camping) ascend the face via broken, eroded rock. Near the summit bear to the W flank; 4 hours.

SOUTHEAST RIDGE: This ridge, clearly visible from the highway, is about 1200 ft in height to the SE summit (7840′+/2390 m), then continues to the true summit. The route is interesting and solid on the hard leads. First ascent by Greg Ball and Bill Fryberger on July 29, 1973.

Take North Cascades Hwy♦ to parking at open area on E (just S of Swamp Creek). Hike W and ford Granite Creek (arduous in early season). Hike up S side of valley to W, then cross to easier N side (no trail, but fairly open except for two slides). Keep in trees to right of brushy open area at valley head; good camp in meadows below E face (5 hours). Begin climb several hundred ft SW of ridge foot. Ascend poorly defined dihedral system to where ridge becomes less steep. Then follow ridge several pitches to SE summit (class 3 and 4 and a few moderate class 5 moves to here). There is a 140-ft notch beyond; down-climb W one pitch (narrow ridge), then make 75-ft rappel. Climb a short wall (class 5-25′) then right on a shelf slope; then up again to easier climbing. Grade II; class 5.5 Time: 6 hours from camp. Descent: via S face; one rappel to gain moderate snow gully; then return E and NE.

Variation: By Philip Kubik, Ian Turnbull, and Edmund Zenger in July 1974. Begin ridge farther N, nearer to snow/ice. Follow ridge closely entire distance. Reported class 3 on lower part, 5.4 and class 4 to SE summit, then 5.4 above notch. Descent on N. Time: road to camp—4 hours; to summit 5 hours; total return 4½ hours.

REPULSE PEAK 7923′/2415 m

A peak of moderate significance, on the Granite-Grizzly Creek divide, between Fisher and Black Peaks, it has a precipitous face on the NE. First ascent by Alan Firey, Joan Firey, Joe Firey, and Jerry Swanson on June 27, 1971.

NORTHWEST ROUTE: From Silent Lakes (see Mt. Arriva) traverse heather and rock on the Grizzly Creek slope of Fisher's S buttress. Ascend to the subsidiary NW peak of Repulse (class 3), then descend into the notch adjacent to the main peak. Ascend the NW ridge from the notch (class 4).

BLACK PEAK 8970′/2734 m

Black is a massive and very important high peak, one of the giants of the North Cascades, on the Granite-Grizzly Creek divide 3.7 mi. W of Rainy Pass. While the rock on the East (highest) Peak is quite loose with much surface scree on S slopes, the West Peak (8820′/2688 m) is of a rugged granitic character (quartz diorite), with a horn-like summit. A smaller peak (8395′/2559 m) ½ mi. NE of Black's summit, has rugged cliffs and small glaciers on its E. Early Forest Service maps (1922, 1926) show a Shelockum Glacier on Black's NW face; the largest body of glacier ice is on this slope, but there are also small glaciers on all flanks but the S. Wing Lake nests in a hollow near the head of the basin SE of the mountain; the barren lake is at the extreme edge of growth and surrounded by snow, glacier remnants and moraine. The first ascent was made by Lage Wernstedt and an unknown companion (possibly Whitey Shull) in late summer, 1926. Hermann Ulrichs climbed Black solo in August 1934 from Lake Ann, finding evidence of the earlier ascent, which he believed had been done via North Fork of Bridge Creek. In these days the trek of Ulrichs, long before the highway, was "A 12-hour trip without a foot of trail—first class pioneering."

BLACK PEAK from east
AUSTIN POST, U.S. GEOLOGICAL SURVEY

CORTEO PK
West Pk.
BLACK PK.
South Slope
East Buttress
N.E. Ridge
Pt. 8395
REPULSE PK.
FISHER PK.
KITLING PK.
GRAY BEARD PK.

References: *A.A.J.*, 1936, p. 472; *Summit,* Nov.-Dec. 1971, pp. 16-17.

SOUTH ROUTE: This route is mainly easy snowfields, talus, moraine, and a rock scramble to the summit, a satisfying ascent of no technical difficulty to a fine vantage height. It is now the most popular way (1934 route). See Lake Ann♦ for route to Wing Lake. Hike around its E, over a moraine, and onto snow. A gentle perennial snowfield in a depression leads to the prominent col on Black's S ridge (est. 7900'); the final 300 ft of snow is moderately steep but rockslides on N provide alternative. A broad gully on the W side of the col (dry scree-talus in late season; snow early) leads to the final summit blocks. At about 150 ft below the false summit traverse E (right) at one of several notches to directly below the final summit; the final 150 ft can be done by several ways (unroped). Time: 3½-4½ hours.

SOUTHWEST ROUTE: This is the easiest route on Black, probably the first climbed. A long hike and scramble up semi-open subalpine slopes, meadows, and scree lead to the notch (8520'+) between the two main peaks (see West Peak). The remainder is scrambling (merge with South Route). One can make the approach via North Fork Bridge Creek (see Bridge Creek Trail♦) and Grizzly Creek, then up Woody Creek for ½-¾ mi. The lower slopes are brushy (see West Peak).

NORTHEAST RIDGE: This route is more technical than the normal way, but not forbidding; the ridge is class 3 and 4 (exposed) with one class 5 pitch. The climbing has had conflicting reports, ranging from fairly solid to fractured and loose. First ascent by Roger Jackson and Michael Kennedy on September 1, 1973. From Wing Lake (see South Route) ascend moraine and a small glacier slope, then make a short rock scramble to the col between the summit and Point 8395. Then climb the NE ridge. Time: 3 hours on ridge. Reference: *Mountaineer,* 1973, p. 83.

EAST BUTTRESS: Ascend from Wing Lake (see South Route). The lower portion is easy, then ascends a gully system. Rock is reported fairly solid, broken as in a stairway. Class 3 and 4.

WEST PEAK 8820'/2688 m

First ascent by Joe Firey, Joan Firey, John Meulemans, and Irene Meulemans on July 8, 1966. For approach see Mt. Logan cross-country route; or use North Fork Bridge Creek-Grizzly Creek. From large meadow at 4800 ft along Grizzly Creek: follow creek until forced into timber, then bear S and rise slightly; into brush ½ hour until junction with long open gully descending directly from Black to Woody Creek. The gully leads nearly to the top of SW shoulder. Then make a climbing traverse across meadows south of Black and ascend to the notch between the East and West Peaks. A traverse (class 3) circles to the left around the West Peak for several hundred ft. Turn a corner and ascend rubble and a series of ledges to the final chimney on the N summit face. Class 4 Reference: *Mountaineer,* 1967, pp. 128-129.

BLACK PEAK from southeast
HERMANN F. ULRICHS

CORTEO PEAK 8080'+/2463 m

Corteo is an interesting rock peak with the unforgettable appearance of a truncated castle. It is 1.8 mi SE of the more dominating Black Peak. Corteo has a small lower N summit and under both the W and N faces is a small body of ice. The Lewis Glacier, NW of the divide, between Corteo and Wing Lake, has a large end moraine; the glacier is much diminished since early in this century. Note: 1926 Forest Service maps show Lewis Glacier on West Fork Maple Creek, not at present location. First ascent by John Lehmann and Hermann F. Ulrichs in July, 1935 (via East Face).

EAST FACE: From Lake Ann♦ hike W across saddle ("Maple Pass"—6600'+); descend 200 ft, then contour westerly (Maple Creek slope) to Horsefly Pass. Make an ascending traverse on heather and talus, to reach the SE spur ridge at est. 6900 ft, then ascend it to cliff band at 7600 ft. Contour N on exposed gravelly ledges (above a wall) until directly beneath N notch (route leads to the black dike, then into the notch between the summits). The final summit tower provides a short solid climb (class 3 and 4). Time: 5 hours from Rainy Pass.

SOUTH FACE: From Maple Creek basin ½ mi. E of Corteo (6000') contour the SE ridge until directly S of the peak. Work up a narrow ridge system to est. 7500 ft to avoid slabby gullies. Follow narrowing fracture lines up, keeping left, on sound granitic rock. From the level promontory below the summit a short descent, then westward climb reaches to the SW ridge a few yds below the summit.

SOUTHWEST RIDGE: First ascent by Marilyn Jensen, Stan Jensen, Joanne Williams, and Norman Winn on July 30, 1972. From Wing Lake follow the long smooth slope of Lewis Glacier (or adjacent terrain) to the ridge extending NW of Corteo at about 7500 ft. Descend 300 ft and traverse into the snow-filled cirque under the W face of the summit. Reach Corteo's SW ridge just E of the SW col via an easy gully. Follow the ridge to the summit; the angle is not steep, but climbing is exposed (class 3 and 4). Reference: *Mountaineer,* 1972, p. 81 (has error).

FRISCO MOUNTAIN 7760'+/2365 m

Frisco is a small attractive pyramidal rock peak 1.1 mi. S of Lake Ann, which together with its southeastern extension—Rainy Peak—culminate the nearly closed loop formed by Maple and upper Bridge Creeks. The saddles on the N (7360'+) and W (est. 7150') are easy to reach. The Lyall Glacier covers part of the eastern flank (7200' to 6400'). First ascent by Lage Wernstedt in summer 1926; in August 1934 Hermann Ulrichs found a summit tin (ascent via N ridge). Reference: *Mountaineer,* 1935, p. 11.

NORTH RIDGE: From Lake Ann♦ cross W at Maple Pass and descend into basin of Maple Creek. Traverse and climb

FRISCO MOUNTAIN from east
LAGE WERNSTEDT, U.S. FOREST SERVICE

to the obvious sharp notch between Frisco and the crag N, then follow the N ridge (exposed class 3). Time 2 hours from pass. An alternative approach is via abandoned Maple Creek Trail to the upper basin, then an ascent to the notch.

Note: the route via Rainy Lake is reported as not advisable; cliff above lake. But it appears satisfactory to hike from the lake's S to the NW margin of Lyall Glacier, and then to the N ridge.

EAST ROUTE: By using part of the Lyall Glacier (see above) a route via the E-NE flank appears very simple, but is not verified. Ascend the easy denuded E slope. Near the summit rock bear left and complete on the E spur.

RAINY PEAK 7768′/2368 m

This small summit, 0.6 mi. SE of and connected to Frisco, is just S of Lyall Glacier and 1 mi. SW of Rainy Lake (on an E-W crest with a short N cliff). There is a long monotonous slope above Bridge Creek Trail♦, but one could also traverse from Frisco. Another route would be Rainy Lake to the NW end of Lyall Glacier, then the NW ridge. There is some cliffy terrain near the lake.

MT. BENZARINO 7720′+/2353 m

A moderately sized peak at the apex of the divide between North Fork Bridge and Maple Creeks. Of the double summits, the SW is highest; a small glacier exists beneath the short N face. An unnamed peak NE of Benzarino is shown at the same altitude contour, but is slightly lower. The first ascent was made by Lage Wernstedt in 1926 during surveying.

ROUTES: The SW slope is easy but long; one could make the ascent from the W via North Fork Bridge Creek. The abandoned Maple Creek Trail offers a route via the NE or E ridge. The S ridge has been done, via Lake Ann and Maple Pass, by John Roper on July 25, 1976.

MT. LOGAN 9087′/2770 m

Mt. Logan, a broad ice-clad massif and one of the largest mountains in the North Cascades, is composed of Skagit gneiss and has three significant glaciers.[81] The true summit is the N peak; there also are the conspicuous middle peak (8960′+/2731 m), S peak (8546′/2605 m), and NE (Thunder) peak. The mountain was named for George Logan, a miner who staked claims and drove tunnels at the headwaters of Thunder Creek, beginning in 1896, and had a cabin 2

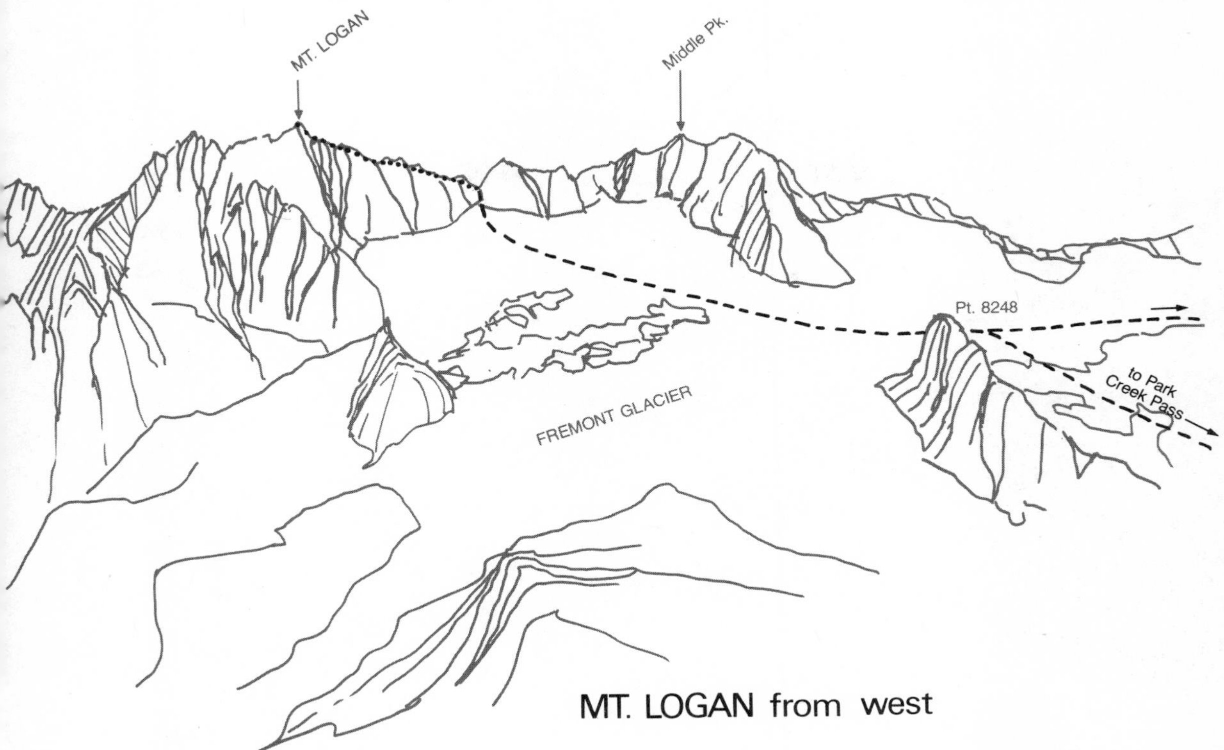

MT. LOGAN from west

mi. from Park Creek Pass. The first ascent was made in summer 1926 by Lage Wernstedt and an unknown companion (possibly Whitey Shull). The next climb was made by Don Blair, Norval Grigg, and Art Winder on July 24, 1934. They found a cairn and stick on the summit, but no record (*Mountaineer,* 1934, pp. 14, 16). Forest Farr and Winder had climbed the South and Middle Peaks on July 28, 1933. The long ridge SE of Logan has pinnacles; the highest of these was climbed by Austin Post in 1947, via North Fork Bridge Creek. References: *Mazama* 30, no. 13 (1948): 16-17; *Mountaineer,* 1934, p. 14, 16; 1935, pp. 11-12; 1964, pp. 12-13; 1972, map p. 42; 1972, pp. 68-69, 80-81. *Summit,* Dec. 1965, pp. 20-23; Nov.-Dec. 1971, pp. 14-15.

SOUTHWEST ROUTE: See Park Creek Pass Trail♦. From the trail at about ¼ mi. N of the pass take an upslope-bearing path through lovely parklands. Then ascend scree and boulders, keeping left of a small basin. The route has flexibility: basic idea is to make an ascending northward traverse of about ½ mi. (partly snow); keep left of large rock outcropping of S peak but right of Point 8248 and reach the Fremont Glacier at its 8000-ft margin. Cross the gentle firn and continue beyond lowest toe of the middle peak, then ascend to upper portion of the glacier. From the large wind cirque climb a short gully with rock corners to a ridge notch N of the middle peak. Begin to follow the ridge, then descend slightly and make an easy rock scramble rising along the E flank of summit ridge (solid but exposed class 2 and 3). An alternate is to first stay on the ridge crest, then on left flank, then cross to the right. Time: 6 hours (4 hours pass to glacier, 1 hour on glacier, 1 hour scrambling).

BANDED GLACIER ROUTE: First ascent by Gary Mellom, John Roper, and Reed Tindall on July 2, 1972. Approach as for Thunder Peak. Ascend upper glacier reach (some crevasses) to the high Banded-Douglas col, then up steeper final glacier slopes. Make final summit ascent from the S. This is mostly a "snow" route, but crampons could be useful.

DOUGLAS GLACIER ROUTE: First ascent by 12 persons of Frank King party August 1972; route had been descended August 1970. See Mt. Logan cross-country route. From Fisher Pass ascend W 1000 ft to tree-covered knoll (some bush). Cross ice sections, then main portion of cre-

Thunder Pk.
MT. LOGAN
BANDED
GLACIER

MT. LOGAN from north
U.S. FOREST SERVICE

MT. LOGAN from southeast
TOM MILLER

vassed Douglas Glacier to high col adjacent Banded Glacier, then per final completion of latter route.

THUNDER PEAK 8800′+/2682 m

The NE peak of Mt. Logan, ½ mi. from the true summit, from which it is conspicuous. First ascent by Gary Mellom, John Roper, and Reed Tindall on July 2, 1972.

Approach via Fisher Creek Trail♦ W of Logan Creek (2 mi. past Rock Cabin), then to lake (5160′+, camping); continue SSE to the pass (est. 7500′; Christmas Tree Col) and down to the Banded Glacier. The climbing route from the glacier is on the rock of the NW face; the hardest pitch is the steep section above the hanging snowpatch; class 3. Descent by N ridge. Reference: *Mountaineer,* 1972, p. 81.

SOUTH PEAK

The climb is not difficult on either S or N flank; the original party (1933) was uncertain which of Logan's peaks was highest, so traversed over both the first and second peaks.

MIDDLE PEAK (Second Peak)

May offer some climbing problems. The first ascent party on July 28, 1933 was uncertain which of Logan's summits was highest, so approached this second peak from the S peak's connecting ridge and reported a strenuous climb; many blocks had to be mantled. They descended a very steep snow slope to the Fremont Glacier.

MT. LOGAN CROSS-COUNTRY ROUTE: From summit: Steep snow slope to Douglas Glacier (crevasse problems and rappels). Descend from moraines at E end of glacier, then contour at about 5300 ft. Some brush en route to Fisher Pass (6480′+). Hike NE along "Spectacular Ridge" and continue ½ mi. to col (6880′+); descend on N to a small glacier (SE fork Fisher Creek drainage) and make diagonal ascent to icy second col (6960′+). Note map error here: the small glacier is really in two parts (eastern part extends to col 6960′+).

A large rockslide can be descended into Grizzly Creek valley; midway down, as vegetation converges, bear N to keep in open; easy creek crossing and pleasant meadow camping at 4800 ft. Hike 3 mi. to upper meadows of Woody Creek (scrub and bush before open meadows). Game trails lead NE to pass SW of Wing Lake.

PEAK 8080 8080′+/2682 m

An unnamed peak of minor importance NW of Storm King. The peak forms the E buttress of Park Creek Pass (0.6 mi. distant). First ascent by Dan O'Brien, Oscar Pennington, Sidney Schmerling, and Hermann Ulrichs in 1932. The ascent is made from the pass, no difficulties.

STORM KING MOUNTAIN 8520′+/2595 m

Storm King is the moderately sized but prominent peak between Park Creek Pass and Mt. Goode. The true summit is the E peak, where there are two prominent towers (eastern highest); the W peak (8515′/2596 m) is about 0.3 mi. distant. The summit area can cause some confusion, for there are four peaks of nearly equal height on an E-W crest. Storm King is flanked on the W and NW by Wyeth Glacier (basin of North Fork Bridge Creek). First ascent by Forest Farr and Art Winder on July 26, 1933. References: *Mountaineer,* 1971, p. 47; *Mazama* 55, no. 13 (1973): 43; *Summit,* Nov.-Dec. 1971, p. 14.

SOUTH ROUTE: Climbed September 4, 1966, but probably same completion as first ascent. Leave Park Creek Pass Trail♦ about ¾ mi. before the pass and ascend. Traverse at 7400 ft to basin S of Storm King. Then ascend deep gully (possible snow). This thins out to a wall of loose rock (falling rock danger). The climb is completed on a short face on the SW side of summit peak (loose class 3 and 4). Time: 4 hours.

Variations: The original party climbed a very steep snow gully from meadows E of Park Creek Pass. The approach has also been described from upper Park Creek where steep consecutive gullies lace the basin. Ascend to a well defined ledge at 6800 ft. Traverse S to a prominent corner and then proceed E (snow in early season or loose talus into basin).

The original party continued on a traverse to Mt. Goode, using the obvious flat ridge which is punctuated with small rock points. Because of loose rubble they did not care to leap the cleft which divided the Storm King massif, so they dropped onto the N face and scaled a sharp ridge which proved difficult, then climbed back to the ridge; a shale slope between rock walls proved to be a muddy area, and in the struggle to get out, Farr injured his knee. The ridge points were found reasonable to climb over or around, but Farr's injury curtailed the Goode attempt.

MT. GOODE 9200′+/2804 m

This magnificent peak of Skagit gneiss[82] dominates not only the Park Creek and North Fork Bridge Creek valleys, but the entire wave of mountains between the head of Lake Chelan and Thunder Creek. On its spectacular glacier-clad NE flace Goode stands 6000 ft closely above the valley floor (1.6 mi.). The opposite face is less stupendous but has precipitous and more puzzling features. While the E and N flanks present a less complex alpine facade, the SW portion of Goode has remarkable breaks which provide natural summit routes. SE of the summit mass a prominent talus gully angles to the long serrate crest which dramatically divides watersheds; nearer to the true summit a deep couloir slices into gigantic grey buttresses, slanting to a notch in the knifed arete. The bold wall beneath the two highest points of the mountain is cleaved by an E-trending fracture that directs one to the notch between the points—a natural climbing route. While the NE, N, and E faces contain steep glacier ice, the absence of

MT. GOODE from southwest
AUSTIN POST, U.S. GEOLOGICAL SURVEY

West Tower
N.W. Ridge
Bedayn Couloir
S.W. Chimney
S.W. Couloir
1940
Black Tooth notch
S.E. Ridge
S.E. Summit
varia.

high moderate slopes has deterred the accumulation of a glacier to match the magnificence of the mountain.[83]

An early mountaineering party concluded from a distance that Goode gives one the impression of being a high jumbled pyramid, and easy mountain meadows extending to the base of its cliffs lure the unsuspecting mountaineer upward to what appears to be a comparatively easy ascent. But perpendicular buttresses and steep narrow chimneys peter out in sheer, smooth walls. Before its first ascent in 1936 Goode had been the object of numerous attempts, one of the most sought-after quests in the range. One is tempted to preserve the myth that the ascent is an enormous route, but knowledge and standards have changed, so that by 1972 forty ascents were recorded, and in 2 years the number had increased to 61.

It was not until nearly the mid-1930s that climbers ventured high on Goode, beginning with a reconnaissance by Forest Farr and Art Winder on July 26, 1933, on the same day as the ascent of Storm King. In 1934 two separate parties came close to success via the 400-ft SW couloir-chimney route that was later climbed on the first ascent. On July 10 Dan O'Brien and Hermann Ulrichs were repulsed by an overhang and smooth rock during roped climbing, then Don Blair and Art Winder reached about the same position, close to success.[84] The following summer Everett Darr and Joe Leuthold attempted the mountain and ascended to about the same location before being turned back.[85] The first ascent was made by Wolf Bauer, Philip Dickert, Joe Halwax, Jack Hossack, and George MacGowan on July 5, 1936, using the route of previous attempts but with superior equipment and more ingenious techniques.[86] The mountain is named after Richard U. Goode, geographer for the U.S. Geological Survey.[87] References: *Mountaineer,* 1934, p. 12; 1936, pp. 13-15; 1964, pp. 11-12; *A.A.J.*, 1936, p. 472; *Mazama* 17, no. 12 (1935): 59-60; 55, no. 13 (1973): 43, *Challenge of the North Cascades,* pp. 26-28.

BEDAYN COULOIR: First ascent by Kenneth Adam, Raffi Bedayn, and W. Kenneth Davis on July 26, 1937. A shortened version of this second ascent route on Goode has now become one of the two most popular routes. The lower portion of the route has several variables, all of which have some problems to give challenging access to the summit gully/chimney. The route has exposure and appeal of a classic line, yet in places a considerable amount of loose rock.[88]

Follow the Park Creek Trail♦ about 4½ mi., turning off at a timbered rib which rises immediately beyond a streambed containing a large alder patch (tree blaze). Ascend the rib to alp slopes, bearing left into a timberline basin (5900′—camping). Ascend the broken rock ridge leading WSW from Goode's NW peak. An alternative is to begin the climbing right (S) of the ridge, from the head of a snowfield basin. Eventually angle slightly right into a couloir-gully dividing the great walls of the NW and main peaks. The couloir is generally a scramble except for one short steep right-bearing pitch, and continues to the notch between the summits. Continue via easy rock to the SE. Class 5 (one pitch); remainder class 3 and 4 (can be more difficult if iced). Time: 7½ hours from Park Creek. Reference: *Sierra Club Bull.* 23, no. 2 (1938): 47-48.

From the summit notch a ridge (class 4) leads to the NW peak.

Variation: Ascend the deep couloir which leads to the notch between NW ridge and West Tower. Part way up the couloir climb right over a shoulder to the couloir system of the route.

NORTHWEST RIDGE (Northwest Buttress): This is a spectacular but quite reasonable route that traverses the NW peak to the main summit. Rock is generally superb on the sustained pitches, and there are great views of the NE face. First ascent by Fred Beckey, William Fix, Don (Claunch) Gordon, Jim Henry, and John Parrott on September 6, 1953. Make the approach per normal route, but when nearing Goode's wall traverse N to a long boulder slope leading toward the deep gap between the NW ridge and the West Tower. Ascend the slope, snow, and then an obvious steep couloir. Below the gap a slightly difficult chockstone is passed. Leaving the gap a piton can protect a leftward traverse; this begins a zigzag system of groove-ramps which are less than the true profile angle, as steep fractured gneiss is climbed to the NW peak. From the summit rappel off the opposite side to a notch, then traverse around gendarmes (on the E) to continue to the main summit. Class 4 and 5 (one piton below gap and one just above). References: *Mountaineer,* 1953, p. 68; *A.A.J.*, 1954, p. 171.

Variation: By Greg Ball and Bill Fryberger on August 20, 1973. Combined with West Tower ascent. The rappels are unpleasant due to loose rock for natural anchors. Time: 11 hours to summit from high camp.

Variation: Lower Northeast Face: By Bob Crawford and Kurt Mendenhall on July 27, 1975. Approach Goode Glacier under face, up glacier, up ice sheet of NE face, cross W over top of rib to ice couloir, traverse three pitches W on ice couloir, and ascend six pitches to gap. Last two pitches steep ice. Time: Half-day, valley to bivouac on rib. Bring crampons and ice screws.

NORTHEAST FACE: This alpine route with its steep glacier and ice sheet and splendid rock face resembles some of the walls in the British Columbia Coast Mountains and the Alps in spectacle and challenge. Rock is solidly jointed, with long slab construction features; the rock in shallow areas is not as reliable for holds. First ascent by Fred Beckey and John Parrott on July 19, 1954; the next climb was not made until 1974.

The basic approach is as per Northeast Buttress route, but

MT. GOODE from northeast
AUSTIN POST, U.S. GEOLOGICAL SURVEY

AGNES MTN.
S.E. Summit
Black Tooth
notch
MT. GOODE
N.W. Summit
West
Tower
1953
N.E.
Buttress
N.E.
Face
1975
GOODE
GLACIER

hike beyond the timber cone until beneath the Goode-Storm King col (possibly cross creek on snow). Find open talus and streambeds on leftward rise. Find ledge systems through cliffs (open rock and bush on denuded glacier slope) to western edge of Goode Glacier. Climb the glacier and steep apron to about 8000 ft. There may be a problem here getting onto rock. The climbing is initially hard to protect, but this improves as the route bears left over a corner, then onto the face and rib (spur) which is the feature of the upper route; follow this upface to notch between main and NW peaks. Grade III-IV; class 4 and 5; take crampons. Time: 7 hours from valley (4 hours on rock); iced conditions will require more time. References: *Mountaineer,* 1954, pp. 65-66; *A.A.J.*, 1955, p. 152; *Appalachia,* Dec. 1954, p. 254.

NORTHEAST BUTTRESS: This elegant and unmistakable buttress rises 2800 ft above Goode Glacier directly to the true summit. It is a magnificent alpine climb, with a certain amount of glacier problem, then a lengthy rock climb ranging from exposed scrambling to class 5; the more difficult portion is about 500 ft beneath the summit, and perhaps at the start, when leaving the ice. The inclination of jointing in the gneiss is favorable for holds. The route is perhaps best done about mid-season while there is snow in the approach gully. The descent can be made by one of the normal routes, or returning via the Goode-Storm King col. First ascent by Fred Beckey and Tom Stewart on August 6, 1966.

Approach via North Fork Bridge Creek (see Bridge Creek Trail♦). Leave trail shortly before opposite timber rib reaches valley. Ford the creek (possibly snow slide cone in early summer) to brief alder-bush area which leads to dry creek bed. Where gradient steepens traverse right through bushes to right-hand watercourse (first stream entering North Fork above 48° 30′) through cliff zone; keep in or adjacent the rock along watercourse for a distance, then bear left in bush to the only stand of conifers. Ascend, then through open-bush area beneath the cliff. Bear left (talus, slabs) and ascend to glacier where it is contoured into a depression (between two major ice cliffs). Bypass rock toe of the buttress on its left, then find the best entry. Grade III or IV; bring crampons, chocks, and runners. Note: second ascent party (Jim Price, Dave Seman, August 10, 1974) estimated 20-25 roped pitches, (eight being low class 5). Time: 6 hours from timberline. References: *A.A.J.*, 1967, p. 352; *Mountaineer,* 1967, p. 129.

SOUTHEAST RIDGE: First ascent by Marilyn Sanford, Alfred F. Tatyrek, and Hassler Whitney on August 1, 1963 (route climbed only to junction with 1940 route). From high meadows S of Goode traverse E across a snowfield. Ascend to the SE ridge via a scree slope at the eastern extremity of the S snowfield. On the ridge the route becomes an ascending traverse (class 4) over broken ledges (some loose) to where the ridge breaks off abruptly over Goode Glacier. Traverse on glacier (steep ice) to continuation of the SE ridge (possible to avoid by easy scramble over scree slope to S side of ridge). The ridge becomes broken, knifed, and exposed; some gendarmes bypassed or climbed over. Hardest gendarme reported at 200 vertical ft below summit—bypass by exposed overhanging hand traverse to right side; traverse on or near ridge to where Southwest Couloir route joins.

Variation: By Marilyn Howisey, Stan Jensen, and Terry Murphy on September 3, 1965. From 7000 ft SW of Goode traverse E to ridge (7240′+) overlooking Greenview Lake. Climb easy ridge N and then traverse NW to gap (8600′+) on the SE summit ridge. Then climb on or near ridge crest (class 3-4) to join Southwest Couloir route. Time: 7 hours from timberline. Reference: *Mountaineer,* 1966, p. 201.

SOUTHWEST COULOIR—UPPER EAST FACE: This route, done on the third ascent of Goode, is now one of the two most used. It was explored in 1936 but not completed until 4 years later. While the route takes a devious pattern to the summit, it is the least technical and exposed on the mountain. First ascent by Everett Darr, Ida Zacher Darr, Kenneth A. Henderson, and Paul Parker on August 4, 1940. From the timbered rib in Park Creek ascend rightward into a talus-snow basin S of the main summit wall. Enter a deep couloir leading toward a notch on the SE summit ridge. At about 8800 ft the couloir constricts to a narrow, vertical chimney (used on first ascent). From this position angle up and right across slab ledges (class 3—some loose rock) to the ridge notch just right of the first prominent black tooth. Note: one can climb from below by the couloir directly up to the black tooth notch. Cross the ridge and take a flat sandy ledge over the E face; there is a tricky awkward mantle at the far end—class 4. Continue to cross and traverse the tooth to reach the runnel between the latter and the summit mass. Then ascend obliquely to the summit. The final 600 linear ft are solid and well broken, with alternating ribs, ledges, and open books—exposed class 3. Time: 7 hours Park Creek Pass to SW face basin; 2-3 hours basin to summit. References: *Harvard Mountaineering,* no. 6 (1943): 37-38; *Appalachia* 24, no. 93 (June 1942): 45-47.

Approach Variation: By original party. From near Park Creek Pass sidehill steeply and in 4-6 hours reach small alp near side-valley gash; may need to drop 500 ft. Route leads to cirque and ridge beyond. This general approach is more tedious, but an old and feasible method of reaching any of W and SW routes on Goode.

SOUTHWEST CHIMNEY: First ascent route. See introduction copy.

Variation: By Donald Bergman and Rosemary Macy, July 5, 1958. At the cul de sac near the top of the chimney (at blank final headwall) traverse left to the W rib of the summit tower (class 4).

WEST TOWER 8760′+/2670 m

Although really positioned NW, it is popularly termed W; 0.3 mi. from the true summit of Goode. There is a deep U-gap between the tower and Northwest Ridge route. First ascent by Fred Beckey and Don (Claunch) Gordon on August 31, 1953.

Use approach per Northwest Ridge. From just beneath the gap continue N along the base of the tower to the ridge extending NW. Ascend gullies and chimneys to the ridge. The hardest portion is the first; make a W-side traverse to a minor notch in order to bypass gendarmes (class 5.5 or 5.6). The remainder of the route stays on or slightly E of the crest (last 50 ft is on crest). The route is class 4 except for the gendarme traverse. References: *A.A.J.*, 1954, p. 171; *Mountaineer,* 1953, pp. 67-68.

MEMALOOSE RIDGE 7265′/2214 m

The high point of this rugged crest extending SE of Goode is 1½ mi. from the Bridge-North Fork junction.

APPROACHES

Roads and trails described in this section are noted in the text by the symbol♦.

The principal wilderness portals are the Skagit River, Suiattle River, and Lake Chelan. The North Cascades Hwy traverses a portion of the section covered in this volume. Services outside the National Park and Recreation Areas include those at Concrete, Marblemount, Winthrop, Twisp, and Chelan. There is a State Park just W of Rockport (camping). A large campground is planned S of Skagit River W of the Newhalem Creek powerhouse. Service facilities are available at Newhalem. Campgrounds are at Colonial Creek (23 mi. E of Marblemount) and Roland Point. Boat landings are on Diablo Lake, Ross Lake, and Lake Chelan; City Light boat landing on Diablo Lake is on N shore (two or more daily runs).

ROADS

Boulder Creek Road (private). At Marblemount cross bridge and turn right in 1 mi. Cross Cascade River bridge, then left onto Boulder Creek Road, which extends over 6 mi.

Cascade River Road No. 3528 extends 23.5 mi. from Marblemount to terminus in N fork (parking area on right fork near end). It is permissable to camp at road's end (Johannesburg). A new plan may provide shuttle buses from a lower parking area. Marble Creek Forest Camp is at 7.1 mi. and Mineral Park Forest Camp at 15.3 mi. The left fork near road's end leads to Value Mine (private).

Marble Creek Road No. 3507 exits at 7.1 mi. and extends 2 mi. (not driveable now).

Sibley Creek Road No. 3503 exits at 9.1 mi. and is 4.2 mi. long (blocked lower by slide).

Found Creek Road No. 354 exits S at 13.3 mi. At 2.6 mi. turn left on Sonny Boy Road No. 3416 (Kindy Creek Trail begins at 0.5 mi.).

Kindy Ridge Road No. 354-A reaches Section 11 by the following route: take Road No. 354 for 4.5 mi. to Section 11, where there is a switchback; road may be closed before this area.

South Fork Road No. 3404 exits at 16.2 mi. and extends 1.7 mi. to trail no. 769.

Grade Creek Road No. 3304 leaves Suiattle River Road♦ at 6.5 mi. and extends 7 mi. (short piece to be added in Section 5).

Green Mountain Road No. 3227 leaves Suiattle River Road♦ at 19 mi. and reaches the trailhead at 5.9 mi.

Illabot Creek Road No. 347 extends 19.9 mi. to the bridge at the upper end of Illabot Lake. Road leaves from East Sauk Road 2.5 mi. S of Rockport on Hwy 20 (road to be extended 2.8 mi.).

Jordan Creek Road is a private road that begins closely E of Marblemount. Jordan and Boulder Creek Roads may be subject to gating and fire closure. To reach Jordan Creek turn S on Cascade-Sauk Hwy 1 mi. across the Marblemount bridge. Continue 1.5 mi. and pass fish hatchery, then left on East Jordan Creek Road. At about 4 mi. (just before crossing Jordan Creek) turn left onto narrow logging road and continue ¾ mi. to parking.

Lake Chelan. See Section II. Stehekin: Campgrounds at Purple Point, Weaver Point. See also Stehekin River Road♦.

Newhalem Creek Road No. 376 extends about 8.5 mi. to Section 14 (can drive only 5 mi. ATP). Distance to trail at 2200 ft is 6 mi. (park at road fork—hike upper spur).

North Cascades Hwy No. 20. Seattle via I-5 to Sedro Woolley turn is 67 mi. Burlington to Marblemount is 47 mi. The new highway at about latitude 48°30′ N is the fifth vehicular route across the Cascade Range in the State. No entrance fee to North Cascades Park and Ross Lake Recreation Area.

Both Diablo and Ross Lakes are visible from the road. Diablo Lake is greenish from the glacial silt carried by Thunder Creek, while Ross Lake is blue.

Stehekin River Road No. 3505. Distances are from Stehekin: High Bridge—11 mi.; Bridge Creek—16 mi.; Park Creek—19.4 mi.; Cottonwood Camp—25.5 mi. Camps at Harlequin, High Bridge (shelter), Tumwater, Shady, Dolly Varden, Bridge Creek (shelter), Park Creek and Cottonwood (fires permitted). Current shuttle bus service in summer: two round trips daily to Cottonwood and two additional to High Bridge.

Suiattle River Road No. 345 extends 23.8 mi. from county road on Sauk River (now ends at Sulphur Creek). Route usually taken via Sauk River Bridge (11 mi. N of Darrington). Northern access is via Concrete-Sauk Hwy. (28.5 mi. from Burlington) or East Sauk Road (38.5 mi. from Burlington).

Tenas Creek Road No. 333 leaves Suiattle River Road♦ at 8 mi. and extends to the N side of Huckleberry Mountain.

TRAILS AND ALPINE HIKING APPROACHES

For use regulations within the Glacier Peak Wilderness, see Trails and Alpine Hiking Approaches, Section I.

For information on North Cascades National Park, see Introduction, Section III.

Agnes Creek Trail (Crest Trail♦) extends from Stehekin River Road♦ (1640′) for 16.9 mi. to Railroad Creek Trail♦. Agnes Creek was named by Lt. Henry H. Pierce in 1882 (but for a period it was shown on maps as Company Creek, so designated by topographer H.H. Gannett). By 1894 prospectors had explored the upper valley, and Deer Fly cabin existed there. The Forest Service built the trail in 1906 and explored the area high on the E side of the valley. The trail divides near the valley head, with one branch E to Cloudy Pass and one branch W to Suiattle Pass (17.8 mi. total). Good camping at Five Mile camp (4.6 mi.), Swamp Creek (7.9 mi.), Cedar Camp (9.7 mi.), and Agnes Meadows (12 mi.).

West Fork Route. Trail No. 1272 leaves at 5 mi. (2400′) and crosses Agnes Creek in 1 mi.; there is a new bridge, but if out a steep log may be found upstream. West fork ford (2155′) is reached at 2 mi. (log ⅛ mi. E of log jam); campsite at 3.2 mi. and Rimrock Creek at 4.5 mi. (trail end). Brush and beaver dam swamps make travel difficult to the valley head (see Dome Peak and Ptarmigan Traverse). The main stream makes an impressive falls, and the entire upper cirque features waterfalls and cascades; the spectacular waterfalls draining Dana Glacier include one of about 150 ft free fall.

Icy Creek Route. A log crossing of the W fork (2400′) is about 1000 ft W of Icy Creek. A route can be taken W of the stream, but it is preferable to take to timber and brush on the E side to a slide alder basin at 4000 ft. A steep section is above: keep to the extreme left of the steep cliff ring, then ascend an 800-ft rock gully (scrambling) on the E flank of the valley to bypass waterfalls (steep snow in early season); one will become acquainted with alder, vine maple, and mountain ash on the route. Above the cliffs ascend snow or talus to the Icy-Spruce Creek pass (6720′); the lake at 6364 ft is just across. W of the Icy Creek valley head a saddle (7640′+) at 0.4 mi. S of Gunsight Peak (.025 mi. N of Point 7875) can be taken for a route to Chickamin Glacier.

Junction Mountain Trail (no. 1239 A) ascends the E ridge of *Junction Mountain* and continues W to the summit (5926′/1806 m). From Stehekin River Road♦ take the W-side Agnes Creek Trail No. 1239; find the mountain trail or a brush-free route on the SE corner of the mountain (trail becomes more pronounced on the ridge).

Cabin Creek Trail No. 1240 (Heather Ridge) ascends a ridge between Agnes and Cabin Creeks; reaches the alpine area of Heather Ridge (uncertain maintenance).

Swamp Creek Trail No. 1242 leaves Agnes Creek Trail at about 8 mi. and extends about 4 mi. into the upper valley of Swamp Creek (maintenance uncertain).

Bridge Creek Trail No. 2000 (Crest Trail♦). This is an old trail, first used by Indians (rebuilt in 1907 by the Forest Service). The trail begins 16 mi. from Stehekin (see Stehekin River Road♦) and extends 14 mi. to Rainy Pass (North Cascades Hwy♦). Much of the trail is among scattered pines, with some open slide areas. Camps (fires permissable) are at North Fork (2½ mi.), Six Mile (4½ mi.), South Fork (6 mi.), Hideaway (8 mi.), and Fireweed (9 mi.).

North Fork Trail No. 1233 leaves at 3 mi.; there is a ford at Grizzly Creek and at 6½ mi. (3800′) are meadows. The trail fades in another mile. Camps (fires permissable) are at Walker Park (2½ mi.) and Grizzly Creek (3½ mi.). Fisher Pass (5480′+) at the head of Fisher Creek (Courtney Creek) was formerly known as Thunder Pass—a route used by miners (the pass and trail shown on 1898-1899 maps). In the prospecting era numerous claims were made in the valley of the North Fork, and cabins were built near the head. (Two creeks of the same name irrigate the map on opposite watersheds; an effort is in progress to apply the name Courtney Creek here.)

Mt. Logan Cross-Country Route: see Mt. Logan.

Cabinet Creek Route. An old trail route (per 1938 maps) began on the S side of Cabinet Creek (see North Cascades Hwy♦), then crossed to the N side and climbed W to Gabriel Pass (6160′+) between Cabinet and Panther Creeks.

Canyon Lake Trail No. 797 branches from Miners Ridge Trail♦ (see Section II) ¼ mi. E of Image Lake and ascends to a saddle (est. 6250′); at 2 mi. cross a branch of Canyon Creek, then a flat (5800′—camping). Sundown Park is the largest of parks along this old sheep trail, which still has some relics from sheep camps. The trail reaches Canyon Lake (est. 5650′) at 5.2 mi. The lake contains boulders high in the center, apparently from rolling down snow, then later settling. Good camp on knoll below lake. The path W above gully and trees contours, then circles to the NE to avoid cliffs enroute to Totem Pass (6500′+).

Chickamin Glacier Route. The pass is easy to cross (perennial snow or small glacier on N slope). Make a moderately steep descent below a rock buttress, then walk on a bouldery rockslide below Bannock Mountain, then the long traverse to Hanging Gardens. Below the Sulphur-Spruce Creek divide, this beautiful W-sloping bench is filled with lakelets, charming floral displays, and the hills and dales of the timberline region. The contrast between the formerly ice-protected alp slopes and forested depths of Sulphur Creek is dramatic.

N of Ross Pass continue on or just W of the divide for 0.8 mi., then descend 400 ft and traverse on the E slope 0.3 mi. to Garden Pass (5840′+). An alternative is to keep W of the divide to the pass. The route then bears NE along or W of the crest; ascend to a notch (est. 7400′), then rise and cross NE onto a broad glacier. It is possible to make a long descending traverse on snow, rock, and heather to the lake (6364′) in the basin of Spruce Creek, and continue to Icy Creek. One can make a rising traverse on the glacier and continuing ice patches to the saddle (7640′+) which leads to the Chickamin Glacier—at 0.4 mi. S of Gunsight Peak. Another crossing is via the ridge above the "Spruce Creek" glacier (est. 7700′), but the opposite descent is steeper.

Cascade Pass Trail No. 744 extends from the parking area at 3600 ft (see Cascade River Road♦) in 3.4 mi. to the pass (5392′). No overnight camping at Cascade Pass, Sahale

Arm, Doubtful Basin, Mixup Arm, or Pelton Basin (Basin Creek is nearest campsite).

Cascade Pass, with its picturesque mountain hemlocks, and dramatic flanking mountain parapets, is one of the most historic passes of the Cascade Range. In early times it was crossed by Indians, then later by explorers—some of whom knew it as "Skagit Pass." An iron post marked "5423" was set at the pass by surveyors in 1897.[89]

A path leads about ¾ mi. up Sahale Arm; a descent of 800 ft on the N slope leads to Doubtful Lake (Reference: *101 Hikes*). The lake's name is because of a doubtful claim location. The Quien Sabe lode was located above (NE) the lake and the Falls lode below (SE) with two cabins. The old Rouse millsite and Pelton wheel below the lake's falls can still be seen. Pershall Mine was established below the lake; its mill machinery and pipeline remnants are evident. Cascade Mining and Smelting Co. built a water-powered sawmill at the lake before 1908, and piped water to supply air compressors.

The Ptarmigan Traverse. The high-level traverse from Sulphur Creek to Cascade Pass popularly takes its name from the Ptarmigan Climbing Club because four of their members were the first to accomplish this alpine trek. *Note: This is not a cross-country hiker's route. It requires ropes, crampons, ice axes, and crevasse rescue ability; only experienced climbers should attempt to follow these directions.* Most of the peak groupings (Magic-Mixup, Spider-Formidable, Le Conte-Sentinel, Spire-Dome) are about a full day's travel apart. Most parties take a minimum of 5 to 7 days for the traverse. Directions for the traverse route are given from a start on Cascade Pass Trail♦. If beginning from the S see Downey Creek Trail♦—Bachelor Creek route, Agnes Creek Trail♦—West Fork route, or Canyon Lake Trail♦—Chickamin Glacier route.

From Cascade Pass make a rising traverse along Mixup Arm, using a path worn into grass and scree on the E slope (snow early season). Round a spur onto the small Cache Glacier, then ascend to Cache Col (eastern and higher of cols—est. 6920'); 2 hours. In late season a moat at the col can be a problem. Then make an easy descending traverse along snow-talus to Kool-Aid Lake (6120'+), a shallow bench pond at the base of perennial snow (camp spots). Continue S to a protruding heather spur with cliff facing; here cross a narrow tongue of steep snow to the entrance of "Red Ledge" (a broad angling ledge leads easily across the spur). Traverse on a slight downtrend across meadows, then across steepish gravel ribs and snow gullies high above the snout of Middle Cascade Glacier. Continue around the shoulder here and bear up talus and snow to the glacier above the main icefall. Then ascend the glacier to Spider-Formidable col (7320'+); the correct col is 100 yds E of the most obvious one. Descend snow on S slope, then bear W.

The route now contours the upper basin of Flat Creek via snow and heather on an easy descent to Yang Yang Lakes (5830')—camping on rise between lakes. From the large rockslide just S of the lakes a goat path climbs through the cliffy area to meadows and the flat ridge crest N of Le Conte Mountain (near Le Conte Pass—6480'+). Continue on contour southward along heather, snowfields, then glacier ice on the E flank of Le Conte (bear SE downward to skirt the lower edge of the black buttress between the route and the Le Conte Glacier; crampons may be needed in this area). Smooth rock terraces lead to the glacier (route may be blocked in late season by crevasses and possibly steep ice at entry). Proceed on firn to the Le Conte-Sentinel saddle (7280'+).

(*Alternative:* From the lakes travel ½ mi. NW to Hahlakl Pass (6400'+)—or take traversing route directly to pass. Continue S and then up steep talus to the ridge crest, then SE to snowfields NE of Le Conte.)

Note: use of the first col SE of Le Conte's summit to the South Cascade Glacier is not a practical route. A good early season shortcut from the Le Conte-Sentinel saddle descends NW toward the lower glacier.

Follow snow below the W flank of Sentinel Peak (keep high) and then to the upper portion of South Cascade Glacier (some loss of altitude necessary—use rock shelves or follow snow). Cross "Lizard Pass" (6800'+) above White Rock Lakes and W of The Lizard. An easy snow-talus descent SW leads to the three lakes (6194'), which nest on a bench. Then descend about 400 ft around a rock spur and traverse easily SW. From the cliff base at the northwestern extremity of Dana Glacier rise to the main glacier, then ascend south to Spire Col (7760'+)—just E of Spire Point. Descend SW to Itswoot Ridge between Spire Creek and Cub Lake (good camp at 6200').

White Rock Lakes to Chickamin Glacier: It is necessary to descend SE into West Fork Agnes Creek valley. By keeping on the N valley slope most of the brush can be avoided (one report advises third and eastern gully—game trails lead to the stream). Cross a thicket to the main stream where there is some gravel. Descend a short distance, then cross thicket and parallel stream to the big talus slope. Traverse E through brush to the open streambed that leads above brush. Climb, then make traverse and slight descent to the meltwater lake at the main glacier lobe snout (4974').

Some parties virtually backpack over Dome Peak (either direction), using the high glacier col. For continuation S of Chickamin Glacier see Canyon Lake Trail♦.

Approach or departure from the center portion of the traverse is also done by South Fork Cascade River Trail (see Cascade River Area♦ or Downey Creek Trail♦). The snow pass (6560'+) W of White Rock Lakes offers a route to Downey Creek; the upper W slope is barren and easy travel—descend to hanging meadow with meandering stream. Another beginning is South Cascade Glaciers and the route past Hoch Joch Spitz to the notch on the Downey Creek drainage. Note: ATP upper Downey Creek is very difficult travel due to abandonment of trail. Rimrock Ridge has been used as another exit from the area. References: *Mountaineer,* 1953, pp. 38-41, 79; 1958, pp. 48-65; 1964, pp. 13-26; 1967, pp. 26-28; 1968, pp. 158-162; 1969, pp. 89-

99; 1971, p. 38; *Mazama* 40, no. 13 (1958): 19-23; *Mazama* 54, no. 13 (1972): 30-31; *Living Wilderness* 24, no. 70 (1959): 1-9; *Backpacker* 16 (1976): 38-41, 67-69.

Cascade River Area

Boston Basin Route. In the mining era the basin was known as "Gilbert's basin"—a "rugged grandeur of tall cliffs and pinnacles towering above broad glaciers, gulches of awful gloom, precipices which no man can scale" (L.K. Hodges, *Seattle Post Intelligencer,* 25 October 1896, p. 18). The glacier (first known as "Boston Glacier") was described as "a huge field of ice", riven by crevasses; "Above it is a line of sawteeth, through which the great Boston ledge cuts" (*ibid*). Indians told of ice breaking from the glacier into the forest, but "All these glaciers are gradually diminishing, for Mr. Landre remembers that six years ago they covered ground which is now bare" (*ibid*). The old miner's trail branched from the State Trail (½ mi. past Gilbert's cabin at 2616′) and switchbacked through heavy steep timber to emerge on a "barren waste of boulders" (it climbed nearly 4000′ in 4 mi. to Boston Mine at 6300′); the trail followed the moraine crest north of "Boston Glacier"—then back to the ice (one leapt from the glacier to the tunnel mouth).

Park at road fork (3200′) leading to the Value Mine and walk the 1-mi. left fork. From the mine (private property) take the old pass trail 0.3 mi. to a path (3800′) beyond a talus; it veers uphill in forest high above the mine (watch for markers). The old path crosses alder slopes, talus, and Midas and Morning Star Creeks (can be difficult in high water). After 1 mi. the path enters old timber, then switchbacks continue to timberline and the moraine (about 3 mi.—5600-5700′). An old tread ascends a moraine crest toward glacier ice. One can readily traverse the meadows of the basins W to Mt. Torment (much up and down) or E to Sahale Arm. Reference: *101 Hikes; Mountaineer,* 1947, pp. 44-46.

Notes: a good spring route keeps E of Midas Creek (if snow covers brush). The route's beginning is sometimes done more directly from the mine cabin, past water hose and stumps to intersect the path higher.

Torment Basin Route. About 50 yds from the North Fork road bridge (near Gilbert's cabin) ascend steep timber E of Eldorado Creek (old trail vanished) for about 1 mi. into the subalpine area. At talus below a horseshoe-shaped ridge bear W through brush about 200 yds, then up talus and meadows into Torment Basin (5-7 hours to campspot). One can hike to the lowest saddle (Torment Col—6640′+) in the ridge; a good ridge campspot is about ¼ mi. W of the col.

Eldorado Glacier Route. This is the most direct approach to Eldorado Peak, Eldorado Glacier, and the area of the Inspiration Glacier. Leave Cascade River Road♦ beyond Roush Creek (est. 2100′), opposite the prominent rocky rib (before 20-mi. marker). Cross the river on large logs, then climb open timber W of Eldorado Creek but within earshot of the creek. A great rockslide on the E slopes of the rocky rib is reached after about 1500-ft gain. Ascend this, passing through one short alder stretch; at slide top a section of heather, scrub trees and mini-cliffs gives way to open meadow (5500-5800′). This basin provides pleasant camping. The great rib on the W is crossed at a level section (est. 6150′), then drop 100 ft into Roush Creek's basin and ascend the Eldorado Glacier. The route continues to Inspiration Glacier (a camp on latter is 6-7 hours from road). Reference: *Mountaineer,* 1966, pp. 199-200.

For traverses in the Eldorado area, see copy following Dean's Spire.

South Fork Cascade River Trail No. 769 leaves road no. 3404 about ½ mi. from its end (1800′)—see Cascade River Road♦. The maintained trail extends about 3 mi. near the river, then the route follows the U.S.G.S. trail in this magnificent wild valley. The trail climbs steeply at about 4 mi. to detour Box Canyon; open timber (4600′) is found near the outlet of Berry Patch Creek's basin. A grade climbs to Mertensia Pass (4940′+)—meadow camping; continue upslope in open forest to Salix Creek and the old lateral moraine at 5200 ft (est. 8 mi. from road). The streamflow gauging station below the lake is government property. Reference: *101 Hikes.*

Middle Fork Cascade River Trail No. 767 departs from South Fork Trail at 0.9 mi. The old trail, shown on the 1899 quadrangle, is also known as Spaulding Mine Trail. ATP the trail is in fair shape for 3 mi. (3200′) where it fades, but does continue to timber fringe. Bars and bush continue on the N side of the stream to the Middle Cascade Glacier (if water low, walk up stream). Reference: *101 Hikes.*

Colonial Creek. This is a good early season route. A rough path exists on the S side of the creek (see Snowfield Peak).

Company Creek Trail No. 1243. This creek was named in the late 1890s, when a mining company from Spokane became interested in claims in the valley. The trail begins just across the bridge on Company Creek NW of the airstrip (spur road from 4½ mi. up Stehekin River Road♦). Reach Courtney cabin at 5 mi., Hilgard Pass (6600′+) at 11.2 mi., and Tenmile Pass (6500′) at 15 mi. A cross-country route via Ten Mile Creek can be taken to Holden; leave at the last meadow on Ten Mile Creek and follow timber in valley, then contour.

Crest Trail. In this section it coincides with Agnes Creek♦ and Bridge Creek Trails♦. A new portion currently from Rainy Pass to Maple Pass is incomplete.

Devore Creek Trail No. 1244 begins at the SE end of the Stehekin airstrip (Stehekin River Road♦); one can also boat to Weaver Point camp and take a way trail to Devore Creek. The trail makes an often-discussed 32 switchbacks; reach Boulder camp at 4.4 mi., Fourth of July Basin at 10.6 mi., and Ten Mile Pass at 12.8 mi. The name is for Dan Devore, packer and prospector who came to Stehekin in 1888. Reference: *Mazama* 23, no. 12 (1941): 43-47.

Downey Creek Trail No. 768 begins from Suiattle River Road♦ at 20.5 mi. (1415′). The valley is a straight deep glacial trough which heads in several large cirques. A footlog leads to the N bank at Sixmile camp (2400′). The trail extends about 3 mi. farther, but becomes overgrown and is very rough travel in the bottomland with its summer brush of ferns, nettles, and salmonberry. Cross a N-forking waterfall stream, then cross through thick brush to open timber. The general plan is to keep in timber as much as possible (bear to the right; snowslide alder and scrub trees to left). First parallel the stream fork, then turn E and continue through heavy timber to an old overgrown slide; cross the stream beyond and ascend ENE up the steep forest cone between main terminal forks to timberline basin. Ascend open slopes NE. A scree gully with pinnacles on its left can be taken to a glacier notch (7080′+) closely NW of Hoch Joch Spitz. Traverse E and cross the firn saddle (0.2 mi.), then descend the glacier arm which joins South Cascade Glacier at 6300 ft (good campsite on ridge above glacier).

An alternative from Downey Creek basin at 5800 ft is to bear E to M M Pond, then from its bench rise steeply NE through a col (6720′+) to a glacier arm E of Hoch Joch Spitz.

The northern fork of Downey Creek directed toward Slim Pass is quite brushy.

Bench Lake Route. Follow the main trail to Goat Creek (log crossing), then in 100 yds bear left to wooded spur crest; this makes a dry but easy, open rise of nearly 3000 ft to above a narrow lake (bypass Point 5226 on its N). Descend heather to the lake, then hike upstream to Bench Lake (5235′)—3 hours from Goat Creek. The lake is not on a bench, but in a rock-rimmed cirque. One can hike around the W flank of Mt. Bruseth through the col (6600′+) to the Bruseth Glacier. Or one can cross the ridge E of the lake and make a traversing route NE to Woods Lake, and onward to Slim Pass and South Cascade Glacier; another long route is to descend to Bruseth Glacier, then make an alpine trek to Sonny Boy Ridge.

Downey Mountain way trail leaves main trail at about 2 mi. and rises steeply E to the N side of Downey Mountain (trail cut by packer and difficult to locate). One can make cross-country treks to the lake N, and to Downey Lake; an easy hike leads to *Downey Mountain* (5924′/1806 m).

Bachelor Creek Route (trail no. 796). From the main trail about ⅛ mi. past Sixmile Camp, cross Downey Creek on a log (trail begins just beyond). The trail crosses Bachelor Creek at 2.7 mi., then climbs to meadow areas at the upper basin; good campsites from 3½ mi. and beyond. The trail becomes a path in the narrow upper valley and crosses Cub Lake Pass (6000′+) at about 5½ mi. A path descends about 0.3 mi. to the lake (5338′); time: 8 hours from road. Cub Lake may have floes all summer; strangely the lake has two outlets, which flow on either side of a high knoll. Camping at the lake should be discouraged; a camp on Itswoot Ridge has water and a rock corral.

Itswoot Lake is a short hike below Cub Lake; it is a deep clear lake with a waterfall entering.

Easy Pass. Reach via Easy Pass Trail♦ or via Fisher Creek Trail♦.

Easy Pass Trail No. 741. From North Cascades Hwy♦ (at 25.5 mi. from Diablo Lake) the distance is 3.5 mi. to Easy Pass (6520′+); no camping.

Falls Creek Route. From parking area (see Jordan Creek Road♦) a path-scramble route goes up the left side of the creek to the falls, then crosses stream on log. Contour ¾ mi. to Falls Creek and then follow uphill about ½ mi. to Falls Lake (4023′) which is in timber near the basin's edge. (4 hours).

From the falls one can continue on the E of the creek to Lower Jordan Lake (4032′—about 4 mi. From here a path can be taken another ½ mi. E to Upper Jordan Lake (4510′), uniquely beautiful. The lakes are both moraine-dammed, now forest covered.

Fisher Creek Trail No. 741 is an old trail, shown on 1922 maps. It leaves from Thunder Creek Trail♦ at 11½ mi. Camping permitted at Thunder junction, Cosho, and Fisher (no fire at latter). The Rock Cabin avalanche, a mile wide, is located on the S slope of Red Mountain (cabin built under the rock). At the valley head a right trail fork leads into Fisher basin, where open terrain offers easy hiking (a route leads to Silent Lakes—6975′); the main trail leads to Easy Pass (10 mi.). A route across the high pass (7440′+) at 1.2 mi. NW of Easy Pass leads onto the Mesahchie Glacier in the Panther Creek drainage; a continuing hike can be taken to Mesahchie Pass (5960′+), between Panther and a branch of Granite Creek.

Flat Creek Trail No. 1271 extends 3.3 mi. from Stehekin River Road♦ (ends just past W fork).

Goode Ridge. At 200 ft W of bridge across Bridge Creek (see Stehekin River Road♦) there is an old trail. The ridge top has been estimated at 8 mi. (over 6000′ altitude).

Granite Lakes Route. Approach by Boulder Creek Road♦. Follow it about 6 mi. and then turn left on a steep spur. Note spur contouring slope on right; drive to its end, where a path begins. Contour about 1 mi. to the first lake (est. 4100′), then follow either Lower or Upper Granite Lake outlet streams (each about ¾ mi.). Lower Granite Lake (4679′—38 acres) has a bizarre narrow shape; there is extensive talus on the SW side. Upper Granite Lake (4543′—144 acres) is usually snow-free in late July but may still have ice floes in August. The lake is unique in the Cascades because it has Arctic grayling.

Continuing routes for alpine hiking or climbing can be made. Whale Lake (SE of Upper Granite Lake; has the outline shape of a whale), can be reached by hiking across the divide.

Green Mountain Trail No. 782, extends to the summit lookout in 4 mi. from Green Mountain Road♦ (3200′); the lookout (6500′) was built in 1933 for sighting fires. Water and camping at 2½ mi.

Buckindy High Route is a spectacular scenic trek with interesting alpine traverses (slippery Hellebore are a succulent nuisance) and an approach to seldom visited summits. One can bypass the final 300 ft of Green Mountain on the E (from where trail reaches S shoulder, take goat path across grass slopes, round a spur, and traverse NE, keeping E of Point 6082 at about 5700 ft). Continue at near 5500 ft to the 5371-ft lake. Continue the slope contour and rise to saddle (5760′+). Go E over (or S of) Point 5890 and follow to the low saddle (5360′+); as shown on 1931 maps, an old trail existed on this Downey Creek slope for several miles.

An alternate (N-side) route can be taken to the same low pass. From the saddle (5960′+) N of Green Mountain, hike N up the steep grassy crest to a 6400-ft shoulder with a few small trees; traverse easily on the E slope about ¼ mi. to a saddle about the same level. Now hike NE about ¼ mi. on the W slope (slightly downward traverse) and cross a slight knoll. Here a 200-ft drop to a series of snowfields on a tilted bench is made; cross them about ¼ mi. and continue downhill traverse to a cliff. Descend about 300 ft to where one can work down and around this rocky spur; a tricky talus descent, then bear down E. Follow trees and steep grass just below a cliff to a snow basin, then up on a rising E traverse to steep grass. Descend the slope to meadows at the W side of the low saddle (above Horse Lake).

Follow goat path leading N up ridge, then traverse the W slope (heather) to just below the large white talus slope. From a high alp descend to the base of the large hidden snowfield, then traverse and climb steep meadows and talus to the SW flank of Mt. Misch. To reach the head of Horse Creek basin (N) aim for moraines and bedrock slab. There is a nice camp spot at the stream (5200′) 0.9 mi. N of Horse Lake.

Snowking Route: From the basin S of Mt. Buckindy detour the S flank of Point 6495 at about 5900 ft and then climb back over the ridge closely W at about 6360 ft (do not hike farther W because of cliffy area on Buck Creek slope).

Traverse the basin slope about 1¼ mi. to the tarn at 5975 ft (just SW of the low point of divide). The best crossing is the Kindy-Buck pass to the NW of the lake (at 6320′+). Descend ice to 5800 ft and then traverse and descend NW (fastest to descend to 5100′, then work up to west Fork Kindy-Buck ridge at saddle (5800′+) N of Point 6305). Ascend N up ridge and then NW closely under the summit of Mutchler Peak. It is easy to reach the ridge near Point 6921 and traverse to Point 6995. The best crossing to the Illabot Creek divide is at the col (6000′+) at 1¼ mi. S of Snowking Mountain, where there is a tarn (from here one can virtually walk the S slope of Snowking). One can continue W along the slope or ridge of Snowking (easy terrain) to reach Illabot Creek Road♦.

Goat Creek Glaciers Traverse Route. From Horse Creek basin cross the notch just N of Peak 7185 onto a glacier. Make a descending traverse to cross the next ridge just W of an obvious wooded spur-point. Descend steep heather to turn a cliff, then hike N onto "Goat Creek" glacier. Make a rising traverse to keep above the wide lower crevasse field and traverse to the next ridge; a rock ramp leads to the edge of Kindy Glacier. The route can be continued into Kindy Creek or across to the Kindy-Buck pass (occasional technical problems). Bring ice axe, crampons, and rope for the traverse.

Hidden Lake Peak Trail No. 745A begins at about 4.2 mi. up Sibley Creek Road (see Cascade River Road♦) at est. 3600′ in a logged clearcut (currently ¼ mi. up track beyond parking). The trail area (East Fork Sibley Creek) presents a sweeping display of mountain flora, but in early season snow cover suggests taking an ice axe for gully crossings. There is a good campsite in the basin (at 3½ mi.). From the saddle overlooking Hidden Lake (est. 6600′) one can descend E to the lake. There are interesting displays of the exposed granodiorite here (Hidden Lake stock shows vertical jointing). The lookout point (6890′) is about ¼ mi. beyond the saddle (cabin, built in 1931, now abandoned).

Hidden Lake Peak (7088′/2160 m) is a short hike of about ½ mi. NE from the saddle.

Sibley Creek Pass (6100′+) is about ½ mi. from the trail; leave where trail re-crosses the creek (5200′—est. 2½ mi.).

Holden Lake Trail No. 1251. From Holden (see Section II—Lake Chelan♦) hike W on the pack road past corral, over two footbridges (est. ½ mi.), then take right-hand road uphill about 200 yds to intersect an old road which turns into trail. The S end of Holden Lake (est. 5250′) is reached in 4 mi. James H. Holden built a 20 x 20-ft cabin there, with stove and bunk bed; a sign long hung over the doorway: "Lord Gordon Holden—1897."

On arriving at the lake follow the path around right, and immediately at the head of the lake cross W on a log; camp can be made at the NW corner in first or second meadow (no camping within 200′ of shore). Reference: *Routes and Rocks,* pp. 193-194.

Holden Pass Route. Follow brush margin out of the basin, around a large rock buttress on right to where the low area of the pass is apparent. Grassy slopes lead to the pass (6300′+)—good camping.

Huckleberry Mountain Trail No. 780 begins from Suiattle River Road♦ (1000′) at 1 mi. W of Buck Creek campground. At 5½ mi. the old lookout trail goes W (1.7 mi. to former lookout). The trail extends to Point 5856 at 1.7 mi. S of Hurricane Peak. A good cross-country route N along the Buck and Tenas-Big Creek divide is an approach to Mt. Chaval. The major hump S of Boulder Lake (6267′) can be bypassed on the E at about 6000 ft. Then bear down to the saddle (5640′+) above Pear Lake for a continuing route NE and N. The entire route is a pleasant high-level traverse.

Hurricane Peak Route can be taken from Tenas Creek Road♦. At 7.2 mi. a spur goes NE; either use the spur or hike directly to Boulder Lake (4975′); this is a good cross-country approach. Crater Lake, Lake Chaval, and Lake Toketie (a dammed cirque lake) are interesting and lovely subalpine lakes of the area. Suiattle Indians once favored this area for autumn berry picking.

Illabot Creek. The Illabot area is now heavily logged, much changed even from 1939 when there were no logging roads in the upper valley; as early as 1913 a trail led up the valley to Illabot Lake and an old trapper's cabin there. It is known that William Leach, a trapper of the Cascade River area, trapped for marten along Jordan and Illabot Creeks with Frank Davis in the winter of 1885. The name of the vivid green lake is derived from the Sauk Indians, in whose language Illabot meant "painted." The valleys of the basin are generally rough travel and brushy (trails do not last long unless maintained). For route up Illabot Creek valley, see Mt. Chaval.

Irene Creek Route. From Cascade River Road♦ shortly beyond Sibley Creek take road fork W (no. 3542) into Irene Creek valley. The valley offers a hiking route, but there are many blowdowns; trail in uncertain condition.

Jug Lake Route leaves Illabot Creek Road♦ at 17 mi. (Arrow Creek). This is a very brushy route; about 5 hours are needed to Lower Jug Lake (3453′), then hike 1 mi. to Jug Lake (3907′) in an attractive basin. A cross-country route can be easily taken to Bluff Lake (4237′). Cross the divide SW from Jug Lake, then make a descending traverse in forested slopes.

A slightly easier route to Jug Lake is to begin 1 mi. farther on the road, before the bridge. Ascend S through the first clearcut above the bridge. Continue through a saddle and pass a small lake E of Point 5522, then descend to the lake (4 hours).

Another route to Bluff Lake is to traverse from Grade Creek Road♦ (where road elbows farthest E in Section 8) to Jug Creek, then follow the drainage to Bluff Lake (6 hours). Cross above Bluff Lake and Cliff Lake for an ascent to the ridge W of Mt. Chaval.

Kindy Creek Trail No. 766. See Found Creek Road (Cascade River Road♦). The trail extends about 5½ mi., but is only in good condition the first 1½ mi. (the trail was built before 1931). In earlier times Kindy Creek was known as Big Creek (per 1899 Glacier Peak quadrangle). The valley is a straight deep glacial trough; near its head are numerous cirques, often on two levels. The glaciers, waterfalls, bedrock slabs, and brush-covered slopes combine to form a dramatic headwaters to this wilderness valley.

Kindy-Found Ridge Route. See Cascade River Road♦—Kindy Ridge Road. Take road no. 354A to near its end (est. 5 mi.) in a logging cut (2200′). Ascend a cat road in slash (see markers) to junction of timber on the E and alder W; a cat track 75 yds E leads to where the trail bears S. Ascend the moderately steep forest (keep on steepest portion) to the knoll at 5116 ft (route bisects old Found Creek Trail—but do not use). Descend 300 ft to a saddle, then to Found Lake (4200′+—4 hours); camping near outlet. This 71-acre lake is turquoise-colored (glacial siltation); Skaro and Neori Lakes are clear. Snowking Lake (4460′) is glacier-fed (and turquoise), while Cyclone Lake is often ice-covered even in August. From Found Lake a route leads to upper Cyclone Lake (est. 5350′)—considerable talus; to reach the Snowking Glacier one can skirt Cyclone Lake on the W, past the outlet.

The best cross-country route to Snowking Mountain is to continue via the Found-Mutchler Creek ridge to about 5600-ft altitude and skirt Cyclone Lake on the E; keep high and follow the divide SW (the route emerges from timber to semi-open parkland with light bush; reasonable travel).

Lake Ann. Trail no. 1274 begins 300 yds W of Rainy Pass (4840′)—see North Cascades Hwy♦. Distance to the 5475-ft lake is 1.4 mi. (no camping within ¼ mi.). A new Crest Trail section has been built to Maple Pass, with uncertain future.

Wing Lake Route. From Lake Ann reach Wing Lake by hiking to the lowest part of Heather Pass (6040′+). Drop gently 200 ft in a traverse in line with Lewis Lake, then cross two prominent rockslides on a traverse; this brings one out at Lewis Lake (5702′) exit stream (¾ mi. from Heather Pass). Bypass the lake on the S, traversing snow slopes and heading for the prominent moraine above the lake; keep N below the moraine, staying in a series of larch meadows to Wing Lake (6905′); good campspots near the lake.

Lookout Mountain Trail No. 743. From Cascade River Road♦ at 6.4 mi. there is a 4½-mi. trail to the summit (5719′). At 3½ mi. on the trail (4200′) there is a junction and campsite. To reach Monogram Lake traverse right (blazes) on a lightly timbered slope. Hike through a meadow, then cross a 5400-ft ridge (1½ mi.), then descend ¾ mi. to the lake (4800′+); camping. Access from here to the T-Bone Ridge area.

Marble Creek Trail No. 630 was shown on 1931 maps, but is now largely overgrown (begin from end of logging spur road—see Cascade River Road♦). Marble Creek remains flat until about 2000 ft, then the basin slope rises nearly 7000 ft in 2¼ mi. The glacial trough of Marble Creek is heavily brushed, but allows a cross-country route to the Eldorado area and peaks on the Marble Creek rim.

Newhalem Creek-Stout Lake Route. A trail once led up Newhalem Creek (shown on 1939 maps). Indian chief Charlie Moses (Marblemount tribe) named Ne-Whalem Creek (meaning "goat snare"). Skagit Indians drove goats off the mountains here and trapped them below the falls by snare.

Hike the upper road spur (Newhalem Creek Road♦) to the N edge of the first stream (½ mi.). Then ascend steep forest slopes. Begin bearing SE at about 4500 ft, then S about ½ mi., then SE again to the lake (5200′+). A steep gully bearing SSW from the SW corner of the lake provides a start for various traverses.

Panther Creek Trail No. 758 leaves Thunder Creek Trail♦ at 0.2 mi. (1.3 mi. from Colonial Creek camp to trail fork). Fourth of July Pass is 3.2 mi. and North Cascades Hwy♦ is 9.7 mi. Camping and fires at Panther Creek and Fourth of July. From the trail pass a non-maintained trail leads 5 mi. to the top of Ruby Mountain.

Park Creek Trail No. 1270 leaves Stehekin River Road♦ 2½ mi. beyond Bridge Creek; in 7.9 mi. the trail reaches the pass (6040′+), a narrow defile, usually snow-covered until late summer. Camping and fires at 2 mi. and 5 mi. (here a branch path leads to Goode Ridge).

From the pass one can contour W in the Park Creek basin toward Mt. Buckner. One can readily contour the N slope ½ mi. through meadows and moraines toward Boston Glacier, but beyond cliffs block the route. Reference to area: *Mazama* 30, no. 13 (1948): 4-14. See Mt. Logan for cross-country traverse to Fisher Pass (*Summit,* Nov.-Dec., 1971).

Pyramid Lake Trail No. 770 leaves North Cascades Hwy♦ ½ mi. E of Gorge Lake bridge (1150′) and reaches the lake

(2600′+) in 2 mi. The route to Pyramid Peak ridge climbs southward, then follows the crest. A formerly used route to the ridge, beginning at Thunder Lake, is less popular, but a reasonable cross-country approach.

Railroad Creek Trail No. 1256. See Section II.

Riddle Peaks Trail begins at 8½ mi. on the road (shortly past Ninemile Creek). It crosses the crest in 3½ mi. (est. 6450′), then descends to Riddle Creek.

Tenmile High Route connects with Devore, Hilgard, and Company Creek. Begin from the road at the E end of mine tailings and ascend NNE to the nose of Martin Ridge; forest and meadows lead to the pass (est. 6650′) to Hilgard Creek (3 hours). W along the ridge is a route to the basin beneath Martin Peak (*Routes and Rocks,* pp. 189-190). To reach Tenmile Pass leave the main route just after crossing Tenmile Creek (4700′) and hike NE (old trail) to the pass (est. 6550′); a pleasant area of timberline larch.

Martin Ridge Route (to Martin Ridge from Holden). Leave E side of town and climb NNE—keep in trees W of Tenmile Creek and later ascend valley to old trail that led between Hilgard and Company Creeks. Then climb N to the pass at 6650 ft and Hilgard Creek. From here it is 11 mi. to Stehekin River Road♦ via Company Creek.

Rainy Lake. Trail no. 1278 makes the 1-mi. hike from North Cascades Hwy♦ (S of Rainy Pass) to the lake (4790′).

Slide Lake Trail No. 635. Take Illabot Creek Road♦ for 20 mi. Here the trail extends 1½ mi. to the lake (3110′). One can follow Otter Creek cross-country; it is best to keep about 200 yds N, above the stream. Enjar Lake is about 3 mi. Various alpine hiking routes can be taken (including Snowking Mountain, only 1½ mi. SE of Enjar Lake). This approach offers a fine ski tour to Snowking.

Sonny Boy Ridge Route is a long high route (no trail). Begin from Sonny Boy Road (est. 1600′)—see Cascade River Road♦. Hike SE up the long wooded ridge (rocky at times); traverse W of the crest near 6000 ft and 5800 ft or on the crest. The route can be followed along the divide E of Kindy Creek and is an approach to the peaks at the western head of South Fork Cascade River, and those near Bench Lake. At the head of Milt Creek it is probably best to stay on the NE slope at about 6000 ft en route toward Long Gone Lake.

Stehekin River Trail No. 1234. From Cottonwood Camp (road end—2760′; see Stehekin River Road♦) the trail reaches Cascade Pass in 4.7 mi. (camping and fires only at Cottonwood and Basin Creek). About 1 mi. up the trail are remains of the massive rockslide of April 1972. At ½ mi. E of Cascade Pass a path leads S into Pelton Basin; the small lake there was called "Spirit Lake" by the 1877 party (Otto Klement) who slept on the pass August 1.

Horseshoe Basin Route. Follow the abandoned mining roadway 2 mi. W of Cottonwood Camp (at 3600′) and ascend 1000 ft to the cirque of Basin Creek. Reach meadows in 1½ mi. The area has many mining relics, though cabins are now demolished by slides. Reach abandoned Black Warrior Mine (in lower basin—2½ mi. from Cottonwood); an old cabin still stands across the stream from the mine. Near the mine is an end of the tramway cable that crosses the lower basin to claims in the upper basin. The original tramway was destroyed by avalanches. In the mine adit are remains of rails of a hand-cart railroad which operated until 1950.

To continue to the upper basin cross the cirque below the mine and ascend amid cliffy areas to the right of walls. Heather knolls abound. An interesting moraine exhibit is below the E margin of the wide, crescent-shaped Davenport Glacier at about 6100-6200 ft.

An early botanist, Martin Gorman, stated that here were dramatic features which were the gems of the Cascade Range: "The lower basin is surrounded by abrupt horseshoe-shaped walls of rock, as the name indicates, and the upper rugged, more or less snow-clad peaks, while in late summer both constitute a veritable flower garden to the botanist." (Section II, footnote 23, *op cit.*). One is impressed by the beauty and size of the waterfalls (one count has 22 falls to the lower basin). William G. Steel, an early writer, rhapsodied on the scene of the upper basin, "Above the snow and ice, the semicircle is surmounted by sharp minarets and peaks . . . like teeth of a saw."

Trapper Lake Route. Once called "Chyall" (for a claim) this dramatic lake is the largest of the high lakes E of the Cascade crest in this section. From about 0.2 mi. past Cottonwood Camp (see Stehekin River Road♦) ford the river and ascend a steep brushy path which leads to the E end of the lake (4165′).

Another approach is from ½ mi. E of Cascade Pass, via Pelton Basin. A path from Pelton Lake leads along open slopes E to a gentle ridge at 5400 ft. From its crest one sees a steep heathery ridge 300 ft higher (connects Pelton Peak with Point 5973). Make a traversing rise to cross here, then descend a steep slope (snow or talus) to the W end of the lake. If one traverses around the lake, the open talus and snow on the S offers an alternative to the wooded N side (suggest take ice axe).

A higher alpine route climbs over the Magic-Pelton Peak col (6480′+); this route can be icy and does involve glacier travel. Reference: *101 Hikes.*

Suiattle Pass Trail. See Section II, Suiattle Trail♦ and Miners Ridge Trail♦. One can hike along the crest of Miners Ridge toward Plummer Mountain.

Sulphur Creek Trail No. 793. "No one who has ever tangled with Sulphur Creek could ever possibly forget it . . . a deep, dark, dank, dreary dismal dungeon with colossal walls." So wrote Hermann Ulrichs, one of the valley's first explorers with mountaineering ambitions. The trail once extended up the valley's magnificent rain forest for over 8 mi. (shown on 1939 maps, but not earlier), but now fades at about 4 mi. in brush and swamp. Occasional climbing parties negotiate the brush of the upper valley to reach Spire Creek or the Dome Peak area; it is most sensible to avoid the slide alder slopes and remain in timber. The rib W of Itswoot Creek, the slope W of Spire Creek, and shoulder E of Spire Creek, and S side of Dome Creek into Dome basin offer routes, but none is easy. The ridge SW of Dome is steep but open; when the trail was good the only brush was the main stream crossing (leave at 1½ mi. past Bath Creek). An old route from ½ mi. past Bath Creek led N and E up a rocky-timbered ridge S of Spire Point (high camp made in upper Spire basin). If the trail is in bad condition, it may be well to recall another Ulrichs comment about the valley: "my only advice would be to absolutely stay out of it."

Sulphur Mountain Trail No. 794 climbs steeply to the ridge crest (6000′+) in 5 mi. Begin 0.3 mi. past Sulphur Creek bridge (1800′)—see Suiattle River Road♦. To reach *Sulphur Mountain* (6735′/2053 m) follow the easy ridge SE (about 1 mi.). Reference: *101 Hikes.* There are great vistas of Glacier Peak. The Sulphur Mountain pluton extends from W of Sulphur Mountain to E of Bath Lakes; the extensive granitoid rock unit extends S to Grassy Point.

There are numerous summits on the Sulphur/Canyon Creek ridge; rock here is mostly granite and gneissic granite. The highest and most dominant is *Peak 7145* (2178 m), 1.3 mi. NE of Sulphur Mountain; the S flank is gentle and the N alpine. Both Peaks 7145 and 7100+ (2178 m and 2164 m) are N of the high route notch.

Bath Lakes High Route begins from the ridge crest at about 6050 ft (route can be taken to Totem Pass or Canyon Lake). The route keeps N of Sulphur Mountain, then rises E up talus, and a basin to cross a high ridge notch (est. 6650′). Here is a rocky table above an unnamed lake in the deep basin S. Continue E near the divide to Bath Lake Pass (est. 5850′), then NE above the basin of Bath Creek to Bath Lake (round shoulder of Peak 6818—S of the high route).

Open basins and an easy slope leads to the lower Bath Lake (5600′+). Cross the ridge; a gully above talus leads to benches above the upper lake (est. 5950′); it is set in a talus basin at timberline. The route to Canyon Lake now largely traverses the S side of the main ridge, and rises to 6900 ft to cross the spur of *Peak 7021* (2140 m). This is the highest of the "Bath Lake Peaks"—just a hike on its S flank.

Make a steep drop into the basin and then traverse below Stonehenge Ridge on the Canyon Creek slopes (heather bench) at about 6200 ft to 6400 ft to beneath Totem Pass; game paths lead down to the lake (11-12 mi. from trail). Bath Lake Pass to Canyon Lake is about 7 mi. Reference: *Routes and Rocks,* pp. 22-28; see also Canyon Lake Trail♦.

Thunder Creek Trail No. 740 begins at Colonial Creek campground (see North Cascades Hwy♦). Reach Middle Cabin in 5 mi., Meadow Cabin in 10 mi., Skagit Queen Creek in 13 mi., and Park Creek Pass in 18 mi. Fisher Creek Trail junction is at 9 mi. Camping and fires allowed at Thunder, Neve, Middle, Junction, Skagit Queen; camping only in Thunder basin.

McAllister Creek, named for William McAllister, who moved into Thunder Creek valley in 1897, has a passable trail extending about 3 mi. (exit ½ mi. beyond Middle Cabin); if trail bridge gone, possible logs upstream. At about ¾ mi. on the trail cross logs to the N side, then follow the near bank about 2½ mi. (partially cross-country). Beyond here, the route is now a jungle (old trail gone). The valley remains low; the glacier tongue is at about 4000 ft. The terminal forks of the valley descend from McAllister Glacier and a series of glaciers on the flanks of Backbone Ridge.

Skagit Queen Creek, the Thunder Creek valley's terminal fork, has a trail about 1 mi., it then fades. The old trail to the mine (4500′) on the E side of the creek is in uncertain condition. The Skagit Queen claims are on steep, rocky slopes on both flanks. The valley is a spectacular setting: a magnificent forest of Douglas fir, silver fir, western hemlock, and western red cedar with a backdrop of cliffs, waterfalls, and the Boston Glacier.

NOTES

[1]Fred H. McNeil, "In the Glacier Peak Region, 1926," *Mazama* 8, no. 12 (1926): 13.

[2]I.C. Russell, "A Preliminary Paper on the Geology of the Cascade Mountains in Northern Washington," *20th Annual Report, U.S. Geological Survey, 1898-1899,* pt. 2 (Washington, 1900), p. 92. He added, "The ground throughout the great forest is encumbered with fallen trunks, sometimes piled one on another, which, owing to the continued moisture, remain undecayed for centuries" (p. 93).

[3]H.B. Ayres, "Washington Forest Reserve," *19th Annual Report, U.S. Geological Survey,* 1897-1898, pt. 5 (Washington, 1899), p. 288. A Forest Service study made in 1928 in the Cascade River watershed showed that the forest types were Douglas fir—18%, western hemlock—37%, silver fir—2+%, and western red cedar—16%.

[4]E of the Cascade crest ponderosa pine grows to 160 ft in the lower reaches of Railroad, Agnes, and Stehekin Valleys. Western red cedar sometimes over 100 ft high, is found in moist valleys. Alaska yellow cedar is common in the Agnes and Stehekin Valley; it is stunted alpine in its upper limits to about 6000 ft in Horseshoe Basin. The Stehekin Valley contains black cottonwood in magnificent proportions up to 100 ft along the rich river bottom; here also is found Oregon maple to 70 ft. Lovely fir is found from about 1800 ft to 5500 ft; subalpine fir from 5000 to 6000 ft. Western hemlock, common in the Stehekin Valley, occurs from 2000 ft to 4700 ft and alpine hemlock, the prevailing tree of Cascade and other passes, normally extends from 2100 ft to 5800 ft. Engelmann spruce has a wide range, from about 2800 ft to 6800 ft on sheltered ridges. Alpine larch grows high, generally from 5800 ft to 7100 ft, favoring the high ridges about Lake Chelan. In the wide valley of Granite Creek it is common to see lodgepole, western white, and ponderosa pine amid meadows.

[5]The great Chelan Valley was considered by Russell to owe its existence mainly to stream corrasion. He believed the length of the Chelan Glacier was about 75 mi. and that it was 2500 to 3000 ft thick in the central portion of its course (Russell, *op. cit.,* p. 162).

[6]Apparently Chelan basin received Cordilleran ice that flowed up Cascade Valley and over Cascade Pass. The pass and its northern shoulder, Sahale Arm, are anomalously broad and rounded up to an altitude of 7400 ft, and both are striated and have perched boulders. Several anomalously broad passes along the Cascade crest and Rainy Pass suggest that the flow of Cordilleran ice into Chelan trough was nearly as common as into the Methow drainage. The largest appears to have been Rainy Pass; the inferred 7400 ft to 7500 ft ice-limits on Tower Mountain and Sahale Arm indicate that the ice stream across Rainy Pass was about 2500 ft deep (Richard B. Waitt, Jr., "Geomorphology and Glacial Geology of the Methow Drainage Basin, Eastern North Cascade Range, Washington," Ph.D. dissert., Univ. of Washington, 1972, p. 107). Because of the ice divide during the Pleistocene lay W of Big Beaver Creek, during this epoch Skagit ice flowed both N and W.

[7]Waitt, *ibid,* p. 142.

[8]Trimline is a term to designate the boundary between differing ages and densities of plants and trees marking the position from which a valley glacier has recently receded. On the highest peaks and ridges the trimline may indicate recent recession of glacial ice by a change in the dark tones on the rock; removal of lichen is often seen by the presence of a conspicuous horizontal line separating distinct tones.

[9]Between 47° and 49° latitude, N- and NE-facing glaciers receive far less solar radiation than glaciers flowing S and SW. Glaciers in the deeper N and NE cirques are further protected, and more drift snow is swept into these cirques by the prevailing winds. Under otherwise similar topographic conditions, the largest percentage of ice is on N- and NE-facing slopes; glaciers draining S are generally much smaller. Most orientation anomalies result from high-altitude topography which favors glacier development in more exposed quadrants.

[10]The summer snowline is not always the same in related months, but generally approximate. Firn limit is a reflection of changes in several climatic variables, the amount of snow accumulation, thermal effectiveness, and temperature gradient. These determine the height to which the annual snowline will migrate each year.

[11]The property of ice tending to freeze to objects in contact is a strong factor in quarrying in the role of bottom slippage. Glaciers shod with coarse frozen rock waste in basal layers friction along the bed, and as the ice moves it dislodges. The weight of glaciers is about 30 tons to the sq. ft. for every thousand ft of thickness.

[12]It is estimated 75 percent of the annual precipitation in western Washington occurs during the period October to March. At altitudes above 2500 ft much of this occurs as snowfall.

[13]A research station and program were set up in 1957 near the glacier at 6040 ft with the purpose of increasing our understanding of how glaciers can be used as climate indicators and how they affect the hydrology of mountain drainage basins; a gauging station has been operated to measure glacier streamflow. The investigation attempts to provide representative information from a localized area, including a study of periodic changes in glacier regimen and the terminus position as related to climatic trends. The study is part of the continuing effort to complete the mosaic that explains the intricate pattern of cause and effect between glaciers and meteorological factors. The observed runoff from the South Cascade Glacier basin for the past 10 years is remarkably independent of winter accumulation. The timely release of water from glaciers during critical warm, dry periods is important in recreation and to the local economy (meltwater runoff during August-September is greatest in those basins that have the glacier-covered area). Increasing evidence shows that glaciers are capable of storing significant amounts of liquid water and releasing it during the summer. This water is a natural phenomena that can be predicted seasonally and is being measured at many stations.

Glaciers are hydrological gauges which respond to the slightest climatic fluctuations, but Meier (1966) has cautioned that changes in ice thickness and volume do not always reflect specific responses to changing climate. The hydrologic significance of annual changes in a glacier's mass is that the effects of streamflow are not synchronized with changes in annual precipitation (this is in direct contrast to the close relationship which exists between annual snowfall and snowmelt in non-glacierized basins). Glaciers are natural moderators of streamflow on both a seasonal and annual basis; summer runoff from glacierized areas has considerably less variance of that from non-glacierized areas. There is a substantial effect on variance with the presence of only a few small glaciers in a large drainage basin. This runoff is the result of snow ablation, firn and ice melt, rain, and release of water stored in the glacier drainage network.

The South Cascade Glacier lies in a drainage basin of nearly 1000 m relief, (basin area 6.25 km^2) and flows in a slightly serpentine N to W direction from its origin at about 2100 m in a depression between The Lizard and Sentinel Peak to its terminus in a lake at 1613 m. The glacier has an area of 2.72 km^2 and a mean altitude of 1870 m. The longitudinal profile is characterized by four flattish reaches, separated by steeper pitches. The glacier has been continuously retreating for many years, possibly because it has a lower altitude than other North Cascade glaciers which were actively advancing or near equilibrium 1953-1961. Snow which is apparently largely wind drift covers the glacier and high basins. This builds up the snowpack to produce a stable shape, regardless of total winter snowfall volume, and excess snow is blown off, deposited elsewhere. Snow line is routinely mapped for several dates during a melt season to help relate precipitation input and water outflow from the basin in a study of area hydrology. High altitude precipitation is difficult to measure because of the effect of wind. Many exposed ridges are swept bare even during the heaviest snowfalls by the common high winter winds; drifting snow accumulates to greater depths in the cirques and gullies of upper slopes. The heavy regional precipitation does not show a consistent relationship with altitude, chiefly because of high-relief precipitation shadowing effects. The local area shows as much as 210 in. annually (Tangborn, p. 27). Additional sources are: R.M. Krimmel and W.V. Tangborn, "South Cascade Glacier: The Moderating Influence of Glaciers on Runoff," *Proc. 42d Annual West. Snow Conf.,* 1974, pp. 9-13.

M.F. Meier, "Research on South Cascade Glacier," *Mountaineer,* 1958, pp. 40-47.

M.F. Meier, "Some Glaciological Interpretations of Remapping Programs on South Cascade Glacier, Nisqually, and Klawatti Glaciers, Washington," *Can Jour. Earth Sciences* 3 (1966): 811-818.

M.F. Meier and W.V. Tangborn, "Net Budget and Flow of South Cascade Glacier, Washington," *Jour. Glaciology* 5, no. 41 (1965): 547-566.

Lowell A. Rasmussen and Wendell V. Tangborn, "Hydrology of the North Cascades, Washington": Part I. Runoff, Precipitation, and Storage Characteristics. U.S. Geological Survey, Tacoma, 1975.

Wendell V. Tangborn, "Glaciological Investigations on South Cascade Glacier," *Mountaineer,* 1962, pp. 25-32.

[14]The Dana and Le Conte Glaciers are high-level firn fields that debouch in spectacular ice walls; these advance over cliffs and send down great ice blocks, which in turn build up ice cones below the cliffs. The Dana Glacier (7600′ to 5800′) terminates on a steep bedrock slope above the West Fork of Agnes Creek; four end moraines built during Neoglaciation extend into the valley. The Le Conte Glacier (7900′ to 6000′), about a mi. in length, has an E orientation and lies on an irregular slope. The glacier terminates on a spectacular wall of ice above Le Conte Lake. Five small end moraines border the lake and record fluctuations during the last four centuries. Typical of the larger glaciers here, it is nourished directly by snowfall and moderate amounts of drift snow.

[15]C.D. Miller, "Chronology of Neoglacial Moraines in the Dome Peak Area, North Cascades, Washington," MS thesis, Univ. of Washington, 1967. The anomalous behavior of the glacier reaching a maximum earlier than nearby glaciers may be a reflection of a higher accumulation area. The main tongue has retreated in the past two decades, but still terminates on cliffs.

The velocity and strain rate patterns in a small temperate glacier display flow effects of channel geometry, ice thickness, surface slope, and ablation. Velocity vectors diverge from the glacier center near the terminus, in response to surface ice loss (but converge toward the glacier center near the firn line because of channel narrowing). This composite valley and slope glacier demonstrates variations that can take place in a single ice mass. The low E tongue has retreated since 1955 when observations began but the terminus on cliffs W advanced in the early 1950s and then stabilized (Inventory of Glaciers, pl. 3).

[16]The McAllister Glacier is a small valley outlet glacier draining the northern slope of the high plateau of the Eldorado Peak area and the W slope of Klawatti Peak. The glacier measures 3.9 km along its longitudinal axis and descends from an elevation of 2530 m to a low terminus at 1200 m (this shows slight retreat); there is a small lake (3920′+) at the foot. The firn edge has a mean elevation of about 2010 m (the average lowest altitude of seasonal snow remaining at the end of the summer melt season). The glacier bifurcates into two icefalls of 250-300 m around a bedrock cliff near the firn edge which separates the lower McAllister Glacier from its principal accumulation basins. Marginal shear on the tongue below the icefalls seems to be strongly asymmetric due to flow westward around a bend. Backbone Glacier and Perdition Glacier (unofficial names) are located on the NE slope of Backbone Ridge W of the snout.

"Austera" Glacier (1.1 mi. in length and trending NW from Klawatti Peak) is the portion of ice NNW of Klawatti Peak identified with McAllister Glacier.

[17]Crevasses form where the greatest extending strain occurs. Longitudinal crevasses superimposed on the marginal shear causes formation of curving transverse crevasses which here are part of an echelon system. The Boston Glacier reaches from 2650 m to 1520 m; its terminus advanced rapidly 1950-1955 and its area increased 17 percent during this period (Inventory of Glaciers, p. A 18 and Pl. 3).

[18]Peter Misch, "Geology of the Northern Cascades of Washington," *Mountaineer* 45 (1952): 4-22. Granitization during Mesozoic metamorphism has been complete (p. 15).

[19]Peter Misch, "Tectonic Evolution of the North Cascades of Washington State—A West Cordilleran Case History," *in* A symposium on tectonic history and mineral deposits of the western cordillera in British Columbia and neighboring parts of the United States, *Canadian Inst. Mining and Metallugy,* Spec. Vol. 8 (1966), pp. 101-148, ref. p. 121.

Peter Misch of the University of Washington began investigating the North Cascades in 1949 and began a systematic study by reconnaissance mapping the geology. See also Rowland W. Tabor, "The Crystalline Geology of the Area South of Cascade Pass, Northern Cascade Mountains, Washington," Ph.D. dissert., Univ. of Washington, 1961.

The maximum of the N-S axis of Late Cenozoic uparching was in the North Cascades, thus exposing the older rocks. Massive crustal uplift exposed the durable gneiss, which with granites were formed during and after periods of folding and compression. Later they were uplifted and stripped of overlying rocks.

[20]Erik H. Erikson, Jr., "Petrology of the Composite Snoqualmie Batholith, Central Cascade Mountains, Washington," *Geol. Soc. Am. Bull.* 80 (1969): 2213. Meta-igneous rocks, exposed in the North Cascades, are part of the complex pre-Jurassic metamorphic basement (Misch, *op. cit.,* 1966).

[21]Tertiary Cascade intrusions predominantly are quartz

dioritic in composition, but emplacement of late-stage magma was commonly quartz monzonite and granite; some plutons are composite. Cascade plutonic rocks were produced in Late Cretaceous and Tertiary periods of granite evolution. Intrusions of igneous bodies continued until about 15 million years ago.

[22]Alan Robert Grant, "Chemical and Physical Controls for Base Metal Deposition in the Cascade Range of Washington," *Wash. Div. Mines and Geology,* Bull. 58 (1969). See also footnote 17, Section I.

[23]R.W. Tabor and D.F. Crowder, "On Batholiths and Volcanism," *U.S. Geological Survey Prof. Paper No. 604* (1969), p. 1. Regional structural trends are predominantly northwesterly. Trends are most easily distinguished by the major alignment of rock belts in metamorphic-plutonic terrain of the North Cascades.

[24]Bruce H. Bryant, "Petrology and Reconnaissance Geology of the Snowking Area, Northern Cascades, Washington," Ph.D. dissert., Univ. of Washington, 1955. The Snowking massif is a NW-trending projection of the granitic core of the North Cascades into the lower grade metamorphic rocks along the regional structural trend. In the western part of the Snowking area the Straight Creek Fault separates major units.

[25]Grant, *op. cit.,* p. 44. The Cascades can be considered primarily a copper province. The principal copper occurrences seem to be along transverse structural zones. Sulphide mineralization is ubiquitous in the Buckindy structure. The transverse zone, continuing across the South Fork Cascade River, exhibits strong shearing, and passes through Horseshoe Basin, Thunder Creek, and Skagit Queen mining districts.

[26]Pictographs on the W bank, near the head of Lake Chelan, apparently were created at an unknown prehistoric time; it has been suggested Indian artists worked from canoes or rafts. Army explorers once commented that the location indicated an earlier higher lake level.

It should be noted that Indians had little practical reason to spend much time in the far reaches of the Cascades, unless such areas were accessible by waterways. The plentiful game in lowland and foothill forests, and fish in rivers and salt water made the non-mountainous areas more attractive.

[27]Judge William C. Brown believed Indian horses came from the SW about 150 years prior to Lewis and Clark's expeditions ("Old Fort Okanogan and the Okanogan Trail," *Oregon Hist. Soc. Quart.* 15 (March 1914): 31). Other observers concluded Indian policy was to go only where the pony took him. The idea of cutting and logging out a trail was repugnant; lines of travel favored sparse ridges where feed and game were plentiful.

[28]George Gibbs, "Physical Geography of the North-Western Boundary of the United States," *Jour. of the Amer. Geog. Soc. of N.Y.* 4 (1873): 332. Sakumihu is the Indian name for what later became Sauk; the boundary map of 1866 depicts this trail via the 'Saakw' (and an eastern branch) via a pass to the lake's head. A sketch of this period clearly shows the legend "Trail to Lake Chelan" with a route-line along "Suiatl R" (Report of Edwin F. Johnson, Engineer-in-Chief, to the Board of Directors, Northern Pacific Railroad, April 1869. Hartford, 1869, Sketch no. 4).

The Sauk-Suiattle tribe supposedly lived near the divide by Glacier Peak in summer, and had large houses at Buck and Tenas Creeks. Their chief, Wa-wet-kin, helped the railroad surveyors in 1870. Gibbs on an 1855 map identified Skagit tribes which lived along the upper river and included the Miskaiwhu, Skaumehu, Ski a lehu, and Nook wach amich (Wheat, *op. cit.,* IV, p. 36). The Skagit Indian, who belonged to the Salishan linguistic stock, probably was only vaguely conceived as a tribe; they lived along the river delta and nearby islands.

[29]This is confirmed in McClellan's report, which indicates he learned of an Indian trail from the Methow to a stream emptying into the head of Lake Chelan, "then to cross very steep and lofty mountains at the head of that stream . . . to the Skagitt" (*Pacific Railroad Reports,* I. Sen. Ex. Doc. No. 178, 33rd Cong., 2d sess., p. 197).

While this suggests the known route over Cascade Pass, another Indian route may have used Bridge and Granite Creeks. The G.L.O. Washington Territory map of 1887 places the legend Sluk-le-ko-kul R at what appears to be Granite Creek.

[30]In October 1880 Lt. Thomas W. Symons conducted troops up the Skagit to protect a public lands survey party whose lives were threatened by Indians; the sudden arrival of soldiers quieted the Indians. Symons and a company of soldiers met with Indians at Baker River to negotiate an agreement for D.S.B. Henry, U.S. Deputy Surveyor ("Report of Lt. Thomas W. Symons, Corps of Engineers, for Fiscal Year ending June 30, 1881." In *Report of the Chief of Engineers, U.S. Army,* House Ex. Docs. (1882), Cong. ser. set 2013, vol. 5. Appendix CCC, pp. 2868-2870).

[31]The Cascade Range was shown on some early maps as one chain, but with somewhat fanciful spurs trending into British territory. See Stevens' "Preliminary Sketch" (Wheat, *op. cit.,* IV, p. 12). The 1853 Map of the proposed Northern Route for a Railroad to the Pacific (Wheat, III, p. 193) shows the line crossing the range in a conjectural fashion N of Barrier (Methow) River.

[32]Report of Lt. Thomas W. Symons, Corps of Engineers, Headquarters, Department of the Columbia. In *Report of the Chief of Engineers, U.S. Army* (1879-1880), House Ex. Doc., 46th Cong., 3d sess., vol. 2, pt. 3, p. 2552. The 1859 map of John Arrowsmith traces the lake conspicuously with lettering "Clearwater or Chelan R & L."

[33]Alexander Ross, *The Fur Hunters of the Far West,* ed. by Kenneth A. Spaulding, Norman (Oklahoma), 1956. Ross presents a minimum of evidence to support unamplified footnotes concerning the conjecture of a route down "Cascade

River." Wishing to carry out a project of discovery, Ross set out with three Indians to follow a trading route, one which becomes hazy beyond lower Methow Valley. A careful reading of the imprecise account raises doubts about the "West River" reached August 4; Ross possibly followed Bridge Creek, Granite Creek, or the Suiattle-Sauk system. The manuscript, first published in London in 1855, lacks the topographic clarity of writings by earlier explorers William Clark and David Thompson.

[34]Otto Klement, "Early Skagit Recollections," *Burlington Farm Journal,* 6 December 1961, typescript p. 8. Also see "Early Historical Incidents of Skagit County," coll. by Ethel Van Fleet Harris, *Mt. Vernon Herald,* 19 October 1926. Klement, Charles Von Pressentin, Jack Rowley, John Duncan, John Sutter, Frank Scott, and Charles and Joe Seaan (Indian guides) hiked from Skagit River to Lake Chelan, where canoes were hidden. On the third day they met 30 Indians and ponies, who had crossed from the E. "Cascade River Pass" was reached on the fifth day. See also Erwin N. Thompson. North Cascades National Park, Ross Lake National Recreation Area and Lake Chelan National Recreation Area Basic History Data. Office of Archeological and Historical Preservation, Washington, 1970.

[35]An old miner he met on the trek told of riches and routes. Henry H. Pierce, "Report of an Expedition from Fort Colville to Puget Sound, Washington Territory by way of Lake Chelan and Skagit River during the months of August and September, 1882," Records of the Office of the Adjutant General, R.G. 94, National Archives, p. 19. See also Fred Beckey, "Across the North Cascades in 1882," *Summit,* Feb./March 1977, pp. 8-13, 38, 40.

[36]Allen E. Hart, "The Unexplored Mountains of North America," *Geog. Review* 7 (June 1919): 403.

[37]The Soldier Boy is one of the historic claims of the district, and here was the cabin where the soldier of Lt. Pierce's party lived with his wife for 2 months when he returned in search of the ledge. Nearby claims were the Ventura and Midas. W of the famed Boston Mine were the Eldorado and King Solomon.

[38]L.K. Hodges, "The Cascade River District," *Seattle Post Intelligencer,* 25 October 1896, p. 18. See also L.K. Hodges, *Mining in the Pacific Northwest,* pp. 54-56.

[39]*Ibid.*

[40]In 1895 the Board of State Road Commissioners made surveys of three cross-state routes; the one chosen led over Cascade Pass, up Bridge Creek and down Twisp River. Work began in 1896, but crews did not widen it even to wagon width between Gilbert's cabin and Gilbert townsite (the entire route was really a pack trail and in a year much slid out. Hodges, *op. cit.*). The route followed the trail cut from Marblemount to the confluence of the N and S forks by A.M. Doty and John McIntosh, who after the Boston discovery located placer claims there and established the mining camp.

In 1897 there were 8 mi. of wagon width from the new cable ferry at Marblemount, then 24 mi. of trail to Cascade Pass. The route was noted for puncheon bridges. Immediately after the discovery of mineral, El Dorado (Mineral Park) featured a hotel, store, and saloon amid an ever-changing population of 90. In 1897 H.B. Ayres reported there were seven cabins en route on the Cascade River in addition to the mining camp (H.B. Ayres, "Washington Forest Reserve," *19th Annual Report U.S. Geological Survey,* 1897-1898 (Washington, 1899, pt. 5, p. 285). While the year 1906 was so active a ranger station site was selected the following summer, within 10 years all the buildings had tumbled. The most lasting and famed human abode was the cabin of Gilbert Landre, 3 mi. from Cascade Pass; it served as hotel, store, and saloon for passing prospectors.

[41]"It can be traced by the red iron stain eastward through the sawteeth to Horseshoe Basin and runs westward through the summit . . . at the side of Boston (sic Quien Sabe) Glacier" (Hodges, *ibid*). Eventually the Rouse boys had a scow on the lake; downslope there was a 54-inch Pelton wheel to power the sawmill (this wheel, shaped like a doughnut, is turned when a water jet is directed on it).

[42]In 1889 the Rouse boys reached Doubtful Lake from Lake Chelan because of the deteriorating Cascade River route; this of course gave notice of their activity and camp. M.M. Kingman and Albert M. Pershall followed their route and soon concluded the veins must cut through the adjacent basin; when they reached the wall above the lower basin they found that the ledge was well mineralized. On June 20 they located the Blue Devil and Black Warrior claims, to mark the beginning of much prospecting in Horseshoe Basin. The next year they discovered and located the famous Davenport group in the upper basin, near the glacier (*Chelan Leader,* 31 August 1897). The Horseshoe galena ledges were traced 12 mi. E to the head of Bridge Creek. Discoveries were made near the head of the N fork, and also in the valleys of Park, Agnes, and Company Creeks.

In what L.K. Hodges called the Lake Chelan district, the North Star group of eight claims were located at the head of Railroad and Agnes Creeks; claim appellations such as North Star, Bonanza, and Mary Green were also applied to important natural features.

[43]Pershall was shown on the Kroll 1899 and the G.L.O. 1909 maps. In the winter of 1909 Henry F. Buckner had a crew of 30 who worked "buried" under snow in Horseshoe Basin. Settlers arrived at Stehekin in 1885, and in 5 years cross-mountain traffic included "Okanogan Smith," who took cattle over Cascade Pass. The first steamboat excursion, by the "Belle of Chelan," was on August 19, 1891. M.E. Field arrived the next year, then opened his noted hotel in 1900. The lake's beauty inspired the name Lucerne for a small settlement, a duplicate of the name of the medieval town and the beautiful lake in Switzerland, the locale of Wilhelm Tell's exploits.

[44]Hodges, *op. cit.*

[45]The Willis and Everette claim was located 1 mi. W of the Skagit Queen camp, where a Pelton wheel ran a generator to power the machine drilling (steep slopes and avalanches precluded a camp near the mine, N of Mt. Buckner). With the discovery of silver and lead along with the gold ore, a modern camp evolved at the junction of Skagit Queen and Thunder Creeks. Real development began in 1905, with a hydroelectric powerhouse built to supply power to camp and the mines. A great investment was spent in development, building trails, surveying a railroad route, and packing in the heavy machinery. Various new companies took the holdings, including the British Mining Co. in 1913. Two of the most famous miners of the district were George Logan, who arrived in 1896 and spent 21 summers driving tunnels on his claims, and William McAllister, who arrived on Thunder Creek in 1897.

[46]James Tilton to Edwin F. Johnson, 7 August 1867. Records of Lake Superior and Puget Sound Company. Minnesota Historical Society. Also Tilton to Thomas H. Canfield, 12 September 1867. Tilton indicated the Skagit was mostly unknown in regard to passes, but the map in Johnson's Report clearly depicts a pass W of the head of Lake Chelan.

[47]D.C. Linsley, "Pioneering in the Cascade Country," *Civil Engineering,* no. 6 (1932), pp. 340-344. Linsley possibly followed an Indian route via Khaiwhat Creek (possibly Sulphur) to Agnes Creek; on the pass to Lake Chelan evidence of a trail was found June 7; further research of Linsley's diary is needed. In July Linsley and John Tennant canoed Lake Chelan and explored into Agnes Creek; the summary of Linsley's achievements by canoe, foot, and horseback seems quite overstated. A cost estimate of $16 million was made for a railroad route from the Skagit River via Lake Chelan to the Columbia River. To the Northern Pacific surveyors in the winters of 1870 and 1871, the "numerous slides of great magnitude" must have been sobering.

[48]Diary of Albert B. Rogers, p. 52. A.B. Rogers Papers, University of Washington Library. J.A. Navarre of Chelan told Rogers that the Upper Skagit had fearful falls and that its canyon would be impossible for a railroad.

[49]John F. Stevens, "Great Northern Railway," *Wash. Hist. Quart.* 20, no. 2(1929): 111-113. Stevens was assisted by Charles Haskell in explorations of that year, which culminated in the discovery of the pass named for him. About this time C.W. Root also explored Indian, Cascade, and Ruby Passes for the Great Northern (Seattle Post Intelligencer, 16 August 1894, p. 3).

[50]*Chelan Falls Leader,* 29 December 1892. In the summer of 1892 surveyors were stated to be thick in Skagit County. Among various schemes was the one of Chelan Transportation and Smelting Co. (1901) for an electric railroad from Stehekin to Horseshoe Basin.

[51]It is apparent that the intrepid surveyors went through the Illabot-Buck-Goat-Downey-Sulphur Creek areas to accurately map the drainages and mark such features as Totem Pass, Bath Lakes, Bench Lake, Found Lake, Jordan Lakes, and Granite Lakes. The equally detailed first Stehekin quadrangle provides an indication of the hardy exploration of the government surveyors. Quixotically the Surveyor General Map of 1906 titles all the mountainous area adjacent the Cascade River, "Unsurveyed."

[52]They marked the summit of Cascade Pass with an iron post (altitude 5423′); see *19th Annual Report U.S. Geological Survey,* pt. 1, pp. 364-365. In the next 2 years Cascade Pass and the area W was surveyed under L.C. Fletcher (*20th Annual Report U.S. Geological Survey,* pt. 1, p. 490). In the summer of 1899 E.C. Barnard mapped the area between the Suiattle, Cascade, and Skagit Rivers. I.C. Russell, on a geological reconnaissance in 1898, saw some of the high regions between Glacier Peak and the Skagit River; he commented about glaciers on "granitic peaks" (*ibid,* pt. 2, p. 193). He believed there were probably several hundred glaciers S of the Canadian border, but only a few in the vicinity of Glacier Peak had been traversed.

[53]The first published Forest Service maps, in 1913, were quite accurate on drainage patterns and summit locations. Such summits as North Star (i.e. Bonanza), Spire, Dome, Agnes, Green, Boston, Logan, Booker, Sahale, Frisco, Needle, Flora, and Castle Rock were shown (but not Mt. Goode).

The wagon road up Railroad Creek and the continuing trail to Cloudy and Suiattle Passes is shown on the Chelan National Forest maps of 1913 and 1916. Some names have vanished from earlier maps (McCallum Mtn. N of Bridge Creek and Copper Mtn. near Twisp Pass—as shown on the Kroll map of 1899). As late as 1926 the Forest Service maps showed no summit names N of Boston Peak's vicinity, and even Eldorado Peak was not named; the entire area on both sides of Thunder Creek was devoid of detail. But some names appeared for the first time in cartographic history—among them Spider, Glory, Magic, Le Conte, Sentinel. By 1931 these maps contained much more detail and nonmenclature. Ragged Ridge was depicted for the first time (this ties in with Wernstedt's fieldwork), and the Mt. Buckindy-Snowking area was detailed.

[54]A.S. Pattullo, "Lake Chelan and Mount Sahale," *Mazama* 2, no. 3 (1903): 138-142. See also W.G. Steel, "Lake Chelan and the Valley of the Stehekin," *Oregon Native Son,* 1, no. 8 (1900): 407-415.

[55]Hermann F. Ulrichs, personal communication, 28 December 1972. "I did not begin to see the range by degrees—I had seen nothing of it, not even a solitary picture . . . . It could not have been arranged more dramatically than by climbing the peak forming the two buttresses of Park Creek Pass and be suddenly confronted with that great complex of mountains."

[56]*Ibid.* In 1936 Ulrichs and Dwight Watson hoped to

climb all the summits between Agnes and Sentinel, but an accident to a third partner curtailed plans. On approaches to such localities Ulrichs found brush so thick that he departed from the traditional custom of traveling the stream valleys and took to the high divides—somewhat of an innovation in the early 1930s. Significantly, the summits of Dome Peak were climbed in 1936 by different approaches by adventurers unknown to each other. A historic early visit to the South Cascade and Le Conte Glaciers was the trek via Downey Creek in July 1938 by Dwight Watson and Herbert Butt.

[57]Continuing the specialized exploration of the high country between Agnes Creek and upper Lake Chelan in 1940 and 1941 the Oregon climbers apparently depended on old maps, leading to some confusion about geographic directions as well as place names.

[58]Russell, *op. cit.*, p. 192.

[59]Various early records and photography depict Isella Glacier as being on the E side of Bonanza, near the Mary Green mine trail and cabins. In the period before 1908 the Crown Glacier was used for the name of the present Isella. Probably names were transposed at about that time and the Crown name eliminated. The name Isella is for a prospector's daughter. Like the Mary Green, the Isella is a severely crevassed, stationary cirque glacier, and ends on a moderate slope. The mean altitude of the 0.6 km^2 glacier is high—limits range from 8700 ft to 7700 ft. The glacier has polished bedrock and bulldozed talus into a gigantic sharp moraine and is actively undercutting its cirque. The exposed SW-facing eastern area of the cirque contains no glacial ice, whereas the W portion is laden with snow and ice. The Dark Glacier (1.1 km^2, 1½ mi. NW of Bonanza) is little known and drains to Swamp Creek. Grant Glacier, a small high body of ice, lies on the N of North Star Mountain. Tenmile Park Glacier, an old name, is the small glacier on the high eastern cirque of Martin Peak.

[60]Martin Gorman wrote that the two mountains at the head of Railroad Creek are known locally as Bonanza and North Star (Martin W. Gorman, "Eastern Part of Washington Forest Reserve," *19th Annual Report, U.S. Geological Survey, 1897-1898*, pt. 5 (Washington, 1899), p. 317). Bonanza was shown as "North Star" on the G.L.O. map of Washington State, 1909 and the Forest Service map of 1913, but on the 1922 map the words Bonanza Peak are shown.

[61]The symbol should have been placed on North Star. Similar triangulation station marks were placed during this period on Pyramid, Reynolds, Sahale, and Glacier Peak (summits occupied). Because the triangulation station was still shown on the Mt. Baker Forest map of 1931, it was supposed that surveyors had climbed the peak. In 1932 when Hermann Ulrichs and John Burnett were at Spider Pass after the climb of Mt. Maude they were interested in an attempt, but interpreted the map to show the summit had been reached. Ulrichs stated he would have gone to Bonanza instead of Fernow later that year. "I wasn't interested in following in the footsteps of the surveyors, and put Bonanza off with Mt. Stuart for my old age" (Hermann F. Ulrichs, interview, 1973).

[62]Mazama, *op. cit.* On June 25 these five made their attempt from the Company Glacier face. Five hours were required to climb 2000 ft of steep snow and ice, capped by a cornice, then climb to Point Two (West Peak). Everett Darr summarized these efforts when he wrote "The very complexity of the mountain necessitated a most complete and exhaustive study and the ascent itself was the culmination of three seasons spent in the area (*The Wy'east Climber*, Bull. 5, no. 6 & 7 (1937), p. 1).

[63]On June 26 the successful route was scouted by Ida Darr and Joe Leuthold. Both Darrs participated in the summit climb on the 28th, but Everett became ill at the base of the rock pitches, and Ida remained behind to assist. The summit trio made the ascent in 12 hours from Holden Lake (23 hours round trip). Interestingly they used Swiss-edge nails on boots in preference to tricouni nails which were the most popular with contemporary Northwest climbers. The second ascent of Bonanza was made by Franklin Bennett and Ward Carithers in July 1938.

[64]W.D. Lyman, "Lake Chelan," *The Overland Monthly* 33 (1899): 201.

[65]The climb from Sulphur Creek to the meadows SW of Dome took an arduous 7½ hours. The Ptarmigan foursome scrambled from Dome's Southwest Peak along the ridge to the Northeast Peak, then from the upper Chickamin Glacier crossed the ice col to the Dana.

[66]*Sierra Club Bull.* 22, no. 1 (1937): 78. The only quadrangles existing at the time were Stehekin and Glacier Peak.

[67]Prof. Paper No. 19, U.S. Geol. Survey, (Washington, 1903), pl. 20. In his album Willis labelled the formation "Pinnacles of the Crest."

[68]Klement, *op. cit.*, footnote 34. L.K. Hodges, the mining journalist who viewed the mountain from Gilbert's basin in 1896, wrote "A roar and rattle draws your attention to the mountain opposite, where every gulch between the unscalable sawteeth is filled with a narrow, tumbling stream of ice, broken into huge waves. The roar is caused by the falling of blocks of ice from the tail of one of these glaciers, to be shattered on the rocks beneath and pour in a white cascade . . . over the precipice beneath." (Hodges, *op. cit.*)

[69]*Ibid.* The mountain clearly should have the name Johnsburg, as derived from the mine. Hodges describes clambering up the steep mine path, which included deep canyons filled with snow and steep brushy rock.

High on Johannesburg Mountain was the Johnsburg group of four claims (Lookout, Ohio, Buckeye Boy); Landre was involved with these. The highest tunnel was 2800 ft above the valley; others were at the 1500-ft and 2000-ft level. They could only be reached by a 1 mi. cable or precipitous trail.

Charles L. Pollard, the Taber brothers, and John Connick (sp.?) prospected in the middle fork valley (Hodges, *op. cit.*). Other adventurers traced the mineral belt from there across the ridge to the S fork. George Leach, an important figure who came to the area in 1894, was active in the middle and S fork regions.

[70]Glee Davis, interview, 8 November 1975. L.K. Hodges visited the Johnsburg claims and wrote, "crossing the creek, (Cascade River) you switchback among the brush up the base of the mountain, and are kept busy sorting out your legs from among the straggling limbs. Some people use strong language . . . " (Seattle Post Intelligencer, 25 October 1896, p. 18). After climbing 1000 ft one emerged on the side of a gulch, whose lower half was filled with icy snow. "You climb through brush again to another gulch, which only needs to be tilted up a little more to attain the perpendicular. Its bed is smooth granite, with only slight occasional projections and is thinly covered with decaying fir needles which have dropped from the overhanging trees . . . . Mr. Landre, missing the trail, started to climb this gulch like a mountain goat and the writer started to follow, but soon found the soil so thin that he was practically stepping on the smooth rock at an angle of 75 degrees." He then accepted a pull from the old pioneer to avoid rolling down "a little matter of 2,000 feet." The ledge cropped on the side of the gulch, and according to Hodges, had been traced along it "over the summit of the mountain."

[71]The names given for the summits of Buckindy Ridge are not official. Some were applied by parties in 1969 and 1972 on traverses of the area, and appear in more than one publication; the names of various crags and pinnacles appear here because of publishing exposure and ready identification, but some names proposed for the larger summits will not be endorsed here.

[72]Forest Service maps of 1922 and 1926 lettered "Buck Creek" on the NE fork (draining Mt. Buckindy—7311'); latter maps placed the name Horse Creek on this fork, and the main N fork became Buck Creek. The route described in the 1961 climbing guide (p. 201) pertains not to Mt. Buckindy but to Mt. Misch.

[73]Ridges are sharp and usually asymmetrical due to mountain glaciation after the last maximum; aretes tend to have cliffs on the NE and be less steep on the opposite side. When there has been no recent glaciation (as to the W of Snowking) the NE slopes are open meadows and at the same altitude the SW is forest. The glacier on the NE has retreated ¼ mi. from the fresh moraine adjacent to alpine firs (near 5000'); the ice now terminates near 6000 ft. Glaciated slabs and recent moraines are apparent on the NE flank of the ridge SE of the SE peak (6995'/2132 m) of Snowking. Recent moraines extend E along the spur from the SE peak to where the ridge declines, far beyond the glacierized area mapped 1897-1899. Lakes nearby (Cyclone, Snowking, etc.) have much suspended rock flour—an indication of glacier activity.

[74]Bruce Bryant thoroughly traversed the Snowking-Chaval-Buckindy ridges in the summer of 1952 in conducting geologic investigations. On July 27 he climbed the W peak of Snowking via Illabot Lake and the W ridge (he found a register with 1938 and 1941 recordings). On July 28 he climbed the main E peak but found no signs of previous visit.

[75]*Washington Miner,* 15 October 1908.

[76]"A sharp rocky point 4 mi. north of Cascase Pass. A red sugar-loaf peak, a little higher, but inaccessible, lies about one-half mile to the north on the same ridge . . . . The Boston mine is at the foot of the peak on the southeast. Four glaciers on the four sides of the peak reach nearly to the summit." *21st Annual Report U.S. Geological Survey, 1899-1900,* pt. 1 (Washington, 1900), p. 367. The Quien Sabe name is from an old mining prospect in the vicinity which extended under the glacier; it may be related to the ledge located by the Rouse boys in Doubtful Basin.

[77]Misch, *op. cit.,* 1952, p. 15. Gneiss on the W face is granodioritic in composition. Multiple intrusion of quartz diorite into gneissic rocks forms migmatites in banded gneiss.

[78]The Klawatti and North Klawatti Glaciers, each 2 to 3 km long, originate at separate points along a N-S ridge and flow easterly to a common terminus. They have exhibited striking and diverse changes in recent years although they are closely adjacent. In 1947 stagnant ice from both glaciers covered the area of Klawatti Lake (1.2 mi. E of Klawatti Peak). At that time Klawatti Glacier ended on a steep cliff which it now descends in a spectacular icefall. Since 1947 ice in the basin has melted; the lake, now 1 km long, has formed, and the Klawatti Glacier has advanced down the cliff. Due to glacier melting, the berg-filled lake is presently about twice the size as shown on the Forbidden Peak quadrangle. The stream draining the lake (Klawatti Creek) flows 1 mi. SE to join the West Fork of Thunder Creek. Meanwhile the North Klawatti Glacier has continued to thin and recede (Glacier Inventory, pl. 3). This glacier is 1.8 mi. long and heads 0.7 mi. W of Primus Peak, to trend SE along the N flank of Austera Towers (the Klawatti Glacier as shown on existing maps is actually two glaciers; this defines the northern one). The Borealis Glacier (0.8 mi. in length) is located on the NE flank of Primus Peak. This is the northernmost glacier in the extensive Eldorado-area glacier complex. Reference: Mark F. Meier, "Some Glaciological Interpretations of Remapping Programs on South Cascade, Nisqually, and Klawatti Glaciers, Washington," *Canadian Jour. of Earth Sciences* 3, no. 6 (1966): 815-817.

[79]To perpetrate such a name would be an injustice to the dramatic landscape, and at a later date Austin Post, involved with glacier studies of the region, applied the name Klawatti.

[80]The names Austera Peak, Austera Towers, and Tepeh Towers, and some glacier identities, were approved on the

April-June 1969 decision list of the U.S. Board on Geographic Names. Both Austin Post and Fred Beckey made a diligent effort to apply logical and sensible names to features in the area N of Eldorado Peak.

[81]The largest glacier is the Douglas (0.9 km^2 and 1.4 km length) at the southern fork of Fisher Creek and opposite the head of North Fork Bridge Creek (shown on 1922 maps), which early photography indicates it spilled into. The Douglas and Banded meet at the high col (8520′+) E of the true summit in merged upper reaches. The Fremont Glacier (1.1 km^2 and 2.4 km length) is on the better known SW slope and the recently named Banded Glacier (conspicuous ice bands) trends NW from the summit. Along the margins recent ice retreat (since the mid-1950s) has left a consistent whitish trimline in contrast with the dark tones of lichened gneiss.

[82]Mt. Goode is located at the eastern border of the gneiss area. Gneisses show gradations into younger massive granodiorite which underlies the Black Peak area to the E. Peter Misch, "Geology of the Northern Cascades of Washington," *Mountaineer,* 1952, p. 17.

[83]The Wyeth Glacier on the E flank of Storm King is larger than present-day glaciers on Mt. Goode. But impressive lateral moraines and glacial scouring of natural features testify to the size of former glaciers. Photographs taken early in the 20th century show far more ice on the Goode Glacier (*Mazama,* 1912, photo p. 16).

[84]An unseasonable blizzard had made conditions poor for both parties. Both O'Brien and Ulrichs attempted to get past this obstacle estimated to be about 100 to 150 ft under the summit, but saw no way around (*A.A.J.,* 1936, p. 472). Shortly after (July 23) an attempt was made by Don Blair, Norval Grigg, and Art Winder from a base camp on Park Creek. This team noted the couloir later used by the Sierra Club party (Bedayn Couloir) but decided not to make an attempt here. They ventured into the deep couloir to the right (S), filled with loose rock, and climbed until it ended in a deep narrow shaded chimney of about 150 ft formed by dike erosion. At the base of the chimney Blair and Winder donned rubber soled shoes and went ahead. A huge chockstone filled with snow blocked the route, so a route was selected along two narrow ledges and across a treacherous face to above the chockstone. Here they found the chimney steeper and narrower than expected, and partly filled with snow and ice. Winder nearly climbed to the summit ridge, but icy rock encountered during stemming forced a halt when the chimney widened; they estimated their position to be within 150 ft of the summit (*Mountaineer,* 1934, p. 12). They reached the area where Bauer later made his finger traverse on the first ascent. After a later conversation with Hermann Ulrichs, Winder apparently concluded Ulrichs had reached a position about 25 ft higher, but in review this appears doubtful. Both parties were limited in their climbing time at the difficulties because they did not make higher camps. The Winder party admittedly left camp too late, and had no days left for alternate routes (Art Winder, written commun., 9 November 1976).

[85]They climbed up the deep chimney several hundred ft until the chockstone stopped them; they had no pitons for a possible pendulum across about 20 ft of smooth rock to where the route appeared to continue (*Mazama,* 1935, pp. 59-60). In June 1936 Darr and companions tried another route, and reached a ridge notch to the SE. For some time it was generally supposed Darr considered the summit nearly inaccessible, but an examination of his faintly suspect account related to later completion of this route fails to remind of the earlier estimate of Goode and his failure.

[86]The party crossed over snowfields to the S of the main summit to the debris-cluttered couloir which veered directly toward the summit. At about 8900 ft it narrowed to the chimney, with its rear wall covered by ice and snow; sidewalls were verglassed and the chimney ended in an overhang. Near the chockstone they stemmed overhanging chimney walls, then scrambled to a ledge beneath a slab, 30 ft higher on the left; about 30 ft higher a break in the ridge appeared to be the solution. First a rope was flipped over a crack or rock spike for an ascent using prusik knots. By climbing with piton protection Bauer was able to make a delicate rightward finger traverse, and this quickly led to the ridge (*Mountaineer,* 1936, p. 14). The appraisal of earlier parties was correct: there was only about 100 ft of climbing remaining. The party felt that their success was not due to superior ability, but to better equipment and technique, as well as an effort molded from teamwork and training classes.

[87]Mountains in the Sierra Nevada and Chugach Range were also named for Goode. He did extensive mapping and triangulation in the Cascade Range at the turn of the century, and later took charge of the topographic branch of the Pacific Division. Mt. Goode was first shown on U.S. Forest Service maps in 1922. At that time Lemolo Creek, a name that has not survived, was shown as a branch of North Fork Bridge Creek between Goode and Storm King.

[88]The climb actually began in a devious fashion, now taken by more direct lines. The party began via the gully which splits the S end of the summit mass, then traversed N in tennis shoes along a narrow, exposed ledge to emerge on a shelf. Because a section was missing they rappelled an overhang of 100 ft, then climbed to the W arete. A wall forced a traverse back via a tiny ledge; then they began up a small chimney. This became a difficult crack which encountered a large smooth chockstone (this portion appears to be on the current normal route). The crux (class 5) was 100 ft of wall which had small sloping holds.

[89]"Appendix to Director's Report," *20th Annual Report, U.S. Geological Survey,* pt. 1 (1899), p. 490.

Index

PEAK	Elevation Feet	Meters	Page
Kololo Peaks	8200+	2500	159
Kopeetah Divide	7723	2354	95
Kyes Peak	7280+	2219	67
Labyrinth	6376	1944	145
Last Devil	6960+	2121	305
Le Conte Mountain	7762	2366	247
Lewis Peak	5608	1709	51
Liberty Cap	6700+	2042	169
Liberty Mountain	5688	1733	104
Lichtenberg Mountain	5844	1781	197
Lime Mountain	6772	2064	96
Little Chief Peak	5280	1609	46
Little Devil Peak	6985	2129	305
Little Johannesburg	7945	2422	317
Little Tack	7400+	2256	319
The Lizard	7400+	2256	243
Lizard Mountain	7400+	2256	243
Mt. Logan	9087	2770	322
Longfellow Mountain	6577	2005	146
Long John Mountain	5697	1736	82
Long Mountain	5111	1558	102
Lookout Mountain	5719	1743	305
Luahna Peak	est. 8450	2576	153
Lumbar Peak	7040+	2146	306
Mt. Lyall	7892	2405	225
Magic Mountain	7610	2320	252
Mantis Peak	7614	2321	309
Marble Needle	8401	2561	299
Marble Peak	5111	1558	40
Marmot Back	7560+	2304	240
Marmot Head	7665	2336	240
Marmot Pyramid	8500+	2591	178
Martin Peak	8511	2594	227
Mt. Mastiff	6741	2055	145
Mt. Maude	9082	2768	176
Maurine Peaks			305
McCall Mountain	5765	1757	148
Meadow Mountain	6324	1928	97
Memaloose Ridge	7265	2214	331
Merchant Peak	6113	1863	35
Mesahchie Peak	8975	2736	315
Meulefire Peak	est. 7930	2417	317
Middle Devil	6960+	2121	305
Mindolluin Crag	7280+	2219	266
Mineral Butte	5255	1602	55
Mt. Misch	7435	2266	264
Mixup Peak	7440+	2268	255
Monte Cristo Peak	7136	2175	66
Morning Star Peak	6020	1835	50
Mutchler Peak	7160+	2182	267
Napeequa Peak	8073	2461	166
The Needle	8040+	2451	309
Needle Peak	7880+	2402	225
Newhalem Peaks	6920+	2109	306
New Morning Peak	7230	2204	315
Neyah Point	8175	2492	153
North Crested Butte	5318	1621	55
North Lake Peak	5445	1660	102
North Star Mountain	8068	2459	218
North Wilmans Spire	6075	1852	60
Old Gib Mountain	7081	2158	175
Old Guard Peak	8240+	2512	244
Oliphant Tower	8120+	2475	302
Orthanc	7040+	2146	267
Overdrive Tower	8560+	2609	239
Oversight Peaks	8280+	2524	226
Painted Mountain	6975	2126	83
Paul Bunyan's Stump	7480+	2280	311
Peak 5144	5144	1568	32
Peak 5193	5193	1583	104
Peak 5335	5335	1626	32
Peak 6103	6103	1860	276
Peak 6356	6356	1937	276
Peak 6364	6364	1940	276
Peak 6400	6400	1951	276
Peak 6559	6559	1999	276
Peak 6720	6720	2048	267
Peak 6840	6840	2085	305
Peak 7021	7021	2140	339
Peak 7100	7100	2164	339
Peak 7145	7145	2178	339
Peak 7185	7185	2190	264
Peak 7280	7280	2219	264
Peak 7340	7340	2237	244
Peak 7690	7690	2344	315
Peak 8080+	8080+	2682	326
Peak 8599	8599	2621	225
Pelton Peak	7120+	2170	252
Perdition Peak	7675	2339	306
Mt. Pilchuck	5324	1623	29
Pilot Peak	7088	2160	243
Piltdown Tower	8120+	2475	303
Pinnacle Mountain	8402	2561	186
Pinnacle Peak	7360+	2243	311
Pirate Peak	6640+	2024	75
Plummer Mountain	7870	2399	227
Poe Mountain	6015	1833	145
Point 5903	5903	1799	110
Point 7598	7598	2316	172
Portal Peak	6999	2133	83
Post Peak	7188	2191	244

ABOUT THE AUTHOR

Fred Beckey has achieved enduring recognition as the most imaginative, persistent and thorough explorer of the Cascade wilderness. He has climbed hundreds of peaks—many of them first ascents—in every part of the Range, establishing countless new and adventurous routes. His intimate knowledge of Cascades topography has been gained through many years of personal wilderness experience and study of thousands of aerial photographs and maps. This knowledge is reflected in two of his other books: *Cascade Alpine Guide: Climbing and High Routes, Columbia River to Stevens Pass,* and *Darrington and Index: Rock Climbing Guide.* His own story, that of a life dedicated to wilderness exploration and climbing, is told in *Challenge of the North Cascades.*

In addition to becoming a legendary climber, Beckey has also earned a reputation as a student of scientific knowledge about the mountains: their natural history, ecology, climatology, geology and glaciology. However, his personal area of concentration, and the one in which he has made his own scholarly contributions, is human history. This includes not only the recent decades of climbing and hiking, but the preceding century of travels by miners, geologists, geographers, surveyors, soldiers, trappers and fur traders, and the previous eons of Indian journeys.

Through keeping abreast of published literature, seeking out and interviewing explorers whose experience in the backcountry dates to the beginning of the century, and investigating documents, maps and other archival materials in libraries of the Northwest, Canada, California and Washington, D.C., Beckey has become widely acknowledged as an authority on Cascade history. His findings have been published in numerous articles in journals and magazines.

OTHER BOOKS FROM THE MOUNTAINEERS:

50 Hikes in Mount Rainier National Park
101 Hikes in the North Cascades
102 Hikes in the Alpine Lakes, South Cascades and Olympics
103 Hikes in Southwestern British Columbia
109 Walks in B.C.'s Lower Mainland
Trips and Trails, 1: Family Camps, Short Hikes and View Roads in the North Cascades
Trips and Trails, 2: Family Camps, Short Hikes and View Roads in the Olympics, Mt. Rainier and South Cascades
Bicycling the Backroads Around Puget Sound
Bicycling the Backroads of Northwest Washington
Discover Southeast Alaska with Pack and Paddle
55 Ways to the Wilderness in Southcentral Alaska
Hikers' Map to the North Cascades: Routes and Rocks in the Mt. Challenger Quadrangle
Guide to Leavenworth Rock Climbing Areas
Cascade Alpine Guide: Climbing and High Routes, Columbia River to Stevens Pass
Climbers' Guide to the Olympic Mountains
Darrington and Index: Rock Climbing Guide
Snow Trails: Ski and Snowshoe Routes in the Cascades
Mountaineering: The Freedom of the Hills
Medicine for Mountaineering
Mountaineering First Aid
Snowshoeing
The South Cascades: The Gifford Pinchot National Forest
Challenge of Mount Rainier
The Unknown Mountain
Fire and Ice: The Cascade Volcanoes
Across the Olympic Mountains: The Press Expedition
Men, Mules and Mountains: Lieutenant O'Neil's Olympic Expeditions
The Coffee Chased Us Up: Monte Cristo Memories
Challenge of the North Cascades
Bicycling Notes
Hiking Notes
Climbing Notes
Mountains of the World
The Mountaineer
Northwest Trees
The Ascent of Denali

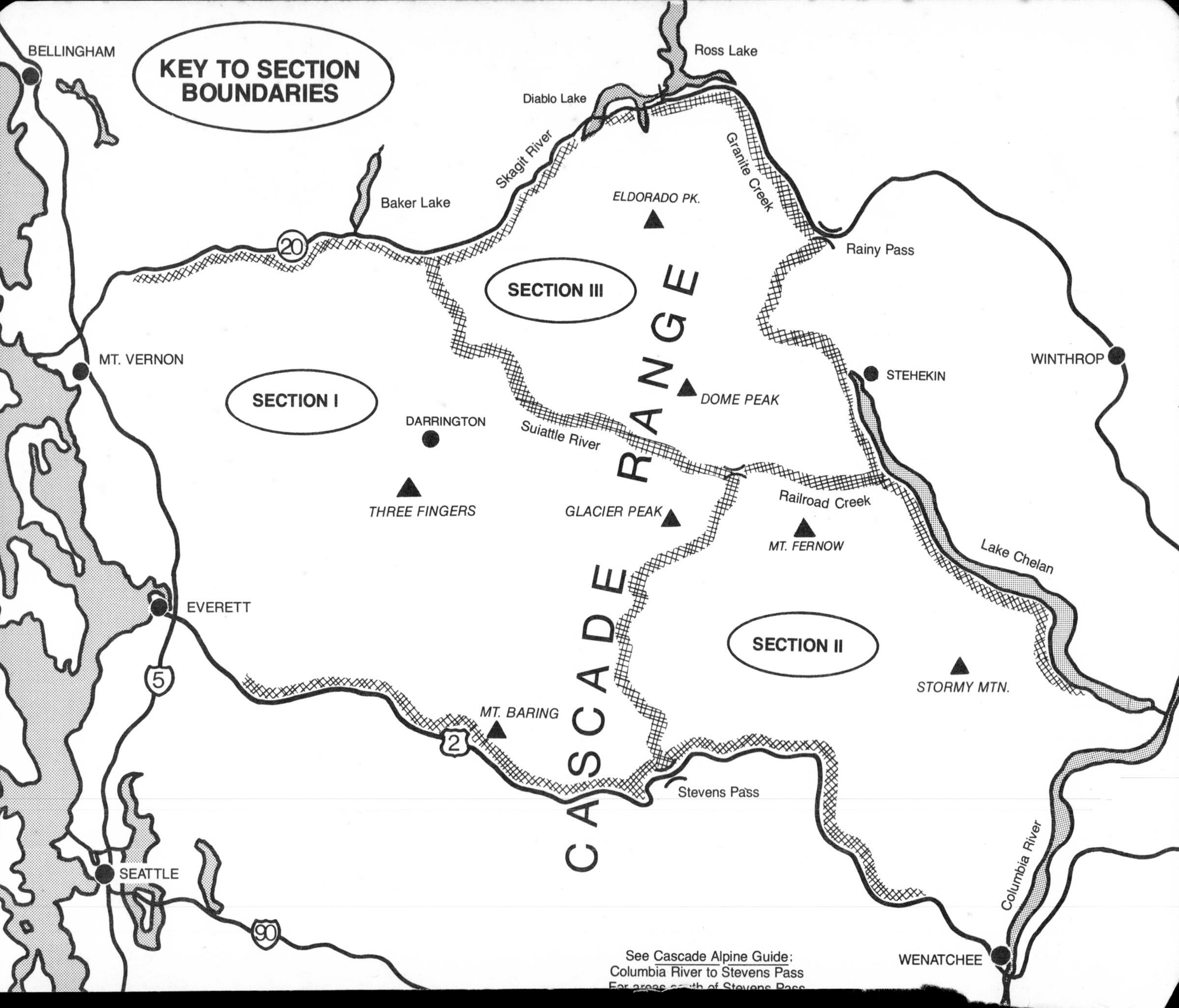

KEY TO SECTION BOUNDARIES
BELLINGHAM
Baker Lake
20
Skagit River
Diablo Lake
Ross Lake
Granite Creek
ELDORADO PK.
Rainy Pass
SECTION III
WINTHROP
STEHEKIN
DOME PEAK
MT. VERNON
SECTION I
DARRINGTON
Suiattle River
THREE FINGERS
GLACIER PEAK
Railroad Creek
MT. FERNOW
Lake Chelan
CASCADE RANGE
EVERETT
5
SECTION II
STORMY MTN.
MT. BARING
2
Stevens Pass
SEATTLE
90
Columbia River
WENATCHEE
See Cascade Alpine Guide:
Columbia River to Stevens Pass